A GUIDE TO
THE MUSIC OF
LATIN AMERICA

AMS PRESS
NEW YORK

A GUIDE TO
THE MUSIC OF
LATIN AMERICA

by

GILBERT CHASE

Second Edition, Revised and Enlarged

A Joint Publication of

THE PAN AMERICAN UNION

AND

THE LIBRARY OF CONGRESS

PAN AMERICAN UNION

GENERAL SECRETARIAT, ORGANIZATION OF AMERICAN STATES

Washington, D. C.—1962

Library of Congress Cataloging in Publication Data

Chase, Gilbert, 1906-
  A guide to the music of Latin America.

  Reprint of the 1962 ed., Second Ed., Revised & Enlarg.
  1945 ed. published under title: Guide to Latin
American music.
  1. Music--Latin America--Bibliography. 2. Music--
Bibliography--Catalogs. I. Pan American Union. Divi-
sion of Music and Visual Arts. II. U.S. Library of
Congress. I. Title.
[ML120.S7C47 1972]   016.7817'8   70-181910
ISBN 0-404-08306-4

From the edition of 1962, Washington, D. C.
First AMS edition published in 1972
Manufactured in the United States of America

AMS PRESS INC.
NEW YORK, N. Y.   10003

Table of Contents

Foreword

A Guide to Latin American Music by Gilbert Chase, issued by the Music Division of the Library of Congress in 1945, has been out of print for many years. The demand for bibliographical guidance in this field, however, has persisted, and, indeed, grown more urgent during the fifteen years since the *Guide* was published.

It is therefore with great indebtedness to the Library of Congress, to Dr. Chase and to the Martha Baird Rockefeller Aid to Music Program, that the Music Division of the Pan American Union presents this second edition of the *Guide to Latin American Music,* under its new title, *A Guide to the Music of Latin America.*

This second edition is intended to bring the first up to date, from July, 1943 to Spring of 1960. More selective than the first edition, it includes as many important monographs as possible. The coverage of periodicals has, however, been limited to some extent by Dr. Chase's other professional commitments which have necessitated his absence from the United States and also by the inaccessibility of certain essential periodicals in the Columbus Library of the Pan American Union.

Thanks are due to Dr. Barbara Krader, who has assisted Dr. Chase in listing and annotating the periodical entries from 1943 through 1959. Likewise the cooperation of Dr. Harold Spivacke and the staff of the Music Division of the Library of Congress, and of the Hispanic Foundation, is gratefully acknowledged. The help of Mrs. Dorothy Harrel is also greatly appreciated.

GUILLERMO ESPINOSA
Chief, Music Division

Preface to the Second Edition

Once again we are in the midst of a great wave of interest for all that concerns the Pan American community of nations. In the musical field, impressive indications of this trend are the Inter-American Music Festivals in Washington, D. C., held in 1958 and 1961, organized by the Inter-American Music Council under the auspices of the Pan American Union: the plan is to make the Festival a biennial event.

The creation of the Inter-American Music Council in 1956, with the Music Division of the Pan American Union as its permanent secretariat and with constituent National Music Councils in most of the American Republics as well as in Canada and Puerto Rico, was another important step in achieving more effective musical interchange in the Americas.

As regards publications of and about the music of Latin America, they have increased in both quantity and quality, with emphasis on the latter. There has been also a notable increase in the number of recordings of music from Latin America, although the problem of distribution has not always been satisfactorily solved. Much has been accomplished, but much remains to be done: in publication, in recording, in performance, in teaching, and above all in research and investigations Latin America is the one great unexplored area remaining for musicology today; thus far there has been little evidence of interest in this extraordinary opportunity for research among musicologists in the United States: but it may be hoped that the younger generation of musical scholars will bring about a change of attitude and will direct more of their effort and attention to the problems and opportunities presented by musicological studies in Latin America.

The vicissitudes of this *Guide* since its original publication in 1945 are illustrative of the difficulties encountered by those working in this field. The *Guide* went out of print shortly after its publication, and Mr. Charles Seeger, at that time Chief of the Music Division of the Pan American Union, made persistent efforts to bring out a new edition. Publication funds were made available, but I was unable to obtain a grant for undertaking the necessary revision. When Mr. Espinosa succeeded Mr. Seeger he took over the project and finally obtained a very modest grant for revision and publication of the *Guide*. Meanwhile, I had rejoined the United States Foreign Service and found myself serving as Cultural Attaché in Brussels. Copy for the revision had to be completed and delivered by the end of the current fiscal year or the grant would be forfeited. Unwilling to let the project lapse by default, I undertook the task of revision under the most unfavorable circumstances that could be conceived. This explanation is

3

given, not by way of alibi, but rather to explain certain features of this second edition that might otherwise appear puzzling, and even perhaps unjustified. There was, in short, no opportunity to undertake a complete and thorough revision of the entire work as a whole: the best that could be done was to correct errors of detail in the original printing and to add supplementary sections bringing the bibliographies and the introductory comments up to date. This accounts for the dual system of numbering, (the items having the small letter "a" affixed to their numerals representing additions to the present edition). In general, I have allowed the original text to stand as it appeared in the first edition, so that any present tense statements occurring in that portion of the *Guide* must be taken to refer to the year 1943.

With the creation, in June 1961, of the Inter-American Institute for Musical Research at Tulune University in New Orleans, conditions vastly more favorable now exist for undertaking scholarly projects in the field of Latin American musical studies. It is regrettable, certainly, that the task of revising the present work could not have been accomplished under these more favorable conditions. Nevertheless, the fact the *Guide to the Music of Latin America* (as it is now called), with nearly 1,100 additional items, is in print again, may serve to encourage others to take up the task of furthering the study of American music throughout the Western Hemisphere. Should it serve such a purpose, the republication of the *Guide,* in spite of its shortcomings and imperfections, will be fully justified.

Tulane University   GILBERT CHASE
New Orleans, La.   *October 10, 1961*

KEY TO NAMES OF COMMENTATORS

A number of entries in this work have been taken from *The Handbook of Latin American Studies* and other bibliographical sources. In such cases, the initials of the commentator usually appear within parentheses immediately following the annotation. The key to these initials is as follows:

R. S. B.: Ralph S. Boggs
R. E. D.: R. E. Dimmick
B. K.: Barbara Krader
S. W. M.: S. W. Mintz
J. H. R.: J. H. Rowe
C. S.: Charles Seeger
D. B. S.: D. B. Stout
R. A. W.: Richard A. Waterman

Preface

THE object of this guide is to provide a means of orientation in the field of Latin American music. The form of an annotated bibliography with introductory comments on each country has been adopted as the most practical for this purpose, since it provides the framework for a general historical survey and at the same time indicates the sources of information for those who wish to pursue more thoroughly any particular phase of the subject. Taken together, the bibliographical annotations and the introductory comments are designed to furnish an essential minimum of information, including the main outlines of the development of music in each country; the nomenclature of the most typical songs, dances and musical instruments; and basic biographical data on the principal composers.

Bibliographies in books and articles have been freely used in the compilation of this work, but as a general rule only those items have been included which were found to be in the Library of Congress and could therefore be checked and annotated. A few exceptions to this general rule have occurred; such items usually bear an indication of their source. The fact that a title is in the Library of Congress is indicated by the presence of a call number, immediately following the pagination, as in the following entry:

> **Almeida, Renato.** História da música brasileira. Rio de Janeiro,
> F. Briguiet & comp., 1926. 238 p. ML232.A6
> **[704]**

Call numbers of periodicals are given in the Key to Periodicals.

For the benefit of readers unacquainted with the idiosyncrasies of Spanish and Latin American personal names, a few words of explanation may be in order. It is customary for persons of the Spanish-speaking world to use two surnames, the penultimate being the patronymic and the last (generally) the matronymic. Sometimes both the patronymic and the matronymic may consist of compound names, as in the case of the Peruvian composer Theodoro Valcárcel Caballero y Martínez del Campo. The patronymic may be joined to the matronymic by the conjunction "y" (and), but both names frequently appear without the conjunction, as in the following: Alcides Prado Quesada. In this case Prado is the paternal surname, what we would call the "last name", and Quesada is the mother's family name. Often the latter is indicated simply by the initial: Alcides Prado Q. In alphabetizing, all Spanish names are entered under the first surname. For instance, the Peruvian composer mentioned above would be entered

7

under Valcárcel, and Prado Quesada will be found under Prado. It is perfectly correct to omit the matronymic in all but the strictest official or legal usage; but it is generally incorrect to refer to a person by the matronymic alone.[1] Thus, one may speak of Alcides Prado, but not of Alcides Quesada, in the case of the individual mentioned above. But a pedantic insistence on the use of the complete name on all occasions is unnecessary and may often lead to needless confusion. Since this is intended to be a practical guide, we have tried to apply the criterion of common sense in this matter. The first composer mentioned above, for example, is always referred to in this work simply as Theodoro Valcárcel. That is the name under which all his writings and compositions appear, and which is always used in writings referring to him. While it would be appropriate to use his complete name in a biographical dictionary, its use in a work such as this would merely be misleading and confusing. In cases where the matronymic is occasionally but not generally used, we have included it with the author's name in the Index of Authors, enclosed within parentheses, thus: Sánchez de Fuentes (y Peláez), Eduardo. In the bibliographical entries, and in the main body of the text, this composer is always referred to as Eduardo Sánchez de Fuentes. There are cases, on the other hand, where individuals use both surnames consistently. Such is the case of the Chilean historian Eugenio Pereira Salas. In general, the form which the author uses in signing his writings or compositions is the one that has been adopted in this work. But we see no point in mystifying the reader by referring to the well-known Mexican composer as Carlos Chávez Ramírez, simply because he signed his name that way in his earliest compositions. To the world at large he is Carlos Chávez, and so he stands in this book.

When we come to Portuguese and Brazilian names, we have no fully established precedent to guide us. The Library of Congress catalogue follows the same principle for Portuguese names that it does for Spanish names, that is, they are entered under the first surname. After considerable deliberation and comparison of various bibliographical sources, including the *Handbook of Latin American studies,* it was decided to enter Portuguese and Brazilian names under the last surname rather than the first. Such a name therefore, as Guilherme Theodoro Pereira de Mello will be entered under Mello. In this procedure we are in accordance with the majority of Brazilian bibliographies, and also with the *Guide to the art of Latin America* edited for the Library of Congress by Dr Robert C. Smith. Inconsistencies will be found in the spelling of Brazilian names and words,

---

[1] Custom or personal preference occasionally sanctions an exception to this rule. A case in point is that of the famous painter Diego Rodríguez de Silva y Velázquez, commonly known as Velázquez.

due to changes in Brazilian orthographic usage. In the case of personal names we have generally followed the spelling established in the Library of Congress catalogue; other spellings are reproduced as they appear in the respective titles and imprints. We should mention the Brazilian custom of referring to prominent men by their first names, e. g., José Mauricio (for José Mauricio Nunes Garcia).

General collections and anthologies of music are included in this bibliography, but not separate pieces of music or collections of music by a single composer. Readers interested in available sources of Latin American music are referred to the *Partial list of Latin American music obtainable in the United States,* compiled by the present writer in the Music Division of the Library of Congress (see items nos. 21 and 21a). This work may also be supplemented by the annual bibliography of music, phonograph records, books and articles appearing in the music section of the *Handbook of Latin American studies,* published under the auspices of the Joint Committee on Latin American Studies (see nos. 1, 5 and 6). Phonograph records are not included in the present work because prevailing conditions make it impossible to guarantee the availability of any given recording. However, guides to recorded music are listed in the bibliography under Discography.

The term "Latin American", adopted for the sake of convenience, is not susceptible of a too-rigid interpretation. Strictly speaking, it does not apply to all the territories lying in the southern sections of the Western Hemisphere. The Guianas, the British and French West Indies, the Republic of Haiti—these can only loosely be caled "Latin American" by virtue of geographical proximity. All that pertains to aboriginal culture before the coming of Columbus is in no sense Latin American, but Amerindian. And in other cases the predominating influence is Afro-American. As a ready working formula, we have grouped under the rubric "Latin America" all of South and Central America, Mexico, the West Indies, and those parts of the United States in which Hispanic influence was once predominant. For the sake of completeness it seemed desirable to include the Bahamas also.

The entries are grouped under the individual countries or territories to which they pertain, but in certain cases such a classification is bound to be more or less arbitrary. For example, references to Incan music will be found under PERU, although the ancient domain of the Incas included parts of what is now Bolivia, Ecuador and Argentina. References to Patagonia will be found under ARGENTINA, though the Patagonian territory extends also into the political boundaries of Chile. Again, Puerto Rico is not included in the section devoted to the United States, but has a separate entry.

The system of subdivision within the various countries has been devised solely with the object of facilitating use of the bibliography. Its application inevitably varies according to the extent and nature of the material available for any particular country. In those countries or territories which have a very limited number of entries, no attempt at subdivision has been made. In general, repetition of the same item under different headings has been practised sparingly, but cross-references have been freely used.

No attempt was made to comb newspaper files systematically, but such newspaper articles as came to our attention were included when deemed of sufficient interest. In this respect it should be pointed out that several of the more important South American dailies, such as *La Prensa* and *La Nación* of Buenos Aires, and *El Comercio* of Lima, often publish important articles on music in addition to reviews of current musical activities.

The emphasis throughout has been on references dealing with Latin American music, but a sampling of musical textbooks, and of writings on theory and aesthetics, has been included in order to give a general idea of Latin American production along these lines. There is also a brief section consisting of Latin American writings on music in the United States.

The preparation and publication of this volume was made possible through an appropriation from the Interdepartmental Committee for Cooperation with the American Republics, Department of State. The compiler wishes to express his appreciation to the Chief of the Division of Cultural Relations, Dr. Charles A. Thomson, for assistance rendered by the Department of State through its representatives in the other American Republics.

The number of individuals in the other American Republics who have cooperated in this work is so large that no list of acknowledgments, however extensive, is certain to cover them all. Though it is difficult to pick out a few names from among so many who have proved helpful, particular gratitude for the furnishing of bibliographical data on the folk music of their respective countries must be conveyed to Dr. Enrique Planchart, Director of the Biblioteca Nacional of Venezuela, and to Dr. Walter Spalding, Director of the Arquivo e Biblioteca da Prefeitura Municipal of Pôrto Alegre, Brazil. Dr. Luis Heitor Corrêa de Azevedo, Professor of National Folklore at the Escola Nacional de Música of Rio de Janeiro, was kind enough to place at my disposal, during his sojourn in Washington, his entire card file on Brazilian folk music. The Ateneo Musical Mexicano, through its secretary, Sr. Estanislao Mejía, sent copious bio-bibliographical data on contemporary Mexican composers. Dr. Jesús C. Romero of Mexico sent us complete files of several Mexican musical periodicals, which he had assembled with considerable difficulty. Dr. Romero also offered to place at our disposal his unpublished bibliography of Mexican music. Though material circumstances prevented us from taking advantage of this offer, we are no less grateful to Dr. Romero for his generosity. Sr. Enio de Freitas e Castro of Pôrto Alegre, Brazil, was instrumental in gathering material on the musical institutions of Rio Grande do Sul—material which it was not found possible to use in this guide to the extent originally anticipated, owing to the necessity for limiting the scope of the work due to wartime restrictions. The same remarks apply to other material on musical institutions submitted to us by Sr. José Ardévol of Havana, Dr. Myron Schaeffer and Sr. Alfredo de Saint-Malo of Panama, the Asociación Amigos del Arte of Santa Fe (Argentina), and the Asociación de Música de Cámara of Buenos Aires. This material will eventually be used to advantage in other publications.

It is gratifying to list the following additional names of persons in the other American Republics who have contributed to this work by sending either bibliographical data or copies of their publications, or both: Renato Almeida, Rosa Mercedes Ayarza de Morales, Gerónimo Baqueiro Fóster, Rodolfo Barbacci, Mariano Antonio Barrenechea, Israel Castellanos, Jesús Castillo, Augusto Raúl Cortazar, Luis A. Delgadillo, Jaime Fonseca Mora, Raúl G. Guerrero, Rudolph Holzmann, Emirto de Lima, Silvio Júlio de Albuquerque Lima, Enrique de Marchena, Vicente T. Mendoza, Fernando Ortiz, Eugenio Pereira Salas, Juan Bautista Plaza, Alcides Prado Quesada, Fernando Romero, Vicente Rossi, Domingo Santa Cruz, Andrés Sas, Federico Schwab, Guillermo Uribe Holguín, Emilio Uzcátegui, José M. Valega, Carlos Vega, Josué Teófilo Wilkes.

Among persons in the United States who made helpful suggestions for this work are Carleton Beals, Gustavo Durán, Leila Fern, Alfred Métraux, Helen H. Roberts, Nicolas Slonimsky and Carleton Sprague Smith. Valuable advice was received from Charles Seeger, Chief of the Music Division of the Pan American Union, who also made available the bibliographical files of his Division. A special word of appreciation is due to the staff of the Hispanic Foundation, in particular to Dr. Lewis Hanke, Dr. David Rubio, Dr. Robert C. Smith and Miss Elizabeth Wilder, for their interest in the progress of this work. Dr. Harold Spivacke and the staff of the Music Division have earned the compiler's sincere gratitude for unflagging encouragement and friendly cooperation at all times. Capable assistance was rendered by Miss Sally Lewis during the final stages of preparing this work for the press.

GILBERT CHASE

June 3, 1943.

Introduction

T HE function of a guide is to show the way through unfamiliar territory. That the territory of Latin American music history is so unfamiliar as to constitute virtually a *terra ignota* will be admitted by all who
have attempted investigation in that direction. Not only are general histories
of the subject lacking, but also, with one or two exceptions, individual histories of music in particular countries. While there exist a few valuable
monographs, especially those treating of musical instruments, the monographic literature is by no means sufficient to form a solid musicological foundation for general studies. If we turn from the literature on music to the
music itself, we find that a large percentage of the latter remains unpublished and therefore inaccessible to the average investigator. Yet those who
have followed recent developments in this field are aware that great forward strides have been made within the past few years in exploring and
charting the vast expanse of Latin American music. This refers not only
to the notable awakening of interest in inter-American musical activities
within the United States itself, but also to the remarkably accelerated mo-
mentum of musicological production among the other American Republics.

The bibliography on any subject is not a rootless and arbitrary growth.
Rather is its growth organic, corresponding to certain fundamental needs
and functions, which in turn arise from basic historical processes. The
retardation of musical development along traditional European lines in the
New World, due to the dislocation caused by exploration, conquest, colonization and revolution, precluded any stimulus toward the development of
a strictly American musical bibliography. Throughout the nineteenth century, the American mind —and by "American" we refer to all the Americas— was conditioned to consider all that was admirable and interesting in
music as emanating from European sources and either faithfully reproducing or closely imitating European models. Excellence in music was judged
only in terms of European acceptance. A case in point is that of the Brazilian composer Carlos Gomes (1836-1896), whose operas, acclaimed in Milan
and other European centers, earned for him a preëminence not approached
by any other Latin American composer of the nineteenth century. There
sprang up, consequently, a fairly copious bibliography on Carlos Gomes
and his works. Among musicians of the United States, an analogous though
less conspicuous case is that of Louis Moreau Gottschalk (1829-1869), of
whom several biographies were written during the nineteenth century, including one published at Havana in 1880.

With very few exceptions the published literature on American music

previous to the twentieth century is negligible. Usually these few exceptions, such as Ramón de La Plaza's essay on Venezuelan music in his
Ensayos sobre el arte en Venezuela (Caracas, 1883), are notable less for
their intrinsic merit than for their rarity. In a field so barren, La Plaza's
85-page study of musical history in Venezuela, preceded by an equally lengthy study of primitive music and instruments, and followed by a musical
supplement of fifty-six pages, stands out as a veritable landmark.

A graph of the bibliography on American music would show a slow
but continuous rise since the beginning of the present century. Within the
past five years the graph-line rises sharply. Its present peak, though tower-
ing far above all previous levels, is certain to be greatly surpassed in the
next decade. Such a hypothetical graph, of course, indicates only the volume
of output, without reference to quality. No doubt a certain amount of in-
consequential matter finds its way into this increased bibliographical production. Yet improvement in quality is a natural function of bibliographical development, especially in new and untried fields, as will be seen
if we turn to a consideration of those historical and cultural processes upon
which this development is based.

The conventional chronological division of American musical history
into three periods—Pre-Columbian, Colonial and Modern—has a certain
superficial usefulness but does not correspond to the basic historical, cultural
and social factors involved in the development of American music. It is
preferable to keep these chronological periods in the background, and to
place the main emphasis upon the fundamental process which has determined the character of music in the western hemisphere. The study of
American music is essentially a study of musical acculturation. The following definition of acculturation was formulated by a committee of the Social
Science Research Council: "Acculturation comprehends those phenomena
which result when groups of individuals having different cultures come into
continuous first-hand contact, with subsequent changes in the original cultural patterns of either or both groups."[1]

Acculturation took place in the Americas before the coming of the Europeans, but the meagre data that we possess concerning the musical results
of such acculturation belong to the realm of archaeology rather than history.
It is only by the study of archaeological remains that we can hope to recon-
struct, even partially and imperfectly, the vanished musical systems developed
by such comparatively high cultures as those of ancient Mexico and Peru, as
represented by the respective civilizations of the Aztecs and the Incas. The

---

[1] *American anthropologist,* v. 38, nº 1 (Jan.-March 1936). Cf. the excellent paper by
Charles Seeger read before the Conference on Inter-American Relations in the Field of Music
[nº 82].

evidence indicates that while music played a highly important social and ritualistic function in the lives of these ancient American peoples, their musical system remained on a somewhat lower level than their achievements in other branches of art, such as architecture, sculpture and script-writing. Curt Sachs has pointed out the similarity that exists between the indigenous musical instruments of America and those of ancient China. This authority states that, "except for a few universal instruments, all relatives of American instruments are exclusively found in a territory comprising China, the area between China and India, the Malay Archipelago and the Pacific Islands". And he concludes: "Ancient Amerian instruments can be classified as 'Pacific'." [2]

Most accounts of American music in Pre-Columbian times are based on the writings of early Spanish chroniclers and historians such as Cervantes de Salazar, Clavijero, Diego Durán, López de Gómara, Toribio de Motolinía, Sahagún and Torquemada. Almost all the early writers on the New World devoted some attention to music, dances and instruments; but these works, written in the sixteenth and seventeenth centuries, are not, of course, Pre-Columbian sources, even when, as in the case of Sahagún's monumental *Historia de las cosas de Nueva España,* they make a conscientious attempt to assemble and record the indigenous traditions. Moreover, these literary descriptions of music and dancing are more interesting from a sociological than a musical point of view, since they tell us more about how the music was used than about how it actually sounded. Even the best literary description of a musical performance is not a satisfactory substitute for musical notation or a detailed technical analysis. The earliest written notation of American Indian music that has còme down to us dates from the last third of the sixteenth century. These are the five melodies of the Tupynambá Indians of Brazil (near Rio de Janeiro) collected by the Frenchman Jean de Léry who went to South America to join Villegaignon in 1557 and who in 1578 published his *Histoire d'un voyage faict en la terre du Brésil, autrement dite Amérique.* It was in the third edition of this work, printed at Geneva in 1585, that the above-mentioned Tupynambá melodies first appeared.[3] There is no guarantee that these tunes have been correctly transcribed or notated.

In addition to all that can be reconstructed from archaeological remains of the Pre-Columbian era (in this connection, consult the introductory sec-

---

[2] Sachs, Curt: *The history of musical instruments* (New York, 1940), p. 202-203.

[3] The Brazilian musicologist Luiz Heitor Corrêa de Azevedo, in a paper read before the American Musicological Society at Minneapolis, 29 Dec. 1941., made a detailed survey of the various editions of Léry's work and analyzed the tunes and their variants as printed by Léry and reproduced by subsequent writers.

tions on Mexico and Peru), and all that can be ascertained from the writings of the first Europeans who undertook to describe the Indian ways
of life, our knowledge of the primitive or indigenous factor in American
music embraces the data gathered in recent times by anthropologists, ethnologists and comparative musicologists working in the field among the
more isolated Indian tribes. Since the end of the last century, interest in
the study of American Indian music has steadily increased throughout the
Americas. However, it is necessary to point out that as the sphere of participation in primitive music gradually diminishes due to the encroachment
of more aggressive cultures, primitive music in the Americas, as elsewhere, may eventually disappear. Fortunately for the purposes of future
study, the scientific recording of primitive music has now reached a high
degree of efficiency. In the Library of Congress, as well as in other centers,
permanent archives of phonographic recordings of American primitive
music—North, South and Central American—are being gradually built up
through scientifically organized field expeditions. In fact, as it becomes
more readily available in recorded form, American primitive music may
possibly become a factor of increasing importance in the development of
American art music.

As soon as the first European colonies were established in the New
World, a complex process of acculturation began. The process varied considerably in degree and character in different regions, according to the
nature of the social groups which came into contact. A strong contrast,
for instance, is presented by the Spanish pattern of colonization and the
English settlements in North America. In determining the pattern of acculturation the religious factor was of prime importance. The Puritans
who settled in New England came to seek religious freedom for themselves. But the Spaniards who came to the New World aimed at a double
conquest, both material and spiritual. They bore the banner of a militant
church which exacted of its adherents the conversion of unbelievers and
imposed on its servants the duty of zealous proselytism, involving a methodical penetration and transformation of the indigenous social structure by
means of an elaborately organized educational system. The New England
settlers were content if they could keep the Indians at a safe distance. In
spite of subsequent sporadic manifestations of proselytism, or of violent
hostility, this remained the fundamental attitude toward the Indian in the
pattern of North American colonization and expansion. It follows that
acculturation between the indigenous population and the European colonizers and immigrants in what is now the United States of North America, has been negligible. There has been a great deal of acculturation in

the United States, but this has involved cultures other than the indigenous, except in isolated instances of minor significance.

Bearing in mind that acculturation arises from continuous first hand contact, it is clear that the proselytism of the Spaniards, with its attendant educational organization, was bound to have the effect of bringing the European and indigenous cultures into first hand contact and was therefore of immense importance in the process of acculturation. It is true that this proselytism had also an element of intolerance, which abetted the violence of the conquerors in the destruction of those indigenous civilizations which were more advanced and therefore more dangerous. The outward civilization of the Aztecs and the Incas, and with it their musical art systems, perished by violent destruction. But the destruction of monuments and political systems did not necessarily mean the destruction of indigenous culture, which survived as a potential force in the indigenes themselves. Only where the native population itself was virtually exterminated, as in the Antilles, did the indigenous element cease to remain as a potent factor of acculturation.

Since the ritual of the Catholic Church required a more or less elaborate musical ceremony, it was natural that much emphasis should be placed on musical training in the educational program of the missionaries. In 1524, only three years after the capture of Mexico City by Cortés, a school for the natives, which included musical training, was established at Texcoco by the Franciscan missionary Fray Pedro de Gante. At this school, which in 1527 was transferred to Mexico City, the Indians were taught to copy European musical notation, to sing the ecclesiastical chant, to construct musical instruments and perform on them, and to compose hymns and masses for the church service. For this aspect of European musical penetration in the New World, the reader may profitably consult the monographs of Lota M. Spell on Fray Pedro de Gante and on the first music books printed in America [see items no. 1790 and no. 1689]. Here we may mention that the first book containing music printed in the New World was an *Ordinarium* (Ordinary of the Mass) issued at Mexico City in 1556. Seven books containing music are known to have been printed in Mexico before 1600.

General histories of missionary activities in Mexico and South America form the indispensable bibliographical foundation for the study of early musical acculturation in the New World. One or two musical monographs are available. There is, for instance, the monograph on the Jesuit musician and missionary H. Luis Berger (1588-1641), published by P. Grenón in 1927 [see item no. 360x]. Berger was active in the La Plata region, in Paraguay and in Chile. Important from another angle, as showing how researches in early American musical history can sometimes shed light on certain details of European musical history, is the monograph by Lauro Ayestarán on Domenico Zipoli [no. 370], the celebrated Italian organist and composer of the eighteenth century, whose *Sonate d'intavolatura per organo o cimbalo* were printed at Rome in 1716. Standard references make no mention of Zipoli's activities after that date. But Ayestarán, starting with clues contained in Guillermo Fúrlong's *Los Jesuítas y la cultura rioplatense,* was able to establish that Zipoli entered the Society of Jesus in 1716 and sailed in the following year for the Rio de la Plata, becoming organist at the Jesuit church in Córdoba (Argentina), where he died in 1726. Further research might uncover hitherto unknown musical manuscripts left by this important composer in Córdoba or Lima.

With the importation of African slaves into the Spanish and Portuguese colonies of America early in the sixteenth century there was introduced into the pattern of New World acculturation another element which has been of tremendous importance in the musical field. The musicality of the Negro developed powerfully under the stimulus of contact with European and (to a lesser extent) indigenous cultures in the New World. As yet the data are lacking for a comprehensive scientific study of Afro-American music in all its ramifications, both in relation to basic African cultures and to varying patterns of acculturation in different sections of the Americas. This is a subject which is receiving increased attention from specialists in this hemisphere, among whom may be mentioned Arthur Ramos in Brazil, Fernando Romero in Peru, Fernando Ortiz in Cuba, and Melville Herskovits in the United States. In addition to a general study of Negro cultures in the New World (*As culturas Negras no novo mundo,* Rio de Janeiro, 1937), Arthur Ramos has published two studies on the Negro in Brazil which treat of music in some detail. These are *O folk-lore negro do Brasil* (1935) and *O Negro brasileiro* (2d ed. 1940), both of which contain examples of Brazilian Negro music. The latter work has been translated into English by Richard Pattee as *The Negro in Brazil* (Washington, 1939), but without the musical examples. For the Negro musical influence in the La Plata region, Vicente Rossi's *Cosas de Negros* [item no. 542] should be consulted. Fernando Ortiz of Havana, who has in preparation a book on Afro-Cuban music, has published several monographs on the subject (see Index of Authors). Brazil, Cuba and Haiti are the Latin American countries in which the musical influence of the Negro is greatest. There are two good books in Englsh dealing with music in Haiti, Harold Courlander's *Haiti singing* (Chapel Hill, 1939), and *The voice of Haiti* (New York, 1938), by Laura Bowman and LeRoy Antoine. The volume entitled *Suriname folklore* (New York, 1936), by Melville and Frances Herskovits, with musical transcriptions and analyses by M. Kolinski [see item no. 1550], is one of the most important contributions to the study of Negro music in the Americas. Here it may be mentioned that the Library of Congress has acquired recordings of Negro music from Haiti, Dutch Guiana (Surinam) and Baía, Brazil.

We come now to the beginning of the twentieth century. Four centuries of acculturation, to which steady waves of immigration have continually added new elements, have produced a wide variety of distinctive musical patterns, most of which find their strongest manifestations in the folk and popular idioms rather than in the fine art forms. *In the course of these four centuries the folk and popular idioms have developed certain characteristic features, which, whatever they may owe to European or African backgrounds, are distinctly of the New World.* In the realm of art music, however, most of the countries, which have long since attained their political independence, remain in a state of colonial dependency upon Europe. Facilities for training professional musicians are generally inadequate. A European musical education, success as a virtuoso in the European capitals, is the goal of all ambitious American musicians. But as the twentieth century advances, the picture gradually changes. Musical nationalism emerges. A new phase of American music begins.

There was no absolute uniformity in the emergence of musical nationalism among the various American countries, but there was a fundamental unity in the basic pattern. In Mexico, for instance, the Revolution of 1910 was a dominant factor in bringing a reawakened national consciousness which found musical leadership and creative expression in such composers as Manuel Ponce and Carlos Chávez, both of whom have been strongly articulate in formulating the aesthetic basis of musical nationalism. In tracing the rise of musical nationalism in the Americas one cannot discount the influence of certain analogous European movements, especially that of the Russian nationalist school as represented by "The Five", and of the Spanish nationalist school which derived its impetus from the doctrines of Felipe Pedrell (1841-1922), who upheld the thesis that each country should build its musical art system on the foundation of its national folk music. Musical nationalism was not exclusively an American doctrine; it was a natural means of self-assertion for all those countries whose musical potentialities, for one reason or another, had long lain dormant.

The first manifestation of musical nationalism is a preoccupation with the elements of national folk music. It is thus that in Brazil, in the second half of the nineteenth century, we find composers such as Itiberê da Cunha and Alexandre Levy utilizing Brazilian folk and popular themes in their compositions. In Mexico a similar tendency is represented by

Julio Ituarte with his *Aires nacionales,* forerunners of Ponce's *Canciones mexicanas.* Even the titles are significant of a trend. In Cuba we have the *Danzas cubanas* of Ignacio Cervantes, models of pianistic stylization. In Brazil, Alberto Nepomuceno writes a *Serie Brasileira* and Luciano Gallet his *Dansa Brasileira.* In Argentina, Julián Aguirre writes his *Danzas Argentinas* and López Buchardo his *Escenas Argentinas.* The list could be continued indefinitely, but it will be sufficient to point out that since the turn of the century the majority of "art music" compositions written in the Latin American countries have made use, more or less freely, of traditional tunes and rhythms. In this connection it is also interesting to observe that the primitive or indigenous element receives its share of attention in this nationalist movement, acquiring a new if vicarious existence. Thus the Brazilian Villa-Lobos makes use of Brazilian Indian themes collected by the anthropologist Roquette Pinto, and the Chilean Carlos Isamitt transcribes Araucanian melodies to incorporate in his symphonic compositions. In Mexico the Instituto Indigenista Interamericano commissions composers to write symphonic works based on recordings of Indian themes. Not only in their creative work, but also in their writing and teaching, the majority of Latin American composers of the present century have given ample evidence of their intense interest in folk and popular music. It is undoubtedly true, as Charles Seeger has stated, that "when the history of music in the New World is written, it will be found that the main concern has been with folk and popular music".

Nevertheless we do not wish to limit the concept of musical nationalism to an exclusive preoccupation with folk and popular idioms. Rather will we extend its application to include all artistic creation produced with a definite consciousness of relation to a specific cultural environment. The creative musician who feels himself spiritually rooted to the land in which he lives will produce work that is of national significance regardless of its subject matter or specific idiomatic content. Chávez is no less a Mexican composer in his *Sinfonía de Antígona* than in his *Sinfonía India.* To be free from all arbitrariness in our survey, we must admit that there are certain composers who profess to be completely cosmopolitan and international in their outlook, displaying no interest in national-folkloristic manifestations. Such isolated exceptions do not alter the predominant pattern of musical nationalism as it has developed in the Americas during the past fifty years or 'so, reaching its greatest intensity in the past two decades. At the same time it may be pointed out that most students of musical trends regard the national-folkloristic movement as a transitional rather than a final phase in creative development. The historical function of folkloristic nationalism appears to be that of enabling musically backward or retarded nations to achieve self-confident expression by the assertion of characteristic traits which derive their force from the cumulative action of native tradition. When this self-confidence and self-knowledge have been acquired the tendency is to evolve toward less restricted forms of expression. Moreover, the preoccupation with folkloristic elements, used at first as a means of nationalistic assertion, leads eventually toward the breakdown of musical nationalism. We mentioned above the Instituto Indigenista Interamericano, which is concerned with fostering the study of Indian culture in the Americas and with stimulating artistic creation based on that culture. This is not a national but an international organization. It commissions composers of any of the American countries, who are interested in the subject, to write works based on Indian themes which may have been collected in any part of the hemisphere from Tierra del Fuego to Alaska. Similarly, a composer in Brazil or in Cuba who draws his material from Negro sources may ultimately find himself more interested in Afro-American music as a whole than in Afro-Brazilian or Afro-Cuban music as such. The tracing of common cultural heritages in the western hemisphere may well lead to the supplanting of musical nationalism by "musical Americanism".

The slogan *americanismo musical* has, indeed, become familiar in recent years to all those working in the inter-American musical field, thanks chiefly to the efforts of Francisco Curt Lange, founder and director of the officially recognized Instituto Interamericano de Musicología at Montevideo. Around 1933 Lange launched his campaign for promoting the musical independence and interdependence of the Americas—that is, independence from Europe and interdependence among themselves. To implement his program Lange founded the *Boletín latinoamericano de música,* an annual publication whose first issue appeared in 1935. Subsequent issues appeared in 1936, 1937, 1938 and 1942 (dated 1941). To form an idea of the scale on which this publication was conceived, volume II consisted of 479 pages, and volume IV of 861 pages. Volumes I, III, IV and V also had extensive musical supplements. The fifth volume, edited in collaboration with Charles Seeger, is dedicated to the United States and the musical supplement consists of works by contemporary United States composers. The five volumes of the *Boletín* thus far published comprise more than 2,600 pages of text and nearly three hundred pages of music in the supplements, forming an impressive bibliographical foundation for the doctrine of *americanismo musical.* At the time of this writing, Lange was planning to publish his sixth volume in Brazil, dedicating it to the music and musicians of that country.

There is another phase of "musical Americanism" which may acquire increasing importance as time goes on. We refer to the use of Latin American themes by composers of the United States, and *vice versa*. Aaron Copland, Henry Cowell, Harl MacDonald, Paul Bowles and Morton Gould are among contemporary United States composers who have drawn upon the folk and popular music of Latin America for some of their compositions. The great vogue of Latin American popular music in the United States has already brought about a fusion of inter-American musical elements which may eventually permeate the field of art music as well.

Returning now to the rise of musical nationalism in the Americas, we undertook to show that the rapid growth of the Latin American musical bibliography during the past few decades is organically related to the growth of that movement. In this broadest interpretation, musical nationalism means simply the definite awareness of the full musical potentialities of a given country, and a deliberate effort to realize those potentialities in every sphere of musical activity. As musical education develops, as facilities for musical performance are increased, and, above all, as composers of talent appear on the scene, the need for intensified bibliographical activity makes itself inevitably felt. Composers and critics seek to formulate in writing the aesthetic bases of nationalism. They discuss the relation of folk music to artistic creation. Outstanding creative personalities stimulate the flow of critical and biographical literature. Consciousness of present achievement leads to interest in historical antecedents. Thus the Chilean historian Pereira Salas affirms that in writing his book on the origins of musical art in Chile he was moved by a desire "to seek the foundations upon which rests the magnificient structure of the contemporary music of Chile". Simultaneously with the rise of the splendid contemporary school of Brazilian composers we see the growth of an admirable critical and historical literature produced by such able and gifted writers as Renato Almeida, Mario de Andrade, Luiz Heitor Corrêa de Azevedo, Luciano Gallet, and many others who have enriched the musical bibliography of Brazil.

Similarly, as interest in inter-American relations has increased, there has been a corresponding increase in the volume of literature intended to inform the people of the United States about the music of the other American republics. It is true that as yet the obvious need for an adequate book in English on the music of Latin America has not been met. Eleanor Hague's little book on the subject, published in 1934, is out of print. Without question this is a need that will be filled within the next few years, entirely by private initiative, since several writers in the United States are known to be at work on books dealing with Latin American music.

Meanwhile, publications such as the present one, and such as those issued by the Music Division of the Pan American Union under the able direction of Charles Seeger, represent an endeavor to meet the most pressing needs for information on Latin American music, which is eagerly being demanded throughout the United States. How real and widespread is this demand is shown by the reception accorded to the two bibliographical publications in the inter-American musical field previously compiled in the Music Division of the Library of Congress. Early in 1941 the writer of these lines compiled a *Partial list of Latin American music obtainable in the United States with a supplementary list of books and a selective list of phonograph records,* which was issued in a mimeographed edition of theree thousand copies (the list was mimeographed and distributed by the Pan American Union). In June 1942 a second edition, revised and augmented, was issued. In all, a total of five thousand copies have been distributed, most of them in response to specific requests.

Of a more specialized nature is the second compilation to which we refer, the *Bibliography of Latin American folk music* issued by the Music Division of the Library of Congress in mimeographed form in April 1942. Containing over eleven hundred entries, most of them annotated, this bibliography has been in wide demand among libraries and universities in the United States. Its primary purpose, however, was to serve as a sort of preliminary study for the present bibliographical guide. Copies were distributed to leading musicologists and folklorists throughout the Americas, with a request for additional data and for corrections. The response, as indicated by the acknowledgments in the Preface to the present work, was gratifying as an example of inter-American intellectual cooperation. All the material originally included in the above-mentioned folk music bibliography has been incorporated in the present work, together with much additional material both on folk music and on other subjects. While this bibliographical *Guide to Latin American Music* still falls far short of completeness or perfection, it nevertheles constitutes an initial step toward the systematic organization of bibliographical materials which may form the basis for a comprehensive study of music in the Americas. If it serves to stimulate and facilitate such study among musicians, music-lovers, students and scholars in this hemisphere, pointing the way toward work still to be done as well as illuminating the path of history through past accomplishment, it will have proved its usefulness in a field which, perhaps more than any other, reveals the possibilities inherent in the cultural community of the Americas.

A Guide to the Music of Latin America

GENERAL BIBLIOGRAPHY

BIBLIOGRAPHIES

Berrien, William. Latin American music in 1939. A selected list of publications which appeared on this subject during the year 1939, with evaluative and informative notes on important items, reprinted from the Handbook of Latin American Studies for 1939. Cambridge, Mass., Harvard university press, 1940. Cover-title, 403-417 p. ML120.S7L3 [1]

Includes a survey of inter-American musical activities for 1939.

Boggs, Ralph Steele. Bibliography of Latin American folklore. New York, H. W. Wilson co., 1940. 109 p. (*Half-title:* Inter-American bibliographical and library association. Publications. ser. I, v. 5) Z5984.L4B7 [2]

"Poetry, music, dance and games", p. 54-64.

——. Folklore. (Running title: Bibliography of Latin American folk music.) 3 p. ML128.F75B5 [3]

Positive photostat from Handbook of Latin American studies, 1936, p. 155-158.

Brooklyn College. Department of music. Outline of lectures, notes and references. The music of Latin America. By Benjamin Grosbayne. New York, Brooklyn college press, 1943. 56 p. [4]

Reproduced from typewritten copy. Contains extensive bibliography, both musical and general.

Chase, Gilbert. Latin American music in 1940. A selected list of publications which appeared on this subject during the year 1940, with evaluative and informative notes on important items, reprinted from the Handbook of Latin

American Studies for 1940. Cambridge, Harvard university press, 1941. Cover-title, 439-452 p. ML120.S7L3 [5]

Includes a resumé of inter-American musical activities for the year 1940. The bibliography includes musical scores and phonograph records.

——. Latin American music in 1941. A selected list of publications which appeared on this subject during the year 1941 ... reprinted from the Handbook of Latin American studies. Cambridge, Harvard university press, 1942. Cover-title, 535-549 p. ML120.S7L3 [6]

Lists about 200 items, including musical scores, phonograph records. Includes a resumé of inter-American musical activities for 1941.

——. Materials for the study of Latin American music. *In* Notes for the Music library association, no. 13 (March 1942), p. 1-12. Mimeographed by the Columbia university libraries, New York. [7]

Reviews the general bibliography of the subject. Cf. item no. 8.

——. Materials for the study of Latin American music. *In* Music and libraries; selected papers of the Music library association presented at its 1942 meetings. Washington, Music library association, American library association, 1943, p. 14-21. [8]

A revised version of item no. 7, brought up to date as of February 1943.

——. The music of Spain. New York, W. W. Norton, 1941. 375 p. il. ML315.C42M8 [9]

Bibliography of Latin American music, p. 334-337.

Chase, Gilbert. La música de España. Buenos Aires, Librería Hachette [1943]. 410 p. il.   **[9x]**

A Spanish translation (by Jaime Pahissa) of the preceding item. Revised and augmented.

Grismer, Raymond Leonard. A new bibliography of the literatures of Spain and Spanish America, including many studies on anthropology, archaeology, art, economics, education, geography, history, law, music, philosophy and other subjects. Minneapolis, Perine book co., 1941.   **[10]**

Partial report of WPA project 11, O. P. 165-1-71-124. Reproduced from typewritten copy.

Handbook of Latin American studies. See nos. 1, 3, 5, 6, 11, 12 and 13.

Labastille, Irma Goebel. The music of Mexico and Central America. Photostat from Handbook of Latin American studies for 1936, Cambridge, Mass., 1937, p. 459-472 (Running title: Guide to Caribbean music). ML128.C18L2   **[11]**

A bibliography. Cf. item no. 12.

———. The music of Mexico and Central America. *In* Hanke, Lewis H., *ed.* Handbook of Latin American studies, 1936. Cambridge, Mass., Harvard university press, 1937, p. 459-472. (Running title: Guide to Caribbean music.)   **[12]**

A miscellaneous bibliography.

Lange, Francisco Curt. Los estudios musicales de la América Latina publicados últimamente. A reprint from the Handbook of Latin American studies for 1937. Cambridge, Mass., Harvard university press, 1938. p. 527-546. ML133.L26E8   **[13]**

———. Programs of Latin American music. Washington, D. C., 1939. 39 p. Reproduced from type-written copy.   **[14]**

Prepared for the Conference on Inter-American relations in the field of music, Washington, D. C. Issued by the Division of cultural relations of the Department of State. Suggested programs of symphonic and chamber music, piano music, voice and piano, and choral music. Sources for the music indicated.

Latin-American music published in the United States by Edward B. Marks music corporation. Piano; vocal; orchestra; band. New York, Edward B. Marks music corp. [1942]. 13 p.   **[15]**

Library of congress. *Division of music.* Bibliography of· Latin American folk music compiled by Gilbert Chase. Washington, Library of Congress, 1942. 141 p. ML120.S7L5. Reproduced from type-written copy.   **[16]**

Contains 1143 items, the majority with brief annotations. This material has been incorporated in the present work.

New York. Public library. The folk music of the Western hemisphere; a list of references in the New York public library, compiled by Julius Mattfeld, Music division. New York, 1925. 74 p. ML136.N5M2 and Z6814.F7N5   **[17]**

Reprinted, with additions, from the Bulletin of the New York public library. November and December 1924. Contains about 230 referencse on Latin America.

Pan American union. *Division of intellectual cooperation.* References on Latin American music, the theatre and the dance. Washington, Division of intellectual coperation. Pan American union, 1941. ML120.L2P2 Reproduced from type-written copy.   **[18]**

———. List of Latin American music (vocal, piano, instrumental, orchestral and band) which can be purchased in the United States. Compiled in the office of the Counselor, Pan American union Washington, D. C., Pan American union, 1933. 2 ed. 60 p. ML120.S7P2 1933. Autographic reproduction of type-written copy.   **[19]**

———. *Music division.* Latin American music published in connection with the editorial project of the Music division of the Pan American union in cooperation with the Music educators national conference and a partial list of other publications of Latin American music and books of Latin American music. Washington, D. C., Pan American union, 1942. 7 p. Reproduced from type-written copy. ML120. S7P29 **[20]**

——. *Music division*. Partial list of Latin American music obtainable in the United States, with a supplementary list of books and a selective list of phonograph records; compiled by Gilbert Chase, Music division, Library of Congress. Washington, D. C., Music division, Pan American union, 1941. 36 p. Reproduced from typewritten copy. ML120.S7P22 (*Its* Music series, no. 1) **[21]**

——. *Music division*. Partial list of Laitn American music obtainable in the United States, with a supplementary list of books and phonograph records; compiled by Gilbert Chase, Music Division, Library of Congress. 2d ed. Washington, D. C., Music division, Pan American union, 1942. 44 p. Reproduced from typewritten copy. ML120.S7-P22 1942 (*Its* Music series, no. 1) **[21x]**

——. *Music division*. Partial list of collections of Latin American songs and references for guidance in planning fiestas. Washington, Pan American union, 1942. 4 p. **[22]**

Reproduced from typewritten copy.

See also nos. 35, 44, 56, 57, 207, 239X.

DISCOGRAPHY

Alvarenga, Oneyda. Pequena contribução ao estudo das questões do organização discotecária. *Bol. lat. am. mús.*, v. 4 (Oct. 1938), p. 267-278. **[23]**

Chase, Gilbert. The music of Spain.

New York, W. W. Norton, 1941. 375 p. il. ML315.C42M8 **[24]**

Recordings of Latin American music, p. 355-356.

Conference on inter-American relations in the field of music, *Washington, D. C., 1939*. Report of the committee. William Berrien, chairman. Washington, D. C., 1940. **[25]**

Includes: *Relação de discos de musica folclorica brasileira*, compiled by Oneyda Alvarenga, p. 117-118; and List of records of Brazilian folk songs and popular music compiled by Mario de Andrade, p. 119-123. Also: List of Brazilian "art" music available on records, p. 124-125.

Ferraz, José Bento Faria. Catálogo dicionário aplicado a uma discoteca, *Rev. arq. mun. São Paulo*, v. 7, no. 73 (1941), p. 151-168. **[26]**

A study of record cataloguing methods, by a staff member of the Discoteca Pública Municipal of São Paulo.

Gramophone shop encyclopedia of recorded music. New York, Simon and Schuster, 1942. 558 p. ML156.G8D3 **[27]**

Supervising editor, George Clark Leslie. Includes recordings by the following Latin American composers; Humberto Allende (Chile), José Ardévol (Cuba), Felipe Boero (Argentina), Julián Carrillo (Mexico) [erroneously spelled Carillo], Carlos Chávez (Mexico), Eduardo Fabini (Uruguay), Oscar Lorenzo Fernandez (Brazil), Antonio Carlos Gomez (Brazil), Francisco Mignone (Brazil), Cayetano Troiani (Argentina), Guillermo Uribe-Holguín (Colombia), Heitor Villa-Lobos (Brazil).

Handbook of Latin American studies. See nos. 1, 5 and 6.

Lange, Francisco Curt. Fonografía pedagógica III—La discoteca nacional. *Bol. lat. am. mús.*, v. 4 (Oct. 1938), p. 99-132 **[28]**

Marsh, William Sewall. From the Rio Grande to Cape Horn; a survey of the recorded music of Latin America. *The phonograph monthy review*. v. 4, no. 12 (Sept. 1930), p. 399-401. **[29]**

——. From the Rio Grande to Cape Horn; the recorded music of Caribbean and South American countries. *The phonograph monthly review,* v. 5, no. 2 (Nov. 1930), p. 42-44.   [30]

Covers Cuba, Porto Rico, Haiti, Santo Domingo and Venezuela.

——. Musical Spain from A to Z as exemplified on phonograph records; with which is also included the music of Hispanic America. Providence, R. I., Campbell music co., 1929. 52 pp. ML 106.S7M3   [31]

Inclues brief references to Latin American musicians and folk music froms.

The other Americas through films and records. Washington, D. C., American council on education, 1942. 37 p.   [32]

Section 3: Music recordings, p. 21-32, compiled by Gustavo Durán of the Pan American Union.

Pan American union. *Music division.* Partial list of Latin American music obtainable in the United States, with a supplementary list of books and a selective list of phonograph records; compiled by Gilbert Chase, Music division, Library of Congress. Washington. D. C., Music division, Pan American union, 1941. 36 p. Reproduced from typewritten copy. ML120.S7P22 (*Its* Music series, no. 1)   [33]

A second revised edition issued in June 1942.

——. *Music division.* Recordings of Latin American songs and dances; an annotated selected list of popular and folk music. By Gustavo Durán. Washington, D. C., Music Division, Pan American union, 1942. 65 p. (*Its* Music series, no 3) ML156.P17R3   [34]

Includes descriptions of dances, notation of rhythms, bibliography and index of terms.

See also nos. 1, 4, 5, 56, 56x, 334, 715, 2691.

GENERAL AND MISCELLANEOUS

Boletín latinoamericano de música. An annual publication. Editor: Francisco Curt Lange. At head of title: Instituto de estudios superiores, Montevideo. Sección de investigaciones musicales. ML199.B64 il.   [35]

Vol. 1 (April 1935) published in Montevideo. 287 p. Suplemento musical, 54 p. [see item no. 297].

Vol. 2 (April 1936) published in Lima. 479 p.

Vol. 3 (April 1937) published in Montevideo. 543 p. Suplemento musical, 25 p. [see item no. 298].

Vol. 4 (Dec. 1938) published in Bogotá. 861 p. Suplemento musical, 135 p. [see item no. 299].

Vol. 5 (Oct. 1941) published in Montevideo. 637 p. Suplemento musical, 167 p. At head of title: Instituto interamericano de musicología.

Concerning Lange and the *Boletin,* see items nos. 76, 78, 79, 80.

See also Introduction.

Buccino, Raúl A., and Luis Benvenuto. La música en Iberoamérica. Buenos Aires, Ferrari hnos., 1938. 156 p. il. (incl. music). ML199.B83M8   [36]

"Adaptada a las exigencias de los programas en vigor en colegios nacionales y liceos de señoritas." Includes illustrations of pre-Hispanic musical instruments. Gives a clear and concise outline of the development of music in the Latin American countries from pre-Hispanic times to the present. A second edition was published in 1939.

Cardeza, María Elena. Historia de la música americana. Buenos Aires, Talleres Gráficos "Buenos Aires", 1938, 86 p. ML199.C17H5   [37]

A summary outline of music in Latin America, for schood use (*3er año*).

Chase, Gilbert. The music of Spain. New York, W. W. Norton, 1941. 375 p. ML315.C42M8   [38]

Chapter 17, p. 257-272—includes: Early history of music in Latin America, both religious and secular, with special reference to the work of Pedro de Gante in Mexico; introduction of the Spanish ballad; first printing of music in America; the dissemination of Christian church music among the Indians; beginnings of lyric theatre in the 18th century; *corrido in* Mexico; musical instruments; Creole songs (with one musical example) and dances (with discussion of the Spanish and folk elements in them), with comments on many dances, including the Argentine *cuando,* the Mexican *huapango* and *jarabe,* the Cuban bolero and *zapateo;* nature of Brazilian music; Hispanic music in the United States, which discusses Spanish music, dances, games and plays found in various parts of the United States. An extensive Bibliography of Chapter 17 is found on p. 334-337; a comprehensive record list of Latin American music, p. 355-356.

――. Piano music by 12 contemporaries. *Int. amer. monthly,* v. 1, no. 5 (Sept. 1942), p. 32-33. **[38x]**
Contains portraits of Villa-Lobos, Ginastera and Guarnieri. This article is a review of *Latin-American art music for the piano,* edited by Francisco Curt Lange [item no. 301].

Chávez, Carlos. Toward a new. music; music and electricity. Translated from the Spanish by Herbert Weinstock. New York, W. W. Norton & co., 1937. 180 p. il. (music) ML1092.C4T6 **[39]**

Coeuroy, André. Panorama de la musique contemporaine. Paris, Simon Kra, 1928. 209 p. ML197.C7 **[40]**
Brief reference to South American music, p. 44-45, with special mention of Alberto Williams, Villa-Lobos and Alfonso Broqua.

Los derechos de los compositores, autores y editores latino-americanos. *Gaceta mus.,* v. 1, nos. 7-8 (July-Aug. 1928), p. 56-57. **[41]**

García, Rolando V., Luciano C. Croatto and Alfredo A. Martín. Historia de la música latinoamericana. Buenos Aires, Librería Perlado, 1938. 231 p. il. (incl. music). ML199.G3H5 **[42]**
An outline of Latin American musical history, designed for use in schools.

González, Manuel Pedro. Racial factors in Latin American music. *Int. amer.*

quart., v. 3, no. 4 (Oct 1941), p. 44-52. **[43]**
Points out that Italian influence was predominant in the music of Latin America during the 19th century. Refers to Gilberto Valdés as "the greatest, perhaps, of all Cuban composers". Valdés is a cultivator of the Afro-Cuban style. A reprint of this article, issued under the title *Latin America, a musical melting pot,* is available from the Pan American Union.

Hague, Eleanor. Latin American music, past and present. Santa Ana, Calif., The Fine arts press, 1934. 98 p. il. (music). ML199.H14 **[44]**
Attempts to cover an immense territory, both in space and time, within five brief chapters; consequently the treatment is often sketchy. More attention is devoted to primitive and folk music than to art music. The chapter on contemporary music (7 pages) is the least satisfactory of the book. The "Partial list of musicians" (p. 85-88) would have been more useful if complete names had been given. There is a chart of "Songs, dances, and instruments of Spanish America" (2 unnumbered pages, preceding p. 85), and a bibliography, p. 91-98. Includes 10 musical examples.

Hellmer, Joseph R. Is it really Latin American? *Panam. mag.* v. 4, no. 1 (Apr. 1943), p. 15-18. **[45]**
Discusses Latin American popular music, especially that well-known in the United States. Contrasts genuine Latin American music and orchestration with Latin American-flavored music composed in the United States.

Lange, Francisco Curt. Colonial music in Latin American lands. *Mus. Amer.,* v. 59, no. 14 (Sept. 1939), p. 8 il. **[46]**
"Religious and secular fields reveal a rich art background."

――. El festival Ibero-Americano de música. *Bol. lat. am. mús.,* v. 4 (Oct. 1938), p. 55-64. **[47]**

Latorre, Medardo Héctor. Músicos y críticos. *Nosotros,* v. 14, no. 136 (Sept. 1920), p. 100-103. **[48]**
Brief mention of Latin American music.

Lima, Emirto de. Música española en

América. *Revista hispanoamericana de ciencias, letras y artes,* v. 2 (May 1932), p. 164-165. [49]

Lualdi, Adriano. Viaggio musicale nel Sud-America. Milano, Istituto editoriale nazionale, 1934. 245 p. [50]

McPhee, Colin. South America once more. *Mod. music,* v. 17, no. 4 (1940), p. 245-246. [51]

Notes on the concert of South American music given by the Schola Cantorum of New York in Carnegie Hall.

Marsh, William Sewall. Musical Spain from A to Z as exemplified on phonograph records; with which is also included the music of Hispanic America. Providence, R. I., Campbell music co., 1929. 52 p. ML106.S7M3 [52]

Includes brief references to Latin American musicians and folk music forms.

Marx, W. Burle. Music of the hemispheres. *Bull. pan amer. union,* v. 69, no. 10 (1935), p. 741-745. il. [53]

Mayer-Serra, Otto. Panorama de la música hispanoamericana (esbozo interpretativo). Separata del tomo II de la Enciclopedia de la música Atlante. México, D. F., Ed. Atlante, 1943. p. 379-440. il. MT6.A885 [54]

This monograph deals succinctly yet comprehensively with the broad development of music in Latin America from pre-Columbian times to the present. It is on the whole the most thoroughly documented general survey of Latin American music at present available. Illustrated with portraits and musical facsimiles. Bibliographical footnotes.

Muñoz Sanz, Juan Pablo. Nacionalismo y americanismo musical. Quito. Imprenta del Ministerio de gobierno, 1938. 41 p. ML199.M85N3 [55]

"América, v. 12, no. 65, 1er trimestre de 1937, suplemento no. 3, Quito, Ecuador"; p. 20-42.

Music of the new world. Handbook, vol. 1, 1942-1943. New York, Published for the National broadcasting company by the Southern music publishing company, inc., 1942. 52 p. MT6.16 [56]

"Research director and author of the Handbook, Gilbert Chase, Music Division, Library of Congress." A listener's manual for the broadcast series of the Inter-American University of the Air. This volume includes background material, with bibliographies and record lists, for the first 15 programs, from Pre-Columbian music to the songs of the wars for Latin American independence.

———. Handbook, vol. 2, 1943. New York, Published for the National broadcasting company by the Southern music publishing company, inc., 1943. 76 p. MT6.16 [56x]

"Research director and author of the Handbook, Gilbert Chase, Music Division, Library of Congress." A listener's manual for the broadcast series of the Inter-American University of the Air. This volume, complete with bibliographies and record lists, embraces American music from the introduction of romanticism to the modern music of today, discussing Negro and Indian influences, the lyric theatre, orchestras, etc.

Narodny, Ivan. Music's place in countries of Latin America. *Mus. Amer.,* v. 18, no. 24 (1913), p. 11, 12. [57]

Nolasco, Flérida de. De música española y otros temas. Santiago de Chile, Ediciones Ercilla, 1939. 106 p. ML315.N78M9 [58]

Pan American union. *Counselor's office.* Music in Latin America, a brief survey compiled by Charles Seeger from various sources. Washington, D. C., Pan American union, 1942. 73 p. (*Its* Club and study series, v. 3, no. 3). Reproduced from typewritten copy. ML199.P2M8 [59]

Compiled "from recent books, articles and unpublished writings by William Berrien, Gilbert Chase, Evans Clark, Harold Courlander, Gustavo Durán, Albert T. Luper and Carleton Sprague Smith." Contents: On pre-Columbian music; The colonial period; The nineteenth century; The music of today in Mexico and Central America; The music of today in South America; The music of today in the Antilles; Summary; Index to persons, countries, and cities. Includes 7 musical illustrations. This is primarily a work of popularization, especially suitable for use in schools, study clubs, etc.

Pedrell, Felipe. Diccionario técnico de la música. Ilustrado con 117 grabados y 51 ejemplos de música y seguido de un suplemento. Barcelona, Impr. de V. Berdós, 1894. 529 p. il. ML108.P37 **[59x]**

See *marimba mexicana, quena, guitarra, flauta de Pan*, etc.

Poole, Gene. "Enciclopedia de swing." Buenos Aires, La Academia americana, 1939. 92 p. il. ML102.S9P5 **[59y]**

Includes music.

Reyes, Alfonso. Los autos sacramentales en España y América. *Bol. acad. arg. letras.* v. 5, no. 19 (July-Sept. 1937), p. 349-359. **[60]**

Mention of dance, p. 354. Also published separately [item no. 61].

———. Los autos sacramentales en España y América. Buenos Aires, "Coni", 1937. p. 349-360. PQ6121.R3R4 **[61]**

A reprint of no. 60.

Ryan, Arthur. Opera in South America. *The opera,* v. 1 no. 13 (27 Nov. 1913), p. 9-11. **[62]**

Description of the Teatro Nacional in Mexico City, the Municipal Theatre in La Paz, the Grand Opera House in Rio de Janeiro, and the Teatro Colón in Buenos Aires.

Salas, Samuel J. A., Pedro I. Pauletto and Pedro J. S. Salas. Historia de la música (América Latina). Buenos Aires, Editorial Araujo, 1938. 176 p. il. (incl. map, music.) ML199.S26H5 **[63]**

A school text.

Sanjuan, Pedro. Música nueva. *Contemporáneos,* v. 5, no. 17 (Oct. 1929), p. 161-175 **[64]**

Contrast between modern music and music of earlier centuries; discusses Honegger's *Pacific 231.*

Sas, André. La musique en Amérique Latine. *L'art musical,* v. 4, no. 96 (7 Oct. 1938), p. 7-9, ports. **[65]**

Deals especially with José Ardévol and Juan Carlos Paz. Reprinted in *Revista brasileira de música,* v. 4, nos. 3-4 (1937), p. 197-201.

Seeger, Charles. The importance to cultural understanding of folk and popular music. *In* Conference on inter-American relations in the field of music, Digest of proceedings, principal addresses. Department of State, Division of cultural relations, Washington, D. C., 1940. F1418.C786 **[66]**

"When the history of music in the new world is written, it will be found that the main concern has been with folk and popular music." Of especial significance is the statement that "the music-acculturation processes operating in the new world from the first conquests to the present time, must eventually exhibit a fundamentally identical pattern".

Slonimsky, Nicolas. Music in South America. *In* Who is who in music. Chicago and New York, Lee Stern press, 1940, p. 518-520. ML105.W5 **[67]**

A general survey.

———. Music since 1900. 2d ed. New York, W. W. Norton & co., 1938. 592 p. ML197.S634M98 **[68]**

Includes a descriptive chronology of music from 1900 to 1937, a concise biographical dictionary af 20th-century musicians, and a section of miscellaneous letters and documents bearing upon modern music. Devotes considerable attention to Latin American music. See the index, under Ayala, Carillo [sic], Carreño, Castro, Caturla, Chávez, Espinosa, Havana Philharmonic Orchestra, Mexican Orquesta Filarmónica, Orquesta Sinfónica Nacional (Bogotá), Paz, Quevedo, Revueltas, Roldán, Sandi, Sanjuán, Villa-Lobos.

Smith, Carleton Sprague. Music libraries in South America. *In* Notes for the Music library association, no. 11 (Aug.

1941), p. 19-31. Mimeographed by the Newberry library, Chicago.   [69]

A survey based on general impressions rather than on extensive research.

——. Music of Latin America. *Progressive education,* v. 18 (Oct. 1941), p. 308.   [70]

——. What not to expect of South America. *Mus. Amer.,* v. 61, no. 3 (10 Feb. 1941), p. 217, 220. port.   [71]

Advice to musicians who expect to visit South America.

Tatum, Louise Terrell. The music of the Spains. *Etude,* v. 53, no. 5 (May 1935), p. 265-266, 310.   [72]

Includes Latin America.

Urquieta, Felipe. Breve reseña histórica de la música americana. *Estudio,* Barcelona, v. 31 (1920), p. 188-192.   [73]

General observations on Latin American music, including folk music.

Valdivia Palma, Ernesto. El nacionalismo en la música ibero-americana. *Rev. mus. cat.,* v. 32, no. 379 (July 1935), p. 298-302.   [74]

General survey of contemporary musical activity in Latin America, listing many composers.

Villa-Lobos, Heitor. A música—fator de comunhão entre os povos. *Anuario brasileiro,* no. 3 (1939), p. 32, 482. PQ9501. A6.   [75]

Music as a factor in international unity.

Williams, Mary Wilhelmine. The people and politics of Latin America. New ed. Boston, New York, etc., Ginn and co., 1938. 888 p. il. F1408.W72 1938.   [75x]

Ch. 32 deals with Hispanic American literature, art and music.

See also nos. 94, 95, 97, 108, 109, 114, 122, 143, 145, 160, 198

INTER-AMERICAN RELATIONS

Berrien, William. Boletín latino-americano de música. *Int. amer. quart.,* v. 1, no. 2 (Apr. 1939), p. 115-118.   [76]

A review of vol. 4 of the Boletín, with a summary of Lange's movement for *Americanismo musical.*

Chase, Gilbert. American relations conference held in capital. *Mus. Amer.,* v. 59, no. 16 (25 Oct. 1939), p. 13. il.   [77]

An account of the Conference on Inter-American Relations in the Field of Music held in the Library of Congress under the auspices of the Division of Cultural Relations. Department of State. See items nº 82 and 83.

——. Americanismo musical. *Mod. music,* v. 20, no. 5 (March-Apr. 1943), p. 214-215.   [78]

A review of *Boletín latino-americano de música,* vol. 5.

——. Francisco Curt Lange and "Americanismo musical". *Int. amer. monthly,* v. 2, no. 5 (May 1943), p. 33. port.   [79]

——. Linking the Americas. *Mus. Amer.,* v. 59, no. 3 (10 Feb. 1939), p. 224. il.   [80]

Deals with the *Boletín latino-americano de música* and the activities of Francisco Curt Lange.

——. Musicological congress puts emphasis on hearing music. *Mus. Amer.,* v. 59, no. 15 (10 Oct. 1939), p. 8, 15. il.   [81]

Refers to Latin American participation in International Congress of the American Musicological Society, held at New York in September 1939.

Conference on inter-American relations in the field of music, *Washington,, D. C., 1939.* Digest of proceedings. Principal addresses. Washington, D. C. Division of cultural relations, Department of state, 1940. Mimeographed. F1418.C786. **[82]**

Includes the addresses of William Berrien, Francisco Curt Lange (Facilitating the exchange of "serious" musical compositions, the role of libraries, music schools and music publishers) and Charles Seeger (The importance to cultural understanding of folk and popular music).

——. Report of the committee. William Berrien, chairman. Washington, D. C., 1940, Reproduced from typewritten copy. 151 p. **[83]**

This important document contains, in addition to the chairman's summary, reports of the subcommittees on the following subjects: Music libraries; comparative musicology; school music; interchange of professors and students; films; copyright; music management; WPA music units; radio; community and recreational music; music recording; concert interchange in the popular field. It also includes an article on Brazilian popular music by Mario de Andrade.

Labastille, Irma Goebel. Americanismo musical. *Mod. music,* v. 14, no. 2 (1937) p. 76-81. **[84]**

Lange, Francisco Curt. Americanismo musical. *Bol. lat. am. mús.,* v. 2 (Apr. 1936), p. 117-130. **[85]**

Also reprinted separately

——. Suma de las relaciones interamericanas en el campo de la música. *Bol. lat. am. mús.,* v. 5 (1941), p. 11-22. **[85x]**

Traces the development of the movement for "Americanismo musical" which Lange launched in 1933, and which received a great impetus following the Conference on Inter-American Relations in the Field of Music held at Washington, D. C., in October 1939 (cf. nos. 82 and 83).

Lawler, Vanett. Latin Americans see our musical life. *Bull. pan Amer. union,* v. 76, no. 7 (July 1942), p. 368-373. **[85y]**

Marx, W. Burle. Musical reciprocity between the Americas. *Mus. Amer.,* v. 59, no. 11 (June 1939), p. 34. ports. **[86]**

Mills, Helen Harrison. Music as a power to weld the Americas. *Mus. Amer.,* v. 61, no. 11 (June 1941), p. 10, 61. **[87]**

Discusses efforts to promote inter-American musical relations through the National Federation of Music Clubs.

Music strengthens Pan American ties. *Mus. Amer.,* v. 63, no. 3 (10 Feb. 1943), p. 174, 175. **[88]**

National committee of the United States of America on international intellectual cooperation. Preliminary survey of inter-American cultural activities in the United States. Nina P. Collier, director. Marjorie Sachs, research assistant. September 25, 1939. Reproduced from typewritten copy. 159 p. **[89]**

Music, p. 126-130. "A marked inadequacy in the material available on music interchange indicates that this field is much neglected."

Pan American union. *Music division.* Notes on the history of music exchange between the Americas before 1940 ... by Eugenio Pereira Salas. Washington, D. C., Pan American union, 1943. 37 p. Reproduced from type-written copy ML198.P2N6 **[90]**

Bibliographical footnotes. Appendix 1: Addenda. Appendix 2: Latin American artists appearing in Pan American union concerts, 1924 through 1939. Appendix 3: Latin American music awards at three North American expositions..

Seeger, Charles. Inter-American relations in the field of music, some basic considerations. *Mus. educ., jour.,* v. 27, no. 5 (1941), p. 17-18, 64-65 **[91]**

Also reprinted separately.

Smith, Carleton Sprague. Musicology as a means of inter-cultural understanding. *In* Proceedings of the Music teachers national association, 35th series, Pittsburgh, 1941, p. 54-57. **[91x]**

Zanzig, Augustus D. Music's good neighborliness in the Americas. *Recrea-*

tion, v. 35, no. 1 (Apr. 1941), p. 3-10,
50.   [92]

See also nos 1, 5, 6, 130

BIOGRAPHY AND CRITICISM

Baker's biographical dictionary of musicians. 4 ed., rev. and enl. New York, G. Schirmer, inc., 1940. 1234 p. ML105. B164 1940.   [93]

Edited by Gustave Reese and Gilbert Chase. Includes several Latin American composers.

Berrien, William. Latin American composers and their problems. Washington, D. C., Pan American union, 1938. 20 p. ML199.B47L3   [94]

Reprinted from the *Modern language forum,* Feb. 1937. Also published in *Bull. pan Amer. union,* Oct. and Nov. 1937. A general survey.

————. Some considerations regarding contemporary Latin American music. *In* Griffith, Charles C., *ed.,* Concerning Latin American culture, New York, Columbia university press, 1940, p. 151-180. F1408.3.G75   [95]

Written by a scholar who is not a musicologist, but who is intimately acquainted with Latin American culture, this survey forms an excellent introduction to the study of the aims, problems, attitudes and achievements of contemporary Latin American composers. The background of colonial and popular music is also lightly sketched. There is no attempt at style criticism or analysis, but the relation of Latin American music to the problems of American art as a whole is ably presented. Among composers prominently mentioned are Carlos Chávez, Villa-Lobos, Domingo Santa Cruz, Juan Carlos Paz, Carlos Gomes, The activities of Francisco Curt Lange receive considerable attention.

Copland, Aaron. The composers of South America. *Mod. music,* v. 19, no. 2 (Jan.-Feb. 1942), p. 75-82.   [96]

Discusses chiefly the contemporary composers of Argentina, Brazil and Chile, with briefer notice of other countries.

Cortijo Alahija, L. La música popular y los músicos célebres de la América Latina. Barcelona, Casa Maucci, 1919. 446 p. il. ML230.C67   [97]

A survey of music and musicians in Latin America. There is also a musical supplement (not in L. C.).

Cowell, Henry. Four little known modern composers. *Aesthete magazine,* v. 1, no. 3 (Aug. 1930), p. 1, 19-20. [98]

Includes Carlos Chávez.

Ewen, David, *ed.* Composers of today. 2 ed. New York, The H. W. Wilson Co., 1936, 332 p. (ports.) ML105.E94C6   [99]

References cited at end of each biography. Includes articles on Juan José Castro (Argentina), Carlos Chávez (México), Reynaldo Hahn (Venezuela) Heitor Villa-Lobos (Brazil).

————. Living musicians. New York, H. W. Wilson co., 1940. 390 p. ML105.-E94L6   [100]

Includes biographical data on the following Latin American musicians: Carlos Chávez, Burle Marx, Claudio Arrau, José Echaniz, Guiomar Novaës, Bernardo Segall, Magda Tagliafero, Bidú Sayão.

Grove's dictionary of music and musicians. 4 ed. Edited by H. C. Colles. Supplementary vol. London, Macmillan & co., 1940. 688 pp. il. [101]

Includes brief articles on the following Latin American composers: Alfonso Broqua, Oscar Lorenzo Fernândez, Melesio Morales (Mexican composer, 1838-1908), Eduardo Sánchez de Fuentes, Domingo Santa Cruz, Guillermo Uribe-Holguín, H. Villa-Lobos and Alberto Williams. Most of the articles are by Nicolas Slonimsky; the article on Villa-Lobos is by Alfred Loewenberg. Carlos Gomes is included in v. 2 of the regular edition.

Hull, Arthur Eaglefied, *ed.* A dictionary of modern music and musicians. London, J. M. Dent & sons; New York, E. P. Dutton & co., 1924. 544 p. ML100. D5   [102]

Includes numerous brief articles on Latin American musicians, also an article on South American Dances.

Lange, Francisco Curt, ed. Latin-American art music for the piano by twelve contemporary composers. New York, G. Schirmer, inc., 1942. 55 pp. **[103]**

The introduction includes 17 pages of biographical data on the following composers: Camargo Guarnieri, Roberto García Morillo, Juan Carlos Paz, Juan B. Plaza, Manuel M. Ponce, Andrés Sas, Carlos Suffern, Heitor Villa-Lobos, José María Castro, Alberto E. Ginastera, René Amengual, Eduardo Fabini.

Martin, Percy Alvin, ed. Who's who in Latin America. 2 ed. Stanford university, Calif., Stanford university, press; London, Humphrey Milford, Oxford university press, 1940. 558 p. F1407. W55 1940 **[104]**

Petit, Raymond. Trois musiciens hispano-américains; Allende, Broqua, Ponce. *Musique*, v. 2, no. 7 (15 Apr. 1929,) p. 844-852. **[105]**

Prat, Domingo. Diccionario biográfico, bibliográfico, histórico, crítico, de guitarras, guitarristas, danzas y cantos. Buenos Aires, Casa Romero y Fernández, 1934. 468 p. ML128.G8P7 **[106]**

Contains many biographical sketches of Latin American guitarists and composers for the guitar.

Salazar, Adolfo. Los modernos compositores sudamericanos. *Unión hispanoamericana,* v. 3 (Nov. 1918), p. 10. **[107]**

Reprinted from *El sol* (Madrid).

Slonimsky, Nicolas. Music under the southern cross. *Christian scien. mon. weekly mag. sec.* (18 Mar. 1939), p. 8-9. il. **[108]**

This article takes us through the South American countries, and discusses the foremost composers and musical activities of each.

———. South American composers. *Mus. Amer.,* v. 60, no. 3 (10 Feb. 1940),

p. 281, 286-287. il. (ports.) Also reprinted separately **[109]**

Brief biographical sketches.

See also nos. 42, 44, 52, 54, 63, 65, 68

AESTHETICS

Barrenechea, Mariano Antonio. Historia estética de la música. 3 ed. Buenos Aires, Editorial Claridad, 1941. 535 p. ML160.B15 **[110]**

Charlot, Jean. Art from the Mayans to Disney. New York and London, Sheed and Ward, 1939. 285 p. N7445.C44 **[111]**

Chapter 5, *Aesthetics of Indian dances,* p. 48-56, studies the elements and composition of Indian dances.

González, Joaquín V. Música y danza nativas. *In his* Obras completas, v. 20, Buenos Aires, Imprenta Mercatali, 1936, p. 21-48. F2846.G628 **[112]**

General discussion of the aesthetics of musical culture among the various modern peoples of South America. Several examples of Indian song texts throughout the article.

Hurtado, Leopoldo. La música contemporánea y sus problemas. Santa Fe, Imp. de la Universidad, 1936. 34 p. ML197.H96M8 **[113]**

Lange, Francisco Curt. Arte musical latino-americano, raza y asimilación. *Bol. lat. am. mús.,* v. 1 (Apr. 1935), p. 13-28 **[114]**

Pahissa, Jaime. Naturaleza de la música y de la creación musical. Santa Fe, Impr. de la Universidad nacional del litoral, 1928. 22 p. (Universidad nacional del litoral. Instituto social. Publicación. Extensión universitaria. no. 38.) ML3800.P24N3 **[115]**

Richard Lavalle, Enrique. La herencia musical. *Correo mus. sud-am.,* v. 1, no. 22 (25 Aug 1915), p 10. **[116]**

Stresses the importance of folk music as material for artistic creation.

Salazar, Adolfo. America, north and south. *Mod. music,* v. 16, no. 2 (1939), p. 75-82.   **[117]**

——. Música y sociedad en el siglo xx, ensayo de crítica y de estética desde el punto de vista de su función social. México, Impreso y distribuido para la Casa de España en México por el Fondo de cultura económica, 1939. 221 p. ML 3795.S23M8   **[118]**

——. Las grandes estructuras de la música. México, La casa de España en México, 1940. 191 p. ML3795.S23G7   **[119]**

——. La rosa de los vientos en la música europea; los conceptos fundamentales en la historia del arte musical. México, D. F., Ediciones de la Orquesta sinfónica de México, 1940. 274 p. (music) ML3800.S16R7   **[120]**

Salinas Cossío, Guillermo. La música en la América Latina y su nacionalización. *Bol. lat. am. mús.,* v. 2 (1936), p. 157-162   **[121]**

Saminsky, Lazare. Below the equator: Indo-Latin forms and figures. *Mus. amer.,* v. 61, no. 3 (10 Feb. 1941), p. 219-220. il.   **[122]**

    The author traces four main currents in South American music: (a) literary folklorism: (b) musical folklorism; (c) cosmopolitan current; (d) radical modernism (Juan Carlos Paz of Argentina and Domingo Santa Cruz of Chile). Pays special attention to the work of Villa-Lobos, in which Saminsky finds a basic Indo-Latin core. There are musical fragments from compositions by Andrés Sas, Lorenzo Fernández, Jacobo Ficher, Juan Carlos Paz, Domingo Santa Cruz and Villa-Lobos.

——. Music of our day; essentials and prophecies. New enl. ed. New York, Thomas Y. Crowell Co., 1939. 390 p. il ML197.S18 1939.   **[123]**

    Includes a section on Latin American music, p. 188-192.

Struckhof, Wadim von. La música como factor de cultura. Buenos Aires,

Librería académica Poblet hermanos, 1936. 101 p. ML3845.S93M88   **[124]**

    First published in German, Buenos Aires, 1935.

Williams, Alberto. Literatura y estética musicales. Obras completas. Buenos Aires, Ed. La quena, 1941. 2 v.   **[125]**

    Vol. 1: Versos líricos; v. 2: Pensamientos sobre la música.

See also nos. 149, 153, 235

EDUCATION

Allende, Pedro Humberto. La educación musical. *Bol. lat. am. mús.,* v. 1 (Apr. 1935), p. 163-175.   **[126]**

Granja, Luis Aníbal. El valor de la música en la educación. *Bol. lat. am. mús.,* v. 4 (Oct. 1938), p. 259-266.   **[127]**

Lange, Francisco Curt. La difusión radio-eléctrica como medio de educación de las masas y como factor de difusión cultural y científica. *Bol. lat. am. mús.,* v. 2 (Apr. 1936), p. 131-142.   **[128]**

Mutschler B., Luis. La exploración de talento musical. *Rev. arte,* v. 4, no. 19 (1938), p. 22-29.   **[129]**

    Scientific and methodical means of determining musical talent. Charts and bibliography.

Ruddick, J. Leon. Music for uniting the Americas. *Mus. educ. jour.,* v. 28, no. 3 (Jan. 1942), p. 10-11.   **[130]**

RADIO

Barbour, Philip L. Commercial and cultural broadcasting in Mexico. *In* Annals of the American academy of political and social science, v. 212 (Mar. 1940), p. 94-102.   **[131]**

——. Open questions in inter-American broadcasting. *In* Annals of the American academy of political and social

science, v. 213 (Jan 1941), p. 116-124.
[132]

Music of the new world. Handbook, vol. 1, 1942-1943. New York, published for the National broadcasting company by the Southern music publishing company, inc., 1942. 52 p. [133]

"Research director and author of the Handbook, Gilbert Chase, Music Division, Library of Congress." A listener's manual for the broadcast series of the Inter-American University of the Air. This volume includes background material, with bibliographies and record lists, for the first 15 programs, from Pre-Columbian music to the songs of the wars for Latin American independence.

——. Handbook, vol. 2, 1943. New York, Published for the National broadcasting company by the Southern music publishing company, inc., 1943. 76 p. [134]

"Research director and author of the Handbook, Gilbert Chase, Music Division, Library of Congress." A listener's manual for the broadcast series of the Inter-American University of the Air. This volume, complete with bibliographies and record lists, embraces American music from the introduction of romanticism to the music of today, discussing Negro and Indian influences, the lyric theatre, orchestras, etc.

See also no. 83.

NATIONAL ANTHEMS

Anthems of the united nations. Compiled and arranged by Felix Guenther. New York, Edward B. Marks music corp., 1942. 56 p. [135]

Includes the national anthems of Brazil, Costa Rica, Cuba, Dominican Republic, El Salvador, Guatemala, Haiti, Honduras, Mexico, Nicaragua, Panama.

Benter, Charles, comp. and arr. Lieut. Charles Benter's book of national airs. New York, Carl Fischer, inc., 1926. [136]

Arranged for band.

Lima, Emirto de. Folklore colombiano. Barranquilla, 1942, 210 p. ML3575.C7 L5 [137]

Los himnos y cantos patrióticos, p. 105-118.

Monserrat, Gabriel. El poema del himno nacional argentino (estudio historial y crítico). Buenos Aires, Librería del Colegio, 1932. 565 p. ML3575.A7M7. [138]

Includes data on the national anthems of all the Latin American countries.

Murillo, Ernesto, ed. National anthems of the countries of North, Central and South America. Chicago, New York, Clayton F. Summy co., 1935. 72 p. M1627.M95N3 [139]

New edition, 1942.

Ofrenda de Venezuela en el primer centenario de la batalla de Ayacucho. Caracas, Litografía del comercio, 1924. 130 p. M1686.035 [140]

Includes the music of the national anthems of Venezuela, Bolivia, Colombia, Ecuador and Peru. Music for voice and piano, and band scores. Includes also the music of the hymns of the Venezuelan states (voice and piano only).

Sousa, John Philip, comp. National patriotic and typical airs of all lands. Philadelphia, Harry Coleman, 1890. 283 p. M1627.S72C [141]

Includes national anthems of most of the Latin American countries.

Treharne, Bryceson. National anthems of the united nations ... Boston, Boston music co., 1943. 132 p. [142]

Music.

FOLK AND PRIMITIVE MUSIC

(A) GENERAL

Adams, Franklin. Indigenous music of Latin America and its modern development. *Mus. advance,* v. 18, no. 3 (Oct. 1930), p. 6-9. ports. [143]

Aretz-Thiele, Isabel. El velorio del angelito. *Folklore,* v. 1, no. 3 (1941), p. 27-28.   **[144]**

With melody and text of one song. When a child under seven deid, it was customary to sing and dance around the corpse. This was to rejoice in the belief that the child would go straight to heaven and immediately become an angel.

Arvey, Verna. M u s i c a l potentialities in Cuba and South America. *Mus. cour.,* v. 112, no. 11 (14 Mar. 1936), p. 6, 27.   **[145]**

Contains n u m e r o u s references to folk music of Cuba, Brazil, Peru, Chile, Colombia and Argentina, especially in its relation to the art music of those countries.

Azevedo, Luiz Heitor Corrêa de. Dois pequenos estudios de folclore musical: Algunas reflexões sobre folcmúsica no Brasil, caminhos da música sul-americana. Rio de Janeiro, Typ. do 'Jornal do commercio", Rodriguez & cia., 1938. 43 p. il. (music) ML3575.C8D6   **[146]**

First part deals with Brazil; 2nd part with Brazil and the other South American countries. Contains 7 musical examples.

Béclard d'Harcourt, Marguerite. Las fuentes de inspiración musical popular en América del Sud. *Rev. música,* v. 2, no. 1 (July 1928), p. 29-33.   **[147]**

Boggs, Ralph Steele. Bibliography of Latin American folklore. New York, H. W. Wilson co., 1940. 109 p. Z5984.-L4B7   **[148]**

"Poetry, music, dance and games", p. 54-64.

Cabrera, Ana S. Rutas de América; el folklore, la música, la historia, la leyenda, las costumbres. Buenos Aires, Peuser, ltda., 1941. 242 p. il. F1408.-3.C2   **[149]**

Part 3, *Panorama de la música folklórica sudamericana,* deals with indigenous and colonial music. Part 4, *Del folklore chileno,* includes *Música popular* and *El arte musical de Araucania.* Part 5 is *La canción y la danza populares en México.*

There are also numerous references to folk dances in Part 6, *Supervivencia del folklore en las costumbres.* There are numerous illustrations of musicians, dancers and instruments. Notation of 9 tunes.

Canal Feijoo, Bernardo. F o l k l o r e. *Bol. lat. am. mus.,* v. 3 (1937), p. 43-46.   **[150]**

Observations on the cultural and aesthetic significance of folklore.

Canciones del terruño. Libro de canciones modernas. Primera edición. Contiene canciones españolas, mexicanas, colombianas, de zarzuelas, operetas, jotas, canciones populares, aires típicos mexicanos, corridos y todas las canciones más escogidas y en boga en la actualidad. Editado por José Gras. Los Ángeles, Calif., Librería española, 1925. 118 p. PQ6210.C3   **[151]**

Celebración del primer congreso musical folklórico del Caribe. *In* Unión interamericana del Caribe. Memorias de la segunda reunión, Ciudad Trujillo, 31 Mayo-6 Junio 1940, p. 143.   **[152]**

Article no. 43. Citation from files of Pan American union.

Chávez, Carlos. El arte popular y el no-popular. *Musicalia,* v. 2, no. 7 (July-Aug. 1929), p. 6-9.   **[153]**

Points out that so-called popular music is "popular" only in relation to an arbitrary standard of values.

Cortijo Alahija, L. La música popular y los músicos célebres de la América Latina. Barcelona, Casa Maucci, 1919. 446 p. il. ML230.C67   **[154]**

General survey of Latin American folk music, with numerous musical examples.

Donostia, José Antonio de. A propos du nombre musical g r é g o r i e n de Dom Mocquereau et de la chanson populaire espagnole et américaine. Paris, Société et l i b r a i r i e Saint-François d'Assise, 1930. 11 p. ML3710.D7   **[155]**

Quotes the song *E n c a n t a d o r a   s i r e n a* from M. Béclard d'Harcourt, *Mélodies populaires indiennes.*

Folk songs and stories of the Americas. *Bul. pan. amer. union,* v. 71, no. 2 (Feb. 1937). **[156]**

Includes music of two *bambucos* from Colombia (Spanish words with English translation), p. 148-149; *jarabe tapatío* and *Las mañanitas costeñas* from Mexico, arranged for piano, with Spanish words and English translation, p. 178-179; and four melodies from Panama, p. 182-183. Also reprinted separately [no. 185].

Frank, Waldo. America hispana; south of us. New York, Garden city publishing co., 1940. 388 p. il. F1408.F863 **[157]**

First published in 1931. Refers to music and dances, p. 29, 30, 42, 44-46, 79, 80, 97, 98, 100, 114-116, 118, 231, 232, 237, 238.

Friedenthal, Albert. Musik, tanz und dichtung bei den Kreolen Amerikas. Berlin-Wilmersdorf, H. Schnippel, 1913. 328 p. il. ML3575.F7 **[158]**

The first part of the author's *Stimmen der völker.* Contains about 100 tunes, some of them harmonized. The text of them only in German translation. Covers Mexico, Central America, the West Indies and South America.

——. Stimmen der völker in liedern, tänzen und charakterstücken. I. abteilung. Die volksmusik der Kreolen Amerikas. Berlin, Schlesinger'sche buch-und musikhandlung (Rob. Lic. nau), 1911. M1680.F84 **[159]**

González, Manuel Pedro. Racial factors in Latin American music. *Int. amer. quart.,* v. 3, no. 4 (Oct. 1941), p. 44-52. **[160]**

Deals with the component elements of Latin American folk music. Also issued as an offprint by the Pan American Union under the title, *Latin America, a musical melting pot.*

Hague, Eleanor. America's indigenous music. *Mex. life,* v. 15, no. 5 (1939), p. 23-25. **[161]**

——. Latin-American folk music. *In* Thompson, Oscar, *ed.* The inernation-

al cycloperia of music and musicians. New York, Dodd Mead & co., 1939, p. 575-576. ML100.T4715 **[162]**

——. Latin American music, past and present. Santa Ana, Calif., The fine arts press, 1934. 98 p. ML199.H14. **[163]**

Contains numerous references to folk music, with many musical examples.

——. Music in Latin America. *Bull. pan amer. union,* v. 68 (1943), p. 556-560. il. **[164]**

Brief discussion of Indian music, and popular songs and dances. Includes illustrations of native musicians, and of a couple dancing the *zamacueca.*

Hare, Maud Cuney. Folk music of the Creoles. *Mus. observer,* v. 19, no. 9 (Sept.-Oct. 1920), p. 16-18; v. 19, no. 10 (Nov. 1920), p. 12-14. **[165]**

Includes a section on Spanish-Creole music.

Hulbert, Winifred. Latin American backgrounds. New York, Friendship press, 1935. 209 p. F1410.H85 **[166]**

Impressions of the folk music, p. 154.

Jijena Sánchez, Rafael. Hilo de oro, hilo de plata; selección ... de letras y cantares infantiles recogidos de la tradición popular hispanoamericana. Buenos Aires, Ediciones Buenos Aires, 1940. 189 p. PZ74.3.15 **[167]**

A collection of folk verses, containing 167 items.

Lange, Francisco Curt. Roberto Lehmann Nitsche. *Bol. lat. am. mús.,* v. 4 Oct 1938), p. 797-798. **[168]**

——. Sistemas de investigación folklórica y el empleo del acervo folklórico en la música artística. *Bol. lat. am. mus.,* v. 2 (1936), p. 143-156. **[169]**

A discussion of basic methods in musicofolkloric investigations.

Lavín, Carlos. El cromatismo en la música indígena sudamericana. *Gaceta mus.,* v. 1, no. 3 (Mar. 1928), p. 28-

34; v. 1, no. 4 (Apr. 1928), p. 21-31.
                                    [170]
Fifteen musical examples.

——. La musique en Amérique latine.
Guide concert, v. 11, nos. 16-23 (1925),
p. 453-454, 485-486, 517-519, 549-550,
581-582, 645-646, 677-679. il.   [171]
A general survey, devoted largely to
pre-Hispanic and primitive music, with 14
musical examples.

Leça, Armando. Do folclorista. *Rev. bras.
mús.* v. 6 (1939), p. 43-44.   [172]
Discusses the rôle of the musical folklorist in terms of methods and objectives.

Lima, Emirto de. Música panamericana. *In* Reys, Emma Romero Santos
Fonseca de Câmara, Divulgaçao musical. Lisboa, 1940. v. 5, p. 405-419.
ML42.L5R6   [173]
Treats of Latin American folk music
in general.

——. Pregones y pregoneros. *Bol. lat.
am. mús.,* v. 4 (Bogotá, 1938), p. 635-
647.   [174]
A description of street-vendors' cries,
with 17 musical examples.

López Vega, C. Poesía popular de la
América española. Madrid, J. Pueyo,
1924. 46 p.   [175]

Mann, W. Volk und kultur Latein-
amerikas. Hamburg, Brochek & co.,
1927. 301 p. F1408.3.M28   [176]
Folk elements and characteristics in the
music of South America, p. 250-251.

Marsh, William Sewall. Musical Spain
from A to Z ... Providence, Campbell
music co., 1929. 52 p. ML106.S7M3
                                    [177]
Includes references to Latin American
folk music forms.

Menéndez Pidal, Ramón. Las primeras
noticias de romances tradicionales en
América, y especialmente en Colombia. *In* Habana, Publicaciones de la

Secretaría de educación, 1935, p. 23-
27. F1787.V31   [178]
Discusses the earliest recorded evidence
of the presence of traditional Spanish ballads in South America.

——. El romancero; teorías e investigaciones. Madrid, Editorial Páez, 1928.
229 p. PQ6089.M28   [179]
Includes: Los romances tradicionales en
América.

——. Los romances de América, y otros
estudios. Buenos Aires-México, Espasa-
Calpe Argentina, S. A., 1939. 187 p.
4 ed. 1945, 188 p. PQ6089.M33 [180]
One of the fundamental studies in the
field of the Spanish-American ballad.

La música a través del tiempo. *Brú-
jula,* San Juan, v. 3, nos. 9-10 (Nov.
1937), p. 182-188.   [181]
A general history of music, with a section at the end, *América,* dealing with folk
and indigenous music of the Western
Hemisphere (mainly South America).

La música en la Habana. Ana S. de
Cabrera, recital de canciones folklóricas sudamericanas. *Musicalia,* no. 15-
16 (Jan.-Apr. 1931), p. 19-21. [182]
Revue of a lecture-recital of South American folksongs by Ana. S. de Cabrera,
with an account of her folkloric investigations.

La música popular latino americana.
México, D. F. Secretaría de educación
pública, 192-? 28 p. Mimeographed.
ML199.S33M8   [183]
Deals with the indigenous music of the
Andean region; classification of Incan
(Peruvian) melodies; rhythms of Indian
music (Andean); folk dances of the In-
dians; folk music in Venezuela (p. 10-
12), Colombia (p. 12), Bolivia (p. 12-15),
Chile (p. 15-16), Argentina (6. 16-22),
Antilles (p. 22-26).

Outes, Felix Faustino. La música y
nuestro folk-lore, respuesta a la encuesta de *Nosotros.* Buenos Aires,
1918. 3 p. F2230.1.M9093   [184]
Reprinted from *Nosotros,* v. 29, p. 230-
233. Considers the definition of folklore,

the development of South American folklore, and the important place of music therein.

Pan American union. Folk songs and stories of the Americas. Washington, D. C., Pan American union, 1943. 62 p. ML3549.P2F6 **[185]**

Includes music. Reprinted from the Feb. 1937 issue of the *Bulletin* of the Pan American union. Cf. item no. 156.

——. *Music division.* Recordings of Latin American songs and dances... By Gustavo Durán. Washington, D. C., Music Division, Pan American union, 1942. 65 p. (*Its* Music series, no. 3.) ML156.P17R3 **[186]**

Arranged alphabetically by countries, each section including a brief description of the principal folk music forms of the country concerned. There are numerous references to musical instruments.

Ratner, Conrad H. Justin Elie and the revival of the music of the natives of Latin America. *Mus. monitor,* v. 14, no. 2 (1923), p. 7-8. **[187]**

Includes one example of a drum rhythm.

Robertson, Willliam Spence. History of the Latin American nations. New York, London, D .Appleton co., 1932. 821 p. F1410.R543 **[188]**

Folk and Indian music, p. 201-202. See index under the various Latin American countries for further material on music and dance.

Rojas, Ricardo. El arte americano. *Mús. de Amér.,* v. 1, no. 1 (Mar. 1920), p. 5-12. **[189]**

References to folk music, p. 11.

——. Cosmópolis. Paris, Ed. Garnier, 1908. 205 p. **[190]**

Includes: Romances tradicionales en América.

Salas Viú, Vicente. Un camino cerrado: el folklore. *Sur,* v. 9 (1939), p. 80-87. **[191]**

The author is a Spanish musician now living in Chile.

Sánchez de Fuentes, Eduardo. La música aborigen de América. Habana, Molina y cía., 1938. 61 p. ML3547. S25M9 **[192]**

Sanjinés, A. El alma de la raza (Interpretación de la música indígena). *Senderos,* v. 3 (1935), p. 367-374. **[193]**

Santos, Carlos. El laud hispano-americano. Contiene las canciones más selectas y modernas. Canciones españolas, mexicanas, colombianas, operetas, zarzuelas. Los Ángeles, Casa Santos, 1921. 160 p. PQ7084.S33 **[194]**

Without music.

Simon, Alicia. Musik in Latein Amerika. *Signale,* v. 85, no. 40 (1927), p. 1368-1370. **[195]**

Deals with the character of South and Central American music, the elements of folk-lore and the African influence. Mentions the names of outstanding Latin American composers.

Slonimsky, Nicolas. The folklore of Latin America's music. *Christian scien. mon. weekly mag. sec.* (18 July 1942), p. 8-9. il. **[196]**

A general survey, with bibliographical data.

——. El folklore musical de la América Latina. *Rev. mus. mex.,* v. 2, no. 4 (21 Aug. 1942), p. 79-82. **[197]**

Originally published in the *Christian Science Monitor.* Cf. no. 196.

Smith, Carleton Sprague. The song makers. *Surv. graph.,* v. 30, no. 3 (Mar. 1941), p. 179-183. **[198]**

Includes brief comments on Latin American folk music and dancing.

Spell, Lota M. Notes on music in South America. *Southw. mus.,* v. 4, no. 2 (1937), p. 4, 12. **[199]**

Brief comments on the chief popular songs and dances.

Telles de Menezes, Julieta. Quelques musiciens et folkloristes d'Amérique espagnole. *Rev. musicale*, v. 12, nos. 117-118 (July-Aug. 1931), p. 205-207. **[200]**

Traversari-Salazar, Pietro P. L'arte in America. Storia dell'arte musicale indigena e popolare. *In* Atti del Congresso internazionale di scienze storiche (Roma, 1-9 Aprile 1903), v. 7, sezione 4 (1905), p. 117-129. D3.A2 1903 **[201]**

Covers Mexico, Cuba, Central and South America. A musical supplement contains 17 tunes from Mexico, Argentina, Peru, Bolivia, Ecuador and Venezuela.

Vallejo, Carlos María de. Los maderos de San Juan; glosario de rondas y canciones infantiles. Cádiz, Impr. de S. Repeto, 1932. 87 p. PZ74.3.V3 **[202]**

Contains music: 9 tunes harmonized by Luis Cluzeau Mortet. "Canciones y rondas trasladadas a América por España, recogidas de memoria en los coros y juegos infantiles, que se conservan por tradición, hasta el presente, en aquellas tierras", p. 81.

Vega, Carlos. Escalas pentatónicas en Sudamérica—Los estudios del músico cuzqueño Leandro Alviña. *La Prensa*, v. 69, no. 24,926 (5 June 1938), sec. 3, p. 2. **[203]**

Includes music.

———. La escala pentatónica en Sudamérica—Cómo fue descubierta. *La Prensa*, v. 69, no. 24,772 (1 Jan. 1938), sec. 2, p. 3. **[204]**

———. Música indígena americana. *An. inst. pop. conf.*, v. 16 (1931), p. 39-56. **[205]**

Includes music.

———. Panorama de la música popular sudamericana. *La Prensa*, v. 60, no. 24,801 (30 Jan. 1938), sec. 2, p. 2. **[206]**

Reprinted in *Ars*, v. 1, no. 2 (Sept. 1940), p. 9-11. Includes music.

Zanzig, Augustus D. Some collections of folk songs in the library of the Pan American union. *In* Conference on inter-American relations in the field of music, Report of the committee, Washington, D. C., 1940, p. 92-93. **[207]**

(B) AMERINDIAN

1. *Pre-Columbian*

Danzel, Theodor Wilhelm. Handbuch der präkolumbischen kulturen in Lateinamerika. Hamburg, Hanseatische verlagsanstalt, 1937. 136 p. il. E65-D253 **[208]**

Illustration of old Peruvian Pan-pipe, p. 122; of old Peruvian trumpet, p. 115. High position of musicians in ancient Mexico, p. 26. Brief references to music and dance in connection with religion.

Harcourt, Raoul d'. Les civilisations disparues, l'Amérique avant Colomb. Paris, Stock, 1925, 152 p. E61.H25 **[209]**

Dance, music and musical instruments, with special reference to those of Mexico and Peru, p. 73-82.

Harcourt, Raoul and Marguerite d'. La musique indienne chez les anciens civilisés d'Amérique *In:* Encyclopédie de la musique et dictionnaire du conservatoire, partie 1, p. 3337-3371, Paris Librairie Delagrave, 1922. ML-100.E5 **[210]**

This article is divided into two parts. Part 1, by Raoul d'Harcourt, is entitled *Les instruments de musique des Mexicains et des Péruviens.—Place que tenait la musique chez ces peuples.* Part 2, by Marguerite Béclard d'Harcourt, is *Le folklore musical de la region andine; Equateur, Pérou, Bolivie.* See separate entries under these authors.

Marchesini, Cesare G. Musica degli antichi popoli americani. *Mus. d'oggi*, v. 22, no. 5 (May 1940), p. 130-131. **[211]**

Mendoza, Vicente T. Música precolombina de América. *Bol. lat. am. mús.*, v. 4 (1938), p. 235-257. **[212]**

Text of a lecture delivered in Mexico,

D. F., on Oct. 24, 1934, with 14 musical examples.

Sentenach y Cabañas, Narciso. Ensayo sobre la América precolombina. Toledo, J. Peláez, 1898. 187 p. E58.S47 **[213]**

Music, p. 67-68. Citation from files of Pan American Union.

See also nos. 44, 54, 56, 59, 170, 192, 203, 204. See under Mexico, *Amerindian,* and Peru, *Amerindian* (Pre-Columbian).

2. *Post-Columbian*

Arguedas, Alcides. Pueblo enfermo. Santiago, Ediciones Ercilla, 1937. 281 p. F3310.A753 **[214]**

Qualities of Indo-hispanic music, p. 97.

Bahlis, Jorge. Artes amerindias. Pôrto Alegre, Edição do autor, 1938. 189 p. il. E59.A7B3 **[215]**

Amerindian dances and musical instruments, p. 91-103.

Barber, Edwin A. Indian music. *Amer. naturalist,* v. 17 (1883), p. 267-274. **[216]**

Includes descriptions of musical instruments of the Indians of Central and South America.

Cappa, Ricardo. Estudios críticos acerca de la dominación española en América. Madrid, G. del Amo, 1889-1897. v. 13, Bellas Artes. F1410.C24 **[217]**

Music, p. 283-341, containing information on: Incan music, *yaravis,* musical education, singing. There is also a chart showing the distribution of musical instruments among the Uruguay, Paraná, Chiquitos, Mojos peoples. Dance, equitation and music, p. 325-330.

Embree, Edwin Rogers. Indians of the Americas. Boston, Houghton, Mifflin co., 1939. 260 p. il. E58.E63 **[218]**

See index for numerous references to music and musical instruments.

García, Gregorio. Origen de los Indios

del nuevo mundo. Valencia, P. P. Mey, 1607. 535 p. E61.G12 **[218x]**

See especially bk. 2, ch. 2, and bk. 3, ch. 3.

Karsten, Rafael. The civilization of the South American Indians, with special reference to magic and religion. London, K. Paul, Trench, Trubner & co., ltd.; New York, A. A. Knopf, 1926. 540 p. F2230.1.R3K2 **[219]**

Description of mask-dances, p. 214-222; musical instruments, p. 223-227.

Krickeberg, Walter. Los Totonaca. México, Talleres Gráficos del Museo Nacional, 1933. 241 p. F1219.K834 **[220]**

Translated from the German by Porfirio Aguirre. References to festivals, music and dancing, with lengthy description of the *juego del volador,* p. 71-75.

Kunike, Hugo. Der fisch als fruchtbarkeitssymbol bei den Waldindianern Südamerikas. *Anthropos,* v. 7 (1912), p. 206-229. **[221]**

Song texts of the magic dances, p. 209-211, with 2 musical examples and words of 3 additional chants (1 translated from the Indian into German).

Lejeal, L. Note sur la musique et la magie des primitifs chez les Américains. *Rev. musicale,* v. 7, no. 7 (1 Apr. 1907), p. 182-184. **[222]**

Mentions several sources of research on music in the religious rites of the Indians. List of instruments used by the magician.

Radin, Paul. Indians of South America. Garden City, Doubleday, Doran & co., 1942. 324 p. front., plates. (The American museum of natural history. Science series.) F2230.R3 **[223]**

Bibliography, p. 307-313. Musical instruments: Drum, p. 122, 124 ff.; flute, p. 135; pan-pipes, p. 122 n. Mask dances, p. 133 ff., 199 ff. (See also references to ceremonies and rituals in index.)

Raygada, Carlos. Indian and mestizan music. *Panam. mag.,* v. 2, no. 4 (July-Sept. 1941), p. 44-47. **[224]**

Rivet, Paul. La musique indienne en Amérique. *La nature*, v. 69 (1927), p. 244-247.   **[225]**

Stern, Philip. La musique des Indiens d'Amérique. *Rev. musicale*, v. 4, no. 8 (1923), p. 167-169.   **[226]**

Review of "Concerts de la Revue Musicale", Paris.

Tastevin, Constant. Le poisson symbole de fécondité ou de fertilité chez les Indiens de l'Amérique du Sud. *Anthropos*, v. 9, nos. 3-4 (May.-Aug. 1914), p. 405-417.   **[227]**

Dances-as celebration of successful hunts, as prayers for abundance, etc., p. 408-413; musical examples of accompaniment to the Pirawawá dance; musical instrument, the *calebasse*, p. 413. 2 Indian chants, with musical examples, p. 415-417.

Wegner, Richard N. Indianer rassen und vergangene kulturen. Stuttgart, F. Enke, 1934. 320 p. F2229.W34 **[228]**

Life of the Indians of Bolivia, Peru, North Argentina, Yucatan, and shorter accounts of Mayan life. Spirit dance, musical instruments, p. 35-52.

Wilkes, Charles. Narrative of the United States exploring expedition. During the years 1838, 1839, 1840, 1841, 1842. Philadelphia, Lea and Blanchard, 1845. 5 v. il. Q115.W66   **[229]**

Vol. 1 has 2 brief tunes, p. 125-127.

Wissler, Clark. The American Indian; an introduction to the anthropology of the New World. New York, D. G. McMurtrie, 1917. 435 p. il. E58.W8 **[230]**

Music and musical instruments, p. 145-148. Later editions published in 1922 and 1938.

See also nos. 44, 54, 149, 183, 192, 203, 204, 205.

(C) DANCES

Akora, C. R. Argentine, Patagonian, and Chilean sketches with a few notes on Uruguay. London, Harrison, 1893. **[231]**

References to dances, p. 45-46.

Blasis, Carlo. Manuel complet de la danse. Paris, Librairie encyclopédique de Roret, 1830, 412 p. ML3420.B64   **[232]**

Spanish dances, p. 31-52, which includes descriptions of the *fandango, bolero* and *cachucha*.

——. Notes upon dancing, historical and practical. London, M. Delaporte, 1847. 190 p. GV1601.D64   **[233]**

The *chica*, p. 24-26; *fandango*, p. 26; *sarao*, p. 32-33; more about Spanish dances, p. 49-55.

Cardoza y Aragón, Luis. Flor y misterio de la danza. *Cuad. Amer.*, v. 1, no. 1 (Jan-Feb. 1942), p. 208-216. **[234]**

Folk dances, of Spanish America. *Bull. pan amer. union*, v. 73, no. 11 (1939), p. 652-658. il.   **[235]**

"Based chiefly on 'Danza' by Luis Alberto Sánchez, published in the 'Revista de Educación, Santiago, Chile." Cf. no. 243.

Includes music of 3 dances: *pericón, huayño* and *sanjuanito*. One of the first writings to emphasize the importance of the dance for the cultural understanding of Latin America.

García, Rolando V., Luciano C. Croatto, and Alfredo A. Martín. Historia de la música latinoamericana. 3er. año nacional. Buenos Aires, Librería "Perlado", 1938. 231 p. il. ML199.G3H5 **[236]**

In this succinct history of Latin American music there are several references to dance, both in its musical and choreographic aspects, viz: Bolivian dances, p. 43-46; the *contradanza*, the *danza* and the *danzón* of Cuba, p. 63-73; native dances of Peru, p. 99-103; characteristic dances of Venezuela and Colombia, p. 116-120; native Indian dances of Mexico, p. 131-136; Mexican folk dances, p. 143-144; native dances of Chile, p. 177-178; Brazilian dances, p. 215-217.

Hughes, R. M. (La Meri). South American dances, *Dancing times*, n. s., nos. 246-252 (Apr.-Sept. 1931), p. 332-335, 421-424, 514-519. il. **[237]**

Labastille, Irma. Under the southern stars. New York, Chicago, Silver, Burdett co., 1941. ML52.L2U5 1941. **[238]**

A pamphlet consisting of 8 scenes dealing with Latin American history and contemporary life. Includes directions for dancing.

Magriel, Paul David. A bibliography of dancing. New York, H. W. Wilson co., 1936. 229 p. front., facsims. Z7514.D2M2 **[239]**

Mexico, p. 58-59; West Indies, p. 59; Central and South America, p. 59; South and Central American Indians, p. 60. For more material on the dances of Mexico, Jamaica, West Indies, Cuba, Central and South America, consult the *Second Cumulated Supplement,* p. 28-29.

Pan American union. *Music division.* Recordings of Latin American songs and dances; an annotated selected list of popular and folk music. By Gustavo Durán. Washington, D. C., Music division, Pan American union, 1942. 65 p. (*Its* Music series, no. 3) ML156.P17R3 **[240]**

Includes descriptions of dances, notation of rhythms, bibliography and index of terms.

Prat, Domingo. Diccionario biográfico, bibliográfico, histórico, crítico, de guitarras, guitarristas, danzas y cantos. Buenos Aires, Casa Romero y Fernández, 1934. 468 p. ML128.G8P7 **[241]**

The section on *Danzas* (p. 425-452) includes many descriptive notes on Latin American folk dances.

Sachs, Curt. World history of the dance. Translated by Bessie Schönberg. New York, W. W Norton & co., 1937. 469 p. il. GV7601.S27 **[242]**

Refers to the American origin of the *chacona* (p. 371) and the *zarabanda* (p. 367). Describes the *batuque* of Brazil, p. 369. References to the *tango,* p. 308, 445; and to the *zamacueca,* p. 96. Consult also the index, under Brazil, Chile, Mexico, etc.

Sánchez, Luis Alberto. Vida y pasión en la cultura de América. Santiago de Chile, Ediciones Ercilla, 1935. 135 p. F1408.3S35 **[243]**

Ch. 5: Danza. Cf. no. 236.

Slonimsky, Nicolas. Whence the dance in Latin America? *Christian scien. mon. weekly mag. sec.* (8 May 1943), p. 4, 14. **[243x]**

Discusses the combination of Negro, Iberian and Indian influences in South American dances, and goes into some detail describing the *habanera,* the *tango,* etc. Illustrations of the *tamborito* (of Panama) and the *marinera* of Peru, as well as a map showing the distribution of Latin American dances.

Talamón, Gastón O. Creación del arte coreográfico argentino. *Mundo mus.* (Apr. 1937), p. 4. **[244]**

Tango. *In* Enciclopedia universal ilustrada europeo-americana. Barcelona, 1921, v. 59, p. 353. **[245]**

Brief article on the origin and form of the tango, with one musical example. Also states that in Honduras "tango" is the name of an indigenous percussion instrument.

See also 44, 149, 164, 183, 198, 199, 215, 219, 220, 221, 227, 228, 276, 280, 281, 290.

(D) INSTRUMENTS

Baglioni, S. Contributo alla conoscenza della musica naturale. *Atti soc. rom. antrop.,* v. 15 (1910), p. 313-360. il. **[246]**

An acoustical study of the marimba, panpipes, and other primitive instruments.

Baker, Theodore. Uber die musik der Nordamerikanischen wilden. Leipzig, Breitkopf & Härtel, 1882. 82 p. ML3557.B161 **[247]**

Percussion instruments in Mexico and Central America, p. 51-54; panpipes in Mexico, Central America and Peru, p. 56; wind instruments among the Mexicans, p. 57; lack of string instruments in Mexico, with a note on the stringed *tinya,* of Peru, p. 57.

Balfour, Henry. The natural history of the bow; a chapter in the development history of stringed instruments of music. Primitive types. Oxford, Clarendon Press, 1899. 87 p. il. ML755.B18 **[248]**

The West Indies, p. 38-47; South America, p. 47-52.

Brown, Mary, and William Adams Brown. Musical instruments and their homes. A complete catalogue of the collection of musical instruments now in the possession of Mrs. J. Crosby Brown. New York, Dodd, Mead and co., 1888. 380 p. il. ML460.B87 **[249]**

Instruments of Mexico, Central and South America, p. 301-329.

Edgerly, Beatrice. From the hunter's bow; the history and romance of musical instruments. New York, G. P. Putnam's sons, 1942. 491 p. il. **[250]**

Ch. 7, Indians of the Americas: A. The Inca (p. 34-41); B. The Chiriqui—Maya—Aztec (Mexico and Central America), p. 41-56.

González Bravo, Antonio. Trompeta, flauta travesera, tambor y charango. *Bol. lat. am. mús.,* v. 4 (1938), p. 167-175. **[251]**

A study of primitive instruments in South America, with 10 illustrations and the notation of 3 tunings.

Izikowitz, Karl Gustav. Musical and other sound instruments of the South American Indians. Göteborgs Kungliga Vetenskaps och Vitterhets-Samhället. Handlingar. Följden 5, ser. A, v. 5 (1936), p. 1-453. il. ML486.I8M8 **[252]**

Jackson, J. Wilfred. Shell-trumpets and their distribution in the old and new world. Memoirs and proceedings of the Manchester library and philosophical society, v. 60, no. 8 (1916), p. 30-69. **[253]**

An important and detailed scientific study, with many bibliographical references.

Janér, Florencio. De los antiguos instrumentos músicos de los Americanos, conservados en el Museo Nacional de Arqueología. *Mus. esp. antig.* (Madrid, 1873), v. 2, p. 265-271. **[254]**

Includes 4 tunes quoted from Brasseur de Bourbourg and a selection of the music from the Rabinal-Achi for 2 trumpets and drum.

Kraus, Alessandro. Catalogo della collezione etnografico-musicale Kraus in Firenze. Sezione istrumenti musicali. Firenze, Tip. di S. Landi, 1901. 29 p. 21 mounted phot. ML462.K91 **[255]**

Primitive musical instruments of Central and South America listed p. 28-29.

Lima, Emirto de. Les flûtes indigènes. *L'art musical,* v. 3, no. 65 (22 Oct. 1937), p. 71-73. **[256]**

Names numerous types of flutes used in the South American countries, with special attention to the *quena* of Peru, the *flauta de millo* of Colombia, the Brazilian *sons,* which imitate birds. 8 musical examples.

——. A guitarra, instrumento romanceiro. *Rev. bras. mus.,* v. 5, no. 1 (1938), p. 48-59. **[257]**

Historical comments for a guitar recital by José Mazzili.

Mason, Otis Tufton. Pre-Columbian music again. *Science,* n. s., v. 8 (New York, 1898), p. 371. **[258]**

Deals with musical instruments.

Métraux, Alfred. Le baton à rhythme, sa contribution à l'étude de la distribution géographique des éléments de culture d'origine mèlanésienne en l'Amérique du Sud. *Journ. soc. Amér.,* n. s., v. 19 (1927), p. 117-120. **[259]**

Map showing distribution of the *baton* and giving explanatory key, p. 121-122. Illustration, p. 118.

Morse, Edward Sylvester. Pre-Columbian musical instruments in America. *Pop. scien. monthly,* v. 54 (1809), p. 712-714. il. **[260]**

Nordenskiöld, Erland. The copper and

bronze ages in South America. Göteborg, Elanders boktryckeri aktiebolag, 1921. 196 p. F2230.N82, v. 4 F2229.-N83 **[261]**

Bells found throughout the Incan empire, p. 50, 56, 57; illustration of bells or rattles of palmnut or metal, p. 148; mention of musical instruments, p. 150. See also p. 40, p. 96-99, 171.

———. Origin of the Indian civilizations in South America. Göteborg, Elanders boktryckeri aktiebolag, 1931. 205 p. il. F2230.N83 no. 9 **[262]**

Musical instruments, p. 74.

Pan American union. *Music division.* Recordings of Latin American songs and dances ... By Gustavo Durán. Washington, D. C., Music Division, Pan American union, 1942. 65 p. (*Its* Music series, no. 3.) **[263]**

Arranged alphabetically by countries, each section including a brief description of the principal folk music forms of the country concerned. There are numerous references to musical instruments.

Peet, Stephen D. The ethnography of art in America. *Amer. antiq.,* v. 26 (1904), p. 201-224. **[264]**

References to musical instruments of the South and Central American Indians, p. 223-224.

Prat, Domingo. Diccionario biográfico, bibliográfico, histórico, crítico, de guitarras, guitarristas, danzas y cantos. Buenos Aires, Casa Romero y Fernández, 1934. 468 p. ML128.G8P7 **[265]**

Includes a glossary of musical instruments.

Puccioni, Nello. Gli oggetti musicali nel Museo nazionale d'antropologia. *Arch. antrop. etnol.,* v. 36 (Florence, 1906), p. 59-84. **[266]**

Brief descriptions of musical instruments of the Indians of South and Central America contained in the National Museum of Anthropology at Florence.

Roth, Walter Edmund. An introductory study of the arts, crafts, and customs

of the Guiana Indians. *In* U. S. Bureau of American ethnology. Thirty-eighth annual report, 1916-1917. Washington, 1924, p. 23-745. il. E51.-U55 38th GN2.U5 38th **[267]**

Musical and other sound instruments, p. 450-469.

Sachs, Curt. Geist und werden der musikinstrumente. Berlin, D. Reimer, 1929. 282 p. il. (incl. music). ML3547.-S2 **[268]**

———. The history of musical instruments. New York, W. W. Norton, 1940. 505 p. il. ML460.S24H5 **[268x]**

Ch. 9, *America,* p. 102-203, discusses Central America (including Mexico) and South America (chiefly Peru). Also contains passing references to South American primitive instruments, especially in ch. 1 (rattles, drums, marimba, etc.).

Schneider, Marius. Bemerkungen über südamerikanische panpfeifen. *Arch. musikf.,* v. 2, no. 4 (1937), p. 496-497. **[269]**

Schünemann, Georg. Musikinstrumente der Indianer; aus der sammlung der Frankfurter Südamerika-expedition (1927-29). *Arch. musikf.,* v. 1, no. 3 (1936), p. 368-382; no. 4, p. 467-483. **[270]**

With 25 illustrations of musical instruments and several tables. The regions covered are northern Argentina, Bolivia, Peru and Yucatan. An important scientific study.

Sellers, Gatty. The organs of South America. *Mus. opinion,* v. 44 (Aug. 1921), p. 934. **[271]**

See also nos. 42, 44, 54, 59, 63, 149, 215, 216, 217, 218, 219, 222, 223, 227, 228, 230

(E) COLLECTIONS (FOLK AND POPULAR)

Berggreen, Andreas Peter. Folke-sange og melodier, faedrelandske og fremmede. Copenhagen, A. C. Reitzels forlag, 1869-71. 11 v. M162.B49 **[272]**

Vol. 10 contains 2 Nicaraguan folk songs arranged for piano (nos. 105-106); also

6 Mexican folk songs (nos. 99-104) and 3 Peruvian folk songs (nos. 110-112), with paino accompaniment.

Botsford, Florence Hudson, comp. Botsford collection of folk-songs, with English versions by American poets. New York, G. Schirmer, inc., 1930-33. 3 v. Published 1921-22 under title: Folk songs of many peoples. M1627.- B72 1930.   **[273]**

"Songs from Latin America", v. 1, p. 72-106, contains ten Mexican songs, 5 songs identified simply as from "Latin Argentina, and a street-cry from "South arranged by Carlos Valderrama.

————. Songs of the Americas. New York, G. Schirmer, inc., 1940. **[274]**

This is v. 1 of the Botsford collection of folk-songs [no. 273].

————. The universal folk songster for home, school and community. New York, G. Schirmer, inc., 1937. 154 p. M1627.B72U5   **[275]**

Includes 2 songs from Mexico, one from Argentina, and a street-cry from "South-America and Mexico".

Brown, James Duff, comp. Characteristic songs and dances of all nations ... The music arranged for the pianoforte by Alfred Moffat. London, Bayley & Ferguson, 1901. 276 p. M1627.- B878   **[276]**

"Songs and dances of South America", p. 206-216. Folk and national songs of Bolivia, Argentina, Chile, Brazil, Paraguay, Peru and Venezuela; also 2 "South American Indian tunes" arranged for piano. 7 numbers are for piano alone. 2 songs have English words.

Canciones Panamericanas; songs of the Americas. New York, Chicago, San Francisco, Silver, Burdett co., 1942. 42 pp. il. M1680.C16   **[277]**

Song texts in English, Spanish and Portuguese. Descriptive notes. Prepared in collaboration with Pan American Union.

Clark, Kenneth Sherman, ed. The "Everybody sing" book. Rev. ed. New York, Paull-pioneer music corp., 1935. 128 p. M1977.C5C25   **[278]**

Includes 5 Latin American songs: *Ay, ay, ay!; Cielito lindo; La cucaracha; La golondrina; La paloma.* English words.

Cugat, Xavier, ed. Collection of Pan American songs, with English and Spanish lyrics. New York, Robbins music corp. 1942. 64 p.   **[279]**

————. The other Americas; an album of typical Central and South American songs and dances. New York, E. B. Marks music corp. 1938. 64 p. M1680.R66Q7   **[280]**

"Descriptive comment: brief notes on the national dances and music of the various Latin American countries." Music mostly by Ricardo Romero.

Friedenthal, Albert, comp. Stimmen der völker in liedern, tänzen und charakterstücken. I. abteilung, Die volksmusik der Kreolen Amerikas. Berlin, Schlesinger'sche buch-und musikhandlung (Rob. Lienau), 1911. M1680.F84   **[281]**

V. 1. Einleitung. Mexiko. V. 2. Zentralamerika, Westindien und Venezuela. V. 3. Ecuador, Peru, Bolivia. V. 4. Chile. V. 5. Die La Plata-Länder. V. 6. Brasilien. Text in German, French and English. These 72 songs, with the introductory matter and commentary, constitute what is on the whole the most important collection of Latin American folk music thus far published. While it does not conform to the scientific standards of the modern folklorist, it is more comprehensive, and more fully documented, than any other similar collection in this field.

Hague, Eleanor. Folk songs from Mexico and South America. Pianoforte accompaniments by Edward Kilenyi. New York, H. W. Gray co., 1914, 37 p. M1682.H25   **[282]**

Contains 12 songs for voice and piano. Spanish words with English translations.

————. *comp.* Spanish-American folksongs. Lancaster, Pa., and New York, The American folk-lore society, 1917.

(G. E. Stechert & co., New York, agents). M1680.H2 **[283]**

95 melodies, with Spanish and English words.

La hora del canto (The hour of singing); canciones escogidas de Latino-América especialmente adaptadas para los estudiantes norte-americanos. Por (by) F. González [pseud. for Felix Guenther]. New York, Edward B. Marks music corp. 1942. 55 p. **[284]**

Publisher's preface in English and Spanish. Songs with piano accompaniment, Spanish words.

Jiménez, Ramón Emilio. La patria en la canción, obra graduada de canto coral en cuatro series. Barcelona, Imprenta hispano-americana, s. a., 1933. 348 p. port. M1681.D8J61 **[285]**

Musical editor: José de Js. Ravelo.

Krone, Beatrice, and Max Krone. Spanish and Latin American songs. Collection of easy arrangements of Spanish, Central & South American folk songs for either mixed voices, two treble voices or two changed voices. Book 1. Chicago, Neil A. Kjos music co., 1942. 48 p. **[286]**

Labastille, Irma, ed. Canciones típicas. New York, Chicago, etc., Silver, Burdett co., 1941. il. **[287]**

19 songs from 16 Latin American countries, with descriptive notes and English translations of the texts.

The Latin-American songbook. Boston, New York, [etc.] Ginn and co., 1942. 128 p. il. M1680.L17 **[288]**

Published in cooperation with the Music division of the Pan American union. List of contributors, p. 2. All the songs have English texts, and for most of them the original Spanish, Portuguese or French text is also given. Includes section on Latin-American dances, by Gustavo Durán, p. 107-111.

Luce, Allena, ed. Canciones populares. Boston, etc. Silver, Burdett & co., 1921. 138 p. M1681.P6L9 **[289]**

Traditional and semi-popular songs edited and arranged for voice and piano. Section 1: 28 songs of Puerto Rico. Section 2: 12 songs of Cuba, Spain and Mexico. Section 4: 22 songs and singing games (unaccompamed melodies and Spanish text).

Molina, Carlos. Carlos Molina's album of Spanish favorites; a collection of unrivalled tangos and other Latin-American successes. With English and Spanish text. New York, E. B. Marks music corp., 1934. 40 p. M1686.-M72 **[290]**

13 songs with piano accompaniment, with arrangements for ukulele and banjo or guitar.

Novoa, Sofía, arr. Cantares españoles. Hastings on Hudson, N. Y., Gessler publishing co., 1942. 24 p. il. M1680.-N6C2 **[291]**

Includes songs of Argentina, Mexico, Peru, Chile and Puerto Rico. Spanish words only. Notes, p. 22-24.

Pedro, Don, comp. Don Pedro . . . Mexican and Spanish songs. Chicago, M. M. Cole publishing co., 1935. 54 p. M1682.P37M3 **[292]**

29 songs with piano accompaniment; with ukulele arrangements. English and Spanish text.

Schindler, Kurt. Folk music and poetry of Spain and Portugal. Música y poesía popular de España y Portugal. New York, Hispanic institute in the United States, 1941. 378 p. (music) ML315.-S25F6 **[293]**

Introduction, "Kurt Schindler and his Spanish work" (in English and Spanish) signed: Federico de Onís. A fundamental work for the study of basic types of Hispanic melody and rhythm.

Stevens, David, ed. Latin American songs for unison and two part singing with piano accompaniments. Boston, C. C. Birchard & co., 1941. 42 p. M1680.S73L2 **[294]**

The countries represented are Brazil, Chile, Costa Rica, Cuba, Mexico, Peru, Venezuela. There are 28 songs, all with English words.

Wilson, Harry Robert, *ed.* Cantemos! New York, Penny press, 1940. 31 p. M1680.W5C2   **[295]**

A collection of Spanish songs for group singing.

Zanzig, Augustus D., *ed.* Singing America, song and chorus book. Boston, C. C. Birchard & co., 1941. M1629.-Z27S5   **[296]**

Includes 13 Latin American songs, with English and Spanish words.

See also nos. 97, 201

COLLECTIONS OF ART MUSIC

Boletín latinoamericano de música. Suplemento musical, v. 1. Montevideo, 1935. 54 p. ML199.B64   **[297]**

Compositions by Juan José Castro, Luis Gianneo, Carlos Isamitt, Juan Carlos Paz, P. Humberto Allende, H. Villa-Lobos, J. T. Wilkes, F. Eduardo Fabini, M. Camargo Guarnieri, O. Lorenzo Fernández, Francisco Mignone, Enrique M. Casella.

——. Suplemento musical, v. 3. Montevideo, 1937. 25 p. ML199.B64.   **[298]**

Compositions by Radamés Gnattali, Luis Cluzeau Mortet, R. Carpio Valdés, Vicente Ascone, Frederico Gerdes. Also 8 of the *Doce canciones coloniales del siglo xvii* originally collected by Fray Gregorio de Zuola; transcribed and harmonized by Josué T. Wilkes.

——. Suplemento musical, v. 4. Bogotá, 1938. 135 p. ML199.B64   **[299]**

Compositions by Honorio Siccardi, Julio Perceval, Carlos Suffern, Roberto García

Morillo, José María Castro, Jacobo Ficher, Isabel Aretz-Thiele, Juan Carlos Paz, Eduardo Caba, Fructuoso Vianna, Heitor Villa-Lobos. Domingo Santa Cruz, Próspero Bisquertt, René Amengual, Samuel Negrete, Carlos Isamitt, Alfonso Leng. P. Humberto Allende, Carlos Sánchez Málaga, Abraham Jurafsky, Alejandro Inzaurraga, Carlos Posada Amador, Guillermo Uribe Holguín, Andrés Sas, Estanislao Mejía.

Guenther, Felix, *ed.* Collection espagnole (Colección de obras españolas e iberoamericanas), from Albéniz to Villa-Lobos, for piano solo. New York, Edward B. Marks music corp., 1941. 96 p.   **[300]**

Ten of the 19 compositions are by Latin American composers, as follows; *Pirilâmpos,* by Oscar Lorenzo Fernândez (Brazil); *Estudio no. 3,* by Carlos Isamitt (Chile); *Danza lucumí* and *La conga de media noche,* by Ernesto Lecuona (Cuba); *El condor pasa,* by Daniel A. Robles (Perú): *La mariposa,* by Miguel Sandoval (Guatemala); *La nostalgia,* by Carlos Suffern (Argentina); *Moreninha, Mulatinha* and *Le polichinelle,* by Heitor Villa-Lobos (Brazil).

Lange, Francisco Curt, *ed.* Latin-American art music for the piano by twelve contemporary composers. New York, G. Schirmer, inc., 1942. 55 pp.   **[301]**

The composers represented are Camargo Guarnieri, Roberto García Morillo, Juan Carlos Paz, Juan B. Plaza, Manuel M. Ponce, Andrés Sás, Carlos Suffern, Heitor Villa-Lobos, José María Castro, Alberto E. Ginastera, René Amengual Astaburuaga, F. Eduardo Fabini. In the preface, Lange traces the development of piano music in Latin America. There are 17 pages of bio-bibliographical data.

SUPPLEMENT TO 1960

A. PRIMITIVE, FOLK, AND POPULAR MUSIC

Aretz-Thiele, Isabel. Músicas pentatónicas en Sudamérica *Arch. ven. folk.,* v. 1, no. 2 July-Dec. 1952, p. 283-309 **[1a]**

Includes 25 musical examples. A technical study of pentatonism in the Indian- and African derived musics of South America. (R.A.W.)

Azevedo, Luiz Heitor Corrêa de. L'heritage africain dans la musique du nouveau monde. *Rev. mus.,* numéro spécial, no. 242 (1958), p. 109-112. **[2a]**

Two photographs of dancers and musicians in Brazil, following article.

Bello, Enrique. Decadencia de la música popular. *Rev. mus. chil.*, v. 13, no. 67 (Sept.-Oct. 1959), p. 62-67. **[3a]**

Points out that popular music of the 20th century is no longer "popular" in origin (i. e., stemming from the people), but popular only through its usage by the people.

Calcaño, José Antonio. Posición del investigador ante la música aborigen. *Acta venez.*, v. 1, no. 3 (Jan.-Mar. 1946), p. 291-297. **[4a]**

Author deals with the attitude the researcher must assume in relation to aboriginal music, and supports Professor Karsten's viewpoint on the role music played among the primitive peoples of America: that among them it was a part of the rituals of common life. He believes that aesthetic or artistic value was not sought, but that to them music was simply a magical influence in wars, hunting, dancing, love-making, sickness, etc., and therefore it is not reasonable to value aboriginal music by the expression believed to be felt in it. Even if it were conceived with the same finality as that sought by the European composers, we could never understand it, and that therefore it should not be considered as an art similar to the musical art of the European culture. (C.S.)

Cortazar, Augusto Raúl. Naturaleza de los fenómenos folklóricos. *Rev. mus. chil.*, v. 5, no. 35-36 (Aug.-Nov. 1949), p. 23-25. **[5a]**

Durán, Gustavo. Recordings of Latin American songs and dances. An annotated selective list of popular and folkpopular music. Second edition, revised and enlarged by Gilbert Chase. Washington, D. C., Pan American union, Department of cultural affairs, Division of music and visual arts, 1950. xii, 92 p. **[6a]**

A revision of item. 34.

Gandía, Enrique de. Cultura y folklore en América. Buenos Aires, Librería y editorial "El Ateneo", 1947. 375 p. **[7a]**

Includes "Música y músicos de los rincones perdidos" (chapter 6) and "Ideas y notas de la música indígena" (chapter 7).

——. Ideas y notas perdidas de la música indígena. *Rev. geog. amer.*, v. 24, no. 147 (Dec. 1945), p. 321-329. **[8a]**

Copious quotations from chroniclers, conquistadores and early travellers relating to music of Indians. (C.S.)

Grases, Pedro. La nomenclatura de bailes y canciones en Hispanoamérica. *Rev. ven. folk.*, v. 1, no. 1 (Jan.-June 1947), p. 123-130. **[9a]**

A scholarly study. (C.S.)

Hague, Eleanor. Latin-American folk music. *In* Thompson, Oscar, *ed.*, The international cyclopedia of music and musicians, 8th ed. rev. New York, Dodd, Mead & Co., 1958, p. 575-576. **[10a]**

With very brief bibliography.

Herrera Carrillo, Pablo. La conquista musical de América por España. *Bol. soc. mex. geog. estad.*, v. 63, no. 3 (May.-June 1947), p. 609-640. **[11a]**

Poses combat of "the scale of Guido d'Arezzo" against "the putative scale". Valiant attempt to envisage total acculturation process of European and American music idioms from Patagonia to Canada. Thoughtful and imaginative. (C.S.)

Klatowsky, Richard. Desde la zarabanda hasta la rumba. *Bol. progr. Col.*, v. 1, no. 187 (Feb. 1960), p. 13-16. **[12a]**

"Apuntes sobre la influencia de la danza hispanoamericana en Europa durante cuatro siglos." With portrait and biographical sketch of the author.

Labastille, Irma. Recuerdo latinoamericano. (Memories of Latin America); album of folksongs for voice and piano, with original Spanish text and English translations; compiled and arranged. New York, E. B. Marks music corp., 1943. 64 p. il. **[13a]**

Liscano, Juan. The feast of St. John; June 24 celebration is rooted in antiquity. *Américas*, v. 8, no. 5 (May. 1956), p. 14-19. **[14a]**

Brief historical background of Catholic cult, then details of customs in Spain and Latin America, particularly in Brazil,

Cuba, Paraguay, and Venezuela. Three song texts, one of Venezuela, two of Brazil. Thirteen illustrations, one of Venezuelan drummer.

Lowie, Robert H. Some problems of geographical distribution. *In* Sudseestudien: Gedenkschrift zur Erinnerung an Felix Speisen, Museum für Völkerkunde und Schweizerischen Museum für Volkskunde, Basel, Switzerland, 1951, p. 11-26.   **[15a]**

Brief discussion, with well-chosen examples, of the question of trans-Pacific influences on pre-Columbian American Indian cultures. (D. B. Stout)

Marti, Samuel. Música aborigen americana, *Sodre,* v.2 (1955), p. 15-20. **[16a]**

Brief summary of structure and functions of Central and South American Indian music. (R.A.W.)

———. Música de las Américas. *Cuad. am.,* v. 56, no. 2 (March-Apr. 1951), p. 153.   **[17a]**

Review of prehistoric musical artifacts and depictions in Middle American art. (Robert Wauchope)

Mendoza, Vicente T. La Navidad en el folklore. *An. soc. folk. Méx.,* v. 8 (1954), p. 105-126.   **[18a]**

General world view, but most details from Mexico, with some from Bolivia, Brazil, Peru. Discusses the carved Nativity Scene in these countries, the *posadas* of Mexico and Peru, the *piñatas,* the *Misa de Aguinaldo* in Mexico and Peru, songs and dances, 4 music examples, three without indication of source or place sung.

———. Pregones y pregoneros. *An. soc. folk. Mex.,* v. 1 (1942), p. 51-68. **[19a]**

Survey of street vendors' cries in Latin America and their Hispanic background, profusely illustrated with texts and music notations.

Menéndez Pidal, Ramón. Los romances de América y otros estudios. 4th ed. Buenos Aires-Mexico, Espasa-Calpe argentina, s. a., 1945. 188 p.   **[20a]**

A fundamental poineer work for the stu-

dy of the Spanish ballad in America. The two essays most pertinent to the subject are "Los romances tradicionales en América" and "Las primeras noticias de romances tradicionales en América". The former was first published in the review *Cultura española,* no. 1 (1906), p. 72-111. The second of these essays first appeared in the volume *Homenaje a Enrique José Varona,* 1935.

Writing in 1905, Menéndez Pidal asserted :"Hasta ahora no se conocía ningún romance tradicional de la América española". He quoted a passage from the *Historia de la literatura en Nueva Granada* (Bogotá, 1867) by José María Vergara, in which this author states that the llaneros of Colombia, "indudablemente tomaron la forma de metro y la idea de los romances españoles; pero desecharon luego todos los originales, y compusieron romances suyos para celebrar sus propias proezas"; that is to say, they discarded the traditional Spanish ballads and composed others in their stead, on the same patterns but dealing with local subjects. In a trip to South America made in 1905, Menéndez Pidal was able to track down a version of "Las señas del marido" in Lima; but it was in Chile that he found survivals of old Spanish ballads in the greatest abundance. There too he met Julio Vicuña Cifuentes (q. v.), who had already collected many Spanish ballads in Chile.

Pan American union. Music division. Selected list of collections of Latin-American songs and references for guidance in planning fiestas. Washington, D. C., Pan American Union, 1949. 7th ed. rev. 11 p.   **[21a]**

Compiled by Leila Fern Thompson.

Pardo Tovar, Andrés. A propósito del pentafonismo anhemetónico. *Bol. interam. mús.,* no. 5 (May 1958), p. 3-8 (music).   **[22a]**

A discussion of pentatonic scales and their use by Latin American composers, with 10 music notations.

Primitive musical instruments. *Americas,* v 1, no. 3 (May 1949), p. 30-32. **[23a]**

Popularly written description of several

instruments, including the *erke, maracas,* panpipes, marimba, Haitian voodoo drums. Good photographs of large Bolivian panpipes, Ecuadorian panpipe player, Guatemalan marimba player, Haitian *vaccines.*

Ramón y Rivera, Luis Felipe. El ritmo sesquialtero, su difusión y su conexión con otros ritmos en América. *Arch. ven. folk.,* v. 2-3, no. 3 (1953-54). **[24a]**

——. Es el ritmo una comprobación? *Rev. ven. folk.,* v. 1, no. 1 (Jan.-June 1947), p. 57-66. (music). **[25a]**

The author rejects generalities regarding Negro influence in American music and insists upon the necessity of studying the music of each song or dance tune in each of its component elements (rhythm, melody, etc.). Recognizing the importance of the N°gro contribution, he nevertheless maintains that the Negro has taken as much from America and from Europe as from Africa, and that this extraordinary mixture is what characterizes the musical panorama of the Americas.

——. La anonimia en el folklore musical. *Educación,* Caracas, v. 6, no. 44 (Aug.-Sept. 1946), p. 108-112. **[26a]** Brief discussion.

——. La veracidad en la investigación. *Bol. inst. folk.,* v. 2, no. 2 (Aug. 1955) p. 41-43. **[27a]**

Essay on the qualities necessary to make a good field collector of folklore and folk music.

——. Los congresos de musicología y la música popular de América Latina. *Bol. inst. folk. ven.,* v. 2, no. 6 (May 1957), p. 193-194. **[28a]**

A plea for the more systematic collection of Latin American folk music.

Romero, Jesús C. La folklorología: Lugar del folklore en los conocimientos humanos. *Orientac. mus.,* v. 5, no. 52 (Oct. 1945), p. 10-11. **[29a]**

Distinction is made between the "encyclopaedists" (Boggs, Mendoza, Cadilla de Martínez, *et al.*) and the "exclusivists" (Romero, Guerrero, Povuña, *et al.*). (C.S.)

Vega, Carlos. Panorama de la música popular argentina con un ensayo sobre la ciencia del folklore. Buenos Aires, Ed. Losada, 1944. 361 p. il. (incl. music). **[30a]**

150 melodic notations, 8 plates, 6 maps. A work of paramount importance in Latin American musicology and folklore. For Vega, "el Folklore es una ciencia histórica", because it studies relics from the past that are "alive" (*vivientes*) in the present: i. e., it studies survivals. Though dealing primarily with folk music of the Argentine, Vega establishes a classification that is applicable to the whole of South America. His two main classifications are the *Cancionero Occidental* and the *Cancionero Oriental,* though he distinguishes eight *cancioneros* (song families or groups) in all (in addition to the *Cancionero Europeo Antiguo*). The list of Vega's publications is a valuable feature of this book.

Waterman, Richard A. African influence on the music of the Americas. *In* Tax, Sol (ed.), Acculturation in the Americas, Proceedings and selected papers of the XXIXth International Congress of Americanisis. Chicago, Ill., Univ. of Chicago Press, 1952, p. 207-218. **[31a]**

An important study, with authoritative analysis and music notations.

Williams, Jane, and Edelmira Roa y Mendoza. La clave panamericana. New York and London, Harper and brothers, 1943. 454 p. il. (incl. music) **[32a]**

Wilson, Betty. Adventures in folk music.' Through the South American hinterland with two musicologists. *Americas,* v. 8, no. 9 (Sept. 1956), p. 15-20. **[33a]**

Fine popular article on the work of Luis Felipe Ramón y Rivera and his wife Isabel Aretz in collecting and studying the folk music of Latin America, particularly about her work in Argentina, and their work together in Venezuela for the Venezuelan National institute of Folklore. Eleven photographs of dances, musicians and instruments.

Zerries, Otto. The bull-roarer among South American Indians. *Rev. museo Paul.*, n. s., v. 7 (1953), p. 275-309. Map.   **[34a]**

A most welcome compilation of the occurrences and uses of the bull-roarer among some 40 tribes and areas of South America. (The bull-roarer is a thin piece of wood with string attached at one end which is whirled about over the head of the user.) The present article is an amplification of part of the author's previous monograph *Das Schwirrholz* (Strecker u. Schröder, Stuttgart, 1942) wherein he discussed the bull-roarer throughout the world. (D. B. Stout)

B. GENERAL AND MISCELLANEOUS

Almeida, Renato. A América e o nacionalismo musical. *Cultura,* Rio de Janeiro, v. 1, no. 1 (Sept.-Dec. 1948), p. 5-46.   **[35a]**

A bold effort to give a synoptic view of the unity and diversity of the music of the American continent, with special emphasis on materials of Brazil and the United States. (C.S.)

Anson, George. Contemporary piano music of the Americas. *Interamer. mus. bull.*, no. 13 (Sept. 1959), p. 4-24. (First part.)   **[36a]**

List of piano works, with most of space given to Canada and Latin American countries. Listing is by countries, and the publisher, the difficulty of the work, and some comment on the type of music are indicated with each piece.

Apel, Willi, ed. Harvard dictionary of music. Cambridge, Mass., Harvard univ. press, 1944, 826 p. il. **[37a]**

Includes articles by Gilbert Chase on music in Argentina, Brazil, Chile, Colombia, Mexico, Peru, Venezuela, also bibliographies under "Central America" and "Latin America", and various individual references to songs, dances, and instruments of Latin America.

Asuar, José Vicente. En el umbral de una nueva era musical. *Rev. mus. chil.*, v. 13, no. 64 (March-April 1959), p. 11-32. il.   **[38a]**

On electronic music.

Azevedo, Heitor Luiz Corrêa de. La création musicale contemporaine en Amérique Latine. *Rev. mus.,* numéro spécial, no. 242 (1958), p. 105-108. **[39a]**

Bauer, Marion, and Claire R. Reis. Twenty-five years with the League of Composers. *Mus. quart.*, v. 34, no. 1 (Jan. 1948), p. 1-14.   **[40a]**

Includes several references to League's interest in Latin American music. Program of March 6, 1932, "probably the first of living Latin American composers to be presented in New York", includes the names of Allende, García Caturla, Chávez, González, Ponce and Villa-Lobos.

Becerra, Gustavo. Crisis de la enseñanza de la composición en occidente *Rev. mus. chil.*, v. 12, no. 58 (Mar-Apr. 1958), p. 9-18.   **[41a]**

Description of the crisis and proposal of a new plan. Interesting because the author is one of most prominent Chilean composers of younger generation.

Breython, John. Diccionario bibliográfico de grandes músicos. Buenos Aires, Editorial E.M.C.A., 1945. 278 p. **[42a]**

Includes very brief information on the following composers: J. Aguirre, F. Boero, C. Gaito, H. Panizza, Blas Parera (Argentina); E. Caba (Bolivia); A. Carlos Gomes, H. Villa-Lobos (Brazil); E. Fabini (Uruguay).

Carvajal Quesada, I. Historia de la música europea y americana, desde sus orígenes hasta hoy. Buenos Aires, Editorial Nacor, 1944. 208 p. il. (Colección Eco universal, v. 1.)   **[43a]**

"La música en América", p. 139-199, and "Suplemento", p. 201-208, include brief sketches of many Latin American and a few North American composers.

Centro Interamericano de música (CIDEM). *Bol. interam. mús.*, no. 4 (March 1958), p. 9-26.   **[44a]**

Proceedings of the First General Assembly of the CIDEM, held in Mexico City from January 21 to 24, 1958.

Chase, Gilbert. A dialectical approach to music history. *Jour. soc. ethnomusicol.* v. 2, no. 1 (Jan 1958), p. 1-9.

Abridged version of a paper read at the annual meeting of the American Musicological Society in Urbana, Illinois, Dec. 30, 1956. After general considerations, the paper deals with the problem of writing the musical history of the New World, and specifically of Latin America.

———. A guide to Latin American music. Washington, D. C., The Library of Congress, Music Division, 1945. 274 p. (Latin American series, no. 5). **[45a]**

Compiled while the author was attached to the Music Division of the Library of Congress (Oct. 1, 1940 to June 30, 1943) under an arrangement with the Interdepartmental Committee for Cooperation with the Other American Republics. The bibliographical entries were closed as of June 1943.

———. America's music: from the pilgrims to the present. New York, McGraw Hill, 1955. xxii, 733 p. (incl. music). **[46a]**

References to Latin American music, especially songs and dances of the West Indies, also to L. M. Gottschalk in South America, are contained in chapter 15.

———. Caracas host to second Latin American festival. *Mus. Amer.,* v. 77, no. 6 (May 1957), p. 11-12. **[47a]**

———. Current musical trends in South American lands. *Mus. Amer.,* v. 77, no. 3 (Feb. 1957), p. 31, 176-179. **[48a]**

Contemporary composers and tendencies. Three photographs.

———. Dialectica e musica. *O Estado de S. Paulo,* Suplemento literario, no. 76 (12 April 1958), p. 5; no. 77 (19 April 1958), p. 5. **[49a]**

Portuguese translation, with revisions, of a paper read at the annual meeting of the American Musicological Society in Urbana, Illinois, in December 1956.

———. Do salmo ao jazz. A música dos Estados Unidos. Rio de Janeiro — São Paulo — Porto Alegre, Editôra Globo, 1958. 674 p. **[50a]**

A Portuguese translation of item no. 46a. Numerous musical examples.

———. Entrevista a Gilbert Chase, por Alberto Ginastera. *B. A. mus.,* v. 10, no. 160 (15 Aug. 1955), p. 5, il. **[51a]**

Deals chiefly with music in the United States.

———. Fundamentos de la cultura musical en Latino-América, *Rev. mus. chil.,* v. 3, nos. 25-26 (Oct.-Nov. 1947), p. 14-23. **[52a]**

Translation of item no. 63a.

———. Hacia una conciencia americana en la música. *Rev. mus. chil.,* v. 12, no. 61 (Sept.-Oct. 1958), p. 49-56. **[53a]**

Epilogue of the book titled *Introducción a la música americana contemporánea.*

———. Introducción a la música americana contemporánea. (Compendios Nova de iniciación cultural, 17). Buenos Aires, Editorial Nova, n. d. (1958). 129 p. **[54a]**

Includes both Latin America and the United States. The author attaches particular importance to the Epilogue: "Hacia una conciencia americana en la música." This book was written originally in Spanish; there is no English translation.

———. La música de los Estados Unidos. Buenos Aires, Editorial Guillermo Kraft, n. d. (1958). 858 p. **[55a]**

Spanish translation of item no. 46a. Prólogo by Alberto Ginastera. Numerous musical examples.

———. Música del Nuevo Mundo. *Boi. interam. mús.,* no. 6 (July 1958), p. 3-5. **[56a]**

"Festival Interamericano en Washington, D. C." Reprint of item no. 58a.

———. Music of Latin America. *Mus. quart.,* v. 32, no. 1 (Jan. 1946), p. 140-143. **[57a]**

A devastatingly detailed review of the book of that title by Nicolas Slonimsky (item 120a), a work which does justice neither to the subject nor to the author.

——. New World music. *Américas*, vol. 10, no. 7 (July 1958), p. 10-13, il. **[58a]**

Describes the First Inter-American Music Festival held in Washington, D. C., in April 1958. The Festival was organized by the Inter-American Music Center in cooperation with the Pan American Union, and with the participation of the National Symphony Orchestras of Mexico and of Washington. New works by the following composers were performed: Roberto Caamaño, Juan Orrego Salas, Alberto Ginastera, Aurelio de la Vega, Rodolfo Halffter, Camargo Guarnieri, José Ardévol, H. Villa-Lobos, Violet Archer, and Quincy Porter.

——. Our smaller neighbors make music. *Mus. Amer.*, v. 66, no. 3 (Feb. 1946), p. 122, 340. **[59a]**

Need for knowledge of Latin American music in U. S. A. Reporting on a trip through Latin America, the author found increased musical activity.

——. Problemática de la música americana actual. *Cuadernos*, no. 30 (May-June 1958), p. 37-41. **[60a]**

Nationalism, folklorism, the 12-tone polemic, and Guarnieri's diatribe against "internationalist" trends in modern music.

——. Radio prominent in musical exchange between Americas. *Mus. Amer*. v. 65, no.3 (Feb. 1945), p. 333, 348. **[61a]**

Traces musical relations between North and South America and emphasizes importance of radio broadcasting as a link.

——. The creative picture in South America. *New York Times*, Sect. 2, X (Sept. 30, 1956), p. 9. **[62a]**

Impressions of a tour of several countries, with comments on compositional trends.

——. The Foundations of musical culture in Latin America. *In* Intellectual trends in Latin America. The university of Texas, Institute of Latin-American studies. Latin-American studies, I.- Austin, The University of Texas Press, 1945, p. 35-43. **[63a]**

——. The music of Spain. 2nd rev. ed. New York, Dover Publications, 1959, 383 p. il. (music). **[64a]**

Chávez, Carlos. Composers and their folk music, *New York Times,* Sect. X (March 3, 1940), p. 7. **[65a]**

——. Los problemas del compositor latinoamericano. *B. A. mus.*, v. 12, no. 197 (Oct. 1, 1957), p. 1. **[66a]**

——. Nacionalismo musical. I-II. El arte popular y el no popular. III. Paralelo entre el arte popular y el no popular. IV. La creación artística. *Música*, México, v. 1, no. 3 (June 1930), p. 28-32; no. 4 (July 1930), p. 18-22; no. 6 (Sept. 1930), p. 3-11. **[67a]**

Comas, Francisco. El arte de bailar, antaño y ogaño. Buenos Aires, Fontana y Traverso (n. d.). 283 p. il. (incl. music). **[68a]**

The author makes an historical survey of the dance in a very popular way. Includes descriptions of the *tango, rumba, ranchera, paso doble* and *maxixe*.

Composers of the Americas. Biographical data and catalogs of their works. Compositores de América. Datos biográficos y catálogos de sus obras. Washington, D. C., Unión Panamericana, Departamento de asuntos culturales, 1955-57. 4 v. il. (ports., facs.) **[69a]**

Vol. 1: José Ardévol (Cuba); Renzo Braceño (Peru); Ricardo Castillo (Guatemala); Aaron Copland (U.S.A.); Alberto Ginastera (Argentina); Carlos Guastavino (*id.*); Juan Orrego Salas (Chile); Manuel M. Ponce (Mexico): Silvestre Revueltas (*id.*); Amadeo Roldán (Cuba); Domingo Santa Cruz (Chile); Enrique Soro (*id.*); Floro M. Ugarte (Argentina); Guillermo Uribe Holguín (Colombia).

Vol. 2: Pedro Humberto Allende (Chile); Luiz Cosme (Brazil); Henry Cowell (U.S.A.); Ruth Crawford Seeger (*id.*); Luis A. Delgadillo (Nicaragua); Eduardo Fabini (Uruguay); Jacobo Ficher (Argentina); Julio Fonseca (Costa Rica); Juan F. García (Dominican Rep.); Rodolfo Halffter (Mexico); Charles Ives (U.S.A.); Alfonso Letelier (Chile); Juan

Carlos Paz (Argentina); Andrés Sas (Peru); Honorio Siccardi (Argentina); Alberto Williams (*id.*).

Vol. 3: Carlos Chávez (Mexico); Alejandro García Chávez (Cuba); Heitor Villa-Lobos (Brazil).

Vol. 4: Juan José Castro (Argentina); Washington Castro (*id.*); Paul Creston (U.S.A.); Luis Gianneo (Argentina); Guillermo Graetzer (Argentina); Camargo Guarnieri (Brazil); Rodolfo Holzmann (Peru); Carlos Lavin (Chile); Francisco Mignone (Brazil); Walter Piston (U.S.A.); Quincy Porter (*id.*); Luis H. Salgado (Ecuador); Enrique Solares (Guatemala); Antonio Maria Valencia (Colombia); Fructuoso Vianna (Brazil).

The introductory texts are bilingual (English and Spanish).

Composers of the Americas. Compositores de las Américas. Washington, D. C., Pan American Union, 1959.
[70a]

Includes short biographies, holographs and lists of compositions (with publishers, duration, names of movements, dates of composition, and date of first performance) of Rodolfo Arizaga (Argentina); Harry Partch, William Schuman, Samuel Barber, Peter Mennin, William Grant Still, Howard Hanson, Elliott Carter, Marc Blitzstein (U.S.A.); John Weinzweig, Pierre Mercure, Robert Turner, Harry Somers, Jean Papineau-Couture (Canada).

Consejo panamericano de la Confederación internacional de sociedades de autores y compositores. Buenos Aires. Información completa del XIV Congreso, realizado en Londres, del 23 al 28 de junio de 1947. Buenos Aires. 115 p. il.
[71a]

Cordero, Roque. ¿Dodecafonismo versus nacionalismo? *Clave,* v. 6, no. 5 (Apr. 1957), p. 13.
[72a]

Brief but thoughtful and trenchant ideas on the subject of nationalism, showing that the attack on 12-tone music by the exponents of musical nationalism is completely illogical and unjustified.

——. ¿Nacionalismo versus dodecafo-

nismo? *Rev. mus. chil.,* v. 13, no. 67 (Sept.-Oct. 1959), p. 28-38.
[73a]

The Panamanian composer discusses musical nationalism in Latin America with rational objectivity and shows that it cannot logically be placed in opposition to 12-tone composition, as has been claimed by several adherents of intransigent nationalism.

Costas, Carlos José. El nacionalismo musical en Hispanoamérica. *B. A. mus.,* v. 10, no. 166 (Nov. 15, 1955), p. 2-4.
[74a]

Devoto, Daniel. La canción tradicional y la música culta. Buenos Aires, Imprenta de la universidad. 1944. (Separata from *Revista de la Universidad de Buenos Aires,* época, v. 2, no. 1 Jan.-March 1944. p. 73-91).
[75a]

Discusses nationalism and its utilization of folk and popular music.

Ewen, David. The complete book of 20th century music. New York, Prentice-Hall, Inc., 1952, xix, 498 p.
[76a]

Includes Carlos Chávez: *Sinfonía de Antígona;* Concerto No. 1 for piano and orchestra; Toccata for percussion instruments. Camargo Guarnieri: *Abertura concertante;* Symphony No. 1. Francisco Mignone: *Congada; Four churches.* Silvestre Revueltas: *Caminos; Sensemaya.* Heitor Villa-Lobos: *Uirapurú* (The Enchanted Bird); *Chôros* Nos. 1-13; *Rudepoêma; Bachianas brasileiras;* Quartet No. 6 in E major (Brazilian Quartet No. 2); *Madona; Mandu-Carara.*

Falabella, Roberto. Problemas estilísticos del joven compositor en América y en Chile. *Rev. mus. chil.,* v. 12, no. 57 (Jan.-Feb. 1958), p. 41-49; no. 58 (March-April 1958), p. 77-93.
[77a]

Stresses the very important rôle of folklore in the art music of Latin America, and the delay in the assimilation of the important European styles by the composers of Latin America. Deals with movements and institutions as well as with composers. The author died in 1958.

Festival of Contemporary music of the Americas. *Interamer. mus. bull.,* no. 9-10 (Jan.-Mar. 1959), p. 3-7.
[78a]

Detailed account of eight-week festival

held in Buenos Aires from September to early November 1958. Much space given to the local newspaper criticism of the compositions played.

First inter-American music festival. Washington, D. C., The Pan American Union, n. d. (1958). 56 p. il.   **[79a]**

The festival was held in Washington, D. C., on April 18, 19 and 20, 1958. Preface by John H a s k i n s. Biographical notes on performes and composers, with portraits. Six pages of photographs at end.

First inter-American music festival. *Interamer. mus. bull.,* no. 5 (May 1958), p. 1-6.   **[80a]**

Account of festival, works performed, with excerpts of the criticisms published in the *New York Times* and *Herald Tribune.* Photographs of composers Roberto Caamaño, Roque Cordero, Alberto Ginastera, Blas Galindo, Violet Archer, Rodolfo Halffter, and Gustavo Becerra.

Garde, Carlos. El Festival de música contemporánea americana. *B. A. mus.,* v. 13, no. 215 (Nov. 16, 1958), p. 2.   **[81a]**

The festival was held in Buenos Aires.

González, Luis A. Critic surveys Latin American scene. *Mus. Amer.,* v. 53, no. 16 (Dec. 1943), p. 5, 15.   **[82a]**

Musical life of Chile, Cali (Colombia), Venezuela, Havana (Cuba).

Haskins, John. Cartagena festival. *Americas,* vol. 11, no. 7 (July 1959), p. 17-20. il.   **[83a]**

Describes the Ninth Festival of Cartagena de Indias, which, after a lapse of 6 years, was held from May 18 to 28, 1959. The Cartagena Festivals were founded in 1945 by Guillermo Espinosa. At first devoted only to music, the Festival now includes all the arts. The National Symphony orchestra of Washington, D. C., under the direction of Howard Mitchell, participated in the 9th Festival. Guillermo Espinosa was guest conductor.

——. El panamericanismo en la música. *B. A. mus.,* v. 12, no. 197 (Oct. 1, 1957), p. 10.   **[84a]**

Traces the work of the Music Divi-

sion of the Pan American Union. Reprinted in *Bol. interam. mus.,* no. 7 (Sept. 1958), p. 3-4.

Lange, Francisco Curt. A manera de prólogo. *Rev. estud. mus.,* v. 1, no. 1 (1949), p. 13-36.   **[85a]**

Reviews tardy development of musicology in Latin America, laments lack of facilities, particularly of libraries, and cites need for organized work. (C.S.)

Latin America in school and college teaching materials. Report. American Council on Education. Committee on the study of teaching materials on Inter-American subjects. Washington, D. C., 1944. 496 p.   **[86a]**

A chapter on "School and College Music" concerned with the divulgation of Latin-American music. Bibliography: p. 489-491.

Lawler, Vanett. A educação musical nas Américas. Washington, D. C., p. 9-13 (Boletin da União panamericana, v. 46, no. 1, Janeiro 1944).   **[87a]**

English text (Bulletin of the Pan American union, v. 77, no. 8, Aug. 1943).

Spanish text (Boletín de la Unión panamericana, v. 77, no. 12, Dic., 1943).

——. Educación musical en 14 repúblicas americanas. Music education in 14 American republics. Washington, D. C., Oficina de música, Unión panamericana, 1945. 34 p. il. (Music series, no. 12.)   **[88a]**

Survey on music education in the following Latin-American countries: Chile, Colombia, Costa Rica, Cuba, Dominican Republic, El Salvador, Guatemala, Haiti, Honduras, Mexico, Nicaragua, Peru, Puerto Rico, Panama and Venezuela.

——. Madurez de la música del Nuevo Mundo. *Rev. mus. chil.,* año 3, no. 24 (September 1947), p. 27-33.   **[89a]**

Lowens, Irving. Current chronicle. Washington, D. C. *Mus. quart.,* v. 44, no. 3 (July 1958), p. 378-382.   **[90a]**

Discusses the works performed at the first Inter-American music festival in Washington, April 18-20, 1958, and picks out Ginastera's 2nd string quartet as "the undoubted sensation of the entire festival".

Lussagnet, Suzanne. Bibliographie américaniste. *Jour. soc. amer.,* n. s., v. 43, 1954, p. 249-349. **[91a]**

Continuation of comprehensive yearly bibliography. Covers physical anthropology, archeology, ethnology and folklore, linguistics, history, geography, and biography. (I. Rouse.)

Martín, Edgardo. Divulgación de la música de América. *Clave,* v. 6, no. 5 (April 1957), p. 15-16. **[92a]**

Matilla, Alfredo. Festival de música de las Américas. *B. A. mus.,* v. 13, no. 204 (May 16, 1958), p. 6. **[93a]**

The First Inter-American Music Festival in Washington, D. C.

Mayer-Serra, Otto. Música y músicos de latinoamérica. México, D. F., Editorial Atlante, 1947. 2 vols. il. (incl. music) **[94a]**

A bio-bibliographical dictionary of music and musicians of Latin America.

———. Panorama de la música hispano-americana en la época actual. *Repr. camp.,* v. 2, no. 5 (Sept.-Oct. 1945), p. 103-118. **[95a]**

Survey of composers of fine-art or concert music during the twentieth century. (C.S.)

Montes, Juan. Ediciones de la unión panamericana. *B. A. mus.,* v. 12, no. 197 (Oct. 1, 1957), p. 3. **[96a]**

Brief reviews of music published by the Pan American Union.

Orchestras and managers of the world: Central America, South America. *Mus. Amer.,* v. 75, no. 4 (Feb. 15, 1955), p. 289-290. **[97a]**

List for Mexico, Argentina and Brazil.

Orchestras of the Americas. *Mus. Amer.,* v. 77, no. 3 (Feb. 1957), p. 290-293. **[98a]**

List of orchestras, their addresses, and also concert managers of Mexico, Argentina, Brazil, Chile, Colombia, and Uruguay, on pages 292-293.

Orrego-Salas, Juan. Hacia un lenguaje musical de latinoamérica. *Clave,* v. 6, no. 5 (April 1957), p. 21-22. **[99a]**

Maintains that an "American tradition" in musical composition should not be identified solely with folklore, or with indigenous and vernacular elements of style, but should be enlarged to include the New World reflections of aesthetic currents originating in Europe. This is a characteristically Chilean point of view, although shared by an increasing number of composers throughout Latin America.

Pan American union. Departamento de asuntos culturales. Sección de música. Directorio musical de la América Latina. Musical directory of Latin America. Conservatorios, academias y escuelas de música, y orquestas sinfónicas. Conservatories, academies and music schools, and symphony orchestras. Washington, D. C., Pan American uion, 1954. 27 p. **[100a]**

A very useful compendium of practical information.

Paz, Juan Carlos. Problemática y creación musical en América. *Bol. progr. Col.,* v. 18, no. 180 (July 1959), p. 1-7. **[101a]**

Mentions Charles Ives and Julián Carrillo as "two extraordinary values in the domains of musical creation and of theoretical speculation, respectively..." Points out the "backwardness" (*retraso*) of Latin American music and asserts that most of the best-known composers of Chile, Brazil, Argentina and Cuba suffer from "a suicidal and painfully premature academicism." In conclusion: "That portion of the history of music embracing the area from Mexico to the end of the southern Continent, still remains to be written."

Pequeno, Mercedes Mouro de. La formación profesional del bibliotecario musical. *Bol. interam. mús.,* no. 3 (Jan. 1958), p. 5-7. **[102a]**

Pimsleur, Paul. Concert busines thrives in Latin America. *Mus. Amer.,* v. 76, no. 11 (Sept. 1956), p. 33-34. **[103a]**

General comment on theaters and audiences, followed by a list of concert managers for Mexico, Guatemala, the Dominican Republic. Puerto Rico, the Dutch West Indies, Cuba, Venezuela, Colombia, Ecuador, Peru, Chile, Argentina, Uruguay and Brazil.

Pineda, Rafael. First festival of music; Venezuelans play host to musicians. *Americas*, v. 7, no. 3 (March 1955), p. 33-36.   **[104a]**

Account of initiation and event of inter-American music festival in Caracas held in November-December 1954. Nine photographs of prominent composers and musicians.

Salazar, Adolfo. La música moderna; las corrientes directrices en el arte musical contemporáneo. B u e n o s Aires, Editorial Losada, 1944. 518 p. il. (incl. music).   **[105a]**

Chapter 30 deals with contemporary Latin Amercian music, chiefly in relation to nationalism. Treatment is summary, with special emphasis on the work of Villa-Lobos and Chávez. The analysis of nationalist trends is harsh but perspicacious. There are s o m e s e r i o u s factual errors.

Sandi, Luis. Problemas del compositor en América. *Nuestra música*, v. 7, no. 25 (Ist trimestre, 1952), p. 62-64.   **[106a]**

Assessment to the plight of the composer in Latin America, where he faces "a thousand problems that the European does not know." Urges state patronage of musicians as the only answer. (R.A.W.)

Santa Cruz, Domingo. Charles Seeger y su obra americanista. *Rev. mus. chil.,* v. 1, no. 2 (June, 1945), p. 12-15.   **[107a]**

Account of the work of Charles Seeger as Chief of the Music Division of the Pan American Union. (B.K.)

——. El segundo festival de música latinoamericana de Caracas. *Rev. mus. chil.,* v. 11, no. 52 (June-July 1957), p. 7-14. il.   **[108a]**

Includes a photograph of the members of the Caracas jury: Santa Cruz, Ginastera, Copland, Chávez, J. B. Plaza.

——. Las normas musicales del Comu-

nismo. *Rev. mus. chil.,* v. 5, no. 34 (June-July 1949), p. 7-25.   **[109a]**

Lucid account of the dogmatism of the 1948 Manifesto of Prague (concerning music), and the Communist Party line on music in general.

——. Los festivales latinoamericanos de música y el festival de Montevideo. *Rev. mus. chil.,* año 11, no. 55 (Oct.-Nov. 1957), p. 37-49.   **[110a]**

Sas, Andrés. La música culta de América. Consideraciones generales sobre su estado actual. *Rev. mus. chil.,* v. 2, no. 11 (May 1946), p. 15-24; no. 12 (June 1946), p. 15-22.   **[111a]**

A strongly critical, thoroughly realistic and slightly pessimistic analysis of the state of m u s i c a l composition in Latin America. Ends on a note of faith in the future.

Seeger, Charles. "A G u i d e to Latin American Music." *Mus. quart.,* v. 32, no. 2 (Apr. 1946), p. 303-305. **[112a]**

An appreciative review of the first edition of this work, by an important authority on the subject.

——. Brief history of the Music division of the Pan American union. Washington, D. C., Music division. Pan American union, 1947. 14 p.   **[113a]**

Reproduced from typewritten copy.

——. Music and society: Some New-World evidence of their relationship. *In* Conference on Latin American Fine Arts, June 14-17, 1951. P r o c e e d i n g s. Austin, Texas, U n i v e r s i t y of Texas, Institute of Latin A m e r i c a n Studies (Latin American Studies, 13), 1952, p. 84-97.   **[114a]**

"The New World ... offers several advantages as a domain in which the influence of society upon music can be studied." Analyzes the process of musical acculturation in the Americas, with special regard to two opposing trends discernible in every culture "one toward integration, the other toward diversification." A scholarly and systematic analysis along sociological lines.

——. Music in the Americas. *Bull. pan amer. union*, v. 79, no. 5 (May 1945), p. 290-293; no. 6 (June 1945), p. 341-344. **[115a]**

Deals on a masterly theoretical level with "Oral and written traditions in the Americas", and the interrelation of the two traditions.

——. Música y musicología en el Nuevo Mundo. *Rev. mus. chil.*, v. 2, no. 14 (Sept. 1946), p. 7-18. **[116a]**

——. Notes on music in the Americas. *Bull. pan Amer. union*, v. 78, no. 8 (Aug. 1944), p. 449-452; no. 9 (Sept. 1944), p. 507-510; no. 10 (Oct. 1944), p. 575-578; no. 11 (Nov. 1944), p. 627-631; no. 12 (Dec. 1944), p. 698-701. **[117a]**

——. Opportunities in the field of music. *In* Doyle, Henry Grattan, ed. A handbook on the teaching of Spanish and Portuguese, with special reference to Latin America. Boston, D. C. Heath, 1945, p. 82-90. **[118a]**

——. Review of inter-American relations in the field of music, 1940-1943. Washington, D. C., Pan American union, 1943. 13 p. **[119a]**

Reproduced from typewritten copy.

Slonimsky, Nicolas. Music of Latin America. New York, Thomas Y. Crowell Company, 1945. vi, 374 p. il. (music). **[120a]**

A superficial, anecdotal survey rather than a seriously critical or scholarly treatment of the subject. The work is divided into 3 parts. The first is largely taken up with the author's experiencies in Latin America as conductor, lecturer, and reporter. Part II consists of an alphabetical survey of musical activity, past and present, in the 20 countries of Latin America, with biographical sketches of composers. Part III is a "Dictionary of Latin American musicians, songs and dances, and musical instruments".

For a detailed review, cf. item no. 57a

——. La música de Latino-América. Buenos Aires. El Ateneo, 1947. **[121a]**

Spanish translation of the preceding item.

Smith, Cecil M. The ABC countries at the Met. *Américas*, v. 3, no. 5 (May 1951), p. 9-12-27. **[122a]**

Particularly on Bidú Sayão of Brazil, Ramón Vinay, tenor of Chile, and Delia Rigal, soprano of Argentina, and their lives and careers at the Metropolitan Opera House in New York.

Solórzano Díaz, Adolfo. IAMC. OAS backs new Inter-American Music Center. *Americas*, v. 9, no. 1 (Jan. 1957), p. 27-30. **[123a]**

Informal account of the aims of Center, more commonly known as CIDEM (Centro interamericano de música). Photographs include eight Latin American composers, and the meeting in Washington at which the Center was organized.

Stevenson, Robert. The first dated mention of sarabande. *Jour. amer. musicol. soc.*, v. 5, no. 1 (Spring 1952), p. 29-31. **[124a]**

Finds a 1579 reference to the *zarabanda* in chapter 99 of Fray Diego Durán's *Historia de las Indias de Nueva España*, which he considers "perfect evidence showing the American provenience of the sarabande".

Thompson, Leila (Fern). Concerts at the Pan American Union, 1946-1947. Washington, Pan American Union, 1947, p. 679-688 (*Bulletin of the Pan American union*, v. 81, no. 12, December 1947). **[125a]**

——. Spanish text. *Boletín de la Unión panamericana*, v. 81, no. 11, noviembre 1947. **[126a]**

——. Portuguese text. *Boletim dar União Panamericana*, v. 49, no. 10, outubro 1947. **[127a]**

——. Partial List of Latin-American music obtainable in the United States. Washington, D. C., Music Division, Pan American union, 1947. 57 p. (Music Series, no. 1.) **[128a]**

A revision of item no. 21.

Trenti Rocamora, J. Luis. El teatro en la América colonial. Prólogo de Guillermo Fúrlong, S. J. Buenos Aires,

Editorial Huares, S. A., 1947. 534 p.
il. facs.   **[129a]**

Part I deals with Argentina, Bolivia, Paraguay and Uruguay; Part II with Brazil, Canada, Colombia, Cuba, Chile, Ecuador, United States, Guatemala, Mexico, Panama, Peru, and Santo Domingo. The Thematic Index has numerous entries under Baile, Canto, Compositores, Entremeses, Guitarras, Loas, Música, Músicos, Óperas, Orquestas, Piezas musicales, Sainetes, Tonadillas, Violines, and Zarzuelas. A work of solid erudition, based largely on primary sources. Copious bibliographical data.

Valenti Ferro, Enzo. El festival de Caracas. *B. A. mus.*, v. 12, no. 187 (May 2, 1957), p. 1, 5. il.   **[130a]**

A critique of each of the 9 concerts of the Caracas Festival of Latin American music held in 1957.

——. El festival de Montevideo. *B. A. mus.*, v. 12, no. 198 (Oct. 16, 1957), p. 1.   **[131a]**

Festival of Latin American Music organized by the S.O.D.R.E. (national broadcasting service).

——. Festival de música contemporánea americana. *B. A. mus.*, v. 13, no. 3 (Sept. 16, 1958), p. 1.   **[132a]**

The festival was held in Buenos Aires, sponsored by the Asociación de Conciertos de Cámara.

——. La música en Latinoamérica. *B. A. mus.*, v. 12, no. 197 (Oct. 1, 1957), p. 1.   **[133a]**

Introducing the special issue of this periodical devoted to contemporary music of Latin America.

——. Música de Latinoamérica en Caracas. *B. A. mus.*, v. 13, no. 186 (Apr. 1. 1957), p. 1, 2.   **[134a]**

——. New Union promotes exchange of music between Americas. *Mus. Amer.*, v. 76, no. 9 (July 1956), p. 24 **[135a]**

On the background and organization of the Inter-American Music Center, founded on April 12, 1956 in Washington. Cites aims of Center, lists officers, and discusses immediate plans.

——. Profesionalismo, amateurismo.

folklorismo. Música de Latinoamérica en Caracas. *B. A. mus.*, v. 12, no. 188 (May 16, 1957), p. 3.   **[136a]**

Objects to the predominance of "folklorism" at the 2nd Festival of Latin American Music in Caracas.

Vega, Aurelio de la. El denominador común. *Música,* v. 1, no. 3 (Oct. 1957), p. 7-8.   **[137a]**

Discussion of contemporary music in the Americas.

——. Problemática de la música latinoamericana actual. *Rev. mus. chil.*, v. 12, no. 61 (Sept.-Oct. 1958), p. 33-38.   **[138a]**

Affirms that the remnants of excessive nationalism are disappearing from the Latin American musical scene, and that the newer composers have a more universal outlook.

——. The negative emotion (an essay on modern music). La Habana, 1950. 37 p.   **[139a]**

Includes brief discussion of Villa-Lobos and Chávez.

Vega, Carlos. La musique en Amérique Latine au XXᵉ siècle. *Rev. mus.*, numéro spécial, no. 242 (1958), p. 101-104.   **[140a]**

——. Voices of the south. *Americas*, v. 3, no. 9 (Sept. 1951), p. 20-23. 41-42.   **[141a]**

Brief but important tracing of Indian, African and European musical influences in South American music. Photographs and 8 music examples. (B.K.)

Villa-Lobos, Heitor. Educação musical. *Bol. lat. am. mus.*, v. 6, 1946, p. 405-588.   **[142a]**

In 1932, in mid-career as a composer of concert music, Villa-Lobos became interested in the music education of children. Initiating a movement "cívico-artístico-educacional" in the schools of the Federal District, he evolved a technique of mass instruction of his own and founded the Conservatorio Nacional de Canto Orfeónico to teach it to prospective teachers. The whole mixture of fantasy, hard-headed realism, and artistic resourcefulness is probably without parallel in 20th century civilization history of music. (C.S.)

ARGENTINA

THOUGH there exists no adequate history of music in Argentina, various phases of the subject, notably folk music and the lyric theatre, have been rather thoroughly covered in several monographs. Carlos Vega's *Danzas y canciones argentinas* [no. 568] is a valuable and comprehensive treatise, containing detailed descriptions of folk dances, and illustrated with numerous musical examples. Vega, who is in charge of the Gabinete de Musicología Indígena of the Museo Argentino de Ciencias Naturales, has a large collection of Argentine folk music, which he plans to publish in the near future. As a preliminary study for this publication, he has explained his method of melodic analysis in two large volumes issued under the auspices of the Instituto de Literatura Argentina [see item no. 526]. Arturo C. Schianca's *Historia de la música argentina* deals almost exclusively with folk music, as does also the book by Juan Álvarez entitled *Orígenes de la música argentina*, which briefly surveys the indigenous and Creole music, and discusses the Negro influence on Argentine music. More important data on the latter subject will be found in Vicente Rossi's *Cosas de Negros*, which, in opposition to Vega's theories, attempts to prove that the *tango* is of Negro origin.

An excellent survey of Argentine folk music, closely integrated with the social and historical background of Argentine life, is to be found in the monumental work of Ricardo Rojas, *La literatura argentina*. Unlike most literary historians, Rojas gives full importance to music in relation to popular poetry. In Part I of his great work, entitled *Los gauchescos* he includes many musical examples to illustrate his account of Gaucho songs and dances [see item no. 514]. Gaucho folk music has also been studied and published by Ventura R. Lynch, Vicente Forte and Jorge M. Furt. For the background of Argentine Gaucho life, English readers may consult *Los payadores Gauchos* by Frederick Mann Page, and *The Gaucho; cattle hunter; cavalryman; ideal of romance*, by Madaline W. Nichols (Duke University Press 1942). The *payadores* were the Gaucho troubadours, whom Page calls "the descendants of the *juglares* of old Spain in La Plata". Such well-known Argentine songs and dances as the *estilo,* the *gato,* the *milonga,* the *pericón* an the *vidala,* are particularly associated with the Gauchos.

The ancient Incan empire, which had its center in Peru, extended to the northern part of what is now Argentina, hence the study of pre-Hispanic music in that country must begin with an examination of the Incan musical system. The Argentine musicologist Juan Giacobbe has attempted to establish the basis for such a study in his article, *Introducción al es-*

63

tudio de una etnofonía argentina, which includes analyses of musical themes collected by Victor Guzmán Cáceres [see items no. 536 and no. 2391x].
As the native Indian races of Argentina have almost died out—there are
some thousands still living in the northern provinces—the indigenous element cannot be considered an important musical factor. In their monograph
on the aborigines of Argentina, Felix F. Outes and Carlos Bruch devote
some attention to music among such surviving tribes as the Matacos, the
Chorotes, the Caingúas and the Patagonians [see item no. 540].

Documents which could serve for a study of the beginning of European
music in Argentina have been assembled by the Jesuit writer, P. Pedro
Grenón, in his monograph *Nuestra primera música instrumental* [no.
360]. Through exhaustive researches in archives, Padre Grenón was able
to locate numerous references to musical instruments dating from the sixteenth, seventeenth and eighteenth centuries. His first entry, dated 1585,
shows that in that year church organs already existed in Santiago del
Estero. Harps, flutes and *vihuelas* (old type of Spanish guitar) are other
instruments mentioned before 1600. The work of the Jesuit missionaries
in teaching European music to the Indians is dealt with by Guillermo
Fúrlong. S. J., in his *Los Jesuítas y la cultura rioplantense,* and by Padre
Grenón in his pamphlet on Padre H. Luis Berger (1588-1641), which gives
a complete list of the musical instruments introduced by the Jesuits [nos.
359 and 360x].

Theatrical activity has long flourished in Argentina, and more operas
have been written and produced there than in any other Latin American
country. In addition to monographs devoted specifically to the lyric theatre,
such as Mariano G. Bosch's *Historia de la ópera en Buenos Aires* and
Fiorda Kelly's *Cronología de las óperas ... en Buenos Aires,* there are
several general historical works on the theatre which contain much interesting information on the history of opera in Argentina. Prominent among
such works are Oscar R. Beltrán's *Los orígenes del teatro argentino,* Bosch's
Historia del teatro en Buenos Aires, and Alfredo Taullard's *Historia de
nuestros viejos teatros.* Not only do these volumes contain numerous details
on the lyric theatre, but often they include data on other musical activities. Taullard, for instance, gives an account of the first orchestral performances in Buenos Aires. The history of Argentina's famed opera house,
the Teatro Colón, is told in a thoroughly documented and profusely illustrated volume entitled *El arte lírico en el teatro Colón (1908-1933),* by
Ernesto de la Guardia and Roberto Herrera [408]. This work also deals
with symphonic concerts given at the Teatro Colón.

Those who do not read Spanish are fortunate in having at hand a convenient introduction to Argentine music in the form of Albert T. Luper's

brief monograph, *The music of Argentina* [no. 333], issued by the Pan American Union as its Music Series No. 5. In addition to a general historical survey, this pamphlet includes a bibliography, a list of Argentine music available in the United States, and a list of recordings.

A fairly large amount of music by modern Argentine composers is available in published form, due chiefly to the activities of the publishing firm of Ricordi in Buenos Aires. The Argentine government, through its Comisión Nacional de Cultura, has also published a number of scores by native composers, including the *Sinfonía Bíblica* by the prominent composer and conductor Juan José Castro (b. 7 March 1895). The Academia Nacional de Bellas Artes has inaugurated the publication of an anthology of Argentine art music, of which the first volume, devoted to *Los precursores,* appeared in 1941 [no. 304]. The three "precursors" whose compositions are included in this volume are Amancio Alcorta (1805-1862), Juan Pedro Esnaola (1808-1878) and Juan Bautista Alberdi (1810-1884). The volume was edited by Alberto Williams, dean of Argentine composers (b. 23 Nov. 1862), whose numerous compositions include nine symphonies (see item no. 389).

Buenos Aires is an important center of musical activity, with many conservatories and musical societies, prominent among the latter being the Asociación Wagneriana, the Asociación del Profesorado Orquestal and the Asociación de Música de Cámara. Among provincial cities, Tucumán, Rosario and Córdoba (see item no. 329) are especially active as music centers.

In the section on Biography and Criticism below will be found the names of many Argentine composers of the present day. For a list of representative works by Argentine composers, the reader is referred to the pamphlet by Luper mentioned above [no. 333]; consult also the *Partial list of Latin American music obtainable in the United States* [no. 21x]. Prominent among contemporary Argentine writers on music are Leopoldo Hurtado, Mauricio Ferrari Nicolay, Mayorino Ferraría and Gastón O. Talamón. Important articles on music appear frequently in the Sunday issues of the leading Argentine dailies, *La Nación* and *La Prensa.*

GENERAL AND MISCELLANEOUS

Alessio, Nicolás Alfredo. Música argentina. *Cultura,* v. 11, no. 83. (July-Aug. 1940), p. 87-88.   **[302]**

André, José. La música argentina. *La Nación* (1 Jan. 1939), sec. 3, p. 2.
                                       [303]

Antología de compositores argentinos; obras para piano y para canto con acompañamiento de piano; escogidas, revisadas y anotadas por Alberto Williams. Cuaderno 1: Los precursores. Buenos Aires, Publicaciones de la Academia nacional de bellas artes, 1941. 123 p. ports. M2.A53
                                       [304]

Compositions by Amancio Alcorta (1805-1862), Juan Pedro Esnaola (1808-1878) and Juan Bautista Alberdi (1810-1884).

Includes biographical sketches and portraits of these three pioneer Argentine composers. All three were amateurs; Alberdi was a prominent man of letters and public figure.

Berrenechea, Mariano Antonio. Historia estética de la música. 3 ed. Buenos Aires, Editorial Claridad, 1941. 535 p. ML160.B15 **[305]**

Deals with Argentine music, p. 387-402. Composers discussed include Arturo Berutti, Pablo Berutti, Julián Aguirre, Constantino Gaito, Ernesto Drangosch, Vicente Forte. R. Peacán del Sar, Joaquín Cortés López, J. Torre Bertucci, E. García Mansilla, A. Rolandone, Pascual de Rogatis, C. López Buchardo, Felipe Boero, José André, Alfredo Schiuma, Ricardo Rodriguez, J. T. Wilkes, Floro Ugarte, Alberto Machado, Alejandro Inzaurraga, Athos Palma, José Gil, Andrés Gaos, Raúl Espoile, Montserrat Campmany.

Beattie, John W., and Louis Woodson Curtis. South American music pilgrimage. IV. Argentina and Uruguay. *Mus. educ. journ.* v. 28, no. 5 (Apr. 1942), p. 22-27. il. **[306]**

Becerra, Martín L. Música nativa; conferencia. Zarate, La Tribuna, 1930. 19 p. **[307]**

Blomberg, Héctor Pedro. Canciones históricas. Buenos Aires, Editorial Tor [1936?]. 172 p. PQ7797.B6C3 **[308]**

Broqua, Alfonso. La musique au Rio de la Plata. *Rev. arg.* v. 1, no. 5 (1935), p. 50-52. **[309]**

The author is a composer of Uruguayan birth.

Calderón de la Barca, E. G. Apuntes de historia de la música. Sud-América. *Correo mus. sud-am.,* v. 1, no. 22 (25 Aug. 1915), p. 4-6. **[310]**

References to music of Brazil, Argentina and Uruguay.

Captain Head's journeys in South America. *In* Stories of popular voyages and travels; South America. London, Charles Tilt, 1829, p. 98-154. F2223.S88 **[311]**

Mention of Argentine music, p. 153.

Cardeza, María Elena. Historia de la música americana. Buenos Aires, Talleres gráficos "Buenos Aires", 1938. 86 p. ML199.C17H5 **[312]**

Apéndice: La música argentina, p. 77-86.

Coeuroy, André. Panorama de la musique contemporaine. Paris, Simon Kra, 1928. 209 p. ML197.C7 **[313]**

Brief reference to Argentine music, p. 44-45.

Composers of Argentina coming to the fore in serious art music. *Mus. Amer.,* v. 49 (25 Nov. 1929), p. 33. **[314]**

Interview with Antonieta S. de Lenhardson, Argentine singer.

Cuarta encuesta de "Nosotros". La música y nuestro folk-lore. *Nosotros,* año 12, v. 28 (Buenos Aires, 1918), p. 525-538; v. 29, p. 227-247. **[315]**

A symposium on the value of folk music in the Argentine as a basis for a national art-music.

Dumesnil, Maurice. Music in Argentina. *Etude,* v. 59, no. 6 (June, 1941), p. 388, 410. il. **[316]**

Ferrari Nicolay, Mauricio. Notas introductoras a la filiación de la cultura musical argentina. *Bol. lat. am. mús.,* v. 3 (Apr. 1937), p. 97-108. **[317]**

Ferraría, Mayorino. Crónica musical. *Nosotros,* v. 64 (1939), p. 115-120. **[318]**

Asociación sinfónica de Buenos Aires, etc.

Forte, Vicente. La canción nacional. *Nativa,* v. 3 (31 July 1926), 2 p. **[319]**

A lecture given by Forte on Argentine music, at which he played some of his own compositions, and María Luisa Carranza sang the music of several outstanding composers.

Guardia, Ernesto de la. La musique et les compositeurs argentins. *Rev. Am. lat.*, v. 7, no. 29 (1924), p. 429-431. **[320]**

Gutiérrez Saenz, Alberto. The evolution of Argentine music. *Mus. digest.* v. 6, no. 5 (20 May 1924), p. 10-11. **[321]**

Huber, Fritz. Aus der geschichte des gesangvereins *Harmonie* in San Carlos Sud, 1876-1926. Buenos Aires, Druckerei Argentinisches, Tageblatt, 1927 [?]. 48 p. **[322]**
New York Public Library.

Jean-Aubry, G. American impressions. *Chesterian*, v. 8, no. 59 (Dec. 1926), p. 79-83. **[323]**
Music in Buenos Aires.

Lagorio, Arturo. Originalité de la musique argentine. *Rev. arg.* (Paris), v. 4 (Sept. 1937), p. 51-56. **[324]**

Luedecke, Hugo Ernesto. Musikbriefe. Buenos Aires. *Neue musikzeitung*, v. 41, no. 13 (Apr. 1920), p. 208-209. **[325]**
Lists numerous musical presentations given in Buenos Aires during 1919, a year cited as one of the most preëminent in the development of music in Buenos Aires.

Lütge, Wilhelm. Deutsche musik in Buenos Aires, *Zeit. musik,* v. 95, no. 9 (Sept. 1928), p. 500-502. **[326]**
Review of German opera, concerts and recitals.

Montés, John. Musikleben in Buenos Aires.. *Signale,* v. 93, no. 3 (16 Jan. 1935), p. 36-37. **[327]**
Notes on musical activities; does not mention any Latin American music.

——. Musikleben in Buenos Aires. *Signale,* v. 94, nos. 32-33 (5 Aug. 1936), p. 473-475. **[328]**
German, Italian and French music, with a comment on Villa-Lobos, p. 475.

Moya, Ismael. El niño y su teatro.
Buenos Aires, Editorial A. Kapelusz y cía. [193-?] 99 p. PQ7797.M73N5 **[329]**
Includes music, p. 13, 41-44, 78.

Moyano López, Rafael. La cultura musical cordobesa. Córdoba, Imprenta de la universidad, 1941, 212 p. ML231. 8.C6M6 **[330]**
A detailed account of musical activity and musical institutions in the city of Córdoba from colonial times to the present.

Oria, José A. La moda, un periódico representativo, 1837-1838; prólogo de la edición facsimilar publicada por la Academia nacional de la historia. Buenos Aires, Guillermo Kraft ltda., 1938. PN5010.M6Q7 **[331]**
La moda, gacetín semanal de música, de poesía, de literatura, de costumbres, was published in Buenos Aires in 1837-38. The writer and musician Juan Bautista Alberdi (see item no. 304) was the leading spirit behind this publication.

Ortiz y San Pelayo, Félix. Nuestra música; o la música española. Buenos Aires, Librería "La facultad" de Juan Roldán. 1920. 198 p. ML231.08N8 **[332]**
Includes: Los orfeones españoles en la Argentina; su pasado, su presente y su porvenir, p. 121-156. Traces the history of Spanish choral groups in Argentina.

Páginas de Sarmiento. De la música argentina. *Rev. amer.,* v. 75 (July-Aug., 1938), p. 25-27. **[333]**
Selection from the writings of the famous Argentine leader Domingo Faustino Sarmiento (1811-1888).

Pan American union. *Music division.* The music of Argentina; by Albert T. Luper, University of Texas. Washington, D. C., Pan American union, 1942. 30 p. Reproduced from typewritten copy. (*Its music series,* no. 5) ML231.L8M8 **[334]**
Includes: Bibliography; a brief list of Argentine music obtainable in the United States; selected list of recordings of Argentine music; guide to music and record sources; index of composers.

Pasqués, Victor A. Texto de música. Buenos Aires, Roque Gaudiosi, n. d. 220 p. **[335]**

A textbook of musical theory for use in secondary schools. Includes bio-bibliographical data on Argentine composers, p. 152-176. A note on the Argentine national anthem (with music), p. 177-183. "El folklore nacional, canciones y danzas nativas." p. 184-195. Portraits of Argentine musicians, 8 p. following p. 208.

Poulet, Gaston. Impressions musicales d'Argentine. *Cour. mus.*, v. 31, no. 9 (1 May 1929), p. 311. **[336]**

Rojas, Ricardo. Eurindia. Buenos Aires, Librería La facultad, Juan Roldán y cía., 1924. 366 p. PQ7797.R7 1922 **[337]**

Dance, p. 228-243; music, p. 244-262. Gives the primitive, colonial and cosmopolitan aspects of these arts, and describes the nationalism of each.

Rubio Piqueras, F. En Argentine: l'activité musicale au Congrès eucharistique de Buenos Aires. *España sacromusical* (Jan. 1935). **[338]**

Citation from files of Pan American Union.

Sarmiento, Domingo Faustino. Obras completas, v. 4. Paris, Belín hermanos. 1909. F2846.S215 **[339]**

Enseñanza de la música, p. 408-412.

Schianca, Arturo C. Historia de la música argentina; origen y características ... Buenos Aires, Establecimiento gráfico argentino [1933?]. 202 p. ML-231.S32 **[340]**

Schiuma, Oreste. La música argentina. *Mundo mus.*, v. 3, no. 34 (July 1941), p. 7-9. **[341]**

Sofía, Pedro. La cultura musical argentina. *Rev. mus. arg.*, v. 1, no. 3 (May 1936), p. 5-9. **[342]**

Includes biographical data on Amancio Alcorta, a composer of the 19th century. Cf. item no. 304.

Talamón, Gastón O. Un año de música argentina. *Nosotros,* ép. 2, v. 2, no. 13 (Apr. 1937), p. 468-478. **[343]**

———. La canción de cámara argentina con texto en idiomas extranjeros. *Rev. música*, v. 3, no. 7 (Jan. 1930), p. 140-148. **[344]**

———. La canción de cámara argentina en la primera mitad del siglo XIX. *Rev. música*, v. 3, no. 2 (Aug. 1929), p. 74-79. **[345]**

Traces the beginning of the art song in Argentina.

———. El cancionero popular y la música culta argentina *Azul*, v. 2 (Jan.-Feb. 1931), p. 15-25. **[346]**

———. Un cuarto de siglo de música argentina. *Nosotros,* año 21, v. 57, no. 219-220 (Aug. 1927), p. 244-284. **[347]**

———. Escuela argentina de música. *Nosotros,* v. 29, no. 112 (Sept. 1918), p. 594-595. **[348]**

Review of auditions.

———. La literatura pianística argentina. *Rev. música*, v. 2, no. 8 (Mar. 1929), p. 5-10. **[349]**

———. La música en Argentina en 1920. *Mús. de Amér.*, v. 2 (Jan. 1921). **[350]**

———. Nuestra música en 1917. *Nosotros,* año 12, v. 28, no. 105 (Jan. 1918), p. 116-124. **[351]**

"En 1917 el movimiento musical argentino ha sido muy importante."

———. Nuestra música en 1918. *Nosotros,* año 13, v. 31, no. 118 (Feb., 1919), p. 281-290. **[352]**

———. Orígenes de la canción de cámara argentina moderna. *Rev. música*, v. 3, no. 5 (Nov. 1929), p. 1-7 **[353]**

Uriarte, José R. de. ed. Los baskos en

la nación argentina. Buenos Aires [pref. 1919]. 482 p. F3021.B2U7 **[354]**

Includes a general account of the Basques, their history, customs, art and music, etc.

Vega, Carlos. La creación en estilo popular. *La Prensa*, v. 68, no. 24,605 (18 July 1937), sec. 2, p. 4. **[355]**

Includes music.

Vicuña Mackenna, Benjamín. La Argentina en el año de 1855. Buenos Aires, Ed. de la revista americana de Buenos Aires, 1936. 255 p. F2815.-V54 **[356]**

References to music, p. 41-43, 205.

See also nos. 44, 54, 59, 95, 97, 384.

COLONIAL MUSIC

Baucke, Florian. Iconografía colonial rioplatense. Buenos Aires, Vian y Zona, 1935. 43 plates. F2841.B38 **[357]**

Introduction by Guillermo Fúrlong. Plate no. 20, *Gran fiesta con chicha, música, bailes y riñas;* plate no. 21, *Otra gran fiesta.*

Buenos Aires. Universidad. Facultad de filosofía y letras. Instituto de literatura argentina. Sección folklore. Primera serie: El canto popular. Vol. 2, no. 1. Música colonial. La música de un códice colonial del siglo XVII. Por Carlos Vega. Buenos Aires, Imprenta de la Universidad, 1931. 93 p. music. facs. ML3575.C2 **[358]**

"El presente opúsculo ofrece al historiador del arte virreinal americano, en notación moderna, el único documento musical erudito de la colonia conocido hasta nuestros días..." This is a critical analysis and transcription into modern notation of a collection of songs found in a manuscript of the 17th century copied by Fray Gregorio de Zuola. Cf. nos. 363-366.

Fúrlong, Guillermo. Los jesuítas y la

cultura rioplatense. Montevideo, Urta y Curbelo, 1933. 161 p. F2831.F86 **[359]**

Chap. 13, *La música y el canto,* p. 78-83. Jesuit work in the field of music goes back to 1609, when P. Diego de Torres ordered that the Indians be taught singing; musical instruments; illustrations of musical progress through the efforts of the Jesuits, are included in this chapter.

Grenón, Pedro. Nuestra primera música instrumental, datos históricos. Buenos Aires, Librería "La Cotizadora económica", de E. Perrot, 1929. 106 p. il. ML231.G7 **[360]**

The most important monograph dealing with music in Argentina in the early colonial period. Beginning with the year 1585, the author cites references to music, instruments and dances found in various sources, chiefly unpublished. His chronology ends with the year 1858, with a description of the organ in the cathedral of Córdoba.

——. Una vida de artista: H. Luis Berger, S. J. (1588-1641). Córdoba, Argentina, A. Biffignandi, 1927. 32 p. il. **[360x]**

Padre Luis Berger (also Verger, Vergier, Vergel, Bergel), of Belgian birth, was a musical leader among the Jesuit missionaries in the Rio de la Plata. He was also active for a time in Chile. Includes an account of his musical teaching among the Indians, and a list of musical instruments introduced by the missionaries. Illustrations of wind instruments, p. 29.

Olivari, Nicolás. La música en el pasado colonial de Buenos Aires. *Rev. música,* v. 2, no. 3 (Sept. 1928), p. 172-176. **[361]**

Concert music in Buenos Aires from 1832 (when the first concert of note was given) to 1855.

Rega Molina, H. La música en Buenos Aires antiguo. *Rev. música,* v. 1, no. 5 (Nov. 1927), p. 27-31. **[362]**

Deals with concert life in Buenos Aires from 1789-1817.

Wilkes, Josué Teófilo. Doce canciones coloniales del siglo XVII recogidas por fray Gregorio de Zuola ... *Bol. lat. am. mús.*, v. 1 (1935), p. 79-109. [363]

Only 4 of the songs are analyzed in this article, with 4 musical examples. Wilkes' arrangement of these 4 songs are published in the musical supplement of the *Boletín* for 1935. See nos. 364 and 365.

——. Doce canciones coloniales del siglo XVII, puestas en notación moderna y armonizadas. Estudio demostrativo de sus relaciones con la morfología de la música grecorromana y el canto gregoriano. (Segunda Parte.) *Bol. lat. am. mús.*, v. 2 (Apr. 1936), p. 21-60. [364]

Cf. nos. 363 and 365.

——. Doce canciones coloniales del siglo XVII, puestas en notación moderna y armonizadas. Estudio demostrativo de sus relaciones con la morfología de la música grecorromana y el canto gregoriano. (Conclusión.) *Bol. lat. am. mús.*, v. 3 (Apr. 1937), p. 143-178. [365]

Wilkes's harmonizations of these songs (nos. 7, 8, 9, 10, 11, 13, 14, 15) are in the musical supplement of the *Boletín*, v. 3.

——. Música colonial. *Nosotros*, año 26, v. 74, no. 273 (Feb. 1932), p. 134-147. [366]

A discussion of Carlos Vega's *La música de un códice colonial del siglo XVII*, with the music of one song and several briefer musical examples. See item no. 358. Cf. also nos. 363, 364 and 365, for Wilkes' analysis and transcriptions of these songs.

See also nos. 46, 370, 403, 404, 405, 422, 457, 514, 568.

BIOGRAPHY AND CRITICISM

Aguirre, Julián. Músicos argentinos. *Miscelánea* (Buenos Aires), v. 1 (1907), p. 13. [367]

Arconada, César N. Folklore mexicano: a propósito de la artista argentina Ana S. de Cabrera. *Gaceta mus.*, v. 1, no. 3 (Mar. 1928), p. 7-10 [368]

Autores modernos: Ricardo Rodríguez. *Rev mus.*, [Guatemala], v. 1, no. 10 (July, 1928), p. 9. [369]

Brief biographical sketch of this Argentine composer (b. 1877), with portrait.

Ayestarán, Lauro. Domenico Zipoli, el gran compositor y organista romano del 1700 en el Río de la Plata. Montevideo, Impresora uruguaya, s. a., 1941. 30 p. ML410.Z62A9 [370]

Reprinted from *Revista histórica*, publicación del Museo histórico nacional, *Montevideo*, año 35 (2ª época), v. 13, no. 37.

Zipoli was an important figure in European organ music of the 18th century. His *Sonate d'intavolatura per organo o cimbalo* were printed in 1716 at Rome, where he was organist of the Jesuit church. Standard authorities (Riemann, Grove, Baker, etc.) give only meagre biographical data, with no mention of Zipoli's activities after 1716. Taking as his point of departure a reference to a certain Domingo Zipoli in Guillermo Fúrlong's *Los Jesuítas y la cultura rioplatense*, who is mentioned as organist of the Jesuit church in Córdoba (Argentina), the author establishes the identity of these two musicians. From records of the Society of Jesus, Ayestarán is able to correct and amplify the biographical data on Zipoli. It appears that Zipoli was born at Prato (Tuscany) on 15 Oct. 1688, not at Nola (Naples) in 1675, as generally stated. In July 1716 he went from Rome to Sevilla (Spain), where he entered the Jesuit Order. On 5 April 1717 he set sail from Cádiz for the Río de la Plata, and from 1718 until his death in 1726 (2 Jan.) he was organist at Córdoba. The possibility that musical MSS. of Zipoli may exist in Córdoba opens up an interesting field for research in Latin American musicology.

Baqueiro Fóster, Gerónimo. Por el mundo de la música: Juan José Castro. *Rev. mus. mex.*, v. 1, no. 7 (7 Apr. 1942), p. 157-158. [371]

Castro's appearance as conductor in Mexico leads to a discussion of contemporary Argentine music.

Chase, Gilbert. Juan José Castro. *Int. amer. monthly*, v. 1, (May. 1942), p. 35. port. [372]

A brief impression, motivated by Castro's appearance as guest conductor of the National Symphony Orchestra in the Pan American Union, Washington, D. C.

Clerise, J. Músicos argentinos. *Música,* no. 16 (15 Aug. 1906). **[373]**

Coeuroy, André. Panorama de la musique contemporaine. Paris, Simon Kra, 1928. 209 p. ML197.C7 **[374]**
Breif reference to South American music, p. 44-45, with special mention of Alberto Williams, Villa-Lobos and Alfonso Broqua.

Del compositor argentino, Alberto E. Ginastera. *La Prensa,* v. 69, no. 24.750 (19 Dec. 1937), sec. 3, p. 4. **[375]**
Short review of his life and works; music to *Danza del viejo boyero,* written especially for *La Prensa.*

Del compositor argentino Antonio de Raco. *La prensa,* v. 69, no. 24,752 (12 Dec. 1937), sec. 2, p. 4. **[376]**
Biographical notes and music to *Prelude* (for piano), written especially for *La Prensa.*

Del compositor argentino, Juan Francisco Giacobbe. *La prensa* (Buenos Aires), v. 69, no. 24,745 (5 Dec. 1937), sec. 2, p. 4. **[377]**
Brief biographical sketch of this composer, with words and music to a song, *Carnaval Calchaquí* written especially for *La Prensa.* Portrait.

Del compositor argentino, Pedro Valenti Costa. *La prensa,* v. 69, no. 24,766 (26 Dec. 1937), sec. 3, p. 3. **[378]**
Words and music to a song written especially for *La Prensa, Caminito de la sierra.* Also biographical data on the composer.

Ferraría, Mayorino. Juan José Castro. *Nosotros,* v. 6, 2d época, no. 65 (Aug. 1941), p. 185-189. **[379]**
Castro, leading Argentine composer and conductor, appeared as guest-conductor of the NBC Orchestra in New York in the winter of 1941.

———. Músicos argentinos: Alberto Wil-

liams. *Mundo mus.,* v. 3, no. 36 (Sept. 1941), p. 1-4. **[380]**
Alberto Williams (b. 1862), is the dean of Argentine composers. See item no. 389.

———. José de Nito. *Mundo mus.,* v. 3, no. 32 (May 1941), p. 3-4. **[381]**
De Nito was born in Rosario on 12 Dec. 1887.

Gallac, Hector I. La obra musical de Juan Carlos Paz. *Bol. lat. am. mús.,* v. 1 (Apr. 1935), p. 33-42. **[382]**

Guardia, Ernesto de la. Julián Aguirre. *Rev. música,* v. 1, no. 3 (15 Sept. 1927), p. 153-155. **[383]**

Hurtado, Leopoldo. Below the equator. *Mod. music,* v. 20, no. 2 (Jan.-Feb. 1943), p. 121-124 **[384]**
Review of recent musical activities in Buenos Aires, by the music critic of *La Prensa.* Mentions especially the concerts of the Grupo Renovación and La Nueva Música, both devoted to modern music. Points out that Washington Castro (younger brother of Juan José and José María) is coming to the fore as a composer.

———. La musique dans la République Argentine. *Rev. mus.,* número especial (Feb.-Mar. 1940), p. 54-57. **[385]**
Stresses the strong cosmopolitan element in Argentine music. Mentions especially the composers Juan José and José María Castro, Luis Gianneo, Jacobo Ficher, Juan Carlos Paz, Honorio Siccardi, R. García Morillo, Antonio de Raco and Alberto Ginastera.

Keller, Eduardo. Juan Carlos Paz. *Mus. viva,* v. 2, no. 10-11, (Apr.-May 1941), p. 1-2. **[386]**
With portrait and list of works.

Lange, Francisco Curt. El compositor argentino Juan Carlos Paz. *Bol. lat. am. mus.,* v. 4 (Bogotá, 1938), p. 799-829. **[387]**

———. Juan Bautista Massa. *Bol. lat. am. mús.,* v. 4 (1938), p. 665-674. **[388]**

Músicos argentinos: Alberto Williams; nota biográfica y catálogo de sus obras. Buenos Aires, Gurina y cía., 1940. 27 p. port. **[389]**

Biographical sketch, p. 5-13. Alberto Williams was born in Buenos Aires, 23 Nov. 1862. He is described as "composer, poet, pianist, conductor and pedagogue". His maternal grandfather was the composer Amancio Alcorta (cf. item no. 304). He studied composition at the Paris Conservatoire, also privately with César Franck. In 1893 he founded the Conservatorio de Buenos Aires (also known as Conservatorio Alberto Williams), of which he was active director until 1940. This Conservatory has many branches throughout the republic; as an organ of the Conservatory, W. founded the review *La Quena*. 112 opus numbers are listed in the catalogue of his works; also several works without opus numbers; numerous didactic works, literary writings, etc. Cf. item no. 125.

Músicos argentinos: Athos Palma. *Preludios,* v. 2, no. 7 (Sept.-Dec. 1939), p. 216-220. **[390]**

Biographical sketch, with a list of his works, and the various positions he has held.

Nesle, Robert de. Un entretien avec... Alberto Williams. *Le guide du concert,* v. 17, no. 22 (6 Mar. 1931), p. 615-617. **[391]**

Prat, Domingo. Diccionario biográfico, bibliográfico, histórico, crítico, de guitarras, guitarristas, danzas y cantos. Buenos Aires, Casa Romero y Fernández, 1934. 468 p. ML128.G8P7 **[392]**

Contains many biographical sketches of Argentine guitarists and composers for the guitar.

Saminsky, Lazare. In the Argentine. *Mod. music,* v. 18, no. 1 (1940), p. 31-36. il. **[393]**

Discusses the work of Juan Carlos Paz, Luis Gianneo, Juan José Castro, José María Castro, Jacobo Ficher, Honorio Siccardi, Alberto Ginastera. The author finds that most of these composers are "frankly anti-folklorist ... and cosmopolitan to the core." He considers J. J. Castro "the premier composer of Argentina".

Schiuma, Oreste. Músicos argentinos: Angel E. Lasala. *Mundo mus.,* v. 4, no. 44 (May. 1942), p. 1-2. **[394]**

Includes a list of works by this composer, who was born in Buenos Aires in 1914.

Slonimsky, Nicolas. Alberto Williams: the father of Argentine music. *Mus. Amer.,* v. 62, no. 1 (10 Jan. 1942), p. 11, 37. il. **[395]**

——. Modern Argentine composers. *Christian scien. mon.,* v. 33, no. 28 (28 Dec. 1940), p. 12; v. 33, no. 39 (11 Jan. 1941), p. 6. **[396]**

The first article deals with Alberto Williams, Pascual de Rogatis, Arturo Luzzatti, Felipe Boero, Gilardo Gilardi and Constantino Gaito. The second discusses José María and Juan José Castro, H. Siccardi, J. Ficher, L. Gianneo, Juan Carlos Paz, Carlos Suffern, R. García Morillo, Julio Perceval, Antonio de Raco.

La sociedad argentina de conciertos. *Rev. amer.,* v. 13, nos. 145-146 (May-June 1936), p. 145-168. il. **[397]**

Includes biographical sketch of Carlos Olivares, founder of this society, which gave its inaugural concert on 17 March 1934.

Sofía, Pedro. Juan Pedro Esnaola. *Rev. mus. arg.,* v. 1, no. 4 (June 1936), p. 8-9. **[398]**

Bio-bibliographical data on this pioneer Argentine composer.

Talamón, Gastón O. Crítica musical; Arturo Berutti y Juan Bautista Massa. *Nosotros,* ép. 2, v. 3, no. 24 (Mar. 1938), p. 354-356. **[399]**

A necrology.

——. El estado actual de la música argentina. *Música,* Chile, v. 2, no. 5 (May 1921), p. 6-11. ports. **[400]**

Deals with Alberto Poggi, Felipe Boero, Alfredo Schiuma, Carlos Pedrell, Julián Aguirre, Ernesto Drangosch, Luis Ochoa, R. Peacán del Sar, Ricardo Rodríguez, Floro Ugarte, Arturo Berutti, Pascual de Rogatis, Vicente Forte, Carlos López Buchardo, Athos Palma, José Gil, Celes-

tino Piaggio, Constantino Gaito, H é c t o r
Panizza, César Stiattessi, Alberto Williams.

——. Músicos argentinos: Alberto Williams. *Rev. música,* v. 2, no. 11 (June,
1929), p. 209-217. **[401]**
With portrait and list of works.

Vega, Carlos. Ana S. de Cabrera. *El
hogar,* año 25, v. 64, no. 1011 (1 Mar.
1929). **[402]**

See also nos. 96, 99, 103.

LYRIC THEATRE

Beltrán, Oscar R. Los orígenes del
teatro argentino, desde el virreinato
hasta el estreno de "Juan Moreira"
(1884). Buenos Aires, Ed. Sopena
argentina, 1941. 155 p. PN2451.B38
[403]
In addition to references on the lyric
theatre, this volume includes a note on the
national anthem of Argentina, p. 62-66.

Bosch, Mariano G. Historia de la ópera
en Buenos Aires. Buenos Aires, Imprenta el comercio, 1905. 256 p. il.
ML1717.8B9B7 **[404]**
Traces the origin of the lyric theatre in
South America from the Spanish *tonadillas*
of the 18th century.

——. Historia del teatro en Buenos
Aires. Buenos Aires, Establ. tip. el
comercio, 1910. 518 p. PN2452.B8B6
[405]
This work contains a copious documentation on the lyric theatre in Argentina. See
esp. chapters 3, 9, 17, 25 (La música y los
conciertos), 29, 33, 34, 35, 38, 39.

Ferrari Nicolay, Mauricio. En torno a
"Las vírgenes del sol", la nueva ópera
argentina. *Estudios,* v. 62 (July-Dec.
1939), p. 29-46. **[406]**

Fiorda Kelly, Alfredo. Cronología de las
óperas, dramas líricos, oratorios, himnos, etc., cantados en Buenos Aires.
Buenos Aires, Imp. Riera y cía., 1834.
83 p. ML1717.8.B9F5 **[407]**

García Velloso, Enrique. Abelardo Lastra y el género chico en Buenos Aires.
Nosotros, v. 5, nos. 52-53 (July-Aug.
1940), p. 5-16. **[408]**
"Capítulo inédito perteneciente al libro
Memorias de un hombre de teatro"—footnote. "Género chico" is the generic term for
the one-act Spanish comedy, which in its
musical form is known as *zarzuela* or
sainete. The one-act zarzuela began to be
popular in Buenos Aires in the 1890's.
"Abelardo Lastra fue el artista español que
mejor encarnó los tipos populares de los
sainetes porteños y de las zarzuelas cam-
peras."

Gómez Carrillo, Enrique. El encanto de
Buenos Aires. Madrid, Perlado Páez
y cía., 1914. 276 p. F3001.G63 (*also
in his* Obras Completas, v. 20, Madrid,
Ed. Mundo latino, 1921). **[409]**
"En los grandes teatros", p. 71-83.

Góngora, Luis. *Chrisanthème* de R a f a e l
Peacán del Sar. *Rev. música,* v. 1, no.
2 (15 Aug. 1927), p. 24-28. **[410]**
Deals with the production of this opera
at the Teatro Colón, Buenos Aires.

**Guardia, Ernesto de la, and Roberto
Herrera.** El arte lírico en el teatro
Colón (1908-1933). Buenos Aires, Ed.
Zea y Tejero, 1933. 513 p. il. ML1717.-
8.B9G9 **[411]**
Includes a detailed description of the
Teatro Colón, with floor plans and photographs. The seating capacity of the Colón
(3,500) is greater than that of the Paris
and Vienna opera houses. Résumé of the
activities of each season from 1908
through 1932, p. 26-52. Plots of all operas
performed at the Colón, with casts, arranged in alphabeticial order, p. 54-336.
Biographical dictionary of opera composers
(with portraits), p. 338-420. Biographical
sketches of composers and notes on compositions performed in concerts at the
Colón, p. 422-450. Among the operas described, the following are by Argentine
composers: *A f r o d i t a,* (Arturo Luzzatti);
La angelical Manuelita, 1 act (Eduardo
García Mansilla); *Ardid de amor,* 1 act
(Carlos Pedrell); *Ariana y Dioniso,* 1 act
(Felipe Boero); *Aurora* (Héctor Panizza);
Chrisanthème, 1 act (R. Peacán del Sar);
Flor de Nieve, 1 act (Constantino Gaito);
Frenos (Raúl H. Espoile); *Los héroes* (A.
Berutti); *Huemac* (Pascual de Rogatis);
Ilse (Gilardo Gilardi); *Ivan,* 1 act (García

Mansilla); *Lázaro* (C. Gaito); *Litigio de amor*, 1 act (Alfredo L. Schiuma); *La Magdalena* (Juan B. Massa); *El matrero* (Felipe Boero); *Nazdha*, 1 act (Athos Palma); *Ollantai* (C. Gaito); *Petronio* (C. Gaito); *Raquela*, 1 act (F. Boero); *Saika*, 1 act (Floro M. Ugarte); *La sangre de las guitarras* (C. Gaito); *El sueño del alma* (Carlos López Buchardo); *Tabaré* (Alfredo Schiuma); *Tucumán*, 1 act (F. Boero).

Hesse-Wartegg, Ernst von. Zwischen Anden und Amazonas. 3d. ed. Stuttgart, etc., Union deutsche verlagsgesellschaft, 1926. 493 p. F2223.H47 **[412]**

Contains such references to music as: opera in Argentina, p. 333; music and dance in Bahia, p. 96; photographs of gauchos with their guitars, p. 357, 359.

Labastille, Irma Goebel. Argentine opera. *New York times*, v. 79, no. 26, 433 (8 June 1930), sec. 9, p. 7. **[413]**

Looks forward to the coming season of opera at the Teatro Colón, at which many foreign stars will sing. Primarily Italian opera expected.

Loewenberg, Alfred. Annals of opera, 1597-1940. With an introduction by Edward J. Dent. Cambridge, W. Heffer & sons, ltd., 1943. 879 p. **[414]**

Chronology of operatic performances. Includes *Nazdah* (1924) by Athos Palma; *El matrero* (1929) by Felipe Boero; 4 operas by Ettore Panizza; *Huemac* (1916) by Pascual de Rogatis; *Cayo Petronio* (1919) by Constantino Gaito; *Tabaré* (1925) by Alfredo Schiuma; *Tarass Bulba* (1895), *Pampa* (1897) and *Gli eroi* (1919) by Arturo Berutti.

Lyman, John W. Opera in the Argentine. *Mus. cour.*, v. 74, no. 2 (11 Jan. 1917), p. 30-31 **[415]**

A general review of opera in Buenos Aires, its popularity, the Teatro Colón, several of the visiting virtuosi, the audience, price of tickets, etc.

Montés, John. Opernleben in Buenos Aires. *Signale*, v. 90, no. 6 (10 Feb. 1932), p. 105-108. **[416]**

Account of the various operas given in Buenos Aires, little mention of South American music.

Morante, Luis Ambrosio. El hijo del Sud, acto alegórico en música. Buenos Aires, "Coni", 1924. 281 p. (Facultad de filosofía y letras de la Universidad de Buenos Aires. Instituto de literatura argentina [Publicaciones]), PQ8497.M68H5 **[417]**

Blank verse, with stage directions for music.

Olivari, Nicolás. La accidentada historia del primer teatro Colón. *Rev. música* (Buenos Aires), v. 3 (Jan. 1930), p. 156-159. **[418]**

Talamón, Gastón O. Evolución de nuestro teatro musical; La Ciudad roja de Raúl H. Espoile. *Nosotros*, ép. 2, v. 1, no. 5 (Aug. 1936), p. 588-597. **[419]**

——. La licitación del teatro Colón. *Mús. de Amér.*, v. 2 (Nov. 1921), 4 p. **[420]**

——. El teatro lírico en Buenos Aires. *Nosotros*, año 9, v. 19, no. 76 (Aug. 1915), p. 196-206. **[421]**

Taullard, Alfredo. Historia de nuestros viejos teatros. Buenos Aires, Imprenta López, 1932. 500 p. PN2452.B8T3 **[422]**

This book is of particular value for study of opera in Buenos Aires. See p. 69-80, 194 ff., 254-270, etc. Also includes much on other musical activities; see *La filarmónica, el teatro del colegio y la Academia de música*, p. 57-63. Contains a description of the orchestra at the *Ranchería* (first theatre in Buenos Aires), p. 18, and tells of the first orchestral performances in that city (the first being 25 May 1813), p. 43-49.

Vázquez Machicado, Humberto. En torno al drama musical; Enrique Mario Casella y sus leyendas líricas. *Nosotros*, ép. 2, v. 3, no. 33 (Dec. 1938), p. 560-566. **[423]**

See also nos. 62, 329.

INSTRUCTION AND THEORY

Campana de Paulsen, María Estela. Pedagogía para la enseñanza del canto. Buenos Aires, "Azul y blanco", 1933. 127 p. il. MT820.P3P3 **[424]**

Palma, Athos. Tratado completo de armonía. Vol. 1. Buenos Aires, Ricordi americana, 1941. 301 p. il. MT50.- P18T7 **[425]**

Rubertis, Victor de. Sistema fácil y racional para la lectura de la música. Buenos Aires, Ricordi americana, 1941. 31 p. il. MT35.R83S5 **[426]**

——. Teoría completa de la música. Buenos Aires, G. Ricordi & c., 1937. 182 p. il. MT7.R89T3 **[427]**

Williams, Alberto. Teoría de la música para servir de texto en el Conservatorio de Buenos Aires. Buenos Aires, Gurina y cía., 1923. 159 p. MT1.W78 **[428]**

For a list of other didactic works by Alberto Williams, see item no. 389.

NATIONAL ANTHEM

Ambrosetti Villa, Victoria. La canción de la patria, lo que simboliza. *Mon. educ. común,* año 31, no. 487, v. 46 (31 July 1913), p. 54-56. **[429]**

Archivo general de la nación argentina. Himno nacional argentino. 11 de mayo 1813. Asamblea general constituyente. Buenos Aires, n. d. M1688.- A7H **[430]**

Facsimile of decree officially adopting the text of the Argentine national anthem.

Ardoino Posse, Alfredo. Himno nacional argentino. Estudio estético de su letra y de su música. *Mon. educ. común,* año 29, no. 446, v. 32, ser. 2, no. 66 (28 Feb. 1910), p. 258-298. **[431]**

Contains words of *La lira argentina,* and the text of the hymn sanctioned on 11 May 1813; also reproductions of Blas Parera's music.

Argentine national anthem. *Mus. cour.* v. 57, no. 27 (1908), p. 34. **[432]**

Beltrán, Oscar R. Los orígenes del teatro argentino, desde el virreinato hasta el estreno de "Juan Moreira" (1884). Buenos Aires, Ed. Sopena argentina, 1941. 155 p. PN2451.B38 **[433]**

In addition to references on the lyric theatre, this volume includes a note on the national anthem of Argentina, p. 62-66.

Bosch, Mariano G. El himno nacional (la canción nacional); no fue compuesta en 1813 ni por orden de la asamblea. Buenos Aires, Librería y editorial "El Ateneo", 1937. 125 p. ML3575.A7B6 **[434]**

A valuable and well-documented study of the origins of the Argentine national anthem, composed in 1812 by Blas Parera.

El centenario del himno. *Nosotros,* v. 7, no. 49 (May 1913), p. 327-329. **[435]**

Quotes *Oración al Himno* given by Dr. Carlos Ibargurén.

Centenario del himno nacional. Actos escolares de conmemoración del centenario. *Mon. educ. común,* año 31, no. 485, v. 45 (31 May 1913), p. 105-137. **[436]**

Tells of the various programs given in the schools and by the government.

Dellepiane, Antonio. Estudios de historia y arte argentinos. Buenos Aires, "El Ateneo", 1929. 252 p. F2831.- D35 **[437]**

El himno nacional argentino, p. 124-234, a comprehensive study of the hymn, with detailed discussions of its relation to *La lira,* and of other musical influences on it. Several musical examples, and excerpts from the verses (no complete score of the hymn).

——. El himno nacional argentino. Buenos Aires, Librería y editorial "La Facultad", Imp. M. Rodríguez Giles, 1927. 105 p. ML3575.D3 **[438]**

Treats of all phases of the National

Hymn, notes on the composer, on other national hymns of Argentina, etc. Photograph of Parera's *Himno nacional* at the end of the book. Many musical examples throughout.

Forte, Vicente. El himno nacional argentino en la tradición y en la música. *In* Instituto popular de conferencias, ciclo 13, 1927, p. 109-123. **[439]**

Gallardo, Guillermo. Juan Pedro Esnaola, el autor del arreglo del himno nacional. *La nación*, no. 24,005 (22 May 1938), sec. 3, p. 1. **[440]**

Gastos para la conmemoración del centenario del himno, Abril 28, 1913. Programa de la celebración del centenario del himno. *Mon. educ. común*, año 31, no. 484, v. 45 Apr. 1913), Sección oficial, p. 10-12. **[441]**

Giménez Pastor, Arturo. El himno nacional. Conferencia para el estudio del himno en su (1) concepto literario; (2) verso; (3) expresión poética; (4) carácter lírico; y (5) música. [Buenos Aires, 19-?] **[442]**
Cf. *Nosotros*, v. 21, no. 217 (June 1927), p. 396.

Guardia, Ernesto de la. Estudio sobre el himno nacional. Buenos Aires, Talleres gráficos de la penitenciaría nacional, 1927. 49 p. ML3575.G7 **[443]**
Includes many musical examples.

Himno nacional. Sancionada por la Asamblea nacional en sesión de 11 de mayo de 1813. *Correo del domingo*, Buenos Aires, v. 1 (22 May 1864), p. 336. **[444]**

Himno nacional argentino; música del maestro Blas Parera; arreglado por d. Juan P. Esnaola (año 1860). Buenos Aires, Machado y cía., n. d. 7 p. M1688.A7P **[445]**
For voice and piano. "Facsímil del ejemplar adquirido por la caja nacional de ahorro postal y donado al museo histórico nacional."

Monserrat, Gabriel. El poema del himno nacional argentino (estudio historial y crítico). Buenos Aires, Librería del Colegio, 1932. 565 p. ML3575.-A7M7 **[446]**
Includes data on the national anthems of all the Latin American countries.

Novillas, Lorenza. Himno nacional argentino. *Mon. educ. común*, año 31, no. 485, v. 45 (31 May 1913), p. 169-171. **[447]**
Dissertation on the merits of the music and text of this hymn.

Ortiz y San Pelayo, Félix. Nuestra música; o la música española. Buenos Aires, Librería "La facultad" de Juan Roldán, 1920. 198 p. ML231.08N8 **[448]**
Contains a section on the Argentine national anthem, p. 183-198, including: El autor de la música del himno nacional argentino; El monumento al himno; Homenaje a Blas Parera; La música del himno nacional.

Parera, Blas. Himno nacional argentino. Versión de Juan P. Esnaola. Buenos Aires, Ediciones de la División de publicidad y propaganda, Ministerio de relaciones exteriores y culto, Dirección de investigaciones, archivo y propaganda. n. d. [1942?]. **[449]**
Band score. "Esta es la versión oficial que distribuye el Ministerio de Justicia e Instrucción Pública de la Nación."

Pedrell, Carlos. La música del himno nacional. *Mon. educ. común*, año 29, no. 446, v. 32, ser. 2, no. 66 (28 Feb. 1910), p. 299-390. **[450]**
Considers the various versions of music from the original by Parera, especially those of Monro and Esnaola. Contains the music of the following: Monro's *Marcha del Rio de la Plata*, Messenmaecker's *Chant national to Buenos Ayres*, the Parera and Esnaola versions of the Argentine national hymn, and the proposed version of the hymn, the piano version by Pedrell, and his full orchestra score.

La reforma del himno nacional, en-

cuesta. *Nosotros,* v. 31, no. 217 (June 1927), p. 395-415. **[450x]**

A symposium on the reform of the Argentine national anthem authorized by official decree and carried out by a commission, consisting of José Andre, Floro M. Ugarte and Carlos López Buchardo. Those participating in the symposium include Arturo Giménez Pastor, Ernesto de La Guardia, Carlos Vega, Raul H. Espoile, Alberto G. del Castillo, Isaac Carvajal and Jorge C. Servetti-Reeves.

Revista de derecho, historia y letras. Cancionero popular de la Revista de derecho, historia y letras, compilado y reimpreso por Estanislao S. Zeballos ... Buenos Aires, Impr. de J. Peuser, 1905. PQ7760.R4 **[451]**

A collection of ballads and songs (words only). "Himno argentino" (words and music): p. 128-143.

Rubertis, Victor de. La fuente temática de la música del himno nacional argentino. Buenos Aires, Ed. Casa grande, 1938. 31 p. ML3575.A7R8 **[452]**

With particular attention paid to the various influences on the music.

Vega, Carlos. El himno nacional hasta 1860. *La prensa,* v. 67, no. 24,187 (24 May 1936), sec. 5, p. 2 **[453]**

Versión auténtica del himno nacional. *La prensa,* v. 70, no. 25, 158 (24 Jan. 1939), p. 11. **[454]**

———. *La prensa,* v. 69, no. 24,896 (6 May 1938), p. 10. **[455]**

Lack of unity in the versions of the Himno Nacional. Since the official text was approved on 25 Sept. 1928, there should no longer be any confusion as to the correct version.

Williams, Alberto. La música del himno nacional argentino. Buenos Aires, Gurina & cía., 1938. 132 p. ML3575.-A7W5 **[456]**

Historical survey of the origins of the Argentine national anthem and analysis of the music in various versions and editions, Music facsimiles. Collation of the music of the following versions: (1) Blas

Parera, (2) *La lira argentina,* (3) Juan Pedro Esnaola, (4) Alberto Williams.

FOLK AND PRIMITIVE MUSIC

(A) GENERAL

Álvarez, Juan. Orígenes de la música argentina. [Rosario?] 1908. 83 p. ML231.A7 **[457]**

Deals briefly with the indigenous music and dances of Argentina, with the folk music of the Argentine Creoles, and with the Negro influence on Argentine folk and popular music. Includes illustrations of primitive musical instruments, and numerous musical examples.

Ambrosetti Villa, Victoria. Rondas escolares. *Mon. educ. común,* año 31, no. 487, v. 46 (31 July 1913), p. 57-129. **[458]**

Includes many pages of music (children's singing games).

Aramburu, Julio. Canciones de la infancia. *La prensa,* v. 66, no. 23,783 (14 Apr. 1935), sec. 3, p. 2. **[459]**

Includes words of several verses.

———. Rondas de niños; recuerdos de provincia. Buenos Aires; C. A. P., 1937. 62 p. **[459x]**

Descriptions of children's games and songs. Cited by Boggs, *Bibliography of Latin American folklore,* p. 56.

Aretz-Thiele, Isabel. Cantos con caja en los valles de Tucumán. *La nación,* v. 72, no. 25,192 (24 Aug. 1941), sec. 2. **[460]**

The *caja* is a kind of small drum. Includes 2 refrains and 4 photographs of musicians.

———. El velorio del angelito. *Folklore,* v. 1, no. 3 (1941), p. 27-28. **[461]**

With melody and text of one song. When a child under seven died, it was customary to sing and dance around the corpse. This was to rejoice in the belief that the child would go straight to heaven and immediately become an angel.

Berdiales, J. La canción de cuna. Buenos Aires, Ed. Futura, 1937. 96 p. **[462]**

Blaya Alende, Joaquín. El folklore musical argentino. *Alma latina,* v. 10, no. 208 (25 Nov. 1939), p. 17, 55.
[462x]

Bonesatti, Tobias. Cuaderno de estética (palabra, sonido, imagen). Primer curso. La Plata, Ediciones Martín Fierro, 1939. 97 p. il. ML3845.B61C8
[463]

"Danzas y canciones nativas", p. 30-39.

Buenos Aires. Universidad. Facultad de filosofía y letras. Instituto de literatura argentina. Sección de bibliografía, tomo I, no. 1. Guía bibliográfica del folklore argentino; primera contribución. Por Augusto Raúl Cortazar. Buenos Aires, Imprenta de la Universidad, 1942. 291 p.
[464]

Contains 867 items, many of them annotated. Appendix: Informes sobre la labor realizada en el seminario de bibliografía folklórica, Cátedra de literatura argentina del doctor Ricardo Rojas, 1940-1941.

Cabrera, Ana S. Elementos teatrales en el folklore nacional. *Cuad. cult. teatral,* no. 9 (1940), p. 45-57.
[465]

Discussion of Argentine folk music and dances from the viewpoint of their dramatic elements and their choreographic possibilities.

————. El folklore musical argentino. *An. inst. pop. conf.,* (1923), p. 226-231.
[466]

Cano, Rafael. Del tiempo de ñaupa (folklore norteño). Buenos Aires, Talleres gráficos argentinos, L. J. Rosso, 1930. 475 p. GR133.A7C3
[467]

Includes words of folk songs.

Carrizo, Juan Alfonso. Algunos aspectos de la poesía popular de Catamarca, Salta y Jujuy. *Humanidades,* v. 21 1930), p. 195-232.
[468]

————. Cancionero popular de Tucumán. Buenos Aires, A. Baiocco y cía, 1937. 2 v. PQ7791.T8C3
[469]

Children's songs, v. 1, p. 537-550.

————. Los cantares tradicionales de La Rioja en su relación con el teatro. *Cuad. cult. teatral,* v. 17, no. 1 (1942), p. 29-38.
[470]

————. Cantares tradicionales del Tucumán; (antología) de los cancioneros de Catamarca, Salta, Jujuy, Tucumán y La Rioja... (Estudio preliminar del doctor Alberto Rougés). Buenos Aires, Imp. A. Baiocco y cía., 1939. 204 p. M1687.A7C2
[471]

A collection of 604 folk songs, with 41 melodies (ballads, children's rhymes, and Christmas carols).

————. Nuestra poesía popular. *Humanidades,* v. 15 (1927), p. 241-342.
[472]

Castex, Eusebio R. Cantos populares (apuntes lexicográficos), Buenos Aires, Talleres gráficos "La Lectura", 1923. 156 p. PC4871.C3
[473]

Contreras, Segundo N. Disertaciones musicales. Buenos Aires, Librería "La Cotizadora económica" de E. Perrot, 1931. 126 p. il. ML60.C8
[474]

Several of the essays deal with folk music, both indigenous and Creole.

Córdoba, Numa. Bajo mi cielo pampa; danzas nativas: La calandria. *Caras y caretas,* v. 39, no. 1962 (9 May 1936), p. 6-7.
[475]

Includes music and words of *La calandria,* "danza del folklore cordobés".

————. *Caras y caretas,* v. 39, no. 1960 (25 Apr. 1936), p. 4-5. il.
[476]

Contains music of the *zamba.*

Dardo López, Albino. La milonga. *Nativa,* v. 3 (31 July 1926), 2 p.
[476x]

Includes verses of a song as arranged for a round.

Demolli, Lida Alicia. Las danzas y canciones populares argentinas. *Quena,* v. 8 (July 1927), p. 8-14.
[477]

Español, Raquel. El pequeño artista. Buenos Aires, Talleres gráficos argentinos, 1932. 151 p. PC4115.E8 [478]

Children's performances. Includes words

and music of *Aria del Zingaro*, p. 40; *Rosas y Mariposas*, p. 50; *¡Patria!*, p. 85; *Estilo Criollo*, p. 115.

Euritmia. Cuadernos de educación y cultura. Series 5, no. 1 (May 1938). Buenos Aires, Biblioteca Euritmia. [479]

Includes two articles on *Vidala o cueca,* one by Ismael Guerrero, the other by J. T. Wilkes, p. 7-13. The first has 3 musical examples, the second has 5.

Fischer, Erich. Patagonische musik. Nach phonographischen aufnahmen. *Anthropos*, v. 3 (1908), p. 941-951. [480]

Includes 3 tunes.

Folk-lore argentino. *Cult. venezolana*, v. 10, no 78 (Jan.-Feb. 1927), p. 125-128. [481]

Text of the *pericón* and *adivinanzas criollas.*

———. *Cult. venezolana*, v. 10, no. 80 (Apr. 1927), p. 107-108. [482]

Words to *El gato.*

———. *Cult. venezolana*, v. 11, no. 74 (Aug. 1926), p. 231-233. [483]

Words to *El baile*, by Julio Díaz Usandivaras.

Furt, Jorge M. Coreografía gauchesca, apuntes, para su estudio. Buenos Aires, "Coni", 1927. 78 p. diagrs. ML3417.-F8. [484]

Includes music (unaccompanied melodies). Contains the musical themes of 10 dances cultivated among the gauchos of Argentina.

Gennero, S. Cantos y danzas de Santiago del Estero. *Ensayos* (Montevideo), no. 6 (1938), p. 190-192. [485]

Giménez Rueda, Julio. Música y bailes criollos de la Argentina. *Mús. de Amér.*, v. 2, no. 8 (1921). [486]

Gómez Carrillo, Manuel. Música aborigen. Conferencias y audiciones sobre el tema (Universidad de Tucumán.

Extensión universitaria, no. 18). Buenos Aires, Impr. Coni, 1920. 30 p. [487]

Gutiérrez Castro, Alberto. Lo que no se escucha; el folklore y los músicos argentinos. *Boletín de la asociación folklórica argentina*, v. 2, no. 9-12 (1940), p. 104-105. [488]

Ibarguren, Carlos. La música popular [argentina]. *Preludios*, v. 4, nos. 13-14 (Apr.-Sept. 1941), p. 457-458. [489]

Reprinted from *Nuestra tierra.*

Instituto de literatura argentina. Sección folklórica. Catálogo de la colección de folklore. Vol. 1, no. 1, El canto popular. Buenos Aires, Imprenta de la universidad, 1925. GR133.A7B8 [490]

Compiled by M. Ugarriza Aráoz. There are occasional references to music in connection with the listing of folk song texts.

Jahn-Ruhnau, Romuald. Das argentinische volkslied. *Ibero-amer. rund.*, v. 3, no. 6 (1937), p. 174-175. [491]

Jijena Sánchez, Rafael. Vidala; letras para cantar con la caja. Buenos Aires, Talleres gráficos San Pablo, 1936. 84 p. PQ7797.J4V5 [492]

With an introduction on the *vidala.*

Latorre, M. El huaso y el gaucho en la poesía popular. *Atenea*, v. 36 (1936), p. 184-205, 380-400. [493]

Leguizamón, Martiniano. El gaucho. Buenos Aires, 1916. 43 p. il. [494]

Includes: Música, cantos y bailes nativos.

Lugones, Leopoldo. La musique populaire en Argentine. *Rev. sud.-am.*, v. 2, no. 5 (1914), p. 183-206. [495]

The article contains 9 musical examples, and there is a musical supplement with 11 "Morceaux de musique populaire argentine" arranged for piano.

———. El payador. 1, Hijo de la pam-

pa. Buenos Aires, Otero & cía., 1916.
267 p. il.   [496]
La música gaucha, p. 97-124, with
music.

Lullo, Orestes di. El espíritu cristiano
en el folklore de Santiago. *Sustancia,*
v. 1, no. 3 (Dec. 1939), p. 351-355.
                                 [497]

——. Villancicos recogidos en La Rioja
y Santiago del Estero. *Folklore,* no. 2
(Dec. 1940), p. 19-20.   [498]

Moglia, R. Sobre J. A. Carrizo, Antiguos
cantos populares argentinos (Cancionero de Catamarca). *Nosotros,* v. 56
(1927), p. 116-118.   [499]

Molina-Téllez, Félix. Tierra madura;
panorama del folklore. Rosario de
Santa Fe, Ed. Ruiz, 1939. 183 p.
GR71.M6   [500]
Among many references to music and
dance, this book includes the following:
Leyenda, quena, y canción (p. 13-23), with
material on the gaucho; *La música* (p. 39-
44), with quotation from an article by
Gastón O. Talamón on folkloric values in
the music of the world; the words of a
gaucho song, *Desesperanza,* p. 52-53; *El
folklore en la escuela* (p. 55-62), with
frequent comments on music, singing and
dance; *El extraño ritual de la Telesita* (p.
83-94), with many notes on the accompanying music and dance; several examples of their songs (no music).

Molins, W. Jaime. Nuestra música aborigen; payador o pallador. *Mús. de.
Amér.* (Buenos Aires), v. 1 (July,
1920), 2 p.   [501]

Montagne, Edmundo. La música gaucha
y la música indígena. *Correo mus.
sud.-am.,* v. 1, no. 9 (25 May 1915), p.
4-5.   [502]

——. Música indígena. *Correo mus. sud.-
am.,* v. 2, no. 67 (5 June 1916), p.
55-56.   [503]
Includes facsimile of the "coro de vírgenes sacras" from the opera *Huemac* by
Rogatis, whose melody is said to be a pure
yaraví.

Morales, Ernesto. Niños y maestros.
Buenos Aires, "El Ateneo", 1939. 180
p. LB775.M84 "El maestro Julián Bello
transcribió la música de las canciones."
—Colophon.   [504]
Includes: Romances, canciones y rondas
de niños.

La música en la Habana. Ana S. Cabrera, recital de canciones folklóricas sudamericanas. *Musicalia,* no. 15-16 (Jan.-
Apr. 1931), p. 19-21.   [505]
Review of a lecture-recital of South
American folk-songs by Ana S. de Cabrera
with an account of her folkloric investigations.

Outes, Félix Faustino. La música y
nuestro folk-lore. Buenos Aires, 1918.
F2230.1.M9O93.   [506]
Reprinted from *Nosotros,* v. 29, p. 230-
233. Cf. item No. 315.

Page, Frederick Mann. Los payadores
gauchos. The descendants of the juglares of old Spain in La Plata; a contribution to the folk-lore and language
of the Argentine Gaucho. Darmstadt,
G. Otto, 1897. 88 p. PQ7680.P3. [507]
Includes data on the folk songs of the
Gauchos.

Palazzolo, Octavio. Ana S. Cabrera y el
folklore. *Nosotros,* ép. 2, v. 3, no. 32
(Nov. 1938), p. 441-446.   [508]

Pan American union. *Music division.*
Recordings of Latin-American songs
and dances ... By Gustavo Durán,
Washington, D. C., Music division, Pan
American union, 1942. 65 p. (*Its* Music
series, no. 3) ML156.P17R3   [509]
Descriptions of Argentine folk songs and
dances. p. 1-10, with notation of rhythmic
patterns.

Pedrell, Felipe. Lírica nacionalizada; es-
tudios sobre folklore musical. Paris, P.
Ollendorf, n. d. [1913]. 298 p. [510]
Includes: Folklore argentino, p. 193-198.

Quiroga, Adán. El folk-lore argentino.
Rev. amer., Rio, v. 7, no. 9 (June
1918), p. 70-91.   [511]
Music, dance, song and muscial instru-

ments, p. 81-82. Cf. *Revista argentina de ciencias políticas* (Buenos Aires), 1918.

Quiroga, Carlos B. Alma popular. Buenos Aires, "Buenos Aires", cooperativa ed. ltda, 1924. 22 p. il. PQ7680.Q5 **[512]**

A study of Argentine folk songs. Includes: La música de la montaña, with music of 2 songs for piano with interlinear text, p. 185-188.

Richard Lavalle, Enrique. Origen de la vidalita. *Correo mus. sud-am.,* v. 1, no. 9 (25 May 1915), p. 6. **[513]**

Attempts to demonstrate that the *vidalita* is of indigenous origin.

Rojas, Ricardo. La literatura argentina; ensayo filosófico sobre la evolución de la cultura en el Plata. Buenos Aires, Impr. de Coni hermanos, 1917-22. 4 v. il. (incl. music), facsims. PQ7611.-R6 **[514]**

Vol. 1, *Los gauchescos,* has numerous references to folk poetry and music, especially Ch. 5, "El folklore de los gauchos"; Ch. 8, "Poesía lírica de nuestros campos"; Ch. 9, "Poesía dramática de nuestros campos"; Ch. 13, "La tradición del romancero". There are tunes (some harmonized) on p. 187, 199, 200, 201, 210, 212, 231, 233-234, 254, 260, 367. Illustrations of musical instruments, p. 189-195.

See also v. 2, *Los coloniales,* which includes references to music in colonial times, with 2 folk tunes, p. 257-258. These are "Las albricias" and "Cantos para el niño dios", transcribed by Andrés Chazarreta.

———. La literatura argentina. 2 ed. Buenos Aires, Librería "La Facultad", J. Roldán y cía., 1924-25. 8 v. il. (music). (Obras ... t. 8-15). PQ7797.R7 1922 t. 8-15 **[515]**

Rojas Paz, Pablo. El arte popular. *Azul,* v. 1, no. 4 (May 1930), p. 113-127. **[516]**

Argentine folk-song, p. 121-122.

Sarmiento, Domingo Faustino. Facundo. La Plata, 1938. 474 p. (Universidad nacional de la Plata. Biblioteca

de autores nacionales y extranjeros, v. 1). F2846.S247 1938a **[517]**

First published in 1845 under title *Civilización y barbarie.* Includes a section on the Gaucho as folk singer, *El cantor,* p. 60-63.

Schiuma, Oreste. Coral folklórica argentina: maestro Felipe Boero. *Mundo mus.,* v. 3, no. 31 (Apr. 1941), p. 5. **[518]**

Discusses the folklore choral society directed by Boero.

Silva Valdés, Fernán. El canto platense. *La Prensa,* Buenos Aires, v. 65, no. 23553 (26 Aug. 1934). **[519]**

Talamón, Gastón O. Por el folklore. *Nosotros,* año 10, v. 23, no. 89 (Sept. 1916), p. 290-297. **[520]**

Trejo Lerdo de Tejada, Carlos. El folklore argentino. México, D. F. Editorial "Cultura", 1941. 62 p. **[521]**

A rather rambling essay on Argentine folk songs and dances. "Bailes populares argentinos", p. 35-62.

Vega, Carlos. Acerca de la canción argentina. *Nosotros,* año 20, v. 54, no. 204 (May 1926), p. 84-90. **[522]**

———. Algo más sobre la canción argentina. *Nosotros,* año 20, v. 54, no. 210 (Nov. 1926), p. 351-367. **[523]**

———. Curiosos cantos indígenas. *Crón. arte,* v. 1, no. 2 (Sept. 1931). **[524]**

Includes music.

———. En torno a las tradiciones orales. *La Prensa,* v. 68, no. 24,570 (13 June 1937), sec. 2, p. 2. **[525]**

Includes music.

———. La música popular argentina. Canciones y danzas criollas. Tomo 2. Fraseología, proposición de un nuevo método para la escritura y análisis de las ideas musicales y su aplicación al canto popular. Buenos Aires, Imprenta de la Universidad, 1941. 2 v. (Universidad de Buenos Aires, Facultad de filosofía y

letras, Instituto de literatura argentina).
ML3577.V4M8   **[526]**

Contains 717 musical examples, of
which only 4 are Latin American tunes
(fragments).

——. Orígenes del arrorró. *Mon. educ.
común*, v. 49, no. 72 (Feb. 1930), p. 72.
[527]

Includes music.

——. La vidala—su forma poética. *La
Prensa*, v. 68, no. 24,408 (1 Jan. 1937),
sec. 2, p. 2.   **[528]**

Videla-Rivero, C. J. A few words on Argentine music. *Bull. pan Amer. union*,
v. 67, no. 10 (Oct. 1933), p. 795-800.
[529]

Treats of the Negro influence on Argentine music. Also gives a short history of
the *fandango, malambo, gato, güella, pericón, cielito, tango*.

Wilkes, Josué T. De algunos aspectos y
particularidades rítmicas del cancionero musical popular argentino. *Bol.
lat. am. mús.*, v. 5 (Oct. 1941), p. 565-
584.   **[530]**

——. Ensayo para una clasificación rítmica del cancionero criollo según la
rítmica clásica. *Bol. lat. am. mus.*, v.
2 (1936), p. 297-313.   **[531]**

Contains the music of 5 songs, besides
some fragmentary rhythmic examples.

See also nos 148, 307, 315, 316, 333, 339,
568.

(B) AMERINDIAN

Ambrosetti, Juan B. Los indios Kain-
gángues de San Pedro (Misiones).
Revista del jardín zoológico (Buenos
Aires), v. 2 (1895).   **[532]**

Music and instruments, p. 318.

Fúrlong, Guillermo. Entre los Lules de
Tucumán. Buenos Aires, Talleres grá-
ficos "San Pablo", 1941. 175 p. F2823.-
L8F8.   **[533]**

Music, p. 113, 115, with note on P. Juan
Fecha, who opened a music school around
1750. Songs and dances of the Lules, p. 25.

——. Entre los Mocobies de Santa Fe.
Buenos Aires, Sebastián de Amorrortu
e hijos, 1938. 233 p. F2823.M6F8.
[534]

Padre Baucke's work in educating the
Indians in music, p. 28, 46, 50, 127, 130.

——. Entre los Vilelas de Salta. Buenos
Aires, Academia literaria del Plata,
1939. 181 p. F2958.F95.   **[535]**

Songs, p. 46, 49; dances and devils, p.
57; indigenous music, p. 58, 125.

Giacobbe, Juan. Introducción al estudio
de una etnofonía argentina. *Bol. lat.
am. mús.*, v. 2 (1936), p. 215-235.
[536]

A study of primitive music in Argentina.
with special reference to pentatonic elements. With 28 brief musical examples,
some of a purely technical nature.

Guinnard, Auguste. Three years' slavery
among the Patagonians. From the 3d
French ed., by Charles S. Cheltnam.
London, R. Bentley and son, 1871.
375 p. F2936.G982.   **[537]**

Ch. 7 deals with music and musical instruments, p. 195-203.

——. Trois ans d'esclavage chez les
Patagons. 2 éd. Paris, P. Brunet, 1864.
340 p. F2936.G98.   **[538]**

Ch. 7 deals with music and musical instruments, p. 177-180.

Lehmann-Nitsche, Robert. Patagonische
gesänge und musikbogen; phonogramm-
aufnahmen und enleitung. *Anthro-
pos*, v. 3 (1908), p. 916-940.   **[539]**

An important scientific study, with 50
musical examples.

**Outes, Felix Faustino, and Carlos
Bruch.** Los aborígenes de la república
argentina. Buenos Aires, A. Estrada y
cía., 1910. 149 p. il. F2821.O93. **[540]**

Songs and dances of the Matacos, p. 70;
music of the Chorotes, p. 74; lack of music and dance among the Charrúas, p. 91;
music of the Caingúas (with illustration
of a guitar), p. 97; dance and music of the
primitive Patagonians, p. 123-124; dearth
of music among the Yamanas, p. 139.

(c) AFRO-AMERICAN

Álvarez, Juan. Orígenes de la música argentina. [Rosario?] 1908. 83 p. ML231.A7 **[541]**

Deals briefly with the indigenous music and dances of Argentina, with the folk music of the Argentine Creoles, and with the Negro influence on Argentine folk and popular music. Includes illustrations of primitive musical instruments, and numerous musical examples.

Rossi, Vicente. Cosas de Negros; los orígenes del tango y otros aportes al folklore rioplatense. Córdoba, Imprenta argentina [Rio de la Plata], 1926. 436 p. il F3021.N3R8 **[542]**

A detailed account of Negro customs in the La Plata region from the time of the importation of the first African slaves, with many references to music and dances, especially the *milonga* and the *tango*. Music of ten Argentine songs and dances showing Negro influence, p. 357-394.

Vega, Carlos. Eliminación del factor africano en la formación del cancionero criollo. *Cursos y conferencias*, v. 10, no. 7 (1936), p. 765-779. **[543]**

Includes music. The author attempts to eliminate the African influence in the development of Argentine folk music. Cf. his book, *Danzas y canciones argentinas* [item no 568]. For a refutation of Vega's thesis, see the article by Fernando Romero, *De la "samba" de África a la "marinera" del Perú* [no. 2353].

(d) DANCES

Abregui Virreira, Carlos. Origen y filosofía de los bailes criollos. *Música y arte* (Buenos Aires), v. 1 (Oct. 1934), p. 9. **[544]**

Barbacci, Rodolfo. El tango. *Amér. mús.*, v. 1, (20 May 1937), p. 83-89. **[545]**

Bonesatti, Tobias. Cuaderno de estética (palabra, sonido, imagen). Primer curso. La Plata, Ediciones Martín Fierro, 1939. 97 p. il. ML3845.B61C8 **[546]**

Danzas y canciones nativas, p. 30-39. Includes a description of the dance *El gato*

quoted from the novel *Don Segundo Sombra* by Ricardo Güiraldes, and a nomenclature of Argentine folk dances.

Bustamante, Perfecto P. Girón de historia. Buenos Aires, Talleres gráficos, J. Crovetto & M. Carrio, 1922. 278 p.il. F2831.B97 **[547]**

Includes: Los bailes; las fiestas tradicionales; las vidalitas.

Castle, Vernon and Irene. Modern dancing. New York, Harper and bros., 1914. 176 p. il. GV1751.C35 **[548]**

Chapter 5, The tango argentine, p. 83-105. Chapter 6, The tango brésilienne or maxixe, p. 107-133. Complete instructions on how to dance each of the steps, with many photographs.

Chazarreta, Andrés A. Coreografía descriptiva de las danzas nativas. Buenos Aires, 1941. 30 p. **[549]**

Deiro, Pietro. Argentine tango rhythms. *Etude*, v. 59, no. 3 (Mar. 1941), p. 205, 208. **[550]**

Hints on playing tango rhythms on the accordion, with 5 musical examples.

Demolli, Lida Alicia. Las danzas y canciones populares argentinas. *La quena*, v. 8 (July 1927), p. 8-14. **[551]**

Folk-lore argentino: El Gato. *Cult. venezolana*, v. 10, no. 80 (1927), p. 107-108. **[552]**

Fúrlong, Guillermo. Entre las pampas de Buenos Aires. Buenos Aires, Talleres gráficos "San Pablo", 1938, 245 p. F2861.F87 **[553]**

Dances, p. 97.

Gómez Carrillo, Enrique. El encanto de Buenos Aires. Madrid, Perlado Páez y cía., 1941. 276 p. F3001.G23 (*also in his* Obras Completas, v. 20, Madrid, Ed. Mundo latino, 1921). **[554]**

"El tango", p. 213-223.

Graham, R. B. Cunninghame. Le tango argentin. *Rev. sud-am.*, v. 1, no. 1 (Jan. 1914), p. 22-30. **[555]**

Impressionistic views on the tango.

Hahn, Bolke von. Argentinische natio-
naltänze and volkslieder. *Lasso,* v. 7,
no. 4 (1939), p. 203-209.　　**[556]**

Martínez Estrada, Ezequiel. El tango
según lo ve un maestro argentino. *Crisol,* v. 11, no. 61 (1934), p. 32-35.
　　　　　　　　　　　　　[557]

Unfavorable reaction to the tango as a
dance.

Pérez-Freire, O. Algo acerca del tango.
Correo mus. sud-am., v. 1, no. 9 (25
May 1915), p. 6.　　　　　　**[558]**

The tango is considered a derivation of
the habanera, and it is stated little has
survived of the original tango save the
name.

Prat, Domingo. Diccionario biográfico,
bibliográfico, histórico, crítico, de guitarras, guitarristas, danzas y cantos.
Buenos Aires, Casa Romero y Fernández, 1934. 468 p. ML128.G8P7 **[559]**

The section on *Danzas* (p. 425-452), includes descriptions of many Argentine
dances. See especially under *Aires, bailecito, cielito, cuando, chacarera, firmeza,
gato, huella, malambo, mariquita, milonga,
pericón, tango argentino, vidalita.*

Rojas, Ricardo. La literatura argentina.
v. 1, Los Gauchescos. Buenos Aires,
Imprenta de Coni hermanos, 1917. 588
p. il. PQ7611.R6　　　　　　**[560]**

The dance is dealt with particularly in
ch. 9, *Poesía dramática de nuestros campos,*
in which typical dances of the Indians and
the gauchos are described. On p. 228 there
is a nomenclature of the best-known Argentine gaucho dances; 24 dances are listed. The dances described in the text are
the zamba (with music), the *firmeza*
(do.) and the *pericón.* There is an illustration of the *huella* and the *gato con relaciones.* p. 225.

———. El país de la selva. (Obras, t. 16).
Paris, Garnier hermanos, 1917. 268 p.
PQ7797.R7P3　　　　　　　　**[561]**
La danza, p. 103-114.

Rossi, Vicente. Martín Fierro, su autor
y su anotador. Rio de la Plata, 1940.

84 p. (Folletos lenguaraces, no. 25).
　　　　　　　　　　　　　[561x]

On reverse of inside title-page: Casa
editora. Imprenta argentina, Córdoba.
Deals with the origins, choreography and
etymology of the *pericón,* p. 52-80. Rossi
states that the *pericón* is a dance of Uruguayan origin, derived from a combination
of the *huella* and the *gato con relaciones.*
Cf. item no. 561y.

———. Teatro nacional rioplatense. Rio
de la Plata, 1910. 198 p. PN2451.R6
　　　　　　　　　　　　　[561y]

Deals with the folk dance *pericón* and its
incorporation in the play *Juan Moreira* by
José J. Podestá. According to Rossi the
pericón was introduced into Argentina
thorugh *Juan Moreira.* Cf. item no. 561x.

Salaverria, José María. Civilización y
criollismo. *Síntesis,* v. 1, no. 7 (Dec.
1927), p. 61-67.　　　　　　**[562]**
Tango and *canciones criollas.*

Scholes, Percy Alfred. The Oxford com-
panion to music. London, New York,
Toronto, Oxford university press, 1938.
ML100.S3709.　　　　　　　**[563]**

Includes an article on the tango by Julio
de Caro "Argentine composer and conductor" in which "the Argentine writer
Eros Nicola Siri" is cited as authority for
the statement that the tango is of African
origin (p. 918).

Toro, M. de. Folklore argentino: el
pericón. *Cult. venezolana,* v. 10 (1927),
p. 125-127.　　　　　　　　**[564]**

Torre Revello, José. Los bailes, las danzas y las máscaras en la colonia. *Bol.
inst. invest. hist.,* v. 11, no. 46 (1930),
p. 434-454.　　　　　　　　**[565]**

———. Los orígenes de la danza, la canción y la música populares argentinas.
Conferencia. Sevilla, 1926. 16 p. **[566]**

Reprinted in *Nativa* (Buenos Aires), v.
6, no. 68 (Aug. 1929), p. 16-21. Partially
reproduced in *Cultura venezolana* (Caracas), v. 12, no. 99 (Nov.-Dec. 1929), p.
310-322.

Trejo Lerdo de Tejada, Carlos. El folk-

lore argentino. México, D. F., Editorial "Cultura", 1941. 62 p. [567]
A rather rambling essay on Argentine folk songs and dances. "Bailes populares argentinos", p. 25-62.

Vega, Carlos. Danzas y canciones argentinas; teorías e investigaciones; un ensayo sobre el tango. Buenos Aires, G. Ricordi y cía., 1936. 309 p. il. ML3575.-V4D2 [568]
An important work. Includes choreographic descriptions and music.

——. Hacia el origen de los bailes criollos. La Prensa, v. 69, no. 24,905 (15 May 1938), sec. 2, p. 2. [569]
This and the 15 following entries (through no. 584) constitute a series of articles in which a single thesis is developed, viz., that the Creole dances cielito, pericón, media caña are derived from the old English contradance and are three Argentine rural dances. The first three articles present the general thesis that the popular dances of today are the aristocratic dances of yesterday. These 16 articles have been placed in this order, rather than in strict alphabetical sequence, at the suggestion of the author, who writes that these articles will be incorporated in a book now in preparation.

——. Ascenso y descenso de las danzas. La Prensa, v. 69, no. 24,947 (26 June 1938), sec. 2, p. 2. [570]

——. Vida y costumbres de las danzas. La Prensa, v. 69, 24,975 (24 July 1938), sec. 2, p. 3. [571]

——. La contradanza. La Prensa, v. 69, no. 24,989 (Aug. 1938). [572]

——. La contradanza en la Argentina. La Prensa, v. 69, no. 25,010 (28 Aug. 1938), sec. 2, p. 4. [573]

——. La contradanza en Sudamérica. La Prensa, v. 69, no. 25,031 (18 Sept. 1938), sec. 3, p. 3. [574]

——. La contradanza en la colonia. La Prensa, v. 70, no. 25,073 (30 Oct. 1938), sec. 3, p. 4. [575]

——. La forma de la contradanza. La Prensa, v. 70, no. 25,594 (20 Nov. 1938), sec. 2, p. 4. [576]
With sketches illustrating the various figures of this dance.

——. La forma del cielito. La Prensa, v. 70, no. 25,142 (8 Jan. 1939), sec. 2, p. 2. [577]
A dissertation upon the character and historical development of the cielito, with detailed descriptions of each figure, and examples of accompanying verses.

——. Contradanza y cielito. La Prensa, v. 70, no. 25,219 (26 Mar. 1939), sec. 3, p. 2. [578]

——. La forma de la media caña. La Prensa, v. 70, no. 25,278 (25 May 1939), sec. 3. [579]

——. Contradanza y media caña. La Prensa, v. 70, no. 25,295 (11 June 1939), sec. 3, p. 2. [580]

——. La forma del pericón. La Prensa, v. 70, no. 25,344 (30 July 1939), sec. 2, p. 2. [581]

——. El pericón del circo. La Prensa, v. 70, no. 25,094 (20 Nov. 1939), sec. 2, p. 2. [582]

——. Contradanza y pericón. La Prensa, v. 70, no. 25,408 (1 Oct. 1939), sec. 2, p. 4. [583]

——. La contradanza y su familia. La Prensa, v. 71, no. 25,443 (5 Nov. 1939), sec. 2, p. 3. [584]

——. Los bailes criollos. Aconcagua, año 1, v. 3, no. 7 (July 1930), p. 33-34. [585]

——. Bailes criollos: la mariquita. La Prensa, v. 64, no. 23,003 (19 Feb. 1933), sec. 3, p. 2. [586]

——. Bailes criollos: La media caña. La Prensa, v. 67, no. 24,027 (15 Dec. 1935), sec. 3, p. 2. [587]
The author writes on the history of

this dance, and includes several strophes from its divers texts; Vega associates this dance closely with the *pericón* and *cielito*.

——. Los bailes criollos en el teatro nacional. *Cuad. cult. teatral,* no. 6 (1937), p. 61-79. [588]

——. Clasificación de las danzas. *La Prensa,* v. 67, no. 24,173 (10 May 1936), sec. 2, p. 4. [589]

Classifies dances according to the following outline: *Bailarines sueltos:* (1) Danzas colectivas: (a) Gimnásticas, (b) mímicas; (2) Danzas individuales: (a) Gimnásticas, (b) Mímicas. *Bailarines en parejas:* (nos. 1 and 2 with sub-divisions are the same): (3) Danzas de pareja suelta: (a) graves, (b) picarescas; (4) Danzas de pareja tomada: (a) enlazadas, (b) abrazadas.

——. En torno al origen de la zamacueca. *La Prensa,* v. 65, no. 23,358 (11 Feb. 1934), sec. 2, p. 4 [590]

——. Folklore criollo: Danzas de trenzar. *La Prensa,* v. 66, no. 23,797 (28 Apr. 1935), sec. 2, p. 2. [591]

Outline of this dance-game, with 3 tunes and the accompanying words to the 4 parts of the *danzas de trenzar.*

Wilkes, Josué Teófilo. Un "discurso sobre la música" bajo el gobierno de Rosas, seguido del comentario gráfico musical que motiva acerca del cielito. *Bol. lat. am. mús.,* v. 4 (Bogotá 1938), p. 279-303. [592]

An historical and analytical study of the *cielito,* Argentine popular dance form, with 17 musical examples.

See also nos. 240, 245, 337, 457, 463, 465, 475, 476, 477, 484, 485, 486, 494, 500, 509, 511, 514, 533, 535, 540, 541, 542.

(E) INSTRUMENTS

1. *Pre-Columbian*

Ambrosetti, Juan Bautista. Exploraciones arqueológicas en la ciudad prehistórica de "La Playa" (valle Calchaquí, provincia de Salta); campañas de 1906 y 1907. Buenos Aires, Facultad de filo-sofía y letras de la Universidad, Sección antropológica. Publicaciones no. 3, part 1-2. M. Biedman e hijo, 1907-08. 2 v. il. F2821.1.S15A6 [593]

Musical instruments, v. 2, p. 488-490.

——. Notas de arqueología Calchaqui. Serie 1, Buenos Aires, Imprenta y litografía "La Buenos Aires", 1899. 244 p. il. [594]

Illustrations of idols with musical instruments, p. 159-163.

Boman, Eric. Antiquités de la région andine de la République Argentine et du désert d'Atacama. Paris, Imprimerie nationale, H. LeSoudier, 1908. 2 v. il. F2821.B68 [595]

Description of musical instruments, v. 2, p. 463-466.

Rusconi, Carlos. Instrumentos oseos trabajados por indígenas prehispánicos de Santiago del Estero. *Rev. soc. amigos arqueol.,* v. 7 (1933) p. 229-250. il. [596]

Objetos musicales, p. 246-248.

Vega, Carlos. La flauta de pan andina. *Actas y trabajos científicos del XXV Congreso internacional de americanistas* (La Plata, 1932), tomo 1 (Buenos Aires, 1934), p. 333-348. [597]

Includes music.

——. La quena. *La Prensa,* v. 71, no. 25,464 (26 Nov. 1939), sec. 3, p. 2. [598]

Includes music.

2. *Post-Columbian*

Gallac, Hector I. El erque — Instrumento del norte argentino. *Bol. lat. am. mús.,* v. 2 (Apr. 1936), p. 67-72. [599]

——. El origen del charango, *Bol. lat. am. mús.,* v. 3 (1937), p. 73-75. [600]

The *charango* is a kind of primitive guitar much used by the natives of northern Argentina.

Grenón, Pedro. Nuestra primera música

instrumental, datos históricos. Buenos Aires, Librería "La Cotizadora económica", de E. Perrot, 1929. 106 p. il. ML231.G7 **[601]**

Contains valuable data on the introduction of European musical instruments in Argentina.

Musters, George Chaworth. At home with the Patagonians. London, J. Murray, 1871. 322 p. il. F2936.M99 **[602]**

Reference to musical instruments, p. 81 (illustrations, p. 177).

Sánchez Aranda, E. La guitarra en la Argentina. *Correo mus. sud.-am.,* v. 1 (25 May 1915), p. 7. **[603]**

Vega, Carlos. Contribución al estudio de la música argentina: los instrumentos indígenas y criollos. *La Prensa,* v. 63, no. 22,591 (1 Jan. 1932), sec. 4, p. 2. **[604]**

——. El erke. *La Prensa,* v. 71, no. 25,562 (3 Mar. 1940), sec. 2, p. 2. **[605]**

Includes music.

——. El erkencho. *La Prensa,* v. 71, no. 25.624 (5 May 1940), sec. 3, p. 2. **[606]**

Includes music.

——. La guitarra artística en el Buenos Aires antiguo. *La Prensa,* v. 66, no. 23,783 (14 Apr. 1935), sec. 3, p. 2. **[607]**

The years of 1821-29 brought forth the first notices of the cult of the artistic guitar in Buenos Aires. Names Esteban Massini, Echeverría. Nicanor Albarellos, Esnaola as outstanding contributors to the growth in popularity of this instrument.

——. Música e instrumentos del norte argentino. *An inst. pop. conf.,* ciclo 18, año 1932, v. 58 (1933), p. 173-181. **[608]**

——. La quena. *La Prensa,* v. 71, no. 25,464 (26 Nov. 1939), sec. 3, p. 2. **[609]**

Includes music.

(F) COLLECTIONS OF MUSIC

Álvarez, Juan. Orígenes de la música argentina. [Rosario?] 1908. 83 p. il. ML231.A7 **[610]**

Music: 30 p. at end (for voice and piano alone), also 34 musical examples (some fragmentary) included with the main text.

Buenos Aires, Universidad, Facultad de filosofía y letras, Instituto de literatura argentina, Sección folklore. 1a. serie, El canto popular, Tomo 1, Música precolombina recogida y armonizada por el maestro Manuel José Benavente y consideraciones preliminares por Vicente Forte. Buenos Aires, Impr. Coni, 1923. 33 p. ML3575.C8 **[611]**

Prologue by Ricardo Rojas. Benavente, who has harmonized these Incan themes for piano, is a Bolivian musician. Of the ten themes in the collection, 3 were collected in La Paz, two in Sucre, four in Cuzco. On p. 14 there are illustrations of four Incan flutes of different sizes, forming a "quartet". These are called (from the smallest to the largest) *conyvi, pinculla, quena* and *chayna.*

Cabrera, Ana S. Cantos nativos y danzas del norte argentino; album para canto y piano. 3 ed. Buenos Aires, G. Ricordi e cía. [1932?]. M1687.A7C12 **[612]**

Six songs in popular style.

Cardoso, Luis. Musa nativa. Album no. 1 de danzas norteñas. Buenos Aires, Gornatti hnos., 1940. M1620 **[613]**

12 compositions for voice and piano (Spanish text only) written in the style of traditional popular forms (*zamba, chacarera, gato,* etc.).

Chazarreta, Andrés A. Primer album de música nativa. 9, ed. Buenos Aires, Romero y Fernández, [194-?] M1687.-A7C413 **[614]**

Chazarreta, Andrés A. Segundo album

de música nativa, 5 ed. Buenos Aires, Romero y Fernández, [194-?] M1687.-A7C42   **[614x]**

——. Tercer album de música nativa, 2. ed. Buenos Aires, Imprenta musical Ortelli hnos., [192-?] M1687.A7C43   **[614y]**

——. Cuarto album de música nativa. Buenos Aires, Imprenta musical Ortelli hnos., [1927.] M1687.A7C44 1927   **[614z]**

——. Quinto album de música nativa. Buenos Aires, N. H. Pirovano [1934.] M1687.A7C45, 1934.   **[615]**

——. Sexto album de música nativa. 2. ed. Buenos Aires, Ed. Natalio Hector Pirovano, [194-?] 34 p. M1687.A7C462   **[615x]**

Instructions for dancing the *gato,* the *chacarera* and the *triunfo,* with choreographic diagrams, p. 31-34.

——. 7⁰ album de música nativa. Buenos Aires, Natalio Hector Pirovano, 1940. 28 p. M1687.A7C47 1940 **[615y]**

Draghi Lucero, Juan. Temas musicales. Mendoza, Best hermanos, 1938. Cover-title, p. 584-626. M1687.A7D7 **[616]**

Separate issue of the "Temas musicales" from item no. 634.

Gómez Carrillo, Manuel. Colección de motivos, danzas y cantos del norte argentino. Buenos Aires, G. Ricordi y cía., [1914?]. 2 v. M1687.A7C3   **[617]**

Vol. 1 contains 7 pieces for piano solo, 9 for voice and piano, and 4 for violin and piano. Vol. 2 contains 9 pieces for piano solo, 10 for voice and piano, and 2 for violin and piano. Includes 3 dance routines.

Lynch, Ventura R. Cancionero bonaerense; reimpresión de "La provincia de Buenos Aires hasta la definición de la cuestión capital de la República" con introducción de Vicente Forte. Buenos

Aires, Imprenta de la Universidad, 1925. 64 p. M1687.A7L9   **[618]**

Reprint of a fundamental work for the study of Gaucho music.

Moreno, J. El cancionero mendocino (album de canciones regionales para canto y piano). Mendoza, J. Peuser, 1936. 49 p.   **[619]**

Novillo Quiroga, Diego. Rasjidos (canciones criollas). Con música de María Suasnábar, Fernando E. Randle, Carlos V. G. Flores, José L. Padula, Adolfo R. Avilés, Alfredo A. Pelaia y Magaldi-Noda. Buenos Aires, J. Peuser [1930?]. 88 p. il. M1687.A7N7   **[620]**

Songs with pianoforte accompaniment, written in the style of Argentine folk forms (cielito, cuando, estilo, gato, pericón, vidala, zamba, etc.).

Rodríguez, Alberto. Cancionero cuyano (canciones y danzas tradicionales) con un breve estudio preliminar de Carlos Vega. Buenos Aires, La editorial "Numen", 1938. 178 p. M1687.A7R6   **[621]**

Rossi, Vicente. Cosas de Negros; los orígenes del tango y otros aportes al folklore rioplatense. Córdoba, Imprenta argentina [Rio de la Plata], 1926. 436 p. il. F3021.N3R8   **[622]**

Music of ten Argentine songs and dances showing Negro influence, p. 357-394.

Valle, Argentino. Estampas argentinas; 6 joyas del folklore argentino. Buenos Aires, Pan American music service corp., 1941. 15 p. il. M1687.A7V2   **[623]**

These are "composed" songs, but they are based on popular themes, and are presented as examples of Argentine "folklore".

See also nos. 457, 469, 471, 484, 495, 568.

(G) COLLECTIONS OF TEXTS

Aprile, Bartolomé R. Relaciones para pericón y gato; floreos. Buenos Aires, Ed. V. Buchieri, 1938. 96 p.   **[624]**

——, **and Apolinario Sierra.** Relaciones. Canciones criollas, recopilación y selección. Buenos Aires, Ed. A. M. Angulo, 1938. 96 p.   **[625]**

Bayo, Ciro. Cantos populares americanos. *Rev. hisp.*, v. 15 (1906), p. 796-809.
                                                    [626]
A collection of folk song texts, with notes.

——. Romancerillo del Plata, contribución al estudio del romancero rioplatense. Madrid, V. Suárez, 1913. 238 p. PQ7680.B3   **[627]**
Contains texts of Argentine ballads and folk songs.

Borde, Victor. Texte aus den la Plata-Gebieten in volkstümlichen Spanisch und Rotwelsch. Leipzig, Ethnologischer verlag. Dr. Friedrich S. Krauss, 1923. 239 p.   **[628]**
Includes text of ballads and songs.

Carrizo, Juan Alfonso, ed. Antiguos cantos populares argentinos. Buenos Aires, Impresores: Silla hermanos, 1925. 258 p. PQ7760.C3   **[629]**
Anthology of folk songs, without music.

——. Cancionero popular de Jujuy, recogido y anotado por Juan Alfonso Carrizo. Tucumán, M. Violetto, 1934. 529 p. Colophon and cover dated 1935. PQ7760.C32   **[630]**
Without music.

——. Cancionero popular de Salta. Buenos Aires, A. Baiocco y cía, 1933. 707 p. PQ7760.C33   **[631]**
No music.

——. Florilegio... (de los cancioneros populares de Catamarca, Salta, Jujuy y Tucumán). Tucumán, M. Violetto, 1934. PQ7760.C35   **[632]**

Consejo nacional de educación. Antología folklórica argentina para las escuelas primarias. Buenos Aires. Ed. Guillermo Kraft, 1940. 250 p. **[633]**
Includes section on children's rimes and cradle songs.

Draghi Lucero, Juan. Cancionero popular cuyano ... (Mendoza, Best hermanos, 1938). 632 p. "Tirajc aparte del material publicado en el VII volumen de Anales del primer Congreso de historia de Cuyo". "Temas musicales": p. 583-626. M1687.A7D7   **[634]**

Ferreyra Videla, Vidal. Cancioneros populares argentinos. *Estudios,* no. 360 (Aug. 1941), p. 345-349.   **[635]**

Furt, Jorge M. Antología gauchesca. Buenos Aires. J. Samet, 1930. 83 p. PQ7760.F77   **[636]**

——. Arte gauchesco; motivos de poesía. Buenos Aires, "Coni", 1924. 203 p. PQ7680.F8   **[637]**
Cover imprint: Buenos Aires, Librería "La Facultad" de J. Roldán y cía.

——. Cancionero popular rioplatense, lírica gauchesca ... Buenos Aires, "Coni", 1923-25, 2 v. Cover imprint of v. 1: Buenos Aires J. Roldán y cía. PQ7760. F8   **[638]**
Without music.

Hölzer, W. Argentinische volksdichtung. Bielefeld, 1912. 32 p.   **[639]**

Jijena Sánchez, Rafael. De nuestra poesía tradicional. Buenos Aires, Ed. Buenos Aires, 1940. (Instituto de cooperación universitaria. Publicaciones del Departamento de folklore). 59 p. PQ7665.15   **[640]**
Many verses of songs throughout the book. Chapter 4, p. 54-59, Juan Alfonso Carrizo.

Joubin Colombes, Eduardo. Romancero tucumano. Tucumán, 1941. 78 p.
                                                    [641]

Lullo, Orestes di. Cancionero popular de Santiago del Estero. Buenos Aires, A. Baiocco, 1940. 520 p. PQ7760.L8
                                                    [642]
Without music.

——. Villancicos recogidos en La Rioja y Santiago del Estero. *Folklore,* no. 2 (Dec. 1940), p. 19-20.   **[643]**

Morales, Ernesto. Lírica popular rioplatense; antología gaucha. Buenos Aires, El Ateneo, 1927. 244 p. PQ7760.M6
[644]

Vacarezza, Alberto B. La Biblia gaucha:

Refranes y consejos del viejo Irala y El romance de Ciriaco Ponce. Buenos Aires, Talleres gráficos argentinos L. J. Rosso, 1936. 252 p. PQ7797. V14B5
[645]

See also nos. 459, 467, 469, 471.

SUPPLEMENT TO 1960

Although the musical history of Argentina still remains to be written, important spade-work has been done by the musicologist Francisco Curt Lange, who for several years was head of the department of musicology at the University of Cuyo in Mendoza. Starting, as is logical, with the foundations of neo-Hispanic music in the area that was to become the Republic of Argentina, and concentrating particularly on the archives of those cities, such as Córdoba and Rosario de Santa Fe, which were the most significant cultural centers during the colonial period, Lange has brought to light an impressive body of documentation, relating chiefly to the practise of ecclesiastical music. His findings have been partially published in the *Revista de estudios musicales* of the National University of Cuyo (item 227a), and in booklets issued in 1956 in Córdoba and in Rosario (items 228a and 229a). Thanks to monographs of this kind, based on primary sources and undertaken with exemplary thoroughness, it is now feasible to write the history of music in Argentina during the colonial period with a considerable degree of exactness and completeness.

To these monographs should be added the valuable work by Guillermo Fúrlong, S. J., *Músicos argentinos durante la dominación hispánica,* published in 1945 and dealing especially with the activities of the Jesuit missionaries in the Rio de la Plata region (item 214a).

In the epoch of independence, more attention has been given to folk-popular music than to the development of art music. Carlos Vega (q. v.) has continued his fruitful labors in this field, publishing not only a series of booklets on Argentine dance forms, but also two important books on this subject, *Las danzas populares argentinas,* which appeared in 1952 (item 189a) and *El orígen de las danzas folklóricas,* published in 1956 (item 188a). Another important work by Vega is his volume on musical instruments in Argentina (with comparative data on the rest of South America), titled *Los instrumentos musicales aborígenes y criollos de la Argentina* and published in 1946 (item 190a).

A scholarly study of the musical structure of Argentine popular forms, particularly those known as *cifras, milongas,* and *estilos* (which are basic types), has been made by Josué Teófilo Wilkes and I. Guerrero Cárpena in their valuable work titled *Formas musicales rioplatenses: su génesis his-*

pánica, which appeared in 1946 (item 199a). The authors' main thesis is summarized in the opening sentence of the first chapter: "Del estudio de las raíces de los cantos y bailables rioplatenses se colige inmediatamente su origen andaluz, como que gran parte de la población rural de aquella región provenía de Andalucía." Some musical notations used in the text were transcribed by Guerrero Cárpena from the singing of an Andalusian family settled in Argentina, in the years 1889-90. There are also arrangements for voice and piano by Wilkes.

The most comprehensive and systematic coverage of Argentine folk music in a single volume is the book by Isabel Aretz, *El folklore musical argentino* (item 144a), published in 1952. Part I covers "Música, instrumentos, poesía, coreografía", and Part II treats of "Canciones, danzas, tocatas". There is a useful analytical chart following p. 266. There are also 91 music notations and 8 photographic plates. Each section has its own bibliography. The study is historical as well as analytical and descriptive.

For contemporary music in Argentina, there is no single reliable source, but the catalogs of individual composer's works published by the Pan American Union are very useful (cf. below, entries for Juan José Castro, Washington Castro, Luis Gianneo). There is also an essay on the music of Ginastera by Gilbert Chase, which appeared in the *Musical quarterly* (item 207a), and a brief historical survey written by García Morillo, *La música en la Argentina* (item 218a). Two important Argentine composers of the immediate past receive extensive biographical consideration in books by Juan F. Giaccobbe and Vicente A. Risolía. The former writes about Julián Aguirre (item 220a), the latter about Alberto Williams (item 238a). To these should be added García Morillo's excellent article on Julián Bautista (1901-61), the composer of Spanish origin who lived in Argentina for many years (item 217a).

A. PRIMITIVE, FOLK AND POPULAR MUSIC

Aretz-Thiele, Isabel. Cantos con caja en los valles de Tucumán. *La nación* (Aug. 24, 1941), sección artes — letras.
[143a]
With 3 music notations and 4 photographs of musicians.

——. El folklore musical argentino. Con 91 ejemplos musicales, 33 esquemas y 8 láminas. Buenos Aires, Ricordi americana, n. d. [1952]. 271 p. il. (music).
[144a]
A valuable and authoritative study. For comment, see introductory section above.

——. El velorio del angelito. *Folklore,* v. 1, no. 3 (March 1941), p. 27-28.
[145a]
Melody and text of a song for the *velorio del angelito* from the province of Tucumán.

——. Música tradicional argentina; Tucumán, historia y folklore. Universidad nacional de Tucumán (Argentina), 1946. 743 p. il. (incl. music). **[146a]**
Includes 795 musical examples in the text, 18 harmonized melodies, 26 drawings, 26 photographs, one map. This scientifically organized monograph is based on five field trips made from 1940 to 1943 (a map shows the itinerary followed).

Part I deals with instruments, dances, and music of Tucumán in pre-colonial and colonial times. Part II deals with music among the folk, in the home, and in public entertainments. Part III comprises the description, analysis and classification of the melodies recorded in the field, with choreographic descriptions of dances. The appendix includes 8 folk tunes arranged for various media from piano to solo voice, piano and string orchestra. Contains extensive bibliography and several indices.

Bates, Hector, and Luis J. Bates. La historia del tango, sus autores. Primer tomo. Buenos Aires, Tall. graf. de la Cía. General fabril financiera, 1936. il. **[147a]**

An informative work on the origin of the *tango* and its development up to the date of publication. The second part of the book is entirely devoted to biographical data on different popular composers.

Carrizo, Juan Alfonso. Cancionero popular de La Rioja, recogido y anotado. Buenos Aires, A. Baiocco y cía., 1942, 3 vols. il. **[148a]**

———. Cantares históricos del norte argentino, recogidos y anotados. Buenos Aires, Centro de instrucción de infantería, 1939. 124 p. (Biblioteca del suboficial, v. 94). **[149a]**

Words only, with extensive explanatory notes, of some 47 songs recorded from oral tradition, chiefly in Salta, Catamarca, Tucumán and Santiago del Estero.

———. Cantares tradicionales del norte. Antología breve. Prólogo del capellán Amancio González Paz. Buenos Aires, Tall. "Optimus" de Cantiello cía., 1939. 49 p. **[150a]**

———, and B. C. Jacovella. Cantares de la tradición bonarense. *Revista del instituto nacional de la tradición*, Buenos Aires (July-Dec. 1948. **[151a]**

Study of two MS notebooks found in an *estancia* in the dictrict of Maipú.

Castagnino, Raúl H. El circo criollo. Datos y documentos para su historia. 1757-1924. Colección Lajouane de folklore argentino. Buenos Aires, Lajouane, 1953. 143 p. il. **[152a]**

Interesting for background on the deve-

lopment of the *gauchesco* tradition, and especialy for details on the origin and diffusion of the popular dance known as the *pericón*.

Folklore puntano. Buenos Aires, Instituto nacional de filología y folklore, 1958. (Anexo a la Academia argentina de letras.) **[153a]**

An account of field trips made to the village of Renca, in the province of San Luis, in the northeast section of Argentina, by a group of folklorists from the Escuela nacional de danzas and the Instituto nacional de filología y folklore of Buenos Aires. They found traces of the well-known forms of Argentine folksong, but also discovered that the traditional songs and dances are fast disappearing even in such a remote place as Renca.

Franco, Alberto. Cancionerillo de amor. Buenos Aires, Editorial Emecé, 1942. 101 p. il. **[154a]**

A popular anthology of 132 Argentine folksongs (without music notation of the melodies), of which ten are in Quechua (with Spanish translation). There is 1 page of music, also notes and a bibliography.

———. Retablo de Navidad; cantares y villancicos. Buenos Aires, Editorial Emecé, 1942. 92 p. il. **[155a]**

Texts of 92 Argentine Christmas songs and carols, some with music.

Inchauspe, Pedro. Voces y costumbres del campo argentino. Buenos Aires, Santiago Rueda, 1942. 265 p. il. **[156a]**

Includes references to Argentine rural songs and dances.

Lullo, Orestes di. El folklore de Santiago del Estero. Tucumán, Universidad Nacional de Tucumán, 1943. 446 p. (Instituto de historia, lingüística y folklore, Departamento de investigaciones regionales.) **[157a]**

Includes fiestas, costumbres, danzas, cantos, etc.

Lupión Castro, Antonio. "La baguala". *Atica*, v. 8, no. 82 (Oct. 1946), p. 18-19. **[158a]**

Description of this *tonada* of northern Argentina, with some stanzas in Spanish. No music. (C.S.)

Moya Ismael. Romancero. Buenos Aires, Imprenta de la universidad, 1941. 2 vols. (Universidad de Buenos Aires, Facultad de filosofía y letras, Instituto de literatura argentina. Estudios sobre materiales de la colección de folklore, no. 1). **[159a]**
Important study of the Spanish ballads and their American variants, their origin and history. No music notations.

Mújica Lainez, Roberto, and Betty Wilson. The tango story; the Argentine dance that swept the world. *Americas,* v. 7, n. 4 (Apr. 195), p. 13-16. **[160a]**
Popular article with some probing of the origins in Argentina, and more about the tango vogue in the United States and Europe. Photographs from motion pictures of Rudolph Valentino and of Carlos Gardel dancing the tango.

Ordaz, Luis. El teatro en el Río de la Plata. Buenos Aires, Editorial Futuro (Colección Eurindia), 1946. 223 p. il. **[161a]**
Passing references to music in the theatre, especially in connection with the *zarzuela* and the *sainete.* On p. 58 mention is made of Ezequiel Soria's *sainete, Justicia Criolla,* produced in 1897, with music by Antonio Reynoso. According to Carlos Vega, this was the work in which the tango was first danced with the characteristic choreography that it acquired in Buenos Aires, as distinct from the Andalusian Tango of Spain. The music for theatre of Antonio Podestá also receives attention.

Pérez del Cerro, Haydee S. B. de, and Raquel Nelli. Compendio de danzas folklóricas argentinas. Historia — coreografía —zapateo. Buenos Aires, Privately printed, 1953. 188 p. il. **[162a]**
A practical treatise, with complete choreographic details, diagrams, and drawings, but no music. Bibliography.

Soiza Reilly, Juan José de. Los bailes criollos a través de cien años. Influencia de las danzas en la formación del alma nacional. *Caras y caretas,* v. 35 (21 May 1932). **[163a]**

Vega Carlos. El bailecito. Buenos Aires,

Ricordi Americana, 1948.. 36 p. il. (music). **[164a]**
One of a series collectively entitled "Bailes tradicionales argentinos", which are hereinafter listed alphabetically. Each booklet follows an identical plan: Historia — Origen — Música — Poesía — Coreografía — Bibliografía.

——. Los aires. Buenos Aires, Editorial ulio Korn, 1953. il. (music). **[165a]**

——. La calandria. Buenos Aires, Ricordi Americana, 1948. 22 p. il. (music) **[166a]**

——. El carnavalito. Buenos Aires, Imprenta de la Universidad de Buenos Aires, 1945. 47 p. il. (music). **[167a]**

——. La chacarera. Buenos Aires, no publisher, 1944. 21 p. **[168a]**

——. El cielito. Buenos Aires, Editorial Julio Korn, 1953. 70 p. **[169a]**

——. La condición. Buenos Aires, Imprenta de la Universidad de Buenos Aires, 1945. 39 p. il. **[170a]**

——. El cuándo. Buenos Aires, Imprenta de la Universidad de Buenos Aires, 1944. 48 p. il. **[171a]**

——. La danza de las cintas. Buenos Aires, Ricordi Americana, 1948. 44 p. il. (music). **[172a]**

——. El escondido. Buenos Aires, Imprenta de la Universidad de Buenos Aires, 1946, 30 p. il. **[173a]**

——. La firmeza Buenos Aires, Editorial Julio Korn, 1953. il. (music). **[174a]**

——. El gato. Buenos Aires, Imprenta de la Universidad de Buenos Aires, 1944.1944. 45 p. il. (music). **[175a]**

——. La huella. Buenos Aires, Ricordi Americana, 1948. 40 p. (music). **[176a]**

——. El malambo. El solo inglés. La campana. Buenos Aires, Editorial Julio Korn, 1953. 42 p. il. (music). **[177a]**

——. La mariquita. El pala pala. Buenos Aires, Imprenta de la Universidad de Buenos Aires, 1946. 47 p. il. (music) **[178a]**

——. La media caña. Buenos Aires, Editorial Julio Korn, 1953, 38 p. il. (music).   [179a]

——. El montonero (el minué federal). Buenos Aires, Editorial Julio Korn, 1953. il. (music).   [180a]

——. El pajarillo. Buenos Aires, Ricordi Americana. 1948. 22 p. il. (music).   [181a]

——. El pala pala. Buenos Aires, Sociedad Argentina de autores y compositores de música, 1946. 6 p. il. (music)   [182a]

——. El pericón. Buenos Aires, Editorial Julio Korn, 1953. 52 p.   [183a]

Apéndice: *Cielito — Pericón — Media caña.*

——. La resbalosa. Buenos Aires, Editorial Julio Korn, 1953. 38 p.   [184a]

——. La sajuriana. Buenos Aires, Ricordi americana, 1948. 40 p. il. (music)   [185a]

——. El triunfo. Buenos Aires, Imprenta de la Universidad de Buenos Aires, 1944. 22 p. il. (music).   [186a]

——. La zamacueca (cueca, zamba, chilena, marinera). La zamba antigua. Buenos Aires, Editorial Julio Korn, 1953. 156 p. il. (music).   [187a]

——. El origen de las danzas folklóricas. Buenos Aires. Ricordi americana, n. d. [1956]. 218 p. il.   [188a]

This is a résumé and reiteration of the author's previous publications and well-known theory on the provenience of the traditional rural dances of Argentina. His thesis may be summed up in the phrase, "from the salons of Paris to the Argentine rural setting". The "itinerary" he outlines is from the salons of France to those of Spain, hence to those of Lima and Buenos Aires. He rejects the Spanish-folkloric origin of these dances, with admixture of Indian and Negro elements.

——. Las danzas populares argentinas. Vol. 1. Buenos Aires. Ministerio de educación de la nación. Dirección general de cultura. Instituto de musicología, 1952. 780 p. il. (music).   [189a]

Illustrated with 19 plates, 138 drawings, and 35 musical examples. A systematic coverage of the subject, including the classification, the history, the origin, the music, the choreography, and the bibliography, of each species studied. An author's note at the end states that "This volume was prepared in haste and under unfavorable circumstances", and that it contains "material *errata* and faults of documentary coordination". No list of *errata* is included.

——. Los instrumentos musicales aborígenes y criollos de la Argentina; con un ensayo sobre las clasificaciones universales; un panorama gráfico de los instrumentos americanos. Buenos Aires, Ediciones centurión, 1946. 331 p. il. (incl. music) "Publicaciones citadas": p. 311-313.   [190a]

Illustrations: 1 citocromía, 1 litografía, 214 dibujos, 56 fotografías, 1 mapa. 39 musical examples. An important scientific work, systematically organized and documented. Valuable for the comparative study of musical instruments in South America, particularly the Andean region.

——. Música sudamericana. Colección Buen aire. Buenos Aires, Emecé editores, 1946. 117 p. il. (music).   [191a]

This small volume is not a handbook on South American music, but unites several disparate essays, on the discovery of the tonal system of the Incas (*sic*), on Argentine dances, on the poetic form of the *vidala,* and on the guitar as an artistic instrument in the Buenos Aires of olden days.

Viggiano Esaín, Julio. Instrumentología musical popular argentina. Vigencias de origen indígena. *Rev. univ. nac. Córdoba,* v. 34, no. 5 (Nov.-Dec. 1947), p. 1237-1294.   [192a]

Author is head of the Gabinete de Musicología, Instituto de Arqueología, Universidad de Córdoba, and a follower of Vega. Elaborates his researches with acoustic instruments. 1 map. 24 illustrations, 2 of them additional maps, and 2 of them music notations. Seems to be first 3 chapters of a larger work. After general introduction, a classificatory scheme deals with flute-type instruments only. Brief distribution studies and scholarly discussion. (C.S.)

Villafuerte, Carlos. El cantar de las

provincias argentinas. Melodías y coplas recogidas por el autor. Anotadas y armonizadas por Óscar Bareilles. Buenos Aires, Editorial "El Ateneo", n. d. [1951]. 105 p. il. (music). **[193a]**

The primary purpose of this collection is educational. It bears the *imprimatur*, "Aprobado por el Ministerio de Educación para el canto escolar". The volume contains songs from each province. The compilers state that all but two of the songs were taken from oral tradition, even when written versions existed. The arrangements are for a single voice with piano accompaniment.

Wilkes, J. T. Dos canciones patrióticas anónimas. *Bol. acad. arg. letras,* v. 14, no. 50 (Jan.-Mar., 1945), p. 137-171.
[194a]

Substantial discussions of early patriotic songs of Argentina from 1810 on, of which "La Azulada Bandera del Plata" is given the date 1818-1820 and "La Marcha de la República Argentina", 1830. Some comparative studies of melodic factors among the national anthem and others. 2 complete music notations; 5 others. (C.S.)

——. La música vernacular y el estado. *Rev. estud. mus.,* v. 1, no. 1 (1949), p. 47-60. **[195a]**

Attempts to trace the rhythms of Argentine folk music from the ancient Greek metrical system, thru the medieval rhythmic modes. Ingenious but overly pedantic.

——. La antigua tonada tucumana "Por esta calle a lo largo" y la seudo vidala de la Virgen Generala. *Rev. estud. mus.,* v. 1, no. 3 (April 1950), p. 11-42.
[196a]

Music and words of the "Antigua vidala tucumana" recorded from oral tradition and harmonized by Wilkes, plus 10 brief notations and an appendix containing musical arrangements by the author of a *Cielito federal, La cautiva (cielito)* and *Vidala.*

——. La rítmica específica del cantar nativo. Buenos Aires, Academia argentina de letras, 1945. 48 p. **[197a]**

A study of classical theories of quantity, proportion and accent in the folk song of the Rio de la Plata region, with 17 fragmentary music notations.

Originally published in *Boletín de la Academia argentina de letras,* v. 13, no. 47 (April-June 1944), p. 390-432. Also reprinted, with slight revisions, in *Rev. estud. mus.,* v. 2, no. 4 (Aug. 1950), p. 11-42 (this article bears the date "enero de 1951").

——. Sintaxis sonora del cantar vernáculo. *Anales de la asociación folklórica argentina,* Buenos Aires (1945), p. 85-87. **[198a]**

——, and I. Guerrero Carpeña. Formas musicales rioplatenses (cifras, estilos y milongas). Su génesis hispánica. Buenos Aires, Publicaciones de estudios hispánicos, 1946. 312 p. il. (music).
[199a]

A very important scholarly work, historicaly and musically, tracing the origins and development of certain types of folk music found in the region of the Rio de la Plata, with 90 brief music notations and some arrangements for voice and piano by Wilkes. Bibliography.

B. ART MUSIC AND MISCELLANEOUS

Barrenechea, Mariano Antonio. Historia estética de la música. 4. ed. definitiva, corregida y aumentada por el autor. Buenos Aires, Editorial Claridad, 1944. 563 p. (Biblioteca de obras famosas, v. 58) **[200a]**

Argentine music: p. 430-445. Composers mentioned but not listed under note to 3rd ed.: César Stiatessi, Juan José Castro, Juan Bautista Massa, Gilardo Gilardi, Enrique M. Casella, Héctor Panizza, A. Williams, Luis Gianneo, Miguel Calvello. (Cf. item. no. 305).

Barbacci, Rodolfo. Documentación para la historia de la música argentina, 1801-1885. *Rev. estud. mus.,* v. 1, no. 2 (1949), p. 11-63. **[201a]**

Extracts, with little comment, from newspapers, among them: *La Gazeta de Buenos Aires, El Argos de Buenos Aires, El Centinela, La Crónica,* and others. Covers only 1801-1829, 1851-1852, 1855. Gap of 1830-1850 (Rosas epoch) notable. Perhaps typographical error on final date in title. (C.S.)

Bosch, Mariano G. La música en la Argentina desde remotos tiempos. *Lyra,* no. 13, (1940), p. 12-18.   **[202a]**

———. La música y los músicos de 1810. Blas Parera y el himno nacional. *Lyra,* no. 23 (1945), p. 17-20.   **[203a]**

Cánepa, Luis. Historia del himno argentino. Buenos Aires, Ed. Linari, 1944. 127 p.   **[204a]**

Castro, Juan José. Classified chronological catalog of the works of the Argentine composer Juan José Castro. *Bol. interam. mús.,* no. 4 (March 1958), p. 67-73.   **[205a]**

Castro was born in Avellaneda, Argentina, on March 7, 1895.

Castro, Washington. Classified chronological catalog of the works of the Argentine composer Washington Castro. *Bol. interam. mús.,* no. 5 (May 1958), p. 57-59.   **[206a]**

Castro was born in Buenos Aires on July 13, 1909.

Chase, Gilbert. Alberto Ginastera: Argentine composer. *Mus. quart.,* v. 43, no. 4 (Oct. 1957), p. 339-460.   **[207a]**

A thorough study of this composer's musical development and of his relation to musical nationalism, which sees him as deeply involved in the emotional symbols of Argentine national culture (such as the *pampa*), while at the same time embracing new international techniques of composition in a strongly individual style. With 14 musical notations and a list of works.

———. Alberto Ginastera: portrait of an Argentine composer. *Tempo,* no. 44 (Summer 1957), p. 11-16.   **[208a]**

With musical examples and a portrait of the composer.

¿Debe ser obligatoria la ejecución de música argentina? *B. A. mus.,* v. 11, no. 181 (16 Oct. 1956), p. 1, 6; no. 182 (1 Nov. 1956), p. 1; no. 183 (16 Nov. 1956), p. 1, 2.   **[209a]**

Among the composers who reply to this

query are Ginastera, Gianneo, Floro M. Ugarte, Gilardi, Caamaño, Fontela, Arizaga, Maragno. Most are affirmative.

D'Urbano, Jorge. Primer festival de música de Santa Fe. *B. A. mus.,* v. 14, no. 230 (Oct. 16, 1959), p. 1, 2. **[210a]**

Famous Argentines. Julián Aguirre. *Arg. news,* no. 80 (1946), p. 38.   **[211a]**

Brief biographical sketch of the composer (1868-1924). Portrait. (C.S.)

Franze, Johannes. Neue argentinische Musik. *Musica* (Kassel), no. 1 (1957), p. 17-18.   **[212a]**

Detailed discussion of music by Juan Carlos Paz, especially the new *Transformaciones Canónicas.*

Fúrlong, Guillermo. La música en el Rio de la Plata con anterioridad a 1810. *Lyra,* no. 11 (1944), p. 3-6.   **[213a]**

———. Músicos argentinos durante la dominación hispánica; exposición sintética precedida de una introducción por Lauro Ayestarán. Buenos Aires, Editorial "Huarpes", 1945. 203 p. il. (Cultura colonial argentina, no. 2.) **[214a]**

The work of a scholarly specialist in the colonial period of Argentine cultural history, this volume summarizes the musical data available for that period, copiously annotated with bibliographical footnotes that are valuable to the student. Shows that the Jesuit missionaries encouraged secular as well as sacred music. The illustrations are exceptionally interesting. Includes a comprehensive bibliography.

Gallac, Héctor. Ensayos musicológicos. Buenos Aires, Ed. Coni, 1939. 122 p.   **[215a]**

Includes studies of two indigenous musical instruments, the *erque* and the *charango* (cf. items nos. 599 and 600).

García Morillo, Roberto. El teatro musical en Argentina. *Rev. Mus. chil.,* v. 5, no. 33 (Apr.-May 1949), p. 40-45.   **[216a]**

Operatic activities in Buenos Aires began

in 1825 with the performance of Rossini's *Barber of Seville.* A brief survey of the 19th and early 20th century repertoire of European opera, then discussion of operas by Argentines through 1947.

——. Julián Bautista. *Rev. mus. chil.,* v. 5, nos. 35-36 (Aug.-Nov. 1949), p. 26-43.   [217a]

Excellent critical appreciation of this important Argentine composer of Spanish origin, with 14 music notations and a list of works, also a portrait of the composer.

——. La música en la Argentina. *Nuestra música,* v. 7, no. 26 (2. trimestre, 1952), p. 81-107.   [218a]

A survey of musical composition in Argentina from the colonial period to the present.

——. Una novità di Castro al Colon di Buenos Aires. *Ricordiana,* v. 2, no. 8 (Oct. 1956), p. 389-393.   [219a]

Discussion of Juan José Castro's new opera *Bodas de Sangre,* based on the drama of F. García Lorca.

Giaccobe, Juan Francisco. Julián Aguirre, ensayo sobre su vida y su obra en su tiempo. Buenos Aires, Ricordi americana, 1945, 97 p. il.   [220a]

Ansermet's orchestrations of Aguirre's two creole dances, *Gato y Huella,* have made the name and music of this Argentine composer widely known —though this knowledge is generally limited to the two abovementioned pieces. Aguirre was brought up in Spain and studied at the Madrid Conservatory. At 19 he returned to Argentina, where he devoted his creative efforts to developing a musical style based on popular models but full of artistic refinement, somewhat in the manner of Albéniz. The author points out that "criollismo" was the essence of Aguirre's art, i. e., a blending of European and American elements. Cf. Margarita del Ponte de Aguirre, *La vida de Julián Aguirre,* in *Revista ars* (no. 2, 1940).

Gianneo, Luis. Classified chronological catalog of the works of the Argentine composer Luis Gianneo. *Bol. interam. mús.,* nos. 9-10 (Jan.-March 1959), p. 51-57.   [221a]

Gianneo was born in Buenos Aires, Jan.

9, 1897. Facsimile of holograph score, p. 50.

Ginastera, Alberto. Eight from the Argentine. *Mod. Music,* v. 23, no. 4 (Fall 1946), p. 226-272.   [222a]

Ginastera regards the three Castros, Ficher, Paz, Suffern, García Morillo and Gianneo as the leaders of contemporary composition in Argentina. We must, of course, add Ginastera himself as ninth. Seven fragmentary music notations. (C.S.)

——. Notas sobre la música moderna argentina, *Rev. mus. chil.,* 4, no. 31 (Oct.-Nov. 1948), p. 21-28.   [223a]

Places the origin of the modern music movement in Argentina among the composers of the 1890s generation, who knew works of Debussy, Ravel, Stravinsky, Schönberg. Discusses works of members of the movement: José María Castro, Juan José Castro, Luis Gianneo, Juan Carlos Paz, Carlos Suffern, Washington Castro, Roberto García Morillo; also European immigrants: Julián Bautista, Jacobo Ficher, Guillermo Graetzer, César Brero. Brief mention of promising young Argentine composers Sergio de Castro, Pía Sebastiani, Rodolfo Arizaga, Tirso de Olazábal and Astor Piazzola.

Grenón, Pedro J. Nuestra primera música instrumental. Datos históricos. Segunda edición. Con un prólogo de Francisco Curt Lange. Mendoza, Universidad nacional de Cuyo, 1951 and 1954. In *Rev. estud. mus.,* v. 2, nos. 5-6, Dec. 1950, April 1951, p. 13-96; v. 3, no. 7, Dec. 1954. p. 173-200. il.   [224a]

New edition of an important monograph, deleting the original illustrations but supplementing many of the bibliographical references. (Cf. item no. 600).

Hurtado, Leopoldo. La nueva música argentina. Seis Cuartetos de cuerdas. *Rev. mus. chil.,* v. 2, no. 10 (April 1946), p. 7-12.   [225a]

Discusses string quartets by J. J. Castro, J. Ficher, Washington Castro, G. Gilardi, J. M. Castro, and L. Gianneo.

Lange, Francisco Curt. Huellas de la

música eclesiástica durante la dominación hispánica. *B. A. mus.,* v. 7, no.
117 (15 Dec. 1952), p. 4.   **[226a]**

——. La música eclesiástica argentina en
el período de la dominación hispánica
(una investigación). Primera parte
(Humahuaca-Jujuy). *Rev. estud. mus.,*
v. 3, no. 7 (Dec. 1954), p. 15-171.
    [227a]
A fundamental study, based on firsthand
research and reproducing in facsimile
many original documents of the period.

——. La música eclesiástica en Córdoba
durante la dominación hispánica. Córdoba, Imprenta de la universidad, 1956.
114 p.   **[228a]**
Documents relating to church music,
found by the author in various archives.

——. La música religiosa en el área de
Rosario de Santa Fe y en el convento
San Carlos de San Lorenzo, durante el
período aproximado de 1770 a 1820.
Rosario, Cursos libres de Portugués y
estudios brasileños, 1956. 62 p. il.
(facs.)   **[229a]**

——. La música eclesiástica en Santa Fe
y Corrientes durante la dominación hispánica. *Universidad,* Santa Fe, no. 34
(Apr. 1957), p. 23-88.   **[230a]**

– ——. La vida musical en la Argentina.
Asomante, v. 3, no. 2 (Apr.-June 1947),
p. 57-65.   **[231a]**
Brief historical sketch of the development
of professional music activities, including
conservatories, folklorists, composers'
groups, choral and orchestral aggregations.
Informative. (C.S.)

——. Órganos y organeros en los con-
ventos franciscanos de la Argentina en
el período de la dominación hispánica.
Meridiano 66, v. 1, no. 2 (1955). Publicación de la Dirección general de
cultura, Catamarca.   **[232a]**

Lyons, James. Argentine virtuoso: globe-
trotting violinist Ricardo Odnoposoff.
Américas, v. 5, no. 10 (Oct. 1953), p.
9-11, 39.   **[233a]**
Account of his life and career. 5 photographs.

Mariz, Vasco. Alberto Ginastera. Cursos
libres de portugués y estudios brasileños. Sección publicaciones. Rosario, Argentina, 1954. 38 p. il. (port.) **[234a]**
Includes a catalog of Ginastera's works
up to 1954, a bibliography, and a list of
recordings. Portrait of the composer and
facsimile of the first page of the score of
Pampeana No. 3.

Pahlen, Kurt. Das Teatro Colón. *Oesterreichische Musikzeitschrift* v. 12, no.
11 (Nov. 1957), p. 419-423.   **[235a]**
First of series of articles on the situation
of the great opera houses of the world.

Paz, Juan Carlos. Música argentina,
1952. *B. A. Lit.* v. 1, no. 3 (Dec. 1952),
p. 7-14.   **[236a]**
A devastating critique of contemporary
Argentine music and musical values.
(R.A.W.)

**Ponce y López Buchardo; dos grandes
pérdidas para la música americana.**
Rev. mus. chil., v. 4, no. 29 (June-
July 1948), p. 6-8.   **[237a]**
Brief biographies of Manuel M. Ponce of
Mexico and Carlos López Buchardo of Ar-
gentina, with appreciations of their music.
(B.K.)

Risolía, Vicente Aníbal. Alberto Williams. Curriculum vitae. Con algunas
anotaciones sobre su obra musical, literaria y didáctica. Buenos Aires, Editorial "La Quena", 1944. 188 p. il.
    [238a]
An important biography of the Argentine composer, profusely illustrated (chiefly with portraits of the subject). Bibliography and catalogue of the works of Alberto Williams (including his writings in
prose and verse).

Rojas, Ricardo. Ollantay, tragedia de los
Andes. 2. ed. Buenos Aires, Editorial
Losada, 1941. 218 p. (Biblioteca con-
temporánea, v. 56.)   **[239a]**
"Coros... compuestos por Gilardo Gi-
lardi", p. 167-191.

Rosés Lacoigne, Zulema. Alberto Williams, músico argentino. Buenos Aires,

Talleres gráficos Della Torre Hnos. 1942. 90 p. **[240a]**

Catálogo de las obras de A. Williams: p. 85-90.

Salazar, Adolfo. El caso de Doménico Zipoli. *Nuestra música,* v. 1, no. 2 (May 1946), p. 80-83. **[241a]**

On the controversial question of whether the Domenico Zipoli who went to Argentina in the early 18th century and died there in 1716, was really the well-known European composer of that name.

Schiuma, Oreste. Música y músicos argentinos. 2ª ed. Buenos Aires, Imp. M. Lorenzo Rañó, 1943. 237 p. **[242a]**

Trenti Rocamora, J. Luis. La cultura en Buenos Aires hasta 1810. Buenos Aires, 1948. 154 p. il. Universidad de Buenos Aires, Departamento de acción social universitaria, Sección publicaciones y biblioteca. Serie Divulgación de nuestra historia — Cuaderno no. 2. **[243a]**

Includes "La música", p. 113-124, with "Bibliografía fundamental".

——. La música en el teatro porteño anterior a 1810. *Rev. estud. mus.,* v. 1, no. 1, (1949) p. 36-46. **[244a]**

Period covered is 1747-1810. Bibliography.

Valenti Ferro, Enzo. Argentina *Mus.*

Amer., v. 73, no. 3 (Feb. 1953), p. 161. **[245a]**

Review of Buenos Aires' musical season of 1952. Much listing of visiting conductors, number of concerts. New Argentine works first performed are listed, including the ballet *Estancia* by Ginastera.

——. El estreno de la Zapatera Prodigiosa. *B. A. mus.,* v. 13, no. 211 (Sept. 1, 1958), p. 1. **[246a]**

An opera by Juan José Castro.

——. New Castro work given et Buenos Aires opera. *Mus. Amer.,* v. 76, no. 13 (Nov. 1, 1956), p. 11. **[247a]**

On *Bodas de Sangre* by Juan José Castro, discussing his earlier operas, and the music, staging and performance of this one. One photograph of opera's final scene.

Viggiano Esain, Julio. La escuela musicológica argentina. Córdoba, Imprenta de la Universidad nacional de Córdoba, 1948. 24 p. il. (Publ. del Instituto de arqueología, lingüística y folklore "Dr. Pablo Cabrera", no. 21.) **[248a]**

Villanueva U., Horacio. Influencia de la música incaica en el cancionero del norte argentino; un nuevo libro de Policarpio Caballero Farfán. *Rev. univ.,* Cuzco, v. 34, nos. 88-89 (1945), p. 189-197. **[249a]**

Williams, Alberto. Amancio Alcorta, compositor. Buenos Aires, 1943. 18 p. **[250a]**

BAHAMAS

Edwards, Charles Lincoln. Bahama songs and stories. Boston and New York, Houghton, Mifflin and co., 1895. 111 p. (*Half-title:* Memoirs of the American folk-lore society. v. 3, 1895). GR1.A5 v. 3. **[646]**

Hurston, Zora. Dance songs and games from the Bahamas. *Jour. amer. folk-*

lore, v. 43, no. 167 (July Oct. 1930), p. 294-312. **[647]**

With 11 tunes.

Lomax, John A. and Alan. Our singing country. New York, The Macmillan company, 1941. xxxiv, 416 p. **[647x]**

"Bahaman Negro songs", p. 80-93.

BOLIVIA

B OLIVIA and its neighbor Paraguay are the only two inland republics
of South America. The music of both countries is very little known
to the outside world. As regards Bolivian music, the chief bibliographical interest has centered on a study of the music of the Indians, who
comprise about one half of the population. In the Andean highlands, where
three fourths of the inhabitants are concentrated, the Indians are mostly
of the Aymara and Quechua stocks. There is a marked difference between
the austere and melancholy music of these highland Indians, and the music
of the Bolivian lowlands, where the Spanish influence predominates. Again,
there are Indian tribes completely isolated in the jungle-like Amazon region,
such as the Tobas and the Lenguas, whose music preserves an entirely primitive quality. The famous Lake Titicaca, center of the Incan civilization
in pre-Hispanic times, lies between Bolivia and Peru, belonging partly to
both countries. Since it once formed part of the Inca empire, Bolivia may
lay claim to its share of the bibliography on Incan music which is listed
under Peru. For example, the comprehensive work on Incan music by
Raoul and Marguerite d'Harcourt, *La musique des Incas et ses survivances*
[no. 2406], is indispensable for a knowledge of the background of Bolivian
folk music.

Two shorter studies by the d'Harcourts on the folk music of the Andean region [nos. 653, 655] constitute our main source of information on
Bolivian folk music. These studies have the advantage of being illustrated
with numerous musical examples. Except for the writings of Rafael Karsten
on the Indians of Bolivia, the references in English are less valuable. English readers will find a brief but convenient survey of folk and popular
music in the section on Bolivia in Gustavo Durán's *Recordings of Latin
American songs and dances* [no. 187]. Many of the songs and dances listed
there—such as the *bailecito, tonada, cueca, estilo, huaiño, triste, yaraví* and
zamba—are common to other South American countries and present only
slight local differences in Bolivia. One of the most characteristic dances of
Bolivia is the *sicuris* which derives its name from the Quechua word for
panpipes (*sicu;* the Aymara word for the same instrument is *antara*).
Another well-known dance of the highland Indians is the *kaluyo,* which
involves shoe tapping (*zapateo*) and is related in its choreography to the
Chilean *cueca.*

The most extensive account of musical life in Bolivia available in English is that contained in Carleton Sprague Smith's *Musical tour through
Latin America* (p. 206-215); this, however, is a confidential document not
accessible to the general public. Brief notes on contemporary Bolivian

composers are included in Slonimsky's article on South American composers published in *Musical America* [no. 109]. The principal composers of "serious" music in Bolivia are Antonio González Bravo (b. 1885), Humberto Viscarra Monje (b. 1898) and José María Velasco Maidana (b. 1899). The last-mentioned is director of the Orquesta Nacional de Conciertos of La Paz, which he founded in 1940. He is the composer of a ballet, *Amerindia* (produced in Berlin, 6 Dec. 1938), of the suite *Indiana* for orchestra, and of several symphonic poems, all unpublished. Simeón Roncal (b. 1872) has written popular dances and marches utilizing Indo-American folk rhythms and themes. Francisco Suárez (b. 1858) is another composer who has specialized in writing dances and marches for military band. Eduardo Caba, a composer of Bolivian birth living in Argentina, has published some attractive Bolivian airs and dances for piano. Prominent in the musical life of Sucre, Mario Estensoro is director of the Sociedad Filarmónica and the Escuela de Música in that city.

GENERAL AND MISCELLANEOUS

Andrade, Victor. La música, voz de la tierra. *Kollasuyo*, v. 1, no. 9 (Sept. 1939), p. 35-44. [648]

Guise, Anselm Verner Lee. Six years in Bolivia. London, T. Fisher Unwin, 1922. 246 p. F3313.G96 [649]
Dance and music, p. 56, 80, 222. For less important references, p. 50, 92.

Paredes, Manuel Rigoberto. Mitos, supersticiones y supervivencias populares de Bolivia. La Paz, Arno hermanos, 1920. 282 p. F3320.2.F6P3 [650]

Wright, Marie Robinson. Bolivia. Philadelphia, George Barrie and sons, 1907. 450 p. F3308.W96 [651]
Music, p. 171-172; names the outstanding Bolivian musicians of the time.

NATIONAL ANTHEM

Vincenti, Benedetto. Himno nacional de Bolivia. *In* Ofrenda de Venezuela en el primer centenario de la batalla de Ayacucho, Caracas, Litografía del comercio, 1924, p. 119-130. M1686.O35 [652]
Words and music.

FOLK AND PRIMITIVE MUSIC

(A) GENERAL

Béclard d'Harcourt, Marguerite. Le folklore musical de la région andine; Équateur, Pérou, Bolivie. *In* Encyclopédie de la musique et dictionnaire du conservatoire, partie 1, p. 3353-3371, Paris, Librairie Delagrave, 1922. ML100.E5 [653]
Contains 36 musical examples; many of them are melodies with native Indian words. An important study.

——. Trois chants des andes avec accompagnement de piano. Milano, G. Ricordi & c., 1926. 8 p. M1686.B45 [654]

Harcourt, Raoul and Marguerite d'. La musique dans la sierra andine de la Paz à Quito. Société des américanistes de Paris. *Journal,* n. s., v. 12 (Paris, 1920), p. 21-53. [655]
There are 22 brief musical examples in the main body of the article, followed by 8 melodies, all but one with text in Kechua.

Mendoza, Jaime. Jula-julas. Sobre el folklore musical boliviano. *Rev. circ. altos estud.,* v. 4, nos. 12-14 (1938), p. 36-38. [656]

——. Motivos folklóricos bolivianos. *Rev. univ. Chuquisaca,* no. 20 (1930), p. 177-193.   **[657]**

Paredes, Manuel Rigoberto. Mitos, supersticiones y supervivencias populares de Bolivia. 2d ed. La Paz, Atenea, 1936. 232 p. F3320.2F6P3   **[658]**

Schallehn, Hellmut. Die grundlagen der volksmusik in Bolivien und Paraguay. *Die brücke zur heimat,* v. 33 (1933), p. 215-231.   **[659]**

Schuller, Rudolph. South American popular poetry. *Jour. amer. folklore,* v. 28, no. 110 (1915), p. 358-364. **[660]**

Includes the text (in Kechua) of 2 folk songs of Bolivia, also of 2 folk poems collected in Uruguay and Argentina.

(B) AMERINDIAN

1. *Music and Dance*

Bandelier, Adolphus Francis. La danse des *Sicuri* des Indiens Aymará de Bolivie. *In* Boas anniversary volume, New York, 1906, p. 272-282. 1 plate. GN4.B66   **[661]**

Bayo, Ciro. El peregrino en Indias. Madrid Librería de los sucesores de Hernando, 1911. 443 p. F3313.B36   **[662]**

Mention of *yaravís* and the *chobena* (a dance), p. 425; Kechua music, p. 54.

Campana, Domenico del. Notizie intorno ai Ciriguani. *Arch. antrop. etnol.,* v. 32 (1902), p. 17-144.   **[663]**

Music, p. 104-109, with melodies, p. 105, 108. Article also includes: musical example of a marriage chant, p. 67; discussion of funeral music (with musical examples), p. 117-118; musical instruments of war, p. 121-123; words of a war-chant, p. 124; bibliography, p. 140-141; illustrations of musical instruments, plates 7, 8.

Cortés, José Domingo. Bolivia. Paris, Tipografía Lahure, 1875. 172 p. F3308.-C82   **[664]**

Music of the Indians, p. 60; *bailes ca-*

seros, p. 72-73; complete description of the *quena,* p. 75-77; *yaraví,* p. 77-78.

Engel, Carl. An introduction to the study of national music; comprising researches into popular songs, traditions, and customs. London, Longmans, Green, Reader, and Dyer, 1866. 435 p. il. (music) ML2545.E57 **[665]**

Includes "Two songs of the Chiquitos" (p. 153-154) first published by d'Orbigny, and "A song of the Indian rowers of the Rio Negro" (p. 154), taken from the collection of Spix and Martius.

Faber, Kurt. Tage und nächte in urwald und sierra. Stuttgart, Robert Lutz, 1926. 311 p. F3423.F177   **[666]**

Music, p. 132, 142-143.

Fourdrignier, Édouard. Musique bolivienne. Société d'anthropologie de Paris. *Bull. mém. soc. anthrop.,* ser. 5, v. 7 (Paris, 1906), p. 450-460. GN2.-S61   **[667]**

Commentary on an audition of phonograms made by Adrien de Mortillet while on a scientific mission in South America (recordings made among the Indians of Bolivia). No music.

Harms Espejo, Carlos. Bolivia en sus diversas fases ... Santiago, Talleres Castro, 1922. 284 p. F3308.H28 **[668]**

Note on the dance and music of the Indians, p. 74.

Karsten, Rafael. Indian dances in the Gran Chaco. *Öfversigt at Finska vetenskaps societetens förhandlingar,* v. 37, afd. b, no. 6 (1914-1915). 35 p. **[669]**

Dancing to cure or prevent disease, at drinking feasts, on occasions of various kinds. Includes 2 musical examples.

——. Indian tribes of the Argentine and Bolivian Chaco. Helsingfors, Finska vetenskapssocieteten, 1932, 236 p. il. F-2822.K28   **[670]**

Description of ceremonial dances and chants, p. 141-152, 161-170. With 3 tunes, p. 139, 144, 148.

Métraux, Alfred. Les Indiens Uro-Chipaya de Carangas. *Journ. soc. Amér.,*

n. s. v. 27, no. 1 (1935), p. 325-415; v. 28, no. 1 (1936), p. 155-207; v. 28, no. 2 (1936), p. 337-394. **[671]**

Vol. 27, no. 2, *Fêtes et rites,* includes information on the largest and most important Chipaya festivals, with the music of several songs, and other musical examples; v. 28, no. 1, *Instruments de musique* (p. 180-188), is a brief resumé of K. G. Izikowitz's article on the Chipayan musical instruments [Item no. 691], and consists of exact descriptions of various drums, trumpets, clarinets and flutes, and the *quena.* He adds that the only stringed instrument possessed by these Indians is the guitar brought from the outside world.

Miller, Leo E. Yuracaré Indians of eastern Bolivia. *Geog. rev.,* v. 4, no. 6 (Dec. 1917), p. 450-464. **[672]**

Notes on music, p. 453, 557.

Nino, Bernardino de. Etnografía chiriguana. La Paz, Tipografía comercial de Ismael Argote, 1912. 332 p. F3319.N7 **[673]**

Chap. 11, p. 254-271, is important for information on festivals, music, dance.

Nordenskiöld, Erland. An ethno-geographical analysis of the material culture of two Indian tribes in the Gran Chaco. Göteborg, Elanders boktryckeri aktiebolag, 1919. 295 p. il. F2230.N82, v. 1 (*His* Comparative ethnographical studies. I). **[674]**

A study of the Chorotes and Ashluslay Indians. Description and illustration of musical instruments, p. 164-183.

——. Forschungen und abenteuer in Südamerika. Stuttgart, Strecker & Schröder, 1924. 338 p. F3313.N835 **[675]**

Muscial instruments among the Huari Indians, p. 232; music to a Cavina Indian piece (for flute, drum and bass drum), p. 270-271; for further reference to music see p. 189, 207, 240, and for dance p. 76, 273.

——. Indianerleben. El gran Chaco. Leipzig, A. Bonnier, 1912. 343 p. il. F3319.N83 **[676]**

Musical instruments, p. 86; illustration

of a musical bow, p. 199; for dance, see pages 17, 78, 85-86, 106, 141, 174, 240, 325. For further references to music and dance, see index under *Pfeife, Trommeln, Gesang,* etc. The Chaco region is divided among Argentina, Paraguay and Bolivia.

Orbigny, Alcide Dessalines d'. Voyage dans l'Amérique Méridionale. Paris, Pitois-Levrault et c^{le}.; Strasbourg, Ve Levrault, 1835-47. F2223.O64 **[677]**

Vol. 3 (7 p. following p. 60) has music: "Chants des Indiens Chiquitos" (9 tunes) and "Chants des Indiens Morotocas" (11 tunes).

Paredes, Manuel Rigoberto. El arte en la altiplanicie (folklore). La Paz, J. M. Gamarra, 1913. 70 p. **[678]**

References to Indian dances and music.

Post, Charles Johnson. Indian music of South America. *Harper's,* v. 112 (1905-06), p. 255-257. **[679]**

Includes 5 tunes.

Reiser, Hans. Einer ging in die wildnis. Leipzig, Paul List, 1936. 327 p. F3423.R46 **[680]**

Incan music, p. 43-44; many references to dance, p. 253-261; words to a folk-song (Spanish), p. 62, with German translation, p. 326.

Ross, Colin. Südamerika, die aufsteigende welt. Leipzig, F. A. Brockhaus, 1922. 318 p. F2223.R316 **[681]**

Music and dance among the Bolivian Indians, p. 223.

Schuller, Rudolph. Tacana Indians of Bolivia. *Amer. anthrop.,* v. 24, no. 2 (Apr.-June 1922), p. 161-170. **[682]**

Mention of flutes, p. 165, 167.

Snethlage, Emil Heinrich. Nachrichten über die Pauserna-Guarayú, die Siriono am Rio Baures und die Simonianes in nähe der Serra San Simon. *Zeit. ethnol.,* v. 67 (1935), p. 278-293. **[683]**

Siriono melody collected by M. Schneider, p. 292, footnote.

Walle, Paul. Bolivia. London, Leipsic, T.

Fisher Unwin, 1914. 407 p. F3308.W19 **[684]**

Music of the Indians, p. 149-153, a discussion of the melancholy character of the music, and a description of many musical instruments with particular reference to the *quena;* mention of several dances. Military bands in La Paz, p. 54-55.

Weddell, Hugues Algernon. Voyage dans le nord de la Bolivie et dans les parties voisines du Pérou. Paris, P. Bertrand, 1853. 571 p. il. F3313.W38 **[685]**

"Waiño, mélodie indienne", p. 199-200.

Wegner, Richard Nikolaus. Zum Sonnenthor durch altes Indianerland. Darmstadt, L. C. Wittich, 1931. 175 p. il. F2223.W43 **[686]**

Description of the *Machetero* (dance of the Mojos Indians), p. 111-112; music of a dance festival, p. 38.

2. *Instruments*

Forbes, David. On the Aymara Indians of Bolivia and Peru. *Journ. ethnol. soc.,* n. s., v. (1870), p. 193-298. **[687]**

Mentions musical instruments, p. 233.

Friç A. V. Die unbekannten stämme des Chaco Boreal. *Globus,* v. 96 (1909), p. 24-28. **[688]**

References to musical instruments.

González Bravo, Antonio. Kenas, pincollos y tarkas. *Bol. lat. am. mús.,* v. 3 (1937), p. 25-32. **[689]**

Description, with illustrations, of 3 musical instruments of the Aymara and Kechua Indians.

——. Sicus. *Bol. lat. am. mús.,* v. 2 (1936), p. 253-256. **[690]**

The syrinx, or panpipes, known in Bolivia as *sicu,* plays an important rôle in the indigenous music of the Andean region.

Izikowitz, Karl Gustav. Les instruments de musique des Indiens Uro-Chipaya. *Rev. inst. etnol. univ. Tucumán,* v. 2 (1931-32), p. 263-291. **[691]**

Métraux, Alfred. Chipayaindianerna.

Ymer, v. 52, nos. 2-3 (1932), p. 233-271. **[692]**

Musical instruments, p. 251-253-254; descriptions of bone flutes, panpipes and clarinets. Illustration, p. 253.

——. La civilisation matérielle des tribus-Guarani. Paris, P. Geuthner, 1928. 331 p. il. F2230.G72M4 **[693]**

Ch. 27 deals with musical instruments, p. 212-226.

Nordenskiöld, Erland. Forschungen und abenteuer in Südamerika. Stuttgart, Strecker & Schröder, 1924. 338 p. F33-13.N835 **[694]**

Musical instruments among the Huari Indians, p. 232; music to a Cavina Indian piece for flute and drums, p. 220-271. For further musical references, see p. 189, 207, 240, for dance, p. 76, 273. Illustrations of musical instruments are plentiful.

——. Indianer und weisse in Nordostbolivien. Stuttgart, Strecker & Schröder, 1923. 220 p. F3320.N83 **[695]**

Note on flutes, p. 60; illustrations of these instruments, p. 62.

Paredes, Manuel Rigoberto. Instrumentos musicales de los Kollas. *Bol. lat. am. mús.,* v. 2 (1936), p. 77-82. **[696]**

The musical instruments of the Kolla Indians are nearly all made from a hollow reed called *chuqui.*

Schmidt, Max. Die Paressí-Kabischí. *Baes.-arch.,* v. 4, nos. 4-5 (1914), p. 167-250. **[697]**

Music and instruments, p. 239-241; six instruments pictured. Four song texts, p. 250.

Snethlage, E. Heinrich. Musikinstrumente der indianer des Guaporégebietes. *Baes.-arch.,* no. 10 (1939). p. 3-38. **[698]**

Catalogue of musical instruments collected by the author among the tribes of northeastern Bolivia (Moré, Itoreauhip, Kumana, Makurap, Mampiapä, Wayoro and Pauserna). The instruments are described and represented by good drawings. In many cases the ceremonies with which they are associated are mentioned. A few instruments are entirely new in South American ethnology: a drum made of the protective sheath of palm leaves, a time-beater consisting of a calabash gliding along a stick, and a sort of double panpipe, the elements of which are whistles. The author leaves open the question of the pre-columbian origin of the clarinet. [Alfred Métraux]

COLLECTIONS OF MUSIC

Béclard d'Harcourt, Marguerite. Mélo-dies populaires indiennes; Équateur, Pérou, Bolivie. Milano, G. Ricordi & c., 1923. M1686.B4 **[699]**

Contains 46 Indian folk songs, for voice with piano or harp accompaniment, and 9 airs for flute with piano. Indian texts and French translations.

Maluschka, Antonia. Canciones para las las escuelas de Bolivia. Tomo 2 [no imprint]. [stamped on title page]: Departamento de educación musical y artística, Bolivia. **[700]**

50 songs (numbered from 5 to 100) for voice and piano (Spanish words), includ-ing 1 "Aire Americano" (Nº 61) and 1 "Aire Boliviano" (Nº 73).

Roncal, Simeón. Música nacional boli-viana. 20 cuecas para piano. Sucre, n. d. 42 p. **[701]**

Zárate, Belisario. Folklore boliviano; 12 piezas vernaculares típicas, piezas para piano. Cochabamba, Imp. Segura, 1938. **[702]**

SUPPLEMENT to 1960

BIBLIOGRAPHY

Alejo, Benjamín. Notas para la historia del arte musical en Bolivia. *In* Bolivia en el centenario de su independencia. New York, The University Society, 1925, p. 357-361. **[251a]**

Anaya A., Franklin. La música indígena de Bolivia. *Rev. fed. estud. Chuqui-saca*, año 1, v. 1, no. 1-2 (1945), p. 213-221. **[252a]**

Reports upon visits of Hans Helfritz to Bolivian highlands (1939-1940) and notice of his albums of piano music based on Ay-maran and Kechuan motifs. (C.S.)

Baudizzone, Luis M., ed. Poesía, músi-ca y danza inca. Buenos Aires, Edito-rial Nova, 1943. 91 p. il. (music) Co-lección Mar Dulce. **[253a]**

A popular handbook with no scholarly pretensions. There are 6 music notations arranged for piano, originally published by the Bolivian musical folklorist Manuel Be-navente (cf. item no. 611). Also 6 fine photographs.

Beltrán, Luis Ramiro. Bolivia's dancing devils. *Américas*, v. 6, no. 1 (Jan. 1954), p. 24-27. **[254a]**

Quite detailed account of devil dances performed traditionally on the Saturday be-fore Ash Wednesday in the mining town of Oruro, Bolivia. Eight striking photo-graphs by Alfredo Linares. Very brief refe-rence to music.

Castrillo, Primo. The dancing Aymaras of Bolivia. *Bolivia* (New York), v. 8, no. 1 (Nov.-Dec. 1940), p. 6-10. **[255a]**

Cerrudo, J. C. Música y poesía indígena. *Bol. de la Sociedad geográfica "Sucre"* (Sucre), v. 42, nos. 423-424 (Sept. 1947), p. 491-497. **[256a]**

Coimbra, Gil. La música y la danza del pueblo aymara. *Rev. geog. amer.*, año 9, v. 16, no. 99 (Dec. 1941), p. 331-338. **[257a]**

Costas Argüedas, José Felipe. Navidad en Sucre, la capital de Bolivia. *An. soc. folk. Méx.*, v. 8 (1954), p. 127-139. **[258a]**

Description of Christmas celebration with brief discussion of musical instruments, and dances. Two song texts, without music.

Fernández Naranjo, Nicolás. La vida musical en La Paz. *In* La Paz en su IV Centenario, 1548-1948, v. 3, p. 259-277. **[259a]**

González Bravo, Antonio. Ciertos detalles de fabricación de algunos instrutos musicales indígenas en relación con el timbre. *Armonía,* v. 2, no. 4, (Sept. 1944), p. 26-30.   **[260a]**
Discussion, mainly of the *pincollo* and *tarka.*

——. Clasificación de los sicus aimaras. *Rev. estud. mus.,* v. 1, no 1 (Aug. 1949), p. 92-101.   **[261a]**
11 types are described, 4 pentaphonic, 7 heptaphonic. Music notations of the scale of each are given. 10 photographs of instruments. "Cabe explicar aún que los sicus forman una verdadera orquesta o familia de instrumentos del mismo género." The types most frequently in use are *taicas, maltas and licus.*

——. Música, instrumentos y danzas indígenas. *In* La Paz en su IV Centenario, 1548-1948, v. 3, p. 403-423. **[262a]**
10 pen-and-ink drawings of instruments, and 35 stylized, full-page color plates, 33 with music notations, by a leading musician. (C.S.)

Helfritz, Hans. Música indígena del Altiplano. *Antártica,* no. 14 (Oct. 1945), p. 94-96.   **[263a]**
Informative. Describes the grand fiesta of Copacabana in August of each year. (C.S.)

Mieses, Elisa. Bolivia supports symphony. *Mus. Amer.,* v. 59, no. 9 (July 1949), p. 23.   **[264a]**
La Paz becomes a musical center for the nation.

Slonimsky, Nicolas. Music in Bolivia. *Christian scien. mon.,* Sept. 25, 1943.   **[265a]**
Data on the musicians Teófilo Vargas, Antonio González Bravo, Humberto Viscarra Monje, and J. M. Velasco Maidana.

Vargas, Teófilo. Aires nacionales de Bolivia, 3 vols. La Paz, 1940.   **[266a]**
A collection of traditional Bolivian songs, and of some original songs by Vargas, "to demonstrate to foreign nations that there is a Bolivian national music".

BRAZIL

THE development of music in Brazil has been traced with admirable thoroughness in the second edition of Renato Almeida's *História da música brasileira* (Rio de Janeiro, 1942), a volume of over five hundred pages, profusely illustrated with musical examples. It is characteristic of a general trend in Latin American musical history that somewhat over half of this book is devoted to primitive and folk music. In Part I of his work, entitled *A música popular brasileira,* Almeida begins by studying the various elements that have gone into the making of Brazilian folk music. Quite naturally, the musical influence of Portugal is found to be predominant, since Brazil was discovered and settled by the Portuguese. A minimum musical influence is ascribed to the Indians of Brazil, who either lost their identity by mixture with other races or remained apart in complete isolation. Much importance, on the other hand, is attributed to the Negroes, who were originally imported from Africa as slaves for the colonists. "Das três raças formadoras da nacionalidade brasileria", writes Almeida, "foi a preta que revelou sempre maiores pendores para a música e a sua influência foi acentuada". On the whole, it is the African influence, modifying the Portuguese and Indian elements, that gives its characteristic stamp to Brazilian music. In his section on the Negro influence in Brazilian music, Almeida quotes such authorities as Arthur Ramos, Manuel Querino, Luciano Gallet and Mario de Andrade, whose writings on the subject should be consulted by those who are interested in a detailed study of the field. A lesser but by no means negligible influence was that of Spanish music. During the colonial period many Spaniards came to Brazil, bringing their typical songs and dances such as the *bolero,* the *fandango,* the *seguidillas* and the *tirana.* During the nineteenth century there was a strong Italian influence, which manifested itself primarily in the lyric theatre but also spread to the folk and popular field. French influence is apparent chiefly in the children's singing games.

Following this introductory survey, Almeida devotes his second chapter to a detailed account of the music, the dances and the instruments of the Indians of Brazil. He begins by quoting from the celebrated book by Jean de Léry, *Histoire d'un voyage faict en la terre du Brésil,* which gives an account of music among the Tupynambá Indians near Rio de Janeiro. Léry was one of the Frenchmen who accompanied the French admiral Nicholas de Villegaignon when the latter attempted to establish a French Huguenot colony in Brazil in 1557. His book, published in several editions and translations, became known all over Europe. It was in the third edition of his book, published at Geneva in 1585, that there appeared those nota-

107

tions of Tupynambá melodies to which reference has already been made. The Brazilian musicologist Luiz Heitor Corrêa de Azevedo made an important contribution to musical bibliography when, in a paper read before the American Musicological Society at Minneapolis in 1941, he studied in detail the various editions of Léry's book containing the musical examples and made a comparative analysis of the melodies in their various versions. Dr. Corrêa de Azevedo found that in most modern works which quote Léry's tunes, the latter appear in a corrupt form. It is interesting to note that one of the tunes collected by Léry has been used by the Brazilian composer Heitor Villa-Lobos in a setting for voice and orchestra entitled *Canidé Ioune*. This is also the place to mention the importantt monograph on Brazilian Indian music by Dr. Corrêa de Azevedo entitled *Escala, ritmo e melodia na música dos Indios brasileiros* [item no. 1037].

In his third chapter, *As cantigas do Brasil*, Almeida describes various Brazilian traditional songs and dances, beginning with the *modinha*. He points out that the *modinha* is not a folk song, but a type of salon music which became so popular during the nineteenth century that it was taken up and imitated by the populace. He describes the *modinha* as "a salon ballad, a sentimental and tearful aria, on the theme of love, modulating capriciously and with a strong influence of Italian cantabile". During the nineteenth century the *modinha* became the favorite type of song of Brazilian society and was cultivated by a host of composers, including such eminent figures as José Mauricio Nunes Garcia and Carlos Gomes. For a detailed study of the *modinha*, with numerous musical examples, see Mario de Andrade's *Modinhas imperiais* [item no. 1176]. Other songs and dances described by Almeida in this section are the *lundú* (or *lundum*), of African origin; the *fado*, which is generally considered a typical Portuguese folk song, but which, according to Almeida and Andrade, originated in Brazil; the *tiranas*, which reached Brazil from the Azores; the *desafio*, a kind of improvised vocal contest, in which one singer challenges another to reply impromptu to some riddle or embarrassing question; traditional ballads, of Portuguese origin, called *romances* and *xácaras*, of which *A nau Catarineta* is a famous example [cf. no. 970]; work songs, street-cries, cradle songs, children's singing games, beggars' songs, etc. Almeida also devotes a few paragraphs to the *chôro*, a generic term with several applications. Its primary designation is an instrumental group consisting generally of a flute, ophicleide, mandolin, clarinet, guitar, *cavaquinho* (a kind of small guitar), *piston* and trombone, with one of the instruments treated as soloist. By extension, compositions written for such an ensemble are caled *chôros*. The name is also applied to certain popular dances.

This chapter closes with brief accounts of popular instruments and popular singers.

Almeida next turns his attention to *Cantos religiosos e fetichistas*, studying the popular religious festivals which are always an occasion for widespread singing and dancing, and the music associated with the practice of fetichism in Brazil. The cult of fetichism was brought from Africa to Brazil by the Negroes and there became mixed with Indian, Catholic and spiritualistic elements. The chief rituals in which this cult is practised among the Brazilian Negroes are the *candomblés, xangós* and *macumbas*. Rituals in which the Amerindian element is predominant are the *catimbó* in the northeast and the *pagélança* in the Amazon region.

The two final chapters in Part I of Almeida's book, consisting of 130 pages, are devoted to the dances of Brazil: *batuque, samba, catereté, miudinho, jongo, recortado, cururú, chulas, fandango, maxixe, frêvo, marcha,* etc. *Samba* is a generic term applied to several types of dances in various regions. The urban *samba* of Rio de Janeiro, which has become known as a ballroom dance in the United States, has nothing in common with the rural *samba*, which is a round dance. In chapter VI, Almeida treats of the popular dramatic dances and ballets, such as the *cheganças, pastorís, reisados, bumba-meu boi, congos, congadas, maracatús,* etc. Some of these popular dramatic dances or ballets with singing are of Portuguese origin and deal with such historical episodes as the voyages of discovery and the struggle against the Moors. Others, among them the *congadas* and *maracatús,* are of African origin, mixed with European-Catholic influences.

This comprehensive survey of the primitive, folk and popular music of Brazil forms a logical introduction to the history of Brazilian art music, which Almeida traces in the second half of his book. In the titles of compositions by modern Brazilian composers we continually come across such terms as *chôros, modinha, ponteio, batuque, reisado*—all taken from the terminology of folk and popular music. It is therefore necessary to have an understanding of these terms and forms in order to understand much of the art music of Brazil, which has developed vigorously since the beginning of the present century. Such composers as Alberto Nepomuceno, Francisco Braga, Oscar Lorenzo Fernândez, Francisco Mignone, Camargo Guarnieri and Heitor Villa-Lobos, have placed Brazil in a musically commanding position among the countries of South America. The prolific Villa-Lobos, in particular, has won wide international recognition as an outstanding creative figure in contemporary music. Numerous brief studies of his music have been published, and Lisa M. Peppercorn of Rio de Janeiro had in preparation a full-length biography.

Composers of the past who occupy a prominent place in Brazilian mu-

sical history are José Mauricio Nunes Garcia (1767-1830), noted especially
as a composer of religious music; Francisco Manoel da Silva (1795-
1865), founder of the conservatory of music in Rio de Janeiro (1841) and
composer of the Brazilian national anthem: and Carlos Gomes (1836-1896),
most famous of all Brazilian composers, who won international renown
when his opera *O Guarany* was acclaimed at Milan in 1870. To commem-
orate the centenary of his birth, in 1936, a special issue of the *Revista*
brasileira de música was devoted to Carlos Gomes, who has also been the
subject of several biographies. Among precursors of the contemporary Brazilian school may be mentioned Leopoldo Miguez (1850-1902), Henrique
Oswald (1854-1931), Arthur Napoleão (1843-1925), Brasilio Itiberê da Cunha
(1848-1913) and Alexandre Levy (1864-1892). The late Luciano Gallet (1893-
1931) was a composer who took a deep interest in Brazilian folk music
and made important contributions to the study of this subject. Of great
importance in the realm of semi-popular music was Ernesto Nazareth (1863-
1934), creator of the Brazilian tango.

The second edition of Almeida's *História da música brasileira* is a greatly
augmented version of a work which first appeared under the same title in
1926. In that year there also appeared another history of music in Brazil,
Storia della musica nel Brasile (Milano, 1926), written by an Italian named
Vicenzo Cernicchiaro who had long been active in Brazilian musical circles.
In this work particular attention is given to the lyric theatre, including
the vogue of foreign operetta in Brazil during the mineteenth century.
Another distinctive feature of Cernicchiaro's book is the thoroughness with
which it covers the activities of virtuosi in Brazil; he deals with players
of every modern instrument, including pianists, violinists, violoncellists,
flautists, clarinettists, oboists, harpists, etc. He also devotes a special chapter
to singers and another to music critics. Among the latter he mentions Rodrigues Barbosa, Oscar Guanabarino, Arturo Imbassahy and Antonio
Cardozo de Menezes. The final chapter of the work is devoted to conservatories and schools of music.

Taking chronological precedence over both these histories is Guilherme
Theodoro Pereira de Mello's *A música no Brasil (desde os tempos coloniaes*
até o primeiro decenio da Republica), published at Baía in 1908. Of special
interest in this work is the section devoted to biographies of composers from
Baía (p. 250-271). In addition, Chapter IV is concerned almost entirely
with an account of musical activities in Baía.

Not a history of Brazilian music, but indispensable to a thorough understanding of the subject, is Mario de Andrade's *Ensaio sôbre música brasi-*
leira [item no. 711], in which the eminent author and musicologist analyzes
the component elements of Brazilian music from the point of view of

rhythm, melody, polyphony, instrumentation and form. This analytical section is followed by a collection of traditional Brazilian tunes, with explanatory comments. The reader should consult the Index of Authors for other writings by Andrade, all of which may be studied with profit. His *Pequena história da música* (São Paulo, 1942), contains two important chapters on Brazilian music [see item no. 715], with lists of pertinent recordings.

Those who do not read Portuguese may have recourse to the articles in English by Andrade, Ceição de Barros Barreto, Eunice J. Gates, Mario Pedrosa and Margaret E. Steward [nos. 966, 723, 746, 772, 1032], for general surveys of Brazilian music. Also available in English are special studies by Burle Marx [no. 890], Lisa M. Peppercorn [no. 891], Nicolas Slonimsky [nos. 830, 895, 897] and Herbert Weinstock [no. 899]. For an account of current popular music in Brazil, see the article by Friede F. Rothe [no. 1173]. The Music Division of the Pan American Union has issued a brief monograph on the music of Brazil by Albert T. Luper, published in May 1943 as Music Series no. 9 [no. 771x]. The same office also prepared for publication a complete annotated list of the works of Villa-Lobos. Sponsored by the Joint Committee on Latin American Studies, a *Bibliographical Handbook of Brazilian Studies* has been compiled under the editorship of Rubens Borba de Moraes and William Berrien; the music section of this handbook was assigned to Luiz Heitor Corrêa de Azevedo.

GENERAL AND MISCELLANEOUS

Almeida, Benedito Pires de. A música em Tieté. *Rev. arq. mun. S. Paulo,* v. 7, no. 74 (1941), p. 49-62.   **[703]**

> Primitive musical collections, musicians, musical bands, orchestras.

Almeida, Renato. História da música brasileira. Rio de Janeiro, F. Briguiet & comp., 1926. 238 p. ML232.A6   **[704]**

Cf. item no. 705.

——. História da música brasileira. 2d ed. Rio de Janeiro, F. Briguiet & comp., 1942. 529 p. ML232.A62   **[705]**

> Greatly enlarged edition of a work first published in 1926 [no. 704]. For comment on this history of Brazilian music, see above. The volume contains 151 musical examples and an extensive bibliography.

Alvarenga, Oneida. O sentimento na

música. Creação musical. Música pura. *Rev. bras. mús.,* v. 2, no. 1 (Mar. 1935), p. 41-47.   **[706]**

Andrade, Mário de. Brasil. S. Paulo. *Rev. música,* v. 1, no. 1 (15 July 1927), p. 40-42.   **[707]**

> Chronicle of musical activity in São Paulo, also brief survey of outstanding composers—Enrique Oswald, Luciano Gallet, Lourenço Fernândez, Villa-Lobos, Mignone—and of Brazilian folk music in relation to the national art music.

——. Chronica musical. *Rev. Brasil,* v. 2, no. 11 (May 1939), p. 88-91 **[708]**

> Includes comments on the singing of Maria Joanna.

——. Compêndio de história da música. 2 ed. São Paulo, L. G. Miranda, 1933. 211 p. il. (music).   **[709]**

Cf. item no. 715.

——. Os compositores e a lingua nacional. *In* Anais do primeiro congresso da

lingua nacional cantada, São Paulo, 1938, p. 95-168.   [710]
An important study of the modern Brazilian art song, with special reference to the work of Luciano Gallet, Francisco Braga, Francisco Mignone, Carlos Gomes, Lorenzo Fernândez, Camargo Guarnieri, João Gomes Junior.

——. Ensaio sôbre música brasileira. São Paulo, I. Chiarato e Cia, 1928. 94 p. ML232.A7E6   [711]
For comment on this important item, see introductory section.

——. Música do Brasil. Curitiba, Ed. Guaira, 1941. 79 p.   [712]

——. Música, doce música. São Paulo, L. G. Miranda, 1934. 358 p. ML160.- A5506   [713]
A collection of essays and articles originally published in newspapers and reviews. The first essay is a brief survey of Brazilian music intended for foreign readers. The six essays in the section on folklore deal with various aspects of Brazilian folk music, with 12 musical examples. The third section, entitled *Música de coração*, deals with various Brazilian composers (Villa-Lobos, Oswald, Gallet, Fernândez, Guarnieri, etc.).

——. A música na república. *Rev. Brasil*, v. 2, no. 17 (Nov. 1939), p. 78-79.   [714]
A short review of Brazilian music, mentioning numerous modern composers.

——. Pequena história da música. São Paulo, Livraria Martins, 1942. 286 p. il. ML160.A6P3   [715]
"Esta Pequena Historia da Música é na realidade uma quarta edição do meu Compêndio, profundamente refundido, em alguns capitulos, apenas modificado e atualizado em outros."—Advertência. Ch. 11, *Música Artística Brasileira*, p. 130-143. Ch. 12. *Música Popular Brasileira*, p. 144-155. Record list for Ch. 11, p. 271-277; for Ch. 12, p. 277-280.

Archanjo, Samuel. Movimiento musical paulistano. *Rev. bras. mús.*, v. 3, nos. 3-4 (1936), p. 540-543.   [716]
Enthusiastic commemoration of the Gomes centenary in São Paulo.

Associaão do quarto centenario do descobrimento do Brasil. Livro do centenario (1500-1900). Rio de Janeiro, Imprensa nacional, 1900-1902. 4 v. F2- 521.A84   [717]
Vol. 2: I. As bellas artes, por Henrique Coelho Netto (77 p.). Reference to Indian music and dances, p. 19-21. Music, p. 62-77, deals with José Mauricio Nunes Garcia; with the Conservatorio de Música established in Rio de Janeiro in 1847 and reorganized in 1881; with Leopoldo Miguez and the Instituto Nacional de Música (1890); and mentions various other Brazilian musicians, among them Carlos Gomes and Alberto Nepomuceno.

Azevedo, Luiz Heitor Corrêa de. Compositores de amanhã; impressão de uma audicão de trabalhos da classe de composição do instituto nacional de música. *Rev. bras. mús.*, v. 3, nos. 3-4 (1936), p. 519-523.   [718]
Among the students in composition at the Escola Nacional, the author singles out Hilda Reis for special mention. Ary Ferreira and Enio de Freitas e Castro also receive considerable attention.

——. Crônicas em varios modos ... *Rev. bras. mús.*, v. 2, no. 3 (Sept. 1935), p. 224-232.   [719]
The topics discussed are: Algumas obras novas brasileiras (works of Gnatalli and Guarnieri); A temporada lyrica (*A Fosca* by Gomes); O chefe ausente the (conductor Burle Marx); scenario actual da música brasileira; "Americanismo Musical" (the work of Francisco Curt Lange).

——. Crônicas em varios modos ... *Rev. bras. mús.*, v. 4, nos. 3-4 (1937), p. 171- 196.   [720]
The topics discussed are: Francisco Manoel e o hino nacional; Pan-Americanismo e música; Francisco Manoel da Silva; Música religiosa; Opera nacional; Oscar Lorenzo Fernândez; "Jupira" (opera by Francisco Braga); Francisco Mignone; A música e o regimen sovietico; Primeiro congresso da lingua nacional cantada; A temporada lírica; A questão do hino nacional; Homenagem a Heitor Villa-Lobos; Nacionalismo musical; Retrospecto (review of the musical season, 1937).

——. Inventario dos periódicos musicais

no Brasil. *Res. mus.* (July-Sept. 1939).
[721]

——. Um jubileu. *Mús. viva,* v. 1, no.
1 (1940). **[722]**

An account of the development of the Instituto Nacional de Música of Rio de Janeiro, on the occasion of the 50th anniversary of its founding. The Instituto is now the Escola Nacional de Música.

Barreto, Ceição de Barros. Brazil mirrors its own nature. *Mod. mus.,* v. 16, no. 3 (1939), p. 168-172. **[723]**

Bento, Waldemar L. A magia no Brasil. Rio de Janeiro, Oficinas gráficas do "Journal do Brasil", 1939. 150 p. BF-1615.B4 **[724]**

Magic of rhythm, p. 41-45.

Brand, Max. A música e o Brasil. *Mús. viva,* v. 1, no. 4 (Sept. 1940), p. 5-7. **[725]**

Refers to the "rich treasure" of Brazilian folk music, upon which the leading composers of Brazil have drawn for their creative materials.

Brasil. Himno de la proclamación de la república. *Repertorio del Diario de Salvador,* año 9, v. 21, no. 126 (15 Nov. 1911), p. 5513. **[725x]**

Portuguese and Castilian words.

Brisolla, Ciro Monteiro. Paisagem da música brasileira. *Revista anual do salão de maio* (São Paulo), no. 1 (1939). **[726]**

A very brief but concise discussion of the outstanding characteristics of Brazilian composers from Levy and Nepomuceno to the present day. The author's reactions are always personal and provocative. Among several individual interpretations, he seeks to identifiy Villa Lobos primarily with the music of the North and Camargo Guarnieri with that of the South, especially the regions around São Paulo. [Wm. Berrien].

Bürger, Otto. Brasilien. Leipzig, Dieterich'sche verlagsbuchhandlungen. 1926. 407 p. F2515.B92 **[727]**

Development of the importation of musi-

cal instruments, p. 268. This is a chart showing figures of 1913 and 1920 of the imports of pianos, victrolas, and other musical instruments from Great Britain, United States, France and Germany.

Calderón de la Barca, E. G. Apuntes de historia de la música. Sud-América. *Correo mus. sud-am.,* v. 1, no. 22 (25 Aug. 1915), p. 4-6. **[728]**

References to music of Brazil, Argentina and Uruguay.

Castro, Enio de Freitas e. Em caminho para a música brasileira. *Bol. lat. am. mus.,* v. 2 (Apr. 1936), p .163-168. **[729]**

——. Melodias alemãs e brasileiras. *Rev. bras. mús.,* v. 5, no. 4 (1938), p. 37-51. **[730]**

——. Strawinsky no Brasil. *Bol. lat. am. mus.,* v. 4, (Dec. 1938), p. 65-69. **[731]**

Catálogo da exposição de documentos musicais. *In* Anais do primeiro congresso da lingua nacional cantada, São Paulo, 1938, p. 753-782. ML3558.C72-A5 **[732]**

Particularly important for Brazilian musical publications of the 19th century.

Cernicchiaro, Vincenzo. Storia della musica nel Brasile, dai tempi coloniali sino ai nostri giorni (1549-1925). Milano, Fratelli Riccioni, 1926. 617 p. il. ML232.C42 **[733]**

Includes 16 musical examples, mostly Indian melodies with native texts. For further comment, sec introduction.

Congresso da lingua nacional cantada, 1º, julho de 1937. *Anais.* São Paulo, Departamento de cultura, 1938. 786 p. il. (maps, diagr., music). ML3558.C72-A5 **[734]**

Contains several articles of importance in the field of musical pedagogy (especially voice culture). There are maps showing the distribution of folk dances in Brazil. The articles of musical interest are entered separately in this bibliography (see nos. 732, 738, 919, 932, 933, 909).

Correia, Leoncio. A verdade histórica sobre o 15 de novembro. Rio de Janeiro, Imprensa nacional, 1939. 312 p. F2536.F66   **[735]**

Includes music: *Deodora,* hymno, canto e coro, letra de Leoncio Corrêa [sic], música de Francisco Braga.

Cortot, Alfred. La jeune musique brésilienne. *Monde mus.,* v. 47, nos. 8-9 (30 Sept. 1936), p. 240.   **[736]**

Reprinted from *Revue française du Brésil.* A general impression.

Coutinho, J. de S. Brazilian music and musicians. *Bull. pan Amer. union,* v. 64, no. 11 (Nov. 1939), p. 119-1125. il.   **[737]**

Cunha, João Itiberê da. Algumas notas. *In* Anais do primeiro congresso da lingua nacional cantada, São Paulo, 1938, p. 565-572. ML3558.C72A5A5   **[738]**

Touches on the interesting question of the pronunciation of regional folk songs when sung in formal concerts.

Downes, Olin. From Brazil; music of South American country at the Museum of modern art. *New York times,* v. 90, no. 30.213 (13 Oct. 1940), sec. 9, p. 7. il.   **[739]**

Deals briefly with development of Brazilian popular music; *Maxixe; charangas* and their instruments; Ernesto Nazareth; Romeo Silva.

Fernândez, Oscar Lorenzo. Considerações sobre a música brasileira. *Weco* (May 1930), p. 11.   **[740]**

A festival of Brazilian music, arranged by Burle Marx in association with Hugh Ross. New York, The Museum of modern art, 1940. 16 p. ML42.N3-M821   **[741]**

Includes an introduction on Brazilian music by Burle Marx, and notes on the music performed.

França, Eurico Nogueira. O espirito néoromantico. *Rev. bras. mús.,* v. 5, no. 2 (1938), p. 21-24.   **[742]**

Fróes, Sylvio Deolindo. Palestras sobre definições curiosas e conceitos extravagantes. *Rev. bras. mús.,* v. 2, no. 3 (Sept. 1935), p. 169-196.   **[743]**

A study of acoustics and the physical basis of musical theory.

Garritano, Assuero. Do estilo e da fórma. *Rev. bras. mús.,* v. 5, no. 1 (1938), p. 77-81.   **[744]**

——. As tendências atuais da música. *Rev. bras. mús.,* v. 4, nos. 1-2 (1937), p. 35-44   **[745]**

Gates, Eunice J. Brazilian music. *Hispania,* v. 22, no. 2 (1939), p .129-135.   **[746]**

Refers especially to the music of O. Lorenzo Fernândez, Camargo Guarnieri, Francisco Mignone and Villa-Lobos.

Gomes, Arlindo. Campinas, sua fundação e sua historia musical. *Rev. bras. mús.,* v. 3, nos. 3-4 (1936), p. 490-495.   **[747]**

The first musician active in Campinas was Manoel José Gomes (1792-1868), founder of a musical dynasty whose most illustrious representative was the great Carlos Gomes. Sant' Anna Gomes was a leader in the musical life of Campinas during the 19th century. The Monteiro family was also musically prominent in Campinas.

Gomes, Tapajos. Brasil. *Rev. música,* v. 1, no. 2 (15 Aug. 1927), p. 36-39.   **[748]**

Deals chiefly with the development of musical regionalism in the modern Brazilian school, from Alexandre Levy to Lorenzo Fernândez.

Graziani, Verbera. Síntese de historia da música brasileira. *Villa-Lobos,* no. 1 (May 1939).   **[749]**

Guerra, Oswald. Les villes musicales: Rio de Janeiro. *Rev. int. mus. danse,* v. 1 (1927), p. 136.   **[750]**

Hesse-Wartegg, Ernst von. Zwischen Anden und Amazonas. 3d. ed. Stuttgart, etc., Union deutsche verlagsgesellschaft, 1926. 493 p. F2223.H47 **[751]**

Contains such references to music as: opera in Argentina, p. 333; music and dance in Bahia, p. 36; photographs of gauchos with their guitars, p. 357, 359.

Hirsh, Lina. Episodios musicais. Rio de Janeiro. Fides Brasiliae, 1935. 175 p. ML60.H66E7 **[752]**

"A origem deste livro foi uma serie de palestras feitas na Radio sociedade do Rio de Janeiro—" Nota inicial.

Instituto histórico e geographico brasileiro. Diccionario histórico, geográphico ethnográphico do Brasil (commemorativo do primeiro centenario da independencia). Rio de Janeiro, Imprenta nacional, 1922. F2504.I57 **[753]**

Music (for piano) and words to the *Hymno da Independencia brasileira,* between p. 304-305; *Hymno da Proclamação da República dos Estados Unidos do Brasil,* between p. 316-317; *Hymno nacional* (Silva), between p. 328-329. *A música no Brasil,* p. 1621-1674, is a general study of Brazilian music, covering all periods of its development. There is a great deal of information about dances and many musical examples are included in these pages.

Itiberê, Brasilio. Andrade Muricy, conferencista. *Rev. bras. mús.,* v. 1, no. 3 (Mar. 1936), p. 16-18. **[754]**

Muricy is a well-known Brazilian writer on music.

Kelsey, Vera. Seven keys to Brazil. Rev. ed. New York and London, Funk & Wagnalls, 1941. 314 p. F2508.K39 **[755]**

Guarani: Novel and opera, p. 268-272, including a biographical sketch of Carlos Gomes and the background of *Guarani;* Indian music and dances, p. 283-285; Negro dance and music, p. 285-289, with material on *macumbas, samba,* "The rhythmic and musical capacities the Negro has instilled in the Brazilians"; transformation of dramas into musical performances; carnival, *bumba-meu-boi.*

Lavenère, Luiz. Graphia musical. *Rev.*

bras. mús., v. 3, no. 1 (Mar. 1936), p. 11-13. **[756]**

Deals with the notation of musical ornaments.

——. A música em Alagoas (conferéncia). Maceió, 1928. **[757]**

Cited by Almeida [item no. 705].

Lima, Souza. A sinfonía do Guaraní sob o ponto de vista pianístico (Ainda o centenario de Carlos Gomes). *Rev. brus. mús.,* v. 5, no. 1 (1938), p. 43-47. **[758]**

Machado, Raphael Coelho. Diccionario musical ... Nova edição, augmentada por Raphael Machado Filho. Rio de Janeiro, B. L. Garnier [1909?], 280 p. **[759]**

McPhee, Colin. Jungles of Brazil. *Mod. music,* v. 18, no. 1 (1940), p. 41-43. **[760]**

Comment on the Festival of Brazilian Music at the Museum of Modern Art.

Marx, Burle. Musical reciprocity between the Americas urged. *Mus. Amer.,* v. 59, no. 11 (June 1939), p. 34. ports. **[761]**

Chiefly a discussion of Brazilian music, commenting on the nationalism of Villa-Lobos.

Matthiesen, Harald. Brazilianische musik. *Iberoamer. rund.* v. 5 (May 1939), p. 70-72. **[762]**

Mello, Guilherme Theodoro Pereira de. A música no Brasil desde os tempos coloniaes até o primeiro decenio da república. Bahia, Typ. de S. Joaquim, 1908. 366 p. facsim. ML232.P48 **[763]**

For comment, see introductory section.

Mignone, Francisco. Forma e conteúdo. *Rev. bras. mús.,* v. 1, no. 2 (June 1934), p. 113-116. **[764]**

A plea for order and fundamental culture in artistic creation, with special reference to the problem of the Brazilian composer.

Miguez, Leopoldo [*composer*]. Hymno proclamação da república dos Estados unidos do Brasil. *In* Paes Barretto, C. X., Feriados do Brasil, 1926, v. 2, p. 119-123. F2521.P12 **[765]**

Includes music, text (by Medeiros e Albuquerque) and *decreto*.

Miranda, Nicanor. Técnica do jôgo infantil organizado. São Paulo, Departamento de cultura, 1940. 83 p. **[766]**

Reprinted from *Revista de arquivo municipal*, v. 71 (Oct. 1940). Music of 4 children's songs, p. 36-40.

Muricy, Andrade. Música brasileira moderna. *Rev. assoc. bras. mús.*, v. 1, no. 1 (1932), p. 2-14 **[767]**

Traces the development of musical nationalism in Brazil through the work of Brasilio Itiberê, Alexandre Levy, Ernesto Nazareth, Alberto Nepomuceno, Mário de Andrade, Luciano Gallet, Oscar Lorenzo Fernândez and Heitor Villa-Lobos.

———. Panorama da música brasileira. *Rev. bras. mús.*, v. 4, nos. 3-4 (1937), p. 95-102. **[768]**

See item no. 769.

Musique brésilienne moderne. Rio de Janeiro, 1937. 100 p. **[769]**

This volume was privately printed by the Brazilian government for the New York World's Fair of 1939. It contains a preface (in French) by Andrade Muricy dealing with the basic elements of Brazilian folk music, and tracing the development of art music in Brazil from the colonial period to the present. The volume contains compositions, mostly for piano, and for voice and piano, by Barrozo Netto, Lorenzo Fernândez, Francisco Mignone, Fructuoso Vianna, Radamés Gnatalli, Camargo Guarnieri, Luciano Gallet, Francisco Braga, Luiz Cosme, Heitor Villa-Lobos. Nine of the compositions were previously published in commercial editions; the others are published here for the first time.

Nohara, W. K. v. Brasilien—Tag und nacht. Berlin, Rowohlt, 1938. 261 p. F2515.N65 **[770]**

Der carioca kann keinen walzer spielen, p. 109-129, includes material on modern concerto in Brazil, Villa-Lobos, Indian mu-

sical of the Europeans, samba, Carmen Miranda, German translation of Indian songs, and a list of records of Brazilian music.

Octaviano, João. Síntese da evolução musical no Brasil (desde 1549 até nossos dias). *Revista militar brasileira*, v. 5, no. 3 (1938), p. 67-80. **[771]**

Citation from files of Pan American Union.

Pan American union. *Music division.* The music of Brazil, by Albert T. Luper, Washington, D. C., Music division, Pan American union, 1943. 40 p. Reproduced from typewritten copy. ML232.L8 (*Its* Music series, no. 9) **[771x]**

Pedrosa, Mário. Brazilian music. *Theatre arts monthly*, v. 23, no. 5 (1939), p. 363-368. **[772]**

General introductory survey, dealing chiefly with folk music forms, instruments and dramatic dances (*bailados*).

Penalva, Gastão. D. Pedro I, músico. *Rev. amer.* (Rio de Janeiro), v. 8, no. 10 (July 1919), p. 155-158. **[773]**

Short review of the benefits to Brazilian music derived from this patron of the arts.

Peyser, H. C. Music flourishing in Brazil. *Mus. Amer.*, v. 23, no. 1 (1915), p. 48. **[774]**

Interview with José Carlos Rodríguez.

Sá Pereira, Antonio. Perspectivas da carreira de musicista. *Rev. bras mús.*, v. 1, no. 4 (Dec. 1934), p. 335-340. **[775]**

Santiago, Oswaldo. A alma harmoniosa de Pernambuco através a música de Nelson Fereira *Weco* (May 1939), p. 15. **[776]**

Santos, Samuel Archanjo Dos. O Natal e a sua música. *Res. mus.*, v. 3, nos. 28-29 (Dec. 1940-Jan. 1941), p. 4-6. **[777]**

Saussine, Renée de. Rythmes et figures

de Brésil. *Rev. musicale,* v. 12 (1931), p. 191-204. **[778]**
Includes music.

Schoenaers, Thomas Aquinas. Drie jaren in Brazilie. Averbode, Drukkerij der Abdij. 1904. 2 v. F2515.S36 **[779]**
Vol. I contains: Brazilian music, p. 64; music and song at St. Norbertus' feast in 1901, with the words of a song in his honor (Flemish and Portuguese), p. 122-123; verse of a Rio Grandense gaucho song (Portuguese and Flemish text), p. 160; dances of the gauchos, p. 166-168. Vol. 2 contains: Bumba-meu-boi and musical instruments, p. 91-94; snakes as music-lovers, p. 97-98.

Steward, Margaret E. Music in Brazil. *Brazil Today,* v. 1, no. 1 (Sept. 1940), p. 7, 19-20. **[780]**
The colonial period; the Brazilian romantic school; the modern school.

——, **and Francisco Mignone.** Historia da música contada á juventude. São Paulo, E. S. Mangione, 1935. 95 p. il. **[781]**
Ch. 12 deals with Brazilian music and dramatic folk dances, p. 79-85.

Toni, Alceo. Musica e musiciste in Brasile. *Mus. d'oggi,* v. 8, nos. 8-9 (Aug.-Sept. 1926), p. 245-247; v. 8, no. 10 (Oct. 1926), p. 284-285. **[782]**

Villa-Lobos, Heitor. A música nacionalista no govêrno Getulio Vargas. Rio de Janeiro, Departamento de imprensa e propaganda [1940?]. 69 p. ML232.V5-M8 **[783]**

Volusia, Eros. Dansa brasileira. A creação do bailado brasileiro. Rio de Janeiro, Ed. Autora, 1939. 61 p. il. **[784]**
A lecture delivered at the Teatro Ginastico, describing the creation of the Brazilian ballet.

See also nos. 799, 826, 830, 833.

BIOGRAPHY AND CRITICISM

(A) GENERAL

Almeida, Renato. Henrique Oswald. *Rev. assoc. bras. mus.,* v. 1, nos. 2-3 (1932), p. 27-35. **[785]**

Andrade, Mário de. A obra póstuma de L. Gallet. *Rev. bras. mús.,* v. 1, no. 1 (Mar. 1934), p 49-53. **[786]**

——. Uma sonata de Camargo Guarnieri. *Rev. bras. mús.,* v. 2, no. 2 (June 1935), p. 131-135. **[787]**
An analysis of Guarnieri's Sonata for cello and piano, with six musical examples.

Assiz, Pedro de. Abdon Milanez. *Rev. bras. mús.,* v. 7, no. 1 (1940), p. 53-61. **[788]**
Milanez (1858-1927) was director of the Escola Nacional de Música from 1916. He composed numerous stage-works, including the opera *Primizie* (1921).

Azevedo, Luiz Heitor Corrêa de. Arquivo de música brasileira. *Rev. bras. mús.,* v. 1, no. 1 (Mar. 1934), p. 61-66. **[789]**
The "Arquivo" consists of musical supplements published by this review. This article deals with Francisco Manoel (1795-1865), whose *Cantico religioso* inaugurates this series of musical publications.

——. *Rev. bras. mús.,* v. 1, no. 2 (June 1934), p. 147-153. **[790]**
Deals with the *Tantum Ergo* of José Mauricio Nunes García (1767-1830) and includes a biographical sketch of this composer.

——. *Rev. bras. mús.,* v. 1, no. 3 (Sept. 1934), p. 229-232. **[791]**
Deals with the *Missa dos defuntos* of José Mauricio, composed in 1809.

——. *Rev. bras. mús.,* v. 2, no. 3 (Sept. 1935), p. 219-223. **[792]**
Deals with the *Missa dos defuntos* of José Mauricio Nunes Garcia and *O Salutaris* of Francisco Manoel, both published as musical supplements of this volume. Includes portrait of José Mauricio and facsimile of the MS. of his Requiem.

Azevedo, Luiz Heitor Corrêa de. José Mauricio Nunes García. *Bol. lat. am. mús.*, v. 1 (Apr. 1935), p. 133-150. **[793]**

——. Luciano Gallet. *Rev. assoc. bras. mús.*, v. 2, no. 4 (1933), p. 1-20. **[794]**

——. Luiz Cosme. *Mús. viva*, v. 1, no. 5 (1940), p. 1-2. **[795]**
Cosme, born in 1908, studied at the Cincinnati Conservatory of Music for 2 years. His reputation as one of the most notable among younger Brazilian composers was established by the performance of his ballet *Salamanca do Jarau* (concert version). This article gives a résumé of his work.

Barbosa, José Rodrigues. Alberto Nepomuceno. *Rev. bras. mús.*, v. 7, no. 1. (1940), p. 19-39. **[796]**
The author, a noted Brazilian music critic who died in 1939, traces the career of Nepomuceno (1864-1920) from his student days in Italy, Germany and France, through his directorship of the Instituto Nacional de Música, his triumphs as composer and executant and also deals sympathetically with his character and private life, with quotations from his letters.

Bettencourt, Gastão de. Compositores brasileiros contemporáneos. Lisbon, 1934. **[797]**
Cited by Almeida (cf. no. 705).

——. Temas de música brasileira, conferências realizadas en Lisboa. Rio de Janeiro, Editôra A Noite. 223 p. ML2-32.B3T3 **[798]**
Deals with Glauco Velázquez, Alexandre Levy, Luciano Gallet, Carlos Gomes, José Mauricio and other Brazilian composers.

Bevilacqua, Octavio. Ernesto Nazareth. *Rev. bras. mús.*, v. no. 1 (Mar. 1934), p. 59-60. **[799]**
Ernesto Nazareth was the creator of the Brazilian tango. As a popular composer his influence was considerable.

——. Leopoldo Miguez e o Instituto nacional de música. *Rev. bras. mús.*, v. 7, no. 1 (1940), p. 6-18. **[800]**
Leopoldo Miguez (1850-1902) was the

first director of the Instituto Nacional de Música (created in 1890), and as such played a very important rôle in the development of musical education in Brazil. As a composer he was one of the leading figures of the modern Brazilian school.

Blake, Sacramento. Diccionario bibliographico brazileiro, Rio de Janeiro, Typographia nacional; Imprensa nacional, 1883-1902. 7 v. Z1681.S12 **[801]**
Among the noted Brazilian musicians of the 19th century whose names appear here, see Antonio Carlos Gomes (v. 1, p. 125-127); Francisco Manoel da Silva (v. 3, p. 37-38); José Mauricio Nunes Garcia (v. 5, p. 93-95).

Castro, Enio de Freitas e. Francisco Braga professor. *Rev. bras. mús.*, v. 3, nos. 3-4 (1936), p. 525-528 **[802]**
Eulogy of Francisco Braga as educator.

——. Kinsman Benjamin. *Rev. bras. mús.*, v. 1, no. 1 (June 1934), p. 143-146. **[803]**
Roberto J. Kinsman Benjamin (1853-1934) was born in Rio de Janeiro of English parents and received his musical education in London and Cologne. He returned to Rio in 1872 and took an active part in its musical life, especially as organizer of the Club Beethoven (1882-1889) and as conductor of symphonic concerts. He was the author of a book, *Esboços musicais* (1884), wihch is a guide to the lyric theatre. See no. 841.

——. "Marabá", de Francisco Braga. *Rev. bras. mús.*, v. 4, nos. 1-2 (1937), p. 12-14. **[804]**
Analysis of a symphonic poem by Braga, with three musical examples.

Chase, Gilbert. Camargo Guarnieri... *Int. amer. monthly*, v. 2, no. 1 (Jan. 1943), p. 30-31. **[805]**
Portrait, music.

——. Impressions of Bidú Sayão. *Int. amer. monthly*, v. 1, no. 6 (Oct. 1942), p. 38-39. **[806]**

——. Interview with Elsie Houston. *Int.*

amer. monthly, v. 1, no. 2 (June 1942), p. 22-23. port. **[807]**

Edições musicias; "Batuque", de Oscar Lorenzo Fernândez. *Rev. bras. mús.,* v. 5, no. 2 (1938), p. 61-66. **[808]**

The *Batuque* is a Negro dance from the orchestral suite *Reisado do pastoreio.*

Gomes, Tapajós. Barroso Netto. Rio de Janeiro, Pongetti Irmãos, 1939. 25 p. **[809]**

The subject of this biographical sketch, Joaquim Barroso Netro, died in Rio de Janeiro, 1 Sept. 1941.

——. Francisco Braga. Rio de Janeiro, Irmãos Pongetti, 1937. 41 p. port. ML 410.B78G6 **[810]**

Antonio Francisco Braga, a prolific composer, was born in Rio de Janeiro, 15 April 1868. List of works, p. 35-41.

Guedes, Paulo. Dois nomes para a história do "lied' artístico brasileiro. *Res. mus.,* v. 3, no. 34-35 (1941), p. 24-25. **[811]**

Discusses the contributions of Mário de Andrade and Camargo Guarnieri to the modern Brazilian art song.

João Gomes de Araujo. *Música sacra,* v. 2, no. 6 (June 1942), p. 106-107; v. 2, no. 7 (July 1942), p. 124-125; v. 2, no. 8 (Aug. 1942), p. 142-144 **[812]**

Biographical sketch of this composer (b. 1846), based largely on material provided by Gomes de Araujo himself.

Lira, Mariza. Chiquinha Gonzaga, grande compositora popular brasileira. Rio de Janeiro, Pap. e. typ. Coelho, 1939. 118 p. ML410.G64L5 **[813]**

Monteiro, Antenor de O. Apontamentos sôbre Mendanha e o hino de 35. *Rev. inst. hist. geog. Rio Grande do Sul,* v. 15, 2d. trimestre (1935), p. 311-329. **[814]**

Contains biographical sketch of Joaquim José de Mendanha, and quotations from press notices about him; words to the *Hino de 35;* music of *Senhor Neto va se*

embor and the similar Mozart aria. Cf. Almeida, *História da música brasileira* [no. 705], p. 367.

Moreira, Lopes. Ernesto Nazareth e suas composições de música popular brasileira. *Aspectos,* v. 5, no. 35 (1941), p. 57-59. **[815]**

Nazareth was the creator of the Brazilian tango. This article describes his pianistic technique, and points out that Nazareth did not merely imitate the popular forms, but succeeded in transferring their spirit integrally to the piano.

Muricy, Andrade. Léo Kessler. *Rev. bras mús.,* v. 5, no. 1 (1938), p. 69-76. **[816]**

The late Léo Kessler, of Swiss origin, was director of the Conservatorio Musical do Paraná.

——. Mário de Andrade, musicólogo. *Rev. bras. mús.,* v. 1, no. 2 (June 1934), p. 128-131. **[817]**

Although known primarily as a creative writer of prose and poetry, Andrade has made very important contributions to Brazilian musicology (cf. INDEX OF AUTHORS).

Native rhythms of Brazilian piano pieces. *Mus. Amer.,* v. 63, no. 3 (10 Feb. 1943), p. 206. **[818]**

A short discussion of four compositions by Francisco Mignone.

Necrologio: Jeronymo Queiroz. *Rev. bras. mús.,* v. 3, nos. 3-4 (1936), p. 590-591. **[819]**

Queiroz (1859-1936) was a pianist, composer and conductor. He composed piano pieces, songs, orchestral works and chamber music.

Octaviano, J. Esboço biographico de Alberto Nepomuceno. *Rev. assoc. bras. mús.,* v. 2, no. 6 (1933), p. 57-65. **[820]**

Oliveira, Clovis de. Arthur Pereira. *Mús. viva,* v. 1, no. 9 (1941), p. 1-2. port. **[821]**

Biographical sketch of this Brazilian composer (born in São Paulo), with a list of his principal works.

———. Concerto sinfonico-vocal. *Rcs. mus.,* v. 3, nos. 32-33 (Apr.-May 1941), p. 6. **[822]**

Deals with the first performance, in São Paulo, of a symphonic poem, *Rainha do Brazil,* by the local composer João Gomes Junior.

———. Concerto sinfónico-vocal. *Res. mus.,* v. 3, nos. 32-33 (Apr.-May 1941), p. 9-10. **[823]**

This review of a recital by the pianist Tagliaferro is especially interesting for its comments on the suite from the ballet *Leilão* by Francisco Mignone, which received its first performance on this occasion.

Pereira, Américo. A obra musical de Francisco Valle. *Rev. bras. mús.,* v. 5, no. 1 (1938), p. 36-42. **[824]**

Francisco Valle (or Vale) was born in 1869 and died (suicide) in 1906. He composed the symphonic poems *Telemaco* and *Depois da Guerra;* the orchestral suite *Bailado da roca;* a sonata for piano, etc.

Sá Pereira, Antônio de. A sonatina de M. Camargo Guarnieri. *Weco* (Oct. 1929), p. 13. **[825]**

Santoro, Claudio. Considerações em torno da música contemporânea nacional. *Mus. viva,* v. 2, nos. 10-11 (Apr.-May 1941), p. 5-7. **[826]**

Discusses the problem of building a national school of composition on the basis of folklore.

Silveira, Carlos da. Alguns músicos de Silveiras, Areias, Queluz, Pinheiro, e circunvizinhanças. *Rev. arq. mun. São Paulo,* v. 7, no. 77 (June-July 1941), p. 231-242. **[827]**

A list of provincial musicians of the 19th and beginning of 20th centuries.

———. De algunos músicos do vale do Paraíba: Francisco Carlos da Silveira. *Res. mus.,* v. 3, no. 36 (1941), p. 5-6. **[828]**

The author, a member of the Instituto Histórico e Geográfico de São Paulo, gives some personal reminiscences of the musician Silveira (1851-1910).

———: Manuel Martins Ferreira de An-

drade. *Res. mus.,* v. 4, no. 38 (1941), p. 5-8. **[829]**

Slonimsky, Nicolas. Modern composers of Brazil. *Christian scien. mon.,* v. 32, no. 276 (19 Oct. 1940), p. 13. **[830]**

Deals with O. Lorenzo Fernández, J. Octaviano, Fructuoso Vianna, Camargo Guarnieri, Radamés Gnatalli, Luiz Cosme. This is the second of two articles (cf. no. 896).

Taunay, Alfredo de Escragnolle. Dous artistas maximos, José Mauricio e Carlos Gomes. São Paulo, Comp. melhoramentos de São Paulo (Weiszflog irmãos incorporada) [pref. 1939], 158 p. ML390.E68 **[831]**

———. Uma grande gloria brasileira, José Mauricio Nunes Garcia (1767-1830). São Paulo, Comp. melhoramentos de São Paulo (Weiszflog irmãos incorporada) [pref. 1930], 129 p. ML410.-N87E8 **[832]**

Wright, Marie Robinson. The new Brazil. Philadelphia, George Barrie and sons, 1908. 2d ed. 494 p. F2508.W96 **[833]**

Pages 165-168 present material on Carlos Gomes, José Mauricio Nunes García, Francisco Manoel da Silva, Nepomuceno, Miguez and Braga. Songs and dances of the country people, p. 493.

See also nos. 703, 705, 707, 710, 713, 715, 717, 718, 726, 733, 737, 741, 748, 754, 763, 767, 769, 782.

(B) ANTONIO CARLOS GOMES

Andrade, Mário de. A Fosca. *Rev. bras. mús.,* v. 1, no. 2 (June 1934), p. 117-124. **[834]**

A study of the opera by Carlos Gomes, with description of principal themes.

———. Fosca (1873). *Rev. bras. mús.,* v. 3, no. 2 (June 1936), p. 254-263. **[835]**

Includes ten musical themes from the score of this opera.

Andrade, Martins de. Carlos Gomes; escorço biographico. Rio de Janeiro, Pon-

getti, 1939. 177 p. ML410.G638M2
[836]

Azevedo, Luiz Heitor Corrêa de. Carlos Gomes e Francisco Manoel. Correspondencia inédita (1864-1865). *Rev. bras. mús.*, v. 3, no. 2 (June 1936), p. 323-338. **[837]**

Luiz Heitor has written the short introduction to these letters, and others pertinent to the correspondence, of da Silva and Gomes.

——. Carlos Gomes folclorista. *Rev. bras. mús.*, v. 3, no. 2 (June 1936), p. 177-184. **[838]**

6 musical examples.

——. Carlos Gomes, sua verdadeira posição no quadro da ópera italiana no séc. XIX e na evolução da música brasileira. *Bol. lat. am. mús.*, v. 3 (Apr. 1937), p. 83-88. **[839]**

——. As primeiras óperas. *Rev. bras. mús.*, v. 3, no. 2 (June 1936), p. 201-245. **[840]**

Data on *A noite do castelo*, 1861 and *Joanna de Flandres*, 1863, with many musical excerpts from the operas.

Benjamin, Roberto J. Kinsman. Esbôços musicaes; guia para o theatro lyrico; obra crítica, analytica e biographica. Rio de Janeiro, G. Lenzinger & filhos, 1884. 359 p. **[841]**

Concerning the author, see item no 803. Includes Carlos Gomes, p. 331-334; *O Guarany*, p. 335-343; *Fosca*, p. 345-352.

Bernadini, Giulia. Carlo Gomes nei ricordi della figlia. *Opere e i giorni* (Genova), 1 Jan. 1937, p. 47-52. **[842]**

Bevilacqua, Octavio. Carlos Gomes—A época e o meio em que viveu Suas modinhas. *Rev. bras. mús.*, v. 3, no. 2 (June 1936), p. 143-159. **[843]**

Includes 8 musical examples of *modinhas*.

Bocanera Junior, Silo. A Baía a Carlos Gomes. Bahia, Oliveira & cia., 1904. 377 pp. **[844]**

Carvalho, Itala Gomes Vaz de. *Colom-*

bo e o tiro de canhão. *Rev. bras. mús.*, v. 3, no. 2 (June 1936), p. 196-198. **[845]**

Discussion of this vocal and symphonic poem, with 1 musical example.

——. A vida de Carlos Gomes. 2 ed. Rio de Janeiro, A Noite, s. a., editora, 1937. 285 p. il. ML410.G638G56 **[846]**

Includes music.

The author is a daughter of Carlos Gomes.

——. Vita di Carlos Gomes, traduzione e adattamento dalla II edizione brasiliana di Cleo Guaranà Caimi. Milano, Casa editrice Oberdan Zucchi s. a., 1937. 115 p. il. ML410.G638G6 **[847]**

Castro, Enio de Freitas e. Carlos Gomes. Pôrto Alegre. Ed. A Nação, 1941. 32 p. ML410.G638F7 **[848]**

Biographies of Carlos Gomes are not lacking, but this little volume, which places him among the *Heróis Brasileiros* (such is the title of the series in which it appears), is welcome as a concise exposition of the life and work of the composer of *O Guarany*.

——. A música vocal de cámara de Carlos Gomes. *Rev. bras. mús.*, v. 3, no. 2 (June 1936), p. 185-187. **[849]**

Cunha, João Itiberê da. Il Guarany (1870). *Rev. bras. mús.* v. 3, no. 2 (June 1936), p. 246-250. **[850]**

Contains 6 musical excepts, and a photograph of a page from the *Guarany* manuscript.

——. Lo Schiavo. *Rev. bras. mús.*, v. 3, no. 2 (June 1936), p. 293-299. **[851]**

Covers the genesis of *Lo Schiavo*, its music and dances, as well as the short history of this opera, first performed in 1889.

Cursino de Moura, Paulo. São Paulo de outr'ora. São Paulo, Comp. Melhoramentos de São Paulo (Weissflog irmãos inc.), 1932 [pref.]. 363 p. il. F2-651.S2C8 **[85]x1**

Includes *Carlos Gomes*, p. 306-310.

França, Eurico Nogueira. Carlos Go‑ mes e a política do seu tempo. *Rev. bras. mús.,* v. 3, no. 2 (June 1936), p. 164‑ 167.   [852]

Gomes, Tapajós. O Scala de Milão acolhe e imortaliza "O Guarany". *Rev. bras. mús.,* v. 3, no. 2 (June 1936), p. 191‑ 195.   [853]

Relates the events of the Milan première of *O Guarany.*

Guimarães, Luiz. A. Carlos Gomes. Rio de Janeiro, Typographia Perseverança, 1870. 71 p. front. (port.) ML410.G638‑ G9   [854]

Jacobina, Alberto Pizarro. Visita à ci‑ dade natal de Carlos Gomes. *Rev. bras. mús.,* v. 3, no. 2 (June 1936), p. 419‑ 428.   [855]

Laner, Leo. Salvator Rosa. *Rev. bras. mús.,* v. 3, no. 2 (June 1936), p. 264‑ 269.   [856]

An analysis of the opera, presented in 1874.

Marchant, Annie d'Armand. Carlos Go‑ mes, great Brazilian composer. *Bull. pan. Amer. union,* v. 70, no. 10 (Oct. 1936), p. 767‑776.   [857]

Menezes, Tobias Barreto de. Obras completas. v. 3. Rio de Janeiro, Edição do estado de Sergipe, 1926. PQ9697.B‑ 35   [858]

Carlos Gomes e a sua opera "Salvator Rosa", p. 305‑314, which is more con‑ cerned with the art and style of Gomes, and the comments on his work by critics, than with this opera itself.

Muricy, Andrade. Côndor (1891). *Rev. bras. mús.,* v. 3, no. 2 (June 1936), p. 300‑307.   [859]

Notas sôbre a estética dessa ópera. Contains 9 musical examples.

Octavio, Rodrigo. Carlos Gomes. *Rev. bras. mús.,* v. 3, no. 2 (1936), p. 128‑ 139.   [860]

Revista brasileira de música; número

especial consagrado ao 1º centenario do nascimento de A. Carlos Gomes. Vol. 3, no. 2 (1936). Publicada pelo Insti‑ tuto nacional de música da Universi‑ dade do Rio de Janeiro. 478 p. il. (mu‑ sic). Musical supplement, 32 p. (Ar‑ chivo de música brasileira, no. 6). ML‑ 410.G638R4   [861]

This special number, issued to com‑ memorate the centenary of the birth of Carlos Gomes (1836), contains articles on the composer classified under the follow‑ ing headings: 1. Personal recollections; 2. The man and his art; 3. The operas; 4. Correspondence; 5. Various contribu‑ tions. The musical supplement consists of selections from the opera *Joanna de Flandres* (produced Rio de Janeiro, 15 Sept. 1863). The more important articles are listed separately in this bibliography.

Reys, Emma Romero Santos Fonseca da Cámara. Divulgação musical. Lis‑ boa, Oficina gráfica da imprêsa do anuario comercial, 1929. 5 v. ML42.‑ L5R6   [862]

Vol. 5, p. 369‑404, *Carlos Gomes.* The story of his life and works, with quota‑ tions from his daughter's biography of him, and from various lectures given on his music.

Rocha, Aluizio. Carlos Gomes em discos e na radiophonia. *Rev. bras. mús.,* v. 3, no. 2 (June 1936), p. 548‑461. [863]

Includes a list of records.

Ruberti, Salvatore. Colombo (1892). *Rev. bras. mús.,* v. 3, no. 2 (June 1936), p. 308‑316.   [864]

A musical analysis of the poem, with musical excerpts from each of the 4 parts.

————. Maneira pela qual não se deve can‑ tar a ária *Come serenamente el mar* de *Lo Schiavo* de Carlos Gomes. *Rev. bras. mús.,* v. 5, (1940), p. 54‑64. [865]

With 16 musical examples.

————. Maria Tudor (1879). *Rev. bras. mús.,* v. 3, no. 2 (June 1936), p. 270‑ 292.   [866]

A complete resumé of the story of the opera, as well as an analysis of the music which includes many excerpts from the score.

Seidl, Roberto. Carlos Gomes, "brasileiro e patriota", 1836-1896. Rio de Janeiro, Imprensa moderna, 1935. 53 p. ML410.B638S4 **[867]**

——. Carlos Gomes (Ensaio de bibliographia). *Rev. bras. mús.*, v. 3, no. 2 (June 1936), p. 445-457. **[868]**

Silva, Egydio de Castro e. Música para piano de Carlos Gomes. *Rev. bras. mús.*, v. 3, no. 2 (June 1936), p. 188-190. **[869]**

Reviews the musical contents of Gomes' *Fogli d'album*, with 1 musical example.

Silva, Paulo. Estudos de contraponto e fuga de Carlos Gomes. *Rev. bras. mús.*, v. 3, no. 2 (June 1936), p. 168-176. **[870]**

One half of the space is taken up by musical examples.

Sodré, Lauro. Carlos Gomes. *Rev. bras. mus.*, v. 3, no. 2 (1936), p. 85-92. **[871]**

Personal reminiscences of the composer.

Souto, Luiz Felippe Vieira. Antonio Carlos Gomes. Rio de Janeiro, Typ. do Jornal do commercio, 1936, 43 p. ML-410.G638V5 **[872]**

Suriani, Romualdo. Carlos Gomes. Subsídios históricos. *Rev. bras. mús.*, v. 3, no. 2 (June 1936), p. 437-444. **[873]**

Includes section of the music and the verse to the *Cantata* from *O Escravo*.

Taunay, Affonso de E. Carlos Gomes e o Visconde de Taunay. *Rev. bras. mús.*, v. 3, no. 2 (June 1936), p. 160-163. **[874]**

Discusses the relationship of the author's father and the Brazilian composer, with comments on Gomes' operas.

Vieira, Hermes. Carlos Gomes e os poetas brasileiros de seu tempo. *Rev.*

bras. mús., v. 3, no. 2 (June 1936), p. 432-436. **[875]**

Quotes several verses of poems written in honor of Gomes.

See also nos. 705, 710, 715, 716, 717, 719, 733, 747, 755, 758, 831, 905, 906, 908.

(c) HEITOR VILLA-LOBOS

Almeida, Renato. História da música brasileira. Rio de Janeiro, F. Briguiet & comp., 1942. 529 p. ML232.A62 **[876]**

Heitor Vila Lobos [*sic*], p. 453-460. Considers the "essentially Brazilian" character of Villa-Lobos' work through a review of his best known composition. See index for further material on this musician.

Acquarone, F. Vila-Lobos e o sentido da música brasileira. *In* Anuario brasileiro de literatura, no. 3 (1939), p. 379-382. port. **[877]**

Impressions of Brazilian music quoted from Villa-Lobos.

Andrade, Mário de. Música, doce música. São Paulo, L. G. Miranda, 1934. 358 p. ML160.A5506 **[878]**

Vila-Lobos versus Vila-Lobos, p. 178-212, contains an analysis of the principal works of this composer.

Azevedo, Luiz Heitor Corrêa de. Villa-Lobos e a criação musical. *Mús. viva*, v. 1, no. 7-8 (1941), p. 2-3. **[879]**

In contrast to the intellectualism of most modern composers, the author finds in Villa-Lobos *um músico simple e copioso como os do século XVIII*.

Carpentier, Alejo. Héctor Villa-Lobos. *Gaceta mus.*, v. 1, nos. 7-8 (July-Aug. 1928), p. 6-13. **[880]**

Casos e fatos importantes sobre H. Villa-Lobos numa biografía autêntica resumida. *Mús. viva*, v. 1, no. 7-8 (1941), p. 11-15. **[881]**

Chronological summary of Villa-Lobos' life and work. The date of birth given in this "offcial" version (1888) differs considerably from that found in the most reliable reference books (1881).

A festival of Brazilian music, arranged by Burle Marx in association with Hugh Ross. New York, Museum of modern art, 1940 16 p.   [882]

The compositions of Villa-Lobos dominate these programs (see particularly program 3 which consists entirely of Villa-Lobos' work). Notes follow the listing of these programs.

Guaspari, Silvia. Considerações em torno da obra pianística de Heitor Villa-Lobos. *Mús viva,* v. 1, no. 7-8 (1941), p. 7-8.   [883]

Iitiberê, Brasilio. A obra de Villa-Lobos e o problema folclórico. *Mús. viva,* v. 1, no. 7-8 (Jan.-Feb. 1941), p. 4-5.   [884]

Discusses the utilization of folk elements in the music of Villa-Lobos.

Lage, Alfredo. Universalidade de Villa-Lobos. *Rev. Brasil,* v. 4, no. 37 (1941), p. 26-33.   [885]

The author finds in the music of Villa-Lobos an ideal fusion of nationalism and universality.

Lange, Francisco Curt, ed. Latin American art music for the piano, by twelve contemporary composers. New York, G. Schirmer, 1942. 55 p.   [886]

Contains a composition of Villa-Lobos, *Dansa (Miudinho), de las "Bachianas Brasileiras No. 4",* and biographical data on this composer, p. xxiii-xxv (English and Spanish text).

———. Villa-Lobos, un pedagogo creador. *Bol. lat. am. mús.,* v. 1 (Apr. 1935), p. 189-196.   [887]

Martin, Percy Albin, ed. Who's who in Latin America. Stanford University, California, Stanford university press, 1940. 558 p. F1407.W55 1940 [888]

Biographical data on Villa-Lobos, p. 541-542.

Marx, Burle. Brazilian portrait; Villa-Lobos. *Mod. music,* v. 17, no. 1 (1939), p. 10-17.   [889]

Mayer-Serra, Otto. Panorama de la música hispanoamericana. Separata del tomo II de la Enciclopedia de la música Atlante. México, D. F., Ed. Atlante, 1943, p. 379-440. il. MT6.A885   [890]

Villa-Lobos, p. 438-440, with portrait, preceding p. 437.

Peppercorn, Lisa M. Some aspects of Villa-Lobos' principles of composition. *Music review,* v. 4, no. 1 (Feb. 1943), p. 28-34.   [891]

The author, a resident of Rio de Janeiro, has for several years been gathering material for a biography of Villa-Lobos. She has had exceptional opportunities for studying the scores of Villa-Lobos, and the present study contains an excellent stylistic analysis of his music.

Rosenfeld, Paul. Current chronicle. *Mus. quart.,* v. 25, no. 4 (Oct. 1939), p. 513-518.   [892]

Includes a discussion of Villa-Lobos.

Schwerké, Irving. Héctor Villa-Lobos. *Musicalia,* v. 2, no. 8 (Sept.-Oct. 1929), p. 54-57. il. (port.)   [893]

———. Kings Jazz and David (Jazz et David, rois). Paris, Les Presses modernes, 1927. ML60.8395   [894]

Includes a chapter on Heitor Villa-Lobos.

Slonimsky, Nicolas. Heitor Villa-Lobos. *In* Thompson Oscar, ed. Great modern composers. New York, Dodd, Mead & co., 1941, p. 375-383. ML390.T39G7   [895]

Most of these essays are reprinted from the *International Cyclopedia of Music and Musicians,* but this article on Villa-Lobos was written especially for the present volume. This is a straightforward, factual account of his life and work, followed by a list of compositions that fills two-and-a half pages. This list, however, is subject to considerable rectification (cf. the list of V.-L.'s works published by the Pan-American Union). For an account of the difficulties involved in ascertaining the correct chronology and titles of V.-L's works, see the article by Lisa M. Peppercorn (item no. 891). The date of the composer's birth given by Slonimsky, 1881, is considerably carlier than the date officially released by V.-L. himself.

———. Modern composers of Brazil. *Christian scien. mon.*, v. 32, no. 258 (28 Sept. 1940), p. 5.   **[896]**

This, the first of two articles, is devoted to Villa-Lobos. For the second article, see item no. 830.

———. A visit with Villa-Lobos. *Mus. Amer.*, v. 61, no. 15 (1941), p. 7, 10. il.   **[897]**

Talamón, Gastón O. Heitor Villa-Lobos. *Mús. de Amér.*, v. 2, no. 12 (1921), 3 p.   **[898]**

Weinstock, Herbert. Heitor Villa-Lobos. *In* Ewen, David, *ed.*, The book of modern composers, New York, 1942, p. 424-429. ML390.E85B6   **[899]**

Includes also a portrait, a biographical note, p. 421-422, and a statement of Villa-Lobos's views on modern composers quoted from an interview published in the *Christian Science Monitor*, p. 423.

LYRIC THEATRE

Azevedo, Luiz Heitor Corrêa de. A imperial academia de música e ópera nacional e o canto em vernáculo. *In* Anais do primeiro congresso da lingua nacional cantada, São Paulo, 1938, p. 587-636. ML3558.C72A5   **[900]**

An important document for the history of opera in Brazil. Includes a table of all operas in the Portuguese language sung in Rio de Janeiro and Niteroi (a suburb) from the years 1857 to 1863. Also the statutes of the Imperial Academia de música e opera nacional (approved by decree of 27 Oct. 1858), etc. Cf. item no. 902.

———. "Malazarte", a new Brazilian opera by Lorenzo Fernandez. *Bull. pan Amer. union*, v. 75, no. 12 (Dec. 1941), p. 686-689.   **[901]**

Short review of the opera. Illustrations of 3 of the settings.

———. Operas brasileiras. *Rev. bras. mús.*, v. 5, no. 2 (1938), p. 1-11.   **[901x]**

For a fuller treatment of Brazilian opera by the same author, see item no. 902.

———. Relação das óperas de autores brasileiros. Rio de Janeiro, Serviço gráfico do ministério da educação e saude, 1938. 116 p. il.   **[902]**

Chronology of operas by Brazilian composers, with biographical, historical and critical data, with an introduction on the opera in Brazil and a supplementary chapter, *A imperial academia de música e ópera nacional e o canto em vernáculo* (cf. item no. 900). Ninety-seven operas are listed.

Brasil-Theatro; revista. Repertório dramático de autores naciones e estrangeiros. Collectanea Pires de Almeida. Annos de 1901-1909. 922 p. il.   **[903]**

This periodical published numerous *modinhas* and theatrical songs of-the time of the Empire. Citation from *Anais do primeiro congreso da lingua nacional cantada* (São Paulo, 1938), p. 768.

Cunha, J. Itiberê da. A morte do "Teatro lírico", *Rev. bras. mús.*, v. 1, no. 1 (Mar. 1934), p. 56-58. il.   **[904]**

Brief sketch of the history of this lyric theatre, on the occasion of its demolition.

Loewenberg, Alfred. Annals of opera, 1597-1940. With an introduction by Edward J. Dent. Cambridge, W. Heffer & sons ltd., 1943. 879 p.   **[905]**

Chronology of operatic performances. Includes the following operas by Antonio Carlos Gomez [sic]: *Notte do Castelo* (1861), *Il Guarany* (1870), *Fosca* (1873), *Salvator Rosa* (1874), *Lo schiavo* (1889).

Martens, Frederick H. A thousand and one nights of opera. New York, D. Appleton and co., 1926. 487 p. MT95.M23   **[906]**

Ch. 7, *New World opera stories,* cites operas dealing with American subjects and gives the plots of the following operas by Latin American composers: *La Doreya,* by Eduardo Sánchez de Fuentes (Cuba), p. 225-226; and *O Guarany* by Carlos Gomes (Brazil), p. 233-234. Briefer mention is made in passing of other Latin American operas.

Ruschenberg, William Samuel Waithman. Three years in the Pacific... Philadelphia, Carey, Lea & Blanchard, 1834. 441 p. F2213.R95 **[907]**

Notes on Brazil include a visit to the opera, with description of the opera house, p. 42-43; Brazilian market cries, p. 61.

Silva, Lafayette. História do teatro brasileiro. Obra premiada pela Comissão do teatro nacional. Rio de Janeiro, Serviço gráfico do Ministerio da educação e saude, 1938. 489 p. PN2471.S5 **[908]**

In addition to numerous references to the lyric theatre throughout the book, there is a special chapter devoted to music (p. 429-468), which deals particularly with the operas of Carlos Gomes and Henrique Alves de Mesquita. Also mentions the founding of the Academia Imperial de Música e Opera Nacional in 1857 (13 April). The guiding spirit of this organization, whose aim was to present operas in the Portuguese language, was José Amat. List of Brazilian operas in alphabetical order, p. 442-444.

See also nos. 705, 720, 755, 763, 834, 835, 839, 840, 841, 850, 851, 853, 858, 866.

EDUCATION

Castro, Enio de Freitas e. Uma escola brasileira de canto. *In* Anais do primeiro congresso da lingua nacional cantada, São Paulo, 1938, p. 429-436. ML3558.C72A5 **[909]**

Côrte-Real, Antonio. A música nas escolas do Rio Grande do Sul. *Rev. bras. mús.*, v. 1, no. 3 (Sept. 1934), p. 218-223. **[910]**

Fernândez, Oscar Lorenzo. O canto coral nas escolas. *Rev. bras. mús.*, v. 5, no. 2 (1938), p. 25-35. **[911]**

Fontainha, Guilherme. A escola nacional de música e a universidade do Brasil. *Rev. bras. mús.*, v. 4, nos. 3-4 (1937), p. 91-94. **[912]**

Guaspari, Silvia. Motivação duma tentativa de iniciação musical. *Rev. bras. mús.*, v. 5, no. 3 (1938), p. 15-22. **[913]**

Lacombe, Laura Jacobina. A iniciação do ensino da música. *Rev. bras. mús.*, v. 1, no. 2 (June 1934), p. 135-142. **[914]**

Lange, Francisco Curt. Villa-Lobos, un pedagogo creador. *Bol. lat. am. mús.*, v. 1 (Apr. 1935), p. 189-196. **[915]**

Moreira, Pedro Lopes. Orientação moderna do ensino de canto. *Rev. bras. mús.*, v. 5, no. 2 (1938), p. 12-20. **[916]**

Pelafsky, Israel. O ensino da música em São Paulo. *Rev. bras. mús.*, v. 3, no. 1 (Mar. 1936), p. 14-15 **[917]**

Peppercorn, Lisa M. Musical education in Brazil. *Bull. pan amer. union*, v. 74, no. 10 (Oct. 1940), p. 689-693. **[918]**

A pronúncia cantada e o problema do nasal brasileiro através dos discos. *In* Anais do primeiro congresso da lingua nacional cantada, São Paulo, 1938, p. 187-208. ML3558.C7A5 **[919]**

Sá Pereira, Antonio. Um test de apreciação musical. *Rev. bras. mús.*, v. 4, nos. 3-4 (1937), p. 130-151. **[920]**

Reprinted from *Revista da Universidade do Rio de Janeiro*, série 2, nos. 4-5.

Santos, B. Nicolau dos. A rítmica no ensino escolar. *Rev. bras. mús.*, v. 5, no. 1 (1938), p. 60-68. **[921]**

São Paulo, Prefeitura do municipio, Departamento de cultura. Seis lendas amazônicas. 1942. il. **[922]**

Description of a children's ballet given under the auspices of the Divisão de educação e recreio of the Departamento de cultura. Includes music, partly from traditional sources and partly from compositions in national style by modern Brazilian composers.

Sodré, Joanidia. Música—a grande arte educativa. *Rev. bras. mús.*, v. 5, no. 2 (1938), p. 47-50. **[923]**

Souza, Antonietta de. Relatório apresentado ao exmo. sr. director do Instituto nacional de música do Rio de Janeiro. Rio de Janeiro, Typ. B. de Souza, 1928. 102 p. ML420.S698A1 **[924]**

Villa-Lobos, Heitor. Programa do ensino de música. Rio de Janeiro, Distrito Federal, oficina gráfica da Secretaria geral de educação e cultura, 1937. 78 p. il. (music) MT936.V75P7 **[925]**

A organisação deste programa foi feita no ano de 1934 pelo maestro H. Villa-Lobos, superintendente de educação musical artística. Edição revista e aumentada em 1937. Serviçoes de publicações do Instituto de pesquizas educacionais. "Algumas obras musicais adotadas no ensino de canto orfeônico no ano de 1937", p. 80-83.

INSTRUCTION AND THEORY

Barreto, Ceição de Barros. Côro orfeão. São Paulo, etc., Comp. melhoramentos de São Paulo (Weiszflog irmãos incorporada), 1939. 171 p. il. (music) MT-915.B17C6 **[926]**

Bevilacqua, Octavio. Pontos de teoria elementar da música. Rio de Janeiro, Casa Arthur Napoleão, Sampaio Araujo & cia., 1921. MT7.B56P6 **[927]**

Castro, Enio de Freitas e. Principios de arquitetura musical; tese de concurso. Pôrto Alegre, Livraria Selbach, 1940. 39 p. il. ML448.F73P7 **[928]**

Includes music.

Lavenère, Luiz. Compendio de teoria musical. 2 ed. Jaraguá, Alagoas, Brasil, Livraria Machado, 1938. 178 p. il. (music) diagrs. MT7.L17C7 **[929]**

Lozano, Fabiano R. Antologia musical, 230 melodias para aulas de solfejo nas escolas normais e estabelecimentos congeneres. 4. ed. S. Paulo, G. Ricordi & c., 1940. MT870.L78A61 **[930]**

Supplements the author's *Alegría das escolas,* no. 1131.

Machado, Raphael Coelho. Breve tratado d'harmonia, contendo o contrapon-

to ou regras da composição musical e o baixo cifrado ou acompanhamento d'orgão. Rio de Janeiro, Casa Arthur Napoleão, Sampaio Araujo & cia. [n. d.] 124 p. il. (music) MT50.C734B7 **[931]**

Original imprint covered by label as above. An edition was published in Paris, 1852. Coelho Machado lived from 1814 to 1887.

Mignone, Francisco. A pronúncia do canto nacional. *In* Anais do primeiro congresso da lingua nacional cantada, São Paulo, 1938, p. 585-496. ML3558.-C72A5 **[932]**

Normas para bôa pronúncia da lingua nacional no canto erudito. *In* Anais do primeiro congresso da lingua nacional cantada, São Paulo, 1938, p. 49-94. ML3558.C72A5 **[933]**

Discusses standards of pronunciation of the Portuguese-Brazilian language in relation to the Brazilian art song, with musical illustrations.

——. *Rev. bras. mús.,* v. 5, no. 1 (1938), p. 1-35. **[934]**

A reprint of the foregoing article.

Octaviano, João. Analyse de contraponto e noções de instrumentação, de acordo com o programma do Instituto nacional de música do Rio de Janeiro. Rio de Janeiro, Casa A. Napoleão, Sampaio Araujo & cia., 1934. il. (music). 46 p. MT55.O3A6 **[935]**

——. Curso de analyse harmónico e construcção musical. Rio de Janeiro. Casa A. Napoleão, Sampaio Araujo & cia. 2 v. MT50.O32C8 **[936]**

——. Noções sobre os pedaes do piano ... Rio de Janeiro, Casa Arthur Napoleão, Sampaio Araujo & cia., 1925. 8 p. MT227.O3N6 **[937]**

——. Técnica pianística, observações. Rio de Janeiro, Casa A. Napoleão, Sampaio Araujo & cia. MT220.O2T3 **[938]**

Ribeiro, Nestor Assis. A técnica do piano. *Rev. bras. mús.,* v. 4, nos. 1-2 (1937), p. 28-34.   [939]

Sá Pereira, Antonio. Ensino moderno de piano. São Paulo, G. Ricordi & c., 1933. 94 p. il. (music). MT220.S12   [940]

Santos, Maria Luiza de Queiroz Amancio dos. Methodo analytico-synthetico do piano. São Paulo, Empreza gráphica da "Revista dos tribunales", 1935. 124 p. il. MT222.Q3M3   [941]
Includes music.

Silva, José Paulo da. Curso de contraponto. 2d ed. Adotado oficialmente na Escola nacional de música da Universidade do Brasil. Rio de Janeiro, C. Wehrs & cia., 1938. 95 p. il. (music) MT55.S4C8 1938   [942]

——. Manual de fuga. Adotado no Instituto nacional de música da Universidade do Rio de Janeiro. Rio de Janeiro, C, Wehrs & cia., 1935. 147 p. il. (music) MT59.S4M2   [944]

Sinzig, Petrus. Os segredos da harmonia desvendados singelamente. Opus 45. 3. ed. Petrópolis, Editora "Vozes", 1937. 176 p. il. (music) diagrs. MT50.-S595S3   [945]

Villa-Lobos, Heitor. Canto orfeônico, v. 1. Rio de Janeiro, Casa Arthur Napoleão. Sampaio Araujo & cia., 1939. M-1994.V74C2   [946]
Songs arranged for school use. Includes "canto dos Indios Parecis" (from the collection of Roquette Pinto; melody with Indian text), p. 69. There are also some work-songs.

——. O ensino popular da música no Brasil; o ensino da música e do canto orfeônico nas escolas ... Rio de Janeiro, Oficina gráfica da Secretaria geral de educação e cultura, 1937. 55 p. M-T3.B7V5   [947]
At head of title: Departamento de educação do Distrito federal (Superintendencia de educação musical e artística) (SEMA)

——. Programa do ensino de música: jardim de infancia, escolas elementar experimental e técnica secundaria ... Rio de Janeiro, Distrito federal, Oficina gráfica da Secretaria geral de educação e cultura, 1937. 78 p. MT936.-V75P7   [948]

——. Solfejos originais e sobre têmas de cantigas populares, para ensino de canto orfeônico, v. 1. São Paulo, E. S. Mangione, 1940. MT870.V79S6 [948x]
163 solfeggi. There is no indication of which are original and which are based on popular themes.

NATIONAL ANTHEM

Azevedo, Luiz Heitor Corrêa de. Chronicas em varios modos ... *Rev. bras. mús.,* v. 3, no 1 (Mar. 1936), p. 25-29.   [949]
Includes: "O Brasil e a música" and "A verdade sobre o hymno nacional." In the former the essential originality and independence of Brazilian music is affirmed. The second section deals with the origin of the national anthem of Brazil, which was written to celebrate the abdication of the emperor D. Pedro I (April 1831), but the exact date of composition is not known. The composer was Francisco Manoel da Silva. The words now used for the anthem were written by Osorio Duque Estrada in 1909 and were officially adopted by the Brazilian government in 1922.

——. Francisco Manoel e o hino nacional., *Rev. bras. mús.,* v. 4, nos. 3-4 (1937), p. 171-172   [950]

Caldeira Filho, João C. Hino de Independencia e hino nacional. São Paulo, Ed. Ricordi americana, 1941. 62 p.   [951]

Carlos Magalhães de Azevedo e o Hino Nacional. *Rev. bras. mús.,* v. 5, no. 2 (1938), p. 42-46.   [952]

Fleiuss, Max. Francisco Manoel e o hiymno nacional; conf. realizada no Instituto histórico e geográfico brasileiro

12 Oct. 1916. Rio de Janeiro, Imp. nacional, 1917. 26 p. ML3575.F5 **[953]**

Discussion of Brazilian national songs. At the end of the book there are the music and words to national hymns written by Marcos Portugal, D. Pedro I, Francisco Manoel da Silva, Carlos Gomes, Leopoldo Miguez, and Francisco Braga. Also contains portraits of many illustrious Brazilian composers.

Hino nacional brasileiro. *Res. mus.*, v. 4, no. 37 (Sept. 1941), supplement no. 6. **[954]**

Hymno nacional brasileiro. Commissão de expansão económica do Brasil. 7 p. M1690.M **[955]**

For voice and piano.

Köhling, Fr. Musik in Brasilien. *Musik*, v. 5, no. 5 (1905-06), p. 319-322. **[956]**

Includes music of Brazilian national anthem.

Meira, Augusto. Hymno nacional brasileiro. *Rev. amer.*, Rio, v. 9, no. 1 (Oct. 1919), p. 149-154. **[957]**

Attempts to explain the allusions, meanings and significance of certain passages in the national hymn.

Or, —— d'. O grande compositor norteamericano Gottschalk e o hymno nacional brasileiro. *In* Brasil-Estados Unidos Rio de Janeiro, Ed. do Diario de noticias, 1939, p. 297-298. E183.8.B7B84 **[958]**

Silva, Francisco Manoel da. Hymno nacional brasileiro. Ministério das relações exteriores, 1929. M1690.M **[959]**

Scores and parts, for string quartet and piano or small orchestra, ad libitum.

FOLK AND PRIMITIVE MUSIC

(A) GENERAL

Almeida, Renato. História da música brasileira, 2d. ed. Rio de Janeiro, F. Briguiet & comp., 1942. ML232.A62 **[959x]**

The first part of this work (p. 3-279)

is devoted to the folk music of Brazil. For further comment, see introductory section.

——. La música popular en el Brasil. *Nosotros*, año 17, v. 45, no. 72 (Sept. 1923), p. 66-74. **[960]**

Alvarenga, Oneyda: "Comentários a alguns cantos e danças do Brasil". *Rev. arq. mun. São Paulo*, ano 7, v. 80 (Nov.-Dec. 1941), p. 209-246. **[961]**

Important detailed study, with bibliography.

Amaral, Amadeu. "Reisado", "Bumba meu Boi" e "Pastorís". *Rev. arq. mun. São Paulo*, v. 6, no. 64 (1940), p. 273-284. **[962]**

Andrade, Mário de. Uma conferencia. *Rev. brasil*, v. 30 (Jan.-Apr. 1925), p. 15-23. **[963]**

Touches on the artistic stylization of folk music, on popular music, etc.

——. Ensaio sôbre música brasileira. São Paulo, I. Chiarato e cia, 1928. 94 p. ML232.A7E6 **[963x]**

An important study of Brazilian folk music from the points of view of rhythm, melody, polyphony, instrumentation and form, also in its relation to the art music of Brazil. The second part is a collection of Brazilian folk tunes, with comments.

——. Folk music and folk song in Brazil. *In* Conference on inter-American relations in the field of music, Report of the committee. Washington, D. C., 1940, p. 98-110. F1418.C7865 and ML35C65R4 **[964]**

"It may be said that there are no *folk songs* in Brazil, although there certainly is a *folk music*. That is to say, we have no traditional folk melodies." Includes a list of records and a 7-page bibliography. For a more complete version of this article, see item no. 966.

——. Folk music in Brazil. *Brazil*, v. 8 (Sept. 1936), p. 6-8. **[965]**

——. *Bull. pan amer. union*, 70, no. 5 (1936), p. 392-399. **[966]**

"Prepared for the International Institute

of Intellectual Cooperation, Paris." Contains an extensive bibliography.

———. Música, doce música. São Paulo, L. G. Miranda, 1934. 358 p. ML60.-A55D6   **[967]**

A collection of essays and articles originally published in newspapers and reviews. The six essays in the section on folklore deal with various aspects of Brazilian folk music, with 12 musical examples.

———. A música e a canção populares no Brasil. Rio de Janeiro, Servicio de co-operação intellectual do Ministério das relações exteriores, 1936. 16 p. **[968]**

———. La música y la canción popular en el Brasil. *Letras,* v. 1, no. 2 (São Paulo, 1937), p. 6-9.   **[969]**

———. A nau Catarineta. *Rev. arq. mun-São Paulo,* v. 7, no. 73 (Jan. 1941), p. 61-76.   **[970]**

Studies the origin and history of a Portuguese ballad which has persisted in Brazilian folk tradition through its incorporation in the final episode of the folk ballet known as *Chegança dos Marujos.* Andrade compares various versions of the ballad.

———. O samba rural paulista. *Rev. arq. mun. São Paulo,* v. 4, no. 41 (Nov. 1937) p. 37-116.   **[971]**

Includes words and music of songs.

Arinos, Afonso. Apontamentos sôbre as festas religiosas do mês de junho no folcolre do Brasil. *Rev. acad. letras,* ano 5, v. 12, no. 34 (1941), p. 35-40.   **[972]**

Describes festival of St. John (June 24) in central Brazil, with verses of some songs.

Arinos, Afonso. Pero sertão. 3 ed. Rio de Janeiro, Paris, Garnier, n. d. 200 p. PQ9597.A8P3 1898a   **[973]**

Words of a song, p. 105-106, 197; notes on music and instruments, p. 138-139.

Azevedo, Luiz Heitor Corrêa de. Dois pequenos estudos de folclore musical: Algunas reflexões sobre folcmúsica no Brasil; caminhos da música sulameri-

cana. Rio de Janeiro, Typ. do "Jornal do commercio", Rodriguez & cia., 1938. 43 p. il. (music) ML3575.C8D6 **[974]**

First part deals with Brazil; 2nd part with Brazil and the other South American countries. Contains 7 musical examples.

———. Introducçã ao curso de folclore nacional de Escola nacional de música da Universidade do Brasil. *Rev. bras. mús.,* v. 6 (1939), p. 1-10.   **[975]**

———. La musique au Brésil. *Rev. musicale,* special number, "La musique dans les pays latins" (Feb.-Mar. 1940), p. 74-81.   **[976]**

Discusses the basic elements of Brazilian folk music (African and Portuguese), pointing out that the Indian factor had very little influence in its formation.

Barroso, Gustavo. Através dos folklores. S. Paulo, Comp. melhoramentos de S. Paulo (Weiszflog irmãos inc.), 1927. 196 p. GR71.B3   **[977]**

"Bibliographia", p. 187-193.

———. O sertão e o mundo. Rio de Janeiro, Ed. Leite Ribeiro, 1923. 301 p.   **[978]**

Includes a version of "Bambu-meu-boi" from Fortaleza.

———. Terra de sol (natureza e costumes do Norte). 3. ed Rio de Janeiro, F. Alves, 1930. 272 p. il. F2515.B282   **[979]**

"Os divertimentos (música e danza)", p. 208-219.

Bennett, Frank. Forty years in Brazil. London, Mills & Boon, ltd., 1914. 271 p. F2515.B47   **[980]**

Reference to music of the gauchos, p. 186-187, with illustration of gaucho playing the guitar.

Cascudo, Luis da Câmara. Vaqueiros e cantadores; folclore poético do sertão de Pernambuco, Paraiba, Rio Grande do Norte e Ceará. Pôrto Alegre, Edição da livraria do globo, 1939. 274 p. ML3575.C17V2   **[981]**

Cezimbra, João Jacques. Assumptos do Rio Grande do Sul. Pôrto Alegre, Officinas gráphicas da escola de engenharia, 1912. 258 p. il. F2621.C42 **[982]**

Text and description of the traditional ballad *A náu Catharineta,* p. 162-165.

Chase, Gilbert. The music of Spain. New York, W. W. Norton, 1941. 375 p. il. ML315.C42M8 **[983]**

Chapter 17, *Hispanic music in the Americas,* includes "Some Brazilian types", p. 270-271.

Costa, Francisco Augusto Pereira da. Apontamentos sôbre as festas religiosas do mês de junho no folclore do Brasil: os festejos do dia de São João em Pernambuco. *Rev. acad. letras,* ano 5, v. 12, no. 34 (1941), p. 25-32. **[984]**

Festival of St. John, with some historical and comparative perspective, with verses of some songs. Comparative notes by Silvio Julio [R. S. Boggs].

———. Folk-lore pernambucano. Rio de Janeiro, Livraria J. Leite, 1907. 641 p. GR133-B6P43 **[985]**

Contents: Superstições populares; A poesia popular; Romanceiro; Cancioneiro; Pastorís; Parlendas e brinquedos infantís; Miscellanea; Quadras populares.

Costa, Luiz Edmundo da. Rio de Janeiro do meu tempo. Rio de Janeiro, Imprensa nacional. 1938. 3 v. il. Paged continuously. F2646.C86 **[986]**

Appendix to v. 3 has 4 tunes with Portuguese words.

Cunha, João Itiberê da. O folklore na música atual. *Ilus. mus.* (Nov. 1930), p. 118. **[987]**

Cunha, José Maria Vaz Pinto Coelho da. Cancionero popular brasileiro. v. 1. Rio de Janeiro, 1879. 207 p. **[988]**

Cited by Magalhães, *O folk-lore no Brasil,* p. 8.

Cunha, Mario Wagner Vieira da. Descripção da festa de bom Jesus de Pirapora. *Rev. arq. mun. São Paulo,* v. 4, no. 41 (Nov. 1937), p 5-136. il. **[989]**

"Résumé" (in French), p. 36: "O Sam-

ba", p. 20-30, with quotation of 35 song texts. Also reprinted separately, together with item no. 971 (cf. item no. 1118).

Dornas Filho, João. Cantiga dos capinadores de rua em Belo Horizonte. *Rev. arq. mun. São Paulo,* ano 5, v. 50 (1938), p. 89-92. **[990]**

Fernandes, Annibal Gonçalves. O folclore mágico do nordeste. Rio de Janeiro, Civilização brasileira, s. a., 1938. 177 p. GR133.B6F4 **[991]**

Includes words and melodies of 13 folk songs, also the words of many others.

Fernandes, João Ribeiro. O folk-lore (estudos de literatura popular). Rio de Janeiro, J. Ribeiro dos Santos, 1919. 328 p. il. (music) GR133.B6R5 **[992]**

Includes numerous references to folk songs, with quotation of texts. *Cf.* especially Ch. 25, *Poesia popular,* p. 166-174, and Ch. 26, *Música e nota ao romance antecedente,* p. 175-179, with music of the Spanish ballad *La bella malmaridada.*

Ferrara, Maria Amorim. Notas de uma profesora de música escolar. Belo Horizonte, Imprensa oficial do estado de Minas Gerais, 1938. **[993]**

Includes 5 folk tunes briefly noted, and *Serra da Piedade, melodia da Montanha,* harmonized by H. Villa-Lobos.

Freitas, A. Tradições e reminiscências paulistanas. São Paulo, Ed. Monteiro Lobato, 1921. **[994]**

Contains unharmonized melodies. Cited by Andrade, *Bull. pan amer. union,* v. 70, p. 396.

———. "Vaqueiros e cantadores". *Rev. bras. mús.,* v. 7, no. 3 (1940-1941), p. 232-248. **[995]**

A detailed critical study of the book by Luiz da Câmara Cascudo, dealing with the literary form of Brazilian folk songs.

Gallet, Luciano. Estudos de folclore. Rio de Janeiro, Carlos Wehrs e cia., 1934. 115 p. ML3575.B7G2 **[996]**

A posthumous collection, edited by Mario de Andrade, who contributes a preface (p. 9-32) dealing with Gallet's life and musical activities. "Catalogo das obras de Luciano Gallet", p. 97-109. Includes: O Indio na música brasileira; O Negro na música brasileira; Cantigas e dansas antigas do estado de Rio; Têmas brasileiros (19 folk tunes). An important study, with illustration of musical instruments and numerous musical examples.

Garritano, Assuero. Do rythmo. *Rev. bras. mús.*, v. 3, n. 1 (Mar. 1936), p. 1-5. **[997]**

Touches briefly on the use of folk themes by Brazilian composers, p. 4.

Haase, Freidrich Wilhelm. Volksmusikalische arbeit in Sudbrasilien. *Musik und volk,* v. 2, no. 2 (Dec. 1934-Jan. 1935), p. 67-69. **[998]**

Hague, Eleanor. Brazilian songs. *Jour. amer. folklore,* v. 25, no. 96 (1912), p. 179-181. **[999]**

Four folk tunes, with Portuguese words.

Houston, Elsie. La musique, la danse et les cérémonies populaires du Brésil. *In* Art Populaire, travaux artistiques et scientifiques du 1er congrès international des arts populaires, Prague, 1928, v. 2, p. 162-164. Paris, Editions Duchartre, 1931. N9201-15 1928. **[1000]**

A summary description of the popular songs, dances and instruments of Brazil.

Itiberê, Brasilio. Uma canção popular religiosa e sua variante. *Mús. viva,* v. 1, no. 1 (May 1940). **[1001]**

Two versions of a Brazilian religious folk song found with different words in different parts of Brazil.

Langsdorff, Georg Heinrich von. Bemerkungen auf einer reise um die welt in den jahren 1803 bis 1807. Frankfurt am Mayn, Friedrich Wilmans, 1812. 2 v. il. G420.K94L19 **[1002]**

Place of Brazilian music in customs, p. 31, 44-45, v. 1. Brazilian song (with music), end of part 1, v. 1.

Leite, Serafim. Cantos, músicas e dan-

ças nas aldeias do Brasil, seculo 16. *Brotería,* Lisboa, v. 24 (1937) p. 42-52. **[1003]**

Citation from files of Music Division, Pan American Union. Also in *Música sacra,* v. 3 ,no. 11 (Nov. 1943), p. 204-205, and no. 12 (Dec. 1943), p. 223-225.

Lima, Francisco Peres de. Folclore acreano. Rio de Janeiro, Tipografía Batista de Souza, 1938. 154 p. GC133.-B6P45 **[1004]**

"Dansa, música e canto", p. 129-138.

Lima, Silvio Julio de Albuquerque. A tirana entre os gauchos. *Rev. acad. letras,* v. 6, no. 39 (Mar.-Apr. 1942). p. 40-49 **1005]**

The *tirana* is a type of Spanish peninsular folk song and dance, in ternary rhythm, which enjoyed a great vogue in the final decades of the 18th century. The *tirana* spread to Latin America, in the early 19th century and became especially acclimated in the Brazilian state of Rio Grande do Sul. This article contains textual examples, but no musical notations.

Lion, André. Impressões da voz e da música nas selvas virgens do Brasil. *Ilus. bras.* (Aug. 1938), p. 12. **[1006]**

Citation from the files of Luiz Heitor Corrêa de Azevedo.

Magalhães, Basilio de. O folk-lore no Brasil. Rio de Janeiro, Livraria Quaresma, 1928. 232 p. GR133.B6M3 **[1007]**

Has copious bibliographical footnotes.

Marcos, Miguel de. Folklore brasileño. *América* (Havana), v. 11, no. 3 (Sept. 1941), p. 67. **[1008]**

One-page article on the visit of Olga Coelho to Havana. Makes a few references to Brazilian folk song.

Monte, Octavio d'. Música popular brasileira. *Weco* (Oct. 1929), p. 22. **[1009]**

Citation from personal files of L.-H. Corrêa de Azevedo.

Moraes, Alexandre José de Mello.

Apontamentos sôbre as festas religiosas do mês de junho no folclore do Brasil: desenvolvimento das festas de São João na vila do Lagarto, Sergipe, Brasil. *Rev. acad. letras,* ano 5, 1. 12, no. 34 (1941), p. 19-25. **[1010]**

Festival of St. John (June 24), especially the eve preceding, with verses of some songs. Comparative notes by Silvio Julio [R. S. Boggs].

——. Festas a tradições populares, do Brazil, Nova ed. rev. e augm., prefácio de Sylvio Romero. Rio de Janeiro, Paris H. Garnier, 1901. 504 p. il. GT433.M4 1901 **[1011]**

——. Serenatas e saráus. Rio de Janeiro, Ed. Garnier, 1901-02. 3 v. **[1012]**

Includes several popular tunes. Citation from presonal files of L. H. Corrêa de Azevedo.

Nova collecção de modinhas brasileiras, tanto amorosas, como sentimentaes, etc. Rio de Janeiro, Livraria Garnier, 1899. **[1013]**

Cited by Magalhães, *O folk-lore no Brasil,* p. 8.

Paranhos, Ulysses. Música popular brasileira. *Res. mus.,* v. 3, nos. 26-27 (Oct.-Nov 1940), p. 3-14. **[1014]**

Pedrosa, Mário. Brazilian music. *Theatre arts monthly,* v. 23, no. 5 (1939), p. 363-368. **[1015]**

General introductory survey, dealing chiefly with folk music forms, instruments and dramatic dances (*bailados*).

Phillips, Grace Darling. Far peoples. Chicago, Illinois, The University of Chicago press, 1929, 274 p. BV2086. P45 and M1627.P6 **[1016]**

Stories, songs with music, poetry, games, etc., Section VI. Brazil. Includes 4 songs reprinted from *Characteristic songs and dances of all nations,* edited by James Duff Brown. "Games", p. 189-193, includes music of singing-game, *Na Bahia tem,* for voice and piano.

Pinto, Alexina Magalhães. Cantigas das

crianças e do povo e danças populares ... Rio de Janeiro, Livraria Francisco Alves, 1911. 208 p. il. **[1017]**

Includes music (unaccompanied melodies).

Querino, Manuel Raymundo. A Bahia de outr'ora, cultos e factos populares. 2 ed. augm. Bahia, Livraria economica, 1922. 301 p. F2651.B15Q4 **[1018]**

Includes a chapter, *Cantor de modinhas,* p. 236-243, and other references to popular songs.

Ramos, H. de Carvalho. Tropas e boiadas. São Paulo, Ed. Monteiro Lobato, 1922. **[1019]**

Rodrigues, João Barbosa. O canto e o dansa selvícola. *Rev. bras.,* ano 3, v. 9 (1881), p. 32-60. **[1020]**

Rodrigues, Felix Contreiras. Amores do capitão Paulo Centeno. Pôrto Alegre, Ed. Globo, 1937. **[1021]**

At the end there are several popular gaucho melodies.

Romero, Sylvio. Uma esperteza: os cantos e contos populares do Brazil e o sr. Theophilo Braga. Rio de Janeiro, S. J. Alves, 1887. 166 p. PQ9689.R76 **[1022]**

——. Estudos sôbre a poesia popular do Brasil. Rio de Janeiro, 188. 368 p. **[1023]**

Cited by Andrade, *Bull, pan, amer. union,* v. 70, p. 398.

Sá Brito, Severino de. Trabalhos e costumes dos gauchos. Pôrto Alegre, Barcellos, Bertaso & cia., 1928. **[1023x]**

Santa-Anna Nery, Frederico José de. Folk-lore brésilien. Poésie populaire. —Contes et légendes.—Fables et mythes.—Poésie, musique, danses et croyances des Indiens. Accompagné de douze morceaux de musique. Paris, Perrin et cie., 1889. 264 p. GR133.B6S3 **[1024]**

——. The land of the Amazons, translated from the French of Baron de

Santa-Anna Nery... by George Humphrey. London, Sands & co., 1901. 405 p. il. F2546.S23 **[1025]**
With 1 tune, p. 256.

——. Le pays des Amazones. Paris, L. Frinzine et cie., 1885. 382 p. li. F2546. S21 **[1026]**
Treats of music and dancing, p. 230-238.

Silva, Egidio Castro e. O samba carioca. *Rev. bras. mús.*, v. 6 (1939), p. 45-50. **[1027]**
Description of an "escola de samba", at Morro da Mangueira, with the musical notation of a samba written down by Duilia Fraezão Guimarães.

Spalding, Walter. Poesia do povo (folclore). *Rev. inst. hist. geog. Rio Grande do Sul*, v. 13 (1933), p. 155-225. **[1028]**
Includes music.

Spix, Johann Baptist von. Brasilianische volkslieder und indianische melodien. Musikbeilage zu Dr. v. Spix und Dr. v. Martius. Reise in Brasilien. [München, 1931?] 15 p. **[1029]**
Cited by Mattfeld, *Folk Music of the Western Hemisphere*, p. 37, with this notation: "Contains 14 tunes, eight arr. for 1 voice with piano acc. and Portuguese words". L. C. has the *Reise in Brasilien*, but without the musical supplement.

——, **and Carl Friedr. Phil. von Martius.** Reise in Brasilien. München, Gedruckt bei H. Lindauer, 1823-31. 3 v. F25--.S75 **[1030]**

Steward, Margaret E. The folk music of Brazil. *Mus. Amer.*, v. 60, no. 6 (25 Mar. 1940), p. 9, 23. il. **[1031]**

Valle, Flausino Rodrigues. Elementos de folk-lore musical brasileiro. São Paulo, Companhia editora nacional, 1936. 165 p. il. ML3575.R6E5 **[1032]**
Includes 13 melodies.

Villa-Lobos, Heitor. Solfejos originais e sobre têmas de cantigas populares ... São Paulo, E. S. Mangione, 1940. v. 1. MT870.V79S6 **[1033]**

——. Tres poêmas indígenas ... I. Canidé. II. Teiurú. III. Iára. Paris, Éditions Max Eschig, 1929. 17 p. M1690.V **[1034]**
Three songs with piano accompaniment, based on Brazilian Indian themes.

Wanderley, E. Apontamentos sôbre as festas religiosas do mês de junho no folclore do Brasil: S. João, S. Pedro e Santo Antônio nas festas populares do Nordeste. *Rev. acads. letras*, ano 5, no 34 (1941), p. 32-35. **[1035]**
Brief descriptions, with words and music of a song to St. Anthony. Comparative notes by Silvio Julio [R. S. Boggs.]

(B) AMERINDIAN

1. Music and Dance

Ambrosetti, Juan B. Los indios Cainguá del alto Paraná. *Bol. inst. geog. arg.*, v. 15 (1894), p. 661-744. **[1036]**
Music and dance, p. 669-674, including a list of musical instruments with brief descriptions of each, notes of their scale, and musical examples of Cainguá songs (opposite p. 672).

Azevedo, Luiz Heitor Corrêa de. Escala, ritmo e melodia na música dos indios brasileiros. Rio de Janeiro, Rodrigues & cia., 1938. 48 p. il. (music). ML3575.-C8L7 **[1037]**
Includes 44 musical examples. "Bibliografia", p. 9-15.

Baldus, Herbert. Indianerstudien im nordöstlichen Chaco. Leipzig, C. L. Hirschfeld, 1931. 230 p. il. F2822.B23 **[1038]**
Deals with musical instruments and songs, p. 102-109.

Borromeu, Carlos. Algumas noções sôbre a música entre os indígenas do Rio Xingú. *Música sacra*, v. 2, no. 7 (July 1942), p. 126-127. il. **[1039]**

Cardim, Fernão. Tratados da terra e gente do Brasil. 2 ed. São Paulo, Companhia editora nacional, 1939. 379 p. F2511.C26 1939. **[1040]**
Modern edition of a work written in

the early part of the 17th century, containing references to musical ceremonies and dances, instruments, etc.

Colbacchini, Antonio. I Bororos orientali, "Orarimugudoge", del Matto Grosso (Brasile). Turin, Soc. editrice internazionale, [192-?] 251, 210 p. il. [1041]

"Canti religiosi", with music of 7 songs, part 5, p. 109-199.

Farabee, William Curtis. The central Arawaks. Philadelphia, The University museum, 1918. 288 p. il. F2380.1.A6F2 [1042]

A study of the Arawaks of northern Brazil and southern British Guiana. Music and dances, p. 160-162, with two tunes.

———. The central Caribs. Philadelphia, The University museum, 1924. 299 p. F2380.1.C2F2 [1043]

A study of the Carib Indians of southern British Guiana and northern Brazil. References to music, instruments and dances, p. 39, 61, 65 ff., 73, 97, 156 ff., 166, 170, 175 ff., 187, 190, 190 ff., 203 ff., 206, 233 ff., 226.

Figueiredo, José de Lima. Indios do Brasil. São Paulo, etc. Companhia editora nacional, 1939. 348 p. il. F2520.L55 [1044]

O indio e a música p. 265-268, covering musical instruments with illustrations; speaks of the slow development of dance and music. Festas e dansas dos tupys, p. 319-324; for further notes on music and dance see Festas under each of the various Indian tribes.

Gallet, Luciano. O indio na música brasileira. Weco (Dec. 1928), p. 9. [1045]

Citation from personal files of L.-H. Corrêa de Azevedo.

Gondim, Zacarias. Música e dansas dos indígenas do Brasil. A República (21 Apr. and 3 May 1900). [1046]

Citation from personal files of L.-H. Corrêa de Azevedo.

Koch-Grünberg, Theodor. Die maskentänze der Indianer des oberen Rio Negro und Yapurá. Arch. für anthrop., v. 32, no. 4 (1906), p. 293-298. [1047]

This article is more concerned with the masks, costumes and characters in the dances than with the choreography and music. Includes many illustrations and 4 strophes of the song accompanying the Jaguar dance.

———. Vom Roroima zum Orinoco. Berlin, D. Reimer, 1917-28. 3 v. F2313.K76 [1048]

"Musik der Masuschi, Taulipáng und Yekuaná von Erich M. v. Hornbostel (aus dem phonogramm-archiv im psychologischen institut der Universität Berlin)"; v. 3, p. 307-440. With music. Description of Indian songs and dances, v. 3, p. 154-166.

———. Zwei jahre bei den Indianern nordwest-Brasiliens. Stuttgart, Strecker und Schröder, 1923. 416 p. il. F2520.K76 [1049]

"Dieses buch ist die überarbeitung eines zweibändigen werkes, das 1909-10 unter dem titel "Zwei jahre unter den Indianern, erschienen."—Vorwort.

Köhler, Fritz. Brasilien heute und morgen. Leipzig, F. U. Brockhaus, 1926. 272 p. F2515.K76 [1050]

Indian dances and song, p. 163, 169-170.

Lachmann, Robert. Die musik der ausseuropäischen natur-und kulturvölker ... Wildpark-Potsdam, Akademische verlagsgesellschaft Athenaion, 1929. 31 p. il. (Added t.-p.: Handbuch der musikwissenschaft, hrsg. von dr. Ernst Bücken). ML160.-B9L2 [1051]

With 3 tunes of the Indians of northern Brazil, taken from Hornbostel's phonograms.

Léry, Jean de. Histoire d'un voyage faict en la terre du Brésil autrement dite Amérique. 3d ed. Genève, Antoine Chuppin, 1585. 427 p. F2511.L61 [1052]

The first edition of this famous work was published at La Rochelle in 1578. The third edition is cited here as being the first to include the musical examples which make this a highly important item in the musical bibliography of Brazil. Léry's work went through numerous editions and translations during the 16th and 17th centuries, and it has been republished in various modern editions. These modern editions do not contain the musical examples, consisting of five melodies of the Tupynambá Indians. In the course of passing from one edition to another the notation of the melodies was considerably altered. Luiz Heitor Corrêa de Azevedo undertook to investigate this matter and ascertain the correct form of the melodies. The results of his research were embodied in a paper read before the New York Chapter of the American Musicological Society, scheduled for publication in the *Musical quarterly*. For a further discussion see introduction.

Manizer, H. H. Música e instrumentos de música de algumas tribus do Brasil (1 Cadiuveos—2. Terenos—3. Faias —4. Caingangs—5. Guaranys—6. Botocudos). *Rev. bras. mús.*, v. 1, no. 4 (1934), p. 303-327. il.   **[1053]**

First published in the bulletin of the Museum of Anthropology and Ethnology, Petrograd, v. 5, no. 1 (1918), p. 319-350. A very important study, with 14 musical examples.

Mattos, Anibal. Das origens da arte brasileira. Bello Horizonte, Edições Apollo, 1936. 266 p. il. F2519.3.A7M3. (*also publ. as* v. 1 *of his* Historia da arte brasileira, 1937).   **[1054]**

"A música entre os indios", p. 131-140. Illustrations of dancers with musical instruments.

Métraux, Alfred. La religion des Tupinamba et ses rapports avec celle des autres tribus Tupi-Guarani. Paris, E. Leroux, 1928. 260 p. il. F2520.1.T94M4   **[1055]**

"Fêtes et danses", p. 189-196, including reference to songs.

Nimuendajú, Curt. The Apinayé. Washington, D. C., The Catholic university of America press, 1939. 189 p. F2520.-1.A65N5   **[1056]**

Dance during the game of log-racing, p. 114-116; masquerade dancing, p. 118-119.

Nordenskiöld, Erland. Forschungen und

abenteuer in Südamerika. Stuttgart, Strecker & Schröder, 1924. 338 p. F33-13.N835   **[1057]**

Musical instruments among the Huari Indians, p. 232; music to a Cavina Indian piece (for flute, drum and bass drum), p. 270-271; for further references to music see p. 189, 207, 240, and for dance p. 76, 273.

Pereda Valdés, Ildefonso. Línea de color. Santiago de Chile, Ed. Ercilla, 1938. 248 p. E185.6P44   **[1058]**

Includes: Dances of the Brazilian Negroes, p. 177-180; Brazilian Indian festivals, p. 158-166, with special reference to dances.

Pinto, Estevão. Os indígenas do nordeste. São Paulo, Companhia editora nacional, 1935-38. 2 v. il. F2519.P56   **[1059]**

"Dansas, cantos, festas", v. 2, p. 272-278, with illustration of a native dance.

Ploetz, Hermann, and Alfred Métraux. La civilisation matérielle et la vie sociale et religieuse des Indiens Zè du Brésil méridional et oriental. *Rev. inst. etnol. univ. Tucumán,* v. 1, no. 2 (1930), p 107-238.   **[1060]**

Resumé of tribal songs and dances, p. 190-194.

Rodrigues, João Barbosa. Rio Jauapery. Pacificação dos Crichanás. Rio de Janeiro, Imprensa nacional, 1885. 274 p. F2519.B24   **[1061]**

Includes music.

Roquette-Pinto, Edgardo. Rondonia: anthropologia; ethnographia. Rio de Janeiro, Imprensa nacional, 1917. 252 p. il. (Added t.-p.: Archivos do Museu nacional do Rio de Janeiro. v. xx). Q-33.R6 vol. 20.   **[1062]**

Includes music: 12 phonograms of native Indian tunes from the interior of Brazil.

———. 3 ed. S. Paulo, Companhia editora nacional, 1935. 401 p. il. (Biblioteca pedagógica brasileira. ser. v. Brasiliana, v. 39) F2520.R67   **[1063]**

Includes music: 12 phonograms of native Indian tunes from the interior of Brazil.

Schmidt, Max. Indianerstudien in Zentralbrasilien. Berlin, Dietrich Reimer, 1905. 456 p. F2519.S34 **[1064]**

Song texts of various Indian tribes (some with German translations), p. 418-425; musical instruments of the Guató children, p. 309, 311; for further references to music, and for comments on the dance, see index under *trommel, tanz-, rohrpfeifenflöten, Ciriri-tanz und gesang, Cururú-tanz und gesang, flöten,* etc.

Snethlage, Emil Heinrich. Nachrichten über die Pauserna-Guarayú, die Siriono am Rio Baures und die Simonianes in nähe der serra S. Simon. *Zeit. ethnol.,* v. 67 (1935), p. 178-293. **[1065]**

Siriono melody collected by M. Schneider, p. 292, footnote.

Speiser, Felix. Im düster des brasilianischen urwalds. Stuttgart, Strecker & Schröder, 1926. 322 p. F2586.S85 **[1066]**

This contains an article by Dr. Arnold Deuber, *Musikinstrumente und musik der Aparai,* p. 320-322, with musical examples of animal music and bird music for maskdances. See p. 249-260 for the preparation of the mask-dances, and other information pertinent to these celebrations.

Steere, Joseph Beal. Narrative of a visit to Indian tribes of the Purus River, Brazil. *In* U. S. National museum, annual report, 1901, Washington, 1903, p. 359-393. F2519.S81 **[1067]**

With 3 tunes, p. 378, 387.

Stehmann, Franz. Paradies und hölle... Stuttgart, Strecker & Schröder, 1926. 247 p. F2515.S82 **[1068]**

Dance in Rio Claro festivals, p. 127-128. Author's pseudonym, Franz Donat, at head of title.

Steinen, Karl von den. Entre os aborígenes do Brasil central; prefácio de Herbert Baldus, tradução de Egon Schaden. São Paulo, Departamento de cultura, 1940. 713 p. il. (incl. maps. music). F2576.S833 **[1069]**

Translation of item no. 1070.

——. Unter den naturvölkern Zentral-Brasiliens. Berlin, D. Reimer (Hoefer & Vohsen), 1894. 570 p. il. F2576.S83 **[1070]**

Treats of music and dance, p. 295-329.

Strelnikov, I. D. La música y la danza de las tribus indias Kaa-ihwua (Guaraní) y Botocudo. *In* International congress of Americanists, Proceedings, v. 23, New York, 1928, p. 796-802. E51.- 1716 **[1071]**

These are the Indians of Matto Grosso, São Paulo, and Paraguay. Discussion of several dances and explanations of their meanings. Includes 6 musical themes.

Tastevin, Constant. Les indiens Mura de la région de l'Autaz. *L'anthropologie,* v. 33, nos. 5-6 (1923), p. 509-533. **[1072]**

Dance, musical instruments and 6 chants (translated into French) sung in accompaniment to the dances, p. 518-522.

Whiffen, Thomas. The north-west Amazons: notes of some months spent among cannibal tribes ... London, Constable and company, ltd., 1915. 319 p. il. F2230.W57 **[1073]**

"The two groups [of Indians] with which we are mainly concerned ... are the Witoto and the Boro."—p. 58. Description of music, instruments and dances, p. 190-217.

2. *Instruments*

Bevilacqua, Octavio. A sirinx no Brasil; exame de exemplares pertencentes à coleção do Museo nacional do Rio de Janeiro. *Rev. bras. mús.,* v. 4, no. 1-2 (1937), p. 1-11. **[1074]**

A detailed study, with 23 illustrations.

Enciclopedia universal ilustrada Europeoamericana. Bilbao, Madrid, Barcelona, Espasa-Calpe, s a., 1925. v. 43, A-E61.E6. **[1075]**

Illustrations of primitive musical instruments of Brazil, p. 434. "La música entre los salvajes", p. 433-438.

Giglioli, Enrico H. Due singolarissime

e rare trombe da guerra guernite di ossa umane dell' America meridionale. *Arch. antrop. etnol.*, v. 26 (Florence, 1896), p. 105-112. [1076]

Description of a sacted war-trumpet of bamboo in use among the Yuruna Indians of Brazil, p. 110-112.

Instrumentos de música dos indios. *O Brasil illustrada*, v 1 (31 Aug. 1856), p. 228. [1076x]

Descriptive nomenclature of 16 instruments.

Kissenberth, Wilhelm. Bei den Canella-Indianern in Zentral-Maranhão. *Baes.-Arch.*, v. 2, no. 1 (1911), p. 45-54. [1077]

List of musical instruments with brief descriptions, p. 51.

Koenigswald, Gustav von. Die Coroados in südlichen Brasilien. *Globus*, v. 94 (1908), p. 27-32, 45-59. [1078]

References to musical instruments, p. 48-49, with illustrations, p. 28, 30.

Krause, Fritz. In den wildnissen Brasiliens. Leipzig, R. Voigtländer, 1911. 512 p. il. F2519.K91 [1079]

Music of the Karajá Indians, p. 315-320, with illustrations of trumpets, rattles and other musical instruments. Mentions the poverty of music among these Indians. Short discussion of the musical instruments of the Savajé, p. 365, with one illustration of a flute.

Nordenskiöld, Erland. Forschungen und abenteuer in Südamerika. Stuttgart, Strecker & Schröder, 1924. 338 p. F3-313.N835 [1080]

Musical instruments among the Huari Indians, p. 232; music to a Cavina Indian piece for flute and drums, p. 220-271. For further musical references, see p. 189, 207, 240, for dance, p. 76, 273. Illustrations of musical instruments are plentiful.

Petrullo, Vincent M. Primitive peoples of Matto Grosso. *Museum jour.*, University Museum, Philadelphia, v. 23 (1932), p. 83-173. [1081]

References to musical instruments, p. 160-163.

Ploetz, Hermann, and Alfred Métraux. La civilisation matérielle et la vie sociale et religieuse des Indiens Zé du Brésil méridional et oriental. *Rev. inst. etnol. univ. Tucumán*, v. 1, no. 2 (1930), p 107-238. [1082]

Brief listings of the musical instruments of various Indian tribes, p. 179-180.

(C) AFRO-BRAZILIAN

Aimes, Herbert H. S. African institutions in America. *Jour. Amer. folklore*, v. 18, no. 68 (Jan.-Mar. 1905), p. 15-32. [1083]

Deals with Brazil and West Indies, p. 20-32, depicting historical background of Negro music and dances.

Bittencourt, Dário de. A libertad religiosa no Brasil: A macumba e o ilegalism em face da lei. *In* Congresso afrobrasileiro, Rio de Janeiro, Civilização brasileira s/a, 1940, p. 169-199. F2659.N4-C65 [1084]

Deals with these festivals from the sociological standpoint, rather than the artistic.

Braga, Ernani. Estudos Afro-Brasileiros. Rio de Janeiro, Ed. Ariel, 1935. [1085]

Includes *Toadas de Xangô do Recife*, with notation of 7 tunes.

Carneiro, Edison. Negros Bantus; notas de ethnographia religiosa e de folklore. Rio de Janeiro, Civilização brasileira, s. a., 1937. 187 p. GR133.B6C3 [1086]

Part 2, "Folk-lore", includes descriptions of such Brazilian Negro dances as the *samba*, the *batuque*, etc.

——. Religiões negras; notas de etnografia religiosa. Rio de Janeiro, Civilização brasileira s. a., 1936. 188 p. BL-2490.C3 [1087]

"Os instrumentos musicais dos negros", p. 107-114. "Os canticos dos òrixas", p. 115-126.

——. Structure of African cults in Bahia. *Jour. amer. folklore*, v. 53 (1940), p. 271-278. [1088]

On organization of *candombles* of Negro

religious societies. Useful for social background of Afro-Brazilian music.

Cascudo, Luis da Câmara. Instrumentos negros do nordeste brasileiro. *Movimento brasileiro*, no. 3 (Mar. 1929). **[1089]**
Cited by Renato Almeida [no. 705], p. 13.

Diegues Jr., Manuel. Dansas negras no nordeste. *In* Congresso afro-brasileiro, Rio de Janeiro, Civilização brasileira s/a, 1940, p. 293-302. F2659.N4C65 **[1090]**
Gives the characteristics of the *côco, quilombo, samba do matuto, frêvo;* also a section on the Negro orchestra and instruments.

Dornas Filho, João. A influência social do Négro brasileiro. *Rev. arq. mun. São Paulo*, v. 5, no. 51 (Oct. 1938), p. 97-134. **[1091]**
Description of dances, pictures of musical instruments, song-texts, notation of 6 melodies of dance-songs.

Finck, Gottlob Wilhelm. Etwas über musik und tanz in Brasilien. *Allgem. mus. zeit.*, v. 35, columns 19-21 (Leipzig, 1833). **[1092]**
Brief description of the music and dances of the Negro in Brazil, and of native musical instruments.

Gomes, António Osmar. A vocação musical do mulato. *Rev. Brasil*, v. 2, no. 10 (1939), p. 33-38. **[1093]**
Attributes great importance to the rôle of the mulatto in Brazilian music.

Machado Filho, Aires de Mata. O negro e o garimpo em Minas Gerais. *Rev. arq. mun. São Paulo*, v. 5, no. 61 (1939), p. 259-284. **[1094]**
Includes music and text of 2 religious songs, p. 271-276.

Mendonça, Renato. O negro e a cultura no Brasil. *In* Congresso afro-brasileiro, Rio de Janeiro, Civilização brasileira s/a, 1940, p. 99-125. F2659-N4C65 **[1095]**
Mention of the *cuíca* and the *batuque.*

Pereda Valdés, Ildefonso. Línea de color. Santiago de Chile, Ed. Ercilla, 1938. 248 p. E185.6.P44 **[1096]**
Includes: Dances of the Brazilian Negroes, p. 177-180.

Querino, Manuel Raymundo. Costumes africanos no Brasil. Rio de Janeiro, Civilização brasileira, s. a., 1938. F2659.-N4Q6 **[1097]**
Dos instrumentos musicaes, p. 105-109, with 4 tunes; also 1 tune, p. 59.

Ramos, Arthur. O folk-lore negro do Brasil. Rio de Janeiro. Civilização brasileira, s. a., 1935. 279 p. il. F2659.N4-R28 **[1098]**
Ch. 5, *A sobrevivencia da dansa e da música,* includes 9 Brazilian Negro melodies.

——. O negro brasileiro. 2 ed. São Paulo, Companhia editora nacional, 1940. 434 p. F2659.N4R35 **[1099]**
A dansa e a música dos Candomblés, p. 223-247, with 6 tunes and 2 drum rhythms.

——. The Negro in Brazil. Washington, D. C., The Associated publishers, inc., 1939 203 p. F2659.N4R34 **[1100]**
Includes a chapter on music, instruments and dances. A translation, by Richard Pattee, of the first edition of item no. 1099.

——. Macumba. Religión y ritual de los negros brasileños. *La prensa*, v. 69, no. 24,905 (15 May 1938), sec. 2, p. 6. **[1101]**
Describes various forms of *macumba,* such as the *candomblé, xangó, orixá, terrero.* Includes several excerpts from choruses and an illustration of the drums used in the *macumba* rites.

Rodrigues, Raymundo Nina. Os africanos no Brasil. São Paulo, Companhia editora nacional, 1932. 409 p. F2659.N4-N6 **[1102]**
Treats of music and dances, p. 233-241; see also descriptions of popular festivals, p. 262-274.

Vidal, Ademar. Costumes e práticas do negro. *In* Congresso afro-brasileiro, Rio de)aneiro, Civilização brasileira s/a, 1940, p. 33-58. F2659.N4C65 **[1103]**

There are sections on music and dance, on the *maracatú,* the *butuque* and other festivals.

Walsh, Robert. Notices of Brazil in 1828 and 1829. Boston, Richardson, Lord & Holbrook; New York, G. & C. & H. Carvill, 1831. 2 v. F2513.W22 **[1104]**

In vol. 2: *Imperial constitutional hymn* (with music), appendix 3. Mention of music, p. 62. Negro music in Brazil (with one musical example), detailed description of instruments and dancing, p. 185-187.

(D) DANCES

Almeida, Renato. A dansa dos tapuios, folguedo tradicional Goiano. *Rev. bras. mús.,* v. 2, no. 4 (Sept. 1942), p. 162-169. **[1105]**

A study based on recording made by L. H. Corrêa de Azevedo.

Andrade, Mário de. Os congos. *Bol. lat. am. mús.,* v. 1, no. 1 (Apr. 1935), p. 57-70. **[1106]**

A study of the Brazilian-Negro type of song and dance known as the *congo,* with 5 musical examples (melodies and text). This dance is connected with the custom among the African slaves in America and their descendants of electing a titular king, as though they wished to preserve at least the outward semblance of their ancient tribal traditions. In Brazil this ceremony became blended with certain elements of popular Catholicism, such as the religious processions, but the predominant spirit of the *congos* or *congadas* is strongly fetichist. In its simplest form the *congos* consist of a procession accompanying the newly-elected king interspersed with singing and dancing. A more elaborate form involves the enactment of a dramatic scene, which follows the singing of various songs (*cantigas*). The central episode in this primitive drama is the sending of an embassy from Queen Ginga to the King of the Congo. The ambassador plans to assassinate the king, but he is thwarted, and this leads to a war between the two factions. The action is accompanied by singing and dancing—it is a kind of rudimentary opera. In spite of the African origin of the *con-*

gos, much of the music has definite European characteristics.

———. *Lanterna verde,* Boletím da sociedade Felipe d'Oliveira, no. 2 (Feb. 1935), p. 36-53. **[1107]**

Same as item no. 1106, without musical examples.

———. Danzas dramáticas del Brasil. *Rev. música,* v. 3 (1930), p. 23-26. **[1108]**

———. Origens das danças-dramáticas brasileiras. *Rev. bras. mús.,* v. 2, no. 1 (Mar. 1935), p. 34-39. **[1109]**

Discusses the origins of the traditional Brazilian dramatic dances, such as the *congos,* whose chief musical elements seem to be derived from the *vilhancicos,* the Portuguese popular religious songs. Other influences are the tribal ceremonies of African origin, blended with the traditional Catholic religious processions; and the Iberian pantomimic dances depicting battles between Christians and Moors.

———. Originalidade do maxixe. *Ilus. mus.* (Sept. 1930). **[1110]**

Cited by Almeida [no. 705], p. xv.

———. O samba rural paulista. *Rev. arq. mun. São Paulo,* v. 4, no. 41 (Nov. 1937), p. 37-116. **[1111]**

Choreography of the samba, with many photographs. Includes words and music of songs. Also reprinted separately, together with item no. 989 (cf. item no. 1118).

———. San Paulo. *Rev. música,* v. 1, no. 6 (15 Dec. 1927), p. 122-126. **[1112]**

Describes a popular musical festival in the Amazon basin, near Teffé on the Solimões River. Deals chiefly with the *Ciranda,* a dance with singing, and quotes 3 tunes (in addition to two Swedish folk tunes for comparison).

Braga, Rubem. Um jongo entre os maratimbas. *Rev. arq. mun. São Paulo,* ano 6, v. 66 (Apr.-May 1940), p. 77-80. **[1113]**

The *maratimbas* are fisherfolk on the southern shore of Espirito Santo. Their characteristic dances, here briefly described, are the *catambá* and the *jongo.*

Castle, Vernon and Irene. Modern dancing. New York, Harper and bros., 1914. 176 p. il. GV1751.C35 **[1114]**
Chapter 6, The tango brésilienne or maxixe, p. 107-133.

Cezimba, João Jacques. Assumptos do Rio Grande do Sul. Pôrto Alegre. Officinas gráphicas da Escola de engenharia, 1912. 258 p. il. F2621.C42 **[1115]**
Part 1: Mention of numerous dances, p. 18-19, 59; illustration of people dancing the fandango, opp. p. 18; words and story of *A náu Catarineta,* p. 162-165.

Costa, Luiz Edmundo da. O Rio de Janeiro no tempo dos vice-reis (1763-1808). Rio de Janeiro, Imprensa nacional, 1932. 549 p. il. F2646.C87 **[1116]**
Description of *congadas,* p. 185-196, with illustrations of musicians and dancers.

——. Rio in the time of the viceroys; introduction by Hugh Gibson; translated from the Portuguese, with epilogue, by Dorothea H. Momsen. Rio de Janeiro, Printed by J. R. de Oliveira & cia., 1936. 353 p. il. F2646.C874 **[1117]**
A translation of item 1116.

Cunha, Mario Wagner Vieira da, and Mario de Andrade. Festa de bom Jesus de Pirapora e o samba rural paulista. São Paulo, Departmento de cultura, 1937. ML3575.V54F4 **[1118]**
Two articles reprinted from *Revista do Arquivo municipal* (see items nos. 989 and 1111).

Fereira, Ascenço. O Maracatú. *Arquivos* (Diretoria de estatística, propaganda e turismo, Prefeitura municipal do Recife), ano 1, no. 11 (Nov. 1942), p. 151-163. **[1118x]**
Includes musical examples and illustrations.

Gomes, António Osmar. A chegança. Rio de Janeiro, Livraria civilização brasileira, 1941. 187 p. GV1637.G6 **[1119]**
Often performed at Christmas, the *che-*

gança has come to mean a folkdrama of legendary material centering around the maritime exploits of the early Portuguese colonists. This dance may be related to *Nau Catarineta* (see item no. 970). There are nine pages of music from Penedo (Alagoas), and the text as it is sung in Vilanova (Sergipe).

——. *Rev. acad. letras,* ano 5, v. 12, no. 34 (1941), p. 56-60. **[1120]**
See item no. 1119 for a more detailed study of this subject.

Lamego, Alberto Ribeiro. A planicie do solar e da senzala. Rio de Janeiro, Livraria católica, 1934. 192 p. F2611.R54 **[1121]**
Contains a detailed chapter on folk dances in the State of Rio.

Pires, Cornélio. Danças populares paulistas. *O estado de São Paulo* (5 May 1937). **[1122]**

Saint-Denis, Émile. Au Brésil. Paris, Imprimerie Ernest Flammarion, 1898. 248 p. F2515.S13 **[1123]**
Batuque, p. 106.

Santos, Marciano dos. A dansa de São Gonçalo. *Rev. arq. mun. São Paulo.* v. 33 (1937), p. 85-116. il. **[1124]**
A description of the dance practised in honor of this saint, with diagrams and quotations of verses.

Vidal, Ademar. Dansas rurais paraibanas. *Rev. Brasil,* v. 4, fase 3, no. 39 (Sept. 1941), p. 11-23. **[1125]**
Describes the *figurada,* the *chanchada,* the *xen-en-en,* the *chorado* and *choradinho.*

(E) COLLECTIONS OF MUSIC

Alvarenga, Oneyda. Cateretês do sul de Minas Gerais. Separata da Revista do Arquivo municipal, v. 30. São Paulo, Departamento de cultura, 1937, p. 33-70. MT950.A39C2 **[1126]**
With music (two-part songs). "Bibliografia", p. 69-70.

Barreto, Ceição de Barros. Cantigas de quando eu era pequenina. Rio de Jan-

eiro, Pimento de Mello e cia., 1931. 65
p. M1687.B7B2   [1127]
15 songs for children, collected in
Pernambuco.

Gallet, Luciano. Canções populares brasileiras. Rio de Janeiro, Carlos Wehrs e
cia., n. d.   [1128]
Issued in 2 series, the first containing
6 songs, the second 12; with piano accompaniments.

Gomes Junior, João. Cantigas da minha
terra. São Paulo, Monteiro Lobato &
co., 1924. M1994.G63C3   [1129]
6 songs for 2 and 3 voices, for school
use. Portuguese text.

——. **and João Baptista Juião.** Ciranda, cirandinha ... collecção de cantigas
populares e brinquedos. São Paulo,
Comp. Melhoramentos de S. Paulo,
1924. 39 p. M1687.B7G6   [1130]
A collection of 50 songs for children.

Lozano, Fabiano R. Alegría das escolas,
primeiros passos no ensino natural da
música, aprovado e adotado nos mais
importantes centros educacionais da
união. 21 ed. São Paulo, G. Ricordi &
cia, 1940. 16 p. MT870.L78A6   [1131]

——. Minhas cantigas ... Primeira parte.
5 ed. São Paulo, G. Ricordi & c., 1941.
55 p. M1994.L89M5   [1132]
25 children's songs, arranged for part-
singing.

——. Minhas cantigas ... 2ª parte. 3
ed. São Paulo, G. Ricordi & c., 1941.
55 p. M1994.L89M5   [1133]
25 part-songs for children, of which 15
are of folk origin.

Mendes, Julia de Brito, comp. Canções
populares do Brazil. Rio de Janeiro, J.
Ribeiro dos Santos, 1911. 336 p. M16-
89.B86   [1134]
Melodies unaccompanied; 131 songs with
text and music on opposite pages.

Moraes, Alexandre José de Mello, ed.
Cantares brasileiros. Rio de Janeiro,

Jacintho Ribeiro Santos, 1900. 2 v. M-
1689.M52   [1135]
Contains 87 songs (for voice alone)
written in folk style by various Brazilian
composers. A few songs are anonymous.

Péret, Elsie (Houston), comp. Chants
populaires du Brésil. 1ᵉʳᵉ série. Paris,
P. Geuthner, 1930. 46 p. ML330.MS sér.
1, t. 1   [1136]
With music (unaccompanied melodies).
Words in Portuguese, followed by French
translation. "Nous publions, avec l'aim-
able autorisation de m. Roquette Pinto ... deux chants des Indiens Parecis
extraits de son livre: Rondonia", p. 27.

Villa-Lobos, Heitor. Chansons typiques
brésiliennes depuis les chants indiens
jusqu'aux chansons populaires du carnaval carioca. Paris, Editions Max
Eschig, 1929-30. 10 v. M1690.V
                               [1137]
Ten songs with piano accompaniment.

(F) COLLECTIONS OF TEXTS

Amaral, Amadeu. Cantos de macumba.
Rev. arq. mun. São Paulo, v. 6, no. 68
(1940), p. 201.   [1138]
The words of 4 Brazilian Negro songs
collected in Quintino Bocaiuva.

——. A poesia da viola. São Paulo, Sociedade editora Olegario Ribeiro, 1921.
                               [1139]

Americano do Brazil, A. Cancioneiro de
trovas do Brasil central. S. Paulo, Cia.
gráphico-editora Monteiro Lobato,
1925. 286 p. PQ9660.A6   [1140]
Without music.

Baptista, Francisco das Chagas. Canta-
dores e poetas populares. Parahyba,
F. C. Baptista irmão, 1929. 255 p. ports.
PQ9660.C5   [1141]
An anthology with biographical notices
of the poets.

Barahona y Vega, Clemente. Trovas y
modinhas populares del Brasil. Santiago de Chile, Impr. i lit. Chile, 1903. 49
p. PQ9663.B   [1142]
Spanish translations of Brazilan popular poetry.

Barroso, Gustavo. Ao som do viola (folk-lore). Rio de Janeiro, Leite Ribeiro, 1921. 733 p. GR133.B6B3 [1143]

A collection of folk songs, without music.

Carvalho, Rodrigues de. Cancioneiro do norte. 2 ad. Parahyba do Norte, Livraria São Paulo, 1928. [1144]

Costa, Francisco Augusto Pereira da. Folk-lore pernambucano. Rio de Janeiro, Livraria J. Leite, n. d. 641 p. GR133.B6P43 [1145]

Includes numerous texts of Brazilian folk songs. No music. Bibliography, p. 639-641.

Duque-Estrada, Osorio. Trovas do norte. *An. bibl. nac.,* v. 60 (1923), p. 203-222. [1146]

Goes, Carlos. Mil quadras populares brasileiras. Rio de Janeiro, F. Briguiet e cia, 1916. 246 p. PQ9660.G6 [1147]

Gomes, Lindolfo. Contos populares ... da tradição oral, no estado de Minas. S. Paulo, Comp. melhoramentos de S. Paulo (Weiszflog irmãos incorporada), 1931[?] 2 v. PQ9691.M5G6 [1148]

Vol. 2 includes "cantigas de adormecer" (lullabies).

Gouveia, Daniel. Folk-lore brasileiro. Rio de Janeiro, Paulo, Pongetti & c., 1926. GR133.B6G6 [1149]

Lima, Silvio Julio de Albuquerque. Terra e povo do Ceará. Rio de Janeiro, R. Carvalho & cia., ltda., 1936. 194 p. il. F2556.A36 [1150]

Includes: A musa anónima do Ceará.

Moraes, Alexandre José de Mello. Cancioneiro dos Ciganos. Rio de Janeiro, Ed. Garnier, 1885. [1151]

Motta, Leonardo. Cantadores (poesia e linguagem do sertão cearense). Rio de Janeiro, Castilho, 1921. 398 p. port. PQ9660.M6 [1152]

Motta, Leonardo. Sertão alegre (poesia e linguagem do sertão nordestino). Bello Horizonte, Imprensa official de Minas, 1928. 302 p. PQ9660.M63 [1153]

——. Violeiros do Norte, poesia e linguagem do sertão nordestino. S. Paulo, Cia. gráphico-editora Monteiro Lobato, 1925. 311 p. PQ9660.M64 [1154]

Neto, Simões Lopes. Cancioneiro Guasca. 2nd ed. Pelotas, Livraria universal, 1917. [1155]

Folk poetry collected in Rio Grande do Sul.

Peixoto, Afranio. Missangas; poesia e folklore. São Paulo, Companhia editoria nacional, 1931. 283 p. GR133.B6P4 [1156]

Includes "trovas populares".

——. Trovas populares brasileiras. Rio de Janeiro, F. Alves, 1919. 316 p. PQ9660.P4 [1157]

Pires, Cornelio. Sambas e cateretês (folclore paulista) modas de viola, recortados, quadrinhas, abecês, etc. São Paulo, Gráfico-editora Unitas Limitada [1933?] 352 p. PQ9691.S4P5 [1158]

A study of the folk songs of the rural inhabitants of São Paulo. Without music.

Rebello, Maroquinha Jacobina. Cantares brasileiros. *Rev. inst. hist. geog. bras.,* v. 107, no. 161 (1930), p. 45-76 "Conferencia realisada no Instituto histórico, em 30 de julho de 1928 ..." [1159]

Folk song texts, without commentary.

Ramos, Arthur. O folklore musical no Brasil. *Bol. Ariel,* v. 3 (May 1934), p. 208. [1160]

Discussion of Gallet's *Estudos de folklore.*

Romero, Sylvio. Cantos populares do Brazil ... acompanhados de introducção e notas comparativas por Theophilo Braga. Lisboa, Nova livraria internacional, 1883. 2 v. PQ9680.R7 [1161]

An anthology of folk songs (without music).

——. 2. ed. melhorada. Rio de Janeiro,
S. Paulo, Livraria classica de Alves &
comp., 1897. 377 p. PQ9689.R7, 1897
                                    [1162]
Nos. 77-96 omitted in paging.

Schuller, Rudolph. Native poetry of northern Brazil. *Jour. amer. folklore,* v. 28,
no. 110 (1915), p. 365-375.   [1163]
Contains the text, in Portuguese, of 5
Brazilian folk songs.

Teixeira, José A. Folclore goiano (cancioneiro, lendas, superstição). São
Paulo, Cia. editora nacional, 1941. 434
p.   [1164]

POPULAR MUSIC

Almeida, Renato. História da música
brasileira. 2d. ed. Rio de Janeiro, F.
Briguiet & comp., 1942. 529 p. ML232.-
A62   [1165]
See esp. p. 191-202; also p. 442-443,
444-446, 447.

Barroso, Sebastião M. Música e cultura.
Mens. jour. com., t. 9, v. 2 (Feb. 1940),
p. 275-279.   [1166]
1. A evolução da música a luz de bio-
logía; porque são guerreados os innova-
dores. 2. A música popular como indice da
cultura e da indole de um povo. The second part includes a discussion of Brazilian
popular music.

Iguassu, J. Canções carnavalescas popu-
lares. *Weco* (Jan. 1929), p. 8. [1167]
Citation from personal files of L.-H.
Corrêa de Azevedo.

Lira, Mariza. Brasil sonoro; géneros e
compositores populares. Rio de Janeiro,
Editorial s. a. A Noite [1938?]. 311 p.
ML3575.B7L6   [1168]

——. A característica brasileira nas in-
terpretações de Callado. *Rev. bras. mús.,*
v. 7, no. 3 (1941), p. 210-218. [1169]
Joaquim Antônio da Silva Callado was a
flutist and the leader of the most celebrated *chôro* (popular instrumental ensemble) in Rio during the second half of the
19th century. He died in 1880, at the age

of 32. Callado composed a *Lundú caracte-
rístico* and other pieces and songs.

Moreira, Lopes. Ernesto Nazareth e suas
composições de música popular brasileira. *Aspectos,* v. 5, no. 35 (1941), p.
57-59.   [1170]
Nazareth was the creator of the Brazilian tango. This article describes his pianistic technique, and points out that Nazareth did not merely imitate the popular
forms, but succeeded in transferring their
spirit integrally to the piano.

Músicas do carnaval do Rio de Janeiro.
Carnival songs of Rio de Janeiro. Rio
de Janeiro, Directoria de turismo e propaganda da Prefeitura do distrito federal, 1936. 28 p. il. M1689.M98
                                      [1171]
Music for piano by various composers,
in popular style; song text (in Portuguese,
English and Spanish) printed at end of
each piece. English version by Nick
Lamer.

Rothe, Friede F. Carnival in Rio. *Mus.
Amer.,* v. 61, no. 4 (25 Feb. 1941), p.
6-7. il.   [1172]
Traces the historical background of the
Carnival and mentions some of the prin-
cipal composers of Carnival music.

——. The popular music of Brazil—
Romeo Silva and his band. *Brazil*
(New York), no. 139 (June 1940), p.
12-16.   [1173]
Includes brief descriptions of Brazilian
popular songs and dances, such as the
samba, carioca, embolada, etc.

Tigre, Heitor Bastos. Carnival in Brazil. *Bull. pan amer. union,* v. 73, no. 11
(1939), p. 649-651.   [1174]
Includes words and music of the carnival song. *Rio, the marvelous City,* by
André Filho.

COLLECTIONS OF MUSIC
(GENERAL)

Album musical; composições de autores
Rio-grandense-do-sul. Pôrto Alegre,
Departamento central de organização

do bicentenario de Pôrto Alegre, 1940. 31 p. M1.A6325 **[1175]**

Contents: *Noturno* for violin and piano, by Antônio T. Corte-Real; *Tarde*, for piano, by Armando Albuquerque; *Meu clarim, meu tambor*, for voice and piano, by Enio de Freitas e Castro; *Oração á Teinaguá*, for violin and piano, by Luiz Cosme; *Paginas do sul* for piano, by Nato Henn; *Noturno*, for piano, by Paulo Guedes; *Arlequinade*, for violin and piano, by Walter Schultz. These are effective and well-soundling compositions, the piece by Cosme presenting the most marked Brazilian characteristics. Corte-Real and Guedes follow post-romantic tendencies, while Albuquerque shows the influence of Debussy. Freitas e Castro and Henn appear to draw upon folkloristic elements.

Andrade, Mário de. Mondinhas imperiaes; ramilhete de 15 preciosas modinhas de salão brasileiras, de tempo do imperio, para canto e piano, seguidas por um delicado lundú para pianoforte, cuidadosamente escolhidas, prefaciadas, anotadas, e dedicadas al seu ilustre e genial amigo, o maestre Heitor Villa-Lobos ... São Paulo, Casa Chiarato, 1930. **[1176]**

Moreno, José Alves. Hymnos escolares ... Collecção apresentada com a respectiva música ao concurso aberto no Pedagogium pela inspectoria da instrução pública. Rio de Janeiro, Buschmann & Guimarães, n. d. **[1177]**

Late 19th century edition of school songs.

Musique brésilienne moderne. Rio de Janeiro, 1937. 100 p. **[1177x]**

Edited by Andrade Muricy. Compositions for piano, and for voice and piano, by modern Brazilians. For further comment, see item no. 769.

Piano music of Brazil. *New music*, v. 16, no. 1 (Oct. 1942). **[1178]**

Contains musical compositions of Oscar Lorenzo Fernândez, Radames Gnattali, Heitor Villa-Lobos, Francisco Mignone. Edited by Nicolas Slonimsky.

SUPPLEMENT to 1960

TWO books by Luiz Heitor Corrêa de Azevedo have particularly enriched the musical bibliography of Brazil during the past decade. The first of these, titled *Música e músicos do Brasil (história — crítica — comenários)*, was published in 1950 and is a collection of articles written by the author over a period of fiteen years, plus some material drawn from the MS. of a work in preparation called *Música nativa (etnografia e folclore)*. In spite of its miscellaneous character, the book is carefully organized to present a panorama of Brazilian musical activity from the 18th century to the presnet. The author maintains that "It is in music, among all artistic activities, that the Brazilian genius succeeded in achieving something strongly original and differentiated from European models".

This book is divided into four main parts. The first consists of three introductory essays dealing with the foundations of musical culture in Brazil. Part II, titled "Past and Present", covers a wide range of topics, such as opera, musical periodicals, religious music, and the teaching of composition. Part III, "Composers and their works", is the most extensive section, dealing with Brazilian composers from José Mauricio Nunes Garcia to Hans Joachim Koellreutter. The final section, "Musical Life", deals mainly with various efforts to raise the level of musical activity in Brazil, such as the founding of the Associação Brasileira de Música, the organization of symphonic concerts, and opera at the Municipal Theatre of Rio de Janeiro.

The second work by Luiz Heitor, titled *150 anos de música no Brasil* (1800-1950), covers somewhat the same ground as the preceding, but in a more systematic maner and with more emphasis opon musical composition. Part I deals with the 19th century, Part II with the 20th. Separate chapters in Part II are devoted to Villa-Lobos, Luciano Gallet ("um compositor em busca de folklore"), Oscar Lorenzo Fernândez (who died in 1948), and Camargo Guarnieri ("A transfiguração da música brasileira na obra de C. G."). The Bibliography is preceded by an introductory note on musicology in Brazil. There are ten classified indices, ranging from Composers to Manufacturers of Musical Instruments.

To these works must be added the important *Bibliografia musical brasileira* (1820-1950), compiled by Luiz Heitor in collaboration with Cleofe Person de Matos and Mercedes de Moura Reis, published in 1952 (item no. 334a).

Vasco Mariz' useful little book, *A canção de câmara no Brasil*, published in 1948, has been superseded by the same author's larger and more comprehensive work, *A canção brasileira* (erudita, folclórica e popular), published in 1959 (item no. 361a). Whereas the first version of this book dealt exclusively with the art-song, the revised work covers in addition folk and popular song. Thus the new work is brought into line with the prevailing norm of Brazilian musicology, which might well serve as a model to the rest of America for the attention it has always given to folklore and popular currents and their relation to art music. As indicated by the subject matter, the book falls into three parts: I, A canção erudita; II, A canção folclórica; III, A canção popular. The first and third receive more extensive coverage than the second. The book includes useful appendices, including a selected list of recordings, a "Selected repertoire of the principal composers", and a reprint of the "Normas para a boa pronuncia da lingua nacional no canto erudito", as adopted by the Primeiro Congresso da Lingua Nacional Cantada at São Paulo in 1937 (cf. item no. 933). This is a valuable contribution to Brazilian musical history and criticism, especially because, in the words of Luiz Heitor, it is in its song literature "that Brazilian music has found its moments of most intimate and effective lyricism, at times its moments of profoundest national affirmation".

For a thorough and systematic account of Brazilian folk music, illustrated with numerous musical notations, we must turn to the work by Oneyda Alvarenga titled *Música popular brasileña* (no. 272a), commissioned by the Fondo de Cultura Económica of Mexico, and therefore originally published in Spanish (in 1947). Here, also, we encounter the troublesome problem posed by the use of the term "popular music" (especially prevalent in French and Spanish terminology) to signify what in English is generally called "folk music". Alvarenga's book, in effect, deals largely with "folk music", although there is a section titled "Música popular urbana" that treats of popular urban types of music, such as the *modinha,* the *maxixe,* and the *samba.* The author divides her subject matter into the following categories: Dramatic Dances; Dances (non-dramatic); Religious music; Work songs; Games; "Cantos puros" (i. e., non-functional); and, as already mentioned, "Música popular urbana". There is a descriptive vocabulary of musical instruments of Portugal and Brazil, a valuable bibliography, a synoptic table of contents, but no index. There are 52 photographic plates illustrating dances and musical instruments. The work is a model of its kind.

With the death of Heitor Villa-Lobos on November 17, 1959, Brazil lost its greatest composer and the world one of the most famous musicians of our time. The biography by Vasco Mariz (item no. 364a), and the essay by Carleton Sprague Smith accompanying the catalog of the composer's works issued by the Pan American Union (item no. 382a), are to date the most comprehensive sources for information about Villa-Lobos and his music. It is discouraging to report that the writer of these lines made numerous and prolonged efforts to find an American publisher who might be interested in bringing out an English translation of Mariz's book on Villa-Lobos, but without success. A biography in English of this great composer is certainly needed.

BIBLIOGRAPHY

A. PRIMITIVE, FOLK, AND POPULAR MUSIC.

A escola nacional de música e as pesquisas de folclore musical no Brasil. Rio de Janeiro, Publicação No. 1 do Centro de pesquisas folclóricas da escola nacional de música, 1943. 43 p. [267a]

Includes the program of the course in national folklore (of Brazil), a description of the Center of folklore research, "Instructions for the collecting of recordings of Brazilian folk music" by Alan Lomax, and a similar set of instructions, designed specifically for the Center in Rio de Janeiro, compiled by Luiz Heitor Corrêa de Azevedo (who also wrote the introduction).

Almeida, Renato. Brazilian folk patterns.

Américas, v. 4, no. 3 (Mar. 1952), p. 28-30, 39. [268a]

On the First Congress of Brazilian Folklore, held in Rio de Janeiro in August 1951, called by the Brazilian Committee for UNESCO, and presided over by Almeida. Brief description of dances performed: *cururú, pau-de-fita, cateretê, batuque, capoeira de Angola.* Photographs of *pau-de-fita* and *capoeira de Angola.* (B. K.)

Alvarenga, Oneyda. Catalogo ilustrado do museu folclórico. São Paulo, Departamento de cultura, 1950. 295 p. il. (Arquivo folclórico da Discoteca publica municipal, v. 2). [269a]

Copiously illustrated with photographs of objects associated with fetish cults of Brazil, including musical instruments, and objects pertaining to popular dramatic dances and popular festivals, also including musical instruments. Much valuable information is contained in the descriptive notes. Bibliography, p. xv-xviii. Thoroughly indexed. A work of impressive scope and quality, dedicated to the memory of Mário de Andrade.

——. Catimbó. Registros sonoros de folclore musical brasileiro, III. Discos FM 28 to FM 38. São Paulo. Prefeitura do município de São Paulo. Secretaria de educação e cultura. Departamento de cultura. Divisão cultural. Discoteca pública municipal, 1949. 217 p.   [270a]

——. Melodias registradas por meios não-mecânicos. São Paulo, Departamento de cultura, 1946 (publ. in 1948). 480 p. il. (incl. music) (Arquivo folclórico da Discoteca pública municipal, v. 1)   [271a]

Contains material collected from 1936 to 1938, consisting of the following collections: Mário de Andrade, Oneyda Alvarenga, Camargo Guarnieri, and Martin Braunweiser (names of the collectors). A total of 570 melodies, without accompaniment, classified by kinds. Numerous informative notes, and copious indices.

——. Música popular brasileña. Colección Tierra firme, 33. Traducción de José Lión Depetre. México-Buenos Aires, Fondo de cultura económica, 1947. 272 p. il. (music).   [272a]

The head of the Discoteca Pública Municipal of São Paulo methodically covers the whole field of Brazilian folk and popular music, including dances, religious music, work and play songs, and urban popular music, such as maxixe, samba, chôro, marcha, frêvo. There is a useful nomenclature of musical instruments in Brazil, and a seven-page bibliography. Illustrated with 52 plates and 121 musical examples. The book is dedicated to Mário de Andrade, who provided many of the musical examples and other previously unpublished documentation.

——. Tambor-de-mina e Tambor-de-crioulo. Registros sonoros de folclore musical brasileiro, II. Discos FM. 15 to 28A. São Paulo. Prefeitura do município de São Paulo. Departamento de

cultura, discoteca pública municipal, 1948. 92 p.   [273a]

——. Xangô. Registros sonoros de folclore musical brasileiro, I. Discos FM. 1 to 14. São Paulo. Prefeitura do município de São Paulo. Departamento de cultura, discoteca pública municipal, 1948. 149 p.   [274a]

The first in a series of monographs in which the distinguished director of the Discoteca Municipal sets forth the texts and other pertinent information related to the collection of recordings of Brazilian folk music in that institution. Musical transcriptions are not included. The material was collected in 1938 by the "Missão de pesquisas folclóricas" headed by Mario de Andrade.

Araújo, Alceu Maynard. Folia de Reis de Cunha. Rev. mus. paulista, nova série, v. 3 (1949), p. 413-464.   [275a]

Complete folklore study of nativity celebration, based upon field observation in 1944 and 1947. 6 music notations, 22 excellent plates, some of musical instruments and musicians. Preface by Renato Almeida. (C. S.)

Azevedo, Luiz Heitor Corrêa de. A "catira" em Golás. Cult. polít., v. 4, no. 36 (Jan. 1944), p. 232-237.   [276a]

The catira or cateretê is a dance not of African but of Amerindian provenience. The argument is based on close analysis of the music and choreography.

——. A escola nacional de música e as pesquisas de folclore musical no Brasil. Cult. polít., v. 3, no. 30 (1943), p. 153-155.   [277a]

On its teaching of folklore, on trips to Goiáz and Ceará where 18 and 75 disc recordings were made, and on plans for collecting, analyzing and classifying folk music recordings by disc or ms., musical instruments, films and photographs of instruments and dances, and bibliography. (R. S. B.)

——. A "moda de viola" no Brasil central. Cult. polít., v. 3, no. 32 (1943), p. 181-184.   [278a]

Brief indications of character of this music of northern São Paulo, western

Minas, southern Mato Grosso and Goiáz, sung by 2 voices or more, accompanied by this string instrument. The "moda" is a ballad (kind of folk newspaper) or folksong (sentimental lyrics) whose music does not follow precisely its melodic line or tempo. (R. S. B.)

——. Côcos de jangadeiros *Cult. polít.,* v. 4, no. 43 (Aug. 1944), p. 239-244.
[279a]

Analysis of four records in the Center of Folklore Research of the National School of Music, made from the rendition of two informants in Ceará. The *cantoria* of the *sertão* are contrasted with the *cocos* of the *praia.* Music takes a second place in the former, a first in the latter. Five notations. (C. S.)

——. La Escuela nacional de música y el folklore musical del Brasil. *Bol. Unión Panamer.,* v. 79, no. 3 (March 1944), p. 152-153.
[280a]

——. Música negra do nordeste. *Cult. polít.,* v. 5, no. 48 (Jan. 1945), p. 183-186.
[281a]

Of the 75 discs recorded by the author in the state of Ceará, 18, comprising 74 items, are positively of Negro origin. There are 9 discs of *Congos,* 7 of *Maracatus,* 2 of *Toadas de Xangô.* (C. S.)

——. Música popular nordestina. *Cult. polít.,* v. 4, no. 40 (May 1944), p. 233-236.
[282a]

Account of a sound-recording collection expedition made by the author and his assistant, Eurico Nogueira França, early in 1943. 75 twelve-inch discs were cut. The recordings were fully documented. (C. S.)

——. O "recortado" na "moda" goiana. *Cult. polít.,* v. 3, no. 33 (Oct. 1943), p. 201-203.
[283a]

——. Violas de Godaz. *Cult. polít.,* v. 3, no 34 (Nov. 1943), p. 293-296.
[284a]

Bettencourt, Gaston de. Flagrantes do folclore do Brasil. Coimbra, Coimbra Editora, 1954. 123 p.
[285a]

The author is a Portuguese student of Brazilian culture. This volume includes a section on "Os desafios, as emboladas", p. 55-60. Also the article "Alguma coisa" by

Mário de Andrade, reprinted from *Correio da Manhã* (Jan. 14, 1945), re Portuguese survivals in Brazilian folklore, especially in children's singing games (p. 118-123).

Braga, Levi. Trovas brasileiras. *Rev. bras.,* v. 6, no. 18 (Dec. 1946), p. 65-82.
[286a]

A comparative study of the words only of 10 Brazilian folk songs. (C. S.)

Brufatto, Wanny. Festa do santo rei ou dos tres reis magos. *Rev. arq. mun. S. Paulo,* v. 15, no. 119 (July-Sept. 1948), p. 45-50.
[287a]

Description of the "festa" as observed in the state of Minas Gerais, with music notations.

Cabral, Osvaldo R. As danças de congos no sul do Brasil. *Prov. S. Pedro,* no. 15 (1951), p. 102-105.
[288a]

African dance survivals in southern Brazil. (R. Dimmick).

Carneiro, Edison. Candomblés da Bahia. Coleção mundo brasileiro, no. 2. 2 ed. (revised and amplified). Rio de Janeiro, Editorial Andes, n. d. (1954), 239 p. il.
[289a]

The author's purpose in this book has been to summarize the results of many year's research, in language accessible to the lay reader, without footnotes, and with no technical complications of any kind. The result is a work of "vulgarisation" in the best sense of the term. The subject is clearly and methodically treated, and the 14 line drawings by Caribé are both attractive and useful as documentation. Also useful is the vocabulary of terms used in the *candomblés* of Bahia.

Caribé. Candomblés of Bahia. *Américas,* v. 11, no. 1 (Jan. 1959), p. 16-19
[290a]

A popular treatment of the Afro-Bahian cults and their music, illustrated with interesting photographs.

Centro de pesquisas folclóricas Mário de Andrade. Folclore nacional; referências sôbre fatos folclóricos de interesse musical apresentados em trabalhos realizados pela classe de 1945 e durante o ano de 1946. São Paulo, Conservatório dramático e musical de São Paulo, 1946 and 1947. 40 and 48 p. (music) **[291a]**

Chiarini, João. Cururu. *Rev. arq. mun. S. Paulo*, v. 13, no. 115 (July-Sep. 1947), p. 81-198. **[292a]**

Description of these poetic song contests. Brief information upon instruments and their players, 6 music notations, Many photographs of contestants, some with instruments (*viola* and *violão*). 2 drawings of instrumentalists. Also issued separately. (C. S.)

Cunha, Euclydes da. Os sertões (campanha de Canudos). Rio de Janeiro, Livraria Francisco Alves, Paulo de Azevedo & C., 1942 (16. edição corregida). 646 p. il. maps. **[293a]**

This classic of Brazilian literature, first published in 1902, contains reference to Brazilian dances and to the *desafios*, p. 130-132.

Ferreira, Noemia. Congada de S. Tomás de Aquino (Minas Gerais). *Rev. arq. mun. S. Paulo*, ano 15, no. 119 (July-Sept. 1948), p. 42-45. **[294a]**

Description of this dramatic dance as observed in the state of Minas Gerais, with music notations.

Giménez, Maria de Lourdes. Congada de Sorocaba (S. Paulo). *Rev. arq. mun. S. Paulo*, ano 15, v. 119 (July-Sept. 1948), p. 30-42. **[295a]**

Description of this dramatic dance as observed in the state of São Paulo, with music notations .

Guedes, Paulo Luiz Vianna. A gaita na música rio-grandense. *Prov. S. Pedro*, no. 1 (June 1945), p. 117-118. **[296a]**

Brief report upon the displacement of the viola (violão, guitar) by the harmonica, which appeared in Rio Grande about 1836. It has had a profound influence upon the folk-popular music of the state. (C. S.)

Herskovits, Melville J. Drums and drummers in Afro-Brazilian cult life. *Mus. quart.*, v. 30, no. 4 (Oct. 1944), p. 477-492. **[297a]**

Based on field work carried out during

1941-42 in Bahia, under a grant from the Rockefeller Foundation. The article gives authoritative account of the drums, the drum-playing, and the religious-social backgrounds of Afro-Brazilian cult music. There are 3 photographs of drummers, and important bibliographical footnotes.

——, **and Richard A. Waterman.** Música de culto afrobahiana. *Rev. estud. mus.*, v. 1, no. 2 (1949), p. 65-127. **[298a]**

The text of this important study is by Herskovits, the musicological analysis by Waterman. The latter also provides 22 musical notations and a table of scales. The data are based on field recordings made by M. J. and F. S. Herskovits in Bahia, Brazil, in 1941-42, in cooperation with the Museu do Estado de Bahia (Salvador). Some of the musical transcriptions are very extensive. The translation into Spanish is by Francisco Curt Lange.

Itiberê, Brasilio. Ernesto Nazareth na música brasileira. *Bol. lat. am. mús.*, v. 6, 1946, p. 300-321. **[299a]**

Sensitive evaluation of the work of this Cariocan composer of popular music (1863-1934). About a dozen music examples, portrait, and several covers. (C. S.)

Lessa, Juiz Carlos. Dancing gauchos. *Américas*, v. 5, no. 2 (Feb. 1953), p. 16-19, 46. **[300a]**

About gaucho dances by Uruguayan and Brazilian gauchos. Details of costumes, gaucho life and function of dancing in it, history, names and descriptions of dances. Four song texts, no music. Five photographs of dances as seen at folk festival in Porto Alegre, Rio Grande do Sul, Brazil.

Lessa, Barbosa. Dancing for St. Benedict; little-known festival of rural Brazil. *Américas*, v. 8, no. 7 (July 1956), p. 11-16. **[301a]**

General remarks on festivals in Brazil, then on Brazilian celebrations of the Feast of St. Benedict, patron saint of the Negroes. Much detail on customs in Aparecida do Norte, halfway between Rio and São Paulo. Nine song texts, in Portuguese and English translation. No music. Ten photographs.

Lima, Rossini Tavares de. Melodia e rítmo no folclore de São Paulo. São

Paulo, Ricordi, n. d. (1954). 143 p. il. (music). [302a]

Deals with the following forms: *cururu, jandango, cateretê, batuque, samba, jongo*. In each case, rhythms are analysed and graphically illustrated. Numerous melodies and song texts are given. The appendices include notes on the indigenous musical instruments of the state of São Paulo; observations on the tuning of the ten-stringed guitar; and photographs of musical instruments.

———. Mitos do estado de S. Paulo e congada de Piracaia. *Rev. arq. mun. São Paulo*, v. 15, no. 119 (1948), p. 1-50. [303a]

Contains 5 music notations, and also separate studies: *Congada de Sorocaba*, by Maria de Lourdes Giménez, with 9 music notations; *Congada de S. Tomás de Aquino*, by Noëmia Ferreira, with 9 music notations; *Festa do Santo Rei* and *Dos três reis magos* (from Minas Gerais) by Wanny Bruffato, with two music notations. (C. S.)

———. Nótulas sobre pesquizas de folclore musical. São Paulo, Ed. Artes gráf. Mangiones, 1945. 39 p. [304a]

Brief introduction on the theory of folklore, with paragraphs on various song forms. 32 music notations. Nos. 16-23 are variants of a single four-measure pattern. Most were collected by students of Conservatório Dramático e Musical de São Paulo.

Melo, Veríssimo de. Rondas infantis brasileiras. *Rev. arq. mun. São Paulo*, v. 19, no. 155 (Jan.-Mar 1953), p. 227-356. [305a]

Study of children's round dances (texts and music), objective, well documented, with some attempt to indicate the origin and distribution of the material gathered by the author. (R. E. D.)

Meyer, Augusto. Cancionero gaúcho. Seleção de poesia popular com notas e um suplemento musical. Coleção provincia vol. 2. Rio de Janeiro, Editora Globo, 1952. XIII, 238 p. (music). [306a]

The Notes contain interesting data on traditional dances and songs. The musical supplement contains 7 examples. There is also a useful bibliography.

———. Introdução ao estudo do cancioneiro gaúcho. *Prov. S. Pedro*, no. 4 (Mar. 1946), p. 24-37. [307a]

Informed discussion. Several texts but no music.

Miranda, Nicanor. Achegas ao folclore musical do Brasil. *Rev. arq. mun. São Paulo*, v. 12, no. 105 (Oct.-Dec. 1945), p. 41-61. [308a]

Informative and reflective. Notations of 5 songs. Two of them given also in arrangement for piano and voice by Martin Braunwieser, collaborating with the author. (C. S.)

———. A marujada. São Paulo, Departamento de cultura, 1940. 28 p. il. (music) (Publ. da Divisão de educação e recreio, no. 11). [309a]

Originally published in *Anais do congresso da lingua nacional cantada*. This traditional dramatic dance, also known as *A nau catarineta*, is described as presented by children in the playgrounds of São Paulo in 1937. Words and music of the songs.

Morais Filho, Melo. Festas e tradições populares do Brasil. 3 ed. Revisão e notas de L. da Camara Cascudo. Rio de Janeiro, F. Briguiet & Cia., 1946. xvi, 551 p. il. [310a?]

O negro no Brasil; trabalhos apresentados ao 2º congresso afro-brasileiro (Bahia). Rio de Janeiro, Civilização brasileira, 1940, 367 p. (Bibliotheca de divulgação scientifica, v. 20). [311a]

Includes 23 papers by various authors, many of them dealing with beliefs, customs, witchraft, folk medicine, folk dances, and other aspects of the folklore of the Negroes in Brazil. (R. S. B.)

Peixe, Guerra. Maracatús do Recife. São Paulo, *Ricordi*, n. d. (1955). 163 p. il. [312a]

The Brazilian composer-turned-folklorist has made a careful and thoroughly documented study of this popular form in the state of Recife, especially valuable for its illustration and analysis of rhythmic patterns. There are numerous musical examples, some charts and drawings, a few photographs, and a bibliography.

Pires, Armando S. Rio and Tin Pan Alley. *Américas*, v. 5, no. 8 (Aug. 1953), p. 9-11, 45.·   **[313a]**

Vivid comparison of lyrics of popular songs in Brazil and those popular in the United States, with some reference to popular songs in the rest of Latin America. No music. (7 photographs).

Prado, José Nascimento de Almeida. Cantadores paulistas de porfia ou desafio. *Rev. arq. mun. S. Paulo*, v. 13, no. 115, (July-Sep. 1947), p. 199-254.   **[314a]**

Description of these question-and-answer contests. Information upon singers of songs, but no musicological analysis. 3 music notations. One illustration of names of strings of *viola*. (C. S.)

———. Trabalhos fúnebres na roça. *Rev. arq. mun. S. Paulo*, v. 13, no. 115, (July-Sep. 1947), p. 11-80.   **[315a]**

Mainly a folklore study, with 58 music notations, but without musicological analysis. This monograph won first prize in a contest held by the Discoteca Pública Municipal of São Paulo in 1946. (C. S.)

Ramos, Arthur. O folclore negro do Brasil. Demopsicologia e psicanalise. 2 ed. Revised. Rio de Janeiro, Livraria-editora da casa do estudante do Brasil, n. d. [1954], 264 p.   **[316a]**

A new edition of this important work by Arthur Ramos (1903-1949), which is indispensable for the sociocultural background of Afro-Brazilian music.

Ribeiro, Darcy. Religião e mitologia Kadiuéu. Rio de Janeiro, Serviço de Proteção aos Índios (Publ. no. 106), 1950. 222 p., plates and musical socres.   **[317a]**

Comprehensive account, based on field work. (C. B. Stout)

Rodrigues, Nina. Os africanos no Brasil. Revisão e prefácio de Homero Pires. 3-ed. São Paulo, Companhia editora nacional, 1945. 435 p. il. (Biblioteca pedagógica brasileira, sér. 5: Brasiliana, v. 9).   **[318a]**

Mentions Negro dances in the northeast of Brazil (p. 251) and refers to following musical instruments used therein; *atabaque*,

canzá, marimbao, matungo, pandeiro, berimbao. Includes detailed description of the *reisado*, followed by discussion of other Afro-Brazilian dances and festivals.

Salazar, Adolfo. "La música popular brasileña." *Nuestra música*, v. 3, no. 9 (19), p. 37-44.   **[319a]**

Detailed and favorable review of the book by Oneyda Alvarenga (q. v.).

Schmidt, Max. Los kayabías en Matto Grosso, Brasil. *Revista de la Sociedad científica del Paraguay*, Asunción, v. 5, no. 6 (1942), p. 1-34. (il).   **[320a]**

Includes description of musical instruments.

Smith, Carleton Sprague. Brazil in songs. *Brazil*, New York, v. 23, no. 3 (March 1949), p. 3-6, 17-18.   **[321a]**

The author, who knows Brazil well, has divided the country into different sections and discusses the songs of each region separately. Includes a list of recordings of Brazilian music available at the time of publication.

Souza, Déa de. Manifestações musicais indígenas. *Brasil mus.*, v. 1, no. 10 (Dec. 1945), p. 18-20.   **[322a]**

Brief descriptions of 31 instruments written under guidance of Luiz Heitor. Nine drawings. (C. S.)

B. ART MUSIC AND MISCELLANEOUS

Almeida, Fernando Mendes de. Histórico do Conservatório dramático e musical de São Paulo (1906-1931) organizado para o relatorio de 1931. São Paulo, Typographia Fiume, 1932 (?). 42 p. il.   **[323a]**

Alvarenga, Oneyda. A discoteca pública municipal. São Paulo, Departamento de cultura, 1942. 98 p. il. (Separata da Revista do Arquivo municipal, no. 87   **[324a]**

A general survey with detailed information on the organization of the "Discoteca". Includes statistical data.

Andrade, Mário de. Música del Brasil. Traducción de Delia Bernabó. Buenos

Aires, Ed. Schapire, 1944. 128 p. il. (Col. Alba, 17). **[325a]**

Spanish translation of a brilliant synthesis of the history of music in Brazil.

——. Pequena história da música. 4 ed. (Obras completas, VIII), São Paulo, Livraria Martins Editora S. A., n. d. [1935]. il. (music). **[326a]**

4th edition of this work, published as Volume VIII of "Obras Completas de Mário de Andrade". Contains 2 chapters on Brazilian music, one on "Música erudita", and one on "Música popular".

Azevedo, Luiz Heitor Corrêa de. 150 anos de musica no Brasil (1800-1950). (Coleção documentos brasileiros). Rio de Janeiro, Livraria José Olympio Editôra, 1956. 423 p. **[327a]**

An historical account of musical composition in Brazil during the 19th and 20th centuries, from José Mauricio to the group "Música Viva". An appendix deals with "A musicografia no Brasil", being a summary of publications on the musical history of Brazil. There is a useful index broken down into ten categories, such as composers, interpreters, schools, organizations, periodicals, publishers, with subdivisions for Brazilian and foreign entries.

——. La música en el Brasil. *Cuad. amer.*, v. 33, no. 3 (May-June 1947), p. 250-273. **[328a]**

——. Música e músicos do Brasil. História — crítica — comentários. Rio de Janeiro, Livraria editôra da casa do estudiante do Brasil, 1950. 410 p. (music). **[329a]**

A miscellany consisting largely of previously published articles and the texts of lectures and speeches. The author states that all the texts have been revised for this volume and that he has endeavoured to organize the material methodically. The book is divided into 4 parts: I, Introduction; II, Past and Present; III, Composers and their works; IV, Muscial life. It includes 46 muical examples. In spite of its miscellaneous character, this is a useful and valuable compendium. In his preface, the author tells us that this is one of 3 books that he is planning to publish, the second dealing with Brazilian "Native Music" (ethnology and folklore), the third with music outside of Brazil and with musical matters

in general (all based on previously published articles).

——. O espírito religioso na obra de José Mauricio. *Brasil mus.*, no. 22 (May-June 1947), p. 9-10. **[330a]**

Critical study of the composer's life as a basis for the evaluation of his compcsitions.

——. O padre José Mauricio. *Brasil mus.*, v. 1, no. 6 (June-July 1945), p. 5, 48. **[331a]**

Biographical informaiton on the composer. The author rectifies the date of birth of the composer, on information given to him by Cleofe Person de Matos.

——. Os hinos cívicos do Brasil. *Cult. polít.*, v. 2, no. 22 (Dec. 1942), p. 166-168. **[332a]**

——. Sigismund Neukomm, an Austrian composer in the new world. *Mus. quart.*, v. 45, no. 4 (Oct. 1959), p. 473-483. il. (port.) **[333a]**

Neukomm went to Rio de Janeiro in 1816 and remained there until 1821.

——, with Cleofe Person de Matos and Mercedes de Moura Reis. Bibliografía musical brasileira (1820-1950). Rio de Janeiro, Ministerio de educação e saúde, Instituto do livro, 1952. 252 p. il. (Coleça B I, *Bibliografía*, ix). **[334a]**

Balliet, Carl, jr. Brazilian man of music. Dynamic composer-conductor Heitor Villa-Lobos sponsors national musical awakening. *Int. Amer.*, v. 3, no. 1 (Jan. 1944), p. 25-27, 47.

Baptista, João. Villa-Lobos. *Brasil mus.*, v. 1, no. 4 (Feb.-Mar. 1945), p. 29-35.

Newsy, but nonetheless a document. (C. S.)

Barreto, Ceição de Barros. Estudo sôbre hinos e bandeirado Brasil. Rio de Janeiro, Carlos Wehrs, 1943. 72 p. il. **[337a]**

Numerous music examples including anthems by Francisco Manoel da Silva, Francisco Braga, Dom Pedro I and Leopoldo Miguez.

Bevilacqua, Octavio. Música sacra de alguns autores brasileiros. *Bal. lat. am. mús.,* v. 6, 1946, p. 331-355.   **[338a]**
24 music examples of José Mauricio, Glauco Velásquez, and others down to Villa-Lobos. Informative. (C. S.)

Boletín latino-americano de música. Suplemento musical, v. 6. Rio de Janeiro, Imprenta Nacional, 1946. 167 p. il.   **[339a]**
Concert works by Brazilian composers Francisco Braga, Heitor Villa-Lobos, Fructuoso Vianna, César Guerra Peixe, Jayme Ovalle, Radamés Gnattali, Oscar Lorenzo Fernández, J. Vieira Brandão, Iberê Lemos, Paulo Silva, Claudio Santoro, Luís Cosme, Francisco Mignone, José Siqueira, Camargo Guarnieri, Brasílio Itiberê, Arthur Pereira, Dinorá de Carvalho.

Diégues Júnior, Manuel. Duels in verse; rural Brazilian troubadours. *Américas,* v. 10, no. 6 (June 1958), p. 29-32.   **[340a]**
On the folk poet-singers of the Brazilian Northeast. 11 song texts. No music. Three photographs, the men nearly all holding musical instruments.

Downes, Olin. Hector (*sic*) Villa-Lobos. *The New York Times,* Music Section, Sunday, Dec. 17, 1944.
"Visiting Brazilian composer discusses sources of nationalism in art."

Estrela, Arnaldo. Música de câmara no Brasil. *Bol. lat. am. mús.,* v. 6, 1946, p. 255-281.   **[342a]**
Concise and informative account of principal composers from Oswald to Cosme. Many music notations. (C. S.)

Fernández, Oscar Lorenzo. A contribuição harmônica de Villa-Lobos para a musica brasileira. *Bol. lat. am. mús.,* v. 6, 1946, p. 283-300.   **[343a]**
85 music notations illustrative of the composer's practice. Influences and tendencies are discerned, but no particular system. (C. S.)

França, Eurico Nogueira. A música no Brasil. Rio de Janeiro, Ministério da educação e saúde. Serviço de documentação, n. d. [1953]. 69 p.   **[344a]**
A useful and compact introduction to the subject, dealing briefly with contemporary composers.

————. Evolución de la música en el Brasil. *B. A. mus.,* v. 12, no. 197 (Oct. 1, 1957), p. 9.   **[345a]**
Brief historical survey and evaluation of leading contemporary composers.

————. Lorenzo Fernández. Compositor brasileiro. Rio de Janeiro, Privately printed, 1959. 93 p. il.   **[346a]**
List of composer's works, 9 unnumbered leaves at end. The material used in this book appeared originally in the form of articles published in the newspaper *Correio da Manhã* of Rio de Janeiro, of which the author is music critic. The frontispiece is an excellent portrait of Oscar Lorenzo Fernández drawn by D. Isamailovitch in 1939. The catalogue of the composer's works includes dates of composition, duration (performing time) of each work, name of publisher, and date and place of first performance. Recordings are also mentioned. All of the composer's important works are critically discussed.

Friedmann, Herbert J. Currency devaluation alters Brazil's musical scene. *Mus. Amer.,* v. 76, no. 5 (Mar. 1956), p. 9.   **[347a]**
Review of 1955 season in Rio de Janeiro.

————. Exchange favors European artists in Brazil. *Mus. Amer.,* v. 75, no. 4 (Feb. 15, 1955), p. 188.   **[348a]**
Reviews second half of season in Rio de Janeiro.

————. Newcomers and favorite artists heard in Rio concert season. *Mus. Amer.,* v. 74, no. 12 (Oct. 1954), p. 10, 33.   **[349a]**
Rather lengthy account of early 1954 season in Rio, and the foreign performers. A violin suite by Paul Creston, performed by Bronislaw Gimpel, almost the only contemporary music mentioned.

Ginastera, Alberto. Homenaje a Villa-Lobos. *B. A. mus.,* v. 14, no. 232 (16 Dec. 1959), p. 1, il. (port.).   **[350a]**
"Villa-Lobos is without doubt one of the great creators of this century and one of the most significant musicians of Amer-

ica, not only by the originality and power of his message, but also because he represents in such a complete way these lands in which we live."

Gomes, Carlos. O escravo. Versão e adaptação brasileiras de C. Paula Barros, segundo o original italiano de Rodolfo Paravicini. Rio de Janeiro, Ministério de educação e saúde, 1939. 130 p. (Coleção brasileira de teatro, série C, v. II). **[351a]**

——. O guaraní; opera baile em quatro atos. Versão e adaptação brasileiras de C. Paula Barros, segundo o original italiano de Antonio Scalvini. Extraido do romance "O guaraní" de José de Alencar. Rio de Janeiro, Ministério de educação e saúde, 1937. 87 p. (Colecção brasileira de teatro, série C, v. I) **[352a]**

Lange, Francisco Curt. Estudios brasileños (Mauricinas) I: Manuscritos de la biblioteca nacional de Rio de Janeiro. *Rev estud. mus.,* v. 1, no. 3 (April 1950), p. 99-194. il. (facs.) **[353a]**
Researches in the National Library at Rio de Janeiro have produced valuable documentation on the life and works of the Brazilian composer José Mauricio Nunes Garcia (q. v.). This is one of the author's many notable contributions to the musical history of Latin America.

——. La música en Minas Gerais, un informe preliminar. *Bol. lat. am. mús.,* v. 6, 1946, p. 409-494. **[354a]**
Account of the discovery of numerous manuscripts dating from about 1710 until 1800, when a decline in the music activity of the state set in. Numerous illustrations and facsimiles of notation. An outstanding achievement. (C. S.)

——. La música en Minas Gerais durante el siglo XVIII. *Estud. amer.,* v. 12, no. 57-58 (June-July 1956), p. 1-26. **[355a]**
An account of "one of the most unusual phenomena of the history of music in the Americas", the fantastic efflorescence of all phases of musical art in the wealthy frontier state of Minas Gerais during the 18th century. (R. A. W.)

——. Die Musik von Minas Gerais. *Musica* (Kassel), no. 7/8 (1957), p. 375-280. **[356a]**
Music of the colonial period in the region of Minas Gerais. (B. K.)

——. Vida y muerte de Louis Moreau Gottschalk en Rio de Janeiro (1869). El ambiente musical en la mitad del segundo imperio. *Rev. estud. mus.,* v. 2, no. 4 (Aug. 1950), p. 43-217; nos. 5-6 (Dec. 1950-April 1951), p. 97-350. **[357a]**
An extraordinarily rich documentation of the activities of Gottschalk (q. v.) in Brazil during the last year of his life, with many contemporary illustrations, including facsimiles.

Leite, Serafim. A música nas escolas jesuíticas do Brasil no século XVI. *Cultura,* Rio de Janeiro, v. 1, no. 2 (Jan.-Apr. 1949), p. 27-39. **[358a]**
Author draws on primary sources and on his *História da Companhia de Jesús no Brasil.* (C. S.)

Luper, Albert T. Lorenzo Fernândez and Camargo Guarnieri: notes toward a mid-century appraisal. *In* Conference on Latin-American Fine Arts, June 14-17, 1951. Proccedings. Austin, Tex., University of Texas, Institute of Latin American Studies (Latin American Studies, 13), 1952, p. 98-114. **[359a]**
A critical evaluation of the lives and works of two modern Brazilian composers. (R. A. W.)

——. The music of Brazil. Washington, D. C., Music Division, the Pan American Union, 1943. 40 p. (Music series no. 9). **[360a]**
Syllabus for popular use. Contains 5 pages of bibliography, list of recordings of Brazilian music, and titles of Brazilian musical compositions available in the United States (16 pages).

Mariz, Vasco. A canção brasileira (erudita, folclórica e popular). Rio de Janeiro, Ministério da educação e cultura, Serviço de documentação, n. d. [1960].

(Coleção "Vida brasileira"). 305 p.
[361a]

A revision, greatly expanded, of the next item. For comment on this valuable publication by an outstanding writer on Brazilian music, see the introduction to this supplementary section, above.

——. A canção de câmara no Brasil. Prefácio de Gastão de Bettencourt. Porto, Editora livraria progredior, 1948. 173 p. il. (music). **[362a]**

This work studies the Brazilian art-song under three main headings: I, the Precursors; II, Nationalism (3 generations); III, The Anti-folkloristic Reaction (Santoro, Guerra-Peixe, and Koellreutter). The appendices comprise notes on the interpreters of the Brazilian *lied*, a record list, and selected repertoires (lyric and dramatic).

——. Figuras da música brasileira contemporânea. Porto, Imprensa portuguesa, 1948. 75 p. il., port., facs., tab. **[363a]**

Brief reviews on the works of the following contemporary Brazilian composers, including lists of their works: Fructuoso Vianna, Brasilio Itiberê, Radamés Gnattali, Luiz Cosme and Claudio Santoro.

——. Heitor Villa-Lobos. Rio de Janeiro, Ministério das relações exteriores, divisão cultural, 1949. 159 p. il. (music). **[364a]**

Divided into the usual two sections of "Life" and "Work", this volume also contains a catalogue of the composer's works up to March 5, 1947 (the exact date is important!), a bibliography, a record list, and several interesting illustrations, including a portrait of Villa-Lobos in his youth, and a facsimile of his baptismal certificate. There are no musical examples.

[**Mignone, Francisco**]. Classified chronological catalog of the works of the Brazilian composer Francisco Mignone. *Bol. interam. mús.*, nos. 9-10 (Jan.-March 1959), p. 67-85. **[365a]**

Mignone was born in São Paulo in 1897.

Moraes, Rubens Borba de, and **William Berrien,** *eds.* Manual bibliográfico de estudos brasileiros. Rio de Janeiro,

Gráfica editora Souza, 1949. 895 p.
[366a]

Muricy, Andrade. Academia brasileira de música. *Música sacra,* Petrópolis, v. 6, no. 1 (an. 1946), p. 13-14. **[367a]**

Account of the establishment of the recently founded academy, with a complete list of members.

——. Caminho de música. 1ª série. Curitiba, S. Paulo, Rio, Editora Guaira, ltda., n. d. 320 p. **[368a]**

A collection of articles, reviews, etc., published on different occasions and covering various aspects of music in Brazil, such as concert life, problems of Brazilian contemporary music and musicians, special articles on Villa-Lobos and other composers.

——. Contribuição do Brasil à música universal. *Panorama,* v. 2, no. 5 (193), p. 42-56. **[369a]**

Discussion of the contributions to Western music made by three Brazilians: Joaquim Manuel, Carlos Gomes, and Heitor Villa-Lobos. (R. A. W.)

——. Contribución del Brasil a la música universal. *B. A. mus.,* v. 12, no. 197 (Oct. 1, 1957), p. 11-12, 14. **[370a]**

Musical composition in Brazil since the early 19th century, including Carlos Gomes and Villa-Lobos. Also reprinted in *Bol. interam. mús.,* no. 3 (Jan. 1958), p. 8-10. Cf. preceding item.

——. Villa-Lobos. *Bull. pan amer. union,* v. 79, no. 1 (Jan. 1945), p. 1-10.
[371a]

Substantial appreciation by a leading critic. (C. S.)

——. **Eurico Nogueira França, Luiz Heitor Corrêa de Azevedo, Renato Almeida, Vasco Mariz.** Música brasileña contemporánea. Versión castellana de Marta Casablanca Rosario, Editorial "Apis", 1952, 211 p. **[372a]**

A useful compendium for Spanish-speaking readers, dealing with the principal figures in contemporary Brazilian composition.

Octaviano, J. Francisco Braga, traços bio-

gráficos. *Brasil. mus.*, v. 1, no. 4 (Feb.-Mar. 1945), p. 6-7. [373a]
Brief biographical note and list of works of this composer (1868-1945), (C. S.)

Paranhos, Ulysses. Historia da música. Vol. I — Música brasileira. São Paulo, E. S. Mangione, 1940. 145 p. il. (incl. music). [374a]
Text book dealing with concert, folk and popular music.

Peppercorn, Lisa M. New academy of music founded in Rio. *Mus. Amer.*, v. 65, no. 16 (Dec.1945), p. 10. [375a]
New music academy founded by Villa-Lobos for composers and musicologists.

Rezende, Carlos Penteado de. Cronologia musical de São Paulo (1800-1870). *In* São Paulo em quatro séculos, v. 2, São Paulo, Instituto histórico e geográfico de São Paulo, 1954, p. 233-268. [376a]
This essay is a completely chronological listing of musical events during the 70-year period treated. Several plates, bibliography. (R. A. W.)

———. O ano de 1859 na vida de Carlos Gomes. *Rev. bras.*, v. 6, no. 20 (Apr. 1948), p. 91-110. [377a]
Detailed study. Bibliography.

Sabin, Robert. Villa-Lobos, man of action, pays first visit to U.S. *Mus. Amer.*, v. 65, no. 1 (Jan. 1945), p. 7. [378a]
Sketch of Villa-Lobos and his ideas about music and music education.

Santos, Isa Queiros. Francisco Manoel. *Brasil mus.*, v. 1, no. 4 (Feb.-Mar. 1945), p. 14-19. [379a]
Commemoration of the 150th anniversary of birth of Francisco Manoel da Silva (1795-1865), composer of National Anthem of Brazil, at the National School of Music, Rio. 10 music notations. (C. S.)

Sá Pereira, Antônio. Psicotécnica do ensino elementar da música. Rio de

Janeiro, Liv. José Olympio editora, 1937. 195 p. il. (incl. music). [380a]

Sette, Mario. Maxambombas e maracatús. Recife, Ed. Livraria Universal, 1941. 310 p. [381a]
Carnival songs and dances, streetcries, etc.

Smith, Carleton Sprague. Heitor Villa-Lobos. *In* Composers of the Americas. Biographical data and catalogs of their works. Washington, D. C., Pan American Union, 1957, v. 3, p. 1-59.[382a]
English text and Spanish translation. Portrait of the composer. The catalog of works, the most complete thus far published, has 727 entries.

———. Song of Brazil. *Américas* v, 2, no. 10 (Oct. 1940), p. 14-16, 43-44. [383a]
About Villa-Lobos, his life and personality and his music. Photographs of Brazil and of Villa-Lobos.

———. Relações musicais entre o Brasil e os Estados Unidos de Norte América. *Bol. lat. am. mús.*, v. 6, 1946, p. 141-148. [384a]
One page of early 19th century printed music. (C. S.)

Teixeira, Carlos. O Escravo. *Brasil. mus.*, no. 5 (March-April 1945), p. 6-11. [385a]
Historical information on the opera of that title by Carlos Gomes, with a résumé of the libretto.

[Vianna, Fructuoso]. Classified chronological catalog of the works of the Brazilian composer Fructuoso Vianna. *Bol. interam. mús.*, no. 3 (Jan. 1958), p. 66-70. [386a]
Born in Itajubá, Minas Gerais, 1896.

Villa-Lobos in the United States. *Bull. pan Amer. union*, v. 79, no. 6 (June 1945), p. 364-365. [387a]

BRITISH GUIANA

Brett, William Henry. The Indian tribes of Guiana London, Bell and Daldy, 1868. 500 p. il. F2380.B834 **[1179]**

Maquarri dance of the Arawaks, p. 154-158 (with illustraiton); Carib flute, p. 133; Arawak dance, p. 349.

Gillen, John. The Barama river Caribs of British Guiana. Cambridge, Mass., The Museum, 1936. 274 p. **[1180]**

Music, p. 69.

Im Thurn, Everard Ferdinand. Among the Indians of Guiana; being sketches chiefly anthropologic from the interior of British Guiana. London, K. Paul, Trench & Co., 1883. 445 p. il. F2380.-13 **[1181]**

Description of musical insrtuments, p. 308, 310.

Rot, Walter Edmund. Additional studies of the arts, crafts, and customs of the Guiana Indians, with special reference to those of southern British Guiana. Washington, U. S. Govt. print. off., 1929. 110 p. il. (Smithsonian institution Bureau of American ethnology. Bulletin 91). E51.U6 no. 91 F2380.R84 **[1182]**

Musical instruments, p. 88-90, with illustrations of bamboo flutes and a flageolet.

BRITISH HONDURAS

British Honduras national anthem (Sub umbra floreo). Melody adapted from Handel by A. J. Baber. M1688.H5B **[1183]**

CENTRAL AMERICA

E ACH of the Central American republics has a separate section in this guide (see under Costa Rica, El Salvador, Guatemala, Honduras, Nicaragua and Panama). In the present section we have assembled the entries that deal with Central America as a whole, or that touch upon the music of several countries. We have also included references to musical aspects of the ancient Maya civilization, which spread over part of Mexico as well as over the greater part of Guatemala and El Salvador (for further references to music of the Maya, see the section on Mexico).

The most comprehensive survey of modern music in Central America is the article by Salvador Reyes Henríquez entitled *Influencia en algunos autores de música en Centro América* [no. 1188]. English readers will find it convenient to consult the articles by Nicolas Slonimsky, especially the one entitled *Viewing a terra incognita of music* [no. 1191].

GENERAL AND MISCELLANEOUS

Adalid y Gamero, Manuel de. La música en Centro América. *Para todos*, v. 3, no. 17 (Aug. 1929), p. 41-44.
[1184]

Reviews the development of music in Central America, noting the introduction of various instruments, the Catholic church and other influences on the growth of the music, etc.

Labastille, Irma Goebel. The music of Mexico and Central America. Photostat from Handbook of Latin American studies for 1936, Cambridge, Mass., 1937, p. 459-472 (Running title: Guide to Caribbean music). ML128.C18L2
[1185]

A bibliography.

Lima, Emirto de. A música na América Central. *Res. mus.*, v. 3, nos. 32-33 (Apr.-May 1941), p. 23-25. **[1186]**

A general survey of musical activity in Central America, mentioning outstanding composers and musical institutions.

Morelet, Arthur. Travels in Central America. New York, Leypoldt, Holt & Williams, 1871. 430 p. il. F1432.M84
[1187]

Part of the original, describing Cuba and

Yucatán has not been translated. "Specimens of music" (unaccompanied melodies), p. 214-215.

Reyes Henríquez, Salvador. Influencia en algunos autores de música en Centro América. *Ateneo*, Salvador, v. 30, 3d época, no. 150 (Jan. 1941), p. 13-20. **[1188]**

A Salvadorean musician discusses the composers of Central America with reference to their classical, romantic and modern tendencies. The long list of names cited by him indicates that Central America is not lacking in composers. The author deals in some detail with Rafael Herrador, Felipe Soto, C. Jesús Alas, Alberto Merino, José de la Cruz Mena and Miguel Pinto.

Slonimsky, Nicolas. Music under the southern cross. *Christian scien. mon.*, weekly magazine section, 18 Mar. 1939), p. 8-9. il. (ports.). **[1189]**

Deals with composers of Central America and Mexico.

———. Music, where the Americas meet. *Christian scien. mon.*, weekly magazine section (8 June 1940), p. 8-9. il.
[1190]

Biographical sketches of Central American and Mexican composers, with portraits.

———. Viewing a *terra incognita* of music. *Mus. Amer.*, v. 61, no. 11 (June 1941), p. 15-17. **[1191]**

A survey of contemporary music in Mexico and Central America, with brief biographical data on many composers and an entire page of portraits.

NATIONAL ANTHEMS

Contamine de Latour, E. Chants nationaux de l'Amérique latine. Montdidier, Imp. E. Carpentier, 1912. 24 p.ML-3575.C7 **[1192]**

Translations into French of the words to the national anthems of the republics of Central and South America, Haiti and Cuba.

Obregón Lizano, Miguel. Geografía general de Costa Rica. San José. Imp. Lines A. Reyes, 1932. v. 1 339 p. [Lecturas geográficas, 3ª ser.] F1544.-O36 **[1193]**

National Hymn of Costa Rica, its history, words and music, p. 12-19. Words to 8 patriotic songs, p. 24-29. National Hymn of Central America (words and music), p. 40-43.

Prado Quesada, Alcides, comp. Cantos de autores nacionales (e himnos de Centro América) para escuelas y colegios. San José de Costa Rica, Imprenta universal, 1942. 48 p. M1684.P7C2 **[1193x]**

Piano accompaniment. Includes the national anthems of Costa Rica, Salvador, Guatemala, Honduras, Nicaragua, and Panama.

FOLK AND PRIMITIVE MUSIC

Barrera Vásquez, Alfredo. La cultura maya. *An. museo nac. arqueol. hist. etnog.*, v. 2 (1937), p. 327-349. **[1194]**

Batres Jauregui, Antonio. Los indios; su historia y su civilización. Guatemala, Tip. la Unión, 1893. 216 p. F1465.-B33 **[1195]**

Devoted chiefly to the Indians of Central America and Mexico. Reference to music and dancing, p. 27-44, 65-72.

Bell, Charles Napier. Tangweera. London, Edward Arnold, 1899. 318 p. il. F1529.M9B4 **[1196]**

Christmas dancing festivities, p. 29, Mosquito Indians: love-songs (words of one song), p. 88-89, death and dirge songs (words of one song), p. 90-91. Use of conch shells, p. 190.

Brasseur de Bourbourg, Charles Étienne. Histoire des nations civilisées du México et de l'Amérique-centrale. Paris. Arthus Bertrand, 1857. 4 v. F12-19.B82 **[1197]**

Vol. 1 includes: Yucatán Indian's dance of the sacred tapir, p. 81; song of the penitence of Acxitl, p. 380-381. Vol. 2: Mayan dances and ballet, p. 61-67; musical instruments, p. 64-65. Vol. 3: Chapter 2, p. 498-540, contains descriptions of fêtes, with many brief references to music, songs and dances, especially p. 522, 524; discussion of the great drum of the temple of Quetzalcohuatl, p. 547; Mexican dances, p. 635; musical instruments, p. 669; *ballet ordinaire* and *ballet grand,* p. 670.

Carpenter, Rhys. The land beyond Mexico. Boston, R. G. Badger, 1920. 181 p. F1432.C29 **[1198]**

Reference to marimba music, p. 60-61.

Dubois, Anthony. La civilisation maya connaissait-elle un système musical? *Bulletin de la société des Américanistes de Belgique,* no. 14 (Aug. 1934), p. 111-117. **[1199]**

Gann, Thomas W. F. How the Maya *satan* corrupted mankind: the Kekchi devil dance. *Illustrated London news,* v. 168, no. 4538 (1926), p. 662, 668-669. **[1200]**

Joyce, Thomas Athol. Central American and West Indian archaeology. London, P. L. Warner, 1916. 270 p. il. F1434.-J89 **[1201]**

Dances and music of the Aztecs, p. 203-204. Illustrations of pottery whistles, p. 148.

López de Gómara, Francisco. Historia general de las Indias. Madrid, Barcelona, Espasa Calpe, s. a., 1932. 2 v. E-141.G635 **[1202]**

Vol. 1 includes mention of dances in Darien, p. 163, and in Cumaná, p. 194-195. This work was written in the 16th century.

Mimenza Castillo, Ricardo. La civilización Maya. Barcelona, Editorial Cervantes, 1929. 80 p. F1435.M65 **[1203]**

La música indígena, p. 33-35, including descriptions of several musical instruments, *baile de las cañas, danza de las banderas*. Reference to music and dance, p. 76.

Morelet, Arthur. Voyage dans l'Amérique Centrale, l'ile de Cuba, et le Yucatan. Paris, Gide et J. Baudry, 1857. 2 v. F1432.M83 **[1204]**

Vol. 1 contains the verse of a song (Spanish words with English translation), p. 295. Vol. 2 includes description of fandango with marimba accompaniment, p. 40-42, with origin, history and complete description of the marimba, p. 42-44; discussion of Indian national songs, and reference to the *chirimiya* (wind instrument), p. 44; 2 pages at the end of the book of *Airs nationaux de l'Amérique Centrale* (2 from Yucatán, 2 *Indian*, 1 from Tabasco, 3 from Petén, and 2 from Honduras). Also music at a Guatemalan child's funeral, p. 193.

Sapper, Karl Theodor. Das nördliche Mittel-Amerika nebst einem ausflug nach dem hochland von Anahuac. Braunschweig, Friedrich Vieweg und sohn, 1897. 436 p. il. F1428.S254 **[1205]**

Contains about 30 Indian melodies of Central America and southern Mexico.

Schlieman, Paul. Strange similarity in music of ancient Egyptians and Mayas. *Mus. Amer.*, v. 18, no. 5 (7 June 1913), p. 29. **[1206]**

Tulane university expedition to middle America, 1925. Tribes and temples. New Orleans, Tulane university, 1926. 2 v. F1219.T91 **[1207]**

Saint-feast of Jaltipán, with description of the dances and the drums; mention of

the *Moors and Christians* dance, v. 1, p. 72-74. Music in funerals, v. 2, p. 142, 361.

INSTRUMENTS

Barber, Edwin A. Indian music. *Amer. naturalist*, v. 17 (1883), p. 267-274. **[1208]**

Includes descriptions of musical instruments of the Indians of Central and South America.

Harcourt, Raoul d'. L'ocarina à cinq sons dans l'Amérique préhispanique. *Jour. soc. amér.*, n. s., v. 22 (1930), p. 347-364. **[1209]**

With numerous illustrations of ocarinas from Central America.

Joyce, L. Elliott. The cuna folk of Darien. *In* Lionel Wafer, A new voyage and description of the isthmus of America, Oxford, Hakluyt society, 1934, no. 73, appendix 3, p. 166-178. G161.H2 **[1210]**

Musical instruments, p. 172. First printed in 1699.

Schwauss, Maria. Tropenspiegel. Leipzig, A. H. Payne verlag, 1940. 192 p. F1464.S3 **[1211]**

Dance, mairmba and other musical instruments, p. 127-130.

Seler, Eduard. Mittelamerikanische musikinstrumente. *Globus*, v. 76 (1899), p. 109-112. il. **[1212]**

Spinden, Herbert Joseph. Ancient civilizations of Mexico and Central America. New York, American museum press, 1922. 242 p. il. (American museum of natural history. Handbook series no. 3 (2d and rev. ed.) F1219.-S766 **[1213]**

"Poetry and music", p. 216-218, with illustrations of ancient Aztec instruments from the *Manuscrit du Cacique*.

—— Ancient civilizations of Mexico

and Central America. New York, 1928. 271 p. il. (American museum of natural history. Handbook series no. 3, 3d and rev. ed.) F1219.S767 **[1214]**

"Poetry and music", p. 239-242, with illustrations of musical instruments.

Stacy-Judd, Robert Benjamin. The ancient Mayas. Los Angeles, Haskell-Travers, inc., n. d. 277 p. F1376.S78
[1215]

Past and present Mayan music, p. 69; musical instruments at the time of the Spanish invasion, p. 152-153.

Tempsky, Gustav Ferdinad von. Mitla. A narrative of incidents and personal adventures on a journey in Mexico, Guatemala, and Salvador in the years 1853 to 1855. London, Longman, Brown, Green, Longmans and Roberts, 1858. 436 p. il. F1213.T28
[1216]

Includes a description of the marimba, p. 384-386.

CHILE

THE musical bibliography of Chile was greatly enriched with the publication in 1941 of the important historical work by Eugenio Pereira Salas, *Los orígenes del arte musical en Chile*. In this volume, which comprises over three hundred pages of text, in addition to several valuable appendices, the author traces the development of musical activity in Chile from pre-Columbian times to about the middle of the nineteenth century. Approximately half of the book is devoted to an account of traditional songs and dances, illustrated with musical examples. The appendices comprise an inventory of Chilean musical production from 1714 to 1800 (p. 304-310); a section of musical facsimiles and other illustrations (p. 313-344); and a copious bibliography (p. 345-356).

In his first chapter, *La música precolombina en Chile,* Pereira deals with the instruments, the dances and the songs of the Araucanians, the aborigines of Chile. He refers to the valuable monograph of Carlos Isamitt on Araucanian musical instruments [item no. 1324], and quotes the descriptions of early writers such as Frézier (*Relation du voyage de la mer du sud*, 1716), Fray A. Sors (*Historia del reino de Chile*, late 18th century), Alonso Ovalle (*Histórica relación del reino de Chile, ca.* 1645) and Carvallo Goyeneche (*Descripción histórico-geográfica del reino de Chile*, 1796).

Two brief chapters suffice to summarize the little that is known about music in Chile during the sixteenth and seventeenth centuries, chiefly in connection with civic or religious festivals and ceremonies. With the advent of the eighteenth century (Chapter IV), a few more details are available. With a Bourbon dynasty ruling in Spain, French influence spread to the Spanish colonies and numerous French families established themselves in Santiago de Chile. Music became an elegant social pastime as well as an adjunct of public and religious ceremonies. Harps, guitars, harpsichords, violins and flutes were heard in the salons of Santiago. The first pianos arrived in Chile towards the end of the century. Outstanding among the musicians of this period was José Campderrós, who came to Chile from Lima and in 1793 obtained the post of choirmaster at the Cathedral of Santiago. Fifteen of his compositions, including two complete Masses, are extant.

In Chapters VI and VII, Pereira deals with the transition from the colonial period to the era of independence. He places the real beginning of musical art in Chile around the year 1819; up to that time musical activity had been either social or functional. A Danish merchant and amateur 'cellist named Carlos Drewetcke organized concerts in Santiago and gave the first performances there of symphonies by Haydn, Mozart and Beethoven. These activities led to the formation of a Philharmonic Society in 1827. The first important composer of independent Chile was Manuel Robles (1780-1837), who composed the country's original national anthem, the *Canción Nacional* of 1820. In 1828 this was superseded as the national anthem by the *Himno Patriótico,* written by the Spanish composer Ramón Carnicer, at that time living in London as a political exile. The most popular Chilean composer of the nineteenth century was José Zapiola (1802-1885), who sprang into fame with his *Himno marcial* in celebration of the battle of Yungay, composed in 1839. In 1852, together with Isidora Zegers (a celebrated singer) and the composer Francisco Oliva, he founded the first Chilean musical periodical, *El semanario musical,* of which eleven issues were published. Zapiola's reminiscences, *Recuerdos de treinta años* [item no. 1242] contain much interesting information on musical life in Chile from 1810 to 1840.

Federico Guzmán (1837-1885) was a celebrated pianist and the composer of over two hundred works, mostly for piano, in romantic vein. In 1866 he received some lessons from the American pianist Louis Moreau Gottschalk while the latter was in Santiago. Aquinas Ried, an amateur composer of Bavarian origin, wrote the first Chilean opera, *La Telésfora,* in 1846. The notable musician José Bernardo Alzedo, a native of Lima (b. 1798), resided in Chile for forty years and was active there as teacher, bandmaster and composer of church music. The first national conservatory of music in Chile, the Escuela y Conservatorio de Música, was established on 17 June 1850.

With Chapter XVII, *El desarrollo histórico de la danza y de la música popular,* begins that part of Pereira's book devoted to the folk and popular music of Chile. Among the subjects covered by the author in this section are the following: Traditional ballads (*romances*), ceremonial dances and songs (popular religious festivals, such as the *Fiesta de Andacollo*); music and social life in the colony (street-cries, *esquinazos,* cradle songs, children's singing games); colonial dances of Spanish origin (*fandango, seguidilla, zapateo, bolero, tirana*); aristocratic dances (*contradanza* or *española,* and *minuet*); popular religious songs (*cantos a lo divino*); creole songs (*triste, vidala, tonada*); songs and dances of the republican era (*el cuando, la zamacueca* or *cueca*).

In the course of this work the author makes frequent reference to an *Antología musical histórica de Chile* which he has compiled in collaboration with the Chilean composer Jorge Urrutia Blondel. This compilation, as yet unpublished, contains descriptive analyses of Chilean musical compositions since colonial times. Its publication would undoubtedly be of considerable importance for the study of Chilean music history.

The contemporary musical scene in Chile is exceptionally interesting as regards both creative production and institutional organization. The former is characterized by the development of a well-equipped and distinctive school of composition, working with modern techniques along cosmopolitan as well as national-folkloristic lines. Representing both these tendencies are such composers as Humberto Allende, Domingo Santa Cruz, Próspero Bisquertt, Carlos Isamitt, Jorge Urrutia, Alfonso Letelier and René Amengual. The work of these composers is discussed in Carleton Sprague Smith's article, *The composers of Chile* [no. 1261].

Besides being an important creative artist, Domingo Santa Cruz has been a key figure in the institutional organization of Chile's musical life. In his article entitled *Cómo se ha enfocado el problema artístico en Chile* [no. 1235], Santa Cruz traces the development of musical education and organization in Chile from about 1928 to 1936, showing how there has been an increased tendency toward centralization through university control. To quote from this article, "The present organization of artistic activities in Chile takes its point of departure from the Laws of Autonomy for Higher Education, called *Estatuto universitario,* which, in 1929 and 1931, provided for the incorporation into the University of a Faculty of Fine Arts." The Conservatorio Nacional de Música became a dependency of the Faculty of Fine Arts of the National University. The Faculty also exercised general supervision over all musical education in the country, both public and private. It published the *Revista de arte,* which gave much attention to modern Chilean music, and it sponsored the Asociación Nacional de Conciertos Sinfónicos, corresponding to a national symphony orchestra, conducted by Armando Carvajal (this organization is now known as the Orquesta Sinfónica de Chile). As there exist little or no commercial facilities for the publication of art music in Chile, the musical publications of the *Revista de arte* have been of special value in making available the music of contemporary Chilean composers.

Since the above mentioned article was written, further important organizational changes have taken place in Chile's musical life, emphasizing still more strongly the policy of centralization. The culminating event was the creation by government decree, on 11 October 1940 (cf. *Diario oficial,* año 63, no. 18,785, Ley no. 6,696), of the Instituto de Extensión Musical, with power to exercise control over all aspects of musical activity in Chile, including education on all levels, symphonic concerts, lyric theatre (opera and ballet), chamber music, radio concerts, etc. The law provides that funds for the maintenance of the Instituto are to be derived from a special tax on amusements. The executive power of the Instituto is vested in a council, presided over, *ex officio,* by the Dean of the Faculty of Fine Arts of the National University. The incumbent of this office, at the time of writing, was Domingo Santa Cruz.

GENERAL AND MISCELLANEOUS

Aldunate C., María. La asociación nacional de conciertos sinfónicos de Chile. *Bol. lat. am. mús.,* v. 3 (Apr. 1937), p. 170-196. **[1217]**

Barros Arana, Diego. Un decenio de la historia de Chile. Santiago, Imp. y encuadernación universitaria, 1905-06. 2 v. F3095.B27 **[1218]**
Vol. 1, mention of music in public festivals, p. 80.

Beattie, John W., and Louis Woodson Curtis. South American music pilgrimage. III. Chile. *Mus. educ. jour.,* v. 28, no. 4 (Feb.-Mar. 1942), p. 16-19. il. **[1219]**

Chase, Gilbert. Chilean music institute. *Mus. Amer.,* v. 61, no. 3 (10 Feb. 1941), p. 220. **[1220]**

Dumesnil, Maurice. Musical romance in Chile. *Etude,* v. 59, no. 5 (May 1941), p. 316, 355, 360. il. **[1221]**

Figueroa, Pedro Pablo. Diccionario biográfico de Chile. 4 ed. Santiago, Impr. y encuadernación Barcelona, 1897-1902. 3 v. F3055.F48 **[1222]**

Garrido, Pablo. Tragedia del músico chileno. Santiago de Chile, Editorial Smirnow, 1940. 20 p. ML3795.G27T7 **[1223]**
Pessimistic survey of the social, economic and artistic position of the Chilean musician.

Huneeus y Gana, Jorge. Cuadro histórico de la producción intelectual de Chile. Santiago, 1908, 863 p. PQ8033.-B5 v. 1 (Biblioteca de escritores de Chile, v. 1) **[1224]**
La música, p. 845-863, includes an article by Saffia y Thompson on the work of Isidora Zegers de Huneeus, other members of the Huneeus family, and Zapiola.

Lira Espejo, Eduardo, and Julio Brieva A. Chilean music. *Andean monthly,* v. 3, no. 9 (Nov. 1940), p. 419-421. **[1225]**

Medina, José Toribio. Romances basados en La Araucana. Santiago, Imp. elzeviriana, 1918. 52 p. PQ6204.M4 **[1226]**
With 76 pages of introduction, historical and explanatory notes on the *romances* (ballads).

Montt, Luis. Bibliografía chilena. Santiago, Imprenta Barcelona, 1904. 4 v. Z1701.M82 **[1227]**
Vol. 2, *Explicación de don Manuel Fernández sobre la canción que publicó en la Aurora* (1814), p. 269-271, which includes a few words of the song.

Música de autores chilenos. *Revista de bibliografía chilena y extranjera,* v. 4, no. 5 (May 1916), p. 302-309. **[1228]**
Numerous titles of music by Chilean composers.

Música, teatro y baile; interesante capítulo del libro de don José Zapiola "Recuerdos de treinta años" [1810-1840]; cuarta edición, año 1881. *Música,* Chile, v. 2, no. 1 (Jan. 1921), p. 12-16; v. 2, no. 2 (Feb. 1921), p. 15-16; v. 2, no. 3 (Mar. 1921), p. 12-16. **[1229]**
Cf. item no. 1242.

Pereira Salas, Eugenio. Los orígenes del arte musical en Chile. Publicaciones de la Universidad de Chile. Santiago, Imprenta universitaria, 1941. 373 p. ML2-32.5.P **[1230]**
For comment, see introduction.

Revista de arte, v. 4, nos. 16-17 (1938), p. 60-70; no. 19 (1938), p. 64-80; no. 21 (1930), p. 60-68. **[1231]**
Music sections of this periodical, con-

taining reviews of concerts, notes on Chilean music in other parts of the world, dance activities, notices of important musical development in other Latin American countries.

Revista de arte, boletín mensual, v. 1, no. 1 (1939), p. 2-5; 1, no. 2 (1939), p. 2-11; v. 1, no. 3 (1940), p. 2-8; v. 1, no. 4 (1940), p. 4-7; v. 1, no. 5 (1940), p. 3-7. **[1232]**

Musical section in these mumbers, with short articles and notices of current musical events.

Ruschenberger, William Samuel Waithman. Three years in the Pacific ... Philadelphia, Carey, Lea & Blanchard, 1834. 441 p. F2213.R95 **[1233]**

Notes on Chile include a comment on Chilean singing, p. 96.

Sandoval y Bustamante, Luis. Reseña histórica del Conservatorio nacional de música y declamación .Santiago de Chile, Impr. Gutenberg, 1911, 91 p. MT-5.S2S2 **[1234]**

Contains data on the students, professors, programs, etc., of the Conservatorio during the years 1849-1911.

Santa Cruz, Domingo. Cómo se ha enfocado el problema artístico en Chile. *Bol. lat. am. mús.,* v. 3 (Apr. 1937), p. 17-24. **[1235]**

Santiago de Chile. Biblioteca nacional. Bibliografía musical; composiciones impresas en Chile y composiciones de autores chilenos publicados en el extranjero. Segunda parte, 1886-1896. Santiago de Chile, Establecimiento poligráfico Roma, 1898. 89 p. ML120.S2-M4 **[1236]**

First published in Anuario de la prensa chilena, 1896. The first part covering material prior to 1886 has not been published. "Fué preparado por Ramón A. Laval."

Silva Cruz, Carlos. Cultura musical en Chile. Santiago, Impr. universitaria, 1915, 13 p. ML3575.S5 **[1237]**

Deals with the general progress of music, and the growth of music appreciation.

Little said concerning South American music.

Urrutia Blondel, Jorge. Apuntes sobre los albores de la historia musical chilena. *Bol. lat. am. mús.,* v. 3 (1937), p. 89-96. **[1238]**

Valenzuela Llanos, Jorge. La música en Chile; conferencia. Viña del Mar, 1921. **[1239]**

Cited by Pereira Salas [no. 1230], p. 355.

Wright, Marie Robinson. The republic of Chile. Philadelphia, George Barrie and sons, 1904. 450 p. F3058.W94 **[1240]**

National Conservatory of Music, p. 168; *zamacueca,* p. 236; picture, *Dancing the cueca,* p. 239.

Zapiola, José. Más apuntes sobre la música en Chile. *Semanario musical,* no. 13 (1852). **[1241]**

Cited by Pereira Salas [no. 1239], p. 356.

——. Recuerdos de treinta años (1810-1840), con prólogo de Ventura Blanco. Santiago, Ediciones Ercilla, 1932. 122 pp. F3094.Z353 **[1242]**

Reminiscences of a celebrated Chilean musician, of considerable historical importance. Ch. 5, "Música, teatro y baile", is an important source for the early musical history of Chile. L. of C. also has the 4th ed. of this work (Santiago, 1881). Cf. item no. 1229.

BIOGRAPHY AND CRITICISM

Amunátegui y Solar, Domingo. Recuerdos biográficos. Santiago, Soc. Imp. y Lit. universo, 1938. 324 p. F3055.A5 **[1243]**

Don Pedro Palazuelos y Astaburuaga, p. 287-324. Mention of his school of music, p. 322.

Chase, Gilbert. Talk with Domingo Santa Cruz, Chilean music leader. *Int. amer. monthly,* v. 1, no. 3 (July (1942), p. 28-29. port. **[1244]**

Fabela, Isidro. Claudio Arrau. *Gaceta mus.,* v. 1, no. 6 (June 1928), p. 17-20. [1245]

Figueroa, Pedro Pablo. Un mago de la música; el compositor Federico Uriarte. Santiago, 1904. [1246]
Cited by Pereira Salas [no. 1230], p. 349.

Greve, Ernesto. Don Guillermo Frick. *Rev. chil. hist. geog.,* v. 88, no. 96 (Jan.-June 1940), p. 28-62. [1247]
Notes on Frick's musical activities, p. 32, 61, 62.

Huneeus, Alejandro. Los Huneeus y los Zegers en Chile. Paris, 1927. [1248]
Cited by Pereira Salas [no. 1230], p. 350, Isidora Zegers de Huneeus was a celebrated Chilean singer of the 19th century. Cf. Pereira Salas, *op. cit.,* p. 94-103. See also Miranda, Marta Eba, *Mujeres chilenas* (Santiago, 1940), p. 91-94.

Isamitt, Carlos. Anotaciones alrededor de Humberto Allende y su obra. *Bol. lat. am. mús.,* v. 2 (Apr. 1936), p. 237-246. [1249]

——. Dos poemas para canto y piano de Santa Cruz. *Rev. arte, bol. mens.,* v. 1, no. 5 (1 May 1940), p. 6-7. [1250]
With 3 musical examples.

——. Tres coros infantiles de Jorge Urrutia. *Rev. arte, bol. mens.,* v. 1, no. 3 (1 Jan. 1940), p. 6-8. [1251]
With 2 musical examples.

Keller, Carlos. Aquinas Ried; leben und werke. Concepción, 1927. [1252]
Cited by Pereira Salas [no. 1230], p. 350. Ried was a composer of religious and dramatic music. He composed the first Chilean opera, *La Telésfora* (1846). Cf. Pereira S., *op. cit.,* p. 135-139.

Orquesta sinfónica de México. Notas por Francisco Agea. Programa 2, temporada 1942, p. 27-28. Cinco piezas breves para orquesta de cuerda [Santa Cruz]. [1253]
These *Cinco piezas breves* by Domingo

Santa Cruz of Chile were first performed by the Asociación nacional de conciertos of Santiago in 1937. The music was incorporated in the repertoire of the American Ballet under the title, *Danzas nobles del Virrey.*

Orrego Salas, Juan A. Chilean composers. *Andean monthly,* v. 3, no. 10 (Dec. 1940), p. 477-484. [1254]

Ried, Alberto. Diario de Aquinas Ried. Santiago, 1927. [1255]
See comment under item no. 1252.

Salas, M. Xavier de. Oscar Nicastro y su arte excepcional. Santiago, Talleres S. Vicente, 1939. 78 p. port. ML418.-X28N5 [1256]
"Obras para violoncelo originales de O. Nicastro", p. 77-78.

Santa Cruz, Domingo. Tres canciones de cuna de Alfonso Letelier. *Rev. arte, bol. mens.,* v. 1, no. 2 (1 Dec. 1939), p. 10-11. [1257]
Contains 2 musical examples.

Slonimsky, Nicolas. Chilean composers show notable and varied talent. *Mus. Amer.,* v. 63, no. 10 (25 May 1938), p. 11. ports. [1258]

——. Humberto Allende, first modernist of Chile. *Mus. Amer.,* v. 62, no. 12 (Aug. 1942), p. 5, 21. il. [1259]
"The historical importance of Allende to the student of Latin American music is that he was the first Chilean to write in a modern idiom."

——. Musicians in Chile. *Christian scien. mon.,* v. 30, no. 256 (27 Sept. 1938), p. 8. [1260]
Sketches the work of Domingo Santa Cruz, Humberto Allende, Próspero Bisquertt, Alfonso Leng, Carlos Isamitt, Samuel Negrete, Hector Melo, Jorge Urrutia, René Amengual, Alfonso Letelier, Armando Carvajal.

Smith, Carleton Sprague. The composers of Chile. *Mod. music,* v. 19, no. 1 (Nov.-Dec. 1941), p. 26-31. ports. [1261]
Discusses the work of Enrique Soro,

Humberto Allende, Domingo Santa Cruz, Próspero Bisquertt, Carlos Isamitt, Jorge Urrutia, Letelier and René Amengual.

Soffia, José Antonio. Biografía de doña Isidora Zegers. [Santiago?], 1866. **[1262]**

Republished by Adolfo Allende in *Aulos*, nos. 3 and 4 (Santiago, 1933).

Suárez, José Bernardo. Plutarco de los jóvenes. París, México, Librería de C. Bouret, 1881. 160 p. E17.S93 **[1263]**

Biographical sketches of Gottschalk, p. 44-45, and of Federico Guzmán (Chilean pianist), p. 48-49.

Urrutia Blondel, Jorge. Alfonso Leng, su obra y su estética. *Rev. arte*, v. 1 (June-July 1934), p. 15-22. **[1264]**

Uzcátegui García, Emilio. La composición musical en Chile. *Música*, Chile, v. 2, no. 1 (Jan. 1921), p. 4-7. **[1265]**

Mentions, *inter alia*, Remigo Acevedo, Enrique Soro, Humberto Allende, Guillermo Farr, Carlos Vásquez.

——. Músicos chilenos contemporáneos (datos biográficos e impresiones sobre sus obras). Santiago, Imprenta y encuadernación América, 1919. 236 p. il. (ports., music) ML385.U9 **[1266]**

Biographical sketches of the following Chilean musicians: Claudio Arrau León [the famous pianist], Teresa Parodi, Lydia Montero, Armando Carvajal, Juan Reyes, Osvaldo Rojo, Américo Tritini, Rosita Renard, Amelia Cocq-Weingand, Marta Canales, María Luisa Sepúlveda, Julio Rossel, Alberto García Guerrero, Humberto Allende, Enrique Soro, Andrés Steinfort, Alfonso Leng, Carlos Lavín, Aníbal Aracena Infanta, Próspero Bisquertt, Javier Rengifo, Celerino Pereira, Eliodoro Ortiz de Zárate.

Valdivia P., A. La voz de las calles, por Pedro Humberto Allende. *Música*, Chile, v. 2, no. 6 (June 1921), p. 8 and 9. **[1267]**

Description of Allende's symphonic poem.

LYRIC THEATRE

Abascal Brunet, Manuel. Apuntes para la historia del teatro en Chile; la zarzuela grande. Santiago, Imprenta universitaria, 1941. 227 p. **[1268]**

——. Apuntes para la historia del teatro en Chile. *Rev. chil. hist. geog.*, v. 88, no. 96 (Jan.-June 1940), p. 161-212; 1. 89, no. 97 (July-Dec. 1940), p. 133-184; v. 90, no. 98 (Jan.-June 1941), p 104-176. **[1268x]**

The first part of this study deals with the *zarzuela grande*. [Cf. item no. 1268].

Amunátegui, Miguel Luis. Las primeras representaciones dramáticas en Chile. Santiago, Imp. nacional, 1888. 398 p. PN2491.A5 **[1269]**

P. 83-89 deal with the first lyric company which came to Chile (1830); Zapiola was director of the orchestra.

Hernández Cornejo, Roberto. Los primeros teatros de Valparaíso ... 1712-1900. Valparaíso, Imprenta San Rafael, 1928. 663 p. PN2492.V3H4 **[1270]**

Many references to music activities throughout the book. See especially *Sobre et baile nacional*, p. 633-640; *La zamacueca*, p. 640-644; *En desagravio del baile nacional*, p. 645-649; biographical sketch of Mateo Martínez Quevedo, famous author and also noted dancer of the *cueca*, p. 650-653; words to Himno porteño, p. 197-198; also p. 187, 189-90, etc.

Loewenberg, Alfred. Annals of opera, 1597-1940. With an introduction by Edward J. Dent. Cambridge, W. Heffer & sons, ltd., 1943. 879 p. ML102.O6L6 **[1271]**

Chronology of operatic performances. Includes *La fioraia di Lugano* by Eleodoro [sic] Ortiz de Zárate (b. 1865), produced in Santiago 1 Nov. 1895. "Probably the first opera by a Chilean composer which was produced in his native country" (p. 617). Concerning the composer, see Uzcátegui's *Músicos chilenos contemporáneos* [no. 1266], p. 215-236.

Ribera, Salvador A., and Luis A. Águila. La ópera. Santiago de Chile,

Imprenta & encuadernación Roma, 1895. 583 p.   [1272]

Cited in *Anuario de la prensa chilena* for 1805.

INSTRUCTION AND THEORY

Allende, Pedro Humberto. Conferencias sobre la música. Santiago de Chile, Imp. Universitaria, 1918. 23 p. MT70.-A6   [1273]

1) Modern orchestra; 2) Pre-modernistic music (with 2 pages of music); 3) Modernistic music. At the end of the book there are 9 pages of instruments of the modern orchestra (pictures and descriptions).

Muñoz Hermosilla, José María and Luisa Maluschka de. La enseñanza del canto en las escuelas primarias. Santiago de Chile, Imprenta Roma, 1896. 42 p. MT935.M94E5   [1274]

NATIONAL ANTHEM

Echeverría Reyes, Anibal, and Agustín Canobio. La canción nacional de Chile. Valparaíso, Babra y cia., 1904. 81 p.   [1275]

FOLK AND PRIMITIVE MUSIC

(A) GENERAL

Acevedo Hernández, Antonio. Canciones populares chilenas; recopilación de cuecas, tonadas, y otras canciones, acompañada de una noticia sobre la materia y sobre los que han cantado para el público chileno. Santiago, Ediciones Ercilla, 1939. 193 p. ML3575.A23C2   [1276]

A collection of folk song texts, with 65 pages of introductory matter.

———. Los cantores populares chilenos. Santiago, Nascimento, 1923. 296 p. PQ-8051.A35   [1277]

Chilean popular poetry.

———. El libro de la tierra chilena, lo que canta y lo que mira el pueblo de Chile.

Santiago de Chile, Ediciones Ercilla, 1935. 136 p. PQ8179.C34R6   [1278]

Allende, Pedro Humberto. Chilean folk music. *Bull. pan Amer. union*, v. 65, no. 9 (Sept. 1931), p. 917-924. il.   [1279]

With 4 musical examples.

———. Música popular chilena. In *Chile y sus riquezas*, v. 1, p. 804-805, Santiago, n. d.   [1280]

Cited by Pereira Salas [no. 1230], p. 346.

———. La musique populaire chilienne. *Art populaire, travaux artistiques et scientifiques du 1er congrès international des arts populaires*, Prague, 1928, v. 2, p. 118-123. Paris, Éditions Duchartre, 1931. N9201.I5 1928.   [1281]

This study is divided into three parts: *La musique des Araucans, La musique populaire créole chilienne*, and *Les cris de la rue*. Includes 17 brief musical examples (children's rhymes and street-cries).

Angulo A., José. Música folklórica chilena. *In* Anuario de la Sociedad folklórica de México, 1941, v. 2, México, D. F., 1943, p. 125-131.   [1282]

Deals with the *cueca, tonada, esquinazo, estilo criollo* and *canción*. Mentions also *mapuchinas* and *araucanas* as new types of songs which contain reminiscences of indigenous music.

Brown, Calvin Smith. Latin songs, classical, medieval, and modern, with music. New York and London, G. P. Putnam's sons, 1914. 135 p. M1980.B8   [1283]

Chilean lullaby, p. 80.

Cabrera, Ana S. Rutas de América; el folklore, la música, la historia, la leyenda, las costumbres. Buenos Aires, Peuser, ltda., 1941. 242 p. il. F1408.3.-C2   [1284]

Part 3. *Panorama de la música folklórica sudamericana*, deals with indigenous and colonial music. Part 4, *Del folklore chileno*, includes *Música popular* and *El arte musical de Araucania*. Part 5, *La canción y la danza populares en México*.

There are also numerous references to folk dances in Part 6, *Supervivencia del folklore en las costumbres*. There are numerous illustrations of musicians, dancers and instruments. Notation of 9 tunes.

Carvallo y Goyeneche, Vicente. Descripción histórica-geográfica del reyno de Chile. Santiago, 1888. (Colección de historiadores de Chile, v. 8.) **[1285]**

Chile. Universidad de Chile. Instituto de extensión musical. Departamento de investigación folklórica. Santiago de Chile, 1943. 53 p. **[1286]**

A collection of Chilean folk music, with commentary by various writers.

Flores, Eliodoro. Nanas o canciones de cuna corrientes en Chile. *Rev. chil. hist. geog.,* v. 16 (1915), p. 386-415. **[1287]**

Includes the melodies of 4 traditional Chilean lullabies.

Garvin, Helen. Fun and festival from Latin America. New York, Friendship press, 1935. 44 p. F1408.3.G176 **[1288]**

Includes music with words of *El tortillero* (Chile).

Hanssen, Frederick. Chilean popular songs. *Amer. jour. philol.,* v. 14 (1893), p. 90-92. **[1289]**

Isamitt, Carlos. Apuntes sobre nuestro folklore musical. *Aulos,* v. 1, no. 1 (Oct. 1932), p. 8-9; v. 1, no. 2 (Nov. 1932), p. 4-6; v. 1, no. 4 (Jan.-Feb. 1933), p. 3-6; v. 1, no. 6 (June-July 1933), p. 6-8. **[1290]**

V. 1, no. 6, has the melody and Araucanian text of the "pürün ül", sung by mothers to their small children.

Laval, Ramón A. Contribución al folklore de Carahue (Chile), Madrid, V. Suárez, 1916-21. 2 v. il. (music). V. 2 has imprint: Santiago de Chile, Imprenta universitaria, 1921. GR133.C5L3 **[1291]**

Vol. 1 has 6 tunes and the words of many folk songs.

———. Sobre dos cantos chilenos derivados de un antiguo romance español. *Rev. chil. hist. geog.,* v. 63, no. 67 (1929), p. 41-47. **[1292]**

Lizana D., Desiderio. Cómo se canta la poesía popular. Santiago de Chile, Imprenta universitaria, 1912. 73 p. ML35-75.L79 **[1293]**

Also published in *Revista de la Sociedad chilena de historia y geografía,* año 2, v. 3, no. 5.

Martial, Louis Ferdinand. Histoire du voyage ... Paris, Gauthier-Villars, 1888. 496 p. il. Q115.M68 **[1294]**

Includes 4 Fuegian tunes, p. 209-211.

Medina, José Toribio. Los romances basados en La Araucana. Santiago de Chile, Imprenta elzeviriana, 1918. 52 p. PQ6204.M4 **[1295]**

The text of various ballads dealing with the period of the Conquest, with commentary.

Pereira Salas, Eugenio. Chilean Christmas carols. *Andean monthly,* v. 2, no. 10 (Dec. 1939), p. 3-6. **[1295x]**

Includes the words and music of a *villancico* by Alfonso Letelier.

———. Los orígenes del arte musical en Chile. Publicaciones de la Universidad de Chile. Santiago, Imprenta universitaria, 1941. 373 p. ML232.5P **[1296]**

Includes numerous references to folk and popular music, esp. p. 1-7, 168-199, 206-303. Music facsimiles; Araucanian tune taken from Frézier; *Boleras,* Antonio Aranaz; *Zapateo,* from Frézier; *El cuando,* from Pöppig; *Canción; Tonadita popular;* 2 *zamacuecas,* etc. Also includes 16 folk tunes with the main text.

Urrutia Blondel, Jorge. Brief notes on Chilean folk music. *Andean monthly,* v. 2, no. 8 (Oct. 1939), p. 23-29. **[1297]**

Contains the words and music to *La ventura,* by Urrutia. There is a biographical sketch of this composer, p. 29-30.

Vicuña Cifuentes, Julio. Instrucciones para recoger de la tradición oral romances populares. *Bol. bim. com. chil. coop.*

intel., v. 3, no 15 (May-June 1939), p. 12-23.   [1298]
Includes specimens of ballad texts.

——. Poesía popular chilena. Santiago de Chile, Imprenta universitaria, 1916. 84 p.   [1299]

——. Romances populares y vulgares, recogidos de la tradición oral chilena. Santiago de Chile. Impr. Barcelona, 1912. 580 p. PQ8089.V5 and PQ8033.-B5 v. 7   [1300]
Text of Chilean-Spanish ballads.

(B) AMERINDIAN

I. *Music and Dance*

Augusta, Félix José de. Zehn Araukanerlieder. *Anthropos*, v. 6 (1911), p. 684-698. (Also reprinted separately.)   [1301]
Contains 10 Indian melodies, with native words and German translation.

Delano, Amasa. A narrative of a voyage and travels ... Boston, E. G. House, 1817. 598 p. port. G440.D32   [1302]
Note on music and dancing of the Araucanians, p. 366.

Frézier, Amédée François. Relation du voyage de la mer du sud fait pendant les années 1712, 1713, 1714. Amsterdam, P. Humbert, 1717. F2221.F86   [1303]
Contains music. First edition published in Paris, 1716. Cf. Pereira Salas, *Los orígenes del arte musical en Chile* [Item no. 1230], p. 313-315.

Guevara, Tomás. Folklore araucano; refranes, cuentos, cantos, etc. Santiago de Chile, Impr. Cervantes, 1911. 288 p. il. F3126.G93   [1304]
"Cantos", p. 119-134. Texts in Araucanian and Spanish. No music.

Gusinde, Martín. Die Feuerland Indianer. v. 1, Die Selk'nam. v. 2, Die Yamana. Mödling bei Wien, Verlag

der internationalen zeitschrift *Anthropos*, 1931-1937. F2986.G96   [1305]
The *kloketen* celebration among the Selk'nam Indians (p. 808-1083) is given a great deal of space in this first volume; the complete history and detailed description of this festival, the significance of each section, the choreography of the dance are here gone into thoroughly and scientifically. This section also includes sketches and 24 musical examples. The singing of the medicine man is described, p. 753-755. Vol. 2, *Die Yamana*, contains information on the song and dance during the festivals for the consecration of youth, p. 917-947. See also p. 1468-1471 for music references, and statements concerning the poverty of music culture among these Indians. The chapters on religions in these 2 volumes, and the index (*Gesang, tanz,* etc.) also provide material on music and dance.

Hornbostel, Erich M. von. Fuegian songs. *Amer. anthrop.*, v. 38, no. 3 (1936), p. 357-367.   [1306]
A scientific study, with 15 tunes.

Isamitt, Carlos. Araucanian art. II, Music. *Bull. pan amer. union*, v. 68, no. 5 (1934), p. 362-364.   [1307]
Describes the author's experiences in collecting Araucanian folk songs.

——. Cantos mágicos de los Araucanos. *Rev. arte*, v. 1, no. 6 (1935), p. 8-13.   [1308]
3 pages of music.

——. La danza entre los araucanos. *Bol. lat. am. mús.*, v. 5 (Oct. 1941), p. 601-606.   [1309]

——. El machitún y sus elementos musicales de carácter mágico. *Rev. arte*, v. 1 (Oct.-Nov. 1934), p. 5-9.   [1310]

Latchman, Ricardo Eduardo. La organización social y las creencias religiosas de los Araucanos. Santiago, Imp. Cervantes, 1924. 626 p. F3126.L36 [1311]
Dance and music in connection with festivities, p. 234; dances p. 250-260, with

succeeding pages which deal with ceremonies.

Lavin, Carlos. La musique des Araucans. *Rev. musicale*, v. 6 (March 1925), p. 247-250. [1312]

Includes 1 tune taken from Frézier, 2 tunes recorded by Felix José de Augusta, and 2 tunes of unstated source.

Lenz, Rudolf. Estudios araucanos. Santiago de Chile, Imprenta Cervantes, 1895-97. 485 p. F3126.L57 [1313]

"Publicados en los Anales de la Universidad de Chile, t. xcvii."

Includes: Cantos de los indios de Chile en lengua mapuche, con traducción literal al castellano.

Medina, José Toribio. Los aboríjenes de Chile. Santiago, Impr. Gutenberg, 1882, 427 p. plates F3069.M49 [1314]

Includes references to the music and dances of the aborigines of Chile, p. 293-302, with 1 tune quoted from Frézier [No. 1303], p. 301. Illustrations of musical instruments, figures 79, 80, 82.

Moesbach, Ernesto Wilhelm de. Vida y costumbres de los indígenas araucanos en la segunda mitad del siglo xix. Santiago de Chile, Imprenta Cervantes, 1930. 464 p. F3126.M64 [1315]

On cover: Prólogo, revisión y notas del dr. Rodolfo Lenz. Santiago de Chile, Imprenta universitaria, 1936. Araucanian and Spanish in parallel columns. Description of festival dances, p. 371-394.

Robles Rodríguez, Eulojio. Costumbres i creencias araucanas. *Rev. folklore chileno*, v. 3, no. 4 (1912), p. 153-181, 251-265. [1316]

Ruiz Aldea, P. Los Araucanos i sus costumbres. Santiago, 1902. [Biblioteca de autores chilenos, v. 5] 84 p. F3051.B-58 v. 5 [1317]

Dance, p. 26-27.

Soustelle, Georgette and Jacques. Folklore chilien. Textes choisis et traduits, avec des annotations. Avantpropos de Gabriela Mistral. Paris, Institut international de coopération intellectuelle, 1938. 230 p. GR133.C5S63 [1318]

Includes: Chants araucans.

Vicuña Cifuentes, Julio. Romances populares y vulgares, recogidos de la tradición oral chilena. Santiago de Chile, Impr. Barcelona, 1912. 580 p. PQ8089.-V5 and PQ8033.B5 v. 7 [1319]

Text of popular ballads.

2. Instruments

Amberga, Jerónimo de. Una flauta de Pan araucana. *Rev. chil. hist. geog.*, v. 37 (1921), p. 98-100 [1320]

Cerruto, Oscar. Instrumentos de la expresión Aymará. *Atenea*, año 13, v. 33, no. 128 (Feb. 1936), p. 172-174. [1321]

Impressionistic definitions of native musical instruments.

House, Émile. Une époppée indienne; les Araucans du Chili, histoire, guerres, croyances, coutumes du xive au xxe siècle. Paris, Plon, 1939. 310 p. il. F3126.H68 [1322]

References to music and musical instruments, with diagram of stone flute, p. 189-193.

Isamitt, Carlos. Cuatro instrumentos musicales araucanos. *Bol. lat. am. mús.*, v. 3 (1937), p. 55-66. [1322x]

Describes the *lolkin, pifülka, küllküll*, and *pinkulwe* with about 10 musical examples and drawings of the instruments.

——. Un instrumento araucano: la trutruka. *Bo. lat. am. mús.*, v. 1 (1935), p. 43-46 [1323]

Detailed description of a primitive wind instrument, illustrated. Includes 5 brief musical examples (scales, rhythms, etc.)

——. Los instrumentos araucanos. *Bol. lat. am. mús.*, v. 4 (1938), p. 305-312. il. [1324]

The following instruments are described: wada, künkülkawe, yüullu, trompe or birimbao, corneta and charango.

Joseph, H. Claude. La vivienda arauca-na. *An. univ. Santiago*, v. 1, parts 1-2 (1931), p. 229-251. **[1325]**

Musical instruments, p. 236-238 (with illustrations).

Knoche, Walter. Los Uti-Krag del Río Doce. *Rev. chil .hist. geog.*, v. 5 (1913), p. 230-240 **[1326]**

"Las flautas nasales que Garbe encontró todavía en 1910, en 1912 ya no existían", p. 235.

Rivadeneira, Ester. Folklore de la provincia de Bio-Bio. *Rev. chil. hist. geog.*, v. 87, no. 95 (July-Dec. 1939), p. 95-161. **[1327]**

Includes description of a native musical instrument, the *trutruca*.

(c) DANCES

Barahona y Vega, Clemente. De la tie-rruca chilena. Santiago de Chile, Imprenta Chile, 1015. 3 v. F3059.B22 **[1328]**

Vol. 1, *La danza popular de Chile y el ABC*, deals with various aspects of the *cueca*.

———. La zamacueca y la rosa en el folklore chileno. 2d ed. augmented. Santiago, 1913. **[1329]**

Reprinted from the *Revista de derecho, historia y letras* (Buenos Aires), v. 38 and v. 39 (1910-11). Contains numerous folk song texts, also descriptions of music and dancing in Chile by travellers of the 19th century.

Barros Grez, Daniel. La zamacueca; estudio de costumbres. Discurso leído en la Academia de bellas letras el 26 de mayo de 1877. Santiago de Chile, F. Schrebler, 1877 16 p. **[1330]**

Cavada, Francisco Javier. Chiloé y los Chilotes. Santiago, Imp. universitaria, 1914. 448 p. F3146.C37 **[1331]**

Chap. 9, *Bailes populares*, p. 163-175; this contains a list of dances with short descriptions of each ,and accompanying refrains and verses.

Durand, Luis. Interpretación de la cueca. *Atenea*, año 16, v. 56, no. 167 (May 1939), p. 258-266. **[1332]**

Literary description of the *cueca*.

Franco Zubicueta, Alfredo. Tratado de baile. 7 ed. Santiago de Chile, 1908. **[1333]**

Cited by Pereira Salas [no. 1230], p. 349.

Hall, Basil. Extracts from a journal, writeen on the coasts of Chili, Peru and Mexico in the years 1820, 1821, 1822. Edinburgh, printed for Archibald Constable and co., Edinburgh; and Hurst, Robinson and co., London, 1824, 2 v. 3d ed. F2213.H15 **[1334]**

Concerning Chile, see p. 13-15 (dances) and music); p. 9-10 (dancing, singing and musical instruments); p. 155-158 (dance), all v. 1, Vol. 2 includes Peruvian harp, p. 103, and Mexican dance, p. 224-225.

Johnston, Samuel Burr. Diario de un tipógrafo yanqui en Chile y Perú. Madrid, Editorial América, 1919. 228 p. F3094.J73 **[1335]**

Music and dance, p. 102; guitar in the possession of every family, p. 204.

Latcham, Ricardo Eduardo. La fiesta de Andacollo y sus danzas. *Rev. folklore chileno*, v. 1, no. 5 (1910), p. 197-219. **[1336]**

Verses sung to the Virgin of Andacollo, p. 210-211. Dances of the festival, p. 214-219.

Lenz, Rodolfo. Diccionario etimológico de las voces chilenas derivadas de lenguas indígenas. Santiago, Imp. Cervantes, 1905-10. 929 p. PC4882.L32 **[1337]**

Under derivatives of *zambo* is a complete delineation of the *zambacueca* or *cueca*, with words to a *zambacueca cantora*, p. 785-788. See also *quena*, p. 657, *yaravi*, p. 781.

Pereira Salas, Eugenio. Danzas y cantos populares de la patria vieja. *Anales de la facultad de filosofía y educación de la Universidad de Chile.*

CHILE 175

Sección de filología. Homenaje a la
memoria del Dr. Rodolfo Lenz. No. 1
(1937-38), p. 58-76.   [1338]
Material incorporated in item no. 1230.

——. Los orígenes del arte musical en
Chile. Publicaciones de la Universidad
de Chile. Santiago, Imprenta universitaria, 1941. 373 p. ML232.5.P
                              [1339]
Includes numerous references to dances,
esp. p. 1-7, 168-199, 206-303. Music facsimiles; Araucanian tune taken from Frézier: *Boleras,* Antonio Aranaz; *Zapateo,*
from Frézier; *El cuando,* from Pöppig;
Canción; Tonadita popular; 2 *zamacuecas,* etc. Also includes 16 folk tunes with
the main text, Illustrations of musical
instruments, dances, etc.

Pöppig, Eduard Friedrich. Reise in
Chile, Peru, und auf dem Amazonen-
ströme während der jahre 1827-
1832. Leipzig, F. Fleischer, 1835-36. 2
v. F2213.P74   [1340]
Vol. 2 has musical appendix, "El cuando, baile nacional de Chile", for voice and
piano, Spanish words.

Raygada, Carlos. Panorama musical del
Perú. *Bol. lat. am. mús.,* v. 2 (1936),
p. 169-214   [1341]
Includes the notation of a *sapateo,*
"danza del Perú y Chile", first printed by
M. Frézier in 1732.

Roco del Campo, Antonio, ed. Panorama y color de Chile; antología litera-
rio-descriptiva del paisaje y las costumbres nacionales, Santiago, Ed. Ercilla,
1939. 332 p.   [1342]
Includes descriptions of dances.

Santelices, Sergio. La cueca-Chile's national dance. *Panam mag.,* v. 4, no. 1
(Apr. 1943), p. 22-23.   [1343]
Description of the *cueca* and the accompanying ceremony, with a brief note on its
origin.

Sedgwick, Ruth. Christmas in Andacollo. *Bull. pan. amer. union,* v. 69, no.

12 (Dec. 1935), p. 910-916. il.
                              [1344]
Describes the dance of the "chinos".

Smith, Edmond Reuel. Los Araucanos.
Santiago de Chile, Imprenta universitaria, 1914. 241 p. F3126.S652
                              [1345]
Zamacueca, p. 28-29, with references to
the musical accompaniment; mention of
dancing, p. 66, 209; musical instruments,
p. 155; improvising of songs (with example
of a few lines), p. 214. First edition in
English, *The Araucanians,* London, 1855.

Sousa, John Philip, comp. National, patriotic and typical airs of all lands.
Philadelphia, Harry Coleman, 1890.
283 p. M1627.C72C   [1345x]
Includes a *cueca* from Chile, p. 62.

Sutcliffe, Thomas. Sixteen years in Chile
and Peru. London, Paris, Fisher, son
and co., 1841. 563 p. F3095.S96
                              [1346]
Chinganas (dancing houses) and instruments played there, p. 362-364.

Vowell, Richard Longeville. Campaigns
and cruises in Venezuela and New
Granada ... London, Longman & co.,
1831. 3 v. F2235.V87   [1347]
Vol. 1: Chilean national dances, p. 310;
words of a revolutionary song of Bolivar's
troops (translated), p. 467; also mention
of music in the following pages, 116, 173,
177, 187. Vol. 2: music, p. 35; words of
La montonera (a serenade) and *La zam-
bullidora,* p. 35-38 (with translations of
these songs in the Notes at the back of the
book); dancing, musical instruments, p.
103.

Zañartu, Sady. La cueca chilena. *Plus
ultra,* v. 14, no. 157 (31 May 1939), 2
p.   [1348]
With photograph and several selections
from verses accompany this dance.

(D) COLLECTIONS OF MUSIC

Alba, Antonio. Cantares del pueblo chileno, arreglados para canto y guitarra.

Santiago, Casa Niemeyer, 1898.
[1349]
Cited by Pereira Salas [no. 1230], p. 303.

Sandoval, Luis. Selección de canciones populares chilenas. Santiago, 1937.
[1351]
Cited by Pereira Salas, *loc. cit.*

Balmaceda, Jorge. Canciones chilenas. Buenos Aires, n. d.   [1350]
Cited by Pereira Salas, *loc. cit.*

Vidales, Pablo. Album de cantos escolares. Santiago, Impr. R. Brías, 1930. 96 p.   [1352]

SUPPLEMENT TO 1960

Continuing his comprehensive study on the history of music in Chile, Dr. Eugenio Pereira Salas published in 1957 the *Historia de la música en Chile*, covering the period from 1850 to 1900 (item no. 478a). A large portion of this work is taken up by an account of operatic performances in Chile, including the long hegemony of Italian opera, the introduction of French *opéra comique*, the vogue of the Spanish *zarzuela*, the impact of the Wagnerin music drama, and the beginnings of a national opera. The first opera by a Chilean composer to be produced at the Teatro Municipal of Santiago was *La Florista de Lugano* by Eleodoro Ortiz de Zárate, on November 2, 1895.

Other chapters (V, IX, XV) deal with musical education in Chile, giving particular attention to the National Conservatory of Music, which began to function in 1851 and whose first director was Adolfo Desjardins. The teaching of music in the public schools was placed on a firm footing following the National Congress of Pedagogy held in 1889.

In accordance with his broad sociological view of musical history, Pereira Salas devotes several chapters (notably VI, XVI, XX) to the place of music in Chilean society, and completes his panoramic survey with chapters on religious music (XVII) and on military music (XVIII).

The concluding chapter deals with "Musical Creation in Chile" from 1850 to 1900, admittedly a rather barren period creatively, and therefore primarily of antiquarian interest. In his final sentence, the author justifies his patient labor and exhaustive research with these words: "We have rendered justice and paid tribute to the many forgotten artists who laid the foundations of the great work that is the magnificent edifice of contemporary musical activity (in Chile)."

Contemporary musical composition in Chile, from 1900 to 1951, is the subject of an important book by Vicente Salas Viu, *La Creación musical en Chile*, published in 1952. The first six chapters of this work deal with musical activities, tendencies, organizations and institutions during the first half of the 20th century. Separate chapters are devoted to the activities of the Sociedad Bach, to the University of Chile and music, and to the Institute of Musical Extension, which since its creation in 1940 has continued to be of increasing importance in the musical life of Chile. Chapter VI discusses "Main trends in contemporary musical creation" (*Tendencias predominantes en la creación musical contemporánea*).

Salas Viu divides the contemporary composers of Chile into three main groups: (1) those who are linked to the Romanticism of the past; (2) those who took Impressionism as their point of departure; (3) those who are involved in the most recent developments of our time. Within these main groups he establishes subdivisions. In the first, are those, on the one hand, who retrocede technically and aesthetically toward the beginnings of Romanticism, and on the other hand, those who move in the forefront of the Post-Romantic movement. In the second group, are those who, starting from Impressionism, follow the direction of nationalist tendencies; and those who, starting from Impressionistic ultra-chromaticism, take up "advanced" positions. In the third group, are musicians who follow tendencies related to Impressionism or Expressionism, i. e., who have Post-Romantic roots; and those who from the beginning tended toward a Neo-Classicism influenced by the later compositions of Falla, Bartok and Stravinsky.

Following these introductory chapters, the bulk of the work consists of biobibliographical entries on forty Chilean composers, arranged alphabetically. Their more important works are described in considerable detail, but without any musical notations. The composers who receive the most attention are Pedro Humberto Allende, René Amengual, Prospero Bisquertt, Carlos Isamitt, Alfonso Leng, Alfonso Letelier, Juan Orrego Salas, Carlos Riesco, Domingo Santa Cruz, and Enrique Soro.

A comprehensive survey of musical trends in Chilean composition of the 20th century, written from the personal viewpoint of the author, is the article by Domingo Santa Cruz titled "Trayectoria musical de Chile", published in *Buenos Aires musical* (item 509a).

Chile suffered the loss of several of her most outstanding composers, notably Enrique Soro, Pedro Humberto Allende, René Amengual, Alfonso Leng and Jorge Urrutia.

BIBLIOGRAPHY

A. PRIMITIVE, FOLK, and POPULAR MUSIC

Barros, Raquel, and Danneman, Manuel. La poesía folklórica de Melpilla. *Rev. mus. chil.,* año 12, no. 60 (July-August 1958), p. 48-70. (music) il.
[388a]
"El departamento de Melipilla puede considerarse, en la actualidad, no sólo como la región más pródiga en poesía folklórica, de la provincia de Santiago, sino como una de las más notables del país." Photographs, song texts, and 5 musical examples.

Centenario del folklore, 22 de agosto de 1946; festividades de la semana del folklore chileno. Santiago, Instituto de investigación del folklore musical, Facultad de bellas artes de la Universidad de Chile, 1946 26 p. il. (incl. music). **[389a]**

Comments on the folk festival by Carlos Isamitt, also data on the Instituto and on the Museo de arte folklórico.

Charlín Ojeda, Carlos. Cantares de la Isla de Pascua. *Atenea,* año 23, v. 85, no. 253-254 (July-Aug. 1946), p. 102-111. **[390a]**

A first-hand study of the folk songs of the people of Easter Island. Words only of 6 songs with Spanish equivalent. (C. S.)

Garrido, Pablo. Biografía de la cueca. Santiago de Chile, Ediciones Ercilla, 1943. 133 p. il. **[391a]**

Though somewhat anecdotal and diffuse in style, this volume contains interesting background material on the history of the *cueca,* together with an analysis if its metrical, melodic and harmonic elements. Cf. Vega, *La Forma de la Cueca Chilena* (item 421a).

Gil, Bonifacio. Juegos infantiles de Extremadura y su folklore musical. *Rev. mus. chil.,* v. 5, no. 33 (Apr.-May 1949), p. 18-39. **[392a]**

The author collected children's songs and games in Spain from 1939, particularly from the regions of Old Castille, Andalucia and Extremadura. The latter region is said to have been of great influence on Chilean and other Latin American folk culture. This study begins with a bibliographical survey then provides previously unpublished texts, comments and music. 33 music examples.

Hornbostel, Erich M. von. Canciones de Tierra del Fuego. *Rev. mus. chil.,* año 7, no. 41 (Autumn 1951), p. 71-84. (music). **[393a]**

Based on material gathered by Martin Gusinde (q. v.) Originally published in English in *Amer. Anthrop.* (see item no. 1306)

Instituto de extensión musical. Santiago, Universidad de Chile, 1943. 53 p. **[394a]**

Perspectiva histórica de la música popular chilena, por Eugenio Pereira Salas. *Tradiciones de la música típica chilena,* por Carlos Lavín. *Palabras del presidente del*

Instituto de extensión musical, por Domingo Santa Cruz. *Comentarios sobre la selección de música folklórica,* por Pablo Garrido. 12 melodías en notación musical y texto. *3 tipos de zamacueca,* por Carlos Lavín. *La música popular de Chile y la española,* por Vicente Salas Viu. *A propósito de investigación folklórica;* lo que dicen Carlos Isamitt, Carlos Lavín, Pablo Garrido, Jorge Urrutia. *Apuntes sobre el problema folklórico,* por Filomena Salas. (R. S. B.)

Isamitt, Carlos. El folklore como elemento básico del liceo renovado. *Rev. mus. chil.,* año 2, no. 13 (July-August 1946), p. 21-24. **[395a]**

Folklore in the schools.

Machiluwn, una danza araucana. *Rev. estud. mus.,* v. 1, no. 1 (Aug. 1949), p. 102-108. **[396a]**

On the ceremony with which a new *machi* (medicine-woman) inaugurated her profession. Some music notations. (C.S.)

Lavín, Carlos. El rabel y los instrumentos chilenos.. *Rev. mus. chil.,* v. 10, no. 48 (Jan. 1955), p. 15-27. **[397a]**

Important article. Much information on instrument makers in Chilean cities, from 1854; descriptions of early colonial instruments in the Chilean folklore archives; reference to contemporary folk instruments (stringed). Bibliography. 4 pages of photographs.

——. El rabel y los instrumentos chilenos. Santiago, Universidad de Chile, Instituto de investigaciones musicales, 1955. (Colección de ensayos, no. 10). **[398a]**

A reprint of the preceding item.

——. La música sacra de Chile. *Rev. mus. chil.,* v. 8, no. 43 (Sept. 1952), p. 76-82. (music) **[399a]**

Includes words and music of *Salve Dolorosa, Via Crucis,* and *Salve Chilota.*

——. Las fiestas rituales de La Candelaria. *Rev. mus. chil.,* v. 5, no. 34 (June-July 1949), p. 26-33. **[400a]**

On the ritual celebrations of Candlemas (February 2) at Copiapo oasis in the Atacama desert, a place of pilgrimage. Gives history, description of attendance, costumes, dances, musical instruments, songs. Two plates, map of Chile. 2 song texts, 2 music examples. (B. K.)

——. La tirana. Fiesta ritual de la provincia de Tarapaca. *Rev. mus. chil.,* v. 6, no. 37 (autumn 1950), p. 12-36. (music).   [401a]

——. La vidalita argentina y el vidalay chileno. *Rev. mus. chil.,* v. 8, no. 43 (Sept. 1952), p. 68-75. (music). [402a]

——. Nuestra Señora de las Peñas; fiesta ritual del norte de Chile. *Rev. mus. chil.,* v. 4, no. 31 (Oct.-Nov. 1948), p. 9-20; no. 32 (Dec. 1948-Jan. 1949), p. 27-40.   [403a]

Careful study of the cult of Our Lady of the Rocks, in northernmost Chile, tracing it to a legendary miracle in 1642 when she appeared before a traveller. The church, not far from Arica, is visited by pilgrims annually in October. Lavín describes the location, the legend, the participants, the instrumental groups in attendance, the ritual ceremony, the songs and dances. Map of Chile showing pilgrimage centers, 5 photographs, 15 music examples, 20 song texts. (B. K.)

——. Nuestra Señora de las Peñas; fiesta ritual del norte de Chile. Santiago de Chile, Instituto de investigaciones musicales, 1949. 25 p. il. (incl. music). (Colección de ensayos, no. 5). [404a]

A reprint of the preceding item.

Mendoza, Vicente T. El cuando. *Nuestra música,* v. 3, no. 11 (July 1948), p. 188-205.   [405a]

Draws a parallel between a Chilean and a Mexican *cuando.* Six music notations and bibliography. (C. S.)

——. La canción chilena en México. Santiago de Chile, Instituto de Investigaciones musicales, 1948. 15 p. music. (Colección de ensayos, no. 4). [406a]

——. La música popular en Chile. *Andean quarterly.* Santiago de Chile (Spring 1944), p. 27-32.   [407a]

Examines various types of musical folklore of Chile, in ballads, songs and dances, and indicates many parallels with si-

milar forms in Mexican folk music, often due to their common Spanish source, though some cases seem to indicate direct influence from Chile to Mexico. (R. S. B.)

Mittelbach Medina, Domingo. De los orígenes de la música vernácula. *Lyra,* v. 4, no. 35-36 (June-July 1946), 2 p. [408a]

Three music notations, Patagonian, Araucanian, Tobas. One drawing of a *violín pampa.* (C. S.)

Pereira Salas, Eugenio. El rincón de la historia. La llegada de los "Negro Spirituals" a Chile. *Rev. mus. chil.,* v. 4, no. 31 (Oct.-Nov.1948), p. 68.[409a]

Establishes date of arrival of Negro spirituals in Chile as 1859 in Valparaiso, and October 1860 in Santiago, sung by a group calling itself the Ethiopian Minstrels, directed by C. Henry. Their program included "Mother dear; I am thinking on; Black smoke; Wasn't that a pull back", and plantation scenes with songs and banjo playing.

——. El rincón de la historia: La primera danza chilena. *Rev. mus. chil.,* v. 1, no. 1 (May 1945), p. 3-39.   [410a]

Two epistolary references, of 1664 and 1668, concerning the dance called *panana,* the first, by the Bishop Fray Diego de Umanzoro, calling it "un baile lascivo", the second, by Lorenzo (*sic*) de Arixabala, refering to it as "un baile infame". (B. K.)

——. La música de la Isla de Pascua. *Rev. mus. chil.,* v. 2, no. 17-1 (Jan. 1947), p. 9-24. (music).   [411a]

Music and texts of 7 songs from Easter Island, with a scholarly discussion of the subject.

——. La música de la isla de Pascua. Santiago de Chile, Instituto de investigaciones musicales, 1947. 16 p. il. (music) (Colección de ensayos, no. 1).   [412a]

This is the first monograph published by the "Institute for musical research" of the University of Chile. The data in this study of primitive music in Easter Island are drawn chiefly from Métraux and Walter Koche. Contains music and texts

of 7 songs, and bibliographical footnotes.
A reprint of the preceding item.

――――. Los estudios folklóricos y el folklore musical en Chile. *Rev. mus. chil.*, v. I, no. I (May 1945), p. 4-12. **[413a]**
Survey of collectors, programs of collection, and publications of or about Chilean folklore and folk music. Useful bibliographic data (B. K.)

Plath, Oreste. Folklore chileno; aspectos populares infantiles. Santiago, Universidad de Chile, 1946. 120 p. **[414a]**
Texts only of 31 cradle songs and of 33 children's singing games.

――――. O pregão chileno. *Rev. bras. mús.*, v. 9 (1944). Also available as reprint (9 p.) **[415a]**

Sepúlveda, María Luisa. Cancionero chileno. Canciones y tonadas chilenas del siglo diecinueve para canto y guitarra. 2ª serie. Recopiladas y armonizadas. Santiago, Casa Amarilla, 1945. 14 p. **[416a]**
Preface by Oreste Plath. 12 folksongs taken from oral tradition, chiefly from Ñuble and Chillán, arranged by the compiler.

――――. Generalidades sobre pregones. *Rev. Mus. chil.*, v. 3, nos. 25-26 (Oct.-Nov. 1947), p. 30-32. **[417a]**
Words and music of 6 *pregones* (street vendors' cries).

――――. La voz del pasado; pregones santiagueños antiguos y otros temas folklóricos. Santiago, Casa Amarilla, 1943 (?) 14 p. il. **[418a]**
Words and music of 11 street vendors' cries and of 2 other folksongs of Chile.

Titiev, Mischa. Social singing among the Mapuche. *In* Museum of anthropology, Anthropological papers, Univ. of Michigan, Ann Arbor, Michigan, 1949. 17 p. **[419a]**
Several Araucanian songs, analyzed for the light they shed on the interrelations of social organizations and personality development. (D. B. S.)

Urrutia Blondel, Jorge. Reportaje de un músico a Rapa-Nui. *Rev. mus. chil.*, v. 12, no. 60 (July-Aug. 1958), p. 547 il. **[420a]**
"Contribución al estudio del folklore musical de Pascua, con motivo de un reciente viaje a la Isla." Includes 6 photographs taken on Easter Island, song texts, but no music.

Vega, Carlos. La forma de la cueca chilena. *Rev. mus. chilena*, v. 3, nos. 20-21 (1947), p. 7-21; nos. 22-23, p. 15-45. **[421a]**
Morphology of the Chilean *cueca*, with musical analysis based on the author's theory of phraseology (cf. item no. 526), illustrated by numerous diagrams and notations. "Cuatro períodos temáticamente iguales o ligeramente variados, y las dos primeras frases de un quinto período, también sobre el tema inicial, integran la forma de composición ... característica de la cueca chilena." The 2nd part of the article studies the poetic form and its effect on the basic musical patterns of the *cueca*. This is the most detailed and complete analytical study of the form of the *cueca* that has thus far b·en published.

――――. La forma de la cueca chilena. Santiago, Universidad de Chile, Instituto de Investigaciones musicales, n. d. [1947]. 46 p. (Colección de ensayos, no. 2). **[422a]**
A reprint of the preceding item.

Violeta Parra, hermana mayor de los cantores populares. *Rev. mus. chil.*, v. 12, no. 60 (July-Aug. 1958), p. 71-77. il. **[423a]**
"Violeta Parra sabe tocar nuestros instrumentos folklóricos, la guitarra y el guitarrón y cantar a lo poeta. Sabe escribir versos a 'lo divino' y a 'lo humano', compone sus propias melodías y puede improvisar unas décimas si la ocasión lo exige." Four photographs, including one with *guitarrón*.

(B) ART MUSIC AND MISCELLANEOUS

Aguilar, Miguel. La evolución estilística en la obra de René Amengual. *Rev.*

mus. chil., v. 9, no. 47 (Oct. 1954), p. 9-17. **[424a]**

Quite detailed accound of the stylistic evolution of the Chilean composer who died in August 1954 at the age of 42. Gives list of 6 reviews of performances of Amengual works appearing in *Rev. mus. chil.*, and cites list of his works (in no. 39, p. 54).

———. Los terceros festivales de música chilena en 1952. *Rev. mus. chil.*, v. 9, no. 44 (Jan. 1954), p. 58-73. **[425a]**

Review and some analysis of large number of new works performed at the Third Festival of Chilean Music, held in November and December of 1952. Especial attention to Free Focke's *Sinfonía de la ópera "Deirdre"*, Sextet for Wind Instruments by René Amengual, *Concierto de Cámara* by Juan Orrego Salas, *Diez Preludios para piano* by Carlos Botto. 8 music examples. Signed "M. A."

Allende Sarón, Adolfo. Momentos musicales. *Rev. Soc. escritores Chile*, v. 1, no. 2 (Autumn 1945), p. 62-72; no. 3 (Winter 1945), p. 50-60 **[426a]**

Anecdotes of Chilean music life. Author believes these are not yet gathered together in one place. (C. S.)

———. Música Araucana. *Antártica*, no. 12 (Aug. 1945), p. 84-88. **[427a]**

The distinguished composer and author traces his experiences of Araucanian music. He is convinced there exists unmistakable aboriginal art music of high artistic value. Three notations of two songs and one dance (for trutruca "by" J. de D. Ñanca, blind mapuche). (C. S.)

———. Datos biográficos de Humberto Allende. Santiago de Chile, Soc. imp. y lit. Universo, 1933. 28 p. il. (port.) **[428a]**

———. Los músicos chilenos y la obra de Pedro Humberto Allende. *Rev. mus. chil.*, v. 1, no. 5 (Sept. 1945), p. 48-56. **[429a]**

In special issue devoted to Allende, tribute is rendered to him by many Chilean musicians. Includes also "Noticia biográfica", p. 5-7; "Los grandes maestros y la obra de P. H. Allende", p. 62-65; and "Catálogo de las obras de P. H. Allen-

de", p. 66-70. Other articles are listed separately. This issue was published on the occasion of the award of the first National Art Prize (1945) presented to a Chilean composer.

Amengual, René. El sentido dramático de Santa Cruz en sus obras para piano. *Rev. mus. chil.*, v. 8, no. 42 (Dec. 1951), p. 90-119. (music). **[430a]**

With 25 musical illustrations.

———. La música vocal [de P. H. Allende]. *Rev. mus. chil.*, v. 1, no. 5 (Sept. 1945), p. 37-47. **[431a]**

Includes music for voice with piano, for voice with orchestra, and unaccompanied choral music.

Asuar, José Vicente. La Sinfonía de Roberto Falabella. *Rev. mus. chil.*, v. 12, no. 61 (Sept.-Oct. 1958), p. 15-32. **[432a]**

This Symphony was first performed in 1956; its composer died in 1958. Asuar considers it very important. Analysis with ten musical examples.

Becerra, Gustavo. El estilo de los "Vitrales de la Anunciación". *Rev. mus. chil.*, v. 12, no. 57 (Jan.Feb. 1958), p. 5-22. **[433a]**

Analysis of a work by Alfonso Letelier, originally written as incidental music for a production of Claudel's *L'annonce faite à Marie* by the Catholic University of Chile Theatre Group in 1949. With 31 musical notations.

———. La música sinfónica de Alfonso Leng. *Rev. mus. chil.*, v. 11, no. 54 (Aug.-Sept. 1957), p. 42-58. (music) **[434a]**

Discusses *Preludios Orquestales* (1912), (originally for piano), *La Muerte de Alsino* (1920-21), and *Fantasía* for piano and orchestra (1926).

———. Los "lieder" de Domingo Santa Cruz. *Rev. mus. chil.*, año 8, no. 42 (Dec. 1951), p. 120-127. (music). **[435a]**

With 7 musical illustrations.

———. Próspero Bisquertt, premio nacional de arte 1954. *Rev. mus. chil.*, v. 9, no. 47 (Oct. 1954), p. 18-29. [436a] Biographical sketch, appraisal of works, and analysis.

——. Roberto Falabella Correa (1926-1958). *Rev. mus. chil.*, v. 12, no. 62 (Nov.-Dec. 1958), p. 59-60. [437a] The untimely death of a promising Chilean composer who was planning an opera on the subject of Sacco and Vanzetti. For an analysis of his First Symphony, see item no. 432a.

Botto, Carlos. Lo que pienso de la segunda sinfonía de Gustavo Becerra. *Rev. mus. chil.*, v. 12, no. 63 (Jan.-Feb. 1959), p. 38-43. (music). [438a] The symphony is based on a 12-tone row.

Cárcamo, F. Enseñanza de la música en las escuelas. *Rev. mus. chil.*, v. 2, no. 10 (April 1946), p. 26-29. [439a]

Chase, Gilbert. Chile: European in culture. *Mus. Amer.*, v. 70, no. 2 (Jan. 1950), p. 10, 53-54. [440a] Deals with musical organization in Chile. Discusses some leading composers, such as Soro, Allende, and Santa Cruz.

Colli, Nino. Las obras de cámara en el segundo festival de música chilena. *Rev. mús. chil.*, v. 6, no. 39 (Spring 1950), p. 65-83. [441a] Discusses works by R. Puelma, A. Montecino, R. Campbell, Amengual, Letelier, Quinteros, Botto, *et alter*. With 14 musical illustrations.

[Festivales de música chilena]. Cuartos festivales de música chilena. *Rev. mus. chil.*, v. 10, no. 48 (Jan. 1955), p. 43-70. [442a] Long review of the fourth Chilean music festival. Analysis with music examples of Free Focke's Symphony, Darwin Vargas' Chamber Cantata, Acario Cotapos' *Imaginación de mi país* (symphonic), a fragment of Alfonso Letelier's opera-oratorio *Tobias and Sara*, Gustavo Becerra's Trio for Flute, violin and piano (no music examples), Carlos Botto's String Quartet, Roberto Falabella's Sonata for violin

and piano. Symphonic analysis signed "A. A. B.", chamber music analysis signed "M. A."

Festivales y concursos de música chilena de 1948. Santiago, Universidad de Chile, Publicaciones del Instituto de extensión musical, n. d. 17 p. [443a] A summary of the festival and the prizes, by Domingo Santa Cruz, p. 3-9.

Gayán, Elisa. La educación musical en Chile. *Rev. mus. chil.*, v. 12, no. 59, (May-June 1958), p. 7-10. [444a]

——. La primera convención de educadores musicales. *Rev. mus. chil.*, v. 4, no. 28 (Apr.-May 1948), p. 22-27. [445a] La Asociación de Educación Musical was founded in 1945, a national organization with almost all the music teachers of Chile as members. Its first convention was held in January 1948. Miss Gayán, the secretary of the Association, describes the attendance, and the resolution on school music, advanced music studies and extracurricular music education, and lists new officers. (B. K.)

Grebe, María Ester. Sexteto de Juan Orrego Salas para clarinete en Si bemol, cuarteto de cuerdas y piano. *Rev. mus. chil.*, v. 12, no. 58 (Mar.-Apr. 1958), p. 59-76. [446a] Analysis, with 30 music examples, of work (Op. 38) commissioned by Samuel Wechsler for the Berkshire music center, and completed in March 1954.

Huneeus Gana, Jorge. Cuadro histórico de la producción intelectual de Chile. (Biblioteca de escritores de Chile, tomo 1. Introducción a la biblioteca). Santiago, Chile, 1910. xvi. 880 p. [447a] Cap. XVII, "Las bellas artes en Chile", p. 785-863; includes section "La música", p. 845-863; with historical data on the development of musical activity in Chile. Mentions the periodicals *El semanario musical* (1852) and *Las bellas artes* (ca. 1869), the latter edited by J. J. Thompson.

Isamitt, Carlos. El folklore en la creación artística de los compositores chilenos.

Rev. mus. chil., v. 11, no. 55 (Oct.-Nov. 1957), p. 24-36.   [448a]

In contrast to Domingo Santa Cruz, who has proclaimed that Chilean composers have no use for folklore, Isamitt shows that many Chilean composers have drawn upon indigenous and *criollo* musical sources for their compositions.

———. En qué consiste la reforma de la educación musical en secundaria. *Rev. mus. chil.,* v. 2, no. 12 (June 1946), p. 23-25.   [449a]

———. La música sinfónica y de cámara (de P. H. Allende). *Rev. mus. chil.,* v. 1, no. 5 (Sept. 1945), p. 32-36. [450a]

———. La música y el niño. *Rev. mus. chil.,* v. 1, no. 3 (July 1945), p. 8-14.   [451a]

Theoretical remarks on musical perception of infants of five months and ten months, based on observations of two children. 14 musical examples. (B. K.)

Labor cumplida en 1957 por el Instituto de extensión musical de la Universidad de Chile. Santiago de Chile, Ediciones del Instituto de extensión musical, n. d. 56 p.   [452a]

[Lavín, Carlos]. Classified chronological catalog of the works of the Chilean composer Carlos Lavín. *Bol. interam. mús.,* no. 8 (Nov. 1958), p. 25-28.   [453a]

Lavín was born in Santiago de Chile in 1883. He has been active as a folklorist as well as composer.

Leng, Alfonso. Domingo Santa Cruz. *Rev. mus. chil.,* v. 8, no. 42 (Dec. 1951), p. 5-10.   [454a]

A general discussion of his work.

———. Pedro Humberto Allende. *Antártica,* no. 12 (Aug. 1945), p. 81-84.   [455a]

Brief critical note upon one distinguished composer by another. (C. S.)

Letelier, Alfonso. Las composiciones corales de Santa Cruz. *Rev. mus. chil.,*

v. 8, no. 42 (Dec. 1951), p. 43-61. (music).   [456a]

Analysis of the choral compositions, with 20 musical examples.

———. Leng en su producción pianística. *Rev. mus. chil.,* v. 11, no. 54 (Aug.-Sept. 1957), p. 27-41. (music). [457a]

An analysis of Leng's music for piano, with 21 musical examples.

———. Mi visita a Paul Claudel. *Rev. mus. chil.* v. 10, no. 49 (Apr. 1955), p. 18-22.   [458a]

Account of visit to Claudel in southern France in 1952, and their discussion of details of his play *L'Histoire de Tobie et de Sara,* on the basis of which Letelier was composing an opera.

Lira Espejo, Eduardo. Raigambre popular en la expresión de Allende. *Rev. mus. chil.,* v. 1, no. 5 (Sept. 1945), p. 8-14.   [459a]

Los primeros festivales chilenos. *Rev. mus. chil.,* v. 4, no. 32 (Dec. 1948-Jan. 1949), p. 11-18.   [460a]

Formal account of foundation of the music festival by the Institute of Musical Extension, the establishment of prizes, the 1948 competition and the award winners.

Lyons, James. A busy fifty years; Claudio Arrau made his debut 47 years ago when he was three. *Mus. Amer.,* v. 73, no. 5 (Apr. 1953), p. 12-13.   [461a]

Biographical sketch of the Chilean pianist. Two photographs.

Margarit, Jorge. Ramón Carnicer y la canción nacional chilena. *Antártica,* no. 12 (Sept. 1945), p. 23-27.   [462a]

Biographical data on composer of the national anthem of Chile. (C. S.)

Margot Loyola, intérprete de la danza y la canción de Chile. *Rev. mus. chil.,* v. 12, no. 59 (May-June 1958), p. 24-28.   [463a]

Meza, Teobaldo. La música en el liceo renovado. *Rev. mus. chil.,* v. 2, no. 15

(Oct. 1946), p. 23-28; no. 16 (Nov. 1946), p. 22-24.   **[464a]**
Points of view on the reform of music education in Chile.

Núñez Navarrete, Pedro. Carlos Lavín, dignificador de la música araucana. *Rev. educ.*, Santiago, v. 7, no. 46 (Nov. 1947), p. 353-354.   **[465a]**
Biographical sketch of the Chilean composer and folklorist.

——. Pedro Humberto Allende; apuntes para una semblanza. *Rev. mus. chil.,* v. 1, no. 3 (July 1945), p. 15-18.
          [466a]
Biographical sketch of the composer, with some critical comments, especially concerning his use of harmony. (B. K.)

——. Pedro Humberto Allende: Premio nacional música 1945. *Rev. educ.* Santiago, v. 5, no. 32 (Oct. 1945), p. 398-401.   **[467a]**
Brief biographical notes on the composer (b. 1885). One music notation, excerpted from his *Método original de iniciación musical* (1932-1939). (C. S.)

Orrego Salas, Juan. Current chronicle: Chile; the string quartets of Domingo Santa Cruz, *Mus. quart.*, v. 34, no. 3 (July 1948), p. 419-423.   **[468a]**
Place of compositions of Santa Cruz in development of Chilean music, and some analysis of first (1930) and second (1947) string quartets. Two music examples.

——. El concierto para arpa y orquesta de René Amengual. *Rev. mus. chil.,* v. 6, no. 39 (Spring 1950), p. 54-64. (music).   **[469a]**
With 9 musical examples illustrating this analysis of one of Amengual's most important works.

——. El empleo de la forma en la música de Soro; la Sinfonía Romántica y el concierto para piano. *Rev. mus. chil.,* v. 4, no. 30 (Aug.-Sept. 1948), p. 18-23.   **[470a]**
Rather technical analysis of the two works. Four music examples.

——. Los cuartetos de cuerdas de Santa

Cruz. *Rev. mus. chil.,* v. 8, no. 42 (Dec. 1951), p. 62-89. (music). **[471a]**
Analysis of the string quartets, with 24 musical examples.

——. Los "lieder" de Alfonso Leng. *Rev. mus. chil.,* v. 11, no. 54 (Aug.-Sept. 1957), p. 59-64.   **[472a]**

Pan American Union. Departamento de asuntos culturales. Sección de música. Directorio musical de la América Latina. Musical directory of Latin America. *Chile.* Washington, D. C., Pan American union, 1954. 44 p.   **[473a]**
One of a series planned to cover the countries of Latin America, this is devoted to musical institutions, organizations and activities in Chile. Includes "The musical organization of Chile" by Vicente Salas Viu (in Spanish and English).

Pereda Valdés, Ildefonso. P. H. Allende en el Uruguay. *Rev. mus. chil.,* v. 1, no. 5 (Sept. 1945), p. 60-61. **[474a]**
Deals with a visit to Uruguay by the Chilean composer.

Pereira Salas, Eugenio. El centenario de la canción nacional de Chile. *Rev. chil. hist. geog.,* no. 110 (July-Dec. 1947), p. 3-17.   **[475a]**
Brief survey of history of national anthem. (C. S.)

——. El centenario de la canción nacional de Chile Santiago de Chile, Imprenta universitaria, 1948. 15 p.
          [476a]
A reprint of the preceding item.

——. El centenario del teatro municipal 1857-1957. *Rev. mus. chil.,* v. 11, no. 52 (June-July 1957), p. 30-35.   **[477a]**

——. Historia de la música en Chile (1850- 1900). Publicaciones de la Universidad de Chile. Santiago, Editorial del Pacífico, S. A., 1957 379. p. il. (music).   **[478a]**
This detailed account of musical activity in Chile during the second half of the 19th century covers mainly opera, ballet, music teaching, religious music, military music, and the place of music in the social life

of the nation. There are 64 illustrations and several brief musical notations, as well as a comprehensive index.

——. La música chilena en los primeros cincuenta años del siglo xx. *Rev. mus. chi.*, v. 6, no. 40 (Summer 1950-1951), p. 63-78. **[479a]**

An important critical and historical survey.

——. La música chilena en los primeros cincuenta años del siglo xx. *In* Desarrollo de Chile en la primera mitad del siglo xx. Univ. de Chile, Santiago, (1952), v. 2, p. 417-439. **[480a]**

A brief history of Chilean music between 1900 and 1950, with particular reference to contemporary composers. (R. A. W.) A reprint of the preceding item.

——. Los primeros años del conservatorio nacional de música. *Rev. mus. chil.*, v. 5, no. 35-36 (Aug.-Nov. 1949), p. 13-23. **[481a]**

——. Los primeros pianos en Chile. *Rev. mus. chil.*, v. 1, no. 3 (July 1945), p. 48-49. **[482a]**

In the early 18th century, Breton merchants introduced to Chile the first *claves* (name used by Chileans for spinet and harpsichord at that time). In December 1790 a ship brought the first *piano-clave*, doubtless made by Juan del Mármol of Seville. (B. K.)

Quiroga, Daniel. Aspectos de la ópera en Chile en el siglo xix. *Rev. mus. chil.*, v. 3, no. 25-26 (Oct.-Nov. 1947), p. 6-13. **[483a]**

——. Las "Doce tonadas" para piano. *Rev. mus. chil.*, v. 1, no. 5 (Sept. 1945), p. 25-31. **[484a]**

Analysis of this work by P. H. Allende, with 4 musical notations. Also brief survey of the composer's musical training and teaching.

——. Las obras sinfónicas en el segundo festival de música chilena. *Rev. mus. chil.*, v. 6, no. 39 (Spring 1950), p. 14-18. **[485a]**

Among the composers whose works are discussed are Cotapos, Orrego Salas, R. Puelma, Santa Cruz.

——. Los hermanos García Guerrero. *Rev. mus. chil.*, v. 2, no. 11 (May. 1946), p. 7-14. **[486a]**

Pioneers in the development of music in Chile.

——. Música de cámara de Soro. *Rev. mus. chil.*, v. 4, no. 30 (Aug.-Sept. 1948), p. 24-30. **[487a]**

Brief but remarkably detailed survey of the composer's chamber works, with comments on their critical reception as well as overall appraisal by Quiroga. (B. K.)

——. The present state of music in Chile. *Interamer. mus. bull.*, no. 9-10 (Jan.-Mar. 1959), p. 1-3. **[488a]**

Article written expressly to emphasize musical activities and movements in Chile which are generally not widely publicized. Author is music critic of *El Debate*. Particular attention to a group called "Tonus".

Reyes, Laura. La enseñanza musical en las escuelas. *Rev. mus. chil.*, v. 2, no. 12 (June 1946), p. 25-27. **[489a]**

Riesco, Carlos. Las canciones corales de Gustavo Becerra. *Rev. mus. chil.*, v. 6, no. 39 (Spring 1950), p. 84-88. **[490a]**

[Salas, Filomena]. El instituto de investigaciones del folklore musical. *Rev. mus. chil.*, v. 1, no. 3 (July 1945), p. 19-27. **[491a]**

Account of foundation, program and activities of the Institute. (B. K.)

Salas Viu, Vicente. Alfonso Leng. Espíritu y estilo. *Rev. mus. chil.*, v. 5, no. 33 (Apr.-May 1949), p. 8-17. **[492a]**

Biographical account with appraisal of compositions. Portrait. No musical examples. Leng is self-taught in music, and at the same time a distinguished dental surgeon.

——. Allende y el nacionalismo musical. *Rev. mus. chil.*, v. 1, no. 5 (Sept. 1945), p. 15-24. **[493a]**

Pedro Humberto Allende's musical nationalism is compared with that of Grieg. Smetana, *et alter*.

——. Enrique Soro en el movimiento musical de Chile. *Rev. mus. chil.*, v. 4, no. 30 (Aug.-Sept. 1948), p. 10-17. **[494a]**

Background of state of Chilean music at end of 19th century, biography of Soro, and appraisal of certain works, especially the Sinfonía Romántica (1920-1921) and the piano concerto in D Major, first performed in 1919. (B. K.)

——. Enrique Soro en el movimiento musical de Chile. *Nuestra música,* v. 3, no. 11 (July 1948), p. 213-221. **[495a]**

A reprint of preceding item.

——. En torno a "La muerte de Alsino". *Rev. mus. chil.*, v. 11, no. 54 (Aug.-Sept. 1957), p. 19-26. **[496a]**

Discusses a symphonic poem by Leng.

——. La creación musical en Chile, 1900-1951. Ediciones de la Universidad de Chile. Santiago, Editorial Universitaria, S. A., n. d. (1952), 477 p. **[497a]**

Bibliography, p. 475-477. "Este libro contiene un panorama de la creación musical contemporánea en Chile, dentro del medio siglo que va corrido, y un estudio, por orden alfabético, biográfico, crítico y analítico, de cada compositor y de sus obras." (Preface). Forty Chilean composers are studied. The first 6 chapters deal with general musical activities and institutions.

——. La égloga, para soprano, coro y orquesta, de Domingo Santa Cruz. *Rev. mus. chil.,* v. 6, no. 39 (Spring 1950), p. 19-32. **[498a]**

Gives the full text of this Eclogue by Lope de Vega, with 11 musical notations to illustrate the setting by Santa Cruz.

——. La organización musical de Chile. *Nuestra música,* v. 6, no. 23 (3. trimestre, 1951), p. 177-189. **[499a]**

Deals with the Faculty of Musical Science and Art, the National Conservatory of Music, the Institute of Musical Extension, the Institute of Musical Research, etc.

——. La primera sinfonía de Santa Cruz. *Rev. mus. chil.*, v. 4, no 29 (June-July 1948), p. 9-14. **[500a]**

The first symphony by a Chilean com-

poser to be performed since the première of the Sinfonía Romántica by Enrique Soro in 1920. Brief review of other works by Santa Cruz and very brief analysis of the symphony. No music examples. (B. K.)

——. Las obras para orquesta de Domingo Santa Cruz. *Rev. mus. chil.,* v. 8, no. 42 Dec. 1951), p. 11-42. (music). **[501a]**

"La personalidad de Domingo Santa Cruz es la más compleja de la música chilena." An analysis of his orchestral works with 32 musical examples.

——. Los festivales de música chilena. ¿Una bella iniciativa en derrota? *Rev. mus. chil.,* v. 13, no. 66 (July-Aug. 1959), p. 6-12; no. 67 (Sept.-Oct. 1959), p. 17-21. **[502a]**

The festivals of Chilean music in a state of crisis.

——. Músicos modernos de Chile. Washington, D. C., Pan American Union, Music division, 1944. (Music series no. 11). 29 p. **[503a]**

After giving a brief historical background, the author writes informatively of some of the leading Chilean composers of the present.

——. Ramón Garnicer, músico y liberal. *Rev. mus. chil.,* v. 10, no. 48 (Jan. 1955), p. 8-14. **[504a]**

On the Spanish composer of the Chilean National Anthem, who died in March 1855, and the political and musical influences of his time.

Santa Cruz, Domingo. Alfonso Leng. *Rev. mus. chil.,* v. 11, no. 54 (Aug.-Sept. 1957), p. 8-18. **[505a]**

"La música de Alfonso Lang es un arte muy especial."

——. El concierto para piano y orquesta en la obra de Juan Orrego Salas. *Rev. mus. chil.,* v. 6, no. 39 (Spring 1950), p. 33-53. (music). il. **[506a]**

A detailed analysis, with 13 musical notations.

——. Mis recuerdos sobre la sociedad Bach. *Rev. mus. chil.,* v. 6, no. 40 (Summer 1950-1951), p. 8-62. il. (music) **[507a]**

———. Nuestra posición en el mundo contemporáneo de la música. *Rev. mus. chil.*, v. 13, no. 64 (March-April 1959), p. 46-60; no. 65 (May-June 1959), p. 31-46. **[508a]**

———. Trayectoria musical de Chile. *B. A. mus.*, v. 12, no. 197 (Oct. 1, 1957), p. 6-7, 14. **[509a]**

A comprehensive survey of musical trends and personalities in the 20th century, illustrated with photographic, portraits of the author and of other Chilean musicians.

———. *Revista musical chilena*, v. 8, no. 42 (Dec. 1951). **[510a]**

Issue devoted almost entirely to the work of Santa Cruz, who was at the time Dean of the Facultad de Ciencias y Artes Musicales of the University of Chile, under whose auspices the *Revista* is published. In addition to the articles that are listed separately herein, the issue contains "Datos biográficos" (p. 128-136), "Lista Completa de las Obras" (p. 137-143), and Opinions on Santa Cruz by musicians of America and Europe (p. 144-167).

Smith, Carleton Sprague. Contemporary music in Chile. *In* Conference on Latin-American Fine Arts, June 14-17, 1951. Proceedings. Austin, Tex., University of Texas, Institute of Latin American Studies (Latin American Studies, 13), 1952, p. 115-123. **[511a]**

A survey of contemporary Chilean composers, with particular reference to Domingo Santa Cruz and those whom he has sponsored. (R. A. W.)

Smith, Cecil. Claudio Arrau, master of the keyboard. *Américas*. v. 4, no. 8 (Aug. 1952), p. 9-11, 28. **[512a]**

Life and career of the Chilean pianist. Photographs.

[Soro, Enrique]. *Revista musical chilena.* Número de homenaje al maestro Enrique Soro, v. 4, no. 30 (Aug.-Sept. 1948). **[513a]**

Opens with an address on Soro and Chilean music by Santa Cruz, a biographical sketch and mention of his first works. Also included are articles (q. v.) by Vicente Salas Viu, Juan Orrego Salas and Daniel Quiroga Novoa, and a catalog of Soro's works (pp. 31-33).

———. El maestro chileno Enrique Soro. 1. Catálogo de sus composiciones publicadas. 2. Algunas críticas extranjeras. Santiago de Chile, Soc. imp. y litografía Universo, (n. d.). 24 p. **[514a]**

Soublette, Luis Gastón. Combinación de "letra" y "entonación" de la cueca chilena. *Rev. mus. chil.*, v. 13, no. 65 (May-June 1959), p. 101-103. (music) **[515a]**

The popular singers of the Chilean *cueca* are accustomed to sing several different texts to the same melody or *entonación*. This article describes the procedure used by the singers to adjust any text to a given melody.

Talamón, Gastón O. P. H. Allende y la música americana. *Rev. mus. chil.*, v. 1, no. 5 (Sept. 1945), p. 57-59. **[516a]**

Emphasizes the Chilean quality in this composer's music, as seen by an Argentine critic.

Urrutia, Jorge. Apuntes sobre Próspero Bisquertt. *Rev. mus. chil.*, v. 13, no. 67 (Sept.-Oct. 1959), p. 56-61. **[517a]**

An appreciation of the Chilean composer, who died in 1959.

———. Gabriela Mistral y los músicos chilenos. *Rev. mus. chil.*, v. 11, no. 52 (April-May 1957), p. 22-25. **[518a]**

COLOMBIA

THE history of music in Colombia has been traced in a monograph of 180 pages written by José Ignacio Perdomo Escobar, a young lawyer and musicologist of Bogotá, and published in the fourth volume of the *Boletín latino americano de música* [item no. 1369]. Stating that the documentation on Colombian music is very scarce, the author acknowledges his indebtedness to three earlier writers on the subject: Juan C. Osorio, Jorge W. Price and Andrés Martínez Montoya [cf. item no. 1364]. In his first four chapters, Perdomo studies the music, the instruments and the dances of the Indians of Colombia, illustrated with tunes collected by Densmore and Garay. With Chapter V he enters upon the colonial period.

Among the early missionaries who distinguished themselves in the realm of music was José Dadey (1574-1660), a Jesuit of Italian origin who came to Colombia in 1604 and shortly thereafter founded a school of music in Santafé de Bogotá. Juan de Herrera y Chumacero, choirmaster of the cathedral of Bogotá in the first half of the seventeenth century, is characterized by Perdomo as "el único músico de la época colonial que merece el título de compositor". The compositions of Herrera were collected and put in order by his pupil Juan de Dios Torres. Most of them are written for several voices with accompaniment of organ, harp, bass and other instruments. Among the compositions listed by Perdomo is a Requiem Mass dated 1704 and copied by Herrera's pupil Luis Bernardo de Jalón.

In Chapters VI and VII our historian describes the general musical atmosphere of the colony, with special reference to music in the church, in the theatre, and in popular festivals. Chapter VIII deals briefly with the transition to the era of independence, stressing the rôle of the military bands in the wars of liberation. The next chapter is devoted mainly to three musicians who were largely responsible for the organization of musical life in the new republic: Juan Antonio Velasco (d. 1859), Nicolas Quevedo Rachadell (1803-1874) and Enrique Price (1819-1863). Velasco introduced to Bogotá the symphonies of Mozart, Haydn and Beethoven. Quevedo was aide-de-camp to Bolívar; after the war he formed an orchestra in Bogotá and performed the works of Rossini, Bellini, Mercadante and other Italian composers. His son, Julio Quevedo, became a noteworthy musician (see below). Enrique Price, born in London, was active for several years as organist and piano teacher in New York before he settled in Bogotá. His most important contribution to the musical life of that capital was the founding of the Sociedad Filarmónica, "que fue la base de todas las instituciones musicales que hemos tenido posteriormente". A list of his compositions is given on p. 451-452. Fourther details concerning the activities of the Sociedad Filarmónica are given in Chapter X.

The next three chapters deal with various musicians of the nineteenth century, prominent among whom were Vicente Vargas de la Rosa (1833-1898), Eugenio Salas (1823-1853), Diego Fallón (1834-1905), José Joaquín Guarín (1825-1854), Julio Quevedo Arvelo (1829-1897), José María Ponce de León (1846-1882) and Oreste Sindici (1837-1904). The last-mentioned was the composer of the national anthem of Colombia, to whose origins and history Perdomo devotes his fourteenth chapter.

Chapter XV contains a general survey of the lyric theatre in Bogotá. The first opera company came to Bogotá in 1849, the second in 1858. A list of opera companies which visited the capital from 1865 to 1895 is given on p. 518 (taken from José Vicente Ortega's book on the theatre in Bogotá). The first opera by a Colombian composer to reach the stage was Ponce de León's *Ester* (1874).

After devoting a chapter to the folk music of Colombia, whose chief types, are the *bambuco,* the *pasillo,* the *guabina* and the *torbellino,* Perdomo brings his study to a close with a survey of the principal contemporary musicians. He begins with Jorge W. Price (b. 1853), founder of the Academia Nacional de Música in 1881 (this later became the Conservatorio Nacional de Música, now affiliated with the Universidad Nacional). Other musicians included in this chapter are Guillermo Uribe Holguín, Andrés Martínez Montoya (1869-1933), Santos Cifuentes (1870-1932), Carlos Umaña Santamaría (1862-1917), and many others, some of whom are listed below.

Several appendices conclude this valuable study. These comprise selected programs of the Sociedad Filarmónica; description of a ceremony in honor of Vargas de la Rosa; description of a function at the Academia Nacional de Música in 1894; programs of concerts at the Academia; facsimile of the *canción nacional,* "El 20 de Julio", by Guarín; bibliography.

Other important sources for the musical history of Colombia are the monographs by Andrés Martínez Montoya and Jorge W. Price [nos. 1364 and 1370]. The autobiography of the eminent composer, conductor and educator Guillermo Uribe Holguín is also a valuable document [no. 1381]. Contemporary composers have been discussed in articles by Nicolas Slonimsky [nos. 1374 and 1375] and Victor J. Rosales [no. 1372]. For a description in English of the folk songs and dances of Colombia, consult the section on that country in Duran's *Recordings of Latin American songs and dances* [no. 187].

GENERAL AND MISCELLANEOUS

Aragón, Arcesio. Fastos payaneses. Bogotá, Imprenta nacional, 1941. 2 v. F-2291.P8A6　　　　**[1353]**

At the end of vol. 1, words and music to *A Popayán;* end of vol. 2, words and music to *Salve a Popoyán.*

Cassani, José. Historia de la compañía de Jesús del nuevo reino de Granada ... Madrid, Impr. M. Fernández, 1741. 2 v. in 1, F2272.C34　　**[1354]**

Cifuentes, Santos. Hacia el americanismo musical. La música en Colombia. *Correo mus. sud.-am.,* v. 1, no. 22 (25 Aug. 1915), p. 4-6, 10-11.　　**[1355]**

The first half of this article deals with folk music and includes about 20 musical examples.

——. Tratado de armonía. Londres y Nueva York, Novello, Ewer y compañía, 1896. 251 p. ML50.C569　　　　**[1356]**

The author was professor at the Academia nacional de música de Bogotá.

Conservatorio nacional de música. *In* Anuario de la universidad nacional de Colombia. Bogotá, Editorial Santa Fe, 1939, p. 257-269.　　**[1357]**

Contains information on the history of this institution, its organization, professors, rates, plans of study, requirements for admission, etc.

Cordovez Moure, José María. De la vida de antaño. Bogotá, Editorial Minerva, s. a., 1936. 159 p. F2291.B6C77　　　　**[1358]**

Description of dances, p. 19-43.

Espinay, Vicomte Dard d'. Colombian and Andean music. *Bull. pan amer. union,* v. 59, no. 5 (May 1925), p. 478-485. (From *Rev. am. lat.,* 1 Sept. 1924.)　　**[1359]**

Includes discussion of indigenous music and instruments, with 4 tunes.

Fernández de Piedrahita, Lucas. Historia general de las conquistas del nuevo reino de Granada. Amberes, J. B. Verdussen, 1688. 599 p. F2272.P61 **[1360]**

Hernández de Alba, Gregorio. De la música en Colombia. La música en las esculturas prehistóricas de San Agustín. Bogotá, Lit. Colombia—editorial, 1938. p. 721-737. il. ML3575.H37-D3　　　　**[1361]**

Reprinted from *Bol. lat. am. mús.,* v. 4 (1938). Cf. items no. 1404 and no. 1405.

Manighetti, Luisa. Apuntes sobre historia y literatura del piano, revisados por Antonio J. Cano ... Medellín, Librería de A. J. Cano, 1941. 176 p. ML650.-M16A7　　　　**[1362]**

Martens, Frederick H. Making Colombia a truly musical nation. *Mus. Amer.,* v. 25, no. 21 (1917), p. 17.　　**[1363]**

Deals with Guillermo Uribe Holguín.

Martínez Montoya, Andrés. Reseña histórica sobre la música en Colombia, desde la época colonial hasta la fundación de la Academia nacional de música. *In* Academia Colombiana de bellas artes, *Bogotá,* Anuario, v. 1 (1932), p. 61-76. N16.A15　　**[1364]**

Mentions the Jesuit Padre José Dadey of Milan, who arrived in 1604, as founder of the first school for music in Colombia. Juan Pérez Materano, dean of the cathedral of Cartagena, obtained license to print a theoretical work entitled *Canto de órgano y canto llano,* in 1554. The outstanding musician of the colonial period was Juan de Herrera, some of whose MSS. are preserved in the archives of the cathedral of Bogotá ("desgraciadamente incompletas y en manuscritos muy deteriorados por la acción del tiempo") During the early 19th century the most noteworthy composers were José María Cancino and Juan Antonio Velasco. José María Ponce de León (1845-1882) was the composser of the first Colombian operas to reach the stage. These were *Ester* (1874) and *Florinda* (1880). In 1882 Jorge Price founded the Academia Nacional de Música.

Monsalva, Diego. Monografía estadística del departamento de Antioquía. Me-

dellín, Imprenta oficial, 1929. 210 p.
F2281.A6M7   [1365]
Hymno antioqueño (music and words),
p. 8-10.

Orquesta sinfónica nacional. Temporada de 1940. Bogotá, 1940.   [1366]
The 6 annotated programs of this orchestra for the 1940 season contain descriptive notes on the following works by Uribe Holguín: *Tres danzas* (op. 21); *Bachica,* symphonic poem (op. 73); *Cantares* (op. 33); and *Improperia* (op. 65), cantata for baritone, chorus and orchestra (first performance, conducted by the composer).

Osorio, Juan C. B r e v e s apuntamientos para la historia de la música en Colombia. *Repertorio colombiano,* no. 15.
                          [1367]
Cited by Martínez Montoya, *op. cit.* [no. 1364].

Otero D'Costa, Enrique. Mon t a ñ a s d e Santander. Bucaramanga, Imprenta del departamento, 1932. 185 p. PQ8179.-O74M7   [1368]
The second part of this book, *Apuntes sobre demosofía colombiana y música nacional,* deals with various aspects of folk and national music in Colombia, quoting numerous texts of folk songs.

Perdomo Escobar, José Ignacio. Esbozo histórico sobre la música colombiana. *Bol. lat. am. mús.,* v. 4 (1938), p. 387-570   [1369]
An outline of the history of Colombian music, with 10 Indian melodies and 3 popular dance tunes. For further comment see introductory section.

Price, Jorge W. Datos para la música en Colombia. *Bol. hist. antigüedades,* v. 22, nos. 254-255 (Sept.-Oct. 1935), p. 623-645.   [1370]
Contains biographical and historical notes on the following; Nicolás Quevedo Rachadell, José Caicedo Rojas, Enrique Price, Joaquín Guarín, Julio Quevedo Arvelo, Carlos Torres, Manuel Rueda, Juan Crisóstomo Osorio Ricaurte, José María Ponce de León, Daniel Figueroa, Manuel M. Párraga, Vicente Vargas de la Rosa, Oreste Sindici, Honorio Alarcón, Andrés Martínez Montoya, Santos Cifuentes Rodríguez; La Academia nacional de música. Also

treats briefly the growing place of women in the field of music, commencing with the year 1887; outstanding musical woman, Carmen Gutiérrez Uricolchea de Osorio.

Restrepo, Jorge M. La música en Colombia. *Tesoro sacro musical,* no. 6 (June 1935).   [1371]

Rosales, Victor Justiniano. Colombian music and musicians. *Bull. pan amer. union,* v. 60, no. 9 (1926), p. 852-859.   [1372]
Includes references to the *bambuco, pasillo, guabina* and other popular forms. Also reprinted separately (ML233.R7C7)

Santos, Gustavo. Informe p r e s e n t a d o por la Dirección Nacional de Bellas Artes al Ministerio de Educación Nacional. *Bol. lat. am. mús.,* v. 4 (Oct. 1938), p. 730-756.   [1373]

Slonimsky, Nicolas. The Colombian composer; his status today. *Mus. Amer.,* v. 59, no. 3 (10 Feb. 1939), p. 116. ports.   [1374]

——. Music in Colombia. *Christian scien. mon.,* v. 30, no. 250 (20 Sept. 1938), p. 12.   [1375]
Mentions Guillermo Uribe Holguín, Emilio Murillo, Alejandro Villalobos, José Rozo Contreras, Jesús Bermudes Silva, E. Giovannetti, Carlos Posada Amador, Adolfo Mejía.

Zamudio, Daniel. Anotaciones sobre la música religiosa en Colombia. *Bol. lat. am. mús.,* v. 4 (Oct. 1938), p. 347-350.   [1376]

BIOGRAPHY AND CRITICISM

Chase, Gilbert. Music and m u s i c i a n s; Gillermo Uribe Holguín, Colombia's greatest composer, tells the story of his life. *Int. Amer. monthly,* v. 1, no. 7 (Nov. 1942), p. 36-37.   [1377]
Chiefly a review of the composer's autobiography, *Vida de un Músico Colombiano.* See item no. 1381.

Lange, Francisco Curt. Guillermo Espinosa y la Orquesta Sinfónica Nacional. *Bol. lat. am. mús.*, v. 4 (Oct. 1938), p. 23-54. il.   [1378]

Guillermo Espinosa (b. Cartagena, 9 Jan. 1905), studied music in Milan and Berlin, and in 1936 became conductor of the Orquesta Sinfónica Nacional of Bogotá. This article is a detailed account of the activities of that orchestra and its affiliated chamber group, the Cuarteto de Cuerdas Bogotá. Considerable attention is given to the children's concerts of the orchestra. Complete table of programs given, p. 46-54.

———. Guillermo Uribe Holguín. *Bol. lat. mús.*, v. 4 (Oct. 1938), p. 757-796.
                                        [1379]

Uribe Holguín (b. 1880) has been a prominent figure in Colombian musical life as composer, educator and conductor. He began his career as a violinist and during his youth spent a year in the United States. From 1907 he studied composition under Vicent d'Indy at the Schola Cantorum in Paris. Since 1910, except for brief intervals of retirement, he has been director of the Conservatorio Nacional de Música (formerly the Academia de Música). He founded and conducted until 1935 the Sociedad de Conciertos Sinfónicos del Conservatorio, which formed the nucleus of the Sinfónica Nacional organized in 1936 (cf. item no. 1378). On p. 767-772 of this article, Lange gives a complete list of compositions performed by this orchestra. The second part of the article comprises an analytical study of Uribe Holguín's compositions (piano; voice and piano; chamber music; symphonic and choral-symphonic works), illustrated with numerous musical examples. Catalogue of Uribe's compositions, p. 793-795 (67 opus numbers). In 1941 Uribe Holguín published his autobiography (item no. 1381).

Lima, Emirto de. Folklore colombiano. Barranquilla, 1942. 210 p. ML3575.C7-L5   [1380]

See the articles on *Calvo, Compositor nacional* (p. 23) and *Compositores y artistas colombianos* (p. 155).

Uribe Holguín, Guillermo. Vida de un músico colombiano. Bogotá, Librería voluntad, s. a., 1941. 284 p. ML410.U
                                        [1381]

The auotbiography of a leading Colombian composer, music educator and con-

ductor. This autobiography gives an interesting picture of musical and social life in Bogotá around the turn of the century and of the development of musical activity in Colombia—a development due in large part to the efforts of Uribe Holguín himself. A considerable portion of the book is polemical, for Uribe Holguín wishes to justify himself against the attacks to which he was subjected during his tenure of office as director of the Conservatory. His book is a significant and valuable chapter of contemporary musical history. Since this volume appeared, Uribe has returned to the directorship of the Conservatorio Nacional.

See also nos. 1363, 1364, 1366, 1369, 1370, 1372, 1374, 1375.

NATIONAL ANTHEM

Mora, Luis María. El alma nacional. Bogotá, 1922.   [1382]

Includes a reference to the national anthem of Colombia.

Ofrenda de Venezuela en el primer centenario de la batalla de Ayacucho. Caracas, Litografía del comercio, 1924. 130 p. M1686.O35   [1383]

Includes music (voice and piano, and band score) of national anthem of Colombia.

Quijano, Arturo. Nuestro himno nacional y la música antigua.   [1384]

An article, cited by Martínez Montoya, *op. cit.*, (No. 1364), p. 76.

Villegas y González, Camilo. Cartilla patriótica; historia y filosofía del himno nacional. Bogotá, Impr. "La luz", 1911. 84 p. 2d ed. plates   [1385]

Words and music of hymn, folded, at end.

FOLK AND PRIMITIVE MUSIC

(A) GENERAL

Lima, Emirto de. Del folklore colombiano. *Bol. lat. am. mús.*, v. 1 (1935), p. 47-55.   [1386]

Describes various folk dances of Colombia, with comments on the music and musical instruments.

———. Folklore colombiano, Barranquilla, 1942. 210 p. ML3575.C7L5 **[1387]**

A collection of essays, articles and lectures, most of them dealing with various aspects of folk music, dances and musical instruments in Colombia. Includes a list of the author's writings and musical compositions. There are numerous musical illustrations.

———. Varias manifestações folklóricas na costa colombiana do Atlántico. *Rev. assoc. bras. mus.,* v. 2, no. 5 (1933), p. 45-47. **[1388]**

Describes the songs, dances and musical instruments of the people inhabiting the coastal region of Colombia.

Mendia, Ciro. En torno a la poesía popular, Medellín, Colombia, A. J. Cano, 1927. 121 p. PQ7084.M4 **[1389]**

Menéndez Pidal, Ramón. Las primeras noticias de romances tradicionales en América, y especialmente en Colombia. *In* Homenaje a Enrique José Varona, Habana, Publicaciones de la Secretaría de educación, 1935, p. 23-27. F17-87.V31 **[1390]**

Discusses the earliest recorded evidence of the presence of traditional Spanish ballads in South America.

Murillo, Emilio. Indigenous music in Colombia. *Bull. pan amer. union,* v. 57, no. 7 (July 1923), p. 34-36. **[1391]**

Peñuela, C. L. Cantos populares de la región de Soatá. *Senderos,* v. 1, (1934), p. 190. **[1392]**

Perdomo Escobar, José Ignacio. Esbozo histórico sobre la música colombiana. *Bol. lat. am. mús.,* v. 4 (1938), p. 387-570. **[1393]**

Includes section on folk music, with 13 musical examples.

Urdaneta, Alberto. La guabina chiquinquirena. *Noticiario colombiano* (San José de Costa Rica), v. 1, no. 9 (Nov. 1939), p. 8-9. **[1394]**

For 2 voices with pianoforte accompaniment, "Original de la gran revista colombiana 'Vida'."

Valencia, Reinaldo. La música popular del Chocó. *Rev. Indias,* v. 1, no. 4 (1936), p. 45-46. **[1395]**

(B) AMERINDIAN

Acuña, Luis Alberto. El arte de los indios colombianos. Bogotá, Escuelas gráficas salesianas, 1935. 77 p. il. F2270.-A7A24 **[1396]**

"Comentos literarios sobre música indígena", p. 13-19. "Tres melodías indígenas de la provincia de Vélez", p. 18-19.

Bolinder, Gustaf. Busitana-Indianernas musikbage, *Ymer,* v. 37, nos. 3-4 (1917), p. 300-308. **[1397]**

Includes notes on African influence on the Indian culture and the predominance of the marimba. Illustrations, p. 302, 303. French summary of the article, p. 308.

———. Die Indianer der tropischen schneegebirge; forschungen im nördlichsten Südamerika. Stuttgart, Strecker und Schröder, 1925. 274 p. il. F2270.B68 **[1398]**

Chapter 5, "Spiele, musikinstrumente und genussmittel", p. 77-93. Chapter 11, "Feste und tänze", p. 159-171. With one tune, p. 58.

Bosse, Fritz. Die musik der Uitoto. *Zeit. vergl. musikw.,* v. 2, no. 1 (1934), p. 1-14; no. 2-3, p. 25-50. il. **[1399]**

A thoroughly documented scientific study, dealing with musical instruments (p. 1-14) and characteristics of the Uitoto songs (p. 25-39), followed by an ethnological analysis (p. 39-50). Appendix: "notenbeispiele", wih 51 tunes, transcribed from recordings, and a supplement of 3 songs from Tierra del Fuego, transcribed by E. von Hornbostel.

Brettes, Joseph de. Les indiens Arhouaques-Kaggabas, *Bull. mém. soc. anthrop.* sér. 5, v. 4 (Paris 1903), p. 318-357. **[1400]**

Describes the music, musical instruments and dances of these Indians. Includes 1 tune arranged for piano (p. 325-328).

Igualada, Francisco de. Musicología indígena de la Amazonia Colombiana. *Bol. lat. am. mús.*, v. 4 (1938), p. 675-808. **[1401]**

Contains 14 Amazonian Indian melodies, most of them with native text. Prologue by Fray Marcelino de Castellón, Capuchin missionary and director of the Centro de Investigaciones Lingüísticas y etnográficas de la Amazonia Colombiana, under the auspices of which this study was carried out. Copiously illustrated with photographs of Indian musicians and dancers. The following points are brought out: The Colombian Amazonia offers a rich storehouse of folkloristic material, and is especially rich in music: "cada tribu tiene un número muy variado de melodías instrumentales o vocales". In its diatonic structure the indigenous music often recalls the ancient Greek and the medieval modes. This music usually presents a marked uniformity of rhythm. The chief manifestation of the indigenous music, both vocal and instrumental, is to be found in connection with the dance. Igualada begins by studying the indigenous musical instruments (p. 687-694). He then takes up the analysis of the melodies (p. 694-703). Bibliography, p. 704-708.

Lima, Emirto de. Apuntes de los cantos y bailes del pueblo costeño. *Bol. lat. am. mús.*, v. 4 (Bogotá 1938), p. 95-98. **[1402]**

With 2 musical examples.

(c) INSTRUMENTS

Closson, Ernest. A propos de la zambumbia colombienne. Internationalen gesellschaft für musikwissenschaft. *Mitteilungen*, v. 2, no. 3 (1930), p. 122. **[1403]**

States that the *zambumbia* is analogous in type to the popular Flemish instrument known as *rommelpot*.

Hernández de Alba, Gregorio. De la música indígena en Colombia. *Bol. lat. am. mús.*, v. 4 (1938), p. 721-731. il. **[1404]**

A well-documented study, with 15 photographs of pre-Columbian musical instruments. Cf. item no. 1361.

———. La música en las esculturas pre-

históricas de San Agustín. *Bol. lat. am. mús.*, v. 4 (1938), p. 733-737. il. **[1405]**

Out of 300 statues of the pre-Columbian epoch found in the department of Huila, Colombia, the author studies two which definitely represent the playing of musical instruments. One of these is a conch shell and the other is a kind of flute or trumpet. Cf. item no. 1361.

Lima, Emirto de. Las flautas indígenas colombianas. *Bol. lat. am. mús.*, v. 3 (1937), p. 67-71. **[1406]**

With 5 musical examples, of which 4 are folk themes.

———. La musique colombienne. Internationalen gesellschaft für musikwissenschaft. *Mitteilungen*, v. 2, no. 3 (1939), p. 91-96. **[1407]**

Deals chiefly with the typical musical instruments of Colombia, with 5 brief musical examples.

See also nos. 1359, 1369, 1397, 1398, 1399, 1400, 1401.

(D) FOLK SONG TEXTS

Forero, M. J. Para el folklore colombiano. *Senderos*, v. 1 (1934), p. 190. **[1408]**

Words of folk songs.

Lima, Emirto de. La copla popular colombiana. *In* Anuario de la Sociedad folklórica de México, 1941, v. 2, México, D. F., 1943, p. 243-247. **[1409]**

Otero Muñoz, Gustavo. La literatura colonial de Colombia, seguida de un cancionerillo popular. La Paz, Imp. artística, 1928. 324 p. PQ8162.07 **[1410]**

Texts of Colombian folk songs.

Quiñones Pardo, Octavio. Cantares de Boyacá; libro de crónicas. Bogotá, Tipografía "Colón", 1937. 222 p. il. PQ8177.B6Q5 **[1411]**

Restrepo, Antonio José. El cancionero

de Antioquia. Con una introducción sobre la poesía popular. Barcelona, Editorial Lux, 1930. 442 p. port. PQ8177.-A6R4 1930 **[1412]**

La semilla colombiana. *Cult. venezola-*

na, v. 11, no. 69 (Jan.-Feb. 1926), p. 99-101. **[1412x]**

Popular-songs of the first years of Colombia.

See also no. 1398.

SUPPLEMENT to 1960

Although published in 1945, Perdomo Escobar's *Historia de la música en Colombia* (item 542a) remains to date the only available general history of music in Colombia. The original version, published in the *Boletín latino-americano de música* (item no. 1369), was fully described in the introductory section on Colombia in the first edition of the Guide (see above).

For the current musical situation in Colombia, there is a useful survey by Andrés Pardo Tovar, *Los problemas de la cultura musical en Colombia,* which appeared in the *Revista musical chilena in* 1959 (item no. 541a). This discusses some of the "precursors" of contemporary music in Colombia (with an interesting note on musical bibliography in the 19th century), the history of the National Conservatory of music (including the reforms of Antonio Valencia in 1936-38), the National Symphony Orchestra (founded by Guillermo Espinosa in 1936), and musical education (which he finds inadequate).

The biography of Don Santos Cifuentes (1870-1932) by Alfonso Cifuentes y Gutiérrez (item no. 537a) sheds much light on the musical history of Colombia in the late 19th and early 20th century, because Cifuentes was involved with most of the developments during this period, including the founding of the "Centro artístico" (1889), and the "Academia Beethoven ' (1903). His *Conferencia sobre estética musical* is printed in the appendix to this work.

BIBLIOGRAPHY

(A) PRIMITIVE, FOLK, AND POPULAR MUSIC

Acuña, Luis Alberto. Folklore del departamento de Santander. *Rev. folklore* (Bogotá),no. 5 (April 1949), p. 97-133. il. **[519a]**

Gives the text of numerous popular refrains and coplas, and discusses their musical setting in the section "Sentimiento y expresión" (p. 131-133), which includes notation of 2 *guabina* melodies as recorded and harmonized by Lelio Olarte.

——. Música indígena colombiana. *Noticia de Colombia* (México, D. F.), no. 9 (May 31, 1942), p. 29-30 (music) **[520a]**

Artel, Jorge. What is the Chocó? *Américas,* v. 9, no. 3 (Mar. 1957), p. 7-10. **[521a]**

On the Chocó Department of Colombia, largely inhabited by Negroes. A description of the *currulao* dance, and the music that accompanies it. Reference to the "Singing wakes", still practised at the death of children. 15 photographs.

Carvajal, Mario. Romancero colonial de

Santiago de Cali. Cali. Carvajal & cia., 1936. 161 p.   **[522a]**

Texts of old Spanish ballads.

Fals-Borda, Orlando. Peasant society in the Colombian Andes. A sociological study of Saucío. Gainsville, University of Florida press, 1955.   **[523a]**

References to music, p. 179 ff.

Lima, Emirto de. Apuntes sobre el folklore de la costa atlántica de Colombia. *Bol. Unión panamer.,* v. 77, no. 1 (Jan. 1943), p. 23-37.   **[524a]**

——. La colaboración de la semana santa en Santo Tomás. *Rev. folklore* (Bogotá), no. 5 (April 1959), p. 159-168.   **[525a]**

Notation of ceremonial music for drum and bell.

Lira Espejo, Eduardo. Crónica del cantar colombiano. *Rev. mus. chil.,* v. 2, no. 10 (April 1946), p. 16-25. **[526a]**

Martinez-Cabana, Carlos. Rugged individualists; these Indians are Guajiros first, Colombians or Venezuelans second. *Américas,* v. 7, no. 7 (July 1955), p. 7-12.   **[527a]**

Includes considerable detail on the *chicha maya* dance. Pictures include one of *chicha-maya* dancers, and two of musical instruments, one a pipe, the other a musical bow.

Pardo Tovar, Andrés. Música autóctona nacional. *Colombia,* nos 6 & 7 (June-July 1944), p. 161-164.   **[528a]**

Includes notes on contemporary Colombian composers.

Quiñones Pardo, Octavio. El cancionero colombiano. Selección de... *Rev. América,* v. 8 ,no. 22 (Oct. 1946), p. 104-107.   **[529a]**

Words only of 10 songs from the provinces of Antioquia, Boyacá, Santander, Litoral Pacífico, Tolima, Cauca, Litoral Atlántico, Llanos Orientales, Cundinamarca and Nariño. (C. S.)

——. Interpretación de la poesía popu-

lar. Bogotá, Biblioteca de folklore colombiano, 1947 (vol. 1). 197 p. **[530a]**

Includes: Profundo sentido del cantar popular; Aguinaldos y villancicos; El himno folklórico de Boyacá; El porro. (Texts of songs only, no music).

Rocha Castilla, Cesáreo. La guabina. *Arte, segunda época,* v. 4, entregas 47-49 (Nov. 1945-Jan. 1946), p. 249-253.   **[531a]**

Comments on this popular folk dance. Two music notations, one for piano. (C. S.)

Tolima (Colombia), Dirección de educación pública. Cartilla de folk-lore tolimense, Ibagué, Imprenta departamental, 1935. 36 p. il.   **[532a]**

"El San Juan en el Tolima", by Cesáreo Rocha C.; "La Patasola", by Ricardo Rocha C.; "Coplas populares" and a musical supplement with five bambucos.

Whiteford, Andrew Hunter. Popayán Christmas; Colombian city clings to tradition. *Américas,* v. 8, no. 12 (Dec. 1956), p. 7-10.   **[533a]**

Account of Christmas celebrations in town of 32,000 in Colombian Andes. Details about *chirimías,* on wandering minstrels, on their instruments and who they are. Six photographs, two of *chirimías.* Author's recordings of *chirimías* have been issued by Folkways Records.

Zamudio, Daniel. El folklore musical en Colombia. *Micro,* v. 4, no. 55 (Jan. 1944), p. 14-16.   **[534a]**

Includes a rhythmic analysis of the *galerón,* with music notations.

——. El folklore musical en Colombia. *Rev. Indias,* v. 35, no. 109 (May-June 1949), suppl. no. 14, 30 pp.   **[535a]**

12 music notations, some fragmentary. (C. S.)

(B) ART MUSIC AND MISCELLANEOUS

[Bravo Márquez, José María]. Obra musical del maestro Bravo Márquez. *Univ. católica bolivariana* (Medellín),

v. 12, no. 43 (Oct.-Nov. 1945), p. 130-138. **[536a]**

Cifuentes y Gutiérrez, Alfonso. Don Santos Cifuentes; notas biográfricas. Bogotá, Editorial Centro, Instituto gráfico ltda., 1947. 162 p. il. **[537a]**
Apéndice: p. 115-158, with lectures and various works written by Don Santos Cifuentes. See Introduction to Supplement, above.

Colombian music congress, Ibagué, 1936. Programa oficial. Bogotá, Imprenta nacional, 1936. 40 p. **[538a]**

Drezner, Manuel T. Native compositions heard in Bogotá. Mus. Amer., v. 59, no. 13 (Nov. 1949), p. 8. **[539a]**
Prize for best symphony based on Colombian themes won by Miguel Angel Zulátegui, for work titled Los de Cahipay. (B. K.)

Pardo Tovar, Andrés. Antonio María Valencia, artista integral. Cali, Imprenta del Departamento, 1958. (Biblioteca vallecaucana, Extensión cultural). 40 p. il. (music). **[540a]**
A study of the life and work, as pianist, composer and educator, of the Colombian musician J. A. Valencia (1902-1952), who was a pipul of Vicent d'Indy at the Schola Cantorum in Paris. The catalog of his work comprises 39 opus numbers, including songs, choral works, chamber music, works for orchestra, piano pieces, and arrangements. Much of his music has a national or regional character.

——. Los problemas de la cultura musical en Colombia. Rev. mus. chil., año 13, no. 64 (March-April 1959), p. 61-

70; no. 65 (May-June 1959), p. 47-56; no. 66 (July-Aug. 1959), p. 61-72. **[541a]**
Sets forth the view that "The problems of the composer, of the musicologist and of the musical educator in Colombia are for the moment, almost insoluble." And this because it has not yet been possible to integrate organically the isolated efforts of professional musicians, nor to coordinate the pedagogical activity of the numerous conservatories and schools of music.

Perdomo Escobar, José Ignacio. Historia de la música en Colombia. Bogotá, Imprenta nacional, 1945. 348 p. (Publicaciones del Ministerio de educación, Biblioteca de cultura colombiana, Historia, v. 19.) **[542a]**
Revision of Esbozo histórico sobre la música colombiana (item no. 1269), minus most of the illustrations.

[Valencia, Antonio María]. Classified chronological catalog of the works of the Colombian composer Antonio María Valencia. Bol. interam. mús., no. 6 (July 1958), p. 3-33. **[543a]**
Valencia was born in 1902 and died in 1952. He was a pupil of Vincent d'Indy at the Schola Cantorum in Paris.

Velasco, Santiago. La vida musical en Colombia. Rev. mus. chil., v. 1, no. 6 (Oct. 1945), p. p. 14-19. **[544a]**
Brief account of musical activity in the principal cities.

Wilson, Betty. Colombian harpsichordist. Américas, v. 9, no. 6 (June 1957), p. 20-21. **[545a]**
Brief account of Rafael Puyana, young artist who studied with Landowska.

COSTA RICA

COSTA RICA is one of the most musically active of the Central American republics. There are three main sources of information on the musicians and musical institutions of Costa Rica, as follows: The eight-page pamphlet by Alcides Prado, *Apuntes sintéticos sobre la historia y producción musical de Costa Rica* [no. 1419]; the article by Julio Fonseca, *Apuntes sobre música costarricense* [no. 1416]; and the seventy-nine page survey by José Rafael Araya, published as an entire number of the review *Educación* [no. 1414]. Of these three sources, the last is the most comprehensive. We summarize here a few points of special interest in Araya's monograph.

In 1853 the president of the republic commissioned Manuel María Gutiérrez to compose the music for a national anthem. The new anthem was first performed on 11 July 1853; it was then a purely instrumental composition, without a vocal part. The first text was written in 1879, the second in 1888. Finally, in 1900 the government organized a contest for the best text, to be officially adopted. The contest was won by José Zeledón, whose version begins.

> Noble patria, tu hermosa bandera,
> expresión de tu vida nos da...

The composer of the hymn, Manuel María Gutiérrez, was born in Heredia in 1829 and died in 1887 after a distinguished career as band leader and composer. His son, Carlos María Gutiérrez Rodríguez (1865-1934), was also a noted musician.

Under the heading *Bibliografía musical,* which mentions the chief musical publications of Costa Rica, Araya states that the republic formerly possessed a plant for the printing of music, which no longer exists. There are seven military bands in the country; that of the capital, San José, has seventy pieces; the others (one in each provincial center) have thirty. There are more than sixty municipal or private musical societies in the country; which the author calls "filarmonías". Each group consists of from 15 to 20 musicians, mostly amateurs.

The Escuela Nacional de Música was founded in 1889. It was succeeded, toward the end of the century, by the Escuela de Música Santa Cecilia, which still exists. The Conservatorio de Música y Declamación, founded in 1912 under the direction of Julio Osma, existed until quite recently. Finally, the government, by a law of 25 March 1941, established the Conservatorio Nacional de Música, under the directorship of Guillermo Aguilar Machado.

The second part of Araya's monograph (p. 31-79) is devoted to biographical sketches of Costa Rican musicians. These are not arranged alphabetically, but in approximate chronological sequence. Among composers most prominently mentioned are the following: Pilar Jiménez Solís (1835-1922), Alejandro Monestel Zamora (b. 26 April 1865), Rafael Chaves Torres (1839-1907), José Campadabal (b. in Spain, 1849; d. 1905), José Joaquín Vargas Calvo (b. 1871; was for some years organist in Detroit), Fernando Murillo Rodríguez (1867-1928), Enrique Jiménez Núñez (1863-1932), Ismael Cardona (b. 1887), Roberto Cantillano (b. 1887), Julio Fonseca Gutiérrez (b. 22 May 1885), José Daniel Zúñiga Zeledón (b. 1889), Roberto Campadabal (1881-1932), José Castro Carazo (b. 1896), Julio Mata Oreamuno (b. Cartago, 9 Dec. 1889), Guillermo Aguilar Machado (b. 1905), Alcides Prado Quesada (b. 1900), Carlos Enrique Vargas Méndez (b. 1919), and Jimmy Fonseca Mora (b. 1916).

Chief among the musical organizations of Costa Rica is the Asociación de Cultura Musical, founded in 1934, which gives from eight to ten concerts annually and which publishes a periodical, the *Revista musical* (no issues of this have been received since 1941).

Turning to the pamphlet by Prado [no. 1419], we find that this begins with a discussion of indigenous music. There have been systematic efforts to investigate and collect this music since 1879, when the author's father, Pedro J. Prado Gómez, made various field trips for this purpose. The Museo Nacional has a valuable collection of native ocarinas. One of these instruments, capable of producing eighteen sounds, has been the object of a detailed study by María Fernández de Tinoco and Guillermo Aguilar Machado [no. 1428]. Mention is also made of a collection of ocarinas assembled by the archaeologist Jorge Lines. Other indigenous instruments mentioned are the *quijongo,* a primitive stringed instrument in the form of a bow, plucked with the fingers; the *chirimía,* a kind of oboe; and the *tambor,* or drum.

Under the heading of *Folklore,* Prado states that the most typical form of national folk music in Costa Rica is the *punto,* and especially the *punto guanacasteco,* from the province of Guanacaste. The *punto* is danced by a man and a woman, dancing apart. It has two steps and two figures. In the first figure, she dances with short steps and he follows. In the second, they stand side by side and advance several steps together; they then turn around and come back to the point of origin. The rhythm of the *punto* is gay and lively. Slower and more sentimental is the *danza,* while the *callejera* lies midway between these two types. The *pasión* is a song which has a melody in binary rhythm (6/8) and an accompaniment in ternary rhythm (3/4).

GENERAL AND MISCELLANEOUS

Aguilar Machado, Alejandro. La reforma musical de la Escuela de Costa Rica. *Bol. lat. am. mús.*, v. 4 (Oct. 1938), p. 351-374. **[1413]**

Araya R., José Rafael. Vida musical de Costa Rica. *Educación*, v. 16, nos. 96-97 (Nov.-Dec. 1942), p. 3-79. **[1414]**
For comment, see introductory section.

Fonseca, Julio. Apuntes sobre música costarricense. *Rev. mus.* Costa Rica, v. 1, no. 3 (Oct. 1940), p. 35-42. **[1415]**
Deals with the folk music, dances and typical instruments of Costa Rica. Includes music of 2 Indian songs and illustrations of indigenous musical instruments. This article has a continuation, dealing with art music [no. 1416].

———. Apuntes sobre música costarricense. *Rev. mus.* Costa Rica, v. 2, no. 4 (1941), p. 64-14. **[1416]**
Deals with musical organization in Costa Rica and gives biographical sketches of the following composers: Manuel Ma. Gutiérrez (1829-1887), who wrote the national anthem of Costa Rica; Rafael Chaves Torres (1838-1907); Pedro Calderón Navarro (1864-1909); Carlos María Gutiérrez (1865-1934); Alejandro Monestel Zamora (1865-); who is considered the composer with the best technical equipment; Emmanuel J. García (1872-); Emilio León Rojas (1877-); Rosendo de J. Valenciano (1876-); Ismael Cardona (1877-); Roberto Campabadal (1881-1931); Julio Fonseca Gutiérrez (1865-); Julio Mata Oreamuno (1889-); César A. Nieto (1892-); José Castro Carazo (1896-).

Mills, John Proctor. The status of music in Costa Rica. *Mus. Amer.*, v. 8, no. 11 (1908), p. 19, 23. **[1417]**

Música nacional de Costa Rica, publicación auspiciada por la Secretaría de educación y por el Club Rotario de Costa Rica. Gran fantasía sinfónica sobre motivos folklóricos. Por Julio Fonseca. San José, Litografía nacional, 1942. 16 p. M35.F **[1418]**
Piano reduction of an orchestral work

which won the Gold Medal in the National Exposition of 1937. Analysis of the score and portrait of the composer, p. 1.

Prado Quesada, Alcides. Apuntes sintéticos sobre la historia y producción musical de Costa Rica. San José, Imprenta nacional, n. d. 8 p. **[1419]**
Pamphlet published *circa* 1941. Contents: Música indígena; folklore; compositores nacionales; autores contemporáneos; intérpretes; agrupaciones musicales.

Segura Méndez, Manuel, and J. Daniel Zúñiga A. Teatro escolar costarricense. San José, Librería e imprenta Lehmann & cía., 1936. 14 p. M1513.S495T3 **[1420]**
Includes music.

Slonimsky, Nicolas. Music, where the Americas meet. *Christian scien. mon. weekly magazine section* (8 June 1940), p. 8-9, il. **[1421]**
Biographical sketches of Central American and Mexican composers, with portraits. Discusses the principal Costa Rican musicians, Alejandro Monestel, Julio Fonseca, Julio Mata, and mentions the names of many others.

NATIONAL ANTHEM

Himno nacional. Letra de José María Zeledón. Música de Manuel María Gutiérrez. San José, Publicaciones de la secretaría de educación pública, Dirección técnica de música, 1931. M1685.-C6G **[1422]**
The words were adopted in 1900, the music composed and adopted in 1853.

Obregón Lizano, Miguel. Geografía general de Costa Rica. San José, Imp., Lines A. Reyes, 1932. v. 1 339 p. [Lecturas geográficas, 3ª ser.] F1544.O36 **[1423]**
National Hymn of Costa Rica, its history, words and music, p. 12-19. Words to 8 patriotic songs, p. 24-29. National Hymn of Central America (words and music), p. 40-43.

Prado Quesada, Alcides, comp. Cantos

de autores nacionales (e himnos de
Centro América) para escuelas y colegios. San José de Costa Rica. Imprenta universal, 1942. 48 p. M1684.-
P7C2 **[1424]**

Piano accompaniment. Includes the na-
tional anthems of Costa Rica. El Salvador,
Guatemala, Honduras, Nicaragua and
Panamá.

See also no. 1439.

AMERINDIAN

Sapper, Karl Theodor. Ein besuch bei
den Chirripó- und Talamanca-India-
nern von Costa Rica. *Globus*, v. 77
(Braunschweig, 1900), p. 1-8. **[1425]**

Includes 1 Indian tune.

——. Ein besuch bei den Guatusos in
Costa Rica. *Globus*, v. 76 (Braunschweig, 1899), p. 348-353. il. **[1426]**

Includes a fragment of a tune.

INSTRUMENTS

Alfaro González, Anatasio. Investigaciones científicas. San José de Costa Rica,
1935. 317 p. QH108.A4 **[1427]**

Musical instruments, p. 111-115.

Fernández de Tinoco, María. Una ocarina huetar de 18 notas del museo nacional de Costa Rica, descripción y dibujos... Técnica musical por Guillermo Aguilar Machado. San José, Imprenta nacional, 1937. 12 p. il. ML480.-
F302 **[1428]**

Includes music.

Meagher, J. T. Costa Rica and its rail-
road. *Overland monthly* (San Francisco), v. 10 (1878), p. 160-173. **[14297**

Reference to the marimba and other musical instruments.

COLLECTIONS OF MUSIC

Campadabal, José. Cantos escolares...
Compuestos para las escuelas comunes

y colegios de 2ª enseñanza. Cartago de
Costa Rica, 1888. M1994.C186 **[1430]**

José Campadabal y Calvet (1849-1906)
was a prominent Costa Rican composer.
The words of these school songs are by
Juan F. Ferraz.

Colegio superior de señoritas, San José.
Cuatro canciones nacionales. San José,
Imprenta Gutenberg, 1935. **[1431]**

Songs for 1 and 2 voices with piano.

——. Canciones nuestras. San José, Ed.
Danzuni, 1938. **[1432]**

Songs for 1 and 2 voices with piano.

Dobles Segreda, Luis. Colección de bailes típicos de la provincia de Guanacaste. San José, Imprenta nacional, 1929.
3 v. **[1433]**

Gamboa, Emma. Canciones populares
para niños... San José de Costa Rica,
Lehmann, 1941. M1992.G16C2 Reproduced from type-written and manuscript copy. **[1434]**

Includes: Children's songs, folk songs
and children's dances.

Secretaría de educación. Canciones escolares para uso de las escuelas oficiales
de la república de Costa Rica; colec-
cionadas y ordenadas por la dirección
técnica de música (Contiene canciones
a una y dos veces, de autores nacionales). San José, Imprenta nacional,
1933. 90 p. **[1435]**

Secretaría de educación pública. Album de la madre. 2d. ed. Selección por
J. Daniel Zúñiga Z. San José, Imp.
universal, Carlos Federspiel & cía.,
1941. **[1436]**

——. Cantos de autores nacionales (e
himnos de Centro América) para escuelas y colegios; seleccionados por
Alcides Prado Q., director técnico de
música. San José, Imprenta universal,
1942. 48 p. M1684.P7C2 **[1437]**

Segura Méndez, Manuel. Lo que se canta en Costa Rica; canciones escolares,
de colegio y populares, himnos de la
América latina. San José, Imprenta y

librería universal, 1937. 151 p. M1634.-
C6845   [1438]

Vargas Calvo, J. J. Cantos escolares para
el uso de las escuelas y colegios oficiales de la República de Costa Rica. 1ª
serie. San José, Costa Rica; Paris, Henry
Lemoine & ca., 1907. 62 p. M1994.C-
167   [1439]
Contains 40 songs for school children

by Costa Rican composers. Includes the
national anthem of Costa Rica.

Zúñiga, J. Daniel, comp. Colección de
bailes típicos de la provincia de Guanacaste. San José, Imprenta nacional.
1929. 23 p. M1685.C6Z   [1440]
Native dances of Costa Rica, for piano
(some with interlinear Spanish words).
Harmonizations by Julio Fonseca.

SUPPLEMENT TO 1960

BIBLIOGRAPHY

Araya, José Rafael R. Vida musical de
Costa Rica. Contiene la primera parte
publicada en la revista "Educación"
Nros. 96-97 del año 1942 y la segunda
parte que ahora se publica año 1957.
San José, Imprenta Nacional, 1957. 142
p.   [546a]
A reprint of item no. 1414, with ad-

ditions bringing the information up to
the year 1956 (in Part 2).

Fonseca, Julio. Referencias sobre música costarricense. *Rev. estud. mus.,* v.
1, no. 3 (April 1950), p. 75-97. [547a]
The article is dated "Agosto 12 de 1939".
With 9 musical notations. Originally published in the *Revista musical* (cf. items
1415 and 1416).

CUBA

THE nearest equivalent to a history of music in Cuba is the work by Serafín Ramírez entitled *La Habana artística,* published in 1891 [item 1455]. This remark applies particularly to the first part of the book; the second part, *Estudios de crítica y literatura musical,* is a collection of miscellaneous essays, dealing in a less systematic manner with musical life in Havana. Although the title implies a survey of all artistic activities, the main emphasis throughout the book is on music and musicians.

In his first chapter, *La Habana de otros tiempos,* the author gives a sketch of the dances and songs current in Havana during the early decades of the 19th century, mentioning, among others, the *boleros, polos, seguidillas* and *tiranas* (all imported from Spain). Numerous musicians active in Havana during this period are mentioned, prominent among them being Enrique González (d. 1877), author of an *Introducción a la ciencia universal deducida de los recientes descubrimientos hechos en la música.* Information on the theatre includes references to early operatic performances, such as that of Grétry's *Zémire et Azor* in 1800.

Other chapters in Part 1 deal with the Condesa de Merlín (a celebrated amateur singer); the piano and pianists in Cuba, devoting special attention to Manuel Saumell, Pablo Desvernine, Fernando Arizti, Nicolás Espadero, Ignacio Cervantes and Manuel Jiménez; Cuban songs and singers; musical societies and institutions from 1830 to 1840; the composer Cristóbal Martínez (d. 1482); the origin of the *contradanza;* Cuban violinsts (Bousquet, Julián Jiménez, J. S. White, Albertini, Brindis); the lyric theatre; the Conservatory founded by Hubert de Blanck in 1885; musical activity from 1840 to 1880. These chapters are followed by a biographical dictionary (p. 363-542), devoted chiefly, but not exclusively, to Cuban musicians.

In Part 2 we need only note the article on Gaspar Villate's opera *Zilia,* produced at the Théâtre des Italiens, Paris, in 1877. Also of interest are the program of various concerts and operatic performances given in Havana from 1831 to 1867. The musical appendix comprises a *guaracha* entitled *El Sungambelo* (1813); a canción from 1820, *La Corina;* a *bolero* from 1815; and a *contradanza* from 1803, *San Pascual Bailón.* The first three are for voice and piano, the last for piano alone.

Serafín Ramírez, the author of this work, was born in Havana in 1883 and died there in 1907. He was a violoncellist as well as a music critic, and the founder of the Sociedad de Música Clásica in 1865. He was also founder and director of *La gaceta musical.* The chapter entitled *La Habana de otros tiempos,* from his *La Habana artística,* was reprinted in Carbonell's *Las bellas artes en Cuba* [no. 1444], a volume which contains several other important articles on music [nos. 1445, 1456, 1532]. Among these is a study of music in Santiago de Cuba by Laureano Fuentes Matóns (1825-1898), taken from his book *Las artes en Santiago de Cuba* (1893). This contains much interesting data on musical activities in Santiago from 1850 to the early decades of the nineteenth century.

In his paper, *La historia y desenvolvimiento del arte musical en Cuba...* [no. 1451], Joaquín Molina y Ramos deals particularly with musical education in Cuba, devoting special attention to the work of Manuel Saumell, Pablo Desvernine, Fernando Arizti, Nicolás Ruiz Espadero, Ignacio Cervantes, Manuel Jiménez, Rafael Salcedo and Hubert de Blanck, who went to Cuba from the United States in 1882. Of these, the most famous as composer (he also excelled as a pianist) was Ignacio Cervantes (b. Havana, 31 July 1847; d. there, 30 April 1905), author of many admirable *Danzas cubanas* and other pieces for piano.

A good introduction to Cuban music for English readers is the essay entitled *Cuban music, guide to its study and understanding,* by Emilio Grenet [no. 1847]. As regards the autochthonous element, Grenet writes: "The Indian who survived colonization in the rest of the Americas practically disappeared in Cuba, and if anything of him survives in our music, it is impossible for us to discern it."

Grenet goes on to show that the main influence on the rhythm of Cuban music is that of the Negro, whereas the chief melodic influence is Spanish. In *Genres of Cuban music* he discusses such popular forms as the *zapateo,* the tytpical dance of the Cuban peasants; the *contradanza* (from which sprang the *danzón*); the *habanera,* "possibly the most universal of our musical genres"; the *canción;* the *son,* which "invaded Havana about 1917" and which "seems bound by a close relationship to the *rumba"*; the *conga* "whose steps have come from the street into the salon" and which is of African origin; and the *rumba,* "the most popular of all our genres." Fortified with numerous musical illustrations, this study is of great value to all students of Cuban music. The collection of eighty compositions in popular style, to which this essay serves as introduction, enables the reader to become acquainted with representative examples of music by Cuban composers, ranging from Ignacio Cervantes and Jorge Anckermann to such contemporaries as Sindo Garay, Eduardo Sánchez de Fuentes, Eliseo Grenet, Ernesto Lecuona and Moisés Simons, many of whose songs have won universal popularity.

Cuban composers, of course, have also written music of a more "serious" type than is represented in this collection. Sánchez de Fuentes, for instance, is the composer of several symphonic works and operas, among the latter being *Kabelia,* produced at the Gran Teatro Nacional on 22 June

1942. Sánchez de Fuentes has also writen extensively on Cuban music. His study, *El folk-lor* [sic] *en la música cubana* [no. 1494] is of special importance.

The Afro-Cuban movement in symphonic music [see item no. 1519] was represented by two gifted composers, both of whom died prematurely: Amadeo Roldán (1900-1939) and Alejandro García Caturla (1906-1940). For an excellent analysis of Caturla's work, see the article by Adolfo Salazar [no. 1471], who has also studied the artistic possibilities of Afro-Cuban music [no. 1531]. For the background of Afro-Cuban culture and music, the writings of Fernando Ortiz and Israel Castellanos should be consulted.

GENERAL AND MISCELLANEOUS

Academia nacional de artes y letras, Habana. Memoria del curso académico 1939-1940, por el Dr. Antonio Iraizoz. Panorama actual de la música cubana, por el Dr. Eduardo Sánchez de Fuentes. Habana, Molina y cía., 1940. 24 p. **[1441]**

Sánchez de Fuentes, dean of Cuban composers, who opposed the development of the African element in Cuban music, gives a pessimistic picture of musical activity in his country.

Arvey, Verna. Musical potentialities in Cuba and South America. *Mus. cour.,* v. 112, no. 11 (14 Mar. 1936), p. 6, 27. **[1442]**

Beals, Carleton. The crime of Cuba. Philadelphia and London, J. B. Lippincott co., 1933. 441 p. il. F1787.B32 **[1443]**

References to music; p. 20, 24, 41-45, 58, 64, 75, Bongó, congó drums, p. 24; p. 47; gourds p. 20-23; anklet-bells, p. 20. Dance; p. 20, 24, 42-54, 156-225, 300.

Carbonell y Rivero, José Manuel, ed. Las bellas artes en Cuba. Habana, Imprenta "El siglo xx", 1938. 451 p. (*His* Evolución de la cultura cubana, v. 18) PQ7371.C3 **[1444]**

Includes a section on music, by various authors, p. 99-202, with biographical sketches of the authors. For details, see entries under Fuentes Matóns (no. 1445). Ramírez (no. 1456), Agüero (no. 1481) and Sánchez de Fuentes (no. 1532).

Fuentes Matóns, Laureano. Las artes en Santiago de Cuba. *In* Carbonell y Rivero, José Manuel, *ed.,* Las bellas artes en Cuba, Habana, 1928, p. 99-111. port. PQ7371.C3 **[1445]**

Short biographical sketch of the author, p. 99-100. Deals with the history of musical activities and personalities in Santiago de Cuba from the late 16th century to the 20th century.

García Caturla, Alejandro. The development of Cuban music. *In* Cowell, Henry, *ed.* American composers on American music. Stanford University press, 1933, p. 173-174. ML200.C87A5 **[1446]**

González, Enrique. Crítica musical. Colección de artículos publicados en la Gaceta de la Habana desde principios de febrero de 1855. Habana, Imprenta del gobierno y capitanía general por S. M., 1855. 20 p. ML1714.GC7 **[1447]**

Lavín, Carlos. Metrópolis musicales: La Habana. *Gaceta mus.,* v. 1, no. 3 (Mar. 1928), p. 40-42. **[1448]**

Loewenberg, Alfred. Annals of opera, 1597-1940. With an introduction by Edward J. Dent. Cambridge, W. Heffer & sons ltd., 1943. 879 p. ML102.O6L6 **[1448x]**

Includes *Dolorosa* (1910) by Eduardo Sánchez de Fuentes.

Martens, Frederick H. A thousand and one nights of opera. New York, D. Ap-

pleton and co., 1926. 487 p. MT95.M23
[1449]

Ch. 7, *New world opera stories,* cites
operas dealing with American subjects and
gives the plots of the following operas by
Latin American composers: *La Doreya,*
by Eduardo Sánchez de Fuentes (Cuba),
p. 225-226; and *O Guarany* by Carlos Gomes (Brazil), p. 233-234. Brief mention is made in passing of other Latin
American operas.

Martínez Moles, Manuel. Una compañía
de ópera italiana en Sancti Spíritus, *In*
Anuario de la Sociedad folklórica mexicana, 1941, v. 2, México, D. F. 1943,
p. 133-137. [1450]

The operatic performances to which reference is made took place in 1868.

Molina y Ramos, Joaquín. La historia y
desenvolvimiento del arte musical en
Cuba y fases de nuestra música nacional. Habana, Imprenta "El siglo XX",
1924. 29 p. ML207.C8M6 [1451]

"Discurso leído ... en la sesión solemne celebrada por la Academia nacional
de artes y letras el día 12 de mayo de
1924 ..." Discurso de contestación por
el Sr. Eduardo S. de Fuentes. For comment, see introduction above.

Morelet, Arthur. Voyage dans l'Amérique Centrale, l'ile de Cuba, et le Yucatán. Paris, Gide et J. Baudry, 1857.
2 v. F1432.M83 [1452]

Vol. 1 contains the verse of a song
(Spanish words with English translation), p. 295. Vol. 2 includes description
of fandango with marimba accompaniment, p. 40-42, with origin, history and
complete description of the marimba, p.
42-44.

Muñoz de Quevedo, María. Orquesta
filarmónica. *Musicalia,* v. 1, no. 3
(Sept.-Oct. 1928), p. 104-109. il.
[1453]

Includes a thematic guide to Amadeo
Roldán's suite for orchestra *Le Rebam-
baramba,* with 15 musical examples.

Piron, Hippolyte. L'ile de Cuba. Paris, E.
Plon et cie., 1876. 325 p. F1763.P672
[1454]

Dance and tamborines in a voodoo

séance, p. 50-52; orchestras of the whites,
those of the mulattos, and those of the
Negroes, p. 134-135; military music, p.
286.

Ramírez, Serafín. La Habana artística.
Habana, Imp. del E. M. de la Capitanía general, 1891. 687 p. ML207.C8R2
[1455]

For comment see introductory section.

———. La Habana de otros tiempos. *In*
Carbonell y Rivero, José Manuel, *ed.,*
Las bellas artes en Cuba, Habana,
1928, p. 112-134. PQ7371.C3 [1456]

A portrait and brief biography of the
author, p. 112-113. This is the first chapter of the author's work, *La Habana artística* [no. 1455].

Remos, Juan José. Doce ensayos. Habana, Molina y cía., 1937. 470 p. PQ73-
89.R44D6 [1457]

Includes: La música.

Roig, Gonzalo. Apuntes históricos sobre
nuestras bandas militares y orquestas.
An. acad. nac. artes let., año 22, v.
18 (July 1936-Mar. 1937), p. 117-131.
[1458]

Mentions especially the Banda de Música
de la Policía (founded 1899), which later
became the Banda Municipal; the Banda
de Música de la Marina Nacional (founded
1912); the Sociedad de Conciertos Populares (1903-05; revived in 1916); the
Orquesta Sinfónica (founded 1922); and
the Orquesta Filarmónica (founded 1924).

Sánchez de Fuentes, Eduardo. La canción cubana; conferencia, 16 Mar.
1930, sesión de la Academia nacional
de artes y letras. Habana, Molina y
cía., 1930. 46 p. ML2514.S22C2
[1459]

With 17 musical examples.

———. Consideraciones sobre la música
cubana, Conferencia, *An. acad. nac. artes let.* año 22, v. 18 (July 1936-Mar.
1937), p. 145-159. [1460]

Discusses chiefly the rhythmic elements
in Cuban music.

Slonimsky, Nicolas. Music in Cuba. *Mus. record.*, v. 1, no. 3 (Aug. 1933), p. 90-93. **[1461]**

Tolón, Edwin T., and Jorge A. González. Óperas cubanas y sus autores. Prólogo de Eduardo H. Alonso. Habana, 1943. 472 p. **[1461x]**
An important authoritative work.

Torre, José María de la. Lo que fuimos y lo que somos, ó La Habana antigua y moderna. Habana, Librería "Cervantes", 1857. 178 p. F1799.H3T62 **[1462]**
"The first reports we have of music in the Island are very unfavorable; it being sufficient to note that negresses sang in the churches and that among the instruments used was the *güiro* which is used today in the *changüis* of the country." Quoted by Grenet, *op. cit.*, [no. 1487], p. xviii.

Vidaurreta, José L. Ensayo sobre la música cubana. *Estud. afrocub.*, v. 2 (1938), p. 72-88. **[1462x]**

BIOGRAPHY AND CRITICISM

Chase, Gilbert. Nin-Culmell, Cuban internationalist. *Int. amer. monthly*, v. 2, no. 3 (Mar. 1943), p. 32. port. **[1463]**
Deals with the pianist and composer Joaquín Nin-Culmell (b. 1908).

Cowell, Henry. Roldán and Caturla of Cuba. *Mod. music*, v. 18, no. 2 (1940), p. 98-99. **[1464]**

González, Manuel Pedro. Racial factors in Latin American music. *Int. amer. quart.*, v. 3, no. 4 (Oct. 1941), p. 44-52. **[1465]**
Refers to Gilberto Valdés as "the greatest. perhaps, of all Cuban composers." Valdés is a cultivator of the Afro-Cuban style. A reprint of this article, issued under the title *Latin America, a musical melting pot*, is available from the Pan American Union.

Guillén, Nicolás. Claudio José Domingo

Brindis de Salas, el rey de las octavas. Habana, Municipio de la Habana, 1935. 43 p. incl. port. (Cuadernos de historia habanera, dirigidos por Emilio Roig de Leuchsenring, no. 3) ML418.B66G9 **[1466]**
Biographical sketch of the celebrated Cuban violinist Brindis de Salas (1852-1911).

Lugo Romero, Américo. José Manuel Jiménez Berroa; el "Liszt de ébano" cubano. *Música*, v. 1, no. 4 (July 1941), p. 87-90. **[1467]**
Personal reminiscences and biographical sketch of the Cuban Negro pianist Jiménez Berroa, a pupil of Moscheles at Leipzig and of Marmontel at the Paris Conservatoire. His career began brilliantly but later declined. He died at Hamburg, Germany, in 1917.

Marchena, Enrique de. Del areito de Anacaona al poema folklórico; Brindis de Salas en Santo Domingo. Ciudad Trujillo, Editora Montalvo, 1942. 95 p. **[1468]**
The second part deals with the Cuban Negro violinist Brindis de Salas.

Muñoz de Quevedo, María. Alejandro García Caturla. *Bol. lat. am. mús.*, v, 5 (Oct. 1941), p 611-618. **[1469]**

Ramírez, Serafín. La Habana artística. Habana, Imp. del E. M. de la Capitanía general, 1891. 687 p. ML207.C8-R2 **[1470]**
Includes a biographical dictionary (p. 363-542), devoted in large part to Cuban musicians and foreign musicians active in Cuba.

Salazar, Adolfo. La obra musical de Alejandro Caturla. *Rev. cub.*, v. 11, no. 31 (Jan. 1938), p. 5-43. **[1471]**
A detailed analytical study of the work of the Cuban composer Alejandro García Caturla (1906-1940), with 30 musical examples and a list of his compositions.

Sánchez de Fuentes, Eduardo. Discurso de contestación al de ingreso del señor Gonzalo Roig. *An. acad. nac. artes* *let.,* año 22, v. 18 (July 1936-Mar. 1937), p. 132-144.   **[1472]**

Includes a biographical sketch of the conductor and composer Gonzalo Roig, and a résumé of the history of instrumental music in Cuba.

————. Ignacio Cervantes K a w a n a g ; su vida, su obra, su talento creador. *An. acad. nac. artes let.,* año 22, v. 18 (July 1936-Mar. 1937), p. 11-25.

[1473]

Ignacio Cervantes (1847-1905) was a noted Cuban pianist and composer, especially known for his *Danzas cubanas* for piano.

————. Ignacio Cervantes Kawanag, pianista y compositor eminente; su vida, su obra, su talento creador. La Habana, Imp. Molina y cía., 1936. 18 p. ML410.C3924S3   **[1474]**

A reprint of item no. 1473.

Slonimsky, Nicolas. C a t u r l a of Cuba. *Mod. music,* v. 17, no. 2 (1940), p. 76-80.   **[1475]**

Includes · facsimile of 2 pages from MS. of *Cuban Dances,* with portrait-sketch of the composer.

EDUCATION

Agüero, Gaspar. Alrededor de la amusia. Habana, Molina y cía., 1938. 30 p. ML64.A4   **[1476]**

At head of title: Academia nacional de artes y letras. Deals with various aspects of musical pedagogy.

Mora, Flora. La música y la humanidad; filosofía de la música en torno a la educación. La Habana, Editorial "Argos", 1941. 289 p. ML3800.M768M9

[1477]

Orbón, Benjamín. La enseñanza musical en Cuba. Memoria que presenta como académico correspondiente a la Real academia de bellas artes de San Fernando. Habana, Tip. musical [1931?]. 23 p.   **[1478]**

Bibliography: p. 23.

Serret, Antonio, and Max Henríquez Ureña. Tratado elemental de música. Primer curso. Santiago de Chile, Ediciones Archipiélago, 1929. 192 p. il. MT7.S38T7   **[1479]**

"Himno de Bayamo", "La bayamesa" and "Himno de la Escuela normal", p. 91-102. Includes music.

NATIONAL ANTHEM

Agüero, Gaspar. Nuestro himno nacional. Necesidad de su revisión. *Revista de bellas artes,* v. 1 (1918), p. 61-65.

[1480]

This article contains a full-page facsimile of a part of Pedro Figueredo's *La Bayamesa,* with musical examples showing how it is officially played; a copy of the hymn; and a copy of a letter proving that Figueredo was the composer of the National Hymn.

FOLK AND PRIMITIVE MUSIC

(A) GENERAL (INCLUDING DANCES)

Agüero, Gaspar. Consideraciones sobre la música popular cubana. *Rev. fac. letras cien.,* v. 32 (La Habana, 1922), p. 33-49.   **[1481]**

Includes 2 melodies (1 arranged for piano) and several fragments. Cf. no. 1481x.

————. Consideraciones sobre la música popular cubana. *In* Carbonell y Rivero, José Manuel, *ed.* Las bellas artes en Cuba, Habana, 1928, p. 135-152. PQ737-1.C3   **[1481x]**

Pages 135-136 contain biographical data on the author. This article includes 8 musical examples, and many examples of verses of popular songs.

Bachiller y Morales, Antonio. Cuba primitiva. 2d. ed. Habana, M. de Villa, 1883. 399 p. F1769.B12.F1781.B12

[1482]

Words and music of an Antillean song, p. 44, 45. Vocabulary, p. 185-395; see *areito, maionauau.*

Calero, José. Breves estudios musicales.

La Habana, Imprenta "El siglo xx", 1926. 194 p. ML60.C16 **[1483]**
"El folklore musical cubano y el maestro Sánchez de Fuentes", p. 51-54.

Capdevila y Melián, Pedro. Apuntes del folklore remediano. *Rev. bim. sub.*, v. 43, no. 2 (1939), p. 220-265. **[1484]**
Discusses boleros, canciones, cantos políticos, parrandas, pregones, rumbas, etc. Numerous textual examples, but no music.

Cowell, Henry. The "sones" of Cuba. *Mod. music,* v. 8, no. 2 (Jan.-Feb. 1931), p. 45-47. **[1485]**

Garrigó, Roque E. Historia documentada de la conspiración de los Soles y rayos de Bolívar. La Habana, Imprenta "El Siglo xx", A. Muñiz y hno., 1929. 2 v. F1783.G24 **[1486]**
"La má Teodora. Folklore musical", plate, v. 1, following p. 166.

Grenet, Emilio, ed. Popular Cuban music; 80 revised and corrected compositions together with an essay on the evolution of music in Cuba... Prologue by dr. Eduardo Sánchez de Fuentes. Translated by R. Phillips. Habana, Carasa & cía., 1939. 199 p. ML207.C8-G7 **[1487]**
"This work has been published under the auspices of Sr. José García Montes, Secretary of agriculture." The valuable introductory essay by Grenet includes over 30 musical illustrations, in addition to numerous rhythm notations.

Martínez-Fortún y Foyo, Carlos A. Las parrandas de Remedios; selección musical por Augustín Jiménez Crespo. [n. p.] 1938. 13 p. ML3565.M2P2 **[1488]**
The *parrandas* are groups of local musicians, each ward or district of the city having its own band and its typical music. The *parrandas* originated in the early years of the 19th century, when it was customary to celebrate the "Misas de Aguinaldo", Masses held in the small hours of the morning from December 16 to Christmas Eve. Groups of youths went about with improvised noise-making instruments to wake the people up in time for the early

Mass. Gradually their musical quality improved, reaching its maximum development toward the end of the 19th century.

Martínez Torner, Eduardo. La rítmica en la música tradicional española. *Música,* Barcelona (Jan. 193), p. 33-34. **[1489]**
Discusses certain Spanish folk rhythms in relation to Cuban and Afro-American influences.

La nueva lira criolla; guarachas, canciones, décimas y cantares de la guerra, por un vueltarribero. 4 ed. Habana, "La Moderna poesía", 1900. 265 p. PQ7384.N8 1900. **[1490]**

Prat, Domingo. Diccionario biográfico, bibliográfico, histórico, crítico, de guitarras, guitarristas, danzas y cantos. Buenos Aires, Casa Romero y Fernández, 1934. 468 p. ML128.G8P7 **[1491]**
Section on *Danzas* (p. 425-452), includes brief descriptions of several Cuban dances. See under *danzón, habanera, guaracha, rumba, son,* etc.

Ramírez, Serafín. La Habana artística. Apuntes históricos. Habana, Imp. del E. M. de la Capitanía general, 1891. 687 p. ML207.C8R2 **[1492]**
"Estudios de crítica y literatura musical": p. 549-654. "Composiciones musicales": p. 671-687. Includes music of *guaracha, canción, bolero* and *contradanza,* the first three for voice and piano, the last for piano alone.

Sagra, Ramón de la. Isla de Cuba. Paris, Librería de L. Hachette, 1861. 250 p. F1763.S13 **[1493]**
Words of a creole song, p. 157-158.

Sánchez de Fuentes, Eduardo. El folklor en la música cubana. La Habana, Imprenta "El Siglo xx", 1923. 191 p. il. ML207.S3F8 **[1494]**
A study of folklore influences in Cuban music, with 35 musical facsimiles.

——. Folklorismo; artículos, notas y críticas musicales. Habana, Imp. Molina y cía., 1928. 343 p. ML60.S22 **[1495]**
The following sections deal with folk

music: *Desarrollo de nuestra música vernácula*, p. 3-6; *El areito de Anacaona*, p. 7-18; *El danzón*, p. 19-32; *Música popular*, p. 37-40; *Al margen de nuestro folklore*, p. 41-46; *Sobre nuestro folklore*, p. 79-108. The musical appendix includes 3 Cuban dances for piano. The notation of an *areito* (from Bachiller y Morales, *Cuba primitiva*) is given on p. 83.

——. La música cubana y sus orígenes. *Bol. lat. am. mús.*, v. 4 (Bogotá 1938), p. 177-182. **[1496]**
Deals with the component folk elements of Cuban music.

——. La riqueza rítmica de la música cubana. Club cubano de bellas artes, Habana. Biblioteca, v. 1. Habana, 1925. **[1497]**

——. Viejos ritmos cubanos; la letra de nuestras canciones. Conferencia. *An. acad. nac. artes let.*, año 22, v. 18 (July 1936-Mar. 1937), p. 204-232. **[1498]**
Traces the origin and development of popular Cuban forms such as the *danza*, the *son*, the *danzón*, the *habanera*, the *guaracha*, etc.

Sanjuan, Pedro. Cuba's popular music. *Mod. mus.*, v. 19, no. 4 (May-June 1942), p. 222-227. **[1499]**
Includes brief musical examples of the *guajira* (identified with the *punto criollo*), *habanera*, *bolero* and *conga*.

Simons, Moisés. Música cubana. *Diario de la marina* (26 June 1927). **[1500]**
Cf. E. Sánchez de Fuentes, *Folklorismo*, p. 79 [No. 1495].

——. Música cubana; la guajira montuna o punto cubano. *Diario de la marina* (24 July 1927). **[1501]**
Cf. E. Sánchez de Fuentes, *Folklorismo*, p. 93.

Sousa, John Philip, comp. National, patriotic and typical airs of all lands. Philadelphia, Harry Coleman, 1890. 283 p. M1627.S72C **[1501x]**
Includes the Cuban "typical airs": *Zapateo, El territorial, El mondonguito* (the first for voice and piano, the others for piano), p. 69-73.

Suzarte, J. Q. Tipos y costumbres de la isla de Cuba. Habana, 1881. **[1502]**
The chapter on *Los guajiros* includes references to dances among the peasants of Cuba.

Ximeno, Dolores M. La guaracha "El Sungambelo", *Arch. folklore cub.*, v. 5, no. 2 (1930), p. 156-159. **[1503]**
Gives the text, with comment, of a very popular Cuban *guaracha* (the music is printed by Sánchez de Fuentes in *El folklor en la música cubana*).

(B) TRADITIONAL BALLADS

Castellanos, Carlos A. "El tema de Delgadina en el folklore de Santiago de Cuba". *Jour. amer. folklore*, v. 33, no. 127 (1920), p. 43-46. **[1504]**
Text and commentary.

Castro Leal, Antonio. Dos romances tradicionales. *Cuba contemporánea*, v. 6, no. 3 (Nov. 1914), p. 237-244. **[1505]**
Discusses survivals of two traditional Spanish ballads in Cuba.

Chacón y Calvo, José María. Ensayos de literatura cubana. Madrid, Editorial "Saturnino Calleja", s. a., 1922. 277 p. PQ7371.C5 **[1506]**
Romances tradicionales, p. 85-186 gives the complete text of several ballads, and selections from many others. Quotes from the work of Ramón Menéndez y Pelayo on the *romance;* it is divided thusly: *Romances de reconocimientos; Romances que refieren tragedias domésticas; Romances hagiográphicos y de sucesos maravillosos; Romances picarescos; Romances líricos.*

——. Nuevos romances en Cuba. *Rev. bim. cub.*, v. 9, no. 3 (1914), p. 169-210. **[1507]**
The ballads discussed are "Gerineldo" and "Conde Olinos" (text and commentary).

——. Romances tradicionales en Cuba; contribución al estudio del folklore cubano. Habana, Imprenta "El Siglo XX", 1914. 85 p. **[1508]**
Reprinted from *Revista de la Facultad*

de letras y ciencias, v. 18 (1914), p. 45-121.

Espinosa, Aurelio M. El tema de Roncesvalles y Bernardo del Carpio en la poesía popular de Cuba. *Arch. folklore cub.,* v. 5, no. 3 (1930), p. 193-198. **[1509]**

Treats of the survival of Carolingian ballad-themes in Cuban folk poetry.

Poncet y de Cárdenas, Carolina. El romance en Cuba. *Rev. fac. letras cien.,* v. 18, no. 2 (Mar. 1914), p. 180-260; v. 18, no. 3 (May 1914), p. 270-321. **[1510]**

Includes texts of numerous traditional ballads, with historical notes and commentary. Also reprinted separately (item no. 1511).

———. El romance en Cuba; consideraciones sobre la poesía popular cubana. Habana, A. Miranda, 1914. 130 p. **[1511]**

An offprint of item no. 1510.

———. Romances de Pasión. Habana, Cultural, s. a., 1930. **[1512]**

Traces the ballads dealing with the Passion, which were brought to Cuba from Spain. Reprinted from *Archivos del folklore cubano,* v. 5, no. 1, p. 5-29.

(c) AFRO-CUBAN

Castellanos, Israel. La brujería y el ñañiguismo en Cuba desde el punto de vista médico-legal. Habana, Imp. de Lloredo y ca., 1916. III p. il. **[1513]**

Ch. 31. *El baile,* deals with the *rumba* (p. 63-67).

———. Instrumentos musicales de los afrocubanos. Habana, Imprenta "El Siglo xx", 1927. 40 p. il. **[1514]**

An excellently documented study of Afro-Cuban musical instruments.

Chase, Gilbert. Some notes on Afro-Cuban music and dancing. *Int. amer. monthly,* v. 1, no. 8 (Dec. 1942), p. 32-33. **[1515]**

Courlander, Harold. Musical instru-

ments of Cuba. *Mus. quart.,* v. 28, no. 2 (Apr. 1942), p. 227-240. **[1516]**

Although mainly occupied with description of the instruments used in the African ceremonies in Cuba, Courlander deals also with the background of the cults. There are 4 plates of illustrations of Afro-Cuban instruments.

García Agüero, Salvador. Presença africana na música nacional de Cuba. *In* Congreso afro-brasileiro, Rio de Janeiro, Civilização brasileira s/a., 1940, p. 305-321. F2659.N4C65 **[1517]**

Besides the general description of music, there are several pages devoted to dances. Cf. item no. 1518.

———. Presencia africana en la música nacional. *Estud. afrocub.,* v. 1 (1937), p. 114-127. **[1518]**

Also published in *Ultra,* v. 1 (1936), p. 519-524. Cf. item no. 1517.

García Caturla, Alejandro. Posibilidades sinfónicas de la música afrocubana. *Musicalia,* v. 2, no. 7 (July-Aug. 1929), p. 15-17. **[1519]**

Stresses the artistic possibilities of Afro-Cuban folk music.

García Garófalo, Juan M. Los orígenes del son "Mamá Inés". *Arch. folklore cub.,* v. 5, no. 2 (1930), p. 160-163. **[1520]**

Lachatañeré, Rómulo. Conga y afrocubanismo de exportación. *Norte,* v. 2, no. 3 (Dec. 1941), p. 30-31. il. **[1521]**

Points out that exported versions of the conga and other Afro-Cuban dances and songs differ greatly from the genuine manifestations.

———. Oh. ¡¡mío Yemaya!! Manzanillo, Cuba, Editorial "El Arte", 1938. 214 p. PQ7389.L23O5 **[1522]**

Gives texts of ritualistic songs of the Yorubá Negroes, known in Cuba as *lucumís.*

Martín, Juan Luis. Los tambores sagrados del ñañiguismo. Cosas de Afro-América. *Orbe,* v. 1 (10 July 1931), p. 28-29. **[1523]**

Ortiz, Fernando. Afro-Cuban music. *Int. amer. quart.,* v. 1, no. 3 (July 1939), p. 66-74.   **[1524]**

"The study of Afro-Cuban music is still to be made" for "As yet there has been no through and methodical study." Ortiz has done much toward laying the foundations for such a study, to which scientific laboratory methods should be applied. "Afro-Cuban music represents the fruitful blend between the musical innovations of various white people of Europe on one hand, and on the other the music of distinct and clearly differentiated groups of Negroes who covered almost an entire continent."

——. La "clave" xilofónica de la música cubana. Habana, Tipografía Molina y cía., 1935. 44 p. pl. ML480.O7C4   **[1525]**

——. De la música afrocubana. *Univ. Habana,* v. 1 (1934), p. 111-125.   **[1526]**

Also reprinted separately.

——. El estudio de la música afrocubana. *Musicalia,* v.1, no. 4 (Nov.-Dec. 1928), p. 115-119; and v. 1, no. 5 (Jan.-Feb. 1929), p. 169-174.   **[1527]**

——. La música sagrada de los negros Yorubá en Cuba. *Ultra* (Habana), v. 3, no. 13 (July 1937), p. 77-86. **[1528]**

"Exposición esquemática de su carácter, historia, instrumentos, músicas, cantos y bailes litúrgicos, documentada con un concierto de tambores, cánticos y bailes religiosos, dirigidos por el maestro Sr. Pablo Roche, *Okilapkua.*" With illustrations of musicians and dancers.

——. La música sagrada de los Negros Yorubá en Cuba. *Estud. afrocub.,* v. 2 (1928), p. 89-104.   **[1529]**

Reynolds, Quentin. Jungle dance. *Collier's* (27 Nov. 1937), p. 12, 45-47.   **[1530]**

The main points of this article are: the discussion of *ñañiguismo;* the rumba as danced by Clarita and Alberto: and the predominant African elements in Cuban dance and festivals.

Salazar, Adolfo. El movimiento africanista en la música de arte cubana.

Estud. afrocub., v. 2 (1938), p. 3-18.   **[1531]**

Studies the relation of Cuban art music to the Negro folklore.

Sánchez de Fuentes, Eduardo. Influencia de los ritmos africanos en nuestro cancionero. In Carbonell y Rivero, José-Manuel, ed., Las bellas artes en Cuba, Habana, 1928, p. 15-202. PQ737.1.C3   **[1532]**

Studies not only the African, but also the indigenous and Spanish elements in Cuban music. Includes 23 musical notations.

COLLECTIONS OF MUSIC

Album de música cubana, Sindo Garay. Album homenaje del Consejo corporativo de educación, sanidad y beneficencia. Habana, 1941. 40 p. **[1533]**

A biographical note on the composer Sindo Garay informs us that he was born in Santiago de Cuba in 1869 and that "ha sido hasta ahora el más popular de nuestros compositores de música vernácula".

Grenet, Emilio, ed. Popular Cuban music; 80 revised and corrected compositions together with an essay on the evolution of music in Cuba... Prologue by Dr. Eduardo Sánchez de Fuentes. Translated by R. Phillips. Habana, Carasa & cía., 1939. 199 p. ML207.C8G7   **[1534]**

"This work has been published under the auspices of Sr. José García Montes, Secretary of agriculture."

Luce, Allena, ed. Canciones populares. Boston, etc., Silver, Burdett & co., 1921. 138 p. M1681.P6L9   **[1535]**

Section 2: 12 songs of Cuba, Spain and Mexico.

Sánchez de Fuentes, Eduardo. Folklorismo; artículos, notas y críticas musicales. Habana, Imp. Molina y cía., 1928. 343 p. il. ML60.S22 **[1536]**

Appendix, p. 335-343, consists of musical examples. "Obras del mismo autor"; 2 leaves at end.

SUPPLEMENT to 1960

THE musical bibliography of Cuba has been remarkably enriched during the past fifteen years, notably by the publications of Fernando Ortiz and Alejo Carpentier, the former in the sphere of Afro-Cuban music, the later in the field of general history. Carpentier's *La música en Cuba* (item 586a), published in 1946, provides us with a history of Cuban music that is objective, based on first-hand sources, and written with the intelligence and insight for which this author is noted (he is a poet and novelist as well as a writer on music).

As Carpentier remarks in his preface, the island of Cuba has had the power of creating its own distinctive type of music, which very soon achieved an extraordinarily rapid diffusion. The musical folklore of Cuba, characterized by a surprising vitality, has received throughout its history a wide variety of elements, which it has blended and transformed. At the same time, Carpentier recognizes that Cuba is part of the cultural zone of the Caribbean, and that its musical formation must therefore be related to this area as a whole. The musical history of Santo Domingo, for instance, is very closely related to that of Cuba.

It goes without saying that Carpentier covers the whole continuum of musical expression and not merely certain arbitrarily selected segments thereof. He makes no *a priori* assumption that one type of music is more important than another. The salon and the street, the theatre and the church, the country and the city, all share his keen observation and his penetrating analysis. All musical facts are viewed in their historical context, and in relation to social, economic and demographic factors. His book is a model of how musical history should be written.

After two initial chapters devoted, respectively, to the 16th and 17th centuries, Carpentier devotes a chapter to the first notable Cuban composer, Esteban Salas, who was born in Havana and became choirmaster at Santiago in 1764. He wrote religious music in the style of the Neapolitan School. His death occurred in 1803.

With his chapter on "The introduction of the contradanza", Carpentier enters the important domain of Antillean popular music, whose rhythms and melodic inflections he carefully analyzes. This leads him to the Negro influence, which he finds decisive in the formation of this music, especially through the dance and its accompanying instruments.

After studying the "classical" composers Antonio Raffelín (1796-1882) and Juan París (1759-1845), Carpentier takes up the beginning of musical nationalism in the work of the composer Manuel Saumell (1817-1870), whose *contradanzas* for piano established an important tradition in Cuban art music. This tradition was continued and perfected by Ignacio Cervantes (1847-1905), "the most important Cuban musician of the 19th century". His *Danzas cubanas* for piano utilize freely the form of the Cuban *contradanza*, without direct borrowings, in a personal and polished style.

Reaching the 20th century, Carpentier traces the rise of the *danzón*, which, until about 1920, may be considered the "national dance" of Cuba because of its extreme popularity. Its chief rival was the *son*, which became of fundamental importance in the development of Cuban popular music. In the words of Carpentier, "the great merit of the *son* resides in the liberty that it offers to spontaneous popular expression, thus stimulating rhythmic invention". He also points out that most of the Cuban dances exported under the name of *rumbas* were in reality *sones*. The *son*, he maintains, is the paradigm of Cuban popular music.

A chapter on Afro-Cubanism in music is followed by a study of the two composers who most successfully cultivated this vein in art music: Roldán and García Caturla. The final chapter surveys "The present state of Cuban music". Much prominence is given to the rôle of José Ardévol (q.v.), founder of the "Grupo Renovación Musical", who came to Havana from Spain in 1930 and quickly assumed a position of leadership. He advocated strict formal discipline along strictly modern lines. Other composers mentioned in this chapter are Julián Orbón (b. 1926), Hilario González, Harold Gramatges, Gisela Hernández, and various members of the "Grupo Renovación". Attention is given to the unusual cases of Carlo Borbolla, Gilberto Valdés, and Pablo Ruiz Castellanos, who have made individual contributions of varying merit outside the mainstream of contemporary music.

The seven-volume work on Afro-Cuban music published by Dr. Fernando Ortiz from 1950 to 1955 is the culmination of a life-time of labor devoted to this subject. The first volume of this tremendous work (item 559a), titled *La africanía de la música folklórica de Cuba*, deals with the nature and antecedents of Afro-Cuban music, and with the musical expression of the Negroes of Africa. The second volume deals with *Los bailes y el teatro de los negros en el folklore de Cuba*, discussing "The Sociality of African Music", "The Dances of the Negroes", "Pantomime Among the Negroes", and "The Theatre Among the Negroes". The following five volumes are devoted to a study of *Los instrumentos de la música afrocubana* (item. 561a). Volume V includes a bibliographical index (pp. 453-478), an index of illustrations (a total of 487), an index of musical instruments and of related terms, and a general synoptical table of contents.

The amount of information assembled in this monumental work is staggering. Yet the author himself disclaims all pretention to having produced a definitive work. He considers this a beginning in a field where very little systematic investigation had previously been done. There is still room for more systematic study and research. Yet the work of Dr. Ortiz will remain as the foundation of all subsequent research that may be undertaken in this important field.

BIBLIOGRAPHY

(A) PRIMITIVE, FOLK, AND POPULAR MUSIC

Carpentier, Alejo. El son en la música y el baile popular *Revista de América* (Bogotá), v. 7, no. 19 (July 1946), p. 124-128.   [548a]

Cuéllar Vizcaíno, Manuel. La revolución del "mambo". *Bohemia*, v. 40, no. 22, (May 30, 1948), p. 20-22, 97-99.
[549a]
Attempts to solve the problem of origin of this contemporary dance. Eight reproductions of photographs. (C. S.)

———. Ochun y Yemaya. *Bohemia*, v. 40, no. 38 (Sept. 19, 1948), p. 22-24, 88-89.   [550a]
Discussion of rites of these two cult deities with special reference to the dances. Six reproductions of photographs and two music notations. (C. S.)

Erminy Arismendi, Santos. Hipótesis sobre el origen y evolución de la rumba. *América*, Habana, v. 15, nos. 2-3 (1942), p. 53-56.   [551a]

Galaor, Don. Sindo Garay, el músico poeta de Cuba. *Bohemia*, v. 40, no. 26 (June 27, 1948), p. 3-4, 98-99, 123.
[552a]
Account of life of this popular composer and guitarist (b. 1870). Six reproductions of photographs. (C. S.)

Gálvez, Zoila. Una melodía negra. *Estud. afrocub.*, v. 4, nos. 1, 2, 3 & 4 (1940), p. 23-26.   [553a]
Refers to the melody of a song by Gilberto Valdés, titled *Ogguere,* which was found to resemble the tune of a "white spiritual" in Tennessee.

León, Argeliers. La canción cubana. *La música*, no. 7 (Oct. 1950), p. 6-7.
[554a]
Historical and aesthetic considerations.

Ortiz, Fernando. Cuban drumbeat. *Américas,* v. 2, no. 11 (Nov. 1950), p. 6-8, 44-46.   [555a]
A useful and authoritative digest of the author's voluminous writings on this subject, for the general reader. Good photographs of musicians playing drums.

———. El güiro de moyubá o jobá. *In* Homenaje al Dr. Alfonso Caso. México, Nuevo Mundo, 1951. p. 299-315.
[556a]
An ethnomusicological analysis of the gourd as used in Afro-Cuban music. (S. W. M.)

———. El kinfuiti. Un tambor para "jalar" muertos. *Bohemia,* v. 42, no. 35 (Aug. 27, 1950), p. 20-21, 131, 140.   [557a]
A variety of friction drum, played in a sitting posture by rubbing a piece of wood attached by a thong to the membrane of the drum. Used in the Afro-Cuban congo cult. Illustrated. (C. S.)

———. La música afrocubana. *Rev. mus. chil.,* v. 8, no. 43 (Sept. 1952), p. 13-33.   [558a]

———. La africanía de la música folklórica de Cuba. Habana, Publicaciones del ministerio de educación, Dirección de cultura, 1950. 477 p. il. (music)
[559a]
The first of a series of 7 volumes dealing with Afro-Cuban music in all its aspects, written by a sociologist who has made a life-long study of the subject. This volume deals mainly with a comparative study of African and Afro-Cuban musical elements. There are 83 musical notations. Bibliography, p. 465-474.

———. Los bailes y el teatro de los negros en el folklore de Cuba. Habana, Publicaciones del ministerio de educación. Dirección de cultura, 1951. 463 p. il. (music).   [560a]
The second volume in the author's monumental study of Afro-Cuban music and

folklore, deals with dance, pantomime, and traditional quasi-theatrical manifestations. There are 123 musical notations. Bibliography, p. 457-463.

———. Los instrumentos de la música afrocubana. Habana, Publicaciones de la dirección de cultura del ministerio de educación, 1952-1955. 5 v. il. (music) (vols. 4 and 5 published by Cárdenas y cía., 1954 and 1955).   [561a]

Vol. 1: Los instrumentos anatómicos y los palos percusivos.

Vol. 2: Los instrumentos sacuditivos, los frotativos y los hierros.

Vol. 3: Los tambores xilofónicos y los membranófonos abiertos (A a N).

Vol. 4: Los membranófonos abiertos, Ñ a Z, los bimembranófonos y otros tambores especiales.

Vol. 5: Los pulsativos, los fricativos y los aeritivos. Índices generales. Índice bibliográfico.

———. La música de las tumbas. *Bohemia*, v. 41 (1949), no. 4 (Jan. 23), p. 22-24, 93, 98, 106; no. 6 (Feb. 6), p. 20-22, 90-91. 97-98.   [562a]

Tumbas francesas are "drums and, by extension, certain dances and songs introduced into Cuba early in the 19th century by the Creole Negroes of Haiti", who were called French. 6 illustrations of these drums. 9 illustrations of dances; 6 music notations (fragmentary). (C. S.)

———. La música y los areítos de los indios de Cuba. *Rev. arqueol. etnol.*, época 2, v. 3, no. 6-7 (1948), p. 115-189.   [563a]

Scholarly refutation of claims, particularly by Sánchez de Fuentes, of survival of Indian music in Cuba. (C. S.)

———. La música y los areítos de los indios de Cuba. Estudio presentado al VIII Congreso histórico nacional de Santiago de Cuba, de 1948. La Habana, Editorial Lex, 1948. 79 p. il. (Sobretirada de la *Revista de arqueología y etnología*)   [564a]

A reprint of preceding item.

———. Miscelánea de estudios dedicados al Dr. Fernando Ortiz por sus discípulos,

colegas y amigos. La Habana, 1956.   [565a]

———. La transculturación blanca de los tambores de los negros. *Arch. ven. folk.*, v. 1, no. 2 (July-Dec. 1952), p. 235-265.   [566a]

General cultural-historical description of the diffusion of percussion instruments of African provenience in Europe and the New World, with special attention to Cuba. (S. W. Mintz).

———. Preludios étnicos de la música afrocubana. *Rev. bim. cub.*, v. 59, no. 1-3 (Jan.-June 1947), p. 5-194; v. 60, no. 1-3 (June-Dec. 1947), p. 123-280.   [567a]

Contains chapters 1-4 of a complete work of 8 chapters. Speculation upon the origin of all music leads into reflections upon Cuban music flavored with an encyclopedic reading. Much first-hand observation. 33 music notations. (C. S.)

———. Preludios étnicos de la música afrocubana. *Rev. bim. cub.*, v. 61, no. 1-3 (Jan.-June, 1948), p. 41-278; v. 62, no. 4-6 (July-Dec. 1948), p. 131-210.   [568a]

Continuation, chapters 5-7. (C. S.)

———. Preludios étnicos de la música afrocubana. *Rev. bim. cub.*, v. 63, no. 1-3 (Jan.-June, 1949), p. 63-208; v. 64, no. 1-3 (July-Dec. 1949), p. 87-194. [569a]

Continuation (Chapters 8 and 9). Copious bibliographical references and music notations, many of these being scores of drumming. (C. S.)

Salazar, Adolfo. Músicas negras. *Nuestra música*, v. 7, no. 26 (2do. trimestre, 1952), p. 134-156.   [570a]

Chiefly a commentary on the work *La africanía de la música folklórica de Cuba* by Fernando Ortiz (q. v.).

Törnberg, Gerda. Musical instruments of the Afro-Cubans. *Ethnos*, v. 19, no. 1-4 (1954), p. 105-126.   [571a]

A description of form and use of a number of Afro-Cuban instruments; the author bases herself largely on the work of Ortíz and others. (S. W. M.)

Vasconcelos, Ramón. Confidencias. *Bohemia*, v. 40, no. 26, (June 27, 1948), p. 40-41, 73.   **[572a]**

Account of life of the popular composer and guitarist Sindo Garay (b. 1870). Two reproductions of photographs. (C. S.)

(B) ART MUSIC AND MISCELLANEOUS

Agüero y Barreras, Gaspar. El compositor Nicolás Ruiz Espadero. *Revista cubana*, La Habana (April-June 1938), p. 160-178.   **[573a]**

Ardévol, José. Breve historia de un grupo de jóvenes músicos cubanos. *Mensuario* (March 1950), p. 11, 14.   **[574a]**

Deals with the organization and aims of the "Grupo de renovación musical".

———. Catálogo de obras de los compositores cubanos contemporáneos, no. 3: José Ardévol. La Habana, Publicado por la oficina de difusión e intercambio del Conservatorio municipal de La Habana, 1946. Pages unnumbered. (Reproduced from typewritten copy).   **[575a]**

"Nota crítico-b i o g r á f i c a" by Harold Gramatges (6 p.), followed by chronological "Lista de obras", Letter from Ardévol to Charles Seeger stating his views on his own development as a composer. Bibliography: "Principales artículos sobre J. Ardévol."

———. El Grupo Renovación de La Habana. *Rev. mus. chil.*, v. 3, no. 27 (Dec. 1947), p. 17-20.   **[576a]**

Discussion of foundation of group in 1924, aims, special personalities of individual members. Stresses at end the lack of facilities, especially for performance. (B. K.)

———. Estado actual de la música en la república. *Mensuario*, (May 1940), p. 7, 22.   **[577a]**

———. Grupo de renovación musical. *In* Anuario cultural de Cuba, 1943 (La Habana, 1944), p. 79-86).   **[578a]**

———. Historia reciente y actualidad. *Estudios*, v. 1, no. 4 (July 1950), p. 13-14, 48.   **[579a]**

Musical education and musical activity in Cuba decried as "reactionary." Portraits of Cuban composers: Argeliers León, Ardévol, Orbón, Edgar Martín, Hilario González, A. García Caturla, H. Gramatges.

———. Nuestro breve y neecsario neoclasicismo. *La música*, no. 8 (April 1951), p. 1-3.   **[580a]**

Claims that the neoclassical trend initiated by Ardévol in Cuban music was a necessary creative discipline, but that "esta etapa, desde hace por lo menos cinco o seis años, está ya completamente superada."

———. Panorama de la música cubana. Síntesis histórica del desarrollo de la música seria en la Antilla mayor. Sus triunfos de ayer y sus posibilidades de mañana. *Norte*, v. 6, no. 10 (Aug. 1946), p. 33, 54.   **[581a]**

Chiefly an evaluation of the work of the younger composers who formed the Grupo de Renovación Musical. (C. S.)

———. Posición del compositor cubano actual. *Conservatorio*, v. 2, no. 5 (Oct.-Dec. 1945), p. 3-8.   **[582a]**

Author is Spanish-born teacher of most of the young composers of the present day. Amplification of the ideas expressed in *Presencia cubana en la música universal*. (Cf. item 599a) Discussion of problems of geography, nationalism, tradition, "importance". (C. S.)

Carpentier, Alejo. Alejandro García Caturla. *In* Composers of the Americas. Biographical data and catalogs of their works. Washington, D. C., Pan American Union, 1957, v. 3, p. 83-95.   **[583a]**

Reprinted from *La música en Cuba* (México, 1946), p. 244-51. Spanish text with English translation.

———. La música contemporánea de Cuba. *Rev. mus. chil.*, v. 3, no. 27 (Dec. 1947), p. 9-17.   **[584a]**

Discussion of the state of music in Cuba in the early 1920s, the need for the attack against Italian opera, the campaign for the recognition of Afro-Cuban folk music waged by Roldán, García Caturla, and the author. At the end, refers to the tragic deaths of Roldán and García Caturla which almost decapitated Cuban music, and of the fortunate emergence of José Ardévol. (B. K.)

——. La música cubana en estos últimos veinte años. *Conservatorio*, v. 1, no. 2 (Jan.-March 1944).   [585a]

An account of concert activity in Havana from 1920 to 1940.

——. La música en Cuba. México, Fondo de cultura económica, 1946. 282 p. (Colección Tierra firme, v. 19.)
[586a]

The first attempt at a systematic historical survey of the origins and development of music in Cuba. Trends and personalities are discussed, and there are chapters on some of the leading figures, such as Esteban Salas, Saumell, Espadero, Cervantes, Roldán and Caturla. The final chapter deals with Cuban music of the present day. There is a bibliography but no index. Musical examples with the text.

——. Music in Cuba (1523-1900). *Mus. quart.*, v. 33, no. 3 (July 1947), p. 365-380.   [587a]

Concerns religious music, music of the salon and theater, and mineteenth century composers. Two plates, one of first violin part of a work by the 18th century Havana composer Esteban Salas y Castro (composer's autograph), and the other a picture of Ignacio Cervantes (1847-1905). Important article. Translated by Ethel S. Cohen.

——. Variations on a Cuban theme. *Américas*, v. 2, no. 2 (Feb. 1950), p. 20-23, 38-39.   [588a]

Short but highly competent account of popular and, especially, serious music in Cuba. Excellent illustrations, photographs of prominent Cuban music figures, modern Cuban paintings of musical subjects.

[**Cervantes, Ignacio**]. Primer centenario del natalicio de Ignacio Cervantes, 1947. La Habana, Editorial Netuno, 1947, 22 p. il. (incl. music).   [589a]

A concise biography of this important 19th-century composer, published under the auspices of the "Servicio feminino para la defensa civil".

Conservatorio Municipal de Música. Resumen de las actividades del Conservatorio municipal desde su fundación hasta la actualidad. Habana, Municipio de La Habana, Depto. de cultura y turismo, 1944, 32 p. [590a]

Educación musical en las escuelas primarias. Cursillo oficial de orientación. Aporte de la Confederación nacional de conservatorios y profesionales de la música a la obra de educación nacional que realiza el Ministerio de educación. La Habana, 1945, 112 p. il.   [591a]

With the following contributions: *Exposición de los fines y propósitos de la educación musical*, by Joaquín Rodríguez Lanza; *Rítmica*, by Ondina Torres Momplet; *Bandas rítmicas infantiles*, by César Pérez Sentenat; *Lectura musical artística y teoría aplicada*, by César Pérez Sentenat; *Didáctica del canto coral*, by Dolores Torres Barrós; *Apreciación musical*, by María Muñoz de Quevedo; *La educación rítmica*, by José Raventós Mestres.

English biographies of Cuban composers. New York, Cuban-American music group, 1946, 16 p.   [592a]

Bio-bibliographical data on 27 Cuban composers, from Cervantes and Saumell to Orbón and Ruiz Castellanos. "The responbility for the adaptation of biographical material and its use is assumed wholly by Erminie Kahn, executive director of the Cuban-American music group."

Figueredo Socarrías, Fernando. Perucho Figueredo y el Himno nacional. *Rev. Habana*, año 4, v. 7, no. 41 (Jan. 1946), p. 437-449.   [593a]

An intimate account of the beginnings of the Cuban revolution in 1876 and the writing of the national anthem, *La Bayamesa*, by Perucho Figueredo. (C. S.)

Gacel, Miguel Agustín. Dos virtuosos del violín: Brindis de Salas y White. *Rev. mus. chil.*, v. 5, no. 35-36 (Aug.-Nov. 1949), p. 44-48.   [594a]

[**García Caturla, Alejandro**]. Chrono-

logical catalog of works by the Cuban composer Alejandro García Caturla. *Bol. mús. artes,* nos. 74-76 (April-June 1956), p. 25-30. **[595a]**
García Caturla was born in 1906 and died in 1940. Facsimile of holograph score, p. 24.

Gay-Calbo, Enrique. La bandera, el escudo y el himno. La Habana, Academia de la Historia de Cuba, 1945. 90 p. il. (incl. music). **[596a]**
Historical information on the Cuban national anthem.

Gramatges, Harold. Bosquejo de la música cubana. *B. A. mus.,* v. 12, no. 197 (Oct. 1, 1957), p. 2. **[597a]**
Begins with the composers of the 19th century, and then discusses various contemporary musicians, among them Ardévol, Roldán, García Caturla, Aurelio de la Vega, Julián Orbón. Cites the names of Nilo Rodriguez, Juan Blanco, Natalia Galán and Carlos Fariñas as "los más representativos de la generación última".

———. Sobre "Nueve pequeñas piezas' de Ardévol, y lo cubano en la música 'de este compositor. *La música,* v. 2, no. 5 (Jan.-March 1949), p. 1-3. **[598a]**
Finds definite Cuban elements in the music of Ardévol.

Grupo de renovación musical. Presencia cubana en la música universal. La Habana, Publicaciones del conservatorio municipal, 1945. 24 p. **[599a]**
Aesthetic manifesto of this group of Cuban composers, headed by José Ardévol. According to the *Noticia preliminar,* "se encomendó a Julián Orbón y a Hilario González la redacción de un a modo de resumen de los principales puntos debatidos por el Grupo". Rejects "nationalism" but finds that a national factor is indispensable in musical creation, in the sense that all artistic expression occurs within a given cultural setting. Therefore the term "Cuban music" has a definite meaning in the creative process.

Guiral Moreno, Mario. Un gran musicógrafo y compositor cubano, Eduardo Sánchez de Fuentes. La Habana, Imp. El Siglo xx, 1944. 31 p. **[600a]**
A review of the personality and work

of Sánchez de Fuentes, born April 3, 1874, died September 7, 1944.

Loynaz del Castillo, Enrique. El Himno invasor. *Rev. Habana,* año 4, v. 7, no. 41 (Jan. 1946), p. 450-461. **[601a]**

Lyons, James. Pianistic pilot... Jorge Bolet takes his instrument with him. *Mus. Amer.,* v. 74, no. 15 (Dec. 1, 1954), p. 12. **[602a]**
Full-page biographical article on Cuban pianist. Two photographs.

Martínez, Orlando, *ed.* Eduardo Sánchez de Fuentes; in memoriam. La Habana, 1944, 18 p. il. (incl. music). **[603a]**
Bio-bibliographical data followed by some notes on the habanera "Tu", Also includes two articles: "Sánchez de Fuentes — un músico, una vida y una canción", by Antonio Quevedo and "E. Sánchez de Fuentes— símbolo y expresión de la música cubana", by the editor.

———. La prensa musical en Cuba. *Alerta,* 16 May, 1949. **[604a]**
Useful references from *El Filarmónico Mensual,* founded in 1812. (C. S.)

Muñoz de Quevedo, María. El maestro Alejandro García Caturla. *Estud. afrocub.,* v. 4, nos. 1, 2, 3 & 4 (1940), p. 58-64. **[605a]**
Reprinted from *Musicalia.*

Salazar, Adolfo. María Muñoz de Quevedo. In memoriam. *Nuestra música,* v. 3, no. 11 (July 1948), p. 206-212. **[606a]**
Tribute to an active figure in the musical life of Cuba, with considerable detail about the outstanding Cuban musicians and composers of the period between the two World Wars.

Torre, Gabriel de la. Mi vida profesional, revisada a los ochenta años. La Habana, Imprenta "Cuba intelectual," 1944. 149 p. il. (incl. music). **[607a]**
The distinguished Cuban music educator, born in 1863, describes his musical studies with Albéniz, Pedrell, Granados, and the concert activities of his wife and daughters.

DOMINICAN REPUBLIC

THE musical bibliography of the Dominican Republic, though not large, is fairly comprehensive. Julio Arzeno's monograph, *Del folklore musical dominicano* [no. 1537], covers the field of folk music with exceptional thoroughness. Profusely illustrated with musical examples, Arzeno's treatise deals with every type of folk and popular music in the Dominican Republic, analyzing each form musically and also relating it to the social background of the people. The principal types of Dominican folk music are the *media tuna*, the *mangulina*, the *carabiné*, and especially the *merengue*, which is the most popular of all. The *merengue* is a dance in binary rhythm (2/4 time) and in moderate tempo. Other types which may be mentioned are the *plena*, the *punto*, the *seis* and the *zapateo*. The *bolero*, imported from Cuba, is also popular.

The above-mentioned study was issued as the first volume of a two-volume work dealing with all aspects of Dominican music. To the best of our knowledge the second volume has not yet been published, but we print herewith the projected table of contents:

TOMO SEGUNDO

Primera Parte

I. Génesis del arte musical Dominicano—Origen—Primeras manifestaciones.
II. Profesores antiguos y modernos—Teóricos.
III. Compositores—Pablo Claudio y sus obras—Nuevos progresos.
IV. Ambiente artístico—Cantantes—Sociedades musicales.
V. Porvenir de la música dominicana.

Segunda Parte

I. Cantares populares—Urbanos—Rurales—Influencia exterior.
II. La música Dominicana—Sus tendencias—Evolución.
III. Su expresión—Rítmo y emoción estética.
IV. La audición.
V. Compositores Dominicanos contemporáneos.

The first volume of Arzeno's work may be supplemented by the more generalized studies of Flérida de Nolasco [no. 1540] and Enrique de Marchena [no. 1539], both of which devote considerable attention to folk music as well as to other aspects of musical activity in the Dominican

Republic. Marchena mentions an unpublished work on Dominican folk music by the late Esteban Peña Morell (1894-1938), "comenzada a editar en el Sindicato nacional de artes gráficas, Santo Domingo." Enrique de Marchena (b. 13 Oct. 1908) has for many years been music critic of the *Listín diario,* oldest Dominican newspaper. He is the Dominican representative of the Sociedad Musical Daniel and has composed various works, among them a *Suite des images* for orchestra. Other contemporary Dominican composers are José D. Cerón, Juan Francisco García, Enrique Mejía Arredondo, Luis Mena, Luis Rivera, etc. The young Spanish composer Enrique Casal Chapí settled in Ciudad Trujillo in 1939 and has taken a prominent part in the musical life of the Republic. He was appointed conductor of the Orquesta Sinfónica Nacional, created in 1941 as a dependency of the Sección de Bellas Artes of the Secretaría de Estado de Educación Pública.

BIBLIOGRAPHY

Arzeno, Julio. Del folk-lore musical dominicano. Santo Domingo, Imp. "La Cuna de América", Roques Roman hnos., 1927. ML3565.A8F7 **[1537]**
With music (unaccompanied melodies). For comment, see introductory section above.

Marchena, Enrique de. Del areito de Anacaona al poema folklórico; Brindis de Salas en Santo Domingo. Ciudad Trujillo, Editora Montalvo, 1942. 95 p. **[1538]**
The first part of this book is concerned chifly with various aspects of Dominican folk music. The music of the so-called "areito de Anacaona", quoted from Bachiller y Morales, is given on p. 25.

Nolasco, Flérida de. El carabiné, el son, el merengue, el danzón, la habanera, los ritmos antillanos, son originarios de Arabia. *Bahoruco,* v. 5, no. 252 (1935), p. 4-5, 30-21. **[1539]**

———. La música en Santo Domingo y otros ensayos. Ciudad Trujillo, Editora Montalvo, 1939. 163 p. M220.-N65M8 **[1540]**
Includes music of a *merengue* and a *mangulina.*

Ramírez-Peralta, José G., comp. Popular airs of the Dominican Republic. Vol. 1. New York, Alpha music, 1941. 26 p. **[1541]**
Includes compositions in popular semifolk style by Julio A. Hernández, Enrique Mejía Arredondo, Enrique de Marchena, Rafael Almanzar, Juan F. García, Mercedes Sagredo de Sánchez, Rafael Petitón Guzmán and Ramón Díaz.

———. Songs and dances of the Dominican Republic; expressly published for the pavilion of the Dominican Republic, New York world's fair .New York, Alpha music, 1940. 32 p. **[1542]**

Ravelo, José de Jesús. Historia de los himnos dominicanos. Conf. leída en el Ateneo dominicano el 25 de febrero de 1934. Santo Domingo, Tall. tip. "La Nación", 1934. 44 p. ML3565.-R25H5 **[1543]**
Words and music to the *Himno de la independencia, Himno de la restauración, Himno* by Reyes and Prud'homme. The hymn composed in 1883 by José Reyes, to words by Emilio Prud'homme, was officially adopted as the national anthem of the Dominican Republic in 1934.

Tejada, Valentín. Música popular dominicana. *América,* v. 7, no. 2 (Aug. 1940). **[1544]**
The most characteristic type of Dominican traditional music is the *merengue,* sung and danced by the peasants.

SUPPLEMENT TO 1960

Two useful publications on music in the Dominican Republic have appeared since the first edition of this Guide was issued. They are *Panorama de la música dominicana* (1947) by Juan Francisco García (item 161a) and *Music and musicians of the Dominican Republic* (1949) by J. M. Coopersmith (item 620a). The latter is available (from the Pan American Union) in both English and Spanish.

García's booklet briefly traces the historical backgrounds of music in the Dominican Republic from the 16th century, when Spanish religious music was first implanted there. Although several earlier composers are mentioned, the first important name is that of Juan Bautista Alfonseca de Baris (1810–1875), "considerado como el padre de la música nacional." He was the composer of the first Dominican patriotic anthem, the "Himno a la Independencia." His pupil José Reyes (1835–1905) composed the official national anthem of the republic in 1833. José María Arredondo (1840–1924) wrote several *zarzuelas* that were produced at the Teatro La Republicana (formerly a Jesuit Convent).

In Chapter V of his booklet, García gives biographical data on numerous Dominican composers who have been active in recent times. These include José de Jesús Ravelo (b. 1876), said to have written over 200 scores, both secular and religious; Esteban Peña Morell (1897-1938), whose compositions are based on the folk music of the Antilles; Luis Emilio Mena (b. 1895), author of *Sinfonía Giocosa* and some 200 other compositions; José D. Cerón (b. 1897), composer of symphonic poems; and Juan Bautista Espínola (1894–1923), composer of more than 500 pieces of popular music. Chapters VI and VII deal with musical activities and organizations in the Dominican Republic.

The monograph by Coopersmith is based on field work undertaken in 1944, which included the recording of 78 discs of folk material. His study was originally published in *The musical quarterly* (v. 31, nos. 1 and 2, Jan. and April 1945). It begins with an historical survey of the music of the Dominican Republic as "an outgrowth of three musical influences: native Indian, Colonial-Hispanic, and Negro." Reference is made to descriptions of native songs and dances by early Spanish chroniclers such as Bartolomé de las Casas and Gonzalo de Oviedo. Indigenous musical instruments are named and described. The music of the so-called *Areíto de Anacoana* is printed "as a curiosity."

Turning to the Colonial period, information is gleaned about the cultivation of both religious and secular music (the latter proceeding mainly from Spanish oral tradition). The origins of the Dominican dances, such as the *tumba* and the *merengue,* are discussed, and some musical notations are given.

Mentioned as "outstanding composers in the second half of the 19th century" are Clodomiro Arredondo Miura (1864–1935), José María Rodríguez Arresón (b. 1875 in Puerto Rico), and Alfredo Máximo Soler, "composer of more than 300 works in the popular idiom." Regarding the contemporary scene, Coopersmith writes: "The composers who comprise the modern, nationalistic school in the Dominican Republic today owe their inspiration and sense of direction to the pioneers, Esteban Peña Morell and Juan Francisco García." The latter demonstrated that "the national dance (*merengue*) could be used in the larger forms of composition." He also originated a new, composite dance-form called the *sambumbia.* "Inspired by García's, example, the younger group of composers have enriched their national music so that now more than twenty major works by them are included in the repertoire of the Orquesta Sinfónica Nacional." There follows an account of these composers and their principal works.

Part 2 of Coopersmith's monograph deals with the musical folklore of the Dominican Republic. The typical musical instruments are listed and carefully described, according to the classification of Curt Sachs. The various types of traditional song are then analyzed, with musical notations. Most songs are based on established melodies, called *tonadas,* to which words are improvised utilizing traditional Spanish verse-forms, such as the *copla* and the *décima.*

The concluding section deals with dances, which "have evolved from African and Spanish prototypes." Among the most popular, besides the *merengue,* is the *baile de los palos* (also known as *baile de los atabales*), which is really not so much a dance in the usual sense as "a song-instrument ritual in which are utilized secular or sacred texts." Other dances are the *carabiné,* the *mangulina,* the *bolero,* the *sarambo,* and two derivatives of the *merengue:* the *pambiche* and the *yuca.* A detailed description is given of the *merengue,* with analysis of the rhythmic patterns.

A valuable feature of Coopersmith's monograph is its wealth of bibliographic references, included in the 311 footnotes which accompany this 60–page work. There are also excellent photographic illustrations of typical musical instruments, and a map showing the itinerary of the author's folklore investigation in the Cibao.

For a detailed study of Dominican folklore, the reader should consult *Folklore de la República Dominicana* by Manuel José Andrade (1948, 2 vols.).

BIBLIOGRAPHY

(A) PRIMITIVE, FOLK, AND POPULAR MUSIC

Boyrie Moya, Émile de. Aparición en la isla de Santo Domingo de los primeros silbatos modulados indígenas, tipo ocarino, encontrados en las Antillas. In *Memorias del V Congreso Histórico Municipal Interamericano*, v. 1. Ciudad Trujillo, 1952, p. 187-188, 6. pl. **[608a]**

Two clay whistles are described and illustrated. One, which is decorated with a human face, comes from excavations at a Taino site. (I. R.)

García, Juan Francisco. Formas de la música folklórica dominicana. *Bol. folk. dom.*, v. 1, no. 1 (June 1946), p. 10-14. **[609a]**

Brief general note. One music notation, melody only. (C. S.)

Garrido, Edna. El aguinaldo. *Bol. folk. dom.*, v. 2, no. 2 (Dec. 1947, i. c., 1948), p. 3-25. **[610a]**

Fifteen music notations of *aguinaldos*. Names of informants listed. (C. S.)

――. El folklore del niño dominicano. Juegos infantiles. *Bol. folk. dom.*, v. 2, no. 2 (Dec. 1947, i. e., 1948), p. 54-64. **[611a]**

Three music notations of children's games. Names of informants listed. (C. S.)

――. El son molinero. *Bol. folk. dom.*, v. l, no. 1 June 1946),p.44-48. **[612a]**

Description, verses and music of three variants of this children's game from Azua, Ciudad Trujillo and Peña, Santiago, Dominican Republic. (C. S.)

――. Versiones dominicanas de romances españoles; recogidos y anotados. Ciudad Trujillo, Pol hermanos, 1946. 110 p. il. (Inc. music). **[613a]**

Valuable as providing another monographic link for the comparative study of the survival and evolution of old Spanish ballads in the New World. Includes 17 *romances* (two of which are not related to the Spanish *romancero*), with melodies, texts, variants, descriptive notes, and map showing geographical distribution.

Morel, Tomás E. Del llano i de la loma; tradiciones, fantasías, criollas, tonadas, copla i cantares cibaeños. Santiago. Dominican Republic, Ed. "Corazón de Jesús" de M. Helú, 1937.120. p. **[614a]**

Nolasco, Flérida de. El carabiné. *Bol. folk. dom.*, v. 1, no. 1 (June 1946), p. 18-24. **[615a]**

Brief discussion of character, origin and manner of dancing what author believes to be typically Dominican dance of Spanish provenience. One music notation for piano. (C. S.)

――. La poesía folklórica en Santo Domingo. Santiago, Dominican Republic, Editorial El Diario, 1946. 367 p. **[616a]**

――. Santo Domingo en el folklore universal. Ciudad Trujillo, Impresora dominicana, 1956. **[617a]**

Includes words of many folksongs and compares them with those found in Spain and in other countries of Latin America.

Rodríguez Demorizi, Emilio. Del romancero dominicano. Santiago, República Dominicana, Editorial El Diario, 1943. 119 p. il. **[618a]**

Surveys briefly history of folk ballad, its transmission to America, and its relatively weak survival among school children of Santo Domingo, where the décima has replaced it as the most popular form. Gives texts of *A los valientes dominicanos* (ms. c. 1763) by Luis J. Peguero, anon. *Romance de las invasiones haitianas* (ms. c. 1830), *Romance* by Juan P. Duarte (1813-1876), *A la palma de la libertad* by José F. Pichardo (1837-1873), *Visita a la Isabela, Bayajá*, and *La internvención*, 1801, by Gastón F. Deligne (1861-1913), and *Santomé*, 1855, by Eulogio C. Cabral (1868-1928) (R. S. B.)

(C) ART MUSIC AND MISCELLANEOUS

Coopersmith, Jacob Maurice. Music and musicians of the Dominican Republic; a survey. *Mus. quart.*, v. 31, no. 1 (Jan. 1945), p. 71-88; no. 2 (Apr. 1945), p. 212-226. **[619a]**

Based on a four-month visit (1944-1945) to the Dominican Republic at the invitation of President Trujillo to prepare a survey of the music resources there. Much historical and biographical data. 4 music examples, photographs of composers Alfonseca, Arredondo, Juan Francisco García and Gerardo Mena, and of author with prominent music figurres. Republished, with additions, in Pan American Union publications. (See next item).

——. Music and musicians of the Dominican republic. Música y músicos de la República Dominicana. Washington, D. C., Pan American Union,

1949. (Department of Cultural affairs, Division of music and visual arts. Music series no. 15). [620a]

An important monograph (bilingual edition). For comment, see the introduction to this section (Supplement to 1960).

García, Juan Francisco. Panorama de la música dominicana. Ciudad Trujillo, Publicaciones de la secretaría de estado de educación y bellas artes, 1947. 46 p. [621a]

For comment, see the introduction to this section (Supplement to 1960).

DUTCH GUIANA

BIBLIOGRAPHY

Benoît, Pierre Jacques. Voyage à Surinam ... Cent dessins pris sur nature par l'auteur, litographiés par Madou et Lauters. Bruxelles Société des Beaux-Arts (De Wasme et Laurent), 1839. [1545]

Illustrations of natives playing musical instruments (plates xix–xli, xlv).

Focke, Hendrik Charles. De Surinaamsche negermuzijk. Bijdragen tot de bevordering van de kennis der Nederlandsch West-Indsche koloniën. Haarlem, A. C. Kruseman, 1855–58. 2 v. F2048.W51 [1546]

Vol. 2 contains a supplement of 15 melodies with text.

Goeje, Claudius Henricus de. Beiträge zur völkerkunde von Surinam. Int. arch. ethnog., v. 19 (Leiden, 1910), p. 1–34. [1547]

Includes 9 tunes.

——. Bijdrage tot de ethnographie der Surinaamsche Indianen. Int. arch. ethnog., v. 17, supl. (Leiden, E. J. Brill, 1906). [1548]

Includes 8 tunes, p. 23-25.

Herskovits, Melville J. and Frances. Rebel destiny; among the bush Negroes of Dutch Guiana. New York and London, Whittlesey house, Mc-

Graw-Hill book co., 1934. 366 p. F2431.N3H36 [1549]

References to dances, p. 8–10, 16–17, 29, 82-83, 163-166, 327. References to songs, p. 28, 50, 83, 87, 105–107, 114–115, 162, 164–166, 232, 235, 237, 244, 245–246, 294, 332, 335. Drums, p. 3, 151, 244 ff., 328 ff.

——. Suriname folk-lore. New York, Columbia university press, 1936. 766 p. F2431.N3H38 [1550]

Includes transcriptions of Suriname songs and musicological analysis, by Dr. M. Kolinski. This is one of the largest and most valuable published collections of South American primitive music.

Panhuys, L. C. Les chansons et la musique de la Guyane néerlandaise. Jour. soc. amér., n. s., v. 9 (Paris, 1912), p. 27-29. [1550x]

Includes 6 melodies.

Penard, Thomas E. and Arthur P. Four Arawak Indian songs. In West-Indische gids, s'Gravenhage, v. 8, 1925–26, p. 497–500. F2141.W52 [1551]

Words and English translation of the four songs, with short introductory discussion.

Schomburgk, Sir Robert. On the natives of Guiana, Jour. ethnol. soc., v. 1 (1948), p. 253–276. [1552]

Contains 2 tunes, opp. p. 274.

ECUADOR

THE most comprehensive survey of Ecuadorian music is *La música en el Ecuador* by Segundo Luis Moreno, a ninety-page monograph published in the second volume of the compilation entitled *El Ecuador en cien años de independencia, 1830–1930* [no. 1556]. A large section of this study is devoted to the folk music of Ecuador, in which there is a strong Indian element. In pre-Hispanic times Ecuador formed part of the Incan empire; there are also pre-Incan archaeological remains which according to some authorities indicate a relationship to the Maya civilization of Central America. From the viewpoint of archaic indigenous culture, the Andean region of Ecuador, Bolivia and Peru may be regarded as a unit. Consult, in this connection, the study by Marguerite Béclard d'Harcourt, *Le folklore musical de la région andine* [no. 1564]. See also the studies on Incan music listed in the pertinent section under Peru. Favorite instrument of the Ecuadorian Indian is the *rondador* (panpipes), known elsewhere in the Andean region as *antara* or *sicu*.

The above-mentioned monograph by Moreno includes numerous musical examples illustrating the various types of Ecuadorian songs and dances, prominent among which are the *danzantes, pasillo, sanjuanito, yaraví, zamba, amorfino* and *danza criolla*. In the Andean region, and in the forested region east of the Andes, the Indian music of Ecuador has preserved its indigenous characteristics almost entirely unaffected by European influences. The blending of Indian and Spanish music produces the so-called *música mestiza,* of which the *danzante* and the *sanjuanito* are examples. The *amorfino* is a Creole or Spanish-American song, without Indian influence. Moreno prints an example of an *amorfino,* however, which shows marked Negro influence in the rhythm and melody; he also gives the music of other Negro dances: *marimba, zamba* and *bomba* (p. 215–217).

Dealing with music in the colony, Moreno mentions the musical teaching of the missionaries (p. 218-220) and reproduces the music of several *danzas criollas* which were typical of the colonial music. Of these, he calls *El costillar* "lo mas bello y mejor desarrollado entre las danzas criollas" (music, p. 225-226). Still more popular is the *danza criolla* entitled *Alza que te han visto* (p. 227-228), which according to Moreno had the widest diffusion in Ecuador.

In tracing the development of musical activity in the republic, Moreno points to Agustín Baldeón (d. 1847) as "uno de los mejores músicos que ha tenido hasta hoy el país". Baldeón, who composed several symphonic works, was director of the first musical society of the republic. On 28 February 1870 the Conservatorio Nacional de Música was established in Quito by government decree (it was housed in the building which later became the Palacio de Justicia). After ceasing to function for a number of years, the conservatory was reëstablished by an executive decree of 26 April 1900. The present director of the conservatory is Pedro Traversari. Segundo Luis Moreno is director of the Conservatorio de Música in Cuenca. His compositions include a *Suite ecuatoriana* on indigenous themes, a *Preludio sinfónico,* two overtures, etc. Another prominent contemporary composer is Sixto M. Durán.

On p. 250-269 of his monograph, Moreno includes data on many Ecuadorian composers, past and present, classified by regions. Among contemporaries who receive prominence are the brothers Luis Humberto Salgado and Gustavo Salgado, the former born in 1903, the latter in 1905.

Juan Pablo Muñoz Sanz is the author of a briefer survey of music in Ecuador, *La música ecuatoriana,* published in 1938 [no. 1557], in which he offers a comprehensive plan for the reorganization of musical education and musical activity in the republic.

GENERAL AND MISCELLANEOUS

Abelardo Guerra, Nicolás. Gramática musical; texto completo para el estudio elemental y superior de la teoría de la música. Quito, Talleres tipográficos nacionales, 1929. 167 p. il. (music). MT7.-A16G7 **[1553]**

"Composiciones musicales, por Nicolás Abelardo Guerra", p. 165-167.

Album de música nativa. No. 1. Guayaquil, 1933. M1687.E24 **[1554]**

Ten pieces of popular Ecuadorian music by Luis del Río and Francisco Paredes Herrera, for piano with interlinear Spanish text.

Beattie, John W., and Louis Woodson Curtis. South American music pilgrimage. II. Ecuador and Peru. *Mus. educ. jour.,* v. 28, no. 3 (Jan. 1942), p. 12-18. il. **[1555]**

Moreno, Segundo Luis. La música en el Ecuador. *In* Orellana, J. Gonzalo, *ed.,* El Ecuador en cien años de independencia, Quito, 1930, v. 2, p. 187-276. **[1556]**

The most comprehensive survey of music in Ecuador, with numerous musical examples. For further comment see introductory section above.

Muñoz Sanz, Juan Pablo. La música ecuatoriana. Quito, Imp. de la Universidad central, 1938. 36 p. ML235.M8-M8 **[1557]**

Deals with indigenous, Spanish and African elements in Ecuadorian music.

Música ecuatoriana. No. 2. Guayaquil, 1935. M1687.E2M **[1558]**

Apparently a continuation of the *Album de música nativa* (*cf.* item no. 1554). Twelve pieces in popular style by L. del Río and F. Paredes Herrera for piano with interlinear Spanish text.

Ruales Laso, Joaquín. Cultura musical. Prólogo de Gustavo Bueno. Quito, Talleres gráficos del Colegio militar, 1940. 226 p. MT6.R91C8 **[1559]**

NATIONAL ANTHEM

Guayas (Ecuador). Dirección de estudios. La bandera, el escudo, el himno patrios para los niños de las escuelas. Guayaquil, Imp. La Reforma, 1917. 37 p. (music) **[1560]**

Mora Bowen, Alfonso. La educación cívica al servicio de la enseñanza. Quito,

Imp. de la Universidad central, 1937. 123 p. F3709..M67   **[1561]**

"Himno nacional del Ecuador" (words and music), p. 96-97.

Ofrenda de Venezuela en el primer centenario de la batalla de Ayacucho. Caracas, Litografía del comercio, 1924. 130 p. M1686.O35   **[1562]**

Includes national anthem of Ecuador. Music for voice and piano; also for band (score).

FOLK AND PRIMITIVE MUSIC

(A) GENERAL

Alvarez, Manuel J. Estudios folklóricos sobre el montuvio y su música. Chone, Impr. "La Esperanza", 1929. 12 p. ML3575.A47E8   **[1563]**

Includes music of 3 songs.

Béclard d'Harcourt, Marguerite. Le folklore musical de la région andine; Équateur, Pérou, Bolivie. *In* Encyclopédie de la musique et dictionnaire du conservatoire, partie 1, p. 3353-3371, Paris, Librairie Delagrave, 1921. ML100.E5   **[1564]**

Contains 36 musical examples. An important study.

Durán, Sixto M. La musique aborigène et populaire de l'Équateur. *In* Art populaire, travaux artistiques et scientifiques du 1er congrès international des arts populaires, Prague, 1928, v. 2, p. 117-118. Paris, Éditions Duchartre, 1931. N920.I5 1928.   **[1565]**

Brief comments on the principal folk music forms of Ecuador.

Harcourt, Raoul and Marguerite d'. La musique dans la sierra andine de la Paz à Quito. Société des américanistes de Paris. *Journal,* n. s., v. 12 (Paris, 1920), p 21-53. E51.S68   **[1566]**

There are 22 brief musical examples in the main body of the article, followed by 8 melodies, all but one with text in Kechua.

Jiménez de la Espada, Marcos. Colección de yaravies quiteños. *In* Congreso internacional de Americanistas, Actas de la cuarta reunión, Madrid, 1881, v. 2, Madrid, Imprenta de Fortanet, 1883. E51.I54   **[1567]**

First part comprises 20 *yaravies* and 4 dances, collected by Espada, one arranged for 3 voices, 1 for voice and piano, 1 for fife and drum, the rest for piano alone. Second part comprises 3 tonadas and a set of "láuchas para bailar", taken from an unpublished history of the diocese of Trujillo compiled at the end of the 18th century. The *tonadas* are for voice with instrumental accompaniment, the *láuchas* for violin and bass.

Mera, Juan León. Cantares del pueblo ecuatoriano. Quito, Imprenta de la Universidad central del Ecuador 1892. (Antología ecuatoriana, tomo 1.)   **[1568]**

An anthology of folk songs, without music.

Moreno, Segundo Luis. La música criolla en el Ecuador. *América,* v. 3, no. 3 (1939), p. 60-62.   **[1569]**

——. La música en la provincia de Imbabura. Quito, Tipografía Salesianas, 1923. 39 p.   **[1570]**

(B) AMERINDIAN

Béclard d'Harcourt, Marguerite. Mélodies populaires indiennes; Équateur, Pérou, Bolivie. Milano, G. Ricordi & c., 1923. M1686.B4   **[1571]**

Contains 46 Indian folk songs, for voice with piano or harp accompaniment, and 9 airs for flute with piano. Indian texts and French translations. The preface contains a general discussion of South American Indian music and an analysis of the songs in the volume.

Harcourt, Raoul and Marguerite d'. La musique des Incas et ses survivances. Paris, P. Geuthner, 1925. 2 v. il. ML3575.H27   **[1572]**

Index bibliographique, v. 1, p. 545-556. Part 4 includes 204 musical examples, of which 141 are from Peru, 54 from Ecuador, and 9 from Bolivia. Most of these are melodies with Kechua text and French translation. A fundamental work, profusely illustrated and thoroughly documented.

Karsten, Rafael. The Colorado Indians of western Ecuador. *Ymer,* v. 44, no. 2 |1924), p 137-152. il.   **[1573]**

Magic, music, instruments, p. 147; *ḳunanú* (drum) and *guazá* (rattle). Mention of dance, p. 149. Music at marriages, p. 143.

———. The head-hunters of Western Amazonas; the life and culture of the Jibaro Indians of eastern Ecuador and Peru... Helsingfors, 1935. 598 p. il. (incl. music). (Finska vetenskapssocieteten, Helsingfors. Commentationes humanarum litterarum. VII. 1). P59. F5 v. 7, no. 1. F3722.1.J5K2 **[1574]**

Poetry and music are discussed in Ch. 14, p. 496-502, with 2 tunes. There are also 9 other tunes: p. 135, 137, 200, 323, 325, 415, 467.

Lasso, Ignacio. Sazón de la canción autóctona. *Atenea,* v. 40, no. 150 (Dec. 1937). p. 422-424.   **[1575]**

Discussion of the characteristics of Indian music, and comparison of it with Negro music.

Monteros, Raimundo M. Música autóctona del oriente ecuatoriano. Quito. Imp. del ministerio de gobierno. 1942. **[1576]**

Sáenz, Moisés. Sobre el indio ecuatoriano y su incorporación al medio nacional. Publicaciones de la Secretaría de educación pública. México, 1933. 195 p. F3722.S23   **[1577]**

Música y danza, p. 79-82 (most of that space being taken up by photographs of Indians playing flutes and drums).

Salgado, Gustavo. Indian music in ancient Ecuador. *Étude,* v. 61, no. 4 (Apr. 1943), p. 244, 272.   **[1578]**

Includes an analysis of the Indian musical scale, and a list, with brief descriptive notes, of musical instruments.

Stirling, Matthew William. Historical and ethnographical material on the Jivaro Indians. Washington, Govt. print. off., 1938. 148 p. il. (Smithsonian institution. Bureau of American ethnology. Bulletin 117). E51.U6 no. 117 F-3722.1.J5S7   **[1579]**

"Musical instruments", p. 92-94, with illustration of *tunduli* or signal drum.

SUPPLEMENT TO 1960

BIBLIOGRAPHY

Bueno del Bosque, R. Letrigrama; ensayo de un nuevo sistema de escribir música. Guayaquil, The author, 1958. 20 p.   **[622a]**

Cevallos García, Gabriel. Intención y paisaje de la música ecuatoriana. Cuenca, Ed. Reed and Reed, 1943. 26 p. **[623a]**

"Disertación pronunciada en el Rotary Club de Cuenca." Brief discussion of pentatonic scale and description of indigenous instruments. Contains list of 41 RCA Victor records of folk and popular music of Ecuador.

Cruz Cobo, Armando. El exagrama de

Clodoveo González. *El Universal* (Guayaquil), 27 April 1956, p. 12. **[624a]**

Reprinted from *Democracia,* Buenos Aires. (Cf. item 627a).

Jijón y Caamaño, Jacinto. Antropología prehispánica del Ecuador. Quito, La prensa católica, 1952. 409 p. **[625a]**

Moreno, Segundo Luis. La música indígena ecuatoriana. *Casa cult. ecuat.,* v. 2, no. 3 (Jan.-Dec. 1946), p. 134-162. **[626a]**

Author claims that in the littoral region all preconquest music traditions have died, but that the Indians of the Sierra since the conquest have preserved their music traditions without external influence. This is due to the Spaniards never teaching the Indians Spanish. Presents system of scales (pentaphonic) and roster of instruments (percussion and wind). The only string instrument was musical bow in teeth. (C. S.)

Musical shortcut. *Américas,* v. 5, no. 6 (June 1953), p. 35. **[627a]**

Report of the González Music System, invented by a young musician, Clodoveo González, of Quito, Ecuador. New system of musical notation: six-line musical staff, top three red, bottom three blue. Musical instruments which have been adapted to system (pianos, accordions, marimbas, xylophones and stringed instruments) have corresponding kyes or strings in corresponding colors. (Spaces are white, so corresponding keys would be white.)

[**Salgado, Luis H.**]. Chronological catalog of the works of the Ecuadorian composer Luis H. Salgado. *Bol. interam. mús.,* no. 1 (Sept. 1957), 45-50. **[628a]**

Salgado was born in Cayambe, on Dec. 10, 1903.

EL SALVADOR

THE main outlines of the history of music in El Salvador have been traced by Rafael González Sol in his monograph, *Datos históricos sobre el arte de la música en El Salvador,* published in 1940 [no. 1585]. The author covers the subject under the following headings:

1. *Nuestras bandas militares.* The two oldest military bands in the country are the Banda del Primer Regimiento de Infantería and the Banda de los Supremos Poderes, the former founded in 1890, the latter in 1841.

2. *Orquestas sinfónicas.* The first symphony orchestra was organized by Escolástico Andrino and Eusebio Castillo in 1860. In 1875 the Sociedad Filarmónica was established, with Manuel Ayala as president and Alejandro Coussin as conductor. From time to time other orchestral societies were formed, the most recent being the Orquesta Sinfónica Salvadoreña conducted by Humberto Pacas.

3. *Publicaciones musicales.* The first musical periodical of El Salvador was founded in 1870 by Alfredo Lowental. In 1883 appeared the *Ilustración musical Centro-Americana,* a fortnightly music review edited by Juan Aberle. Mention is made of a work entitled *Principios elementales de música,* by Raúl Santamaría, published in 1920.

4. *Escuelas de música.* A private school of music was founded in 1846 by Escolástico Andrino, called "the father of music in El Salvador". The Academia de Bellas Artes created an Escuela de Música in 1864, and later a Conservatorio Nacional de Música was established.

5. *Compositores nacionales.* Salvadorean composers have written mostly dances and marches. Composers mentioned in this section include Vicente Blanco, Felipe Soto (the "waltz king" of El Salvador), David Flavio Pineda, Tomás Moreira, Wenceslao García, Pedro J. Guillén (author of a waltz entitled *Saint Louis,* after the American city of that name), Domingo Santos, Natalia Ramos (composer of a *Polonesa triunfal* and other works for piano), María de Baratta and Jesús Alas.

6. *Instrumentos de música indígenas.* Includes illustrations of a *teponaztli* or slit-drum, of indigenous flutes, and of musicians playing various typical instruments, including the marimba (primitive and modern).

7. *Música regional.* States that there is no genuine regional folk music in El Salvador. Mentions the popular composer Pancho Lara, whose song *El carbonero* is widely known.

8. *Virtuosos o solistas.* Mentions outstanding virtuosi, including the violonists Rafael Olmedo and Abel Ayala Bonilla, and the pianists Natalia Ramos and Angela García Peña.

9. *El teatro nacional (funciones y conciertos).* The Teatro Nacional

has been the scene of performances by Italian opera companies, and performances of Spanish *zarzuelas* (comic operas).

10. *Exhibiciones populares musicalizadas de origen colonial.* Describes the traditional dramatic festival with music called *Historia de Moros y Cristianos,* a survival from colonial times. Includes five illustrations of the *Historia.*

11. *Obras musicales de compositores salvadoreños.* Music of seven compositions by Salvadorean composers, for piano.

The composer María de Baratta (b. 27 Feb. 1894), who has written numerous works based on Salvadorean themes, has taken a special interest in the musical folklore of her native country. She is the author of an interesting article on methods of investigating indigenous music [no. 1581]. Ciriaco Jesús Alas (b. 7 April 1866) has published a collection of music for schools [no. 1580] and Francisco Espinosa has published two collections of folk songs (without music).

BIBLIOGRAPHY

Alas, Ciriaco Jesús. Cartillas musicales para uso de las escuelas de la república de El Salvador. San Salvador, 1926.
[1580]

Baratta, María de. Danza. *Rev. min. instruc. púb.,* v. 1, no. 2 (Apr.-May June 1942), p. 47-53. [1580a]
Primarily concerned with the aestheties of primitive dance.

——. Orientaciones para la investigación de la música autóctona. *Ateneo,* v. 28, no. 147 (Jan.-May 1940), p. 28-41.
[1581]
Discusses the qualifications of the musical archaeologist, methods of investigation, and classification of melodies according to period and type. Also contains references to musical instruments.

Espinosa, Francisco. Canciones populares. San Salvador, Ed. Cisneros, 1941. 40 p. (Folklore salvadoreño, cuaderno 3.) [1582]
Spanish words only of 25 texts. Alfonso Rochac's introduction includes interesting notes on folkdrama survival. [R. S. B.]

——. Cantos de cuna. San Salvador,

Impr. de la Ocallquina, 1932. 36 p. PQ7536.E75 [1583]
Folk-lore salvadoreño. Cuaderno núm. 1.

——. Folklore salvadoreño, bombas. *Rev. amer.,* v. 52 (1934), p. 126-136, 170-171. [1584]

González Sol, Rafael. Datos históricos sobre el arte de la música en El Salvador. San Salvador, Imprenta mercurio, 1940. 74 p. ML220.S1G6 [1585]
For comment see introductory section above.

——. Instrumentos de música indígena en El Salvador. *Fomento agric.,* v. 1 (Nov. 1938), p. 31-35. il. [1586]

——. Instruments of Salvadorean music. *El Salvador* (Feb.-Apr. 1939), p. 19-22. [1587]

——. Nuestras exhibiciones populares musicalizadas de origen colonial. *Fomento agric.,* v. 1 (Nov. 1938), p. 29-31. [1588]

Plan para la investigación del folklore musical de El Salvador. *Rev. min. instruc. púb.,* v. 1, no. 1 (Jan.-Feb.-Mar. 1942), p. 53-58. [1589]
A systematic outline of the main points to be considered in folkloristic music,

with a list of forms to be included under indigenous and creole music, dance and song.

Planes para la investigación del folklore nacional y arte típico salvadoreño. San Salvador, Ministerio de instrucción pública, 1941. 39 p. Mimeographed. **[1590]**

Investigación del folklore musical de El Salvador, p. 20–33. See item no. 1588a.

Slonimsky, Nicolas. Music, where 'the Americas meet. *Christian scien. mon. weekly magazine section* (8 June 1940), p. 8-9. il. **[1591]**

Biographical sketches of Central American and Mexican composers, with portraits. Commends the work of the Salvadorean musicians María de Baratta and Jesús Alas.

See also no. 1424.

SUPPLEMENT TO 1960

Although El Salvador is one of the smallest countries of Latin America, it has been endowed with one of the largest and most impressive works ever devoted to the music and folklore of any of these countries. This is the two-volume work by María de Baratta, titled *Cuzcatlán típico* (item no. 629a), which takes its name from the ancient Indian appellation for the region that the Spaniards called El Salvador. The furit of many years of patient research and enthusiastic devotion to her subject, María de Baratta's prodigious compendium is truly "a labor of love". While lacking somewhat in systematic organization, the wealth of material it contains is enormous. After introductory sections on folklore studies in El Salvador, and on the historical and ethnic-linguistic backgrounds of the indigenous population, the author deals with "Músicos y cantantes" in the pre-Hispanic period; this is followed by sections on "Danzas" and on "La canción autóctona." The section titled "Ensayo sobre etnofonía de El Salvador" contains detailed descriptions, with photographs and music notations, of indigenous instruments, including archaic flutes. Pentatonic scales are discussed, and classification is undertaken of indigenous melodies. In the next section, on musical folklore, there is an account of the "Orígenes y fuentes de nuestro folklore." Finally, Part I concludes with an extensive "Panorama de la danza indo-Americana."

Part II begins with the "Época de la Conquista", of which the main section is a detailed study of the "Historia de Moros y Cristianos," illustrated with numerous photographs, 15 music notations, and complete text. The section on the "Época de la Conquista" is devoted mainly to various types of folksong, including religious ones. The final section consists of "Estilizaciones folklóricas sobre temas autóctonos y folklóricos", by the author (for piano, or for voice and piano).

Especially worthy of note are the reproductions in color, from various early codices, illustrating pre-Hispanic musical instruments and rituals, contained in Part I of this work. The volumes (pages numbered continuously) are not indexed.

BIBLIOGRAPHY

Baratta, María de. Cuzcatlán típico. Ensayo sobre etnofonía de El Salvador. Folklore, folkwisa y folkway, 2. vols. San Salvador, Publicaciones del ministerio le cultura, n. d. (1951?). 740 p. il. (music). **[629a]**

This work contains a wealth of material on music, dances, and musical instruments, as well as on the customs, rituals, and folkways, of the peoples who have inhabited the area since pre-Hispanic times.

——. La yegüita, son indígena. *Rev. del Min. de instrucción pública* (San Salvador), v. 2, no. 7, (July-Sept. 1943), p. 125-129). **[630a]**

——. Música indígena de El Salvador *Rev. estud. mus.,* v. 1, no. 3 (April 1950), p. 61-74. **[631a]**

Texts and music of several indigenous songs. With 9 musical notations. The article is dated 1939.

Byers, Margaret Chapman. El Salvador fosters its own music. *Mus.Amer.,* v.64, no. 3 (Feb. 1944), p. 238-239. **[632a]**

Salvadorean typical music and Philharmonic orchestra of San Salvador provide varied musical fare.

Comité de investigaciones del folklore nacional y arte típico salvadoreño. Recopilación de materiales folklóricos salvadoreños. Primera parte. San Salvador, Imprenta nacional, 1944. 412 p. il. (Publicaciones del Ministerio de instrucción pública). **[633a]**

This committee was created in 1941

and has been engaged in collecting materials for an archive of Salvadorean folklore. Contains texts only of many types of folksong.

Espinosa, Francisco. Folklore salvadoreño. San Salvador, Impr. Cisneros, 1946. 126 p. **[634a]**

Contains words only of folksongs from El Salvador, including cradle songs and *bombas*.

González Sol, Rafael. Datos históricos sobre el arte de la música en El Salvador. *An. museo nac.,* v. 1, no. 4 (Oct.-Dec., 1950), p. 42-68. **[635a]**

Band (from 1841), orchestra (from 1860), publication (from 1870), school (from 1864), composers, performing groups, indigenous and other instruments, briefly mentioned. Author states that El Salvador does not have "música propia o regional." (C. S.)

Homenaje del Ateneo de El Salvador a compositores nacionales fallecidos. *Ateneo,* Salvador, tercera época, v. 35, no. 178 (Apr.-June 1948), p. 1-9. **[636a]**

Very brief biographies of eleven composers. (C. S.)

Lardé y Larín, Jorge. Historia del himno nacional de El Salvador. *Anales mus. nac.,* v. 2, no. 8 (Oct.-Dec. 1951), p. 37-44. **[637a]**

A brief account of the history and vicissitudes of El Salvador's national anthem. (R. A. W.)

FRENCH GUIANA

Saint Quentin, Auguste. Introduction à l'histoire de Cayenne. Antibes, J. Marchand, 1872. 208 p. PM7854.F7S3 **[1592]**

Pages 73–97, *Fables et chansons*, with French translation on one side, Creole on the other.

GUATEMALA

GUATEMALA ranks as a pioneer country in Latin American musical bibliography, for a history of music in Guatemala was published as early as 1878. This is the *Historia de la música guatemalteca* by José Sáenz Poggio [no. 1596]. Though consisting of only eighty pages, this monograph goes into considerable detail and gives the names of numerous musicians who were active in Guatemala from colonial times to the third quarter of the nineteenth century. One of the most important of the earlier composers was Vicente Sáenz, who died in 1841 at the age of eighty-five. His *Villancicos de Pascua* (Christmas Carols) were especially popular. His son, Benedicto Sáenz, became organist of the cathedral of Guatemala City in 1803 (he died in 1831). The latter, in turn, had a son of the same name, several of whose compositions were published in Paris. Sáenz Poggio also treats of military bands in Guatemala, of the lyric theatre, of music in private society, of music schools, and of Indian music, describing the following instruments: *atabal, tum, caramba, chirimía* and *marimba.* The *zarabanda* he describes as an "orchestra" composed of a harp, a guitar, a *rabel* (primitive three-stringed violin), and square drum, called *aduf* by the Indians.

A more recent study of Guatemalan musical history is contained in the work by Victor Miguel Díaz, *Las bellas artes en Guatemala,* published in 1934. The musical section of this comprises seventy-seven pages. The complete table of contents is given under the entry for this volume [no. 1593]. J. Antonio Villacorta's *Índice analítico de la historia de la capitanía general de Guatemala* [no. 1598] points to some very valuable source material for the study of music in Guatemala during the colonial period. The part dealing with music is Libro II, Capítulo VI, Sección 6 (*La música durante la colonia*).

In pre-Hispanic times the culture of the Mayas spread over most of what is now Guatemala. The Quiché Indians are the chief representatives of this ancient Maya stock in Guatemala. The composer Jesús Castillo (b. Quetzaltenango, 9 Sept. 1877) has made a lifelong study of Maya-Quiché music and has published several monographs on the subject, of which the most comprehensive is *La música Maya-Quiché,* published in 1941 [no. 1630]. This monograph of eighty-six pages is illustrated with photographs of indigenous instruments and with examples of Indian melodies transcribed by the author. On p. 57 are photographs of two pre-Hispanic jade inscriptions which Castillo believes represent a form of musical notation—the first to be discovered in America.

Biographical data on Guatemalan composers are available in the files of the *Revista musical of Guatemala* (see bibliography below, under the heading Biography). Biographical sketches of contemporary composers will also be found in Slonimsky's article, *Music, where the Americas meet* [no. 1613]. Outstanding among contemporary composers of Guatemala are José Castañeda (b. 24 May 1898), Jesús Castillo (d. 1946), Ricardo Castillo (b. 1 Oct. 1891), Salvador Ley (b. 2 Jan. 1907), Paniagua Martínez (b. 5 Sept. 1856), Alberto Mendoza (b. 30 March 1889), Felipe Siliézar (b. 1 May 1903), Mariano Valverde (b. 20 Nov. 1884).

GENERAL AND MISCELLANEOUS

Díaz, Victor Miguel. Las bellas artes en Guatemala. Folletín del Diario de Centro América. Guatemala, Tipografía nacional, 1934. 600 p. il. N6576.D5 **[1593]**

La música, p. 518–595. Contents: Misioneros en el drama de La Conquista de Guatemala; Las estrofas místicas cantadas en las regiones de Tezulutlán; Cantantes que vinieron a Guatemala; Instrumentos musicales; Instrumento indígena—La marimba; Organistas en los primeros tiempos de la Colonia; La música en las grandes fiestas—Lejanías de la Colonia; Desarrollo de la música en la Nueva Guatemala de la Asunción; Vida artística en Guatemala; Los filarmónicos de las Bandas; Fomentadores de la música; El Himno Nacional; El teatro en Guatemala; La música italiana era la predilecta en Guatemala; El baile en Guatemala; Los guitarristas; Canciones populares; los villancicos de Pascua; Cantos de Navidad; Las canciones místicas; La música en las fiestas religiosas y profanas; Las cantantes nacionales; Conservatorio de Música; El arte musical.

La pintura, la escultura y la música en Guatemala, by José Martí, p. 85–89 (*música,* p. 88–89).

La Farge, Oliver, and Douglas Byers. The year bearer's people. New Orleans, Tulane university, Department of middle American research, 1931. 379 p. F1421.T95 no. 3 **[1594]**

Music, p. 67–68, 97; marimbas, p. 110; dances, p. 99–111, with several photographs and charts; special reference to the marimba dance and the use of that instrument in this and other dances; picture of musical instruments, p. 65; musical instruments, p. 67–68 (only men make and play the instruments).

Lee, Thomas F. Guatemala—land of volcanos and progress. *Nat. geog. mag.,* v. 50, no. 5 (Nov. 1926), p. 599–648. **[1595]**

Description of marimba, p. 609 (with illustration, pl. 2); illustration of costumes used in the dance of the Conquistadores, pl. 1, 11.

Sáenz Poggio, José. Historia de la música guatemalteca desde la monarquía española, hasta fines del año de 1877. Guatemala, Imprenta de la Aurora, 1878. 80 p. ML220.S2 **[1596]**

For comment see introductory section above.

Stoll, Otto. Guatemala. Leipzig, F. A. Brockhaus, 1886. 518 p. F1464.S87 **[1597]**

Complete data on the marimba (with illustration), p. 7–11, with further references to this instrument in connection with dances, p. 371–377. This section on dances points out particularly the *baile del venado, baile de los moros;* description of the *chirimía,* p. 375. There is a discussion of songs and guitars, p. 395-396.

Villacorta C., J. Antonio. Índice analítico de la historia de la capitanía general de Guatemala. *An. soc. geog. hist. Guatemala,* v. 16, no. 5 (Sept. 1940), p. 341–383. **[1598]**

La música durante la Colonia, p. 369, naming several outstanding Guatemalan musicians of the 17th and 18th centuries.

BIOGRAPHY AND CRITICISM

Batres Jauregui, A. Notas biográficas del maestro Rafael Álvarez. *Rev. mus., Guatemala,* v. 1, no. 2 (Aug. 1928), p. 1, 24. **[1599]**

Álvarez was the composer of the national anthem of Guatemala.

Datos biográficos acerca del compositor señor Jesús Castillo. *Rev. mus., Guatemala,* v. 1, no. 7 (Apr. 1928), p. 3. **[1600]**

Portrait on front cover.

Díaz, Víctor Miguel. El arte musical en Guatemala. *Rev. mus., Guatemala,* v. 1, no. 2 (Aug. 1928), p. 3, 22. **[1601]**

Concerned largely with the career of Rafael Álvarez.

——. Fabián Rodríguez. *Rev. mus., Guatemala,* v. 2, no. 19 (June 1929), p. 4, 23. **[1602]**

Portrait on front cover.

——. Maestro Lorenzo Morales. *Rev. mus., Guatemala,* v. 1, no. 2 (Nov. 1927), p. 16-17. port. **[1603]**

Germán Alcántara. *Rev. mus., Guatemala,* v. 2, no. 14 (Jan. 1929), p. 2, 16. **[1604]**

Biographical sketch of this Guatemalan composer by Victor Miguel Díaz. Alcántara was conductor of the Martial Band and Director of the National Conservatory of Music. His portrait is on the front cover.

Luis Felipe Arias, el gran maestro malogrado. *Rev. mus., Guatemala,* v. 1, no. 4 (Jan. 1928), p. 2. **[1605]**

Arias (1870-1908) was a celebrated Guatemalan pianist.

El maestro Alvarado; su vida, su muerte. *Rev. mus., Guatemala,* v. 1, no. 2 (Nov. 1927), p. 2-3. port. **[1606]**

El maestro Castro Carazo y su labor musical. *Rev. mus., Guatemala,* v. 2, no. 22 (1929), p. 16. **[1607]**

El maestro Miguel Espinosa. *Rev. mus., Guatemala,* v. 1, no. 1 (Sept. 1927), p. 2. **[1608]**

Meany Ariza, Guillermo. José Joaquín Palma, su vida y su obra. *Rev. mus., Guatemala,* v. 1, no. 11 (Aug. 1928), p. 2, 22. port. **[1609]**

Palma wrote the words of the national anthem of Guatemala.

Monteforte Toledo, Mario. La música guatemalteca del maestro Jesús Castillo. *Rev. fac. cien. jur. soc.,* ép. 3, v. 2, no. 2 (May.-June 1939), p. 258-263. **[1610]**

Rodríguez Beteta, Virgilio. El maestro Jesús Silva. *Rev. mus. Guatemala,* año 1, no. 11 (Aug. 1928), p. 5, 29. port. **[1611]**

Silva (1858-1928) was active as pianist, bandmaster and composer.

Samayoa Aguilar, Carlos. El compositor Alfredo Wyld. *Rev. mus., Guatemala,* v. 2, no. 21 (1929), p. 7, 23-24. port. **[1612]**

Slonimsky, Nicolas. Music, where the Americas meet. *Christian scien. mon. weekly magazine section* (8 June 1940), p. 8-9. il. **[1613]**

Biographical sketches of Central American and Mexican composers, with portraits. Guatemala: Julián Paniagua Martínez, Jesús Mariano Valverde, Alberto Mendoza, José Castañeda.

NATIONAL ANTHEM

Bonilla Ruano, José María. Anotaciones críticodidácticas sobre el poema del himno nacional de Guatemala. Guatemala. Unión tipográfica, 1935. 351 p. ML3572.B72S6 **[1614]**

"Himno nacional de Guatemala, letra de J. J. Palma, música de Rafael Álvarez", facsim. (p. 15-18).

"Himnario universal; poemas de himnos nacionales centroamericanos y extranjeros", p. 281-337.

Himno nacional de Guatemala. Guate-

mala, Impreso en la tipografía nacional, 1808. M1685.G9A   [1615]

Adoptado por acuerdos gubernativos de
28 de octubre de 1896 y 19 de febrero
de 1897. Letra anónima; música de Rafael
Álvarez.

——. *Rev. mus. Guatemala,* v. 1, no. 11
(Aug. 28), p. 6-7, 28.   [1616]

——. Música original de Rafael Álvarez.
An. soc. geog. hist. Guatemala, v. 8
(Dec. 1931), p. 131-135.   [1617]

Narváez, Arturo. A propósito de nuestro
himno nacional. *Rev. mus. Guatemala,*
v. 2, no. 20 (July 1929), p. 1, 5. [1618]

See also nos. 1424, 1599, 1906.

FOLK AND PRIMITIVE MUSIC

(A) GENERAL (INCLUDING DANCE)

Fergusson, Erna. Guatemala. New
York and London, A. A. Knopf, 1937.
320 p. il. F1464.F47   [1619]

Refers to music and dances, p. 229–235,
271–273.

Huxley, Aldous. Beyond the Mexique
Bay. New York and London, Harper
& brothers, 1934. 295 p. il. F1432.H89
                              [1620]

Impressions of Guatemala. References to
the *Baile de los Conquistadores,* p. 154–
156, and to the *Bull Dance,* p. 158. Reference to music, p. 203.

**Kelsey, Vera, and Lilly de Jongh Os-
borne.** Four keys to Guatemala. New
York and London, Funk & Wagnalls,
1939. 382 p. il. F1403.K45. [1621]

Deals with development of dance forms,
p. 102–110. Includes music.

Maler, Teobert. Explorations in the department of Petén, Guatemala. *Memoirs, Peabody museum of American
archeology and ethnology, Harvard
university,* v. 4, no. 3 (1910), p. 131–
170.   [1622]

Marimba music in the *paseo de las flores,* p. 158.

Mérida Carlos. The dance of the little
bulls. *Mex. folkways,* v. 1. no. 4 (Dec.–
Ian. 1925), p. 10-13 [Span. transl. p.
13–14].   [1623]

Description of a dramatic folk dance of
Guatemala, with music (arr. for piano)
collected by Jesús Castillo.

——. Folk arts of Guatemala. *In* Herring, Hubert C., and Katherine Ter-
rill, *ed.,* The genius of Mexico, New
York, 1931, p. 95–103. F1208.H56.
                              [1624]

The second part of this essay deals with
native music, instruments and dances.

Muñoz, Joaquín, and Anna Bell Ward.
Guatemala, ancient and modern. New
York, Pyramid press publishers, 1940.
308 p. F1463.M86   [1625]

Marimba, p. 27, 148, 149, 223; music
and dance of a village fiesta, p. 36; game
of *Palo volador,* p. 160–161; ceremonial
dances, p. 162–163.

Recinos, Adrián. Algunas observaciones
sobre el folk-lore de Guatemala. *Jour.
amer. folklore,* v. 29, no. 114 (1916),
p. 559–566.   [1626]

Includes the words (Spanish only) of
some Christmas songs and popular coplas.

Tejada, Lucía de. Cantos y rondas infantiles. Guatemala, Tipografía nacional, 1934. 130 p.   [1627]

(B) AMERINDIAN

1. Music and Dances

Castillo, Jesús. Authochthonic music.
Bull. pan amer. union, v. 62, no. 4
(1928), p. 356–364.   [1628]

Description of musical instruments. Includes 2 tunes: "Songs of the Cenzontles"
and indigenous melody of Maya-Quiché
Indians.

——. La música autóctona. *An. soc.
geog. hist. Guatemala,* v. 4, no. 1 (Sept.
1927), p. 14–24.   [1629]

2 musical examples. See item no. 1628.

——. La música Maya-Quiché (región
guatemalteca). Quetzaltenango, Tip. E.

Cifientes, 1941. il. 86 p. ML3547.C3 [1630]

Prologue by María de Baratta. Amplifies and supersedes the author's previous studies on this subject. Includes several musical examples and illustrations of musical instruments. Attempts to establish the authenticity of an indigenous Guatemalan musical system.

———. La música Maya-Quiché; sección guatemalteca. *An. Soc. geog. hist. Guatemala*, v. 15, no. 3 (1939), p. 291-295. [1631]

Attempts to investigate the causes of the regional complexity of the indigenous music of Guatemala.

Dutton, Bertha P. All saints' day ceremonies in Todos Santos, Guatemala. *Palacio*, v. 46, no. 8 (Aug. 1939), p. 169-182; v. 46, no. 9 (Sept. 1939), p. 205-217. [1632]

Includes remarks on music and musical instruments.

Heinitz, Wilhelm. Chirimía- und tambor —phonogramme aus Nordwest— Guatemala. *Vox*, v. 19 (1933), p. 4-12. [1633]

Pilet, Raymond. Mélodies populaires des Indiens du Guatémala. *In* Congrés international des Américanistes. Compterendu de la huitième session tenue à Paris en 1890, Paris, Ernest Leroux, éd., 1892, p. 463-480. [1634]

Contains 5 melodies arranged for piano, and one for trumpet solo.

Rodas N., Flavio. Música regional. *Rev. mus.*, v. 2, no. 18 (1929), p. 5. [1635]

Primitive music and musical instruments in Guatemala.

Termer, Franz. Los bailes de culebra entre los Indios Quichés en Guatemala. *In* International congress of Americanists, v. 23, New York, 1928, p. 661-667. il. E51.1716 [1636]

Contains a list of the Guatemalan dances still practiced, with comments on the types of dance in the various departments of Guatemala; account of the *fiesta del*

Atamalqualiztli. Description of marimba, p. 665-666.

See also nos. 1643, 1644.

2. Instruments

Castillo, Jesús. Autochthonic music. *Bull. pan amer. union*, v. 62, no. 4 (Apr. 1928), p. 356-364. [1637]

1) The autochthonic instruments are the *xul* or *zu*, the *caracol*, the *tambor* and the *tun*. Attempts to prove that these indigenous instruments have never existed in any other part of the world. 2) Natural melodies heard by the Indian since the time of his birth; the relation of Indian music to that of the birds. Influence of this music on "imported" music. 2 musical notations.

Díaz, Victor Miguel. Las bellas artes en Guatemala. Guatemala, Tip. nacional, 1934. 600 p. il. N6576.D5 [1638]

La música, p. 518-595. Includes a section on native musical instruments.

Habel, Simeon. The sculptures of Santa Lucia Cosumalwhuapa in Guatemala. With an account of travels in Central America and on the western coast of South America. Washington, D. C. Smithsonian institution, 1878. 90 p. Q11.S68 [Q11.S68 v. 22] F1465.H12 [1639]

References to musical instruments. p. 31, 45.

Notes sur les musiques exotiques. II. Les instruments au Guatémala. *Rev. musicale*, v. 5, no. 19 (15 Oct. 1905), p. 471-473. il. [1640]

A letter writen from Guatemala by E. Enion, Ministre de la légation de France. Describes the marimba, chirimía and sarabanda, guitarilla and harpa, the tamborón, zambonba and tun.

Recinos, Adrián. Los instrumentos musicales de los Indios de Guatemala. *Actualidades* (24 Feb. 1917). [1641]

Saville, Marshall Howard. Terracotta whistle from Guatemala. *Indian notes,*

v. 1, no. 1 (Jan. 1924), p. 16, 19-20.
[1642]
Detailled description of this instrument, and a photograph of it.

Wisdom, Charles. The Chorti Indians of Guatemala. Chicago, University of Chicago press, 1940. 490 p. F1465.2.C-5W6   **[1643]**

Making of musical instruments, p. 174-177, principally the *tun* drum, metal rattles and flutes; playing of the ceremonial musical instruments, a set of which is owned by every chief and used only by

professional musicians, p. 379-380. For additional items on music, see p. 383, 415, 452, and for items on dance, see index.

Wyld Ospina, Carlos. La tierra de las Nahuyacas. Guatemala, Tipografía nacional, 1933. 303 p. PQ7499.W8T5
[1644]

"El Rito", p. 54-59, with many references to the musical instruments used in the dance procession.

See also nos. 1628, 1630, 1632, 1633, 1635, 1636.

SUPPLEMENT TO 1960

BIBLIOGRAPHY

Borhegyi, Stephen F. Un raro cascabel de barro del período primitivo preclásico en Guatemala. *Antrop. hist. Guat.,* v. 9, no. 1 (Jan. 1957), p. 9-12, i..   **[638a]**

Breve historia de la música en Guatemala. *Bol. museos bibl.,* segunda época, v. 3, no. 3 (Oct. 1943), p. 112-121; no. 4 (Jan. 1944), p. 147-154; v. 4, no. 1 (April 1944) p. 20-28; no. 2 (July 1944), p. 56-74; no. 3 (Oct. 1944), p. 87-94.   **[639a]**

This is the complete listing of an important serial article. The last installment mentioned above closes with "continuará", but publication of the Boletín ceased with segunda época, v. 4, no. 3. In February 1945 the *Revista del Museo nacional* de Guatemala began to appear, issued by the same institution and director. No continuation of the *Breve Historia* has been found. However, in no. 2 of the new publication a catalog of the compositions of Guatemalan composers begins anew but in a different form. (C.S.)

Castellanos, J. Humberto. El "son" en Guatemala. Danza y melodía. *ECA,* v. 4, no. 35-36 (Oct.-Dec. 1949), p. 1372-1387.   **[640a]**

Brief description of more than a dozen dances. (C. S.)

Catálogo de las composiciones musicales de autores Guatemaltecos que se conservan en el archivo musical del museo. *Rev. museo. nac. Guatemala,* época 3, no. 2 (Apr.–June, 1945), p. 61-64; no. 3 (July-Sept. 1945), p. 118-127.   **[641a]**

First two instalments. (C. S.)

Continuación del catálogo de las composiciones musicales de autores guatemaltecos que se conservan en el archivo del museo. *Rev. museo Nac. Guatemala,* época 3, no. 1-4 (Dec. 1946), p. 60-68.   **[642a]**

Ley, Salvador. Cultural aspects of music life in Guatemala. *In* Conference on Latin–American Fine Arts, June 14-17, 1951. Proceedings. Austin, Tex., University of Texas, Institute of Latin American Studies (Latin American Studies, 13), 1952, p. 78-83.   **[643a]**

"The only well-defined Guatemalan dance is the one which is called *son,* a mixture of Indian and Spanish rhythm in a rather short and jumpy six-eighth measure. It is an authentic expression of Guatemalan folk music."

The composers of Guatemala may be divided into two groups: "those who seek inspiration in the Indian world, past and present ... and those who write the universal idiom, influenced by different European trends of contemporary composers."

Among composers mentioned are Jesús Castillo, Ricardo Castillo, Enrique Solares, Manuel Herrarte, and the author himself. Also discusses some musical organizations.

Kahan, Solomon. Guatemala government fosters musical renaissance. *Mus. Amer.,* v. 56, no. 2 (Jan. 25, 1946), p. 5, 34, il. **[644a]**
"National conservatory plays key role."

Memoria del Maestro Jesús Castillo. *Rev. museo nac. Guatemala,* época 3, no. 1-4 (Dec. 1946), p. 3-12. **[645a]**
Brief biography of a leading Guatemalan musician (1877-1946). (C. S.)

Reynolds, Dorothy. Guatemalan dances at colorful highland festivals. *Américas.* v. 8, no. 1 (Jan. 1956), p. 31-35. **[646a]**
Popular account, but with considerable

detail, of special dances, usually associated with festivals of patron saints, in villages of Guatemala. Ten photographs, two showing instrumentalists: a) playing a large marimba; b) playing a drum and chirimía.

Sáenz Poggio, José. Historia de la música guatemalteca desde la monarquía española hasta fines del año de 1877. *An. soc. geog. hist. Guatemala,* v. 22, no. 1-2 (Mar.-June 1947), p. 6-54. **[647a]**
A reprint of item no. 1596.

Severin, Kurt. Marimba-maker. *Américas,* vol. 10, no. 11 (Nov. 1958), p. 19-20. il. **[648a]**
Describes the making of marimbas, with 9 photographic illustrations.

HAITI

THE Republic of Haiti occupies the western third of the Caribbean island which Columbus called La Española (Hispaniola) and which later became known as Santo Domingo. The rest of the island constitutes the Dominican Republic (q. v.). The original Indian population disappeared during the Spanish domination. Toward the end of the seventeenth century the French established a colony on the island which they called Saint Domingue. The present population of Haiti is Negro and the official language is French, though most of the people speak a local *patois* (Creole).

Among recent books in English dealing with Haiti, there are two that treat incidentally of music in relation to the social and historical background of the country. These are James G. Leyburn's *The Haitian people* [no. 1653] and Melville J. Herskovits' *Life in a Haitian valley* [no. 1652]. Herskovits is an anthropologist with a keen interest in music and his remarks on the subject are always illuminating. There are also two books published in the United States dealing exclusively with the music of Haiti. These are *The voice of Haiti* by Laura Bowman and LeRoy Antoine [no. 1645] and *Haiti singing* by Harold Courlander [no. 1647]. The former is essentially a collection of music: "original native ceremonial songs, voodoo chants, drum beats." The latter, in addition to the words and music of 126 songs and the notation of numerous drum rhythms, contains a detailed account of the folkways and ceremonials of the Haitian people, with special reference to the songs, dances and rituals associated with vodoun (commonly called voodoo).

As interpreted by Courlander, "Vodoun today means many things. It means dancing, singing, rituals for the living and the dead, drums; it means an attitude towards life and death, a concept of ancestors and the afterworld, and understanding of the forces which control man and his activities ..." He devotes three chapters to the ceremonies, the songs and the dances of Vodoun, and then deals with "Non-Vodoun sources of folk music." His book includes a glossary of common Creole terms. Courlander has also written a valuable article on the musical instruments of Haiti [no. 1649]

Noted Haitian folklorists who have made important contributions to the study of Haitian music are Jean Price-Mars [no. 1655] and Suzanne Comhaire-Sylvain [no. 1646]. The Library of Congress has a collection of recordings of Haitian music made by Alan Lomax in 1937 (for an account of Lomax's experiencies in Haiti, see item no. 1654). The most popular dance of Haiti is the *merengue*. The Haitian composer Justin Elie has published a collection of *merengues* arranged and harmonized for piano [no. 1651].

BIBLIOGRAPHY

Bowman, Laura, and Le Roy Antoine. The voice of Haiti; original native ceremonial songs, voodoo chants, drum beats, stories of traditions, etc. of the Haitian people. New York, Clarence Williams music. pub. co., 1938. M1681.-H15B7   **[1645]**
Includes "La Dessalinienne", national anthem, with piano accompaniment; melodies of other songs unaccompanied. Words of the songs in French and English.

Comhaire-Sylvain, Suzanne. Creole tales from Haiti.. *Jour amer. folklore*, v. 51, no. 201 (July-Sept. 1938), p. 219-346.   **[1646]**
Includes 17 melodies of narrative songs.

Courlander, Harold. Haiti singing. Chapel Hill, The University of North Carolina press, 1939. 273 p. il. (incl. map, music). ML3565.C68H2   **[1647]**
Words of the songs in Creole and English. "Drum music for two dances"; p. 177-181. "Music for the songs" (unaccompanied melodies): p, 183-226.

——. Haiti's political folksongs. *Opportunity*, v. 19 (1941), p. 114-118.   **[1648]**

——. Musical intruments of Haiti. *Mus. quart.*, v. 27, no. 3 (1941), p. 371-383. il.   **[1649]**
A well-documented study.

Dunham, Katherine. The dances of Haiti; a study of their material aspect, organization, form, and function. [1938?] 66 p. diagrams. ML3565.D85-D3   **[1650]**
Microfilm of typewritten copy.

Elie, Justin, arr. Meringues populaires haitiennes. New York, 1920. 7 p. M16-81.E   **[1651]**
Arranged and harmonized for the piano.

Herskovits, Melville Jean. Life in a Haitian valley. New York, London, A. A. Knopf, 1937. 350 p. F1926.H47   **[1652]**
Chapt. 10 (p. 177-198) includes references to songs, instruments and dances.

Leyburn, James Graham. The Haitian people. New Haven, Yale university press; London, H. Milford, Oxford university press, 1941. 342 p. F1921.L6   **[1653]**
Bibliography, p. 322-336.
Dance: p. 39, 68, 72, 133, 137, 139-140, 144, 153, 154, 181, 296. Brief references.

Lomax, Alan. Haitian journey. ... *Southwest rev.*, v. 23, no. 2 (Jan. 1938), p. 125-147.   **[1654]**
Experiences on a recording expedition in Haiti.

Merwin, B. W. A voodoo drum from Haiti. *Museum jour.*, v. 8 (1917), p. 123-125.   **[1655]**

Price-Mars, Jean. Ainsi parla l'oncle ...; essais d'ethnographic. Port-au-Prince, Imprimerie de Compiègne, 1928. 243 p. il. (music) GR121.H3M3   **[1656]**
Songs, including types of colonial songs and rounds (with many verses and several musical examples), p. 16-25. Words and music of a song used in African religious rites, p. 117. Notes on the Voodoo dance and music, p. 116, 118, 121, 197, etc., with words and music of a song, p. 198.

Simpson, George Eaton. Peasant songs and dances of northern Haiti. *Jour. Negro hist.*, v. 25 (1940), p. 203-215.   **[1657]**
Bibliographical footnotes. Gives Creole text and English translation of 7 *coumbite* songs, followed by remarks on the chief popular dances and musical instruments. A *coumbite* is a "cooperative enterprise not unlike the American husking-bee".

——. The vodun service in northern Haiti. *Amer. anthrop.*, v. 42, no. 2 (Apr.-June 1940), p. 236-254. [1658]

The author follows the ceremony through the verses of the chants. He emphasizes the important place of musical instruments (drums, rattles, triangles, bells, etc.) in the service, and describes the general characteristics of the dance.

Steedman, Mabel. Unknown to the world, Haiti. London, Hurst and Blackett, ltd., Toronto, Ryerson press, 1939. 287 p. F1926.S8 [1659]

Includes a section on voodooism with references to the dance and to drum rhythms.

Tiersot, Julien. Chansons nègres, recueillies, traduites et harmonisées. Paris, Heugel, 1933. 94 p. Each part has separate paging. M1627.T47C4 [1660]

Includes: Chansons des anciennes colonies françaises (Louisiane, Ile Maurice, Haiti).

White, C. C. Musical pilgrimage to Haiti, the island of beauty, mystery and rhythm. *Etude,* v. 47, no. 7 (July 1929), p. 505-506. il. [1661]

With 2 brief musical notations.

SUPPLEMENT TO 1960

BIBLIOGRAPHY

Bastien, Rémy. Anthologie du folklore haïtien. *Acta anthrop.*, v. 1, no. 4 (1946), 118 p. [649a]

Includes 12 songs with music.

Courlander, Harold. Profane songs of the Haitian people. *Jour. Negro hist.,* v. 27 (1942), p. 320-344. [650a]

——. The drum and the hoe. Berkeley, the university of California press, 1960. 371 p. il. [651a]

Comprehensive study of traditional song and dance in Haiti, with numerous notations of music and excellent photographs.

Jaeferhuber, Werner A. Les origines de la musique folklorique haïtienne. *Cahiers d'Haiti.* Port-au-Prince (Dec. 1943), p. 53, 55. [652a]

Métraux, Alfred. Chants vodou. *Les temps modernes* (Paris), v. 5, no. 52 (Feb. 1950), p. 1386-1983. [653a]

Words only of songs, with commentary, by a noted anthropologist.

Paul, Emmanuel Casséus. Notes sur le folklore d'Haiti; proverbes et chansons. Port-au-Prince, Imp. Télhomme, 1946. 80 p. [654a]

Discusses Haitian folksongs, including lullabies, rounds, game-songs, etc.

Quirino dos Santos, Benedicta. Haiti sings. *Américas,* v. 3, no. 6 (June 1951), p. 30-31. [655a]

Mme. Lina Blanchet's troupe of singers and dancers, called *Haiti chante.* Photographs.

Roumain, Jacques. Le sacrifice du tambour-Assoto(r). Port-au-Prince. Imprimerie de l'état, 1943. (Publications du Bureau d'ethnologie de la République d'Haiti, no. 2). [656a]

Simpson, George E. Peasant children's games in northern Haiti. *Folk-lore,* v. 65 (Sept. 1954), p. 65-73. [657a]

A description of children's games from the Bassin section of the commune of Plaisance. The author believes those games, some of them sung in French rather than in Creole, have changed little since colonial times. (S. W. M.)

HONDURAS

MANUEL de Adalid y Gamero (b. 1872), prominent composer, organist and music educator, is the author of a survey of the development of music in Honduras, published in the *Revista del archivo y biblioteca nacional* [no. 1662]. In commenting briefly on pre-Columbian Indian music, the author mentions *ocarinas* and flute-like instruments which were common to the indigenous cultures of Mexico and Central America. The autochthonous music was virtually effaced after the coming of the Spaniards. The indigenes quickly learned to play European musical instruments as well as African instruments introduced by the Negro slaves of the Spaniards. As the author writes, "Up to the present our musical folklore consists of old Spanish songs and tunes, lightly modified by time and by the peculiar temperament of the *mestizo.*"

The first military band in Honduras was organized by Marco Aurelio Soto in 1876, under a French conductor named Linier, with instruments imported from Paris. In 1915, Adalid y Gamero was appointed conductor of this band. He was succeded by Benigno Coello. Adalid y Gamero was then given the task of organizing the Banda de los Supremos Poderes, as a concert band, also a smaller Banda Marcial. Francisco R. Díaz Zelaya is another prominent band leader.

The first opera company came to Tegucigalpa, the capital, in 1930.

Compositions by Adalid y Gamero include the orchestral works *Una noche en Honduras* and *Suite tropical*. Rafael Coello Ramos, inspector of musical education in the primary schools, is known as a composer of school songs; he has also written dance music. Other contemporary composers are Camilio Rivera (b. 21 July 1878), Ramón Ruiz V. (b. in Nicaragua, 28 Feb. 1894) and Ignacio Villanueva Galeano (b. 1 Feb. 1885).

BIBLIOGRAPHY

Adalid y Gamero, Manuel de. La música en Honduras. *Rev. arch. bibl. nac.,* v. 17, no. 5 (30 Nov. 1938), p. 299-301; v 17, no. 7 (31 Jan. 1939), p. 500-501; v. 17, no. 8 (28 Feb. 1939), p. 594-596. **[1662]**

For comment see introductory section above.

Coello Ramos, Rafael. La cultura musical del pueblo hondureño. *Bol. lat. am. mús.,* v. 4 (Bogotá, 1938), p. 91-94. **[1663]**

Conzemius, Eduard. Ethnographical survey of the Miskito and Sumu Indians of Honduras and Nicaragua. Washington, U. S. Govt. print. off., 1932. 191 p. (Smithsonian institution. Bureau of American ethnology. Bulletin 106). E-51.U6 no. 100 F1520.M9C7 **[1664]**

References to music, instruments and dances, p. 111-115, 162, 164.

Himno. *Rev. univ. cent.,* v. 1, no. 4 (15 Apr. 1909), p. 256. **[1665]**

Note to the effect that Colonel Marcial Maradiaga has set to music the *Himno a Honduras*. The words and music of this hymn appear at the end of this volume. Between p. 804-805 is the music to *Camilita*, a waltz (for piano) by Maradiaga.

Himno nacional de Honduras. Decreto no. 42. *Rev. univ. cent.*, v. 7 (1915), p. 746-747.   [1666]
Words by Augusto C. Coello, music by Carlos Härtling.

Mason, Otis Tufton. Music in Honduras. *Amer. anthrop.*, v. 10 (188), p. 158.
[1667]

Quiñonez A., Alfredo. Cancionero escolar. Tegucigalpa, Tall. tip. nacionales, 1941.   [1668]

Rodríguez, Saturnino. Música hondureña. Juicios de un músico venezolano. *Rev. univ. cent.*, v. 2, no. 1 (1 Jan. 1910), p. 61.   [1669]
Comments on *Villancico a la muerte*

del Redentor, by U. Ugarte, *Marcha fúnebre*, by Felipe Pineda, and *Polka*, by Fernando Blanco.

Slonimsky, Nicolas. Music, where the Americas meet. *Christian scien. mon. weekly magazine section* (8 June 1940), p. 8-9. il.   [1670]
Biographical sketches of Central American and Mexican composers, with portraits. Discusses the state of musical culture in Honduras; mentions the names of Camilo Rivera, Ignacio Galeano, Francisco Díaz Zelaya.

Wells, William Vincent. Explorations and adventures in Honduras. New York, Harper & brothers, 1857. 588 p. il. F1504.W45   [1671]
References to music and dances, p. 154-155, 208-209, 337-338, 410.

See also no. 1424.

SUPPLEMENT TO 1960

BIBLIOGRAPHY

Adalid y Gamero, Manuel de. La evolución de la música en Honduras. *Honduras rotaria* (Tegucigalpa), v. 2, no. 1 (Sept. 1944), p. 2, 17.

———. Música popular hondureña. *América unida* (Tegucigalpa), v. 2, no. 19 (Nov. 12, 1943), p. 8.

Hartling, Guadalupe V. de. Himno nacional de Honduras. *Rev. arch. bibl.*

nac., v. 23, no. 7-8 (Jan.-Feb. 1945), p. 418-422.
Brief historical notes. (C.S.)

Himnología hondureña. *Rev. arch. bibl. nac.*, Tegucigalpa, v. 24, no. 11-12 (May-June 1946), p. 567-572; v. 25, no. 1-2 (July-Aug. 1946), p. 88-93; no. 3-4 (Sept.-Oct. 1946), p. 185-188; no. 5-6 (Nov.-Dec. 1946), p. 274-278.
Source material for history of national anthem of Honduras. Spanish texts only. No music. (C.S.)

JAMAICA

Beckwith, Martha Warren. Black road-
ways; a study of Jamaican folk life.
Chapel Hill, University of North Carolina press, 1929. 243 p. il. F1879.B-
39   **[1672]**
   Includes songs with music.

——. Christmas nummings in Jamaica.
With music recorded in the field by
Helen H. Roberts. Poughkeepsie, N. Y.,
Vassar college, 1923. 46 p. il. (Publi-
cations of the Folk-lore foundation.
no. 2) GT4985.B4 GR15.V3 no. 2.
                             [1673]

——. Folk-games of Jamaica ... with
music recorded in the field by Helen
H. Roberts. Poughkeepsie, N. Y., Vassar College, 1922. 79 p. M1681.J3B4
                             [1674]
   Words, tunes, and descriptions of games.

——. The Hussay festival in Jamaica.
With music recorded by pronograph.
Poughkeepsie, N. Y., Vassar college,
1924. 17 p. il. (Publications of the Folklore foundation, no. 4.) GT4827.B4
and GR15.V3 no. 4.   **[1675]**

Jekyll, Walter. Jamaican song and story:

Annancy stories, digging sings, ring
tunes, and dancing tunes, with an introduction by Alice Werner, and appendices on traces of African melody
in Jamaica by C. S. Myers, and on English airs and motifs in Jamaica by Lucy
E. Broadwood ... London, Pub. for the
Folk-lore society by D. Nutt, 1907. 288
p. il. (music) GR121.J2J4   **[1676]**

McKay, Claude. Songs from Jamaica.
London, Augener ltd., 1912. 12 p. M-
1681.J3M2   **[1677]**
   With piano accompaniments.

Roberts, Helen H. Possible survivals of
African song in Jamaica. *Mus. quart.,*
v. 12, no. 3 (July 1926), p. 340-358.
                             [1678]
   Includes music.

——. Some drums and drum rhythms of
Jamaica. *Natural history,* v. 24, no. 2
(1924), p. 241-251.   **[1679]**
   Includes music.

——. A study of folksong variants based
on field work in Jamaica. *Jour. amer.
folklore,* v. 38, no. 148 (1927), p. 1-149.
                             [1680]
   Includes music.

MEXICO

THE musical bibliography of Mexico is exceptionally rich and full. There are two comprehensive histories of music in Mexico, the late Miguel Galindo's *Nociones de historia de la música mejicana,* published in 1933, and Gabriel Saldívar's *Historia de la música en México,* limited to the pre-Cortesian and colonial periods, which was published in 1934 by the Departamento de Bellas Artes. Otto Mayer-Serra's *Panorama de la música mexicana* (1941) covers the subject from the Independence up to the present, and *El arte musical en México* by Alba Herrera y Ogazón, dating from 1917, deals chiefly with modern musicians. The field of folk and popular music, which receives considerable attention in the above-mentioned histories is also comprensively covered in monographs by Rubén M. Campos and Vicente T. Mendoza [nos. 1919 and 2023].

Among the ancient nations of America, none has left a name more capable of arousing the imagination than the Aztecs. Tradition has it that this people came from a legendary region in the north called Aztlan, settled in the fertile valley of Mexico, or Anáhuac, toward the beginning of the twelfth century A. D., and challenged the power of its former inhabitants, the Toltecs, whom they soon overcame. In the year 1325 they founded the city of Mexico, or Tenochtitlán, which at first was merely an insignificant settlement on a marshy island on Lake Tezcuco. The Aztec power expanded through conquest so that eventually they dominated the surrounding tribes and even held sway as far as what is now Central America. By the early sixteenth century Tenochtitlán had grown to be a flourishing capital, with a population of perhaps one hundred thousand, with imposing temples and palaces and markets—a city which aroused the wonder and admiration of the Spaniards under Cortés when they first beheld it.

The Aztecs attained to a relatively high degree of civilization. They used a calendar and an elaborate hieroglyphic script (many of their musical instruments are depicted in this picture-writing). They excelled in the arts of architecture and sculpture. Though their rituals were stained by human sacrifice, they were sensitive to the most delicate manifestations of beauty in many forms. They loved flowers and were adept at ornamentation, especially with featherwork designs. Their lyrical poetry was of a high order (see items 2177-2188). The social, political and religious activities of the Aztecs were regulated by a complex system of ritual and ceremony, of which music formed an integral part.

As the Aztecs had no written musical notation, the exact nature of their musical system remains a matter of speculation. Carlos Chávez believes that "the Aztecs understood and applied the natural phenomenon

of harmonics". He bases this conclusion on a study of the sounds produced
by the marine snail-shell, which the ancient Mexicans used as a musical
instrument. Chávez states that a shell preserved in the Museo Nacional
in Mexico City produces the following scale:

Concerning this scale he writes: "The first harmonic is not produced;
those indicated between parentheses are produced with difficulty. The rest
are beautifully and powerfully sounded with great ease. With this instrument the Indians of our America discovered a natural scale, that of the
so-called natural harmonics. This scale obeys a series of acoustic laws which
are the basis of the musical system of the occident. The Indians based on
this scale the foundation (conscious or instinctive) of a musical system using
octaves, fifths, and thirds. Applying this knowledge, they obtained their
pentatonic scale without semitones."

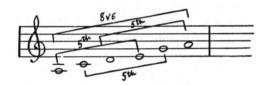

And Chávez adds "Not one of the Aztec instruments produces sounds outside this system." The foregoing quotations are taken from the introduction which Chávez wrote for the concert of Mexican music given by the
Museum of Modern Art, New York, in 1940 [no. 1711]. This theory represents the view of one who is a creative musical artist rather than a musicologist, but who has also given considerable attention to the science of
acoustics, as evinced in his book, *Toward a New Music* [no. 2264]. For
a general description of the part that music played in the life of the Aztecs,
the reader may consult the vividly written though unscientific article by
Frederick H. Martens [no. 2162]. H. T. Craesson, writing in 1883, claimed
that the Astec musical system was not limited to the pentatonic scale
[item no. 2197]. Highly important from the musicological viewpoint are
the studies of Aztec instruments by Castañeda and Mendoza [nos. 2195,
2195x, 2196].

The Aztecs, like other pre-Columbian American peoples, had no stringed instruments. They had only drums, rattles, bells and wind instruments of various kinds. Their chief melodic instrument was a small flute called çoçoloctli or huilacapitzle, made of bone or baked clay, with three, four or five finger holes. The upper end of these flutes was sharpened to form a sort of beak. The Aztecs also had whistle pipes without finger holes, probably older than the flutes. It is likely that most of the bone flutes had no finger holes and were therefore not melodic. There were also tubular trumpets made of wood, cane or clay.

The numerous rattles used by the ancient Mexicans may be divided into two main groups: rattling vessels and rattling sticks. The former were made from gourds or were molded of unglazed terra cotta. The rattling sticks were used in ritualistic ceremonies, often connected with fertility rites, Notched bones scraped with a stick were used as musical instruments, producing, in the words of a Spanish chronicler, "música muy triste." Of a similar nature was the turtle shell or ayotl, played with a stag's antler.

The Aztecs had two principal types of drums. One of these was the huehuetl, a cylindrical drum about two feet in diameter and about five or six feet high. It was generally made of a single piece of hollowed-out wood, and was placed vertically when played. Authorities differ as to whether it was played with a stick or with the bare hands; the greater weight of authority seems to bear toward the latter theory.

The teponaztle (teponaxtle) or slit-drum was shorter, was placed horizontally, and was beaten at the center instead of at the end. Its distinguishing feature was that it had a narrow slit on the top, in the form of a capital letter H, which formed two tongues facing each other. As they were chiseled off on the inside to different thicknesses, each of these tongues, when struck by a stick, produced a different tone. Strictly speaking, therefore, the teponaztli was not a drum at all, but a kind of kylophone with variety of pitch limited to fewer tones. The teponaztli, often elaborately carved to represent some human or animal figure, was placed on a tripod to avoid the deadening contact with the ground. Tradition has it that the teponaztli was invented by Quetzalcoatl, the gentle Toltec divinity, the Orpheus of the Mexican pantheon, who is also credited with having taught mankind to sing.

With the arrival of the Spaniards, who took possession of Mexico City in 1521, there commenced the active diffusion of European music in Mexico to which reference has already been made in the general introduction to this work. Now, to understand the nature of this diffusion of neo-Hispanic musical culture in the New World, some knowledge of the historical background of Spanish peninsular music is required (cf. itm no. 1697). In his history of Mexican music [no. 1702] Galindo discusses the background of

Spanish music in considerable detail (see the section of this work entitled *La música española del siglo XVI*), dealing with the religious, the secular and the folk elements. To the music of the colonial period he applies the term "Neo-Hispanic."

A printing press, the first in the New World, was established at Mexico City in 1539. The first book containing musical notation to be printed in America was issued at Mexico City in 1556 (*Ordinarium Sacri Heremitarum Sancti Augustini Episcopi...*). The Library of Congress has a *Graduale Dominicale* printed at Mexico City by Pedro Ocharte in 1576 (for a detailed description of this work, see Emilio Waltón, *Impresos mexicanos del siglo XVI*, México, 1935, p. 133-146). In 1604 the printer López Dávalos issued a volume containing the liturgical music for Holy Week compiled by Fray Juan Navarro of the Franciscan Order. The title of his work is *Liber in quo quatuor passiones Christi Domini continentur* ... On the title page the compiler is called *Gaditanus*, that is, a native of Cádiz in Spain, and is described as a "vicaro de choro" (chorister) in the diocese of Michoacán. The authorship of this work has been erroneously attributed to the Spanish composer Juan Navarro (*ca.* 1525-1580), choirmaster successively at Salamanca, Ciudad Rodrigo and Palencia, in Spain. This Navarro was an eminent church composer, a collection of whose psalms and hymns was printed posthumously at Rome in 1591. When the Spanish musicologist Mitjana found a copy of the Mexican *Liber* of 1604 in the British Museum, he at once assumed that it was a work by the Spanish Juan Navarro, and put forth the hypothesis that Navarro had journeyed to Mexico, "car c'est dans l'ancienne capitale de Moctezuma qu'il donna aux presses son service pour la Semaine Sainte." At the time when Mitjana wrote (1914), the date of Juan Navarro's death was not known (this was only established by the Spanish musicologists Elústiza and Castrillo in 1933). Various lexicographers turned Mitjana's hypothesis into established fact. This in Riemann's *Musik Lexikon* (11th ed., 1929. p. 1251), we find the following, referring to Navarro, "1604 wanderte er nach Mexiko aus, wo er ein Buch homophoner Passionen und Lamentationen publizierte (1604) und gestorben ist." Thus, on the mere strength of a title page, the famous Spanish composer is transported to Mexico and made to die there. The error is faithfully repeated in other lexicons. In Grove's Dictionary (4th ed., 1940, v. 3, p. 608), we read "Navarro afterwards emigrated to Mexico, where, in 1604, he published a book of Passions and Lamentations ..." It suffices to read the *licencia* of the Mexican *Liber* of 1604 to ascertain that its compiler, the Franciscan Fray Juan Navarro, was living at the time when his book was published ("Por quanto Fray Ioan Nauarro ... me à hecho relació que el à compuesto con mucha diligencia, y cuydado

vn libro, etc."). The exclusive privilege is granted to Fray Juan Navarro
to print and sell his book for a period of twelve years. From this alone
it is evident that Fray Juan Navarro of Michoacán, author of the *Liber*
of 1604, was not the Spanish church musician Juan Navarro *Hispalensis,*
who died at Palencia on 25 September 1580 without ever having gone to
Mexico.

The history of colonial music in Mexico is treated with considerable
thoroughness in the above-mentioned histories by Galindo and Saldívar.
For a survey of Mexican music since the achievement of independence we
may turn to Otto Mayer-Serra's *Panorama de la música mexicana* [no.
1706]. The first chapter studies various aspects of music and society in
Mexico during the nineteenth century, emphasizing the predominance of
the amateur over the professional and the rôle of the musical salon in the
formation of taste. The author also gives attention to music in the church
and the theatre, and to the rise of public concerts after 1840. The second
chapter deals with Mexican musical production in the nineteenth century,
studying the work of such composers as Felipe Larios (b. 1817), Aniceto
Ortega (1823–1875), Luis Baca (b. 1826), Tomás León (1826–1893), Melesio Morales (1838–1908), Julio Ituarte (1845–1905). Numerous examples
of their music are quoted. The third and final chapter traces the development of musical nationalism in México, including an account of the traditional songs and dances from which that nationalism drew its sustenance.
Importance is given to the collection of national music by Julio Ituarte
entitled *Ecos de México.* Among composers who figure prominently in this
section are Ernesto Elorduy, Felipe Villanueva (1863–1893), Gustavo E.
Campa (1863-1934), Ricardo Castro (1864-1907), Manuel M .Ponce (b.
1886), José Rolón (b. 1883), Candelario Huízar (b. 1888), Silvestre Revueltas (1899–1940) and Carlos Chávez (b. 1899). Those mentioned among
the younger men include Luis Sandi (b. 1905), Daniel Ayala (b. 1908),
Blas Galindo (b. 1911) and Salvador Contreras (b. 1912).

BIBLIOGRAPHIES

Alarcón P., Esperanza. Notas e informaciones. *Rev. mus. mex.,* v. 1. no. 2
(21 Jan. 1942), *et seq.*   [1681]

This department, a regular feature of
this review, contains a calendar of current musical events in Mexico City, and
a bibliography of periodical references on
music. Occasionally this department is
devoted to musical events of the past,
with extensive quotations from articles
dealing with music.

Baqueiro Fóster, Gerónimo. Aporta-

ción musical de México para la formación de la biblioteca americana de
Caracas, 1882-1883. *Rev. mus. mex.,* v.
2, no. 2 (21 July 1942), p. 27-32.
                                    [1682]

A list of the Mexican music that was
sent to Caracas, Venezuela, on the oc-
cassion of the Bolívar centenary (July 24,
1883). There are 391 compositions by
more than a hundred composers. This is
an important document for the study of
Mexican music in the 19th century.

Boggs, Ralph Steele. Bibliografía del

folklore mexicano. *Bol. bibl. antrop. amer.,* v. 3, no. 3 (Sept.-Dec. 1939), apéndice, p. 1-121. **[1683]**
247 bibliographical entries, many annotated, including music and dances.

Guichot y Sierra, Alejandro. Noticia histórica del folklore en todos los países hasta 1890 ... Sevilla, Hijos de Guillermo Álvarez, 1922, 256 p. GR80.-G8 **[1684]**
Bibliographical notes. *América del norte,* p. 110–111, includes Mexico. *América central,* p. 112. *América del sur,* p. 112–114. The references to musical sources are few.

Labastille, Irma Goebel. The music of Mexico and Central America. Photostat from Handbook of Latin American studies for 1936, Cambridge, Mass., 1937, p. 459-472 (Running title: Guide to Caribbean music). ML128.C18L2 **[1685]**
A bibliography.

Mayer-Serra, Otto. Bibliografía. *Rev. mus. mex.,* v. 1, no. 2 (21 Jan. 1942), p. 31-42. **[1686]**
A review of the Latin American items published in the educational piano series "Masters of our day" (Carl Fischer, Inc., New York).

———. Bibliografía. *Rev. mus. mex.,* v. 1, no. 11 (7 June 1942), p. 256-257. **[1687]**
Includes a discussion of the policy of the Editorial Cooperativa Interamericana de Compositores of Montevideo, directed by Francisco Curt Lange.

Monterde García Icazbalceta, Francisco. Bibliografía del teatro en México. México, D. F., Imprenta de la Secretaría de relaciones exteriores, 1933. 649 p. (Monografías bibliográficas mexicanas, núm. 28). Z1424.D7M7 **[1688]**
An appendix lists operas and popular patriotic dialogues. The introduction by Rodolfo Usugli contains an historical account of the Mexican theatre.

Spell, Lotta M. The first music books

printed in America. *Mus. quart.,* v. 15, no. 1 (Jan. 1929), p. 50-54. **[1689]**
16th century music-books printed in Mexico (illustrations).

Toussaint, Manuel. Documentos para la historia de la música en Méjico. *Rev. mus. mex.,* v. 1, no. 11 (31 Mar. 1920), p. 17-21. **[1690]**
Contains important bibliographical data.

See also nos. 1702, 1706, 1723.

GENERAL

Barajas, Manuel. México y la cultura musical. México, D. F., Departamento autónomo de prensa y publicidad, 1938. 35 p. ML210.B22M3 **[1691]**

Bermejo, Manuel. Fraudulente campaña sobre nuestro nacionalismo musical. *Méx. mus.,* v. 4, no. 8 (Aug. 1934), p. 1-2, 4. **[1692]**

Campa, Gustavo E. Escritos y composiciones musicales. México, Ed. cultura, 1917. 68 p. incl. music. **[1693]**

Carrillo, Julián. Pláticas musicales. 2⁹ volumen. México, D. F., 1923. 320 p. port. facs. ML60.C2 **[1694]**
The following sections deal with music in Mexico : Felipe Villanueva ; Escuela de música sacra (proyecto de fundación) ; La enseñanza de la música en México ; Informe en el Conservatorio nacional, en la inauguración de los cursos, el año académico de 1921; Himno nacional; Dictámen acerca del ejemplar auténtico; *El sonido 13;* la Orquesta sinfónica "America" de Nueva York y un paréntesis en defensa de la Orquesta sinfónica nacional.

Castañeda, Daniel. Las academias del conservatorio nacional de música. *Música,* v. 1, no. 1 (1930), p. 6-13. **[1695]**
Sets forth the program of folklore investigation of the Conservatorio Nacional.

———. La música y la revolución mexicana. *Bol. lat. am. mús.,* v. 5 (Oct. 1941), p. 437-448. **[1696]**

Chase, Gilbert. The music of Spain. New York, W. W. Norton, 1941. 375 p. il. ML315.C42M8   **[1697]**

Chapter 17, *Hispanic Music in the Americas,* p. 257–272, contains considerable material on music in Mexico, especially with reference to the music school of Pedro de Gante in the 16th century, the first printing of music books, the *corrido* and other types of folk music, the work of Carlos Chávez and Silvestre Revueltas, etc.

Chavero, Alfredo. México a través de los siglos. México, 1939. 4 v. F1226.R62   **[1698]**

Las danzas sagradas, v. 1, bk. 1, ch 4, p. 100; refrain of a funeral chant, p. 104; dance of victory. Musical instruments and dance, v. 1, bk, 1, ch. 13, p. 186; singing, bk. 2, ch. 10. Originally published in the late 19th century.

Chávez, Carlos. The function of the concert. *Mod. music,* v. 15 (Jan.–Feb. 1938), p. 71–75.   **[1699]**

———. The two persons. *Mus. quart.,* v. 15, no. 2 (Apr. 1929), p. 153–159.   **[1700]**

On musical interpretation.

Fétis, François Joseph. Histoire générale de la musique. Paris, Firmin Didot frères, fils et cie., 1869–76, 5 v. il. ML160.F42   **[1701]**

Vol. 1 contains an account of music in Mexico and Peru, with 4 tunes (p. 94–106).

Galindo, Miguel. Nociones de historia de la música mejicana. Tomo 1. Colima, Tip. de "El dragón," 1933. 636 p. il. ML210.G3N6   **[1702]**

Covers Mexican musical history under the following main sections: La música precortesiana; la música española del siglo XVI; la música española del siglo XVII; la música neo-hispánica del siglo XVIII; la música mexicana del siglo XIX. Includes numerous musical notations, chiefly of folk music. The author died 3 Feb. 1942, without having published the second volume of this work.

Herrera y Ogazón, Alba. El arte musical en México. México, Departamento editorial de la dirección general de bellas artes, 1917. 227 p. ML210.H3.   **[1703]**

Part 1: Antecedentes. Deals briefly with the background of pre-Hispanic and Colonial music. Part 2: El conservatorio. Traces the history of the Conservatorio Nacional de Música, which grew out of the Conservatorio de la Sociedad Filarmónica Mexicana, founded 14 Jan. 1866. Part 3: Compositores e intérpretes. A survey of musical activity in Mexico from about 1840 to 1915.

———. Puntos de vista. Ensayos de crítica. México, Secretaría de gobernación, Dirección de talleres gráficos, 1920. 196 p. port.   ML60.H4985P8   **[1704]**

Contents: El modernismo musical; La crítica de arte; Problemas de la crítica.

Herring, Hubert Clinton, and Herbert Weinstock, eds. Renascent Mexico; introduction by Ernest Gruening. New York, Covici, Friede, 1935. 322 p. F1208.H57   **[1705]**

The following chapters deal with music: *Mexican folk dances* by Frances Toor; *Mexican music* by Carlos Chávez; *The fiesta as a work of art* by René d'Harnoncourt.

Mayer-Serra, Otto. Panorama de la música mexicana desde la independencia hasta la actualidad. México, El Colegio de México, 1941. 196 p. il. (music) ML210. M19P2   **[1706]**

For comment see introductory section. *Bibliografía,* p. 179-185.

Mendoza, Vicente T. La obra de los compositores mexicanos y la tendencia nacionalista. *Orientación musical,* v. 1, no. 10 (Apr. 1941), p. 8–10. **[1707]**

Traces the growth of musical nationalism in Mexico; among contemporaries, special attention is given to Manuel Tinoco and Estanislao Meiía.

Michaca, Pedro. El nacionalismo musical en México. *Orientación musical,*

v. 1, no. 5 (Nov. 1941), p. 9–10
[1708]
Discusses the musical nationalism of Mexico in its technical, aesthetic and sociological aspects.

Montenegro, Marco A. La música popular mexicana. *Claridad,* v. 19, no. 342 (1940), p. 81–95. [1709]
General survey of Mexican music from pre-Cortesian times to present. Quotes text of *El corrido de los trenes eléctricos.* No music.

Nagel, H., sucesores. Calendario para el año de 1887 ... México, D. F. 1887. 100 p. [1710]
Includes *Historia de la Sociedad filarmónica mexicana* by Enrique de Olavarria y Ferrari (p. 44–45), an article originally published in the *Revista de Andalucía,* Madrid (1876). Also *Piezas de música,* p. 67–100. New York Public Library.

New York, Museum of modern art. Mexican music: notes by Herbert Weinstock for concerts arranged by Carlos Chávez as part of the exhibition: twenty centuries of Mexican art. Printed for the trustees of the Museum of modern art by William E. Rudge's sons, New York, 1940. 31 p. il. (music) ML42.N3M82 [1711]
Includes a general survey of Mexican music by Chávez (p. 5–11).

Noll, Arthur Howard. Musical Mexico. *Lippincott's mag.,* v. 60 (1897), p. 424–428. [1712]

Orozco y Berra, Manuel. Historia de la dominación española en México, con una advertencia por Genaro Estrada. México, Antigua Librería Robredo, de J. Porrúa e hijos, 1938. 4 v. F1220.-077 [1713]
Vol. 1, ch. 9, includes "Canto y música". This work was originally published in the 19th century.

Ponce, Manuel M. Apuntes sobre música mexicana. *Bol. lat. am. mús.,* v. 3 (1937), p. 73–42. [1714]

——. La canción mexicana. *Revista de revistas,* v. 4 (21 Dec. 1913), p. 17–18. [1715]

——. Escritos y composiciones musicales. México, Ed. Cultura, 1917. [1716]
"Estudios sobre la música mexicana," includes 3 tunes.

——. Estudio sobre la música mexicana. *Mús. de Amér.,* v. 1, nos. 7, 8, 9 (1920). [1717]

Poore, Charles. Mexico finds art a nationalizing force. *The musician,* v. 46, no. 1 (Jan. 1941), p. 6. [1718]

Priestley, Herbert Ingram. The Mexican nation. New York, The Macmillan co., 1923. 507 p. F1226.P92 [1719]
References to music, p. 158–162.

Rolón, José. La música autóctona mexicana y la técnica moderna. *Música,* v. 1 (15 Aug. 1930), p. 16–19. [1720]

——. Organización musical en México. *Bol. lat. am. mús.,* v. 3 (Apr. 1937), p. 77–80. [1721]

Romero, Jesús C. La historia crítica de la música en México, como única justificación de la música nacional. México, Talleres linotipográficos Rodarte, 1927. [1722]
Pamphlet.

Saldívar, Gabriel, and Elisa Osorio Bolio. Historia de la música en México (épocas pre-cortesiana y colonial). México, Editorial "Cvltvra", 1934. 324 p. il. (Secretaría de Educación pública. Publicaciones del Departamento de bellas artes). ML210.S16H5 [1723]
Contains 60 musical examples, incl. Indian melodies, children's singing-games, folk dances, etc. This work, dealing with the pre-Cortesian and colonial periods of Mexican musical history, is divided into three parts: 1, La música indígena; 2, La música europea; 3, La música popular. The first part contains 9 chapters de-

voted to music in the pre-Cortesian period, including a chapter on musical instruments. It also contains 3 chapters on the music and dances of the Indian tribes of Mexico since the conquest. Part 2 traces the introduction of European music in Mexico and the development of musical activity along European lines in that country through the 18th century. Part 3 treats of various types of folk music, viz., children's singing games, the *corrido* (Mexican ballad), the *son, jarabe, huapango* and songs of various kinds, with numerous m u s i c a l illustrations. Bibliography, p. 311-320.

Sartorius, Christian Carl. Zustand der musik in Mexiko. *Caecilia,* v. 7 (1828), p. 199–222. **[1724]**

Indian music, p. 199–206; opera and ballet in Mexico, p. 207–208; church music, p. 209–209; also comments on the Instituto filarmónico, military music, public concerts, musical instruments (with illustrations), songs (with examples of 2 verses, translated into German, p. 216–217); music and words of 3 Mexican songs, with German translation, p. 218–222.

Teschner, Isidoro W. Music in Mexico. *Mus. cour.,* national edition, v. 37, no. 23 [whole no. 978] (7 Dec. 1898), p. 127-129. il. **[1725]**

Wright, Marie Robinson. Mexico, a history of its progress and development in 100 years. Philadelphia, George Barrie and sons, 1911. 511 p. il. F1208.W94. **[1726]**

Music, p. 231–232; National Conservatory of Music, p. 261; bands in Jalisco, p. 413; dance, p. 491.

———. Picturesque Mexico. Philadelphia, J. B. Lippincott co., 1897. 445 p. F1215.W85. **[1727]**

Musical instruments of the Aztecs, p. 34; mention of dance, p. 41; *Posadas,* p. 48.

COLONIAL MUSIC

Bernal Jiménez, Miguel. El archivo musical del Colegio de Santa Rosa de

Santa María de Valladolid, siglo XVIII, Morelia colonial. Sociedad Amigos de la música. [Morelia] Universidad michoacana de San Nicolás, 1939. 45 p. ML3570.B4A7. **[1728]**

Includes music.
"Bibliografía," p. 45.

Bretón Fontecilla, Cecilia. Una obra musical de fray Juan Navarro. *Schola cantorum,* v. 4, no. 8 (Aug. 1942), p. 111–117. il. (facs.) **[1729]**

Deals with the *Liber in quo quatuor Passiones Christi Domini continentur* (México, 1604) compiled by Fray Juan Navarro of the Franciscan Order, a chorister at the cathedral of Michoacán (not to be confused with the Spanish composer Juan Navarro, d. 1580). The copy studied by the author was found in the Biblioteca de Hacienda in México, D. F.

Clavigero, Francisco Saverio. Historia antigua de Mégico. London, México, etc., R. Ackermann, 1826. 2 v. il. F1219.C624 **[1730]**

Music, p. 359–360, with illustration of Mexicans playing musical instruments. Dance, p. 360–362, with short discussions of several dances. Description of the *Volador* dance, p. 362–363, with illustration. First edition published in Cesena, G. Biasini, 1780–1781.

Durán, Diego. Historia de las Indias. México, Imprenta de J. M. Andrade y F. Escalante, 1867–1880. 2 v. F1219.D94 **[1731]**

Ch. 99—"De la relación del Dios de los bailes y de las escuelas de danza que había en México en los templos para servicio de los dioses," p. 225-233. This deals in part with all kinds of dances, both religious and secular. Durán wrote in the 16th century.

Espinosa, Isidro Félix. Crónica de la provincia frasciscana de los apóstoles S. Pedro y San Pablo de Michoacán. México, Imprenta de "El Tiempo", 1899. 574 p. F1306.E77 **[1732]**

Mention of organ and singing in religious choruses, bk. 2, ch. 6, p. 169.

Landa, Diego de. Relación de las cosas

de Yucatán. México, Editorial P. Robredo, 1938. 411 p. il. F1376.L246 1938 **[1733]**

Dances and musical instruments of the Indians, p. 109, 110. (Journey was made during the middle 16th century).

López de Gómara, Francisco. Historia de las conquistas de Hernando Cortés. México, Imprenta de la testamentaría de Ontiveros, 1826. 2 v. F1230.G618. **[1734]**

Vol. 1 includes: Dancing as part of the coronation ceremony (ch. 70, p. 140); custom of singing of the death of the king as his burial (ch. 73, p. 147; ch. 74, p. 149); dancing and singing at marriages (ch. 78, p. 158-159); Mexican dances (ch. 94, p. 217-218).

Vol. 2 includes: Dances in honor of Cortés (ch. 27, p. 63; ch. 57, p. 154). First edition printed in Venice, 1560.

Romero, Jesús C. Estado de la cultura musical de España durante el siglo XVI. *Orientación musical,* v. 1, no. 6 (Dec. 1941), p. 5-6. **[1735]**

While the musical culture of Spain reached a very high level in the 16th century, this culture, says Romero, was not transmitted to New Spain, where the musical instruction imparted by the early missionaries remained in a very elementary stage.

Sahagún, Bernardino de. Historia de las cosas de nueva España. México, Imprenta del ciudadano, A. Valdés, 1829-30. 3 v. F1219.S13. **[1736]**

Vol. 1, bk. 2, p. 41-193: On festivals with music and dance; appendix to bk. 2: "Relación de los cantares que se decían a honra de los dioses de los templos, y fuera de ellos", p. 226-227. Many other references, *passim*. Sahagún went to Mexico as a missionary in 1529.

Saldívar, Gabriel. Una tablatura mexicana. *Rev. mus. mex.,* v. 2, no. 2 (21 July 1942), p. 36-39. **[1737]**

Facsimile of a tablature (6 pages in MS.) probably dating from the 17th century, in which mention is made of a composer, Antonio Carrasio, who was active in Peru ("en el Perú fue Maestro"). For facsimiles of pages 3 to 6, see the two following issues of the *Revista*.

BIOGRAPHY

Altamirano, Ignacio M. Biografías de músicos mexicanos: Don Melesio Morales. *Rev. mus. mex.,* v. 3, no. 1 (7 Jan. 1943), p. 10-13; v. 3, no. 2 (7 Feb. 1943), p. 35-38; v. 3, no. 3 (7 March 1943), p. 63-65; v. 3, no. 5 (7 May 1943), p. 110-112. **[1738]**

Altamirano (1834-1893), a noted Mexican writer, was a contemporary of Morales (1839-1909).

Aranda, Hugo. Nuestros músicos. Alva Herrera y Ogazón. *Méx. mus.* ,v. 3, no. 9 (Sept. 1933), p. 4-6. **[1739]**

Review of the career of this pianist-musicologist.

Bermejo, Manuel M. Carlos J. Meneses, su vida y su obra; ensayo crítico. México, D. A. P. P., 1939. 82 p. ML423 M44B4 **[1740]**

An account of the life and work of the well-known Mexican music educator, long associated with the Conservatorio Nacional, and to whose training and inspiration many of the leading Mexican pianists and teachers of the 1890's and early 1900's were greatly indebted. [Wm. Berrien]

Biografías de músicos mexicanos: Felipe Larios. *Rev. mus. mex.,* v. 2, no. 2 (21 July 1942), p. 40-41. **[1741]**

Interesting not only for its biographical data on Larios (b. 1817), but also for the list of his numerous pupils.

Bowles, Paul. Silvestre Revueltas. *Mod. music,* v. 18, no. 1 (1940), p. 12-14. port. **[1742]**

Brenner, Leah. Silvestre Revueltas. *New York times,* v. 90, no. 30,283 (22 Dec. 1940), sec. 9, p. 7. **[1743]**

Necrology of Revueltas. Notes on his life, personality and works. A brief description of his last composition, the ballet *La Coronela*.

Campa, Gustavo E. Críticas musicales.

Paris, Librería Paul Ollendorff, 1911. 352 p. ML60.C165C7. **[1744]**

Includes a chapter on Ricardo Castro (p. 340–350) and another on that composer's opera *La leyenda de Rudel* (p. 310–318).

——. Nuestros músicos. Felipe Villanueva. *Méx. mus.,* v. 1, no. 3 (Mar. 1931). p. 13. **[1745]**

Biographical sketch, including titles of many of his works.

Campos, Rubén M. El folklore y la música mexicana México, D. F., Talleres gráficos de la nación, 1928. 351 p. il. (Publicaciones de la Secretaría de educación pública.) ML3570.C2 **[1745x]**

Part 3, *La música mexicana* discusses the development of modern Mexican art music, the rise of musical institutions, orchestras, concerts, etc.; includes biographical data on modern composers, with portraits.

——. Máscaras musicales: Alberto Villaseñor. *Rev. mus. mex.,* v. 1, no. 3 (15 July 1919), p. 21–22. **[1746]**

——. Máscaras musicales: Ernesto Elorduy. *Rev. mus. mex.,* v. 1, no. 5 (15 Sept. 1919), p. 13–14. **[1747]**

——. Máscaras musicales: Felipe Villanueva. *Rev. mus. mex.,* v. 1, no. 4 (15 Aug. 1919), p. 11–12. port. **[1748]**
Personal recollections.

——. Máscaras musicales: Ricardo Castro. *Rev. mus. mex.,* v. 1, no. 7 (15 Nov. 1919), p. 7–8. **[1749]**

——. Nuestros músicos: Angela Peralta. *Méx. mus.,* v. 1, no. 10 (Oct. 1931), p. 11–12. **[1750]**

Peralta (1845–1883) was a famous operatic soprano.

——. Nuestros músicos. Ernesto Elorduy. *Méx. mus.,* v. 2, no. 1 (Jan. 1932), p. 8. **[1751]**

Castañeda, Daniel. Balance de Agustín

Lara. México, D. F., Ediciones libres, 1941. 229 p. ML410.L284C2 **[1752]**

Musicologists have too long neglected the field of popular music, hence this study by a leading Mexican musicologist of Mexico's most successful composer in the popular field is doubly welcome. In the first part of his book, the author studies Lara's work as writer of song texts, and in the second part he deals with Lara as composer. At the end there is a biographical sketch from which we learn that Agustín Lara was born in Tlacotalpan, Vera Cruz, in 1903.

Copland, Aaron. Carlos Chávez—Mexican composer. *In* Cowell, Henry, ed., American composers on American music, Stanford university press. 1933, p. 102–106. ML60.C87A5 **[1753]**

Cowell, Henry. Carlos Chávez, *In* Ewen, David, *ed.,* The book of modern composers, New York, 1942, p. 441–446. ML390.E85B6 **[1754]**

Includes also a portrait, a biographical sketch, p. 433, and a statement of Chávez's views on music quoted from his book *Toward a new music* (p. 434-440).

——. ——. *Pro-música,* v. 6, no. 4 (June 1928), p. 19–23. **[1755]**
Biographical sketch.

Cremdell, Rosane. Lecciones y pensamientos. Felipe Villanueva. *Méx. mus.,* v. 3, no. 7 (July 1933), p. 2–3. **[1756]**
Biographical data.

Frías, José D. El maestro músico Agustín González. *Gaceta mus.,* v. 1, no. 1 (Jan. 1928), p. 41–44. **[1757]**
Obituary of this musician of Querétaro.

——. Nuestros músicos. Agustín González. *Méx. mus.,* v. 1, no. 6 (June 1931), p. 7-9. **[1758]**
González worked particularly in the field of religious music.

Gandara, Francisco. Ernesto Elorduy. *Méx. mus.,* v. 3, no. 4 (Apr. 1933), p. 10–11. **[1759]**
Biographical data.

Herrera y Ogazón, Alba. Historia de la música. México, D. F., 1931. 504 p. il. (music) ML160.H53.   **[1760]**

At head of title: Universidad nacional de México autónoma. "Biografa de la señorita Alba Herrera y Ogazón [por Hugo Aranda]": p. 9–12.

Isla, Ezequiel de la. El padre J. Guadalupe Velázquez, primer director de la escuela de música sagrada de Querétaro. *Rev. mus. mex.,* v. 1, no. 4 (21 Feb. 1942), p. 87–89.   **[1761]**

The Escuela de Música Sagrada of Querétaro was founded on 18 Feb. 1892. On p. 82 of this issue there is a portrait of Padre Guadalupe Velázquez, and on p. 83–86 a facsimile of two MS. compositions by him, an *Ave Maria* and an *Ave Maris Stella,* both for four mixed voices.

Lange, Francisco Curt, ed. Latin-American art music for the piano by twelve contemporary composers New York, G. Schirmer, inc., 1942. 55 p.   **[1762]**

Includes a biographical sketch of Manuel Ponce, p. xix–xx, with mention of his most important works. Ponce was born in Fresnillo, State of Zacatecas, 8 Dec. 1886.

Mayer-Serra, Otto. Carlos Chávez; una monografía crítica. *Rev. mus. mex.,* v. 1, no. (7 Jan. 1942), p. 5–7; no. 2 (21 Jan. 1942), p. 35–38; no. 3 (7 Feb. 1942), p. 61–63; no. 4 (21 Feb. 1942), p. 75–79.   **[1763]**

The author views the career and the work of Chávez as representing a decisive phase in the modern history of Mexico. He traces the career of Chávez as conductor and educator in considerable detail, but devotes only a brief paragraph to his work as composer.

——. Music made in Mexico. *Rotarian,* v. 60, no. 1 (Jan. 1942), p. 29–30.   **[1764]**

Short review of the history of music in Mexico, with brief biographies of Ponce, Revueltas, Chávez and Galindo. Accompanying photographs of these men.

——. Silvestre Revueltas and musical nationalism in Mexico. *Mus. quart.,* v.

27, no. 2 (Apr. 1941), p. 123-145. port.   **[1765]**

With 19 musical examples and a list of principal works.

——. Silvestres Revueltas y el nacionalismo musical en México. *Bol. lat. am. mús.,* v. 5 (Oct. 1941), p. 543–564.   **[1766]**

A more complete version of the foregoing.

Orquesta sinfónica de México. Notas por Francisco Agea. Programa 2, temporada 1942, p. 24–35. Blas Galindo.   **[1767]**

Brief biographical note on this young Mexican composer, who appeared as conductor at this program.

——. Notas por Francisco Agea. Programa 3, temporada 1942, p. 41. Eduardo Hernández Moncada.   **[1768]**

Biographical sketch of Hernández Moncada, assistant conductor of this orchestra. He is the composer of a symphony, of the ballet *Procesional,* the cantata *Poemontaje,* piano pieces, school songs, etc.

——. Notas por Francisco Agea. Programa 4, temporada 1942, p. 59–61. Planos, danza geométrica (Revueltas).   **[1769]**

This note includes a biographical sketch of Revueltas and a list of his principal works.

Palau R., Antonio. Pianistas mexicanos: Ramón Cardona. *Cosmos,* v. 2 (June 1913,) p. 392–394.   **[1770]**

Ponce, Manuel M. Nuestros músicos. Gustavo E. Campa. *Méx. mús.,* v. 2, no. 3 (Mar. 1932), p. 8–9.   **-[1771]**

Short review of the work of Campa as conductor, educator and musicologist.

Poore, Charles. Daniel Ayala and racial music. *Musician,* v. 45, no. 7 (July 1940), p. 122–123.   **[1772]**

Translated from the Spanish and reprinted from the *Diario Sureste* of Mérida, Yucatán.

——. *comp.* The musician's encyclopedia of contemporary Mexican composers. *Musician,* v. 47, no. 2 (Feb. 1942), p. 23. **[1773]**
Brief sketch of Carlos Chávez, with partial list of works.

Revilla, Manuel G. Biografías de músicos mexicanos: Antonio Valle. *Rev. mus. mex.,* v. 2, no. 6 (21 Sept. 1942), p. 129-133; no. 7 (7 Oct. 1942), p. 157-159. **[1774]**
Antonio Valle (d. 1876) was a violinist and composer of religious music.

——. Biografías de músicos mexicanos: Cenobio Paniagua. *Rev. mus. mex.,* v. 2, no. 8 (21 Oct. 1942), p. 178-182; no. 9 (7 Nov. 1942), p. 202-204; no. 10 (21 Nov. 1942), p. 216; no. 11 (7 Dec. 1942), p. 234; no. 12 (21 Dec. 1942), p. 251-252. **[1775]**
Paniagua (1821-1882), was the first Mexican composer to have an opera produced. This was *Catalina de Guisa* (29 Sept. 1859).

——. Biografías de músicos mexicanos: D. Julio Ituarte. *Rev. mus. mex.,* v. 2, no. 4 (21 Aug. 1942), p. 83-86; no. 5 (7 Sept. 1942), p. 113-115. **[1776]**
Ituarte (1845-1905) was one of the most outstanding Mexican composers of the 19th century. He was also noted as a pianist. His *Aires nacionales* for piano is one of the pioneer landmarks in Mexican musical nationalism. This biographical study was written in 1904 and is reprinted from the *Obras* of Revilla (v. 1).

Romero, Jesús C. José Mariano Elizaga. México, Ediciones del Palacio de bellas artes, 1934. 156 p. facs. (incl. music). ML429.E43R5 **[1777]**
Elizaga is described as "Fundador del primer conservatorio de América; 'autor del primer libro mexicano de didáctica musical impreso en México, e introductor entre nosotros de la imprenta de música profana." He was born in 1786 and at the age of six became known for his precocious musical gifts. In 1822 he was appointed master of the Imperial Chapel by Iturbide, and in 1823 he published his theoretical work, *Elementos de música.*

He founded in 1824 the first Sociedad Filarmónica in Mexico, and in conjunction with this he established a conservatory of music in 1825 (17 April). Elizaga died in 1842.

Rosenfeld, Paul. Carlos Chávez. *In his* An hour with American music, Philadelphia, J. B. Lippincott, 1929, p. 144-159. ML200.R7H7 **[1778]**

——. Carlos Chávez. *Mod. music,* v. 9, no. 4 (May-June 1932), p. 153-159. **[1779]**

Slonimsky, Nicolas. Music, where the Americas meet. *Christian scien. mon. weekly magazine section* (8 June 1940), p. 8-9. il. **[1780]**
Biographical sketches of Central American and Mexican composers, with portraits. Lists the outstanding Mexican musicians, Carlos Chávez, Silvestre Revueltas, Luis Sandi, Daniel Ayala, Pablo Moncayo, Salvador Contreras, Blas Galindo, Manuel Ponce, José Rolón, Candelario Huízar, Juan Bautista Fuentes, Julián Carrillo.

——. Viewing a *terra incognita* of music. *Mus. Amer.,* v. 61, no. 11 (June 1941), p. 15-17. **[1781]**
A survey of contemporary music in Mexico and Central America, with brief biographical data on many composers and an entire page of portraits.

Soria, Fernando. Galería de músicos mexicanos. *Méx. mus.,* v. 2, no. 9 (Sept. 1932), p. 7-10. **[1782]**
Deals with Luis Adorno, José Alcalá, Luis Baca, Agustín Balderas, Joaquín Beristain, Sr., Lauro Beristain, José María Bustamante (sic), Agustín Caballero, Gustavo Campa, Antonio María Campos, Canales, Ramón Cardona, Alfredo Carrasco, José María Carrasco, Julián Carrillo, Carlos del Castillo, Ricardo Castro, Sor Juana Inés de la Cruz, Alejandro Cuevas, Ana María Charles, Esperanza Dimarias, Mariano Elizaga, Ernesto Elorduy, Alberto Flascheba.

——. Galería de músicos mexicanos. *Méx. mus.,* v. 2, no. 10 (Oct. 1932), p 14 **[1783]**
Deals with Eduardo Gariel, Baltazar

Gómez, José Antonio Gómez, Juan Hernández Acevedo, Alejo Infante, Julio Ituarte.

——. Galería de músicos mexicanos. *Méx. mus.,* v. 2, no. 11 (Nov. 1932), p. 7–8. [1784]

Deals with Felipe Larios, Tomás León, Joaquín Luna, Abundio Martínez, Luis Medina, Estanislao Mejía, Carlos Meneses, Miguel Meneses, Arnulfo Miramontes, Melesio Morales, Alba Herrera y Ogazón, Aniceto Ortega, Cenobio Paniagua, Angela Peralta.

——. Galería de músicos mexicanos. *Méx. mus.,* v, 2, no. 12 (Dec. 1932), p. 13. –[1785]

Treats of Miguel Planas, Manuel Ponce, Velino M. Preza, José Rivas, Jesús Rivera, Juventino Rosas.

——. Galería de músicos mexicanos. *Méx. mus.,* v. 3, no. 1 (Jan. 1933), p. 11–12. [1786]

Contains notes on Rosendo Sánchez, Fernando Soria (autobiografía).

——. Galería de músicos mexicanos. *Méx. mus.,* v. 3, no. 3 (Mar. 1933), p. 11. –[1787]

Deals with Isabel Soria, Ignacio Tejada, Miguel Lerdo de Tejada, Rafael Tello, José Ignacio Torres, José J. Trujeque, Antonio Valle, Octaviano Valle.

——. Galería de músicos mexicanos. *Méx. mus.,* v. 3, no. 4 (Apr. 1933), p. 9. [1788]

Ramón Vega, Felipe Villanueva, Alberto Villaseñor, Octaviano Yañez, María de Jesús Cepeda y Cosío, and lists of *Compositores e instrumentistas, Pianistas, Violinistas* and *Cantantes,* are included.

Sosa, Francisco. Biografías de mexicanos distinguidos. México, Ed. de la sección de fomento mexicano, Oficina tipográfica de la sección de fomento, 1884. 1115 p. F1205.S71 [1789]

Contains materials on Luis Baca (músico), p. 109–113; Joaquín Beristain (músico), 143–146; José María Bustamante (músico), 170–172; José Mara Carrasco (músico), p. 207–210; María de

J. Cepeda y Cosío (cantatriz), p. 244–246; Mariano Elízaga (músico), p. 331–334; Antonio Gómez (músico), p. 414–417; Aniceto Ortega (músico), p. 768–773.

Spell, Lota M. The first teacher of European music in America. *Catholic historical review,* n. s. v. 2, no. 3 (Oct. 1922), p. 372–378. [1790]

Pedro de Gante, a missionary in Mexico, was the first teacher of European music in America. This article tells of his work there, the studies he taught, etc. Also gives a list of instruments used in the Mexican churches in the 16th century. De Gante landed in Mexico on 30 Aug. 1523.

——. The first teacher of European music in America. Austin, Texas, 1922. 7 p. ML210.S7F4 [1791]

A reprint of item no. 1790.

Tablada José Juan. Elorduy, el músico jovial. *Méx. mus.,* v. 3, no. 4 (Apr. 1933), p. 3, 8. [1792]

Necrology.

Urbina, Luis G. La muerte de Ricardo Castro. *Méx. mus.,* v. 1, no. 11 (Nov. 1931), p. 6–8. [1793]

Personal impressions of the death of this composer.

——. Nuestros músicos. Alberto Villaseñor. *Méx. mus.,* v. 2, no. 2 (Feb. 1932), p. 8–9. –[1794]

Impressionistic account of this pianist.

CRITICISM AND ANALYSIS

Baqueiro Fóster, Gerónimo. Hernández Moncada, el compositor en turno. *Rev. mus. mex.,* v. 2, no. 4 (21 Aug. 1942), p. 87–88. [1795]

Deals with the fourth symphony of Eduardo Hernández Moncada, which utilizes folk themes, including some tunes of the Cora Indians collected by Romero Téllez Girón.

Barbacci, Rodolfo. Julián Carrillo e a revolução musical do som 13. *Rev.*

bras. mus., v. 7, no. 3 (1941), p. 219-
225.   **[1796]**

Carrillo, a Mexican composer, has
evolved a system of composition based
upon the division of each tone into 16
equal parts, making a total of 96 different
sounds within the octave. Several of his
works have been widely performed.

Copland, Aaron. Our new music. New
York, Whittlesey house, McGraw-Hill
book co., 1941. 305 p.   **[1797]**

Includes: "Composer from Mexico: Carlos Chávez," p. 202–211. Points to
Chávez as "one of the examples of a
thoroughly contemporary composer." Copland feels that "no other composer has
succeeded so well in using folk material in
its pure form while at the same time solv-
ing the problem of its complete amalgama-
tion into an art form." Comparing him
with Revueltas, "there is no doubt whatever that Chávez is the more mature musician in every way."

González Flores, Manuel. Un gran ballet mexicano. *Lux,* Mexico, v. 14
(Jan. 1941), p. 26–27.   **[1798]**

Deals with *La danza de las fuerzas
nuevas.* Ten illustrations.

Hewes, Harry L. The Mexican ballet
symphony "H. P." *Bull. pan amer.
union,* v. 66, no. 6 (June 1932), p.
421–424.   **-[1799]**

A description of Chávez's ballet, in connection with its performance at Philadelphia on 31 March 1932.

Orquesta sinfónica de México. Notas
por Francisco Agea. Programa 1, temporada 1936, p. 16. Sinfonía india [Chá-
vez]. MT125.M3O7   **[1800]**

Chávez composed the *Sinfonía India*
during a visit to the United States in
1935, and the work was first performed at
a concert of the Columbia Broadcasting
System on 23 Jan. 1936. The performance given at this concert (31 July 1936)
was the first in Mexico. This is the first
composition in which Chávez used indigenous themes.

———. ———. Programa 11, temporada
1936. p. 3–5. "Lamento" y "El rey

poeta" [Campa]. MT125.M3O7
                                         [1801]

Gustavo E. Campa (1863-1934) was
professor of composition at the Conservatorio Nacional of Mexico from 1907 to
1925 (he was also director of the Conservatorio from 1907–1913). From its
founding in 1896 until its discontinuance
in 1914, he was editor of the *Gaceta musical.* His opera *El rey poeta* was produced on 9 Nov. 1901.

———. ———. Programa 2, temporada
1937, p. 9-10. Pueblerinas [Huízar].
MT125.M3O7   **[1802]**

Pueblerinas by Candelario Huízar was
composed in 1913 and first performed on 6
November of that year by the Orquesta
Sinfónica de México. Its three movements are: *Allegro moderato, larghetto,
allegro final.* The first movement uses
the theme of a *jarabe* called *Los panaderos,* and the last movement employs the
theme of another folk dance, *El sauce y
la palma.*

———. ———. Programa 7, temporada
1937, p. 9-10. El Festín de los enanos
[Rolón]. HT125.M3O7   **[1803]**

This is a small symphonic poem written
in 1925 and based on popular themes. The
subject is from a children's tale by Alfonso Gutiérrez Hermosillo. Rolón was a
pupil of Paul Dukas in Paris.

———. ———. Programa 10, temporada
1937, p. 16–17. H. P., sinfonía de baile
[Chávez]. MT125.M3O7   **[1804]**

This work was originally written as a
ballet for small orchestra in 1926. In its
revised version for large orchestra it was
produced by the Philadelphia Opera Company at the Philadelphia Metropolitan
Opera House, under Stokowski on 31
March 1932. At the present concert the
first concert suite from the ballet, consisting of four numbers, was performed.

———. ———. Programa 5, temporada
1937, p. 9-10. Vals poético [Villa-
nueva]. MT125.M3O7   **[1805]**

Felipe Villanueva (1862-1893), a gifted
composer and pianist, was one of the
founders of the Instituto Musical in 1887.
This *Vals poético* was orchestrated by
Gustavo E. Campa.

———. ———. Programa 6, temporada 1938, p. 6–7. Tercera sinfonía [Huízar]. MT125.M3O7   [1806]

Except for the first movement, this symphony has a national character, though not all the themes are taken from traditional sources. First performance in Mexico.

———. Comentarios de la crítica americana sobre Carlos Chávez. Temporada 1938. MT125.M3O7   [1807]

Excerpts (in Spanish and English) from press comments on Carlos Chávez as conductor and composer during his appearances in the United States, 1936–1938.

———. Notas por Francisco Agea. Programa 5, temporada 1939, p. 76. Concertino para cello y orquesta [Adame]. MT125.M3O7   [1808]

Rafael G. Adame, violoncellist, guitarist and composer, was born in the state of Jalisco. He was the first to write concertos for guitar and orchestra. The present work, composed in 1929, is based on a cyclic theme "of psychological Mexican character."

———. ———. Programa 10, temporada 1939, p. 155. Concerto para cuatro cornos y orquestas [Chávez]. MT125. M3O7   [1809]

This work was originally written as a sonata for four horns in 1930, and in this form was played at a concert of the Conservatorio Nacional de Música in May 1931. The revised version of the first and second movements was performed at the Coolidge Chamber Music Festival in Washington, July 1937. The third movement was completed in 1939, and the work received its first complete performance at the present concert (1 Sept. 1939).

———. ———. Programa 3, temporada 1942, p. 45–46. Concerto en la mayor para violín y orquesta [R. Halffter]. [1810]

Rodolfo Halffter (b. Madrid, 1900) has lived in Mexico since 1939, when he began to write this concerto, composed especially for the violinist Samuel Dushkin.

———. ———. Programa 4, temporada

1942, p. 59–61. Planos, danza geométrica [Revueltas].   [1811]

In contrast to most compositions of Revueltas, Planos does not draw upon traditional Mexican sources, but is conceived along abstract lines. The composer himself described it as "functional" architecture in music, but pointed out that this did not exclude sentiment. This note includes a biographical sketch of Revueltas and a list of his principal works.

———. ———. Programa 5, temporada 1942, p. 8–10. Sinfonía de Antígona [Chávez]. MT125.M3O7   [1812]

The original nucleus of this symphony consisted of incidental music which Chávez wrote for a performance of the Antigone of Sophocles (condensed version by Jean Cocteau) in Mexico City in 1933. Revised for large orchestra in 1933, the work was first performed by the Orquesta Sinfónica in that year. The symphony is one movement and in classical sonata form.

———. ———. Programa 7, temporada 1942, p. 104–106. Concerto para piano y orquesta [Galindo]. MT125.M3O7   [1813]

Galindo (b. San Gabriel, Jalisco, 1910) was a pupil of Chávez, Rolón and Huízar. In the summer of 1941 he attended the music school of the Berkshire Festival (Massachusetts), and returned there in 1942. This concerto was originally written for two pianos in 1937 and was entitled Concertino. It utilizes stylized folk material.

———. ———. Programa 8, temporada 1942, p. 120–121. Sinfonía [Hernández Moncada]. MT125.M3O7 [1814]

First performance of this symphony (31 July 1942), which is in four movements: Lento, allegro; Lento sostenuto; Allegro vivace; Allegro.

———. ———. Programa 9, temporada 1942, p. 137–138. Sinfonía núm. 4 [Huízar]. MT125.M3O7   [1815]

First performance in Mexico of Candelario Huízar's 4th Symphony, based entirely on themes of the Cora and Huichol Indians of the Sierra de Nayarit (states of Zacatecas and Jalisco). Huízar was born in Jerez, Zacatecas, in 1889. He studied composition with Gustavo E. Campa at the Conservatorio Nacional de Mexico, where he now teaches musical analysis and composition. Principal works listed on p. 138.

———. Notas por Francisco Agea. Programa 12, temporada 1942, p. 201-203. Concerto para piano y orquesta [Ponce]. MT125.M3O7 **[1816]**

Quotes extensively from an article on Ponce by Marc Pincherle, published in Paris in 1934. This concerto was written in 1910 and was first performed in Mexico City on 7 July 1912, with the composer as soloist. The work shows both romantic and nationalist tendencies.

———. ———. Programa 12, temporada 1942, p. 203-204. Paisajes: Pastoral, cortejos [Adolfo Salazar]. MT125. M3O7 **[1817]**

Salazar is a prominent Spanish critic who has lived in Mexico since 1939. These orchestral pieces were composed in 1926 and 1929, respectively, and received their first Mexican performance on this occasion (28 Aug. 1942).

———. ———. Programa 13, temporada 1942, p. 216-217. Concerto en mi menor para piano y orquesta [Rolón]. MT125.M3O7 **[1818]**

This concerto by José Rolón (b. Ciudad Guzmán, Jalisco, 1883) was written in 1935 for the pianist Salvador Ordóñez. It was first performed at Guadalajara on 31 Jan. 1936, with Ana de la Cueva as soloist. The work is in three movements, played without interruption. A list of Rolón's principal works in on p. 217. On p. 217-218 there is a biographical sketch of the pianist Salvador Ordóñez, the soloist on this occasion.

———. ———. Concierto en Morelia, temporada 1942, p. 8-9. Noche en Morelia [Bernal Jiménez]. MT125.M3O7 **[1819]**

Miguel Bernal Jiménez (b. Morelia, Michoacán, 1910) studied at the Pontifical Institute of Sacred Music in Rome. He composed the opera *Tata Vasco* (Pátzcuaro, 1941).

Two movements from the ballet-symphony, "H. P." [by] Carlos Chávez. *Jour. Phila. orch.*, season 1935-36 (Mar. 20-21-24), p. 821-822. **[1820]**

Program note based on information supplied by Chávez.

See also nos. 1694, 1702, 1703, 1704, 1706, 1707, 1723.

CONTEMPORARY MUSICAL ACTIVITY

Arvey, Verna. Mexico's significance in present day music. *Etude,* v. 54, no. 2 (Feb. 1936), p. 79-80, 128. il. (ports). **[1821]**

With 8 musical examples.

Baqueiro Fóster, Gerónimo. Quinceava temporada, a pesar de todo. *Rev. mus, mex.,* v. 1, no. 11 (7 June 1942), p. 243-244. **[8122]**

In defense of Carlos Chávez and the Orquesta Sinfónica de México.

———. Por el mundo de la música; tres directores en el cuarto concierto de la sinfónica de México. *Rev. mus. mex.,* v. 2, no. 1 (7 July 1942), p. 16-16. **[8123]**

Deals with Jesús Reyes, Mario Alberto Ferrigno and Carlos Chávez as conductors.

Barros Sierra, José. Pan-American festival held in Mexico. *Mus., Amer.,* v. 57, no. 14 (Sept. 1937), p. 8, 27. il. **[8124]**

An account of the Coolidge chamber music festival in Mexico City.

Bowles, Paul. Letter from Mexico. *Mod. music,* v. 19, no. 1 (Nov.-Dec. 1941), p. 36-39. **[1825]**

Discusses the economic plight of Mexican composers (who recently grouped themselves into a professional organization called the Sindicato de Autores, Compositores y Editores de Música); radio and cinema music, and current concerts.

Brenner, Leah. Below the Rio Grande. *Mod. music,* v. 20, no. 2 (Jan.-Feb. 1943), p. 124-125. **[1826]**

A review of the 1942 concert season in

Mexico City. Among the Mexican compositions mentioned are piano concertos by Manuel Ponce, Blas Galindo and José Rolón; folkloristic symphonies by Eduardo Hernández Moncada and Candelario Huízar; and *Planos* by the late Silvestre Revueltas.

Chávez, Carlos. Mexican music. *In* Herring, Hubert C., and Herbert Weinstock, *eds.,* Renascent Mexico, New York, 1935. F1208. H57 **[1827]**

——. Music in Mexican test tube. *Mex. life.* v. 15, no. 9 (1939). **[1828]**

——. The music of Mexico. *In* Cowell, Henry, *ed.,* American composers on American music. Stanford university press, 1933, p. 167–172. ML60.C87A5 **[1829]**

——. ——. *In* Herring, Hubert C., and Katherine Terril, *eds.,* The genius of Mexico, New York, 1931, p. 104–107. **[1830]**

Points out that Mexico lacks a well-established cultural tradition. Yet "a Mexican music exists" and "it has a character and vigor of its own." In order to discover and identify themselves with this musical tradition, Mexican composers must cease to think primarily in terms of European standards. Chávez divides the music of Mexico into three epochs: 1, The aboriginal culture; 2, The *mestizaje* or intermixing of Indians and Spanish; 3, The nationalism of the Revolution. He writes: "'We deny the *professional Mexican music* prior to our own epoch for it is not the fruit of the true Mexican tradition."

——. Revolt in Mexico. *Mod. music,* v. 13, no. 3 (1936), p. 35–40. **[1831]**

——. Sinfonías en México. *Bol. O. S. M.,* v. 2, no.1 (1941), p. 3–13. –**[1832]**

An exposition of the social and cultural function of orchestral concerts, with special reference to the ideals and aims that motivate the director of the Orquesta Sinfónica de México.

Daniel, Oliver. Down to Mexico. *Etude,* v. 58, no. 3 (Mar. 1940), p. 150–151, 198. il. **[1833]**

——. Today in Mexican music. *Christian scien. mon.,* v. 31, no. 237 (2 Sept. 1939), p. 7; v. 31, no. 254 (23 Sept. 1939), p. 10. **[1834]**

The first article discusses Chávez and Revueltas; the contrast between the two composers, and between their works; Revueltas' *Homenaje a Federico García Lorca.* The second article covers the work of Manuel Ponce, José Rolón, Candelario Huízar, and mentions a number of lesser known Mexican musicians.

Del Rio, Alfonso. El coro de madrigalistas (antecedentes), *Rev. mus. mex.,* v. 2, no. 7 (7 Oct. 1942), p. 154–157. **[1835]**

Deals with the formation and early activities of the choral group founded by Luis Sandi in 1940.

Fles, Barthold. Chávez lights new music with old fires. *Mus. Amer.,* v. 48, no. 22 (15 Sept. 1928), p. 5, 21. **[1836]**

González Flores, Manuel. Un gran ballet mexicano. *Lux.* v. 14 (Juna, 1941), p. 26–27. **[1837]**

Deals with the ballet *La danza de las fuerzas nuevas,* music by Blas Galindo, with 10 illustrations.

Jennings, James Richard. Mexico's great strides in music during the last decade. *American music journal,* v. 6, no. 11 (1907), p. 28–30. **[1838]**

Kahan, Solomón. En la hora crítica de la sinfónica. *Rev. mus. mex.,* v. 1 no. 9 (7 May 1942), p. 206–207. **[1839]**

Discusses the status of the Orquesta Sinfónica de México in relation to the artistic personality of Carlos Chávez.

——. Reflejos musicales. México, 1938. **[1840]**

Includes: "Carlos Chávez, dirigiendo la novena sinfonía," p. 199–201.

——. El sueño de una orquesta permanente. *Rev. mus. mex.,* v. 1, no. 7 (7 Apr. 1942), p. 155–156. **[1841]**

Discusses the question of a permanent government-subsidized symphony orchestra in Mexico.

———. "Via crucis" y triunfo del americanismo musical. *Rev. mus. mex.,* v. 2, no. 11 (7 Dec. 1942), p. 232-234. **[1842]**

A discussion of the aesthetic position of the American composer.

Kauffmann, Helen L. Carlos Chávez: decidedly no "mañana" Mexican. *Mus. Amer.,* v. 56, no. 14 (Sept. 1936), p. 11, 26. **[1843]**

Latin-American composer gaining wide recognition. Daniel Ayala, newly-appointed head of esthetics in Michoacán re-creates Mayan lore. *Mus. Amer.,* v. 58, no. 16 (25 Oct. 1938), p. 14. **[1844]**

Langenus, Gustave. Mexico's musical life seen as vital. *Mus. Amer.,* v. 55, no. 13 (Aug. 1935), p. 7, 15. il. **[1845]**

Malvaez, Luis G. Music in Mexico. Translated by K. V. Dufourcq. *New mus. rev.,* v. 19, no. 219 (1920), p. 85-86. **[1846]**

Mariscal, Juan León. La música moderna en México. *Bol. lat. am. mús.,* v. 3 (Apr. 1937), p. 109–112. **[1847]**

Millan, Verna Carleton. Mexico City's orchestra plays under baton of Carlos Chávez. *Mus. cour.,* v. 118, no. 5 (1 Sept. 1938), p. 16. **[1848]**

Nancarrow, Conlon. Mexican music—a developing nationalism. *Mod. music,* v. 19, no. 1 (Nov.–Dec. 1941), p. 67-69. **[1849]**

A detailed review of Otto Mayer-Serra's *Panorama de la música mexicana* [no. 1706].

Orosa Díaz, Jaime. La música en Yucatán y Daniel Ayala. *Rev. mus. mex.,* v. 2, no. 10 (21 Nov. 1942), p. 214–215. **[1850]**

Ayala is conductor of the Banda de Música del Estado de Yucatán, also founder and Conductor of the Orquesta Típica Regional "Yukalpetén".

Orquesta sinfónica de México. Notas por Francisco Agea. Programa 11, temporada 1938, p. 6–7. X aniversario. MT125M3O7 **[1851]**

Reproduces the article written by Chávez for the inaugural concert of the Orquesta Sinfónica in 1928, with some additional comments.

Paz, Juan Carlos. Panorama de la música mexicana. *Rev. mus. mex.,* v. 1 no. 11 (7 June 1942), p. 254–255. **[1852]**

An Argentine modernist reviews the book of the above title by Otto Mayer-Serra [Cf. item no. 1706].

Perkins, Francis D. Music from Mexico. *New York herald tribune,* v. 100, no. 34,151 (17 May 1940), p. 17. **[1853]**

Review of the program of Mexican music given at the Museum of modern art, Carlos Chávez directing. Includes Chávez's comments on the character of Mexican music.

Plenn, Abel. Musical notes. *Mex. life,* v. 9, no. 11 (Nov. 1933), p. 37–38. **[1854]**

Deals with new works by Mexican composers, with special attention to the works of Blas Galindo and Revueltas' *Janitzio.*

Plenn, J. H. Mexico's music program *Mus. digest,* v. 18, no. 9 (Feb. 1934), p. 6, 22. **[1855]**

Ponce, Manuel M. La música después de la guerra. *Rev. mus. mex.,* v. 1, no. 1. (15 May 1919), p. 5-9. **[1856]**

Poore, Charles. Mexico has its nationalists. *Musician,* v. 46. n⁰ 2 (Feb. 1941), p. 25, 34. **[1857]**

Deals with "El grupo de los cuatro": Blas Galindo, J. Pablo Moncayo, Salvador Contreras and Daniel Ayala.

———. The pope's staff buds anew in Mexico. *Musician,* v. 47, no. 5 (May-June 1942), p. 73, 74. **[1858]**

Deals briefly with musical activities of radio stations.

Salas, Ángel E. Mexican music and mu-

sicians—Música y músicos mexicanos. *Mex. folkways,* v. 7, no. 3 (1932), p. 142-147. il.   **[1859]**
Spanish and English text in parallel columns. Discusses Carlos Chávez, Silvestre Revueltas, José Rolón, José Pomas, and Candelario Huízar.

Sandi, Luis. Music in Mexico, 1934. *Mod. music, v.* 12, no. 1 (1934), p. 39-4-. **[1860]**

Spier, William. Advanced musicians in Mexico use quarter-tone and new notation. *Mus. Amer.,* v. 41, no. 24 (4 Apr. 1925), p. 9.   **[1861]**
Interview with Adolf Schmid. Deals chiefly with Julián Carrillo.

Tena Ruiz, Eugenio. El arte y el arte musical en México. Conferencia. *An. acad. nac. artes let.,* año 22, v. 18 (July 1936-Mar. 1937), p. 251-267. **[1862]**
Gives special attention to the composers Manuel M. Ponce, Esparza Oteo, Agustín Lara, Julián Carrillo.

Weinstock, Herbert. Music in Mexico. *In* Who is who in music, Chicago and New York, Lee Stern press, 1940, p. 520-521. ML105.W5   **[1863]**
Deals chiefly with the concert of Mexican music given at the Museum of Modern Art, New York, in May 1940, and devotes special attention to Carlos Chávez and Silvestre Revueltas.

See also nos. 1694, 1706, 1707, 1718, 1721

LYRIC THEATRE

Barros Sierra, José. "Tata Vasco" y su partitura. *Romance,* v. 2, no. 23 (22 Apr. 1941).   **[1864]**
A review of the opera by Miguel Bernal Jiménez, based on the life of Vasco de Quiroga (ca. 1470-1565), first bishop of Michoacán, who was called "Tata Vasco'" by the Indians. Cf. item no. 1865.

Bernal Jiménez, Miguel. "Tata Vasco"; drama sinfónico en cinco cuadros.

Pátzcuaro, 1941. cover-title, 50 p. il. (incl. music).   **[1865]**
" 'Tata Vasco'... libreto de Manuel Muñoz y música de Miguel Bernal Jiménez fue compuesto para celebrar el iv centenario de la llegada a Pátzcuaro del primer obispo de Michoacán, don Vasco de Quiroga."—p. 11.

Campa, Gustavo E. Críticas musicales. Paris, Librería Paul Ollendorff, 1911. 352 p. ML60.C165C7   **[1866]**
Includes a chapter on Ricardo Castro (p. 340-350) and another on that composer's opera *La leyenda de Rudel* (p. 310-318).

Castillo Ledón, Luis. Los mexicanos autores de óperas. *An. museo nac. arqueol. hist. etnol.,* v. 2, nos. 6-8 (Nov. 1910-Jan. 1911), p. 315-354. il. (ports.) **[1867]**
The first Mexican musician definitely known to have composed an opera was Manuel Zumaya. The libretto of his opera *La Partenope* was printed by Rivera in 1711 (a copy is in the Biblioteca Nacional). Castillo Ledón credits Manuel de Arenzana with being the first Mexican composer to have an opera produced in a public theatre. Arenzana's two-act opera *El extranjero* was performed at the Coliseo Nuevo on 25 Nov. 1806. The first to compose operas in the period of Independence was Luis Baca (1826-1855); his operas, however, were not produced. Cenobio Paniagua's opera *Catalina de Guisa* was produced at the Teatro Nacional on 29 Sept. 1859. This was the first Mexican opera produced in the period of Independence. Other Mexican opera composers of the 19th century were Melesio Morales, Octaviano Valle, Mateo Torres Serratos, Leonardo Canales, Miguel Planas, Ramón Vega, Miguel Meneses, Felipe Villanueva, Ricardo Castro, Gustavo E. Campa and Ernesto Elorduy. The activities of the three last-mentioned composers extended into the early years of the 20th century. Among the contemporary composers, only Rafael J. Tello is cited as being active in the field of opera.

Cole, M. R., ed. Los pastores, a Mexican play of the nativity. Boston and New York, Houghton, Mifflin, and co., 1907. 234 p. (Memoirs of the Amer-

ican folklore society. v. 9, 1097).
GR1.A5 v. 9 PQ729.A1P2   [1868]
Text and music, with English translation and notes.

Garcidueñas, José Rojas. Piezas teatrales y representaciones en Nueva España en el siglo XVI. *Revista de literatura mexicana*, 1, no. 1 (July-Sept. 1940), p. 148-154.   [1869]
There is no mention of music in this list of dramatic presentations; however, since these dramas were for the most part religious, it is probable that many of them contain music, or directions for music.

Guillermo, Víctor Manuel. The opera in Mexico. *Mex. life*, v. 10 (Dec. 1934), p. 39-40, 45-47.   [1870]

Loewenberg, Alfred. Annals of opera, 1597-1940. With an introduction by Edward J. Dent. Cambridge, W. Heffer & sons, ltd., 1943. 879 p. [1871]
Chronology of operatic performances. Includes *Ildegonda* (1865) and *Cleopatra* (1891) by Melesio Morales (1838-1908); *Keofar* by Felipe Villanueva (1863-1893).

Mayer-Serra, Otto. Tata Vasco. *The commonweal*, 1. 34, no. 21 (12 Sept. 1941), p. 486-488.   [1872]
Reviews and gives the background of this opera by Miguel Bernal Jiménez. Vasco de Quiroga, called "Tata" Vasco, was the first bishop of Michoacán. Cf. item no. 1865.

Michel, Concha. Pastorela o coloquio. *Mex. folkways*, v. 7, no. 1 (1932), p. 5-30. il.   [1873]
Spanish and English text in parallel columns. Text and description of a popular religious mystery play, with 11 harmonized melodies.

Monterde García Icazbalceta, Francisco. Bibliografía del teatro en México. México, Imp. de la Sección de relaciones exteriores, 1933. 649 p. (Monografías bibliográficas mexicanas, no. 28). Z1424.D7M7   [1874]
Músicos autores de óperas, p. 603-613.

———. Pastorals and popular performan-

ces. The drama of viceregal Mexico. *Theatre arts monthly*, 1. 22 (Aug. 1938), p. 597-602.   [1875]

Olavarria y Ferrari, Enrique. Reseña histórica del teatro en México. 2d ed. México, Casa editorial "La Europea", 1895. 4 v. in 2. PN2311.04   [1876]
This compendious work is of the utmost importance for the study of the lyric theatre in Mexico, from 1538 to 1896. Virtually every chapter contains references to operatic performances in Mexico, hence it is impractical to cite any particular passages here. The synoptical table of contents and the chronological arrangement of the chapters facilitate reference. Not only are all lyrico-dramatic performances thoroughly covered, but there also are numerous accounts of concert activities, with details of performances by local orchestral societies, visiting virtuosi, etc. See, for example, v. 1, part 1, ch. 16, which deals with concerts in 1839-1840.

Plenn, Abel. The stage. *Mex. life*, v. 11, no. 12 (Dec. 1933), p. 39.   [1877]

See also nos. 1702, 1706, 1723, 1724, 1917

INSTRUCTION AND THEORY

Baqueiro Fóster, Gerónimo. Curso completo de solfeo. México, Talleres Gráficos de la Nación, 1939. v. 1. MT870. B256C8   [1878]

Carrillo, Julián. Music without tones and semitones. *Mus. advance*, v. 12, no. 11 (June 1925), p. 1-2.   [1879]

———. La revolución musical del "Sonido 13". *Musicalia*, v. 1, no. 3 (Sept.—Oct. 1928), p. 77-82. il   [1880]

———. Revolución musical del sonido 13. *Bol. lat. am. mús.*, v. 4 (Bogotá, 1938), p. 149-158.   [1881]

———. Teoría lógica de la música. México, D. F., Tip. E. Pardo e hijos, 1938. 136 p. il. (music) diagrs. MT7.C265T3   [1882]
On inside title-page; Sonido 13. An exposition of Carrillo's musical system in-

volving fractional tones and a new method of nation. "Que la música se escriba tan fácilmente como una carta y se lea con igual facilidad que un periódico; es uno de los ideales que persigo."

——. Tratado sintético de canón y fuga. México, D. F., 1921. 56 p. MT59.C2 **[1883]**

——. Tratado sintético de contrapunto. 2d ed. México, D. F., Aztlan editores, 1925. 43 p. MT55.C2 **[884]**

——. Tratado sintético de harmonía. 2d ed. New York, G. Schirmer, 1915. 102 p. il. (music). MT50.C29 **[1885]**

Castañeda, Daniel. Las matemáticas y el principio de las relaciones sencillas aplicado a la escala musical. *Rev. mus. mex.*, 1. 2, no. 11 (7 Dec. 1942), p. 230-231; no. 12 (21 Dec. 1942), p. 245-250. **[1886]**
A paper presented at the Primer Congreso Nacional de Matemáticas at Saltillo, 1-7 Nov. 1942.

——. Música de mañana—Ensayo sobre una nueva teoría musical. *Bol. lat. am. mús.*, v. 4 (Oct. 1938), p. 313–346. **[1887]**

Cordero, Juan N. La música razonada. Vol. V. Estética teórica y aplicada. México, D. F. La Europa, 1897. 278 p. **[1888]**

——. Origen del sistema diatónico; breves consideraciones filosóficas. México, Oficina tip. de la Secretaría de fomento, 1896. 54 p. ML3809.C7 **[1889]**

Gómez Anda, Antonio. Bases técnicas de la música moderna. *Rev. mus. mex.*, v. no. 3 (15 July 1919), p. 7–10. **[1890]**

Guisa, Marcelino. Escuelas diocesanas de música sagrada en la república mexicana. *Schola cantorum*, v. 5, no. 2 (Feb. 1943), p. 27–31. **[1891]**
Information about schools for sacred music in Aguascalientes, Querétaro, Gua-

dalajara, Jalapa, México, D. F., Morelia, León, Oaxaca, Tulancingo.

Martí, Samuel. Técnica básica para violín y viola. Basic violin-viola technique. Mérida, Yucatán, Editor: Orquesta sinfónica de Yucatán, 1938. 74 p. il. MT260.M355T3 **[1892]**
Spanish and English text.

Ponce, Manuel M. La enseñanza actual en la técnica pianista es deficiente. *Rev. mus. mex.*, v. 1, no. 11 (31 Mar. 1920), p. 5–6. **[1893]**

——. A propósito de los exámenes. *Rev. mus. mex.*, v. 1, no. 6 (15 Otc. 1919), p. 5–9. **[1894]**

Santos, Domingo. Tratado sintético de instrumentación ... del maestro mexicano Julián Carrillo. *Rev. mus. mex.*, v. 3, no. 1 (7 Jan. 1943), p. 15–17. **[1895]**
A Salvadorean composer and bandmaster comments on Carrillo's treatise on instrumentation.

Universidad nacional de México. *Facultad de música.* Preludio—Cinco estudios ... by A. Novaro. México, 1933. 15 p. **[1895x]**

NATIONAL ANTHEM

Beltrán, Bernardino. Historia del himno nacional mexicano y narraciones históricas de sus autores, d. Francisco González Bocanegra y d. Jaime Nunó. México, D. F., Departamento autónomo de prensa y publicidad, 1939. 182 p. **[1896]**

Carrillo, Julián. Himno nacional. *El sonido 13*, v. 1, no. 9 (Sept. 1924), p. 1, 21-34. **[1897]**
Photographs of the music of the hymn, p. 23–26, 30, 32.

——. El himno nacional. *El Universal*, año 25, v. 98, no. 9,403 (26 June 1941), p. 8, 9. **[1898]**
Takes up some of the points raised in

Jacobo Delavuelta's interview with Carlos Chávez more arguments over the dates of the various instrumentations.

Galindo y Villa, Jesús. El himno nacional mexicano. *An. museo nac. arqueol. his. etnol.,* v. 22 (1927), p. 60–75. **[1899]**

Himno nacional mexicano y 12 cantos revolucionarios y deportivos. México, D. A. P. P., 1939. 14 p. **[1900]**

Olavarria y Ferrari, Enrique. Historia del himno nacional. México, D. F, Eduardo Dublan, 1901. 20 p. ML410.-N906 **[1901]**
Contains biographical data on Jaime Nunó, and the words to the National Hymn. Reprinted from the author's *Reseña histórica del teatro en México* [no. 1876].

Orquesta sinfónica de México. Notas por Francisco Agea. Programa 1, temporada 1942, p. 7–9. Himno nacional mexicano. MT125.M307 **[1902]**
The national anthem of Mexico was composed in 1853 by a music teacher named Jaime Nunó (b. Gerona, Spain, 1825; d. Bay Side, N. J., 1908). Following a contest for the best national anthem, in which 15 compositions were submitted, Nunó's hymn was afficially adopted on 12 Aug. 1854. This program note was motivated by Carlos Chávez's orchestration of Nunó's anthem.

Rosales, Hernán. Rectificaciones técnicas al himno nacional. *Todo* (México), 6 July 1942. **[1903]**

Sosa, Francisco. El himno nacional mexicano; noticias históricas. *Montevideo musical,* v. 19, no. 255 (1 May 1904), p. 2–4. **[1904]**

FOLK MUSIC
(OTHER THAN INDIAN)

(A) GENERAL

Alarcón P., Esperanza. Notas e informaciones (de los tiempos pasados). *Rev. mus .mex.,* v. 1, no. 7 (7 Apr.

1942), p. 159–160; no. 9 (7 May 1942), p. 210–211. **[1905]**
Quotes from an article on "La música en los entierros" originally published in the *Diario de México* of 8 Feb. 1806, and reproduces a lengthy extract on Aztec burial customs from the *Memoriales* of Fray Toribio de Motolinia (16th century). Includes music of a *Despedida* and of the *Mañanitas de difuntos,* both traditionally associated with Mexican burial customs.

Amador, Armando C. Poetry of Mexican folksongs. *Panam. mag.,* v. 43 (1930), p. 361–363. **[1906]**

Ancona, Eligio. Historia de Yucatán. Mérida, Impr. de M. Heredia Argüelles, 1878–1905. 5 v. F1376.A55 **[1907]**
Vol. 1 has brief section on music and the dance, p. 146–147.

Baqueiro Fóster, Gerónimo. El huapango. *Rev. mus. mex.,* v. 1, no. 8 (21 Apr. 1942), p. 174–183 **[1908]**
The *huapango* is a traditional Mexican type of music and dancing, accompanied by a special combination of instruments, comprising generally harps, *jaranas* (small five-stringed guitar), *guitarras jabalinas* (a kind of four-stringed guitar played with a plectrum) and violins. The music used for the *huapango* is called a *son.* This is a detailed study of the *huapango,* with 15 musical examples. Most of the *sones de huapango* are derived from Spanish music; some show Negro influence.

———. Los Xtoles. Canción al sol de los guerreros mayas. *Mex. folkways,* v. 8 (1933), p. 83. **[1909]**
Indian text only, with music.

Bernal, Rafael. Las tres canciones de la tierra fría. *Rev. mus. mex.,* v. 1, no. 7 (7 Apr. 1942), p. 148–150. **[1910]**
Discusses the popular festivals of the Nevado de Toluca, and reproduces the text of several folk songs.

Bowles, Paul. On Mexico's popular music. *Mod. music,* v. 18, no. 4 (May-June 1941), p. 225–230. **[1911]**
Discusses the principal popular forms of Mexican music, such as the *son* and

the *huapango*, with six notations of *son* rhythms.

Brondo, Whitt, E. Hilitos de oro. *In* Anuario de la Sociedad folklórica de México, 1941. v. 2, México, D. F., 1943, p. 113–116. **[1912]**
Description of a children's singing game.

Cabrera, Ana S. Canciones populares mejicanas. *La Nación* (2 Feb. 1936), **[1913]**

——. Rutas de América; el folklore, la música, la historia, la leyenda, las costumbres. Buenos Aires, Peuser, ltda., 1941. 242 p. il. F1408.3.C2. **[1914]**
Part 5 is *La canción y la danza populares en México.* There are also numerous references to folk dances in Part 6, *Supervivencia del folklore en las costumbres.* There are numerous illustrations of musicians, dancers and instruments. Notation of 9 tunes.

Calderón de la Barca, Frances Erskine (Inglis). Life in Mexico during a residence of two years in that country. With an introduction by Henry Baerlein. New York, E. P. Dutton and co., 1931. 542 p. F1213.C146 **[1915]**
Impressions of Mexico in 1842. Patriotic Hymn, p. 56–58 (with English translation); street cries, p. 64-66; "El Palomo," p. 120; two Mexican songs, p. 157-159; "Mexican airs," with music, p. 267-268; music in Mexico, p. 365.

Campos, Rubén M. El folklore literario de México. Publicaciones de la Secretaría de educación pública., México, D. F., Talleres gráficos de la nación, 1929. 690 p. il. GR115.C3 **[1916]**
"Canciones mexicanas de antaño," words and music of 20 Mexican songs, p. 307-335. Also includes other brief musical examples.

——. El folklore musical de las ciudades. México, Publicaciones de la Secretaría de educación pública, Talleres linotipográficos "El Modelo", 1930. 457 p. il. ML3570.C2F52. **[1917]**
Appendix, "Composiciones musicales mexicanas para bailar y cantar," p. 295-443. This book covers a much wider territory than is generally comprised under the term "folk music." The musical examples contained in the appendix are mostly of "composed" music, with or without folkloristic elements. The first part of the book deals with musical culture in Mexico during the 19th century, with copious data on the lyric theatre. The subtitle of the work, "Investigación acerca de la música mexicana para bailar y cantar," gives a better idea of the contents than does the main title. This is one of the most important printed sources for Mexican music of the 19th century. The volume is profusely illustrated.

——. El folklore musical de México. *Bol. lat. am. mús.*, v. 3 (1937), p. 137-142. **[1918]**
Mentions the rise of typical Mexican songs ("sonecitos del país") in the early 19th century.

——. El folklore y la música mexicana. México, D. F., Talleres gráficos de la nación, 1928. 351 p. il. (Publicaciones de la Secretaría de educación pública) ML3570.C2 **[1919]**
This book is divided into three parts. The first, *Las fuentes del folklore mexicano,* deals with the musical practices and traditions of the ancient Mexicans, their musical instruments, dances, and rituals; it also deals with the musical activities of Fray Pedro de Gante, and with music and musical instruments of the early colonial period. Part 2, *La producción folklórica,* deals especially with the development of folk and popular music during the 19th century, illustrated with examples. Part 3, *La música mexicana* discusses the development of modern Mexican art music, the rise of musical institutions, orchestras, concerts, etc.; includes biographical data on modern composers, with portraits. The musical appendix comprises the music of 100 Mexican folk songs and dances (for piano, some with interlinear text). In addition there are 20 musical examples in the main body of the text. The volume is profusely illustrated.

——. Tradiciones y leyendas mexicanas. *An. museo nac. arqueol. hist. etnog.,* ép. 5, v. 2 (1937), p. 71-191. **[1920]**
Includes "Cómo eran 'las Posadas' en 1836."

Castañeda, Daniel. La música y la revolución mexicana. *Bol. lat. am. mús.,* v. 5 (Oct. 1941), p. 437-448. **[1921]**

Discusses the component elements of Mexican folk music, the role of this music in the Revolution (1910), and the influence that the Revolution had on the folk and popular music of Mexico.

Chase, Gilbert. The music of Spain New York, W. W. Norton, 1941. 375 p. il. ML315.C42M8 **[1922]**

Chapter 17, *Hispanic Music in the Americas,* p. 257–272, contains considerable material on music in Mexico, including the *corrido* and other types of folk music.

Cisneros, María Guadalupe. De la literatura jalisciense: El folklore literario musical, etc. México, D. F., 1933. 133 p. PQ7291.J3C5. **[1923]**

Domínguez, Francisco. Dos sones zapotecos, *Neza,* supl. v. 4, no. 1 (1939), p. 4. **[1924]**

Contains music of two folksongs from Juchitán, Mexico.

Dromundo, Baltasar. Las canciones revolucionarias. *El libro y el pueblo,* v. 12 (1934), p. 419–430. **[1925]**

——. Los cantos de la revolución mexicana. *Univ. Méx.,* v. 2 (1931), p. 213-222. **[1926]**

Cf. item no. 1927.

——. In Homenaje a Enrique José Varona. Habana, Publicaciones de la Secretaría de educación, 1935. p. 429-438. F1787.V31 **[1927]**

A study of the popular songs of the Mexican Revolution of 1910, with 10 textual examples.

Esteva, Guillermo A. La música oaxaqueña. Oaxaca, Talleres tipográficos del Gobierno, 1931. **[1928]**

Cited by Boggs, *Bibliografa del folklore mexicano,* p. 55.

——. La zandunga. *Neza,* v. 1, no. 9 (Feb. 1936), p. 2. **[1929]**

Folk tune from Juchitán.

Gaines, Ruth Louise. Little Light (Lucita), a child's story of old Mexico. Chicago, New York, Rand, McNally & co., 1913. 99 p. il. PZ7.G165L. **[1930]**

Music of Mexican lullaby at end.

Galindo, Miguel. El alma de la raza, afinidades hispanoamericanas. *Bol. soc. mex. geog. estad.,* ép. 5, v. 12 (v. 38), p. 321-347. il. **[1931]**

References to music, p. 334–347, with 3 tunes. Also reprinted separately (F1408. 3.G175).

——. La música popular y el sentimiento de la patria. Colima, Impr. "El Dragón", 1923. **[1932]**

Cited by Boggs, *Bibliografía del folklore mexicano,* p. 55.

——. Nociones de historia de la música mejicana. Colima, Tip. de "El Dragón," 1933. 636 p. il. ML210.G3N6. **[1933]**

Contains about 30 brief musical examples (folk and Indian melodies). Includes copious data on Mexican folk and primitive music.

Gallop, Rodney. Mexican mosaic. London, Faber and Faber, ltd., 1939. 299 p. il. F1234.G166. **[1934]**

Travel impressions of a well-known musical folklorist. Includes music.

Gamio, Gabriel. Leyenda y canción recogidas en México, D. F. *Jour. amer. folklore,* v. 31 (1918), p. 549–550. **[1935]**

García Cubas, Antonio. El libro de mis recuerdos; narraciones históricas, anecdóticas y de costumbres, mexicanas. 2 ed. México, Imprenta Manuel León Sánchez, 1934. 639 p. il. F1386.G22 **[1936]**

Includes 25 tunes, with text of many folk songs.

——. The republic of Mexico in 1876. Tr. by George F. Henderson. México, "La Enseñanza" printing office, 1876. 130 p. F1208.G26 **[1937]**

Contains specimens of popular music.

Garret, Eudora. Mexican folk music. *Palacio*, v. 46 (1939), p. 133-136. **[1938]**
A general discussion.

Gatschet, Albert S. Popular rimes from Mexico. *Jour., Amer. folklore*, v. 2 (1889), p. 48-53. **[1939]**
Gives the words of 4 love songs (Spanish text with English translation).

Henestrosa, Andrés. Las canciones del istmo de Tehuantepec. *Univ. Méx.*, v. 1, no. 6 (1936), p. 6-7. **[1940]**
Discusses *La sandunga, La llorona, El huipilito,* etc.

——. Las canciones del istmo de Tehuantepec. *Mercurio mus.*, v. 5, no. 61 (1936), p. 18-19. **[1941]**

——. Música mestiza de Tehuantepec. *Rev. mus. mex.*, v. 1, no. 5 (7 Mar. 1942), p. 107-109; no. 7 (7 Apr 1942), p. 151-154. **[1942]**
The author states there is, strictly speaking, no indigenous music in the Isthmus of Tehuantepec. The music of this region, be affirms, is a mixture of Spanish and Indian elements. He gives the music of a *fandango yucateco* and of a "composed" waltz, *Para neti naaha* (p. 152).

——. Tres canciones juchitecas y una glosa. *América* (México), v. 2, no. 6 (Mar. 1941), p. 42-43. **[1943]**
Discusses the strong mestizo element in this music, with *Para netl naaha* (words and music) as an example.

Islas García, Luis. Children's games— Juegos de niños. *Mex. folkways*, v. 7, no. 2 (1932), p. 63-74. il. **[1944]**
Spanish and English text in parallel columns. Description of 12 children's games, with 6 tunes.

——. Juegos infantiles. *Mex. folkways*, v. 5 (1929), p. 79-85. **[1945]**
Description and text of children's singing games.

Landazuri, Elena. Why we are different.

Survey, v. 52, no. 3 (1 May 1924), p. 159-160. **[1946]**
Contains 2 melodies (music and Spanish words).

Lanuza, Agustín. Romances, tradiciones y leyendas guanajuatenses. México, Eusebio Gómez de la Puente, n. d. **[1947]**
Cited by Boggs, *Bibliografía del folklore mexicano,* p. 60, who also mentions another edition: México, La Europea, ca. 1906.

Larreba, A. El cantar popular. *Rev. mus. mex.*, v. 1, no. 9 (7 May 1942), p. 200-204. **[1948]**
A literary study, with textual examples, of a form of lirical poetry which is frequently found in Latin American folklore. Originally published in the *Diario del hogar* (México, D. F.), 6 Jan. 1884.

León, Nicolás. El negrito poeta mexicano y sus populares versos. Contribución para el folk-lore nacional. México, Imprenta del Museo nacional 1912. 234 p. PQ7297.L4N3 **[1949]**

Maqueos Castellanos, Esteban. La zandunga, *Neza*, v. 1, no. 8 (Jan. 1936), p. 3, 5, 6. **[1950]**

Matus, Vicente E. Los sones zapotecos. *Neza*, v. 1, no. 7 (Dec. 1935), p. 1, 4. **[1951]**

Mayer-Serra, Otto. Mexican musical folklore. *Étude*, v. 61, no. 1 (Jan. 1943), p. 17, 58, 72; no. 2 (Feb. 1943), p. 89, 137, 139. **[1952]**
The first section of this article deals primarily with the *corrido;* several musical examples, and parts of *corrido* verses. The second section is devoted principally to *mariachis* (with an example of a *son mariachi* transcribed by Blas Galindo), and the *jarabe*. Note that the article was to be continued in the Mar. 1943 issue, but did not appear.

Mazari, Manuel. Un canto arcaico. *An. museo nac. arqueol. hist. etnol.*, ép. 4, v. 5 (1927), p. 55-59. **[1953]**

Mechling, William Hubbs. Stories and songs from the southern Atlantic region of Mexico. *Jour. amer. folklore,* v. 29, no. 114 (1916), p. 547-558.
[1954]
Includes the text (Spanish only) of 5 songs collected by the author in Mexico. among them a version of the well-known ballad of Macario Romero.

Mendizábal, Miguel O. de. La poesía indígena y las canciones populares *Bol. mus. arq. hist. etnog.,* ép. 4, v. 2 (1923-1924), p. 79-84.
[1955]

Mendoza, Vicente T. El album de 24 canciones mexicanas. *Bol. lat. am. mús.,* v. 5 (Oct. 1941), p. 515-542.
[1956]

——. La canción de mayo en México. *Bol. lat. am. mús.,* v. 5 (Oct. 1941), p. 491-514.
[1957]

——. Una canción provenzal en México. *An. inst. invest. est.,* v. 2 (1940), p. 57-76.
[1958]
Contains regional variants of the Mexican folk song *O blanca virgen,* which is believed to be derived from the Provençal *Magali.*

——. Los cantos de arada en España y México. *Rev. mex. soc.,* v. 2, no. 1 (1940), p. 45-55.
[1959]
Includes 2 tunes.

——. Los cantos populares religiosos de México. *Schola cantorum,* v. 4, nos. 2-3 (Jan-Feb. 1942), p. 19-21.
[1960]
With 2 tunes.

——. Origen de dos canciones mexicanas. *In* Anuario de la Sociedad folklórica de México, 1941, v. 2, México, D. F., 1943, p. 145-172.
[1961]
Deals with musical settings of the Ten Commandments. Includes music.

——. Origen de tres juegos mexicanos. *In* Anuario de la Sociedad folklórica de México, 1941, v. 2, México, D. F., 1943, p. 77-89. il. (music)
[1962]
Deals with three well-known children's singing games of Spanish origin: *La víbora de la mar; Al ánimo, al ánimo; Pasen,*

pasen caballeros. Includes the text and music of each.

Michaca, Pedro. El nacionalismo musical mexicano. México, Universidad nacional de México, Sección editorial, 1931. 23 p. il. ML3570.M62N3 [1963]
A detailed analysis of the Mexican folk song *Las mañanitas.*

Michel, Concha. La Eulalia. *Mex. folkways,* v. 2, no. 4 (1926), p. 7. [1964]
Words and music of a Mexican song.

——. Pastorela o coloquio. *Mex. folkways,* v. 7, no. 1 (1932), p. 5-30. il.
[1965]
Spanish and English text in parallel columns. Text and description of a popular religious mystery play, with 11 harmonized melodies.

——. Tristes recuerdos. *Mex. folkways,* v. 2, no. 3 (1926), p. 10-11. [1966]
Words and music of a song collected in Guanajuato by Manuel Hernández Galván.

——, and **Ignacio Fernández Esperón** (Tata Nacho). Me voy para Mazatlán. De la colección de C. M. Arreglo para piano de I. F. E. *Mex. folkways,* v. 4 (1928), p. 204-205.
[1967]

Montenegro, Marco Arturo. La música popular mexicana. *Claridad,* año 19, v. 19, no. 342 (Apr. 1940)), p. 81-95.
[1968]
Deals not only with the folk music of Mexico, but offers in effect a panorama of musical trends in Mexico from pre-Cortesian times to the present, with special relation to the historical and social background. Gives text of *El corrido de los trenes eléctricos.*

Montes lóbregos. Arreglo de Carmen Herrera de Mendizábal. *Mex. folkways,* v. 3, no. 3 (1927), p. 151-153.
[1969]
Music arranged for piano, with interlinear Spanish text.

Murillo, Gerardo. Las artes populares en México. México, Editorial "Cvltvra", 1922. 2d. ed. 2 v. il. (Publicaciones de la

Sría. de industria y comercio). NK844.-
M8 1922   **[1970]**

Vol. 2, p. 197-216, contains 9 folk
songs (3 for one voice, 3 for two voices
and 3 with piano accompaniment). Author's pseudonym, Dr. Atl, at head of
title.

Muro Méndez, José. El alabado. *Mex.
folkways,* v. 2, no. 5 (Dec. 1926-Jan.
1927), p. 46-48.   **[1971]**

Transcribed from the singing of a farm
laborer in Bajía. English and Spanish
text.

Music of "little" Mexico. *Modern Mexico,* v. 7, no. 4 (1935), p. 20. (Reprinted from New York *Herald Tribune*)
                                      [1972]

Discusses native regional music.

New York, Museum of modern art.
Mexican music; notes by Herbert Weinstock for concerts arranged by Carlos
Chávez as part of the exhibition: twenty centuries of Mexican art. Printed
for the trustees of the Museum of modern art by William E. Rudge's sons,
New York, 1940. 31 p. il. (music) M-
L42.N3M82   **[1973]**

Includes important material on Mexican
folk and popular music.

Núñez y Domínguez, José de J. The
alabado and alabanzas. *Mex. folkways,*
v. 2, no. 5 (Dec.-Jan. 1926), p. 12-17.
(See also p. 17-22 and 46-48). **[1974]**

Notes on the bymns in praise of the
Sacrament taught to the natives by the ear-
ly Spanish missionaries, especially Fray
Antonio Margil de Jesús.

Obregón, Luis Felipe. Recreación física
para escuelas y comunidades rurales.
México, Secretaría de educación pública, Talleres gráficos de la nación, 1935.
169 p.   **[1975]**

Includes rounds and traditional games
with music, p. 35-57.

Orcillo, Rubén S. La canción mexicana.
Rev. Españas, v. 5 (1930), p. 185-192,
247-251.   **[1976]**

Ortiz Vidales, Salvador. La arriería en
México. México, Imprenta del Museo
nacional, 1929. 100 p. il.   **[1977]**

Life and customs of the Mexican mule-
teers, including references to their songs.

**Picazo de Murray, Elena, and Paul V.
Murray.** The charm of Mexico's popular music. *Etude,* v. 55, no. 8 (Aug.
1937), p. 508, 546. il.   **[1978]**

Includes discussion of aboriginal music
and musical instruments.

Plenn, Abel. Mexico's folk music. *Mex.
life,* v. 10, no. 7 (1934), p. 15-16, 43-
44.   **[1979]**

Ponce, Manuel M. El folklore musical
mexicano: lo que se ha hecho, lo que
puede hacerse. *Rev. mus. mex.,* v. 1,
no. 5 (15 Sept. 1919), p. 5-9. **[1980]**

Points out the great influence that folk
music has exerted in the evolution of
modern Mexican music, and upholds the
thesis that Mexican folk song contains
the indispensable elements for constitut-
ing a national artistic music.

Prieto, Guillermo. Memorias de mis
tiempos. París, México, Vda. de C.
Bouret, 1906. 2 v. port. F1232.P94
                                      [1981]

Includes numerous references to folk
songs and dances. Vol. 1 covers the
period from 1828-40, v. 2 from 1840-53.
The author was a prominent Mexican writer (1818-1897).

Quevedo, Francisco. Lírica popular ta-
basqueña; cantares yucatecos; estudios
folklóricos. Tabasco, Talleres del Gobierno constitucionalista, 1916. 111 p.
                                      [1982]

Rodríguez Marín, Francisco. Las pete-
neras. *Rev. mus. mex.,* v. 1, no. 12
(21 June 1942), p. 267-269.   **[1983]**

Deals with origin of the *petenera,* a
type of *cante flamenco* from Andalusia.

Romero, Jesús C. El estudio de nuestra
prehistoria musical, como factor impor-
tantísimo en la especulación folklórica
de México. México, 1928. 16 p.
                                      [1984]

Romero Flores, Jesús. Costumbres típicas de Michoacán. México, Departamento de bellas artes, Sección de música, 1935. 6 p. Mimeographed.
[1985]
Includes references to music and dances.

Secretaría de agricultura y fomento. Dirección de antropología. Poblaciones regionales de la república mexicana. La población del valle de Teotihuacan ... Quinta parte, La población contemporánea. Director de las investigaciones, Manuel Gamio. México, D. F., Talleres gráficos de la Secretaría de educación pública, 1932. 2 v. F1301.M63
[1986]
The "quinta parte" corresponds to Tomo II. Chapter 9, *Folk-lore* (p. 283-418), contains numerous references to folk music and dances. For detailed references to these subjects, consult the index to chapter 9, p. 285-286. See especially section 4, *canto y música* (p. 396-401). Seventeen pages of music inserted between p. 296 and p. 297. Eleven pages of music inserted between p. 300 and p. 301. Illustrations of musical instruments and musicians, facing p. 294. Frontispiece: *Danzantes indígenas* (in color), pastel by F. Goytia. The section on *Literatura popular de carácter religioso* (p. 326-396), which quotes the texts of several *loas* (traditional religious plays), is also of great importance for the study of musical folklore in Mexico.

Teja Zabre, Alfonso. Un ciclo de cultura criolla. México, Música primitiva. *Ruta,* v. 4 (15 Nov. 1938), p. 5-16.
[1987]
From his *Historia y música.*

Tejera, Humberto. Canciones de Zirahuén. *Eurindia,* v. 5, nos. 6-7 (June-July 1934), p. 34-40.
[1988]
Texts of folk songs from Michoacán.

Téllez, Jesús L. The huapango in weddings—El huapango en los casamientos. *Mex. folkways,* v. 7, no. 4 (1932), p. 199-200.
[1989]
Spanish and English text in parallel columns.

——. Huapangos, sones. *Mex. folkways,* v. 7, no. 4 (1932), p. 169-184.
[1990]
Arrangements for voice and piano of *Cielito lindo, La azucena, Los panaderos, La guasanga, El fandanguito, El caimán.* Spanish words with the music, Spanish and English text below.

——. Xochipitzahua. *Mex. folkways,* v. 7, no. 4 (1932), p. 198. **[1991]**
Arrangement for voice and piano of a *son de huapango.* Spanish words with the music, English translation below.

Toor, Frances. Calavera histórico-religiosa. *Mex. folkways,* v. 2, no. 4 (1926), p. 8-11. **[1992]**
Text only.

——. Note on huapangos—Nota sobre los huapangos. *Mex. folkways,* v. 7, no. 4 (1932), p. 168. **[1993]**
Spanish and English text in parallel columns.

Torre, Matilde de la. El canto de la Maya en Pujayo de Iguña. *Rev. mus. mex.,* v. 1, no. 6 (21 Mar. 1942), p. 123-127. **[1994]**
Deals with a folk ceremony as practised in Santander, Spain, and reproduces one tune.

——. Del folklore religioso; notas sobre el villancico y los romances de reyes. *Rev. mus. mex.,* v. 1, no. 3 (7 Feb. 1942), p. 57-60. **[1995]**
Deals with Christmas songs collected in Spain, with 2 tunes.

Toussaint, Manuel. Estudios folklóricos. *Rev. mus. Méx.,* v. 1, no. 3 (15 July 1919), p. 23-25. **[1996]**
First of a series of articles on Hispanic-Mexican folk music. Quotes text of *La canción de Mambrú.*

——. Folklore histórico; la canción de Mambrú. *Rev. mex. estud. hist.,* v. 1 (1927), p. 101-104. **[1997]**
Reprinted in *Arch. folklore cub.,* v. 3 (1928), p. 16-20.

Trabajos técnicos del primer congreso nacional de música y reseña de los concursos musicales organizados por la comisión permanente bajo el patrocinio de la Universidad nacional y El Universal. México, D. F., Talleres Gráficos de la Nación, 1928. 326 p. (Publicaciones de la Secretaría de Educación Pública, v. 19, no. 5). **[1998]**

In section E, *Folklore*, Gerónimo Baqueiro Fóster and Daniel Castañeda discuss "Principios técnicos para el folklore en general".

Vázquez Santa Ana, Higinio, ed. Canciones, cantares y corridos mexicanos. México, Imp. M. León Sánchez, 1926. 274 p. PQ7260.V3 **[1999]**

A few of the songs accompanied by melodies.

――――. Historia de la canción mexicana. Canciones, cantares y corridos. Talleres Gráficos de la Nación, 1931. **[2000]**

See also nos. 1709, 1720, 1723.

(B) CHRISTMAS (POSADAS)

Shambaugh, Mary Effie. Folk festivals for schools and playgrounds; folk dances and melodies... music arranged by Anna Pearl Allison. New York, A. S. Barnes & co., 1932. 155 p. il., diagrs. GV1743.S54 M1450.S4 **[2001]**

"Fiestas of the Spanish and Mexicans in California", p. 31-48, with music for *La Contradansa* and for *La Jota*, arranged for piano by A. Pearl Allison. "A Mexican Christmas", p. 49-57, with music for *La Jesucita* and *La Cucaracha*. "Bibliography on Mexico", p. 58-59.

Tercero, José. Christmas in Mexico. *Bull. pan amer. union*, v. 65, no. 12 (Dec. 1931), p. 1232-1236. **[2002]**

Describes the *posadas*, with music (for piano, with interlinear Spanish text) taken from *Mex. folkways*.

Toledano, Miguel Ríos. Las posadas y la Noche Buena en México. México, H. Nagel sucesores [18—]. 13 p. M1683.T. **[2003]**

A potpourri for voice and piano, and for piano alone, of traditional Mexican Christmas songs.

Toor, Frances. Christmas in Mexico. *Mex. folkways*, v. 2, no. 5 (Dec.-Jan. 1926), p. 31-43. **[2004]**

Description of the posadas, with 8 musical examples (melodies and Spanish words).

――――. Neighborhood Christmas in Mexico City. *Mex. folkways*, v. 1, no. 4 (1925), p. 16-21 (Spanish translation, p. 18-19). **[2005]**

A description of the "Posadas", with music (voice and piano) for the verses sung "To receive the Holy Family", p. 21.

See also nos. 1920, 2073, 2491.

(C) BALLADS (CORRIDOS)

Bal y Gay, Jesús. Romance y corrido. *Bol. inst. musicología*, v. 1, no. 1 (1940), p. 5-9. **[2006]**

This is a commentary, by a Spanish musicologist now living in Mexico, on Mendoza's highly important book, *El romance español y el corrido mexicano* [item no. 2023]. The author attempts mainly to clarify the terminology of the various types of narrative poetry whose most representative forms are the Spanish *romance* and the Mexican *corrido*. He finds that such terms as *coplas, relaciones, tratado, ejemplos,* and *tragedias* were arbitrarily applied at various times to compositions of the *romance* type, and he thinks that Mendoza has not entirely cleared up this confusion of terminology.

Brenner, Anita. Mexican ballads. *Mex. folkways*, v. 1, no. 5 (Feb.-Mar. 1926), p. 11-13. **[2007]**

Spanish translation of this article, p. 13-14. Includes some of the words and music of two songs, *La Polla* and *Zihualteco de mi vida*. English and Spanish words of the *corrido*, *The Death of Felipe Carrillo Puerto*, martyr of Yucatán, follow the article.

Canales, María. Corrido del Bajío. *Mex. folkways*, v. 2, no. 5 (1926), p. 30. **[2008]**

Text (Spanish only) of a ballad.

Chávez Orozco, Luis. El romance en México. *Contemporáneos* (June 1930), p. 266-267. **[2009]**

Díaz, E. El corrido de Octaviano Méndez y Juan Higuera. *Letras*, suplemento, no. 3 (1934), p. 45-53. **[2010]**

Disselhoff, Hans Lietrich. Zwei mexikanische corridos aus Colima. *Iberoamer. archiv.*, v. 11 (1937), p. 98-106. **[2011]**
Text and commentary.

Duvalier, Vauquelin. Romance y corrido. *Crisol*, ép. 3 ,no. 84 (June 1937), p. 37-43. **[2012]**
A literary study of the ballad, with textual examples.

Las esperanzas de la patria por la rendición de Villa. *Mex. folkways*, v. 3. no. 2 (1927), p. 70-76. **[2013]**
These pages include both English and Spanish versions of this *corrido*, and illustrations.

González Casanova, Pablo. Un corrido "macarrónico" hispano-azteca. *Investig. ling.*, v. 2 (1934), p. 20-23. (Reprint from *An. museo nac. arqueol. hist. etnol.*, ép. 4, v. 8 (1933), p. 93-96). **[2014]**
A ballad with a mixture of Aztec words and phrases in the Spanish verses.

Guerrero, Eduardo. Corridos de amor y canciones sentimentales del pueblo mexicano. México, 1931. **[2015]**

——. Corridos históricos de la Revolución mexicana desde 1910 a 1930 y otros notables de varias épocas. México, 1931. **[2016]**

Gutiérrez Cruz, Carlos. El 30-30, corrido of the agraristas. *Mex. folkways*, v. 3, no. 4 (1927), p. 188-190. **[2017]**
Melody of a political ballad, with Spanish and English text.

Enríquez Ureña, Pedro, and Bertram D. Wolfe. Romances tradicionales en Méjico. *In* Homenaje ofrecido a Menéndez Pidal, Madrid, 1925, v. 2, p. 375-390. PC14.M4. **[2017x]**
Contains the texts of several traditional Spanish ballads (*romances*) found in Mexico, also the text of a Mexican ballad (*corrido*) entitled *Corrido de doña Elena*, which Henríquez Ureña believes shows Spanish traditional influences. There are comparative bibliographical notes.

Herrera Frimont, Celestino. Los corridos y la Revolución. *El libro y el pueblo*, v. 12 (1934), p. 326-335. **[2018]**

Mendizábal, Miguel O. de. Las montañas principales. *Mex. folkways*, v. 1, no. 1 (1925), p. 5. **[2019]**
Text of ballad recorded in Guayameso, district of Mina, State of Guerrero.

Mendoza, Vicente T. El corrido en México. *Universidad*, v. 3, no. 15 (1937), p. 28-33. **[2020]**

——. Un ejemplo de romance de relación en México. El casamiento del Huitlacoche. *An. inst. invest. est.*, v. 1, no. 1 (1937), p. 15-27. **[2021]**
This Mexican ballad is compared with two traditional ballads from Spain.

——. El romance de las señas del esposo. *Boletín de la asociación folklórica argentina*, v. 3, no. 1-2 (1940), p.10-14. **[2022]**
Deals with a traditional Spanish ballad widely distributed in Latin America.

——. El romance español y el corrido mexicano; estudio comparativo. México, Ediciones de la Universidad Nacional autónoma, 1939. 832 p. il. ML3570. M36R5. **[2023]**
Most of the "Romances" p. 235-419) and "Corridos" (p. 423-782) are accompanied by melodies. "Lista de romances impresos en México durante la época colonial": p. 783-785. "Lista de corridos que no aparecen en esta obra": p. 786-792. "Bibliografía": p. 793-799. A fundamental work.

Moreno, Delfino C. El bandido Agustín

Lorenzo. *Mex. folkways,* v. 5 (1929), p. 86-88. **[2024]**

Quotes part of a ballad dealing with the exploits of this bandit.

Munguía, Enrique. Corrido de la muerte de Emilio Carranza. *Mex. folkways,* v. 4 (1928), p. 130-132. **[2025]**

Text of a modern corrido.

———. Trágica muerte del general Obregón. *Mex. folkways,* v. 4 (1928), p. 116-118. **[2026]**

Text of a modern corrido.

Novo, Salvador. Literatura del pueblo. *Mex. folkways,* v. 5 (1929), p. 132-145. **[2027]**

Deals with the corrido and gives the text of *La amiga de Bernal Francés* and *Corrido de doña Elena.*

Pérez Martínez, Héctor. Trayectoria del corrido. México, 1935. 99 p. PQ2760.94. **[2028]**

Music, p. 36.

Porter, Katherine Anne. Corridos. *Survey,* I. 52, no. 3 (1 May 1924), p. 157-159. **[2029]**

Deals with the character and history of the *corrido,* names several popular *corrido* heroes of the revolution, and relates the story of the *corrido, Marbella and the newly-born,* p. 159.

Toor, Frances. Corrido que cantan los presos de la cárcel de San Juan de los Lagos. La maquinita. *Mex. folkways,* v. 1, no. 5 (1926), p. 27-28 **[2030]**

Text of a prison ballad.

———. La Gran Calavera de Emiliano Zapata. *Mex. folkways,* v. 1, no. 3 (1925), p. 22. **[2031]**

Spanish text of a well-known corrido.

———. Triste despedida de Emiliano Zapata. *Mex. folkways, v.* 6 (1930), p. 197-200. **[2032]**

Text only of this corrido.

Whatley, W. A. A Mexican popular ballad. *In* Publications of the Texas folklore society, no. 4 (1925), p. 10-17. GR1.T4. **[2033]**

Contains the words (Spanish, with English translation) of a bandit ballad, with the melody and guitar accompaniment.

Wood, Ben D. A Mexican border ballad. *In* Publications of the Texas folklore society, no. 1 (1916), p. 55-57. GR1.-T4 **[2034]**

Text of a Mexican song taken from a broadside found in Laredo, Texas.

(D) COLLECTIONS OF MUSIC

Album "México". México, D. F., A. Wagner y Levien sucs., 1933. M1682.-A34 **[2035]**

Arrangements or compositions in traditional forms by modern composers. Ten numbers for voice and piano, 2 for piano solo.

Arista, A. S. Canciones mexicanas. 2d. ed. Buenos Aires, Ed. Fidelio [192?]. 20 p. **[2036]**

Arranged for piano with superlinear Spanish words.

Arzoz, P. Colección de cantos sagrados populares. Tlalpan, D. F., Tip. del asilo "Patricio Sanz", 1911. **[2037]**

Cited by Boggs, *Bibliografía del folklore mexicano,* p. 49.

Berggreen, Andreas Peter. Folkesange og melodier, faedrelandske og fremmede. Copenhagen, A. C. Reitzeis forlag, 1869-71. 11 v. M1627.B49 **[2038]**

Vol. 10 contains 2 Nicaraguan folk songs arranged for piano (nos. 105-106); also 6 Mexican folk songs (nos. 99-104)

Bernal, Gregorio. Aires populares. México, 1895. **[2039]**

Cited by Boggs, *Bibliografía del folklore mexicano,* p. 50.

Bertman, Julio. Brisas mexicanas. 21 Mexican folk songs freely arranged. For voice without accompaniment. In Ms., typewritten text. M1682.B54. **[2040]**

Botsford, Florence Hudson, comp. Botsford collection of folk-songs, with English versions by American poets. New York, G. Schirmer, inc., 1930-33. 3 v. Published 1921-22 under title: Folk songs of many peoples. M1627.B72 1930. **[2041]**

"Songs from Latin America", v. 1, p. 72-106, contains ten Mexican songs.

Cabello, Fernando. Mexican music Spanish music. El Paso, Texas, International music publishing co., 1929. M-1682.C15N3 **[2042]**

"12 new popular songs with Spanish words". For voice with piano.

Campos, Rubén M. El folklore y la música mexicana. México, D. F., Talleres gráficos de la nación, 1928. 351 p. il. (Publicaciones de la Secretaría de educación pública). ML3570.C2 **[2043]**

The appendix includes the music of 100 *sones, jarabes* and songs from the musical folklore of Mexico (for piano, some with interlinear text). The main body of the text also includes 20 musical examples.

Canciones mexicanas. Colección Carmen García Cornejo. New York, Mexican song publishing co., 1919. 20 v. M16-82.C2 **[2044]**

Contains 20 songs in separate sheet form. Music arranged by Guillermo Posadas.

Collection of Mexican music. Vocal. Instrumental. 21 little songs of the country. Boston, Oliver Ditson & co., 1866. 17 p. M1682.C7D4 **[2045]**

Songs with piano accompaniment. English and Spanish text.

Domínguez, Francisco. Album musical de Michoacán. Melodías recopiladas, armonizadas y transcritas para piano y canto y piano solo. México, D. F., Secretaría de educación pública, 1941. **[2046]**

The *Notas preliminarias* (1 page) give data on the background of these songs, and there is an additional note (1 page) on the antecedents of *Las Canacuas*.

——. Sones, canciones y corridos michoacanos. México, Talleres gráficos de la nación [192-?]. 24 p. (Edición de la Secretaría de educación pública, Departamento de bellas artes). **[2047]**

Ten folk songs from the state of Michoacán, arranged for piano and voice and piano solo.

Flores y Parra, José. Colección de 12 canciones mexicanas populares, México, A. Wagner Y. Levien sucs., n. d. M1682.F67 **[2048]**

12 Mexican folk songs, arranged for piano solo and for voice and piano.

Hague, Eleanor. Mexican folk songs. *Jour. amer. folklore,* v. 25, no. 117 (July-Sept. 1912), p. 261-267. **[2049]**

Contains the words (Spanish only) and melodies of 8 songs, and 2 tunes without words.

Hurtado G., Nabor. Sones, canciones y corridos de Nayarit. México, Departamento de enseñanza agrícola y normal rural, Secretaría de educación pública, 1935. 25 p. Mimeographed. **[2050]**

Words, music and commentary.

Iñurreta, José Luis. Una docena de sones tabasqueños; motivos de folklore nacional. México, Editorial moderna, 1938. 46 p. **[2051]**

La Forge, Frank, arr. Mexican songs for voice and piano. New York, (G. Ricordi & co., 1922-1926. 6 v. M1683.L **[2052]**

Luce, Allena, ed. Canciones populares. Boston, etc., Silver, Burdett & co., 1921. 138 p. M1681.P6L9 **[2053]**

Section 2: 12 songs of Cuba, Spain, and Mexico.

Manney, Charles Fonteyn. Mexican and Spanish songs. The English texts by Frederick H. Martens. With piano accompaniments. Boston, Oliver Ditson co., 1928. 43 p. M1682.M28M3. **[2054]**

Martínez, José de J. Canciones mexicanas. México, E. Munguía, 1916. 2 v. M1683.M **[2055]**

Includes *Valentina, La cucaracha, Adelita, Bonitas las tapatías.*

Michel, Concha. Corridos revolucionarios. n. i. [México?], 1938. 13 p. **[2056]**

Cited by Boggs, Bibliografía del folklore mexicano, p. 62, Contains words (in Spanish) and music of 6 corridos: *El niño proletario, Los agraristas, Ley proletaria, Unión, Gocen de su abril y mayo, Lo que digo lo sostengo.*

Primer album de música indígena. México, Departamento de asuntos indígenas, 1940. Mimeographed. **[2057]**

Songs and dances collected among the Aztec and Otomi Indians.

El ruiseñor mexicano (Colección de canciones populares). San Antonio, Texas, Casa editorial Lozano, 1924. **[2058]**

Saldívar, Gabriel. El jarabe, baile popular mexicano; prólogo de Manuel M. Ponce. México, Talleres gráficos de la nación, 1937. 22 pp. 15 pl. (incl. facsims, music). ML370-S18J3 **[2059]**

Includes the music of 15 *jarabes* reproduced from the collection of Toledano [no. 2065].

Sandburg, Carl. The American songbag. New York, Harcourt, Brace & co., 1927. 495 p. il. M1629.S213A5 **[2060]**

Includes 7 "Mexican border songs", p. 289-304, comprising *La cucaracha, Mañanitas, Lo que digo, El abandonado, Cielito lindo, Adelita, Versos de Montalgo.* For voice and piano. All songs except *Cielito lindo* have Spanish words and English translations.

Secretaría de educación pública, sección de música. Mexican folk music. México, D. F. Mimeographed. **[2061]**

37 songs (corridos, etc.) for voice and piano.

Spizzy, Mabel Seeds. The Mabel Spizzy collection of Mexican songs. Santa Ana,

Calif., 1936. 48 p. Mimeographed. M1682.S **[2062]**

Includes music and choreographic directions for 2 dances.

Téllez, Jesús L. Huapangos, sones. *Mex. folkways,* v. 1, no. 4 (1932), p. 169-184. **[2063]**

Arrangements for voice and piano of *Cielito lindo, La Azucena, Los panaderos, La guasanga, El fandanguito, El caimán.* Spanish words with the music, Spanish and English text below.

Téllez Girón, Roberto. La sierra norte de Puebla. *Bol. inst. musicol.,* v. 1, no. 1 (Jan. 1940), p. 35-66. **[2064]**

Includes 39 folk tunes collected in the States of Puebla and Veracruz, with analytical and descriptive commentary.

Toledano, Miguel Ríos. Al pueblo mexicano. Única y auténtica colección de treinta jarabes, sones principales y más populares aires nacionales. México, H. Nagel sucres. [18-]. 84 p. M1683.T **[2065]**

One of the earliest and most famous collections of Mexican traditional music Arranged for voice and piano.

Toor, Frances. Cancionero mexicano de Mexican folkways. Arreglos para piano o guitarra por Graciela Amador y Angel E. Salas. México, 1931. 36 p. **[2066]**

Contains 18 songs grouped under the following headings; Corridos; Canciones de amor; Sones; Canciones revolucionarias. Spanish words only.

——. Canciones populares. *Mex. folkways,* v. 2, no. 2 (1926), p. 23-30. **[2067]**

Words and music of various folk songs.

——. El jarabe. *Mex. folkways,* v. 6 (1930), p. 4-37. **[2068]**

Includes words and music of 30 jarabes.

——. Nuestro número de canciones (our song number). *Mex. folkways,* v. 3, no. 2 (1927), p. 78-108. il. **[2069]**

The introductory section (p. 78-85) has

the Spanish and English texts in parallel columns. This is followed by 12 songs with music (for piano with interlinear text). With one exception, these have Spanish text only.

El trovador mexicano (La colección más completa de canciones populares). San Antonio, Texas, Librería de Quiroga.   **[2070]**

Urquieta, Felipe. 21 sonecitos del país, arreglados para piano y canto ó piano solo. México, A. Wagner y Levien sucs. [191-?]. 11 p.   **[2071]**

Music for piano, with interlinear Spanish words.

Vázquez Santa Ana, Higinio. Sones, corridos y canciones para canto y piano. [Printed in México, D. F., n. d.]   **[2072]**

Ten anonymous songs, arranged for voice and piano (Spanish text only).

Wagner, Max L. Algunas apuntaciones sobre el folklore mexicano. *Jour. amer. folklore,* v. 40, no. 156 (1927), p. 105-143.   **[2073]**

Includes the melodies and words (Spanish only; 2 tunes have no text) of 23 sones colected in 1914 in the State of Veracruz, also the words of 22 songs collected in Córdoba, and of 3 songs originating in Cuauhtlixco (Morelos); also the music of a *posada.*

Xavier Cugat's favorite collection of tangos and rhumbas, including Mexican and Spanish songs and dances. New York, Robbins music corp., 1936. 80 p. il.   **[2074]**

Includes *Jarabe tapatío, La cucaracha, La golondrina* and *La paloma.*

(E) COLLECTIONS OF TEXTS

Boas, Franz. Notes on Mexican folklore. *Jour. amer. folklore,* v. 25 (1912), p. 204-260.   **[2075]**

Includes text of 20 folk songs (in Spanish).

Guerrero, Eduardo. Canciones y corri-

dos populares. v. 1. México, Impr. Guerrero, 1924.   **[2076]**

A collection of 230 loose sheets bound together in 1 volume. Cited by Boggs, *Bibliografía del folklore mexicano,* p. 56.

Herrera Frimont, Celestino, ed. Corridos de la revolución. Pachuca, Hgo., Instituto científico y literario, 1934. 169 p. PQ7260.H4   **[2077]**

Music: p. 165-169. A collection of ballad texts, with a musical supplement of 3 tunes arranged for piano.

Pardo, Ramón. Poesía de los negros oaxaqueños. *Mex. folkways,* v. 4 (1928), p. 28-30.   **[2078]**

Pérez Martínez, Héctor. Diez corridos mexicanos. México, Publicaciones del Departamento de bibliotecas de la Secretaría de educación pública, 1935. 64 p. (Biblioteca del obrero y campesino, v. 9).   **[2079]**

Cited by Boggs, *Bibliografía del folklore mexicano,* p. 64. Modern political ballads.

P. G. C. Nanas o coplas de cuna. *Ethnos,* ép. 1, v .1 (1920-22), p. 88-93.   **[2080]**

Text of cradle songs.

Prieto, Guillermo. Musa callejera; poesías festivas nacionales. México, D. F., Tip. literaria de F. Mata, 1883, 3 v. in 1. (Biblioteca de autores mexicanos). PQ7297.P8M8   **[2081]**

——. El romancero nacional. México, D. F., Oficina tipográfica de la Secretaría de fomento, 1885.   **[2082]**

Silva y Aceves, M. La colección folklórica de la biblioteca del museo nacional *An. museo nac. arqueol. hist. etnol.,* ép. 4, v. 3 (1925), p. 269-320. **[2083]**

The collection includes broadsides of *corridos, aguinaldos,* etc.

(F) DANCES

Adán, Elfego. Las danzas de Coatetelco. *An. museo nac. arqueol. hist. etnol.,*

v. 2, nos. 3-5 (1910), p. 133-194. 7 plates. **[2084]**

Describes indigenous dances, *Las contradanzas, Los vaqueros, Los moros* and *Los tecuanes,* with 48 brief tunes. "Comparaciones de las danzas presentes con las danzas religiosas de los Aztecas" (p. 191-194).

Alcaraz, Angela. The canacuas. *Mex. folkways,* v. 6 (1930), p. 117-118. **[2085]**
The music of a Mexican folk dance.

Álvarez de Toledo, Federico C. Danzas primitivas de los indios mejicanos. *La nación,* no. 23,022 (8 Sept. 1935), sec. 3, p. 3. **[2086]**

Amador, Graciela. Danzas rituales mejicanas. *Mercurio mus.,* v. 7 (May (1938), p. 22, 23. **[2087]**

Basauri, Carlos. Creencias y prácticas de los Tarahumaras. Beliefs and practices of the Tarahumaras. *Mex. folkways,* v. 3, no. 4 (Aug.-Sept. 1927), p. 218-234. **[2088]**
English and Spanish text in parallel columns. Descriptions of Mexican folk dances, with music.

Brasseur de Bourbourg, Charles Étienne. Histoire des nations civilisées du Méxique et de l'Amérique-centrale. Paris, Arthus Bertrand, 1857. 4 v. F12-19.B82 **[2089]**
Vol. 1 includes: Yucatán Indians' dance of the sacred tapir. Vol. 2: Mayan dances and ballet, p. 64-67. Vol. 3, p. 498-540, contains numerous brief references to dances in festivals; Mexican dances, p. 665, 670.

Breton, Adela C. Survival of ceremonial dances among Mexican Indians. *In* Compte rendu du Congrès international des Américanistes, v. 16, Vienna, 1908, p. 531-520. il. **[2090]**
Photographs and descriptions of the performance of the *Volador,* as well as brief notes on other dances.

Brewster, Mela Sedillo. Mexican and New Mexican folk-dances. n. p., 1937.

50 p. il. Mimeographed. MT950.B84M3 **[2091]**
With the music for the New Mexican dances. Includes detailed dancing directions and costume sketches.

Campobello, Nellie and Gloria. Ritmos indígenas de México. México, D. F., 1940. 246 p. il. **[2092]**
A detailed study of the choreographic elements of Indian art in Mexico, with numerous figure drawings and rhythm notations.

Campos, Rubén M. Las danzas. *Nuestro México,* v. 1 (Apr. 1932), p. 25. **[2093]**

——. Las danzas aztecas. *Gaceta mus.,* v. 1, no. 2 (Feb. 1928), p. 8-14; v. 1, no. 3 (Mar. 1928), p. 19-24. **[2094]**
Reproduced from *El folklore y la música mexicana* [no. 1919].
Gives text of two Nahoa dance songs. Includes two tunes,

Coester, Alfred. The "danza de los conquistadores" at Chichicastenango. *Hispania,* v. 24, no. 1 (Feb. 1941), p. 95-100. **[2095]**
Interesting for a comparison of the same dance in Mexico.

Commenda, Hans. Der bandltanz in alt-Mexiko. *Das deutsche volkslied,* v. 32 (1930), p. 70-71. **[2096]**

Cordero, Juan N. La música razonada. Vol. V. Estética teórica y aplicada. México, D. F., La Europea, 1897. 278 p. **[2097]**
Part 2, section 4, *Formas típicas,* includes an analysis of the *danzón* and the *jarabe.*

Dalton, Vane C. Folk dances in Mexico, *Bull. pan am. union,* v. 73, no. 2 (Feb. 1939), p. 96-99. **[2098]**
Includes music of the *jarabe.* This article was reprinted in *Modern Mexico* (Apr. 1939), p. 17-20.

La danza del venadito. *Nuestro México,* v. 1 (Mar. 1932), p. 27-29, 74-77. il. **[2099]**

Delza, Sophia. The dance in Mexico. *New theatre,* v. 3, no. 1 (Jan. 1936), p. 26-28. il.   **[2100]**

Departamento de Asuntos Indígenas. Primer álbum de música indígena. México, D. F., 1940. Reproduced from type-written copy.   **[2101]**

Part 1: Recopilación del prof. Santiago Arias Navarro, realizada durante sus jiras de inspección y estudio en los Estados de S. Luis Potosí y Zacatecas (razas: Azteca y Otomí). Description of the dance *Los Indios,* from the state of Zacatecas, with choreographic diagrams. Music of various *sones.*

Part 2: Recopilación del prof. Arturo Flores Quintana. Región Tarahumara, Estado de Chihuahua. Choreography of Indian dances.

Domínguez, Francisco. Canacuas, danza antigua de Guaris. *Mex. folkways,* v. 6, no. 3 (1930), p. 110-116. il. **[2102]**

Etchings of native dances by Magdalena Casa Madrid. *Mex. life,* v. 16 no. 11 (1940), p. 26-28.   **[2103]**

Fergusson, Erna. Fiesta in Mexico. New York, A. A. Knopf, 1934. 267 p. il. F1215.F34   **[2104]**

Includes impressionistic descriptions of Mexican dances, with brief references to music.

Fernández, Justino. Danzas de los concheros en San Miguel de Allende; estudio histórico, costumbrista, coreográfico de Justino Fernández; recolección y estudio de textos musicales de Vicente T. Mendoza; con ocho estampas de Antonio Rodríguez Luna. México, El Colegio de México, 1941. 49 p. il. GV1627.F4   **[2105]**

This is an admirably illustrated volume, containing, besides descriptions of the dances and costumes, many musical examples, and sketches, as well as textual explanation of the choreography of the most important dances. There is background material on these Mexican festivals, and a section devoted entirely to the music used therein. *Bibliografía,* p. 42.

Fernández Ledesma, Gabriel. Five folkloric dances. *Mexican art and life* (Apr. 1939), p. 16-19. il.   **[2106]**

Folk dances in Mexico. *Bull. pan amer. union,* v. 73, no. 2 (Feb. 1939), p. 96-99. (Repr. from *Mex. Art and Life*).   **[2107]**

Includes music for the *jarabe,* for piano, with superlinear Spanish text.

Galindo, Miguel. Nociones de historia de la música mejicana. Colima, Tip. de "El Dragón", 1933. 636 p. il. ML210.G3N6   **[2108]**

This work contains about 30 brief musical examples (folk tunes and Indian melodies), and a complete description of the *Volador* dance. The author also discusses other indigenous dances of Mexico (p. 113-118), quoting 4 typical rhythms. After an extensive discussion of 16th-century Spanish music and dances in their relation to the music and dancing of the New World, he deals with the development of the principal Mexican dances, devoting special attention to the subject in the chapter on *La música bailable y el canto popular* (p. 551-579). There are musical examples of the *jarabe* and other Mexican folk dances.

Gallop, Rodney. Aerial dances of the Otomis. *Geographical magazine,* v. 4 (Edinburgh, 1936), p. 73-88. il.   **[2109]**

———. Indian drums in Mexico. *Month. mus. record,* v. 68, no. 797 (June 1938), p. 134-138.   **[2110]**

Contains a good description of the *juego de los voladores,* the flying game, as practised by the Otomi Indians of southern Mexico.

Génin, Auguste. The ancient and modern dances of Mexico. *Mex. mag.,* v. 3 (1927), p. 7-33. il.   **[2111]**

González, Carlos. The dance of the *sonaja,* or of the *señor. Mex. folkways,* v. 1, no. 2 (Aug.-Sept. 1925), p. 13-14.   **[2112]**

This is one of the various dances dramatizing the conflict between Christians and infidels. Spanish translation, p. 15.

Guzmán, M. E. El origen de la "zandunga" no es oaxaqueño, sino chiapaneco. *El Universal* (19 Sept. 1937). **[2113]**

Hague, Eleanor. Five danzas from Mexico. *Jour. amer. folklore,* v. 28, no. 110 (Lancaster, Pa., 1915), p. 382-389. **[2114]**
Includes 5 tunes, unharmonized, with Spanish words and English translation.

———. Five Mexican dances. *Jour. amer. folklore,* v. 28, no. 110 (1915), p. 379-381. **[2115]**
Includes 5 tunes.

Harnoncourt, René d'. The fiesta as a work of art. *In* Herring, Hubert C., and Herbert Weinstock, *eds.,* Renascent Mexico, New York, 1935. F1208.-H57 **[2116]**
Includes references to folk dances.

Helfritz, H. Der tanz der voladores. *Atlantis,* v. 11 (1939), p. 246-249. **[2117]**

Herrera Frimont, Humberto. Las danzas típicas de Guerrero. *Letras* (14 Nov. 1937), p. 4. **[2118]**

Infanzón Garrido, Aquileo. El origen de la zandunga. *Neza,* v. 2, no. 13 (June 1936), p. 2. **[2119]**
The author states that this tune was formerly known as *El Quirio* in the State of Chiapas.

Jiménez, Guillermo. The dance in Mexico. *Bull. pan amer. union,* v. 75, no. 6 (June 1941), p. 317-324. il. **[2120]**
Deals chiefly with Indian dances.

———. La danse au Méxique, *Rev. Amér. lat.,* v. 22, no. 120 (1931), p. 489-491; v. 21, 1-3 (1931), p. 343-346. **[2121]**

———. La danza en México. *El libro de la cultura,* v. 4 (Barcelona, 1936), p. 376-392. **[2122]**

Johnston, Edith. Regional dances of Mexico. Dallas, B. Upshaw and co.,

1935. 78 p. il. GV1627.J6 MT950.J6R4 **[2123]**
Includes music with words.

La Farge, Oliver, and Douglas Byers. The year bearer's people. New Orleans, Tulane university, Department of middle American research, 1931. 397 p. F1421.T95 no. 3 **[2124]**
Music, p. 67-68, 97; marimbas, p. 110; dances, p. 99-111, with several photographs and charts; special reference to the marimba dance and the use of that instrument in this and other dances; picture of musical instruments, p. 65; musical instruments, p. 67-68 (only men make and play the instruments).

Landenberger, Emil. Wanderjahre in Mexiko. Leipzig, F. A. Brockhaus, 1925. 304 p. F1215.L24 **[2125]**
Tanzfeste der Yaquis, p. 244-257, choreography, description of dances and musical instruments.

Menéndez, Miguel Ángel. La música y las danzas entre Coras y Huicholes. *Rev. mus. mex.,* v. 1, no. 1 (7 Jan. 1942), p. 17-19. **[2126]**
A novelist writes impressionistically about the songs and dances of the Mexican Indians, quoting text of an Indian song. *Las pachitas.*

Mishnun, Virginia. The dances of Mexico. *The Nation,* v. 150, no. 4 (27 Jan. 1940), p. 107-109. **[2127]**
Descriptions of various dances—*volador, Moors and Christians, King's dance, huapango;* discussion of the influences on Mexican dances.

———. Las danzas de México. *Romance,* v. 1 (1 June 1940), p. 15. **[2128]**
Discusses the *danzón,* the *volador,* "moros y cristianos" and other Mexican dances of Spanish origin.

Montes de Oca, José G. Danzas indígenas mexicanas. Tlaxcala, México, Imprenta de Gobierno del Estado, 1926. 44 p. il. **[2129]**

———. El jarabe tapatío. *Quetzalcoatl,* v. 1, no. 2 (May 1929), p. 10-14. **[2130]**

———. Mirador. México-Tenochtitlán, Imprenta moderna, 1936. 2 v. **[2131]**

Includes references to *El jarabe tapatío* and *Las mañanitas.*

Mullican, Hazel Armstrong, and Bennie Warren. A pageant of the Americas. Dallas, Tardy publishing co., 1935. 34 p. il. E19.M85 MT950.M96P3 **[2132]**

"A ... program for Pan American day." —Pref. Includes music and dance patterns for the *jarabe tapatío.*

Núñez y Domínguez, José de J. Los huapangos. *Mex. folkways,* v. 7, no. 4 (1932), p. 185-197. il. **[2133]**

Spanish and English text in parallel columns. Detailed description of these popular dances.

Ontañón, Eduardo de. Ballet mexicano. *Hoy* (28 Sept. 1940), p. 43-47. **[2134]**

Ricard, Robert. Contribution à l'étude des fêtes de *moros y cristianos* au Méxique. *Jour. soc. amér.,* n. s., v. 24 (1932), p. 51-84. **[2135]**

Detailed account of this festival in the Teotihuacán valley, with quotations from the text (Spanish).

Rivas, Guillermo. A pictorial record of the Mexican fiesta. *Mex. life.* v. 10, no. 11 (Nov. 1934), p. 25-27. **[2136]**

Five illustrations of Mexican folk dances by the Mexican artist Miguel Alonso Machado: *Dance of Jicaras, dance of old men, dance of the deer* and *los matachines.*

Saavedra, R. M. Danzas indias mexicanas: los negritos. *El libro y el pueblo,* v. 12 (1934), p. 379-385. **[2137]**

Saldívar, Gabriel. Las danzas mexicanas. *Nuestro México,* v. 1 (1932), p 17-24. **[2138]**

Saravia, Emma. Colorful dresses for a colorful country. *Modern Mexico,* v. 7, no. 4 (Sept. 1935), p. 7, 24. il. **[2139]**

Describes the costume of the *china,* which is worn by the woman in Mexico's national dance, the jarabe, to which passing reference is made.

Schwendener, Norma, and Averil Tibbels. Legends & dances of Old Mexico. New York, A. S. Barnes and co., 1934. 111 p. il. GV1627.S35 MT950.S38 **[2140]**

Includes music. "The dances are of the Mexican Spanish and Mexican Indian types."

Solorzano, Armando, and Raul G. Guerrero. Ensayo para un estudio sobre la "Danza de los Concheros de la Gran Tenochtitlán". *Bol. lat. am. mús.,* v. 5 (Oct. 1941), p. 449-476. **[2141]**

Spratling, William. Little Mexico. New York, J. Cape & H. Smith, 1932. 198 p. il. ports. F1215.S74 **[2142]**

Fiesta Mexicana, p. 68-85, a chapter describing Mexican dances, and giving a brief history of them.

Starr, Frederick. Popular celebrations in Mexico. *Jour. amer. folklore,* v. 9 (1936), p. 161-169. **[2143]**

Includes description of Mexican dances.

———. The tastoanes. *Jour. amer. folklore,* v. 15, no. 57 (Apr.-June 1902), p. 73-83. il. **[2144]**

Description of this popular drama, which reveals a mixture of Spanish and Aztec elements. Both the play itself and the masked dancers who participate in it are called *Los Tastoanes* (the term is of Aztec origin). Cf. an article by the same author in *Outlook* for 18 Jan. 1896.

Toor, Frances. Mexican folk dances. *In* Herring, Hubert C., and Herbert Weinstock, *eds.,* Renascent Mexico, New York, 1935. F1208.H57 **[2145]**

Toro, Alfonso. The "Morismas"—the Indian dances of the Moors and Christians. *Mex. folkways,* v. 1, no. 2 (Aug.-Sept. 1925), p. 8-9 (Spanish translation, p. 10). **[2146]**

This is a dramatic dance depicting battles between the Moors and Christians, obviously of very old Spanish origin. The author writes with special reference to the

"Morisma" of Zacatecas, celebrated annually in honor of St. John the Baptist. "The festival, which is a real sham battle, lasts three days or longer."

Torres Quintero, Gregorio. Fiestas y costumbres aztecas. México, Herrero hermanos sucesores, 1927. 232 p. il. 11 col. pl. F1219.T695 **[2147]**

"La danza entre los Aztecas", p. 21-26.

Vasconcelos, José. La zandunga. *Neza,* v. 2, no. 12 (May 1936) p. 1, 5. **[2148]**

Vázquez Santa Ana, Higinio, and J. Ignacio Dávila Garibi. El carnaval. México, Talleres Gráficos de la Nación, 1931. 134 p. il. GT4214.V3 **[2149]**

Very little mention of music, many references to dances.

———. La danza de los concheros. *Rev. nac. turismo,* 1. 2 (Jan. 1931), p. 11-13, 53-56. il. **[2150]**

See also nos. 1334, 1698, 1702, 1711, 1723, 1726, 1727, 1730, 1731, 1733, 1734, 1736, 1907, 1908, 1911, 1914, 1917, 1919, 1941, 1950, 1952, 1981, 1985, 1986, 1989, 1993, 2059.

AMERINDIAN

(A) PRE-COLUMBIAN

1. *Music and Dance*

Baqueiro Fóster, Gerónimo. El secreto armónico y modal do un antiguo aire maya. *Rev. mus. mex.,* no. 1 (7 Jan. 1942), p. 11-16. **[2151]**

With music of "Canto de los Xtoles". p. 16. First published in *Los Mayas antiguos* by César Lizardi Ramos (1941).

Biart, Lucien. The Aztecs; their history, manners and customs. Tr. by J. L. Garner. Chicago, A. C. McClurg and co., 1887. 343 p. il. F1219.B57. **[2152]**

References to music, p. 304-305. The 5th edition of this work appeared in 1905. This is a translation of item no. 2153.

———. Les Aztèques; histoire, moeurs, coutumes. Paris, **A.** Hennuyer, 1885. 304 p. il. F1219.B56 **[2153]**

Brief references to music, p. 230.

———. Games of the Aztecs. *Mex. mag.,* v. 2, no. 1 (June 1926), p. 8-10, 34-35. il. **[2154]**

Includes a description and an illustration of the dance or game of the *volador.*

Campos, Rubén M. Las fuentes del folklore mexicano. *Rev. mus. Méx.,* v. 1, no. 1 (15 May 1919), p. 18-23. **[2155]**

Deals with traditional background of Aztec music and attempts a historical reproduction of the Feast of Macuilxochitl, god of music. Upholds the thesis that the spirit of Aztec poetry and music survives in the folk song of Mexico, having blended with the music of medieval Spain. Quotes texts of various Mexican folk songs.

Gann, Thomas William Francis, and J. Eric Thompson. The history of the Maya from the earliest times to the present day. New York, C. Scribner's sons, 1931. 264 p. il. F1435.G175. **[2156]**

Reference to music, p. 184, and to musical instruments, p. 231.

Génin, Auguste. The arts and fashions of ancient Mexico. *Mex. mag.,* v. 2, no. 3 (Aug. 1926), p. 7-28. **[2157]**

Includes a section on ornaments worn by nobles in their religious dances.

———. Notes on the dances, music, and songs of the ancient and modern Mexicans *In* Smithsoman institution. Annual report, 1920. Washington, 1922, p. 657-677. Q11.S66 1920. ML3415.G33 **[2158]**

"Translated ... from the *Revue d'ethnographie et de sociologie,* 1913."

Guzmán, Eulalia. Caracteres esenciales del arte antiguo mexicano. *Univ. Méx.,* v. 5, nos. 27-28 (Jan.-Feb. 1933), p. 117-155; v. 5, nos. 29-30 (Mar.-Apr. 1933), p. 408-429. **[2159]**

Music and dance as a most important part in consistent rhythm and repetition of motif in art, p. 133-135; dance as the most beautifully and peculiarly stylized form of indigenous art, p. 153-154; dance in symbolism, p. 416; magic religious consciousness in music, song, and dance, p. 417-418, 420.

Hubbard, William Lines, ed. The American history and encyclopedia of music. Toledo and New York, I. Squire. 1908. ML160.A5 **[2160]**

History of foreign music includes "Music of primitive peoples" by Frederick Starr, with a discussion of music among the Aztecs, p. 1-15; also "Mexico" by E. Mosley Lampe, p. 66-70.

Lach, Robert. Die musikalischen konstruktionsprinzipien der altmexikanischen tempelgesänge. *In* Festschrift für Johannes Wolf, Berlin, 1929, p. 88-96. ML55.W58M8 **[2161]**

Martens, Frederick H. Music in the life of the Aztecs. *Mus. quart.,* v. 14, no. 3 (1928), p. 413-437. **[2162]**

Martínez G., Raúl. Los Aztecas. Breve estudio histórico-social. *Rev. mex. soc.,* v. 1 (July-Aug. 1939), p. 41-63. **[2163]**

Mena, Ramón, and J. J. Arriaga. Educación intelectual y física entre los Nahuas y Mayas pre-Colombianos, México, 1930. 75 p. **[2164]**

Includes reference to the dance among the Nahuas and Mayas of Mexico in pre-Columbian times.

Mendoza, Vicente T. Música indígena; canciones guerreras, amatorias, de animales, etc. *Orientación musical,* v. 1, no. 5 (Nov. 1941), p. 7-8. **[2165]**

Discusses 6 types of songs among the Aztecs.

Mérida, Carlos. Pre-hispanic dance and theatre. *Mex. life* (Oct. 1939), p. 25-27. il. **[2166]**

Música, danzas y cantos del antiguo México. *La prensa,* v. 67, no. 24,027 (15 Dec. 1935), sec. 3, p. 2. **[2167]**

Names particular characteristics of certain dances, and musical instruments used in ancient Mexico.

New York, Museum of modern art. Mexican music; notes by Herbert Weinstock for concerts arranged by Carlos Chávez as part of the exhibition: twenty centuries of Mexican art. Printed for the trustees of the Museum of modern art by William E. Rudge's sons, New York, 1940. 31 p. il. (music) ML42.N3M82 **[2168]**

Chávez contributes a valuable introduction (p. 5-11) in which he analyzes the musical system of the Aztecs and quotes a lengthy account of music and dancing among the Aztecs from Juan de Torquemada's *Monarquía indiana* (16th century).

Nuttall, Zelia. A penitential rite of the ancient Mexicans. *In* Harvard University, Peabody museum. Archaeological papers, v. 1, no. 7 (1904), p. 437-462. E51.H337 vol. 7. F1219.3.R38N9 **[2169]**

Brief references to music, p. 440, 441, 447.

Spell, Lota M. Music and instruments of the Aztecs; the beginning of musical education in North America. *In* Music teachers' national association, Papers and proceedings, 49th year, Hartford, Conn., 1926, p. 98-105. **[2170]**

Spencer, Herbert. Los antiguos Mexicanos. México, D. F., Oficina tip. de la Secretaría de fomento, 1896. 229 p. F1219.S76 **[2171]**

A translation of that part of Spencer's *Descriptive sociology* relating to the ancient Mexicans. Reference to music and dance, p. 225-229.

Spinden, Herbert Joseph. Ancient civilizations of Mexico and Central America. New York, 1928. 271 p. il. (American museum of natural history. Handbook series no. 3, 3d. and rev. ed.) F1219.S767 **[2172]**

"Poetry and music", p. 239-242.

Thompson, John Eric. La civilisation

aztèque. Paris, Payot, 1934. 230 p. il.
F1219.T465   [2173]
Music and the dance, p. 182-186.

———. The civilization of the Mayas.
Chicago, Field museum of natural history, 1927. 110 p. il. (Field museum
of natural history. Anthropology leaflet
25). GN2.F5 no. 25. F1435.T49
                                 [2174]
Brief reference to music and dance, p.
78.

———. Mexico before Cortez. New York,
London, C. Scribner's sons, 1933. 298
p. il. F1219.T46   [2175]
Treats of music and dance, p. 238-243.

Vaillant, George Clapp. Aztecs of Mexico; origin, rise and fall of the Aztec
nation. Garden City, N. Y., Doubleday,
Doran & co., 1941. 340 p. il. F1219.V-
13   [2176]
References to music, p. 146, 155, 167,
168, 228. Instruments, p. 145, 165, 229,
238. Dance, p. 114, 155, 167, 168, 187,
201, 202.

See also nos. 1701, 1702, 1703, 1706, 1723,
1919.

2. Lyrical Texts

Brinton, Daniel Garrison. Ancient Nahuatl poetry. Philadelphia, D. G. Brinton, 1887. 177 p. PM4068.B7   [2177]
Discusses the musical accompaniment of
these ancient Mexican poems, p. 21-26. Includes translation, notes and vocabulary.

———. Rig Veda americanus. Sacred
songs of the ancient Mexicans. Philadelphia. D. G. Brinton, 1890. 95 p. PM-
4068.B74   [2178]

Campos, Rubén M. La producción literaria de los aztecas. México, D. F., Talleres gráficos del Museo nacional de
arqueología, historia y etnografía, 1936.
464 p. PM4068.C17   [2179]

**Cantares en idioma mexicano; reproducción facsimiliaria del manuscrito
orginal existente en la Biblioteca
nacional.** México, Oficina tipográfica

de la Seccretaría de fomento, 1904. 27
p. PM4068.A1 1904.   [2180]

A collection of Aztec songs in the original,reduced to the Spanish alphabet,
apparently compiled by a Spanish priest
during the 17th century. In the opinion
of the editor, Dr. Peñafiel, many of the
songs date from before the conquest. 27
of them were translated into English by
Daniel G. Brinton and published in his
Ancient Nahuatl poetry [2177], Philadelphia, 1887. The original manuscript includes, besides the songs, a Mexican calendar and several sermons and other religions
works. Cf. "Noticia histórica". Pages 23-27
contain seven cantos, translated into Spanish verse by C. A. Robelo.

Castillo Ledón, Luis. Antigua literatura
indígena mexicana. México, Imprenta
Victoria, 1917. 61 p. (Cultura, t. v, no.
4). PM4068.C25.   [2181]
Contents. —Prólogo. —Himnos. —Cantares. —Oraciones. —Cantos de Netzahualcóyotl.

Cornyn, John Hubert. El canto de
Quetzalcoatl. *Mex. folkways,* v. 4
(1928), p. 78-90.   [2182]
Translations in English and Spanish of
portions of the famous Aztec poem.

———. The song of Quetzalcoatl, translated from the Aztec. 2d. ed. Yellow
Springs, O., The Antioch press, 1931.
207 p. 11 pl. PM4068.9E5C6 1931.
                                 [2183]
Poems composed by Indian poets before
the Spanish conquest; colored illustrations
made by Indian artists four centuries ago.

Génin, Auguste. Légendes et récits du
Mexique ancien; texte définitif des
Poèmes aztèques. Paris, Editions G.
Crès & cie [1923?] 255 p. PQ2613.S.-
63L4 1923 b.   [2184]

Lehmann, Walter. Ein tolteken-klagegesang. *In* Festschrift Eduard Seler ...
zum 70 geburtstag, Stuttgart, 1922, p.
281-319. E57.S46   [2185]
Includes the song itself and several strophes of similar songs, with German translations and no music. The emphasis is

placed on the etymological, rather than the musical or ethnological value.

Pesado, José Joaquín. Los Aztecas. Poesías tomadas de los antiguos cantares mexicanos. México, Vicente Segura Argüelles, 1864. (Documentos para la Historia de México, 1a. serie, tomo 9). **[2186]**

Schottelius, Justus Wolfram, and Richard Freund. Altmexikanische hymnen. Jena, E. Diederichs, 1928. 110 p. PM4068.9.G5S4 **[2187]**

Tozzer, Alfred Marston. A comparative study of the Mayas and the Lacandones, New York, London, Publ. for the Archaeological institute of America by the Macmillan company, 1907. 195 p. il. L51.A63 1902-05 F1435.T35 **[2188]**

Text and translation of chants, p. 169-189. Musical instruments, p. 73-76.

3. *Instruments*

Beals, Ralph L. Aboriginal survivals in Maya culture. *Amer. anthrop.,* v. 34, no. 1 (Jan.-Mar. 1932), p. 28-39. **[2189]**

List of Mayan musical instruments, p. 32.

Beyer, Hermann. Mexican bone rattles. New Orleans, Department of middle American research, Tulane university of Louisiana, 1934, p. 329-349. il. F14-21.T95 no. 5 (Middle American pamphlets, no. 7 of publication no. 5 in the "Middle American research series"). **[2190]**

Includes "An authentic representation of the use of the *omichicahuaztli*".

Bruehl, Gustav. Die culturvolker Alt-Amerikas. New York, Verlag von Benziger bros, 1875-87. 516 p. Issued as "I.XX. abtheilung", in 4 parts, paged continuously. E61.B88 **[2191]**

Describes the musical instruments of the Indians of Mexico, p. 422-423, and of the Mayas, p. 445.

Campos, Rubén M. The musical instruments of the ancient Mexicans. *Bull. pan amer. union,* v. 60 (1926), p. 380-389. **[2192]**

Capitan, Louis. L'omichicahuatzli mexicain et son ancêtre de l'époque du renne en Gaule. *In* Compte rendu du Congrès international des Américanistes, v. 16, Vienna, 1908, p. 107-109. E51.I67 **[2193]**

Deals with Aztec musical instruments used in religious ceremonies, with illustration.

Castañeda, Daniel. Una flauta de la cultura tarasca. *Rev. mus. mex.* ,v. 1, no. 5 (7 Mar. 1942), p. 110-113. **[2194]**

Detailed description and illustration of a pre-Columbian earthenware flute of the Tarascan culture. The instrument, discovered in 1938, is 235 mm. long and has four finger holes.

——— ,and **Vicente T. Mendoza.** Los huehuetls en las civilizaciones precortesianas. *An. museo nac. arqueol. hist. etnog.,* época 4, v. 8, no. 2 [tomo 25 de la colección] (Apr.-June 1933), p. 287-310. il. (25 plates between p. 310 and p. 311). **[2195]**

A detailed scientific study of pre-Cortesian Mexican drums, thoroughly documented and profusely illustrated.

———. Instrumental precortesiano. Vol. 1. Instrumentos de percusión. México, D. F., Imprenta del Museo nacional de arqueología historia y etnografía, 1933. Investigaciones de la Academia de música mexicana del Conservatorio nacional de música, no. 15). **[2195x]**

———. Los percutores precortesianos. *An. museo nac. arqueol. hist. etnog,.* época 4, v. 8, no. 2 [tomo 25 de la colección] (Apr.-June 1933), p. 275-286. il. **[2195y]**

A study of the *teponaztli* (slit drum) and of various rattling instruments of the pre-Cortesian era in Mexico.

———. Los teponaztlis en las civilizaciones precortesianas *An. museo nac. arqueol. hist. etnog.,* época 4, v. 8, no.

1 [tomo 25 de la colección] (1933), p. 5-80. il. **[2196]**

Cresson, H. T. Aztec music. Proceedings of the Academy of sciences of Philadelphia, 1883, no. 35 (1884), p. 86-94. **[2197]**

General discussion of musical instruments, with particular attention paid to flageolets which are capable of producing the entire chromatic scale. Cresson claims that the Aztecs were not limited to the pentatonic scale.

Galpin, F. W. Aztec influence on American Indian instruments. *Samlb. int. mus. gesell.,* v. 4 (1903), p. 661-670. **[2198]**

Génin, Auguste. The musical instruments of the ancient Mexicans. *Mex. mag.,* v. 3, no. 7 (July 1927), p. 355-362. il. **[2199]**

Includes 12 photographs of ancient Mexican instruments, and the notation of 6 dance tunes (p. 362).

Hamy, Jules Théodore Ernest. Galerie américaine du Musée d'ethnographie du Trocadéro. Paris, E. Leroux, 1897. 118 p. il. E56.H24 **[2200]**

Plate 18, p. 35-36, shows musical instruments of the Mexicans. In 2 portfolios.

Harcourt, Raoul d'. Les instruments de musique des Mexicains et des Péruviens; place que tenait la musique chez ces peuples. *In* Encyclopédie de la musique et dictionnaire du conservatoire, partie 1, p. 3337-3353, Paris, Librairie Delagrave, 1922. il. ML100.E5 **[2201]**

This is part of a general study entitled *La musique indienne chez les anciens civilisés d'Amérique* [cf. item no. 210]. It consists of a detailed account of the musical instruments of the ancient Mexicans and Peruvians, with numerous illustrations, followed by a general survey of music and dancing in relation to the social organization of these peoples.

Joyce, Thomas Athol. Mexican archaeology. London, P. L. Warner, 1914. 384 p. il. 1219.J89 **[2202]**

References to musical instruments, p. 167-168, 300-301.

Kollman, J. Flöten und pfeifen aus Alt-Mexiko. *In* Festschrift für Adolf Bastien zu seinem 70. Geburtstage, Berlin, D. Reimer, 1896, p. 559-574. GN4.B3 **[2203]**

Many illustrations of carved pipes and flutes, with comprehensive discussions of the formation, the tone and method of playing each of the instruments. Also gives historical data on the instruments.

Kunike, Hugo. Musikinstrumente aus dem alten Michoacan. *Baes.-Arch.,* v. 2 (Leipzig, 1912), p. 282-284. **[2204]**

Mendoza, Vicente T. Tres instrumentos musicales prehispánicos. *An. inst. invest. est.,* v. 2, no. 7, no. 7 (1941), p. 71-86. **[2205]**

Able, full study of ancient Mexican wind instruments, especially of the flute type.

Muñoz Camargo, Diego. Historia de Tlaxcala. México, Oficina tip. de la Secretaría de fomento, 1892. 278 p. F-1366.M96 **[2206]**

Book I treats of indigenous musical instruments, p. 135.

Peabody, Charles. A prehistoric wind-instrument from Pecos, New Mexico. *Amer. anthrop.,* n. s.,v. 19, (1917), p. 30-33. **[2207]**

Description of a bone flute.

Ruth-Sommer, Hermann. Alte musikinstrumente, ein leitfaden für sammler. 2d ed. Berlin, R. C. Schmidt & co., 1920. 214 p. il. ML489.R92 **[2208]**

Includes illustrations of Mexican and Peruvian flutes, p. 94-95.

Saville, M. H. The musical bow in ancient Mexico. *Amer. anthrop.,* v. 2 (1897), p. 280-284. **[2209]**

——. A primitive Maya musical instrument. *Amer. anthrop.,* v. 10 (1897), p. 272-273. **[2210]**

Seler, Eduard. Altmexikanische knochenrasseln. *Globus,* v. 74 (1898), p. 85-39. **[2211]**

Description and illustration of Mexican bone rattles.

Stacy-Judd, Robert Benjamín. The ancient Mayas. Los Angeles, Haskell-Travers, inc., n. d. 277 p. F1376.S78.
[2212]
Past and present Mayan music, p. 69; musical instruments at the time of the Spanish invasion, p. 152-153.

Starr, Frederick. More notched bone rattles. Davenport academy of sciences. *Proceedings,* 1901-03, v. 9 (Davenport, Ia., 1904), p. 181-184. il.   [2213]

——. Notched bones from Mexico. Davenport academy of sciences. *Proceedings,* 1897-99, v. 1 (Davenport, Ia., 1899), p. 101-107. il.   [2214]

See also nos. 1702, 1723, 2156, 2158, 2160, 2167, 2168, 2170, 2176.

(B) POST-COLUMBIAN

Boulton, Laura C. The conference on Indian life and culture: México, 1940. *In* Music teachers national association, Proceedings for 1940. Pittsburgh, 1941, p. 58-59.   [2215]
Brief account of personal experiences in recording Mexican Indian music.

Brasseur de Bourbourg, Charles Étienne. Histoire des nations civilisées du Mexique et de l'Amérique-centrale. Paris, Arthus Bertrand, 1857, 4 v. F12-19.B82   [2216]
Vol. 1 includes: Yucatán Indians' dance of the sacred tapir, p. 81; song of the penitence of Acxitl, p. 380-381. Vol 2: Mayan dances and ballet, p. 61-67; musical instruments, p. 64-65. Vol. 3: Chapter 2, p. 498-540, contains descriptions of fêtes, with many brief references to music, songs and dances, especially p. 522, 524; discussion of the great drum of the temple of Quetzalcohuatl, p. 547; Mexican dances. p. 665; musical instruments, p. 669; *ballet ordinaire* and *ballet grand,* p. 670.

Brenner, Anita, ed. Canción de los Indios a la Guadalupana. *Mex. folkways,* v. 1, no. 4 (1925), p. 8-9.   [2217]
A song recorded in the Villa de Guadalupe. Text only.

Coolidge, Dane, and Mary Roberts Rinehart. The last of the Seris. New York, E. P. Dutton & co., 1939. 264 p. il. F1221.S43C7   [2218]
Description of musical instruments, p. 207-211, with illustration of an Indian playing the musical bow.

Densmore, Frances. Yuman and Yaqui music. Washington, U. S. Govt. print. off., 1932. 216 p. il. (Smithsonian institution. Bureau of American ethnology. Bulletin 110) E51.U6 no. 110 ML-3557.D36V8   [2219]
"The songs of a group of tribes living along the Colorado river and in northwestern Mexico."—Foreword. Contains music.

Diguet, León. Contribution à l'étude ethnographique des races primitives du Mexique. La sierra de Nayarit et ses indigènes. *Nouv. arch. miss. scien. litt.,* v. 9 (1899), p. 571-630.   [2220]
Discusses the ceremonial music of the Huichols; with 4 musical examples, p. 603-610.

Domínguez, Francisco. Costumbres Yaquis. *Mex. folkways,* special Yaqui number (July 1937, p. 6-25.   [2221]
Includes description of songs and dances of the Yaqui Indians.

——. Música yaqui, *Mex. folkways,* special Yaqui number (July 1937), p. 32-44.   [2222]
Music recorded in Pótam during the celebration of Holy Week.

Fábila, Alfonso. Las tribus yaquis de Sonora; su cultura y anhelada autodeterminación. México, Departamento de asuntos indígenas, 1940. 313 p. il. E99.-Y3F2   [2223]
Music: p. 213-15.

Gallop, Rodney. Indian drums in Mexico. *Month. mus. record,* v. 68, no. 797 (June 1938), p. 134-138. [2224]

——. Music and magic in Southern Mexico. *Month. mus. record,* v. 69, no. 803 (May 1939), p. 104-107. [2225]
Includes 6 tunes collected among the Otomi Indians.

——. Otomi Indian music from Mexico. *Mus. quart.*, v. 26, no. 1 (Jan. 1940), p. 87-100.   **[2227]**

With 30 tunes, 4 accompanied by a free English translation of the texts.

González Bonilla, Luis A. Los Yaquis. *Rev. mex. soc.*, v. 2, no. 1 (1940), p. 57-87.   **[2228]**

Festivals and dances, p. 69-71. Folklore and music of one song, p. 72.

Guerrero, Raúl G. Consideraciones sobre la música tarasca. *Bol. lat. am. mús.*, v. 5 (Oct. 1941), p. 477-490.   **[2229]**

——. La música zapoteca. Una revelación de la cultura. *Neza*, v. 4, no. 1 (1940), p. 16-20.   **[2230]**

Klineberg, Otto. Notes on the Huichol. *Amer. anthrop.*, v. 36 (1934), p. 446-460. il.   **[2231]**

Description of fiestas, with 5 tunes.

Lejeal, L. Note sur la musique et la magie des primitifs chez les Américains. *Rev. musicale*, no. 7 (1907), p. 182-184.   **[2232]**

Chiefly a discussion of Lumholtz's *Unknown Mexico*.

López Chiñas, Gabriel. Canto del niño a la luna. *Neza*, v. 3 (1937), p. 40.   **[2233]**

Zapotec words of a song that the children sing on moonlit nights, lying in their beds.

——. La música aborigen de Juchitán. *Neza*, v. 4, no. 1 (1939), p. 25-27.   **[2234]**

López y Fuentes, Gregorio. El indio, novela. mexicana, 2d. México, Ediciones Botas, 1937. 269 p. PQ7297.L-685.15   **[2235]**

A prize-winning novel of Indian life in Mexico, with passing references to music and dances, especially in the chapter entitled *Música, danza y alcohol*.

Lumholtz, Karl Sofus. El México desconocido; cinco años de exploración en-

tre las tribus de la Sierra Madre occidental, etc. New York, C. Scribner's sons, 1904, 2 v. il. F1215.L932 **[2236]**

Vol. 2, ch. 1, treats of music and dances, with 4 tunes.

——. Unknown Mexico; a record of five years' exploration among the tribes of the western Sierra Madre; in the tierra caliente of Tepic and Jalisco; and among the Tarascos of Michoacan. New York, C. Scribner's sons, 1902, 2 v. il. F1215.L93 **[2237]**

Includes 13 tunes, v. 1, p. 267, 336, 338-340, 371, 425, 523; v. 2, p. 278.

Maillefert, Eugenio Gómez. La marihuana en México. *Jour. amer. folklore*, v. 33, no. 127 (1920), p. 28-33. **[2238]**

Includes 4 tunes with Spanish words.

Mendieta, Gerónimo de. Historia eclesiástica indiana. México, Impr. Librería, 1870. 790 p. F1219.M53 **[2239]**

Bk. 2, ch. 3, p. 80-81: References to music and dance; ch. 14, p. 97-99; Festivals in honor of the fods, with brief notes on dance; ch. 15, p. 99-100: Mention of dance in religious rites; ch. 25, p. 127-128: Dance and music in the Indian religious ceremonies; ch. 31, p. 140-143: Descriptions of the time, place and characters in certain religious dances; ch. 41: Mentionn of music and dance in connection with festivals; bk. 4, ch. 14, p. 410-414: The early teachers of music and voice in Mexico; mention of musical instruments before the Christians; supremacy of the organ since advent of Christians; secular instruments.

Mendizábal, Miguel O. de. Los cantares y la música indígena, las canciones y bailables populares de México. *Mex. folkways*, v. 3, no. (1927), p. 109-121. **[2240]**

Includes Spanish translations of 2 Nahuatl songs, and 9 illustrations showing native musicians and musical instruments.

Mimenza Castillo, Ricardo. La civilización maya. Barcelona, Editorial Cervantes, 1929. 80 p. il. F1435.M65 **[2241]**

Refers to indigenous dances and music, p. 33-35.

Montes de Oca, José G. Manchas de color. México-Tenochtitlán. México, D. F., Imprenta M. León Sánchez, 1939, 156 p. [2242]

Deals with the music, dances and customs of the Mexican Indians.

Motolinía, Toribio. Historia de los indios de la Nueva España. Barcelona, Herederos de J. Gili, 1914. 282 p. F-1219.M92 [2243]

Ch. 12 treats of religious music. Notes on the changes in the Indian music since the advent of the missionaries, p. 214-215. Written in the 16th century.

Musiques exotiques. *Rev. musicale,* no. 7 (1907), p. 181-182. [2244]

Discussion of primitive music in America. Quotes notation of "Huichol rainsong" taken from Lumholtz's *Unknown Mexico.*

Osorio Bolio de Saldívar, Elsa. La música, zapoteca de Juchitlán. *Neza,* v. 4, no. 1 (1939), p. 5-8. [2245]

Pimentel, Francisco. Memoria sobre las causas que han originado la situación actual de la raza indígena de México ... México, Impr. de Andrade y Escalante, 1864. 241 p. F1219.P34 [2246]

Poesía, música, canto, p. 57-61.

Preuss, Konrad Theodor. Au sujet du caractère des mythes et des chants huichols que j'ai recueillis. *Rev. inst. etnol. univ. Tucumán,* v. 2 (1931-1932), p. 445-457. [2247-48]

———. Ethnographische ergebnisse einer reise in die mexikanische Sierra Madre. *Zeit. ethnol.,* v. 40 (Berlín, 1908), p. 582-604. [2249]

Description of Mexican Indian ceremonial songs.

———. Die Nayarit-expedition. Liepzig. B. G. Teubner, 1912. 396 p. F1220.P-67 [2250]

Many comments on music, dance and song; see index under *tanz, gesänge,* etc. For material on the musical bow, see p. XC, CIV, 139, 219, 223. Melodies of 2

songs and analysis of their form, p. 367-376; "Zwei gesänge der Cora-Indianer (aus dem phonogramarchiv des psychologischen instituts der Universität Berlin)."

———. Reise zu den stämmen der westlichen Sierra Madre zu Mexiko. *In* Gesellschaft für erdkunde zu Berlin. *Zeitschrift* (1908), p. 147-167. [2251]

References to Cora and Huichol songs, p. 160.

Redfield, Robert. Tepoztlan, a Mexican village; a study of folk life. Chicago, University of Chicago press, 1930. 27 p. il. F1391.T3R31 [2252]

Gives text of numerous folk songs, also 4 tunes (p. 97, 111, 177, 188). Appendix: Nahuatl text of a *relación,* with English translation.

———, and Alfonso Villa R. Chan Kom, a Maya village. Washington, D. C., Carnegie institution of Washington, 1934. 387 p. il. F1435.1.C47R3 [2253]

With 1 tune, p. 133.

Rojas González, Francisco. Los Mazahuas. *Rev. mex. soc.,* v. 1 (Sept.-Dec. 1939), p. 114-117 [2254]

Music and dance, p. 114-117. Includes music.

Rundall, W. H. A curious musical instrument. *Mus. times,* v. 42 (1901), p. 310-312. [2255]

Description and illustration of the *zapo-tecano* (marimba).

Salas, Ángel. El valor íntimo de la música aborigen mexicana. *Rev. mus. mex.* v. 2, no. 5 (7 Sept. 1942), p. 106-109. [2256]

This is a chapter from a book entitled *La música aborigen,* which the author has in preparation.

Saldívar, Gabriel. Música india; semejanza entre una melodía maya y otra otomí. *Investg. ling.,* v. 5, no. 1-2 (1938), p. 98-101. [2257]

Two musical examples, p. 101.

Sartorius, Christian Carl. Musikalische

leichenfeir und tänze der Mexico-Indianer (mit musikbeilagen). *Caecilia,* v. 8 (Mainz, 1828), p. 1-16. [2258]

Soustelle, Jacques. La música indígena mexicana—los Otomíes. *Ecos mundiales* (México), v. 2 (Sept. 1937), p. 31-32. [2259]

Starr, Frederick. In Indian Mexico. Chicago, Forbes & company, 1908. 125 p. plates. F1219.S78 [2260]
References to music and dances, p. 24, 30, 91, 265, 287, 318, 325, 358.

——. Notes upon the ethnography of southern Mexico. Davenport, Ia., Putnam memorial publication fund, 1900-1902, 2 v. F1220.S793 [2261]
Tlaxcaltecan (song of Tlaxcala state), p. 25-27. Aztec musical instruments, p. 35-37 (illustrations, p. 91, figures 17, 18). Pastores and Snake Dance of the Tepehuas, p. 85-86.

Weitlaner, Roberto J., and Jacques Soustelle. Canciones Otomíes. *Jour. soc. amer.,* n. s., v. 27 (1935), p. 303-324. [2262]
Text only (in Otomí), with Spanish translations of the words of 14 songs.

MISCELLANEOUS

Blanquel, Simón. Calendario de canciones nuevas. México, T. F. Neve, 1869. [2263]

Chávez, Carlos. Toward a new music; music and electricity. Translated from the Spanish by Herbert Weinstock. New York, W. W. Norton & co., 1937. 180 p. il. (music) ML1092.C4T6 [2264]

Departamento de asuntos indígenas. Oficina de educación indígena. Mesa de música. Plan general de actividades de los promotores y maestros de música de las misiones de mejoramiento indígena. México, D. F., 1 Jan. 1941. 8 p. Mimeographed. [2265]

Gabriel, Eduardo. La música y los colo-res. *Rev. mus. Mex.,* v. 1, no. 2 (15 June 1919), p. 17-19. [2266]

Goldsmith, Alfred N. Chávez on music and electricity. *Mod. mus.,* v. 14, no. 3 (1937), p. 164-166. [2267]
A discussion of Chávez's book, *Toward a new music* [no. 2264].

Ponce, Manuel M. Iniciativa de un congreso musical. *Rev. mus. Méx.,* v. 1, no. 2 (15 June 1919), p. 5-7. [2268]
A project for a musical congress to study and discuss problems relating to the development of music in Mexico.

——. El problema de los compositores. *Rev. mus. Méx.* v. 1, no. 3 (15 July 1919), p. 5-6. [2269]

Primeros anales del Conservatorio nacional de música. Formulados y redactados por los profesores y el director, Dr. Adalberto García de Mendoza. v. 1. México, D. F., Ed. "Amigos del conservatorio", 1941. 343 p. il. MT5.M-4C6 [2270]
These *Anales* are intended to serve as the basis for a history of the Conservatorio Nacional, which was founded in 1866. This first volume deals chiefly with the plan of studies offered at the Conservatorio, giving an outline of each course.

Proyecto del plan de estudios de la facultad de música de la universidad nacional. *Rev. mus. Méx.,* v. 1, no. 10 (29 Feb. 1920), p. 23-25. [2271]

Sandi, Luis. El coro de madrigalistas (su estilo interpretativo) *Rev. mus. mex.,* v. 2, no. 9 (7 Nov. 1942), p. 195-196. [2272]
Sandi is the founder and leader of this choral group, formed in 1940.

——. Dos incidentes. *Rev. mus. mex.,* v. 1, no. 5 (7 Mar. 1942), p. 99-101. [2273]
A defense of Carlos Chávez and the Orquesta Sinfónica de México.

Téllez Girón, Roberto. El coro de madrigalistas (su repertorio—su actividad educativa). *Rev. mus. mex.,* v. 2, no. 8 (21 Oct. 1942), p 171-173. [2274]

SUPPLEMENT to 1960

It is fortunate that the first book in English on the history of music in Mexico was undertaken by an American musicologist fully qualified or the task: Dr. Robert Stevenson, of the University of California in Los Angeles. His book, *Music in Mexico: a historical survey* (item 862a), published in 1952, is based on research undertaken in Mexico in 1950 on a grant awarded under terms of the Buenos Aires Convention for the Promotion of Inter-American Cultural Relations.

Dr. Stevenson's book follows a chronological pattern, beginning with "Early aboriginal music in Mexico". In this initial chapter he draws extensively upon the writings of the early Spanish historians, such as Motolinía, Sahagún, López de Gomara, Landa, Mendieta, *et alter*. As he points out, the absence of musical quotations in the 16th-century chronicles leaves the melodic system of the Pre-Conquest era in the realm of conjecture. He believes, however, that the prevailing shape of Aztec melody might be deduced from a study of the pitch inflections of Nahuatl poetry, correlated with the pitch patterns for the *teponaztli* accompaniment. Actually, the Mexican scholar Vicente Mendoza has been working along these lines; but his results are as yet inconclusive. Stevenson also argues for the validity of utilizing contemporary aboriginal melodies of Mexico for the *approximate* reconstruction of the Pre-Conquest melodic system, provided that such a method is used with caution and that its limitations are fully appreciated. In this connection, he quotes melodies of various tribes, such as the Tarahumaras, the Tepenhuane and Huichol Indians, and a presumably "native Maya melody", the *Xtoles,* from Mérida. In conclusion, he states, "The Mexicans all agree that whatever may be ascertained regarding the melodic system of the Pre-Conquest peoples must be inferred from examples recently collected".

Chapter 2 deals with "The transplanting of European musical culture", through the training of Indian singers and instrumentalists (they showed remarkable aptitude), the printing of music, and general development of Neo-Hispanic polyphony and instrumental music in the New World. Chapter 3 continues this phase with an account of "The culmination and decline of Neo-Hispanic music" in Mexico, including the religious compositions of Hernando Franco, music in Puebla, Michoacán, and other provincial centers, and music at the Cathedral of Mexico City (from Salazar to Aldana). Brief consideration is also given to Neo-Hispanic folk music.

The next chapter takes up "The operatic nineteenth century", with attention to the work of such composers as Paniagua, Melesio Morales, Aniceto Ortega. By way of introduction there is a section on "Dance types popular at the end of the viceregal period", and an interesting description of the musical activities of José Mariano Elízaga, "A pioneer during the revolutionary epoch" both as composer and as musical educator (his rôle being comparable to that of Lowell Mason in the United States).

The fifth and final chapter is titled "Fulfillment during the twentieth century". It begins with an account of the older composers —Gustavo E. Campa, Julián Carrillo, Manuel M. Ponce— and then takes up the leading figures of the present time, among them Carlos Chávez, Silvestre Revueltas, Candelario Huízar, Luis Sandi, and Blas Galindo. The stylistic analysis is illustrated with musical quotations. Copious notes, an extensive bibliography, and an index, complete this extremely useful work.

Since the emphasis in Dr. Stevenson's book is primarily on art music, it is admirably complemented by several recent publications of the Mexican scholar Vicente T. Mendoza, in which the "traditional" music of Mexico receives thorough attention. The most comprehensive of these works is the *Panorama de la música tradicional de México* (item 726a), which appeared in 1956. The author's position is clearly stated when he writes: "La música folklórica de mi país es llamada por antonomasia música mexicana. Es ella la forma genuina de expresión de nuestro pueblo". An introductory section traces the "Desarrollo histórico de la música tradicional de México" from the Pre-Conquest era to the Revolution.

Chapter I deals with indigenous music, and contains a particularly valuable discussion of the rhythmic elements in the Mexican songs (*Cantares Mexicanos*) collected by Sahagún (words only). Chapter II treats of Spanish music of the 16th, 17th, and 18th centuries, with comments on popular religious forms (*alabado, cantos de posadas, pastorelas, etc.*), and on traditional secular forms (*romance, copla, pregones, tonadilla*). Chapter III deals with that the author calls "Mexican music", i. e., music which, whatever its origin, has been modified by the cultural ambience of the land. The principal types of this music are the *son*, the *jarabe*, the *huapango*, the *valona*, the *canción*, the *danza habanera*, and the *corrido*.

The second part of Mendoza's book consists of 231 musical notations to illustrate all the types mentioned above. The third part consists of the complete texts of all the songs quoted in the preceding section. The fourth part is made up of 49 photographic reproductions, showing musical instruments of the Pre-Conquest era, of the Spanish period, and of the present-day aborigenes; and typical musical groups of the kind that can be found in Mexico today. Specialized bibliographies add to the usefulness of this valuable publication.

Two other works by Mendoza must be mentioned here, because of their importance for the study of Mexican traditional music. They are *El corrido mexicano* (1954) and *Glosas y décimas de México* (1957) [items 702a and 709a]. The first of these, supplementing the author's earlier work *El romance español y el corrido mexicano* (item 2023), is an anthology of the Mexican popular ballad or *corrido,* containing 172 texts, classified by subject, and 70 musical notations, with a list of sources for each ballad. The introduction traces the origin and evolution of the *corrido,* which Mendoza considers relatively recent (last quarter of the 19th century).

The second of these books follows the same general pattern as the first. The introduction traces the origins of the *décima,* a Spanish literary form that flourished in the 16th century and that passed into the oral tradition of Hispanic America from Colorado and New Mexico to Argentina. The main body of the book contains the text of 184 *décimas,* classified by subject. Unfortunately, there are very few musical notations. As usual, Mendoza carefully gives the source for each *décima.*

In a more specialized field, which verges on archaelogy, Samuel Martí has published *Instrumentos musicales precortesianos* (1955), valuable above all for its numerous illustrations of Pre-Conquest musical instruments (see item 691a). There is also a section on "Instrumentos indígenas actuales de origen precortesiano". There are numerous musical notations of indigenous melodies collected by various field workers in recent times.

A useful compendium on Mexican folk music, in the form of a discography, is the pamphlet issued by the Department of Music of the Instituto Nacional de Bellas Artes, titled *Música folklórica mexicana: Inventario de discos grabados por la sección de investigaciones musicales del I.N.B.A.* (item 737a), with a foreword by Carlos Chávez. This lists 924 recordings of Mexican folk music, together with the pertinent data as to date, place, informant, etc.

In the realm of biography, Carlos Chávez is the subject of a thoroughly documented book by the Argentine composer and critic Roberto García Morillo, published in 1960: *Carlos Chávez: Vida y Obra* (item 801a). This is an "authorized" biography in the sense that Chávez cooperated fully with the author in providing information and in furnishing personal and technical data. It analyzes all of the composer's principal works and some of the minor ones also, and concludes with a general discussion of his style, his technique, his use of form, and his aesthetic position. There is a complete catalogue of compositions by Chávez and a bibliography of his published writings, as well as a discography. It would be highly desirable to have this work available in an English translation.

BIBLIOGRAPHY

A. PRIMITIVE FOLK, AND POPULAR MUSIC

Álvarez de la Cadena, Luis, ed. México; leyendas y costumbres, trajes y danzas; prólogo por Nemesio García Naranjo; selección y comentarios por Luis Álvarez de la Cadena; viñetas por Jesús Nieto Hernández; cuadros en color por Pastor Velázquez, Nieto Hernández, Muñoz López, Devaux, Espino Barros y Torres Palomar. México, D. F., 1945. 458 p. il. (music) **[662a]**

Amézquita Borja, Francisco. Colección de cantos y bailes regionales, Puebla, México, Imprenta cinematográfica "Lux", 1943. 22 pp. **[663a]**

——. Música y danza; algunos aspectos de la música y danza de la sierra norte del estado de Puebla. Puebla, 1943. 101 p. il. (music). **[664a]**

Brief descriptions including steps, costumes, music (44 tunes) and numerous illustrations of the following dances; *El Huapango, Danza de los Quetzales, Danza de los voladores, Danza de los negros, Danza de los toreadores, Danza de los patrianos.*

Baqueiro Fóster, Gerónimo. Aspectos de la música popular yucateca en tres siglos. *Rev. mus. mex.,* v. 4, no. 1 (1944), p. 3-7. **[665a]**

Beltrame, Andrés. El conejito,baile popular mexicano; música y letra, modo de bailarse. Buenos Aires, 1946. 4 p. **[666a]**

Campos, Rubén M. El folklore literario y musical de México. Selección y notas preliminares por Alfredo Ramos Espinosa. México, D. F., Secretaría de Educación Pública, 1946. 95 p. (Biblioteca enciclopédica popular, v. 126) **[667a]**

Selections from 2 important books by Campos: *El folklore literario musical de México* (no. 1916) and *El folklore y la música mexicana* (no. 1919), with introductory comments by Ramos Espinosa.

——. La música popular de México. *Rev. estud. mus.,* v. 1, no. 1 (Aug. 1949), 81-91. **[668a]**

Deals with *"la música típicamente mexicana",* from pre-Hispanic times.

Cárcer, Mariano de. Posibles orígenes de las típicas posadas mexicanas. *An. soc. folk. mex.,* v. 5 (1944, pub. 1945), p. 287-297. **[669a]**

Several texts of songs but no music.

Carochi, Horacio. Arte de la lengua mexicana... Iuan Rvyz. Año de 1645. Reimpreso por el Museo nacional de México. México, D. F., Imprenta del Museo nacional, 1892, *In* Colección de gramáticas de la lengua mexicana, México, 1904, v. 1, p. 395-538). **[670a]**

Book 4, chapter 1, treats of indigenous music.

Castañeda, Daniel. El corrido mexicano, su técnica literaria y musical. México, D. F., Ed. Surco, 1943. 124 p. il. (music). **[671a]**

Begins with comparative study of Mexican and peninsular ballads, as regards metrical structure. Describes the formulas used by the maker of corridos. Traces origins and themes and attempts a classification by subject.

——. Las flautas en las civilizaciones azteca y tarasca. (*Música,* México, Nov. 15, 1930), p. 3-29. **[672a]**

——. Sinopsis de la investigación en el corrido mexicano. *Letras,* año 7, v. 1, no. 7 (July 15, 1943), p. 4-5. **[673a]**

Castillo, Ignacio Manuel del. Los cantares mexicanos. *Rev. mex. estud. antrop.* v. 4, no. 1-2 (1940), p. 129-140. **[674a]**

Discusses a collection of more than 60 folksongs in Nahuatl, noted down by an anonymous missionary and published in 1904. Some are of colonial, others of pre-Columbian times, probably sung in festivals and to accompany dances. Gives Spanish translation of 2 songs. (R. K.)

Chinchilla Aguilar, Ernesto. La danza

del tum-teleche o loj-tum. *Antr. hist.,*
v. 3, no. 1 (Jan. 1951), p. 17–20.
[675a]
Brief study based on early 17th century documents.

Cogen, John. Four folksongs from Jalisco. *Calif. folklore quart.,* v. 4 (1945), p. 411–415.   [676a]
Words and music.

Dávila Garibi, J. I. La toponimia mexicana en boca de nuestros pregones, copleros, cancioneros y otros ingenios populares. México, D. F., Ed. San Ignacio de Loyola, 1946. 121 p.   [677a]

Gillmor, Frances. The dance dramas of Mexican villages. Tucson, University of Arizona, 1943. 28 p. il. (Humanities bulletin, no. 5)   [678a]
Description of "The Moors and Christians" dance drama and its different variations. No music is included, only the literary text with an English translation.

Guerrero, José E. Danzas chontalpeñas, (Tabasco). *Nuestra música.* v. 2, no. 8 (Oct. 1947), p. 192–198. (music)
[679a]
With 3 musical notations.

———. El zapateado tabasqueño. *Orientac. mus.,* v. 5, no. 50 (Aug. 1945), p. 8–10; no. 51 (Sep. 1945), p. 8–10.
[680a]

———. El zapateado tabasqueño. *Nuestra música,* v. 3, no. 10 (Apr. 1958), p. 82-89.   [681a]
The most popular dance of Tabasco is called *zapateado.* Article describes the *zapateado* of Spain, variations in Cuba and Chile, treats that of Tabasco in detail. Three texts, one with music.

Guerrero, Raúl G. Aspectos folklóricos en dos danzas indígenas del estado de Durango. *Mem. cong. mex. hist.,* 1949, p. 127-139.   [682a]
Treats briefly of 2 dances: *La Pluma* and *Matachines,* or *Indios.* 5 music notations and 4 good photographs of dancers. Bibliography. (C. S.)

———. Música de Chiapas. *Rev. estud. mus.,* v. 1, no. 2 (Dec. 1949), p. 129–150.   [683a]
Fragment of report on 1942 field trip for the Museo Nacional de Antropología of Mexico City. Lists places visited, groups recorded, instruments used, etc. The tunings of 4 harps and 3 guitars are given. 9 notations of complete melodies. (C. S.)

———. Prehispanic Indian music and dance. *This week in Mexico and information about U. S.,* México, D. F. (Feb. 19-25, 1944), p. 25-38) [684a]
Text in English and Spanish. Includes musical instruments and other related aspects of folklore. Good descriptive notes. (R. S. B.)

Haro y Tamariz, Jesús. Un poco de folklore del Istmo. *An. soc. folk. Mex.,* v. 5 (1944, pub. 1945), p. 255–273.
[685a]
Reference to *sones populares,* page 271-273. (C. S.)

Hurtado, Nabor. La música purépecha. *Rev. mus. chil.,* v. 13, no. 66 (July-Aug. 1959), p. 55-60.   [686a]
Music of the Tarascan Indians in Mexico, with 4 photographs of dancers and 4 music notations.

Johnson, Jean B. The huapango: a Mexican song contest. *Calif. folklore quart.,* v. 1 (1942), p. 233-244.
[687a]
Good account of this folksong form of mestizo southern Veracruz, Mexico, which is accompanied by dance and musical instruments, and is suitable for improvisation. Spanish verses only and approximate English translation of 41 from Tlacotalpan, Veracruz. (R. S. B.)

Kaplan, Bernice A. Changing functions of the Huanancha dance at the Corpus Christi festival in Paracho, Michoacán, Mexico. *Jour. amer. folklore.,* v. 64, no. 254 (Oct.-Dec. 1951), p. 383-392.
[688a]

Kurath, Gertrude Prokosch. Los concheros. *Journ. amer. folklore,* v. 59, no. 234 (Oct.–Dec. 1946), p. 387–399. [689a]

Detailed though brief survey by a careful observer. List of 12 outstanding fiestas. Group organization, costumes, music, dance and its steps (in a shorthand). Fifteen music notations. (C. S.)

Márquez, Luis. Pahuatlán. Danzantes y hechiceros. La danza del volador. *Hoy*, México, no. 503 (Oct. 12, 1946), p. 36-43. [690a]

Thirteen fine photographs in rotogravure of the *volador*, the *rehilete humano* (a variant of the *quetzales*) and related rituals. Informative comment. (C. S.)

Martí, Samuel. Instrumentos musicales precortesianos. México. Instituto nacional de antropología, 1954. 227 p. [691a]

The numerous illustrations are the most valuable feature of this book.

———. Música precortesiana. *Cuad. am.*, v. 78, no. 6 (Nov.–Dec. 1954), p. 149-155. [692a]

———. Música prehispánica. *In* Guía de la sala de música prehispánica, Museo nacional de antropología, México, D. F., n. d. [1954], 15 p. il. [693a]

Melgarejo Vivanco, José Luis. La décima en Veracruz. *An. soc. folk. Mex.*, v. 4 (1943), p. 61-72. [694a]

Brief description of the social customs accompanying the *décima* singing with the texts of 12, from the coast of Actopan, Alto Lucero and Vega de Alatorre. No music.

Mendoza, Vicente T. Algo del folklore negro en México. Tirada aparte de la *Miscelánea de estudios dedicados al Dr. Fernando Ortiz por sus discípulos, colegas y amigos*. La Habana, 1956. 19 p. il. (music). [695a]

Studies the origin and evolution of the "Danza de los negritos", with citation of texts and several musical notations.

———. Breves notas sobre la petenera.

Nuestra música, v. 4, no. 14 (Apr. 1949), p. 114-134. [696a]

La Petenera is one of the songs of Mexico which is "of pure Andalusian stock." Notes four principal types of the song in Spain. Discusses several examples from many parts of Mexico, including Jalisco, Tabasco, Guerrero, and the coast of Veracruz. Traces it back as far as 1830s in Mexico. 25 song texts, 12 music examples, one with melody and piano accompaniment. Bibliography, 23 items.

———. Canciones mexicanas (Mexican folk songs) seleccionadas y armonizadas. New York, Hispanic Institute in the United States, 1948. 126 p. music. [697a]

———. Cincuenta romances, escogidos y armonizados. México, D. F., E.D.I.A.-P.S.A., n. d. [1940], 111 p. (music). (Ediciones musicales EDIAPSA, no. 2). [698a]

The 50 ballads, taken for the most part from Spanish collections, are grouped in 11 classifications. The harmonizations are purposely simple and in keeping with the traditional Hispanic character of the ballads. The selection is interesting, and the texts include several versions collected by the author in Mexico. Published by the Secretaría de Educación Pública of México.

———. Derivaciones de la canción de Mambrú en México. v. 1 (1942), p. 91-101. [699a]

Gives 5 texts with music.

———. El casamiento del piojo y la pulga. *An. inst. invest. est.*, v. 2, no. 6 (1940), p. 65-85. [700a]

Believes this children's song originated in late 18th century, in Spain, where he finds it first printed in the 19th century. Gives 1 version from New Mexico, 10 from Mexico, scattered from Zacatecas to Yucatán, and each from Perú and Chile. Includes Spanish text of these 13 versions, 6 with music notation, dating from the mid 19th century to the present, deduces some comparative notes, and concludes with the Mayan text and music of another version received from Yucatán. Bibliography. (R. S. B.)

——. El corrido de la revolución mexicana. México, D. F., Biblioteca del
instituto nacional de estudios históricos de la revolución mexicana, 1956.
151 p.   [701a]
Traces the history of the *corrido* from
the beginning of the M e x i c a n Revolution in 1910 until 1938, in a series of
six "Lessons," based on a course given
by the author at the "Instituto Nacional
de Estudios Históricos de la Revolución
Mexicana". Numerous texts, but no musical notations. Bibliography, p. 151.

——. El corrido mexicano. Antología,
introducción y notas. Colección letras
mexicanas, no. 15. México, D. F., Fondo de Cultura Económica, 1954. xliv.
467 p. (music).   [702a]
"La presente obra aspira solamente a
proporcionar al lector una visión panorá-
mica condensada de uno de los géneros
líricos-musicales que el pueblo de México
ha venido cultivando con amor desde
hace cerca de un siglo: el corrido. Pre-
tende también lograr una revisión de los
conceptos vertidos por mí en la obra:
El romance español y el corrido mexicano,
pues no en balde han transcurrido catorce
años desde su aparición y se hace preciso
agregar ciertos detalles impuestos por observaciones mas hondas logradas a través de
varios años de enseñanza del tema." (Introducción). Contains the text of 172
corridos, with 70 musical notations. The
Introduction traces the antecedents, the origin, and the development of the *corrido.*

——. El cuándo. *Nuestra música.* v. 3
no. 11 (July 1948), p. 188–205.
                                    [703a]
Discussion of *cuándo* in México, New
Mexico, Chile and Argentina. Believes it
was well-known in the Mexican states of
México, Veracruz, Tabasco, Jalisco and
Zacatecas throughout the 19th century,
flourishing in the 1840s. 17 texts, six with
music. Bibliography of 8 items.

——. "El Dormido", jarabe que durmió
un siglo. *Nuestra música,* v. 3, no. 9
(Jan. 1948), p. 26-36.   [704a]
Cites references to the *Jarabe* in Mexican
writings of the 1780s. and to "El Dormido" as being danced in 1830; believes
that "El Dormido" and "El Trompito"
are identical, and cites several texts of the

latter, from Mexico, Nicaragua and Peru.
Threee music examples. One plate, a portrait of the governor of Virrey in 1787,
don Manuel Flores. Bibliography.

——. El grupo musical mexicano lla-
mado "mariachi". *Revista universitaria,*
Guadalajara, Jalisco, México, v. 1, no.
2 (1943), p. 87-89.   [705a]
Found chiefly in Nayarit, Jalisco, Colima, Michoacán, Guerrero and part of
Oaxaca, Mexico. Criollo, of Spanish origin. Group of some 4 to 6, playing chiefly string instruments, sometimes percussion or wind. Maybe name originated
during French intervention, from "maria-
ge", since these groups played so often
at weddings Players sing wide variety of
songs. Characterizes rhythm, melody and
harmony of this music. (R. S. B.)

——. El olé Charandel. Una tonadilla
olvidada. *Nuestra música.* v. 6, no. 22
(2. trimestre, 1951), p. 100–118. (music).   [706a]
Further evidence in support of the
author's thesis that much of the popular
music of Latin America is derived from
the Spanish *tonadilla.* With 7 musical
notations.

——. El romance tradicional de Delgadina en México.. *Univ. Mex.,* v. 6, no.
69 (Sept. 1952), p. 8, 17, map [707a]
The distribution i n M e x i c o of this
widely diffused Spanish folksong theme of
incestuous love, both as a *romance* and
as a *corrido.* (R. A. W.)

——. El tango en México. *Nuestra música,* v. 5, no. 18 (2. trimestre, 1950),
p. 138-154. (music).   [708a]
An important study, with 13 musical
notations and bibliographical notes. Treats
of the Mexican derivations of the *tango
andaluz,* which is believed to have originated in Cádiz.

——. Glosas y décimas de México. Introducción y selección. Colección letras mexicanas, no. 32. México, D. F.,
1957. 371 p.   [709a]
Traces the evolution "de una literatura
que fue del dominio de·los eruditos y que
ahora se halla en poder de las gentes del
campo." Two main currents may be per-

ceived within the tradition of the *décima en México*. The first is of classical origin, brought to México by learned writers following the Conquest. The second is of a lyrical, declamatory and musical order, and was brought to México by the soldiers sent from Spain in the 18th century to reinforce the local militia. The first was erudite, the second popular. There is a close relationship between the two, not only in form, but also in vocabulary, since the popular versions employ a number of Latinisms and other literary artifices derived from the erudite tradition.

——. La cachucha en México. *Nuestra música*, v. 5, no. 20 (4. trimestre, 1950), p. 289-310. (music).   [710a]

With 11 musical notations, 24 footnotes, and bibliography.

——. La canción chilena en México. Colección de ensayos, Nº 4. Santiago, Universidad de Chile, Instituto de investigaciones musicales. Facultad de bellas artes, n. d. (1948) 15 p. (music)

The type of Chilean song known as *chilena* is widely diffused in Mexico, doubtless due to the frequent contact between Mexico and Chile during and after the colonial period, especially through traffic between the ports of Valparaiso and Acapulco. During the California "gold rush" of the mid-19th century, many Chilean ships called at Acapulco on the way to San Francisco. The *chilena* is found most frequently in the states of Guerrero and Oaxaca. Mendoza's monograph includes 8 musical examples, including *La Sanmarqueña* from Guerrero.

——. La canción del gato en México. *Folklore*, Buenos Aires, 1er. trimestre, no. 5 (1942), p. 47-48.   [712a]

——. La copla musical en México. *An. soc. folk. Méx.,* v. 5 (1944, pub. 1945), p. 189-202.   [713a]

Authoritative discussion of this poetic form. Numerous examples. Five music notations, melodies only. (C. S.)

——. La música otomí.. Una investigación en el valle del Mezquital, 1936 (primera parte). *Rev. estud. mus.,* v. 2, nos. 5-6 (Dec. 1950–April 1951),

p. 351-580; no. 7 (Dec. 1954), p. 221-246.   [714a]

A very important study, with numerous musical notations.

——. La solterita, tonadilla que se cantaba en el Coliseo de México y que aún perdura. *An. inst. invest. est.,* v. 4, no. 13 (1945), p. 85-92.   [715a]

Includes music notation of songs.

——. México aún canta seguidillas. *An. soc. folk. Méx.,* v. 5 (1944), p. 203-217.   [716a]

Traces this popular folksong form from Spain to Mexico, with several examples. Also in *Previsión y Seguridad*, Monterrey, México, 1946, X, p. 97-101, 104.

——. La danza de las cintas o de la trenza. *An. soc. folklórica de México,* v. 6, 1945 (pub. 1947), p. 113-137, il.)   [717a]

Serious attempt to open way for a broad comparative study of this ancient and worldwide fertility circular or Maypole dance, examining documentary evidence with descriptions, illustrations and music from Mexico, Spain and other parts of Europe. (R. S. B.)

——. Música de Navidad en México. *Méx. en el arte,* no. 6 (Dec. 1948), n. p.   [718a]

After a brief survey (with one reproduction of a music manuscript dated 1797), music notations of 13 songs collected in various parts of the country by the author are given. (C. S.)

——. Música indígena; teorías migratorias, influencias asiáticas, de las islas del Océano Pacífico, posibles influencias del oriente y del sur, instrumentos exóticos que aparecen en México, el por qué de su persistencia. *Revista universitaria,* Guadalajara, Jalisco, México, v. 1, no. 3 (1943), p. 27-31. (il.)   [719a]

Study of surviving musical instruments and their portrayal on pottery, etc., of ancient Indians of Mexico shows a complex cultural pattern, with movements from north to south and west to east. Sees Oriental influences (Chinese, Polynesian), also African, Egyptian and Palestinian parallels, most plainly among Indians who have resisted Spanish influences. (R. S. B.)

——. Música popular del Bajío. *Mex. en el arte*, no. 7 (Spring, 1949), p. 87-99. **[720a]**

The "granary of the Republic" and the State of Guanajuato are particularly rich in folksong. Includes 12 music notations and bibliography. (C.S.)

——. Música tradicional de Guerrero. *Nuestra música*, v. 4, no. 15 (July 1949), p. 198-214. **[721a]**

Clamis to be first study of the folk music of the State of Guerrero, Includes 6 music notations and 5 illustrations. (C.S.)

——. Música en el coliseo de México. *Nuestra música*, v. 7, no. 26 (2 trimestre, 1952) p. 108-113. (music). **[722a]**

A study of the *tonadilla* in Mexico with 7 musical notations. "Es indudable que la tonadilla existió en México en las mismas circunstancias que en España, aunque ligeramente rezagada en el tiempo debido a la dificultad de comunicación" (p. 114).

——. Música indígena en México. *Mex. en el arte*, no. 9 (1950), p. 55-64. **[723a]**

Maintains thesis that pre-Conquest music traditions still survive. Brief review of study since Lumholtz (1904). Five plates, three in color, two of them being copies of frescoes at Bonampak. Six music notations. Bibliography. (C.S.)

——. Origen de la canción mexicana. *Previsión y Seguridad*, Monterrey (1945), p. 75-78. **[724a]**

——. Páginas musicales de los siglos xvii y xviii. *Bol. arch. gen. México*, v. 16, no. 4 (Oct.-Dec. 1945), suplemento. **[725a]**

Manuscripts of two *solos humanos*, one by Manuel de Villa-flor, the other by Antonio Literes (d. 1747) are reproduced in facsimile (voice and figured bass parts separate). 2 pages of tablatures for Spanish *vihuela*. (C.S.)

——. Panorama de la música tradicional

de México. Instituto de investigaciones estéticas. Universidad nacional autónoma de México. Estudios y fuentes del arte en México, VII. México, Imprenta universitaria, 1956. 258 p. (music). **[726a]**

By "traditional music" the author means the music that has a vital organic relation to the national culture of a people. At its core is folk music. "La música folklórica de mi país es llamada por antonomasia música mexicana. Es ella la forma genuina de expresión de nuestro pueblo". This book deals with the indigenous music of Mexico, with neo-Hispanic music of the 16th, 17th and 18th centuries, and with "Mexican Music" as defined above (folk and popular currents). There are 231 musical notations, 49 plates, and several bibliographies. An extremely valuable work.

——. Supervivencias de la cultura azteca; la canción y el baile del Xochipzahua, *Rev. mex. soc.*, v. 4, no. 4 (1942), p. 87-98. **[727a]**

An important study, with music notations.

——. Un juego español del siglo xvi entre los otomíes *An. inst. invest. est.*, v. 3, no. 10 (1943), p. 59-74. **[728a]**

Includes music notations.

——. Un romance castellano que vive en México. *An. soc. folk. Méx.*, v. 1 (1942), p. 69-78. **[729a]**

The ballad is "El enamorado y la muerte'". Includes music notations.

——. Una adoración de pastores en Chipalcingo. Teatro tradicional. *An. inst. invest. est.*, no. 18 (1950), p. 35-62. **[730a]**

15 music notations of complete melodíes taken at dictation from informant "que es ha dado al trabajo de alentar esta clase de representaciones religiosas. . ." and who possessed the written (speech) text of this *adoración*. (C.S.)

——. Una canción estremeña. *Rev. hisp. mod.*, v. 10, nos. 1-2 (1944), p. 174-179). **[731a]**

Gives words and music of 2 variants of a Christmas carol as an example of a song of Extremaduran origin in Spain, which appears in Mexico in a zone of Andalusian influence (Jalisco). (R.S.B.)

——. Una canción isabelina en México. *Divulgación histórica.* México, D. F., v. 4, no. 4 (Feb. 15, 1943), p. 214-220. [732a]

Gives verses only and examines variants of ballad "Dónde vas Isabel?" from Jalisco, Michoacán, Sinaloa and Nuevo León, México, and compares it with an Andalusian children's game "La ponchada" printed in Mexico first *c.* 1840. Concludes this ballad, of political implications, refers to queen Isabel II, was produced *c.* 1837, and became current in Mexico, also with political implications, toward the middle of the century. (R.S.B.)

——, and Manuel García Matos. Las flautas de tres perforaciones que usan los indígenas de México son de origen hispano. *An. soc. folk. Méx.,* v. 5 (1944, pub. 1945), p. 183-187. [733a]

Mendoza's letter of inquiry and García Mato's reply deal with the world-wide distribution of this instrument. One music notation, one photograph. (C. S.)

——, and Virginia Rodríguez Rivera de Mendoza. Folklore de San Pedro Piedra Gorda. México, D. F., Talleres gráficos de la nación, 1952. [734a]

The work is divided into 2 parts: I, La literatura popular, la música, los juegos infantiles y el teatro tradicional; II, la narración tradicional, que incluye leyendas, tradiciones y cuentos; vida, costumbre y fiesta; artes y oficios, comidas y bebidas, creencias, habla popular, refranes y adivinanzas.

Monguió, Luis. El corrido mexicano, canto de libertad. *Rev. América.* v. 4, no. 11 (Nov. 1945), p. 257-266. [735a]

Brief historical review of revolutionary themes and their use in wars of independence and reform, down to the international oil issue and the war against the Axis (1942).

Mora Carlos. Sinfónica del pueblo. La nota picaresca y alegre en las tardes de la provincia. Generaciones de músicos. Una tradición inalterable. Las charan-

gas. La serenata. La feria. Las corridas de toros pueblerinas. Evocaciones de López Velarde. El Mexicano eterno reflejado en la música popular. *Hoy,* México, no. 492, (July 27 1946), p. 37-45. [736a]

Brief comments accompanying 20 fine photographs of an aspect of contemporary community music life rarely reported.

Música folklórica mexicana; inventario de discos grabados por la sección de investigaciones musicales del I.N.B.A. México, D. F., Instituto nacional de bellas artes, 1952. 78 p. [737a]

Pugh, Grace Thompson. Mexican folk dances (2d ed.) Workshop in the Inter-American education summer session, 1944. Southwest Texas, State Teachers college, San Marcos, Texas, in cooperation with Office of Inter-American affairs. New York, Curriculum service bureau for international studies, inc., 1947, 36 p. [738a]

Very brief explanations of different Mexican folk dances, classified by regions. Bibliography: p. 35-36.

Rodríguez Rivera, Virginia. La copla mexicana; estudio preliminar. *An. soc. folk. Méx.,* v. 1 (1942), p. 103-121. [739a]

Good general survey of this typically Spanish concise octosyllabic quatrain and its variant types in Mexico, with examples, 3 with music. (R.S.B.)

Romero, Jesús C. Durango en la evolución musical de México. *Mem. cong. mex. hist.,* 1949, p. 273-316. [740a]

Points to the neglect of study of the music of Durango. After brief historical review, 3-5 pages are given to each of nine composers born between 1826 and 1903, including Silvestre Revueltas. Lists of works are given. (C. S.)

——. El folklore en México. *Bol. soc. mex. geog. estad.,* v. 63, no. 3 (May-June 1947), p. 657-798. [741a]

Largely a theoretical discussion of the doctrinal basis of the "science of Folklore", with historical and polemical injections. The author's definition of folklore (p.

686) is built on the concepts of the vernacular, the spontaneous, and the anonymous as contrasted with what he calls "una cultura universal" (i.e., learned or cultivated tradition), within which folklore evolves. An enormous footnote (pp. 782-786) is useful for bio-bibliographical data on Vicente T. Mendoza (b. Cholula, Puebla, Jan. 27, 1894), a leading Mexican folklorist (q. v.). The article makes special reference to musical folklore and the various organizations in Mexico concerned with it. Also printed separately.

———. Música precortesiana; estudio histórico-crítico de nuestra proto-historia musical *Orientac, mus.*, v. 2, no. 19 (Jan. 1943), p. 12-13; no. 20 (Feb. 1943) p. 8-10, 16; no. 21 (March 1943), p. 8-9; no. 22 (April 1943), p. 12-13; no. 23 (May 1943), p. 8-9, 17; no. 24 (June 1943), p. 7-8, 20.   [742a]

Ruiz Maza, Vicente. Fiestas de la Candelaria en Medellín, Ver., y otras celebraciones en el estado. *An. soc. falk. Méx.* v. 8 (1954), p. 41-55.   [743a]
Brief account of customs, a few details on musicians, with 6 melodies and song texts, for most of which informant, place and time of collection are indicated. Two photographs of 1951 celebration.

Saldívar, Gabriel. Mariano Elízaga y las canciones de la Independencia. *Bol. soc. mex. geog. estad.*, v. 63, no. 3 (May-June 1947), p. 641-656.   [744a]
Historical study of titles and texts only.

Sánchez García, Julio. La Virgen de San Juan de los Lagos en México; fiesta el 1 y 2 de febrero de 1947. *An. Soc. folk. Méx.*, v. 8 (1954), p. 57-79.   [745a]
Account of a new sanctuary just outside Mexico City, and its first major celebration. Description of community, church, also of festival as celebrated at San Juan de los Lagos, in Jalisco, long a place of pilgrimage. Details about dances, especially that representing the Wars against the French. 7 photographs, one music example, bibliography.

Selvas, Eduardo J. La música de la val-

diviana. *Ateneo,* Chiapas, v. 3, no. 4 Apr.-June 1952), p. 77-82.   [746a]
Deals briefly with the popular marimba music of the valleys of Cintalpa and Jiquilpilas and the dances associated with it. Includes three musical notations. (R.A.W.)

Sinclair, Ward. Salinas and Songs; Mexico's leading guitar makers. *Américas,* v. 9, no. 12 (Dec. 1957), p. 13-15.   [747a]
With 4 photographs.

Toor, Frances. A treasury of Mexican folkways. The customs, myths, folklore, traditions, beliefs, fiestas, dances and songs of the Mexican people. Illustrated with 10 color plates, 100 drawings by Carlos Mérida, and 170 photographs. New York, Crown publishers, 1947. 566 p. il. (music).   [748a]
Part III is devoted to music and dance, with copious musical notations (cf. esp. p. 377-453).

Vázquez Santa Ana, Higinio. Fiestas y costumbres mexicanas. Tomo I. México, D. F. Ed. Botas, 1940. 381 p.   [749a]
Incidental comments on folk music and dances.

Yurchenco, Henrietta. Grabación de música indígena. *Nuestra música.* v. 2, no. 2 (May 1945), p. 65-78, il. [750a]
The author has done extensive field recording in Mexico. Two interesting photographs of native musicians.

———. La música indígena en Chiapas, México. *Amér. indígena*, v. 3, no. 4 (Oct. 1943), p. 305-311.   [751a]
Report upon an expedition under the auspices of the Inter-American Indian Institute with cooperation of the Music Division of the Library of Congress, which made sound recordings on discs of the music of the Zoque, Tzotzil, Chiapaneco and Tojolobal Indian groups. 100 *sones* were recorded and 700 feet of 16 mm. film made. One music notation. (C.S.)

———. La recopilación de música indígena. *Amér. indígena* ,v. 6, no. 4 (Oct. 1946), p. 321-331.   [752a]
Observations upon field collection tech-

niques with sound recording on discs, based upon experience over a period of four years among Tarascan, Cora, Huichol, Seri, Tzeltal, Tzotzil, Tarahumaran and Yaqui groups. The 15 original discs are deposited in the Archive of American Folksong of the Library of Congress. (C.S.)

B. ART MUSIC AND MISCELLANEOUS

Agea, Francisco. Blas Galindo. *Méx. en el arte,* no. 5 (Nov. 1948), n. p. **[753a]**
Brief account of the life and work of the composer (b. 1910). Classified list of works in chronological order (C.S.)

Bal y Gay, Jesús. El nacionalismo y la música mexicana de hoy. *Nuestra música,* v. 4, no. 14 (Apr. 1949), p. 107-113. **[754a]**
Traces evolution of Mexican nationalism in music from its early *pintoresquismo,* thorugh literal folklorism to the absorption of the spirit of the music of the people (C. S.)

———. "La Hija de Cólquide" de Carlos Chávez. *Nuestra música,* v. 5, no. 19 (3, trimestre, 1950), p. 207-216. (music). **[755a]**
Analysis, with 15 musical notations.

———. Rodolof Halffter. *Nuestra música.* v. 1, no. 3 (July 1946), p. 141-146. (music). il. **[756a]**
Photograph of the composer with Carlos Chávez and Samuel Dushkin (the interpreter of his Violin Concerto), facsimile of holograph score of one page of the ballet *Don Lindo de Almería,* and list of works.

———. La "Sinfonía de Antígona" de Carlos Chávez. *Nuestra música.* v. 5, no. 17 (1. trimestre, 1950), p. 5-17. (music) **[757a]**
Analysis, with 12 musical notations and reproduction of a page of the score.

———. Los conciertos de la O.S.N.C. *Nuestra música,* v. 4, no. 14 (Apr. 1949), p. 153-156. **[758a]**
Review of several concerts given by the National Symphony Orchestra of the Conservatory, conducted by José Pablo Moncayo, and guest conductors. Listing of works

by Mexican composers played (Mariscal, Moncayo, Chávez, Jiménez Mabarak and Rolón), without details.

Baqueiro Fóster, Gerónimo. El pasado y el presente del Conservatorio nacional. *Numen,* v. 1, no. 3 (June 1946), p. 11-17. **[759a]**
Brief history, with suggestions for reorganization. (C.S.)

Barajas, Manuel. El himno nacional mexicano, su historia y la búsqueda del original, las deformaciones sufridas. México, Secretaría de Educación Pública, 1942. 8 p. il. (incl. music). **[760a]**

Barbacci, Rodolfo. Julián Carrillo y la revolución musical del sonido 13. *Bellas Artes* (Lima), v. 6, no. 4 (1846), p. 9-10.
Cf. item 1796.

Bermejo, Manuel M. La escuela libre de música y declamación, 1920-1945. Esbozo sintético sobre su fundación y actividades. *Rev. mus. mex.,* v. 5, no. 4 (Apr. 1945), p. 75-79. **[761a]**

Bernal Jiménez, Miguel. La música en Valladolid de Michoacán. *Nuestra música,* v. 6, no. 23 (3. trimestre, 1951), p. 153-176. **[762a]**
Deals with musical institutions in the 18th century, with 5 illustrations.

———. La música en Valladolid de Michoacán, 2. Archivos. *Nuestra música,* v. 7, no. 25 (1. trimestre 1952), p. 5-16. **[763a]**
An appraisal of the musical holdings of six archives and two other collections in Valladolid de Michoacán. (R.A.S.)

Brenner, Leah. Chávez ends Mexican series. *Mus. Amer.,* v. 63, no. 1 (Jan. 1943), p. 11. **[764a]**
First performances during season of Mexico Symphony include Galindo's Concerto for piano and orchestra, Moncada's *Sinfonia,* Huízar's 4th Symphony, and Rolón's Concerto in E minor for piano and orchestra.

Campos, Rubén M. D. Jaime Nunó,

autor del himno nacional mexicano. *An. museo nac. arq. hist. etnogr.*, 5. época, v. 2 (1935), p. 165-168.

[765a]

——. Juventino Rosas y la música popular de su época (1880-1890). *Anales del Instituto nacional de antropología e historia* (México), v. I (1939/40-1945) p. 237-353.

[767a]

Carrillo, Julián. Leyes de metamorfosis musicales. Escritas en Nueva York en el año de 1927, y publicadas en México en 1949. México, D. F. Privately printed, 1949. 89 p. (music).

[768a]

"Escritas en Nueva York en el año de 1927" (title-page). A system for the "metamorphosis" of any and all music that has ever been written, "without adding or subtracting a single note of the original composition". The system is based on "the laws of relations and proportions", since it derives from the relations and proportions of the intervals, in both their melodic and their harmonic aspects. Under this system, the 9 symphonies of Beethoven, multiplied by 34,260 (the number of possible metamorphoses) give a total of 308,340 symphonies. The 11 operas of Wagner would yield 276, 860 metamorphoses. The formula is fully explained in the text.

——. Pláticas musicales. 3 ed. México, D. F., Privately printed, 1930. 157 p. il.

[769a]

A miscellany. Of special interest for Mexican music are the sections on Alberto Villaseñor and Juan Hernández Acevedo, as well as on the project for a Conservatory of Music in Mexico City. The prologue is dated, "México, septiembre de 1913", and is signed José L. del Castillo.

——. "Pre-sonido 13". Rectificación básica en el sistema musical clásico. Análisis físico-músico. Segunda edición. San Luis Potosí, Editorial del sonido 13, 1930. 62 p. (music).

[770a]

"Obra escrita en New York en 1926" (title-page). The author's thesis is that "The classical musical system is based on the greatest error ever committed in the entire history of music, namely, the impurity of intervals". He announces "a general rectification of the musical culture of the world". He maintains that the terms "tone"

and "semitone" should never have been used, because "technically there have never been either tones or semitones". Also, "The classical musical theory of consonance and dissonance is absolutely false". Therefore, "In order to avoid the repetition of these secular errors, the Revolution of the *Sonido 13* has supressed the names of all the sounds hitherto used, and which are illogical, confused, insufficient and, above all, unnecessary".

——. "Sonido 13". Fundamento científico e histórico. México, Privately printed, 1948. 67 p. (music).

[771a]

The author writes: "In 1895 I succeeded in dividing the classical tone into 16 equal intervals, and with that experiment was broken the cycle of the 12 sounds in the octave in which music had been enclosed during centuries. Upon the breaking of this cycle, the number of musical sounds increased so extraordinarily that, instead of the 12 that existed, they reached in an instant the number of 96 (within the octave)". The term "Sonido 13" was applied to the new system because 13 was the first number, in numerical order, that followed the existing 12 sounds of the octave and which thus "broke the the classical cycle, opening the breach for the present musical revolution". This new sound was produced at the distance of 1/16th of a tone above the note G of the fourth string of the violin. Its mathematical ratio is 1.007246.

——. Teoría lógica de la música. Segunda edición. México, D. F. Privately printed, 1954. 150 p. (music). [772a]

This work is presented "con criterio absolutamente revolucionario". The Author's program: "That music should be written as easily as a letter and be read as easily as a newspaper, is one of the ideals that I seek"; and: "With this new musical notation based on 12 numerals from O to 11 —the whole of mankind will be enabled to write and read music". Each of the 12 notes of the octave is represented by an invariable number. But the system also provides for numerical notations based on various other divisions of the octave, from 3rds to 16ths of a tone (i. e., from 18 to 96 different sounds). "All the rules stated for the writing of music with 12 sounds... can be applied to all other systems, no matter what may be the number of sounds in a given cycle."

Cervantes de Salazar, Francisco. Crónicas de Nueva España, escrita por el
Dr. y maestro Francisco Cervantes de
Salazar cronista de la ciudad de México. Manuscrto 2011 de la Biblioteca nacional de Madrid, letra de la mitad del
siglo xvi. Madrid, Hauser y Menet,
1914. (Papeles de Nueva España, com-
pilados y publicados por Francisco del
Paso y Troncoso. 3. ser. Historia).
                                [773a]
Cf. Book I, chapters 16, 20, 23, 24,
27, 28. Another edition, edited by M.
Magallón, was published by the Hispanic society of America, Madrid, 1914.

Chávez, Carlos. Blas Galindo. *Nuestra
música.* v. 1, no. 1. (March 1946), p.
7-13. il.   [774a]
"Blas Galindo es un caso espléndido de
la fuerza creadora de México." Photographic portrait of the composer and his
family, facsimile of the holograph score
of the first page of his Sonata for violin
and piano, and list of compositions.

——. Blas Galindo *Bol. progr. Col.,* v.
19, no. 187 (Feb. 1960), p. 4-6. [775a]
Brief appreciation of the work and personality of this Mexican composer, illustrated with portrait. Reprinted from *Nuestra Música.*

——. Carlos Chávez. Catalog of his
works with a preface by Herbert
Weinstock. Catálogo de sus obras, con
un prólogo de Herbert Weinstock.
Washington, D. C., Pan American
union, Music division, 1944. xxxii, 15
p. (Music series no. 11).   [776a]
The introduction by Weinstock was first
published in *Musical quarterly,* v. 32, no.
4 (Oct. 1936), and is reprinted here with
some modifications made by the author
(cf. item no. 868a). The bibliography is
in 3 parts: I, Published writings of Carlos
Chávez. II, Works about Carlos Chávez.
III, Some sources of portraits of Carlos
Chávez. The catalog of works is in 4
parts: I, Chronological list; II, Juvenilia;
III. Classified list: IV. Recordings. The
frontispiece is an informal camera portrait of the composer.

——. Carta a Antonio Rodríguez. *Nues-*

tra música, v. 3, no. 10 (Apr. 1948),
p. 100-198.   [777a]
Reply, in the form of an open letter,
to an "imaginary interview" entitled
"Las extrañas contradicciones del maestro
Chávez", published by Rodríguez in the
review *Mañana* of March 20 1948. Defends
his activities in Mexican musical life.

——. 50 años de música en México. *Mex.
en el Arte,* no. 10-11 (1951), p. 201-
238. il.   [778a]
A section from a book currently in preparation, to be called *La música en México,* this essay reviews the history of
Mexican music from 1900 to 1950 in three
epochs (1900-1915, 1915-1928, and 1928-
1950), with special attention to composers. (R.A.W.)

——. Chronological catalog of works by
the Mexican composer Carlos Chávez.
Bol. mus. artes, nos. 71-73 (Jan., Feb.,
March. 1956), p. 37-44.   [779a]

——. Discurso de Carlos Chávez pronun-
ciado con motivo de la inauguración
del nuevo edificio del Conservatorio.
Nuestra música, v. 4, no. 14 (Apr.
1949), p. 142–146.   [780a]
Historical sketch of the Conservatory
from its beginnnings in the middle of the
nineteenth century, and views concerning
the rôle the government should play at
present in supporting music, and art in
general.

——. Iniciación a la dirección de orquesta. *Nuestra música,* v. 3, no. 9 (Jan.
1948), p. 5-10 (continuación). [781a]
Part 11, on psychology involved in orchestra conducting.

——. La música mexicana. *Univ. Habana,* v. 13, no. 76-81 (1948), p. 213-
244.   [782a]
On the difference between the music of
Mexico and the music *in* Mexico. Three
music notations. (C.S.)

——. La ópera como forma. *Méx. en el
arte,* no. 4 (Oct. 1948), n. p. [783a]
Brief survey of the present situation
in Mexico, attitudes of composer and public, nationalism in opera, opera in the
palace of Bellas Artes, possibilities of a

national Mexican opera. Eight fine illustrations. (C.S.)

——. La sinfónica nacional. *Nuestra música*, v. 5, no. 18 (2. trimestre, 1950), p. 111-137.   [784a]

The "Sinfónica Nacional" of Mexico was established by Presidential Decree published in the *Diario Oficial* of July 18, 1947. It was then officially named "Orquesta Sinfónica del Conservatorio Nacional". In April 1949 a new decree changed the name to "Orquesta Sinfónica Nacional". The article is a detailed account of the organization and functioning of the orchestra, with mention of its historical antecedents.

——. Luis Sandi. *Nuestra música*, v. 4, no. 15 (July 1949), p. 175-179. il. (port.)   [785a]

——. Mexican music. *Mexican life* (México), v. 23, no. 9 (Sept. 1947), p. 21-22,56.   [786a]

Chávez quits post as leader of Mexico symphony. *Mus. Amer.*, v. 59, no. 4 (March 1949), p. 3.   [787a]

Chávez resigns and association of National Symphony orchestra is dissolved.

Cheiner, Sophie. Silvestre Revueltas. *Rev. I.F.A.L.*, v. 1, no. 1 (June 1945), p. 161-170.   [788a]

Appreciative biographical notice of composer (1899-1940). Half-tone facsimiles of two pages each of autograph scores of "Redes" and of "Ventanas". (C.S.)

Copland, Aaron. Música y músicos contemporáneos. Buenos Aires, Editorial Losada, 1945. 269 p.   [789a]

Spanish translation by Néstor Rodríguez Oderigo of item no. 1797. Brief evaluation of the music of Carlos Chávez followed by a list of recordings of his compositions, p. 187-193.

Correspondencia cruzada entre la señora Clema Maurel de Ponce y el Dr. Jesús C. Romero a propósito de las *Efemérides de Manuel M. Ponce.* *Nuestra música*, v. 6, no. 21 (1. trimestre, 1951), p. 48-59.   [790a]

A polemic concerning certain biographical data.

Critilo. (pseud.) Bonampak, ballet de Luis Sandi. *Nuestra música*, v. 7, no. 26 (2º trimestre, 1952), p. 157-159.   [791a]

——. Dos obras instrumentales. *Nuestra música*, v. 4, no. 15 (July 1949), p. 215-219. (music).   [792a]

Comment on Luis Sandi's *Fátima* (*Suite Galante* for guitar and Rodolfo Halffter's *Pastorale* for violin and piano, with 9 fragmentary musical notations.

——. Orquesta sinfónica nacional. *Nuestra música*, v. 3, no. 12 (Oct. 1948), p. 271-274.   [793a]

Review of the orchestra's second season. Mention of works played, with amplification on the works by the young Mexican composers Pablo Moncayo (*Tres Piezas para orquesta*), Carlos Jiménez Mabarak (*Primera Sinfonía*), and Luis Herrera de la Fuente (*Dos Movimientos para orquesta*).

Del Río, Alfonso. El "Coro de Madrigalistas": cómo nació esta agrupación. *Nuestra música*, v. 3, no. 12 (Oct. 1948), p. 251-264.   [794a]

Record of the founding of the Chorus in 1938, its original membership, its concert activities, with some financial details. Several programs are listed.

Díaz de León, Rafael. Los autores del himno nacional. San Luis Potosí, S. L. P., México, Editorial "Valores humanos", 1937. 61 p. il. (incl. music).   [795a]

Booklet with historical information on the authors of both music and words.

Field, Michael Greet. La segunda sonata para piano, de Rodolfo Halffter. *Nuestra música*, v. 7, no. 27-28 (3, trimestre, 1952), p. 208-211.   [796a]

Halffter's Piano Sonata Nº 2 was first performed by Miguel García Mora on Aug. 4, 1952.

——. Las "Once Bagatelas" de Rodolfo Halffter. *Nuestra música*, v. 6, no. 21 (1. trimestre, 1951), p. 44-48. (music)   [797a]

Eleven pieces for piano, written with pedagogical intent.

——. Two-world composer; Rodolfo Halffter, Spaniard living in Mexico, thinks music should be melodious. *Américas,* v. 7, no. 10 (Oct. 1955), p. 10-14. il.   [798a]

Biography with extensive comment on compositions, and musical life in Mexico.

Galindo, Blas. Compositores de mi generación. *Nuestra música,* v. 3, no. 10 (Apr. 1948), p. 73-81.   [799a]

Primarily about the "Grupo de los cuatro", Salvador Contreras, Daniel Ayala, José Pablo Moncayo and Galindo. Discusses the group's training and careers, and provides a brief biography and review and critique of the compositions of each of the other three. Mentions Carlos Jiménez Mabarak briefly as another outstanding Mexican composer in his 30s. Photograph of the four.

——. C. Huízar. *Nuestra música.* v. 1, no. 2 (May 1946), p. 57-64. (music). il.   [800a]

The Mexican composer Candelario Huízar was born in 1888. List of his works, portrait of the composer, and facsimile of the first page of the holograph score of his Symphony N⁰ 4.

García Morillo, Roberto. Carlos Chávez: vida y obra. México-Buenos Aires, 1960. 241p. il. (music).   [801a]

González de Mendoza, J. M. "Música de Cámara de México" y su labor. *Bol. sem. cult. mex.,* v. 2, no. 4 (Sept. 1945), p. 31-35.   [802a]

Account of the activity of the society founded early in 1944. (C.S.)

Herrera de la Fuente, Luis. La ópera de Bellas Artes. *Nuestra música,* v. 3, no. 12 (Oct. 1948), p. 268-271. [803a]

Brief introduction on the state of opera in Mexico ("muy raquítica, casi inerte"). Then reviews the season's performances of *Mefistofele* of Boito, *Carmen* and *La Traviata.*

——. Óperas mexicanas. *Nuestra música,* v. 4, no. 13 (Jan. 1949), p. 45-48.   [804a]

Discussion of three new Mexican operas:

Carlota by Luis Sandi, *La Mulata de Córdoba* by José Pablo Moncayo, and *Elena* by Eduardo Hernández Moncada, all commissioned b ythe Instituto de Bellas Artes, and produced shortly before this writing.

Ibarra, Alfredo, Jr. Vicente T. Mendoza. *An. soc.folk. Méx.,* v. 4 (1943), p. 9-23.   [805a]

An appreciation of Mendoza's work on the occasion of his 50th birthday, followed by biobibliographic data, list of published writings, music compositions, and lectures.

Ichaso, Francisco. Carlos Chávez en La Habana. *Nuestra música,* v. 3, no. 12 (Oct. 1948), p. 265-268.   [806a]

Reprinted from *Diario de la Marina.* Highly laudatory account of Chávez' performance as visiting conductor of the Philharmonic Orchestra of Havana.

Kahan, Solomon. México; Toward development of the seeds of nationalism. *Mus. Amer.,* v. 70, no. 2 (Jan. 1950), p. 29, 72.   [807a]

Review of trends in Mexican composition. Plans for the new season (1950). Growth of the provincial orchestras. (B.K.)

——. Native opera enters Mexican repertoire. *Mus. Amer.,* v. 59, no. 14 (Nov. 1949), p. 10.   [808a]

Review of season. One native opera successfully produced: *Tata Vasco* by Miguel Bernal Jiménez. (B.K.)

Kelemen, Pál. Church organs in colonial Mexico. *Bull pan. Amer. union,* v. 76, no. 3 (March 1942), p. 121-132. (il.)   [809a]

La XXI Temporada de la orquesta sinfónica de México. *Nuestra música,* v. 3, no. 10 (Apr. 1948), p. 113-116.   [810a]

Brief account of the successes of the season which was organized by Chávez, followed by a list of the works performed.

Ley que crea el Instituto nacional de bellas artes y literatura. *Diario ofi-*

cial, México, v. 159, no. 50, sec. 4ª (Dec. 31, 1946), p. 9-11.   **[811a]**

The objects of the Institute are to cultivate, promote and stimulate creation and research in music, painting, sculpture, architecture, theatre, dance and belles lettres. Its administration depends upon the Secretaría de Educación Pública. Carlos Chávez was the first director. (C. S.)

Limón, José. Music is the strongest ally to a dancer's way of life. *Mus. Amer.,* v. 75, no. 4 (Feb. 15, 1955), p. 10-11.   **[812a]**

Mostly on relationship of music and dance; some comment on dancing to music of Mexican composers Chávez and Revueltas, and on seasons performing in Mexico, Rio de Janeiro and São Paulo.

María y Campos, Armando de. Una temporada de ópera italiana en Oaxaca (crónica). Ilustrada con programas, viñetas y hojas impresas de la época, de los archivos del autor. México, D. F., Compañía de ediciones populares, S. A., 1939. 189 p. il.   **[813a]**

Mayer-Serra, Otto. The present state of music in Mexico. Translated into English by Frank Jellinek. Washington, D. C., Music division, Pan American union, 1946. 47 p. (Music series no. 14) Bilingual text (Spanish and English).   **[814a]**

Contents: 1, The present and the past: general survey. 2, Art music: importation and imitation. 3, Folk music, 4, The development of musical nationalism. 5, Towards universalization. 6, Conclusion: the future. Foreword by Charles Seeger. The author views the future of Mexican music in terms of "a receptive nationalism" (phrase coined by Carlos Chávez).

Mendoza, Vicente T. La música en la época de la reforma, la intervención y el imperio. (Separata do *Douro Litoral Boletim da Comissão de Etnografia e Historia — Oitava Serie* — I-II). Porto, 1957. 36 p. (music).   **[815a]**

Studies both popular and "erudite" music, with citation of numerous texts and several musical notations. Includes brief

bibliography. The period covered is from 1850 to 1867.

——. Técnica de Carlos Chávez. *An. inst. invest. est.,* v. 3 (1939), p. 21-24.   **[816a]**

Muñoz, Peggy. Growth of Mexican concerts. *Mus. Amer.,* v. 75, no. 5 (Mar. 1955), p. 12.   **[817a]**

Review of concerts in Mexico City in 1954.

——. In recent years Mexico City has grown into an international center of music. *Mus. Amer.,* v. 75, no. 4 (Mar. 1953), p. 8.   **[818a]**

Full page survey of musical and dance activities in city, indicating when various institutions and groups began. and giving a sense of the development.

——. Mexico. *Mus. Amer.,* v. 74, no. 4 (Feb. 15, 1954), p. 164, 168.   **[819a]**

Extensive review of 1953 season in Mexico City, with attention to contemporary music.

——. Musical events in Mexico reach new heights during recent months *Mus. Amer.,* v. 74, no. 13 (Nov. 1, 1954), p. 22.   **[820a]**

Review of summer and fall concert season in Mexico City, also of orchestras of Guanajuato (José Rodríguez Fraust [*sic*] conductor), and Guadalajara (Abel Eisenberg conductor).

——. On with the dance; the startling career of Mexican-born José Limón. *Américas,* v. 5, no. 4 (Apr. 1953), p. 13-16, 44.   **[821a]**

Includes references to Limón's doing the choreography for Chávez' ballet *Los Cuatro Soles,* for *Redes,* to music by Silvestre Revueltas, and for *Antigone,* also by Chávez. Five photographs, one of Limón in *Redes.*

——. Opportunity for conductor comparison presented by spring season in Mexico. *Mus. Amer.,* v. 73, no. 10 (Aug. 1953), p. 23.   **[822a]**

Includes critical comments on first performance in Mexico of Chávez' Fourth symphony and Julián Carrillo's *Horizontes* for orchestra.

——. Reorganized Mexican symphony memorable. *Mus. Amer.*, v. 76, no. 4 (Feb. 15, 1956), p. 180. **[823a]**

On 1955 season of reorganized National Symphony of Mexico; also on ballet.

——. Silvestre Revueltas. *Mus. Amer.*, v. 78, no. 3 (Feb. 1958), p. 17, 133-134, 156. il. (port.) **[824a]**

A rather superficial sketch, including the backgrounds of musical nationalism in Mexico, with numerous quotations from unidentified sources.

——. Symphony tours Mexico in decentralization program. *Mus. Amer.*, v. 76, no. 14 (Nov. 15, 1956), p. 29. **[825a]**

Review of summer season of National Symphony, University Symphony and other concerts.

——. Young voices of Morelia. Mexican boys' choir scores international hit. *Américas*, v. 7, no. 9 (Sept. 1955), p. 9-13. **[826a]**

Acount of founding, travel experiences, repertoire. Nine photographs.

Osorio, Adolfo. La orquesta sinfónica de Xalapa. *Nuestra música*, v. 3, no. 12 (Oct. 1948), p. 274-276. **[827a]**

Account of the activities of the orchestra in 1945-1948.

Paes, Mariano. Ópera en México de 1800 a 1890. *Car. mus.*, v. 8 (1952): no. 3 (March), p. 100-101; no. 4 (Apr.), p. 156-157; no. 5 (May), p. 220-221; no. 6 (June), p. 291-292; no. 8 (Aug.), p. 381-384. **[828a]**

Brief treatise on the history of the opera in 19th-century Mexico. (R.A.W)

Perucho, Arturo. Ballet moderno en México. *Nuestra música*, v. 2, no. 8 (Oct. 1947), p. 177-191. il. **[829a]**

Photographs of two scenes from ballets by Revueltas, *La Coronela* and *El Renacuajo paseador*.

Pincherle, Marc. A la memoria de Manuel M. Ponce. *Nuestra música*, v. 5,

no. 18 (2. trimestre, 1950), p. 160-163. il. **[830a]**

Biographical sketch and critical appreciation, with a photographic portrait of the composer and his wife.

Ponce, Manuel M. La música y la educación. *Repr. camp.*, año 2, v. 3 (May-June 1945), p. 13-19. **[831a]**

A conservative leader recommends avoidance of the "disorder" of styles of the last 20 years and avoidance of "ritmos vulgares..., las canciones de subido color erótico" and "lo cursi". (C.S.)

Ponce y López Buchardo; dos grandes pérdidas para la música americana. *Rev. mus. chil.*, v. 4, no. 29 (June-July 1948), p. 6-8. **[832a]**

Brief biographies of Manuel Ponce of Mexico and Carlos López Buchardo of Argentina, with appreciations of their music. (B.K.)

Pope, Isabel. Documentos relacionados con la historia de la música en México. *Nuestra música*, v. 6, no. 21 (1. trimestre 1951), p. 5-28. **[833a]**

Biographical data on Pre-Cortesian music and folklore; Music as an instrument of religious conversion; Official and ecclesiastical documents related to music; Music in civic and religious festivals; and miscellaneous.

——. Documentos relacionados con la historia de la música en México, existentes en los archivos y bibliotecas españoles. *Nuestra música*, v. 6, no. 24 (4 trimestre 1951), p. 245-253. **[834a]**

Extracts from three manuscripts concerning pre-Conquest Mexican music in the Biblioteca Nacional, Madrid. (R.A.W.)

Pulido, Esperanza. Música mexicana. *Rev. mus. chil.*, v. 13, no. 65 (May-June 1959), p. 57-62, no. 66 (July-Aug. 1959), p. 73-79. **[835a]**

Deals with Manuel Ponce and other Mexican composers.

Revueltas, Silvestre. Notas y escritos. (Fragmentos). *Nuestra música*, v. 2, no. 3 (July 1946), p. 147-152. **[836a]**

Random comments that reveal the composer's agile and paradoxical thought.

——. Chronological catalog of works by the Mexican composer Silvestre Revueltas. *Bol. mus. artes,* no. 40 (June 1953), p. 23-24.   [837a]

Reyes Meave, Manuel. Psicobiografía de Silvestre Revueltas. *Nuestra música,* v. 7, no. 27-28 (3.-4. trimestres, 1952), p. 173-187.   [838a]

Interpretation of Revueltas' career and his music in terms of opposing forces in his personality. Has a chronology of his life as composer, violinist, conductor, and painter. (R.A.W.)

Romero, Jesús C. Candelario Huízar. *Nuestra música,* v. 7, no. 25 (1. trimestre, 1952), p. 45-61.   [839a]

Chronological and classified list of the composer's works, p. 58-61.

——. Efemérides de Manuel (María) Ponce. *Nuestra música,* v. 5, no. 18 (2, trimestre, 1950), p. 164-202. [840a]

Chronology of the life and works of the Mexican composer. Cf. item 790a.

——. El francesismo en la evolución musical de México. *Car. mus.,* v. 5, no. 4 (July 1949), supl. no. 1, 12 p. [841a]

Excellent study, tracing the influence of French music from 1841 to, roughly, the second decade of the 20th century. (C.S.)

——. El inicio del chopinismo en México. *Mem. r. ac. nac. cien.,* v. 57, nos. 1-2 (1952), p. 181-240.   [842a]

A detailed study of the origins and development of the cult of Chopin in Mexico. (R.A.W.)

——. El periodismo musical mexicano en el siglo xx. *Car. mus.,* v. 9, no. 9, no. 3 (March 1952), p. 138-147.   [843a]

A comprehensive list of musical periodicals published in Mexico, with particulars concerning publishers, prices, dates of publication, etc. (R.A.W.)

——. Galería de maestros mexicanos de música: Rafael J Tello. *Bol. dep. mús. inst. nac.* no. 4 (Feb. 1947), p. 38-40.   [844a]

Tello was born in 1872 and died in 1946.

——. Galería de músicos mexicanos. *Car. mus.,* v. 8, nos. 1-12 (1952), p. 12-13, 63-64, 122, 192-193, 235, 264, 341-344, 388-389, 431-432, 458, 535, 558. [845a]

A series of short biographies of Miguel Bernal Jiménez, José Briseño, Guadalupe Barroeta, Gerónimo Baqueiro Fóster, Carmen Bretón Fontecilla, Francisco Cuervo, Arturo Cosgaya Caballos, José María Carrasco, and Ramón Cardona, in the order named. (R.A.W.)

——. Historia del conservatorio. *Nuestra música.* v. 1, no. 3 (July 1946), p. 153-194. il.   [486a]

——. Historia del conservatorio. Capítulo II. *Nuestra música,* v. 1, no. 4 (Sept. 1946), p. 251-275.   [847a]

Deals especially with the Sociedad Filarmónica.

——. La ópera en Yucatán México, Ediciones "Guión de América", 1947. 103 p.   [848a]

In spite of the localization indicated in the title, this monograph surveys briefly the entire evolution of opera, with special refrence to Spain and Mexico. Points to the economic factor as a major obstacle in the path of operatic development in Mexico.

——. Manuel M. Ponce, premio nacional. *Nuestra música,* v. 3, no. 10 (Apr. 1948), p. 90-99.   [849a]

Account of the history of the prize, the presentation of it to maestro Ponce, the speeches by Chávez (as Director General of the Institute of Fine Arts) and by Ponce, and a final brief word of praise for Ponce by Romero.

——. Melesio Morales, estudio bibliográfico. *Rev. mus. mex.,* v. 3, no. 11 (7 nov., 1943), p. 248-252.   [850a]

Bio-bibliographical list.

——. Rafael J. Tello. *Nuestra música,* v. 2, no. 3 (Jan. 1947), p. 33-39. [851a]

"Tello fue el último valor representativo de nuestra etapa romántico-francesista... que nos desarraigó del italianismo..."

——. Reseña histórica de la fundación del Conservatorio nacional de música. *Orientac. mus.,* v. 3, no. 25 (julio), p.

9; no. 26 (agosto), p. 7; no. 27 (sept), p. 6-7, 20; no. 28 (oct.), p. 8; no. 29 (nov.), p. 13-14; no. 30 (dic.), p. 11, 15: no. 31 (enero) p. 9-10; no. 32 (feb.), p. 8-9; no. 33 (marzo), p. 8-9; no. 34 (abril), p. 11, 19; no. 35 (mayo 1944), p. 11. [852a]

———. Ricardo Castro. Su biografía en más de cien efemérides musicales. *Nuestra música,* v. 4, no. 14 (Apr. 1949), p. 156-168. [853a]

Valuable compilation of biographical data on Castro (1864-1907).

———. Una ópera Cervantina en México. *Nuestra música,* v. 2, no. 8 (Oct. 1947), p. 211-216. [854a]

A study of the opera *La Venta Encantada,* "ópera mexicana en tres actos", by Miguel Planas, produced in 1871.

Rosenfeld, Paul. By way of art. New York, Coward-McCann, inc., 1928. [855a]

Includes "The Americanism of Carlos Chávez", p. 273-283.

———. The new American music. *Scribners magazine,* v. 89, no. 6 (June 1931), p. 624-632. [856a]

References to the music of Carlos Chávez.

Sandi, Luis. Cincuenta años de música en México, *Nuestra música,* v. 6, no. 23, (3. trimestre, 1951), p. 222-238. [857a]

An historical synthesis in which numerous composers are briefly mentioned.

———. La educación musical en México. *Nuestra música,* v. 4, no. 14 (Apr. 1949), p. 135-140. [858a]

Account of music education in Mexico, including the problems involved, and such achievements as the Mexican Symphony Orchestra, the Coro de Madrigalistas, and other orchestras in the country.

———. Problemas de la música sinfónica en México. *Nuestra música,* v. 3, no. 9 (Jan. 1948), p. 44-47. [859a]

Problems divided into three types: performance, audience, and production (composing). Calls for more orchestras, more

concert performers, more audience, more publication of the music of Mexican composers.

———. Struggle in Mexico. *Mod. music,* v. 20, no. 4 (May-June, 1943), p. 273-276. [860a]

Up-hill work in school music education in Mexico.

Spell, Lota M. La música en la catedral de México en el siglo xvi. *Rev. estud. mus.,* v. 2, no. 4 (Aug. 1950), p. 217-255. [861a]

A valuable study, with several illustrations. Translated from the English by Francisco Curt Lange. Three plates of the grand organ. Originally published in English in *Hisp. am. hist. rev.* v. 26, no. 3 (Aug. 1946).

Stevenson, Robert. Music in Mexico. A historical survey. New York, Thomas Y. Crowell company, 1952. v. 300 p., il. (music). [862a]

"This book is the first in English devoted to the history of music in Mexico". Its 5 chapters cover Early aboriginal music in Mexico; The transplanting of European musical culture; the culmination and decline of neo-Hispanic music; The operatic 19th century; Fulfillment during the 29th century. Extensive bibliography, index, and numerous musical illustrations.

———. The "distinguished maestro" of New Spain: Juan Gutiérrez de Padilla. *Hisp. amer. hist. rev.,* v. 35, no. 3 (Aug. 1955), p. 363-373. [863a]

Gutiérrez de Padilla was music director at Puebla from 1629 until his death in 1664.

Tesoro de la música polifónica en México. I, El códice del convento del Carmen. Transcripción y notas de Jesús Bal y Gay. México, D. F., Instituto nacional de bellas artes, sección de investigaciones musicales, 1952. xxiii, 234 p. il. (music, facs.). [864a]

Tuckman, William. Source materials for the correlation of Mexican music with our secondary school curriculum... Workshop in Inter-American education, summer session, 1945, Teachers College, Columbia university, New York, Curriculum service bureau for international studies, inc., 1945. 69 p. il. (incl. music).   **[865a]**

Useful lists of music, recordings, books. 18 notations of (complete) melodies, some in two voices, one in piano arrangement. Some excellent illustrations of instrumental groups and dancing.

Valadez S., pbro. Dr. José E. Los Cabildos y el servicio coral. Morelia, México. Escuela superior de Música sagrada, 1945. 204 p. (music).   **[866a]**

Velasco Urda, José. Julián Carrillo, su vida y su obra. México, D. F., Edición del "Grupo 13 metropolitano", 1945. 423 p. il.   **[867a]**

Based on a series of interviews with the originator of the revolutionary musical system known as "Sonido 13". The origins

of the "Revolución Musical del Sonido 13" are recounted in Chapter 14. According to Carrillo, his "discovery" of the division of the octave into intervals of 16ths of a tone dates from 1895.

Weinstock, Herbert. Carlos Chávez. *In* Composers of the Americas, Biographical data and catalogs of their works. Washington, D. C., Pan American Union, 1957, v. 3, p. 60-82.   **[868a]**

First published in *The musical quarterly,* v. 22, no. 4 (Oct. 1936). Reprinted with modifications made by the author in 1944 and 1956. Text in English with Spanish translation. Portrait of the composer. The list of works is the most complete published up to this time. Cf. item 776a.

———. Music by Chávez. *Américas,* v. 3, no. 3 (Mar. 1951), p. 10-12, 44-46.   **[869a]**

Personal account of Chávez as a human being and as a conductor. Photographs.

NICARAGUA

THE chief representative of contemporary musical activity in Nicaragua is the composer Luis A. Delgadillo (b. 1887), who has written about four hundred musical works, many of them based on the indigenous music of his native country. Such, for example, are his *Sinfonía Nicaragüense* and his *Aires populares de Nicaragua*. Delgadillo has also composed an opera, *Mavaltayán*, dealing with a Nicaraguan Indian subject. For a brief survey of Nicaraguan folk music written by Delgadillo, see item no. 2280. Other contemporary Nicaraguan composers who may be mentioned are Manual Ibarra, J. Francisco Rosales and Antonio Zapata.

In view of the scarcity of material in English on the music of Nicaragua, we quote the following passages from the compilation *Music in Latin America* [no. 59]: "Indian music is still heard in the provinces of Segovia, Chontales, and Matagalpa. It has very simple melodic patterns and a pentatonic scale is used. In the city of Masaya, the feast-day of the patron saint, Saint Gerónimo, is celebrated by natives from all the neighboring villages. The most popular dances, in which only men take part, are the *toro venado*, the *toro huaco*, and the *mantudos*... Another folk dance is the *zopilote* (buzzard), in which the performers dress like birds of prey and dance to a gay rhythm, at the same time singing ironic verses about the politicians— who are suposed to be the birds of prey".

For the indigenous tradition of folk drama and music, Daniel G. Brinton's study of the *Güegüence* [no. 2277] is of extreme interest.

BIBLIOGRAPHY

Berggreen, Andreas Peter. Folkesange og melodier... Copenhagen, A. C. Reitzels forlag, 1869-71. 11 v. M1627.-B49 **[2275]**

Vol. 10 includes 2 Nicaraguan folk songs arranged for piano (nos. 105, 106).

Brasseur de Bourbourg, Charles Étienne. Gramática de la lengua Quiché. Paris, A. Bertrand, 1862. PM4231.B7 **[2276]**

The appendix to the second part contains 4 native tunes gathered in Nicaragua; the first three have what is called a "Spanish accompaniment", while the fourth is set for flute and "zambor".

Brinton, Daniel Garrison, ed. The Güegüence, a comedy-ballet in the Nahuatl-Spanish dialect of Nicaragua. Philadelphia, D. G. Brinton, 1883. PM4070.-Z77 **[2277]**

Includes a discussion of "Nicaraguan musical instruments and music", with 5 tunes.

Conzemius, Eduard. Ethnographical survey of the Miskito and Samu Indians of Honduras and Nicaragua. Washington, U. S. Govt. print. off., 1932. 191 p. (Smithsonian institution. Bureau of American ethnology. Bulletin 106). E5-1.U6 no. 100 **[2278]**

References to music, instruments and dances, p. 111-115, 162, 164.

Cuadra, Pablo Antonio. Horizonte pa-

317

triótico del folklore. *Folklore,* no. 2 (Dec. 1940), p. 23.   **[2279]**

Deals especially with Spanish ballad survivals in Nicaragua.

Delgadillo, Luis A. Del folklore musical en Nicaragua. *Gaceta mus.,* v. 1, no. 9 (Sept. 1928), p. 24-26.   **[2280]**

——. Del folklore musical en Nicaragua. *Música* (Bogotá), v. 1, no. 3 (June 1941), p. 57-58.   **[2281]**

Fletes Bolaños, Anselmo. Regionales. Managua, Nicaragua, Tip. y encuader-

nación nacionales, 1922. 105 p. il. PQ-7519.F6R4   **[2282]**

Includes *Cantares y jalalelas.*

Slonimsky, Nicolas. Music, where the Americas meet. *Christian scien. mon. weekly magazine section* (8 June 1940), p. 8-9. il.   **[2283]**

Biographical sketches of Central American and Mexican composers, with portraits. Brief notes on the Nicaraguan composers Luis A. Delgadillo and J. Francisco Rosales.

See also no. 1424.

SUPPLEMENT TO 1960

BIBLIOGRAPHY

Acuña Escobar, Franco. De la música popular nicaragüense. *Elite* (Managua), v. 5, no. 60 (Aug. 1945), no. 62 (Oct. 1945).   **[870a]**

Brief notes on *sones* for marimba. Three notations (melodies only). (C.S.)

——. De la música popular nicaragüense. *Elite* (Managua), v. 6, no. 65 (Jan. 1946), p. 23-35.   **[871a]**

"Lengua de vaca, perritos y sones pascuales." Brief discussion. Two music notations.

——. De la música popular nicaragüense: San Sebastián. *Elite* (Managua), v. 6, no. 66 (Feb. 1946), p. 27-31.   **[872a]**

——. De la música popular nicaragüense. Violines de talalate. *Elite* (Managua), v. 6, no. 62 (Oct. 1945), p. 10-13. (music).   **[873a]**

——. Música regional nicaragüense. *Elite.* (Managua), v. 4, no. 42 (Feb. 1944), p. 3-5.   **[874a]**

Borgen, José Francisco. Letra y música de la canción folklórica. Bajo los auspicios del Ministerio de instrucción pública se prepara una compilación del acervo vernacular de Nicaragua. Publicaciones del Ministerio de instrucción

pública de Nicaragua (Managua), v. 1, no. 3 (Feb.-July 1944), p. 14-20.   **[875a]**

Cardenal Argüello, Salvador. Música indígena para marimba. *Cuadernos del taller San Lucas* (Granada, Nicaragua), v. 3 (1943), p. 82-83; v. 4 (1944), p. 75-81.   **[876a]**

Includes music notations, musical analysis, and description of dances.

Delgadillo, Luis A. La música indígena y colonial en Nicaragua. *Rev. estud. mus.,* v. 1, no. 3 (April 1950), p. 43-60.   **[877a]**

With 14 musical notations. The article is dated 1939.

——. Por mi honor musical. Polémica sobre el Sonido 13. Páginas históricas de mi vida artística. Managua, Publicación patrocinada por el Ministerio de la gobernación, 1957. 56 p.   **[878a]**

The author attacks the views and the statements concerning himself put forth by Julián Carrillo (q. v.), the Mexican composer and exponent of the musical system known as "Sonido 13".

García, Fr. Secundino, O. P. Cancionero folklórico nicaragüense. Tomo primero. Managua, Publicaciones del ministerio de instrucción pública, 1945. 79 p. (music).   **[879a]**

Contains 85 of the 500 songs that the

compiler states he has collected from oral tradition in Nicaragua. Only the melodies are transcribed, with no accompaniment or added harmonization. Many of the melodies are sung in thirds. This volume contains religious songs exclusively (songs referring to the Child Jesus).

Harcourt, Raoul d'. Ocarinas de Nicaragua. *Jour. soc. amer.,* n. s., v. 40 (1951), p. 242-244. **[880a]**

Mejía Sánchez, Ernesto. Romances y corridos nicaragüenses. México, D. F., Imprenta universitaria, 1946. 123 p. il., map. **[881a]**

Includes a valuable historical introduction (p. 9-26), especially rich in bibliographical references. Points out that the term *corrido* occurs 4 times in the text of the comedy-ballet *El Güegüence,* dating from colonial times. The American Peter F. Stout heard a "romance del Cid" sung by a woman in Nicaragua in 1850. The author classifies his material into two main headings: I) *Los romances tradicionales profanos* (subdivision: *Infantiles*); II) *Los corridos nacionales amorosos* (subdivision: De animales). Variant texts are included. There are 23 tunes. Originally published in *An. soc. folk. Mex.,* v. 5 (1944), p. 69-86.

Vega Miranda, Gilberto. Alejandro Vega Matus, 1875-1935. *Elite,* v. 5, no. 64 (Dec. 1945). **[882a]**

Brief biographical notice. 7 music notations. Also an "Intermezzo", apparently for piano (1 page). (C.S.)

———. Breviario del recuerdo; antología de músicos nicaragüenses. Managua, D. N. Nicaragua, 1945. 212 p. il. (incl. music). **[883a]**

With this is bound his *La canción nicaragüense, compilación de cantos populares,* containing words and music.

———. De la música nicaragüense. *Elite* (Managua), v. 7, no. 75 (Nov. 1946), p. 11-12. **[884a]**

Brief remarks upon folk music of Nicaragua. Three music notations, melodies only. (C.S.)

———. José de la Cruz Mena, 1874-1907. *Elite,* v. 5, no. 62 (Oct. 1945). **[885a]**

From a book in press "Breviario del Recuerdo" (*Autografía de músicos nicaragüenses*). Brief biographical notes. 6 music notations. (C.S.)

———. Música y músicos contemporáneos. *Elite,* Managua, v. 6, no. 71 (July 1946), p. 14-15. **[886a]**

———. Pablo Vega y Raudes. *Elite,* v. 5, no. 63 (Nov. 1945). **[887a]**

From a book in press "Breviario del Recuerdo" (*Autografía de Músicos Nicaragüenses*). 3 music notations followed by "Alabado al sagrado corazón de Jesús" by Vega y Raudes. (C.S.)

———. Un matrimonio indígena en Nicaragua. *Elite* (Managua), v. 6, no. 72 (Aug. 1946), p. 3-5. **[888a]**

Brief description. Two music notations, melodies only. (C.S.)

PANAMA

THE folk music of Panama has been comprehensively surveyed, with copious musical documentation, in Narciso Garay's *Tradiciones y cantares de Panamá* [no. 2285]. This profusely illustrated volume of over two hundred pages deals with the traditions and customs of Panama as well as with the native songs and dances. The numerous musical examples make of it a rich source of material for the folklorist and the musician. The best-known songs and dances of Panama are the *mejorana*, the *tamborito* and the *punto*. All these are of Spanish origin. The chief popular instrument is the *mejoranera*, a guitar with five gut strings. The *rabel* is a primitive violin with three strings. There are three sizes of drums: *tambora* (large), *pujador* (medium) and *repicador* (small). Other instruments used in the typical popular orchestra are the *guáchara*, a gourd rattle, and the *almirez*, a brass mortar.

The Indians in the interior of the country have their own types of music, dances and instrument. Frances Densmore, the well-known authority on Indian music, has written a monograph on the music of the Tule Indians of Panamá, illustrated with musical examples [no 2284]. Garay also devotes much attention to the music and dances of the Indians.

In addition to Narciso Garay (b. 1876), the chief contemporary composers of Panama are Herbert de Castro (b. 18 Jan. 1906), Ricardo Fábrega (b. 28 Jan. 1905), Alberto Galimany (b. Villafranca, Spain, 31 Dec. 1889), and Roque Cordero (b. 1917). Among composers of popular music, mention should be made of the late Máximo Arrates Boza (d. 9 Aug. 1936), a native of Cuba, composer of the universally known danzón entitled *Pescao* and teacher of many Panamanian musicians.

Densmore, Frances. Music of the Tule Indians of Panama. Washington, Smithsonian institution, 1926. 39 p. il. F1565.-3.M9D3   **[2284]**
Includes six musical examples.

Garay, Narciso. Tradiciones y cantares de Panamá. Ensayo folklórico. Bruxelles, Presses de l"expansion, 1930. 203 p. il. ML3572.G2   **[2285]**
Description of the customs and musical folklore of Panama, interspersed with numerous musical examples.

Holmes, William Henry. The use of gold and other metals among ancient inhabitants of Chiriqui, isthmus of Darien. Washington, Govt. print. off., 1887. 27 p. il. (Smithsonian institution. Bureau of ethnology. Bulletin no. 3). F1569.C5H75   **[2286]**
References to the bronze bells found among the Indians of Panama, with 4 illustrations.

Schaeffer, Myron. At the world's crossroads: Panama. *Mod. mus.* v. 20, no. 3 (March-Apr. 1943), p. 202-203. **[2287]**
Review of current musical activity in Panama by the American musicologist and composer who heads the music department of the National University of Panama.

Slonimsky, Nicolas. Music, where the Americas meet. *Christian scien. mon. weekly magazine section* (8 June 1940), p. 8-9. il. **[2288]**

Biographical sketches of Central American and Mexican composers, with portraits. Panama: Alberto Galimany, Ricardo Fábregas, Narciso Garay.

See also no. 1424.

SUPPLEMENT to 1960

BIBLIOGRAPHY

Castilleto R., Ernesto J. Orígenes del himno nacional panameño. *Armonía*, año 1, v. 1, no. 4 (Nov. 1943), p. 7-10. **[889a]**

Chase, Gilbert. Composed by Cordero. *Américas*, v. 10, no. 6 (June 1958), p. 7-11. il. **[890a]**

A study of the Panamanian composer Roque Cordero (b. 1917), whose Second Symphony won a prize at the Caracas Festival of Latin American Music in 1957. He studied composition with Ernst Krenek in the U.S.A. and has also been active as a conductor.

Cordero, Roque. Actualidad musical en Panamá. *B. A. mus.*, v. 12, no. 197 (Oct. 1, 1957), p. 5. **[891a]**

Brief survey of musical activities and institutions, with mention of some leading musicians. An extensive editorial note gives biographical data on the author.

Cramer, Louise. Songs of West Indian negroes in the Canal Zone. *Calif. folklore quart.*, v. 5, no. 3 (July 1946), p. 243-272. **[892a]**

Author believes this is the first serious study of folk elements found in the Canal Zone. Utilises recordings made by Myron Schaeffer, Director of the Institute of Folklore Research of the Inter-American University of Panama. The discs are now deposited in the Archive of American Folksong of the Library of Congress. Texts of 31 songs. No music notations. (C.S.)

Rubio, Angel. The land and the people; intimate glimpses of Panama. *Américas*, v. 5, no. 10 (Oct. 1943), p. 6-8, 41-43. **[893a]**

Considerable reference to folklore and folk music, with names of dances and some description. 12 photographs include one of band with typical instruments.

Schaeffer, Myron, *et alter*. Catorce tamboritos panameños. *Bol. inst. invest. folk.*, v. 1, no. 1 (1944), p. 2-29. **[894a]**

With 14 music notations.

——. La mejorana, canción típica panameña. *Bol. inst. invest. folk.*, v. 1, no. 2 (1944), p. 1-50. **[895a]**

An important study, with 6 music notations transcribed by Schaeffer.

Zárate, Manuel F. Brevario de folklore. Panamá, 1958. **[896a]**

A practical and theoretical guide, intended as an aid to the collection of the folklore of Panama.

——, **and Dora Pérez de.** La décima y la copla en Panamá. Panamá, 1953. 548 p. **[897a]**

A very valuable work, although undertaken primarily from a literary rather than a musical point of view.

Zárate, Dora Pérez de. Nanas, rimas y juegos infantiles que se practican en Panamá. Panamá, 1957. **[898a]**

Includes music of children's games, transcribed by Gonzalo Brenes C. An excellent study.

PARAGUAY

A GLANCE at the bibliography below will make it apparent that the main emphasis is on the music, the dances and the instruments of the Indians of Paraguay, chief among whom are the Guaranís. Special attention is drawn to item no. 2320, an interesting bibliographical item dating from 1793, written in Latin and describing the introduction of European music among the Indians. In early colonial times the missions of Paraguay were important centers for the dissemination of European culture in the new world. The indigenous music of the Guaraní Indians of Paraguay has been studied with considerable thoroughness by Franz P. Müller [no. 2301]. Another valuable study, dealing with the music of the Lenguas and including five tunes, is the monograph by Alfredo Kamprad [no. 2298].

Juan Carlos Moreno González, author of a brief study on the music of the Guaranís [no. 2300], is one of the small group of contemporary Paraguayan composers who are now beginning the serious cultivation of art music in their country. Prominent among the composers is Fernando Centurión de Zayas (b. Asunción, 14 March 1886), director of the Conservatorio de Música in Asunción, founder of the Haydn Quartet, and first conductor of the Orquesta Sinfónica, founded by government decree in 1936. The present conductor of this orchestra is José Asunción Flores, considered the oustanding living composer of Paraguay. Other contemporary composers are Samuel Aguayo, Salvador Dentice (director of the Banda de Policía), Aristóbulo Domínguez, Pablo Maldonado, Agustín Olivetti, Roselio C. Recalde, and Juan Vicente Benítez.

GENERAL AND MISCELLANEOUS

Aguayo, Samuel. Bajo el cielo del Paraguay. Álbum de cinco hermosas melodías del folklore paraguayo. Buenos Aires, Ed. Fermata, 1941. 11 p.
[2289]

Bürger, Otto. Paraguay. Leipzig, Dieterich'sche verlagsbuchhandlungen, 1927. 280 p. F2675.B93 [2290]

Music and dance, p. 57-58; importation of musical instruments, p. 158 (for explanation of this, see item no. 727).

Dreidemie, Óscar J. Los orígenes del teatro en las regiones del Río de la Plata; la obra de los Jesuítas de la provincia del Paraguay. *Estudios*, v. 57 (1937), p. 61-80. [2291]

Important for the study of the early lyric theatre in America. Includes bibliography.

Hernández, Pablo. Misiones del Paraguay. Organización social de las doctrinas guaranís de la compañía de Jesús. Barcelona, Gustavo Gili, 1913. 2 v. F2684.H27 [2292]

Vol. 1: *Música*, p. 301-303, with a list of the instruments used; *Danzas*, p. 303-305.

Schallehn, Hellmut. Die grundlagen der volksmusik in Bolivien und Paraguay. *Die brücke zur heimat*, v. 33 (1933), p. 215-231. [2293]

NATIONAL ANTHEM

Encuesta del Instituto paraguayo. Himno nacional del Paraguay. Su letra y su música. Buenos Aires. 56 p. **[2294]**
Citation from the files of Pan American Union.

Scarone, Arturo. La letra del himno del Paraguay. Montevideo, Renacimiento, 1924. 11 p. PQ8519.A33Z8 **[2295]**
"Himno patriótico por Francisco Acuña de Figueroa", p. 3-6.

Schuster, Adolf N. Paraguay; land, volk, geschichte, wirtschaftsleben und kolonisation. Stuttgart, Strecker und Schröder, 1929. 667 p. F2668.S39 **[2296]**
Die paraguayische nationalhymne, with music: p. 262-265.

AMERINDIAN

Grubb, W. Barbrooke. An unknown people in an unknown land. London, Seeley, Service & co., 1913. 330 p F-2679.G88 **[2297]**
Making of Lengua musical instruments. p. 75; chanting and dancing at feasts (with words to one chant), p. 177-187.

Kamprad, Alfredo. La música entre los indios Lenguas. *Rev. geog. amer.,* año 2, v. 3, no. 17 (1935), p. 129-134. **[2298]**
With 5 tunes transcribed by the author, who claims that these Indians react very favorably to European music.

Métraux, Alfred. La religion des Tupinamba et ses rapports avec celle des autres tribus Tupi-Guarani. Paris, E. Leroux, 1928. 260 p. il. F2520.1.T94M-4 **[2299]**
"Fêtes et danses", p. 189-196, including reference to songs.

Moreno González, Juan C. Los Guaraníes y la música. *Bol. lat. am. mús.,* v. 4 (1938), p. 81-86. **[2300]**
With 2 musical examples.

Müller, P. Franz. Beitrage zur ethnologie der Guarani-Indianer in östlichen waldgebiet von Paraguay. *Anthropos,* v. 29, nos. 1-2 (1934), p. 177-208; nos. 3-4 (1934), p. 441-460; nos. 5-6 (1934), p. 635-702; v. 30, nos. 1-2 (1935), p. 433-450; nos. 5-6 (1935), p. 767-783. il. **[2301]**
Musical instruments, p. 458; illustrations of flutes, rattles, bells and hollow bamboo reeds, plate 4. Musical instruments and song texts, p. 696-702, with illustrations of flutes, rattles, bells and hollow plates 7-8.

Peramas, Josephi Emmanuelis. De vita et moribus tredecim virorum paraguaycorum. Faventiae, Ex typographia archii, 1793. 462 p. E2684.P43 **[2302]**
Music among the Guarani Indians, p. 13. 49-50; choruses, 51-54. It is interesting to note that the author, in his discussion of music, restricts himself almost entirely to music as practiced by the converted Indians, with European musical instruments, etc.

Schuster, Adolf N. Paraguay. Stuttgart, Strecker & Schröder, 1929. 667 p. F26-68.S39 **[2303]**
Musical instruments of the Indians, p. 295, 296 (with musical examples of drum beats), p. 306 (with illustrations).

Strelnikov, I. D. La música y la danza de las tribus indias Kaa-ihwua (Guaraní) y Botocudo. *In* International congress of Amreicanists, Proceedings, v. 23, New York, 1928, p. 796-862. **[2304]**
These are the Indians of Matto Grosso, São Paulo, and Paraguay. Discussion of several dances and explanations of their meanings. Includes 6 musical themes.

Talía, Santiago M. Aporte al estudio del folklore guaraní. *Asunción, Revista de informaciones paraguayas* (Buenos Aires), v. 2, no. 4 (1941), p. 17. **[2305]**

SUPPLEMENT TO 1960

The late Dr. Juan Max Boettner, medical doctor by profession, composer and musicologist by avocation, patiently assembled a mass of documentation concerning music and musicians in Paraguay, from pre-Columbian times to the present, which he published in a book titled *Música y músicos del Paraguay* (item 900a). This work deals with music of the aborigenes, music in the Jesuit missions and during the Spanish domination, music under the dictatorships of Dr. de Francia (1814-1840), and the López family, during the War of the Triple Alliance (1865-1870), in the difficult post-war period (1870-1899), and in the 20th century. There are also chapters dealing with the national anthem of Paraguay, popular music, dances, guitarrists, harpists, and musical activities and organizations. The final section consists of a *Biographical index of musicians of Paraguay*. The bibliography contains 242 items, and is actually a list of sources, including personal interviews. There is no index.

The illustrations in Dr. Boettner's book consist of 55 photographic reproductions and line drawings (mostly of musical instruments), of musical notations, and facsimiles. The author goes thoroughly into the ethnic, social and historical backgrounds of musical activity in Paraguay. Although the indigenous population (Indian) is only about 2% of the total population of the country, and is slowly but surely disappearing, the Guaraní language is a very important cultural factor, and Paraguay is essentially a bi-lingual nation (Spanish and Guaraní). Many of the popular songs have Guaraní words, and the most typical form of popular music, developed by José Asunción Flores (b. 1904), is called *guarania*.

Among "Compositores de música culta" active at present, the author mentions, in addition to those cited in the original introduction to this section of the *Guide* (see above), Remberto Giménez, violinist and composer, born in Asunción in 1899. He has written the official version of the national anthem of Paraguay and has composed a *Rapsodia paraguaya* for orchestra based on popular regional melodies. The first important composer, who wrote chiefly for guitar, was Agustín Pío Barrios (1885-1944).

BIBLIOGRAPHY

Benítez, Leopoldo A. Guahu tetâriguá-ra. Himno nacional, versión guaraní. Prólogo de d. Juan E. O'Leary; glosario del dr. Tomás Osuna. Asunción del Paraguay, Imp. y librería la Mundial, 1925. 43 p. il. (Biblioteca de cultura guaraní, v. 1)   **[899a]**

Boettner, Juan Max. Música y músicos del Paraguay. Asunción, Edición de autores paraguayos asociados, n. d. [1957?], 294 p. il. (music).   **[900a]**

For comment on this work, see introductory section to Supplement, above.

Hensler, Haven. The music of the Paraguayan people. [1943?], 39 p. (Reproduced from typewritten copy). [901a]

One of the first attempts in English to study the folk music and instruments of Paraguay. Includes a bibliography and examples (music notation)of Paraguayan popular music. Available for consultation in the Music Division of the Pan American Union, Washington, D. C.

Kamprad, Alfredo. La música entre los indios lenguas. *Rev. educ.,* Asunción,

v. 1, no. 2 (Oct. 1945), p. 112-116. [902a]

Brief account by a visiting violinist. 6 music notations (without speech-text), one of which is played by the *violín lengua,* of which there is a half-tone cut. (C.S.)

Moreno González, Juan Carlos. Datos para la historia de la música en el Paraguay. *Revista del Ateneo Paraguayo, Asunción,* v. 2, no. 8 (Nov. 1943), p. 6-22. [903a]

A pioneer effort by the editor of the *Revista.*

PERU

A LARGE section of the bibliography on Peruvian music centers around the character of the music known to the inhabitants of the famous Inca Empire in pre-Columbian times, and around the controversial question of the extent and purity of pre-Columbian musical survivals among the Indians of modern Peru. An American scholar, Charles W. Mead, published in 1924 a monograph [no. 2446] on the musical instruments of the Incas, based on a study of the ancient Peruvian collections in the American Museum of Natural History. We quote from the introduction to this monograph: "The Inca had no written language, and no small part of our knowledge of their customs has been derived from their practice of representing the scenes of daily life in the decoration of their pottery vessels. In the study of the musical instruments, in particular, the decorations on the pottery of the ancient Peruvians is important, because the Spanish conquerors and their followers have left in their accounts but little information bearing on the subject. From the pottery and other objects found in the ancient tombs and burial places, therefore, we have derived most of our knowledge of the musical instruments of the Inca". Mead reproduces decorations from ancient Peruvian terra cotta vessels showing musical instruments in use. He also has illustrations of drums, rattles, bells and cymbals (plate vi); whistles, panpipes syrinx and trumpet (plate viii); and twenty-six flutes of various types (plate ix). Another important inconography of Incan musical intruments is the second volume of the work by Raoul and Marguerite d'Harcourt, *La musique des Incas et ses survivances* [no. 2406], a fundamental study based on extensive field work and research in Peru. Because of its many musical examples (over two hundred) this work is also an extremely important source of Andean folk music.

While most of the evidence seems to point toward the use of the pentatonic scale as the basis of the musical system of the Inca, some authorities, and in particular the Argentine musicologist Carlos Vega [see item no. 2429], have upheld the theory that scales with semitones were also used by the ancient Peruvians. The melodic instruments employed by the Peruvian Indians in pre-Hispanic times were the *quena* (*kena*), a vertical flute, which by many is considered the most perfect musical instrument of the western hemisphere; the *antara* (syrinx or panpipes); and the *pinkullo,* a kind of ocarina. The *quena* and the *antara* (called *sicu* by the Aymará Indians) are still used by the Quechua Indians of Peru, descendants of the ancient Inca. Often, however, the tuning of these indigenous instruments has been adapted to the playing of European music. In fact, we learn from the chronicler Garcilaso de la Vega *El Inca,* whose *Royal commentaries of*

Peru contains numerous references to music, that as early as 1560 there was in Cuzco a group of five Indians who were adept at reading European music and playing it on their native flutes. W. E. Safford, traveling in Peru in the second decade of the present century, found at Puno, on Lake Titicaca, an orchestra composed entirely of panpipes, which played the national air of Peru in a creditable manner (cf. Mead, *op. cit.,* p. 326).

According to Francisco Curt Lange (*Boletín latino americano de música,* v. 4, p. 847-848) the pentatonic basis of the Inca musical system was discovered by José Castro in 1897 and scientifically set forth in a paper published in 1910 [no. 2393]. Castro's investigations were supplemented by the studies of Leandro Alviña, Alberto Villaba Muñoz, Daniel Alomía Robles, Policarpio Caballero and other Peruvian musicians. More recently, Andrés Sas has written several articles on Inca music, as well as a monograph on Nazca music [no. 2422]. The Nazca (or Nasca) culture was a pre-Inca culture of the coastal region of Peru. In 1931 an American musician, Winthrop Sargeant, visited central Peru and collected a large number of Quechua melodies, some of which he published, with interesting comments, in two articles [nos. 2462 and 2463]. The Peruvian composer and folklorist Daniel Alomía Robles (1871-1942) assembled a large collection of Peruvian Indian music, most of which remains as yet unpublished. Another large collection of melodies was assembled by the folklorist Policarpio Caballero, whose book, *Rítmica incaica,* containing over four hundred tunes, was published at Buenos Aires in 1942 (at the time of writing, a copy of this work had not yet reached the hands of this editor).

An attempt to trace the main outlines of the development of music in Peru was made by Carlos Raygada in a monograph entitled *Panorama musical del Perú,* published in the *Boletín latinoamericano de música* [no. 2317]. Outstanding among musicians of the nineteenth century was José Bernardo Alzedo (Alcedo) (1798-1878), composer of the national anthem of Peru (1821) and of much religious music. He published a didactic work entitled *Filosofía elemental de la música* (Lima, 1869), For forty years Alzedo lived in Santiago, Chile, where he was choirmaster of the cathedral. A composer who gave a notable impulse to the movement for musical nationalism in Peru was José María Valle Riestra (1859-1925), a pupil of Gédalge in Paris. His opera *Ollanta* (1901) was the first opera written by a Peruvian composer; it purports to use so-called "Inca" themes (for a polemic which arose on the authenticity of these themes, see item no. 2393). Valle Riestra also wrote the operas *Atahualpa* (3 acts) and *Las rosas de Jamaica* (one act). The tradition of musical nationalism based on Peruvian Indian themes was carried on by Daniel Alomía Robles (1871-1942) and Theodoro Valcárcel (1902-1942). The former wrote the opera *Illa-Cori*

(3 acts), several symponic poems, many songs and piano pieces; the latter wrote the ballet-opera *Suray-Surita,* two symphonic suites, the symphonic poem *En las ruínas del templo del sol,* and numerous songs and piano pieces based on Indian themes (for a complete catalogue of Valcárcel's compositions, see item no. 2312).

In addition to those mentioned above, contemporary Peruvian composers include Pablo Chávez Aguilar (b. 1899), Federico Gerdes (b. 1873), Carlos Sánchez Málaga (b. 1904), Roberto Carpio (b. 1900), Raoul de Verneuil (b. 1901), Carlos Valderrama, Alfonso de Silva and Rosa Mercedes Ayarza de Morales. Among musicians of foreign birth who have settled in Lima and have contributed actively to the musical life of that capital are Rodolfo Barbacci (b. Buenos Aires, 1911), Theo Buchwald (b. Vienna, 1902), Enrique Fava Ninci (b. Spezia, Italy, 1883), Rudolph Holzmann (b. Breslau, 1910), Andrés (or André) Sas (b. Paris, 1900), Vicente Stea (b. Italy, 1884). Buchwald became conductor of the Orquesta Sinfónica de Lima. Abraham Vizcarra Rozas is the author of an important monograph on the folk and primitive music of Peru [no. 2363]. Guillermo Salinas Cossío and César Arróspide de la Flor are other noteworthy writers on music.

For a description of Peruvian folk dances and songs, among which are the *cachua,* the *huaiño* the *marinera,* the *tondero* and the *yaraví,* see Durán's pamphlet, *Recordings of Latin American songs and dances* [no. 187]. The Peruvian folklorist Fernando Romero has published as excellent study of the *marinera* (which was derived from the *zamacueca*), tracing the Negro influence in this dance [no. 2379].

GENERAL AND MISCELLANEOUS

Alzedo, José Bernardo. Filosofía elemental de la música, ó sea La exégesis de las doctrinas conducentes a su mejor inteligencia. Lima, Imprenta liberal, 1869. 212 p. MT6.A49   **[2306]**

Dumesnil, Maurice. Music in Peru, the land of the Incas. *Etude,* v. 59, no. 4 (Apr. 1941), p. 223, 280-281. **[2307]**
Includes music of a *yaraví* from the collection of D. Alomía Robles.

Enciclopedia universal ilustrada Europea-americana. Bilbao, Madrid, Barcelona, Espasa-Calpe, s. a., 1921, v. 43, p. 1305-1306   **[2308]**
Under *Perú,* subsection *Música,* there is a discussion of Peruvian and Incan music, based on data supplied by Felipe L. Urquieta.

Fétis, François Joseph. Histoire générale de la musique, Paris, Firmin Didot frères, fils et cie., 1869-76. 5 v. il. ML-160.F42   **[2309]**
Vol. 1 contains an account of music in Mexico and Peru, with 4 tunes (p. 94-106).

Finot, Enrique. La cultura colonial española en el alto Perú. *Rev. arte,* v. 4, no. 21 (1939), p. 1-16.   **[2310]**
Music, p. 15-16.

Gibson, Percy. Coca, alcohol, música incaica y periodismo. Arequipa, Tipografía Sanguinetti, 1920.   **[2311]**
A lecture delivered on 15 Aug. 1920.

Holzmann, Rodolfo. Catálogo de las obras de Theodoro Valcárcel. *Bol. bi-*

bliog., Lima, v. 15, nos. 3-4 (Dec. 1942), p. 135-140. **[2312]**

Of the 44 compositions listed, only five are published. The compiler states that this is the first complete bibliography of the works of a Peruvian composer. He advocates the creation of a national archive for the preservation of musical manuscripts.

Jazz in prehistoric Peru; did Inca host at siege of Cuzco attempt to rout Pizarro with blare of oboes? *South American,* New York (June 1921), p. 14-15. **[2313]**

Lange, Francisco Curt. The state of music in Peru. *New York times,* v. 89, no. 30,122 (14 July 1940), sec. 9, p. 5. **[2314]**

Musical progress in Peru under Theo Buchwald, conductor of the National Orchestra. References to André Sas, Daniel Alomia Robles, Sánchez Málaga, Chávez Aguilar, Rosa Mercedes Ayarza de Morales, Raoul de Verneuil, Alberto Villalba Muñoz.

Lohmann Villena, Guillermo. Apuntaciones sobre el arte dramático en Lima durante el virreinato. Lima, Editorial Lumen, s. a., 1941. 32 p. PN2532.L5L6 **[2315]**

During the viceregal period Lima was an important center of musico-dramatic activity.

Perry, Charlotte. The feast of Raymi. A Peruvian play for children with choreography and music. Musical settings by D. H. Decker. New York, J. Fischer & bro., 1942. **[2316]**

Raygada, Carlos. Panorama musical del Perú. *Bol. lat. am. mús.,* v. 2 (1936), p. 169-214. **[2317]**

A general historical survey of music in Peru.

Sánchez Málaga, Carlos. Peruvian music. *Bull. pan amer. union,* v. 65 (1931). p. 606-611. il. **[2318]**

Includes illustration of a group of Peruvian Indian musicians. Musical themes of Indian character quoted from compositions of Valle-Riestra, also setting of an Incan hymn by Alberto Mejía.

Sas, Andrés. Aires y danzas indios del Perú, para niños. Paris, Bruxelles, H. Lemoine & cia., 1934. 17 p. M1692.S **[2319]**

For piano.

——. O Perú musical contemporâneo. *Res. mus.,* v. 3, no. 34-35 (June-July 1941), p. 2-5. **[2320]**

Schwerké, Irving. Enter Peru. *Mus. digest,* v. 15, no. 10 (Oct. 1930), p. 15. **[2321]**

Deals with Theodoro Valcárcel.

Slonimsky, Nicolas. Composers of Peru. *Mod. music,* v. 18, no. 3 (1941), p. 155-158. il. (ports.) **[2322]**

Discusses chiefly Andrés Sas, Theodoro Valcárcel, and Raoul de Verneuil.

——. Modern Peruvian composers. *Christian scien. mon.* (24 Aug. 1940). **[2323]**

Deals with André Sas, Theodoro Valcárcel, Raoul de Verneuil, Daniel Alomía Robles, E. López Mindreau, E. W. Stubbs, Pablo Chávez Aguilar, Carlos Sánchez Málaga.

Weyland, Ch. Peru. Weimar, F. R. pr. Landes-Industrie-Comptoirs, 1807. 574 p. F3411.P47 **[2324]**

Peruvian music, p. 20, 267.

Where Peru gets its music. *Lit. digest,* v. 110, no. 3 (18 July 1931). **[2325]**

Commenting on an article by Sánchez Málaga.

Wright, Marie Robinson. The old and new Peru. Philadelphia, George Barrie and sons, 1908. 456 p. F3408.W95 **[2326]**

Preservation of Incan musical compositions, p. 224; philharmonic societies of Lima and Arequipa; contemporary musicians, p. 230.

See also nos. 1335, 2338, 2363.

NATIONAL ANTHEM

Ofrenda de Venezuela en el primer centenario de la batalla de Ayacu-

cho. Caracas, Litografía del comercio, 1924. 130 p. M1686.V35 **[2327]**
Includes music (voice and piano; band score) of national anthem of Peru.

Raygada, Carlos. Historia crítica del himno nacional. *Revista militar del Perú* (Nov. 1938), p. 61-81. **[2328]**

FOLK AND PRIMITIVE MUSIC

(A) GENERAL

Arguedas, José María. La aurora de la canción popular en el Perú. *Romance*, v. 1 (June 1940), p. 10. **[2329]**
Stresses the native element in Peruvian folk song.

——. La canción popular mestiza en el Perú. *La Prensa* (Buenos Aires) (23 Feb. 1941), sec. 2, p. 2. **[2330]**

——. Simbolismo y poesía de dos canciones populares Kechwas. *La prensa*, v. 70, no. 25,101 (27 Nov. 1938), sec. 3, p. 1. **[2331]**
With the Indian words to the songs, and Spanish translation.

Arias Anduaga, Clotilde. La música peruana. *Alma latina*, v. 8, no. 139 (30 July 1938), p. 18, 22. **[2332]**
Of slight value.

Arias-Larreta, Abraham. Fisonomía lírica y musical de la *chica o serranita*. *Turismo*, v. 15, no. 154 (Aug. 1940). **[2333]**
A study of a north Peruvian folk song and dance, with 2 musical examples.

Armitage, Marie Teresa, ed. Folk songs and art songs for intermediate grades. Accomp. by H. W. Loomis. Boston, C. C. Birchard & co., 1925. 2 v. M1994.-A71F4 **[2334]**
Contains one Peruvian tune, v. 2, p. 10.

Arona, Juan de. Diccionario de peruanismos. Lima, Imprenta de J. Francisco Solis, 1883. 518 p. PC4902.P2 **[2335]**
See *sub voce* Cáchua, p. 80-81; Yaraví,

p. 507-509; etc. Also reprinted in Biblioteca de cultura peruana, Primera serie, No. 10, Paris, Desclée de Brouwer, 1938.

Ayarza de Morales, Rosa Mercedes. Antiguos pregones de Lima. Lima. "La Crónica" y "Variedades" s. a. ltda., 1939. 40 p. M1692.A97A5 **[2336]**
For one voice with piano accompaniment.
Contents.—La ramilletera.—El negro frutero.—La sanguera.—La picaronera.—La causera.—El listín de toros.—La tisanera.—Revolución caliente.—El cholo frutero.—La tamalera.

Ballón Landa, Alberto. Los hombres de la selva. Lima, Oficina tipográfica de "La Opinión nacional", 1917. 325 p. F3451.M2B35 **[2337]**
P. 91-92, discussion of songs and musical instruments; mentions use of the accordion and guitar, p. 184-191, music, song and dance. The district covered is the department of Madre de Dios.

Beals, Carleton. Fire on the Andes. Philadelphia, London, J. B. Lippincott co., 1934. 481 p. il. F3408.B32 **[2338]**
Music, dances and instruments, p. 343-348. For other items, see numerous references in index, under music, musical instruments, dance, festivals, etc.

Béclard d'Harcourt, Marguerite. Le folklore musical de la région andine; Équateur, Pérou, Bolivie. *In* Encyclopédie de la musique et dictionnaire du conservatoire, partie 1, p. 3353-3371, Paris, Librairie Delagrave, 1921. ML100.-E5 **[2339]**
Contains 36 musical examples. An important study.

——. Mélodies populaires indiennes. Équateur, Pérou, Bolivie. Milano, G. Ricordi & c., 1923. M1686.B4 **[2340]**
Contains 46 Indian folk songs of Ecuador, Peru and Bolivia, for voice with piano or harp accompaniment, and 9 airs for flute with piano. Native texts with French translations.

——. Traditional music in the land of the Incas. *Pro-música* (Oct. 1925), p. 7-13. **[2341]**

Béjar Pacheco, M. Vestigios de arte Ccolla. *Antara*, v. 1, no. 3 (Oct. 1930), p. 2. [2342]

Points out that in the province of Melgar (formerly Ayaviri), and especially in the districts of Nuñoa and Orurillo, there are indigenous inhabitants who appear to be descendants of the ancient Colla or Aymará Indians, and who have preserved their tribal traditions with greater purity than the Indians in other parts of Peru. Gives a brief description of their songs and dances.

Berggreen, Andreas Peter. Folkesange og melodier ... Copenhagen, A. C. Reitzels forlag, 1869-71. 11 v. M1627.-B49 [2343]

Vol. 10 includes 3 Peruvian folk songs with piano accompaniment (nos. 10-112).

Carrey, Émile. Le Pérou. Paris, Garnier, 1875. 511 p. F3408.C31 [2344]

Indigenous music, p. 404-406, including a French translation of a *yaraví*.

Castro Pozo, Hildebrando. Nuestra comunidad indígena. Lima, Editorial "El Lucero', 1924. 408 p. F3430.C33 [2345]

Dance and song in the marriage ceremony, including 3 strophes of the song accompanying the *Pirhualla-pirhua* dance, p. 136-139; funeral dances and music, p. 159-166; *el cantor* in religious activities, p. 231-233. For important source of information on music, dance and song, see chap. 9, p. 309-390, which includes; Música indígena, baile, bailes mímicos, el de los corcobados ó *jerga cunos,* los de los tunantes chunclos, aquilinos mexicanos y el del cóndor; el del pavo, en Piura—Bailes rítmicos, danzas, cachuas, huaynos, cachaspares, tonderos y marineros, cantares, cumananas, *décimas, yaravíes,* canciones ó *tristes* (with words of many verses and songs).

Enock, Charles Reginald. The Andes and the Amazon. Life and travel in Peru. New York, C. Scribner's sons, 1907. 379 p. F3423.E59 [2346]

Cholo-Quechua music, p. 141, 147-149. Dance, p. 103.

Harcourt, Raoul d'. La música en la sie-

rra andina. *Rev. arqueol. Lima,* v. 2, (Apr.-June 1924). [2347]

——, and Marguerite d'. Chants populaires de Pérou. *Rev. musicale,* v. 6 (May 1925), p. 145-151. [2348]

Material included in *La Musique des Incas et ses survivances* [no. 2349].

——. La musique des Incas et ses survivances. Paris, P. Geuthner, 1925. 2 v. il. ML3575.H27 [2349]

Index bibliographique, v. 1, p. 545-556, Part 4 includes 204 musical examples, of which 141 are from Peru, 54 from Ecuador, and 9 from Bolivia. Most of these are melodies with Kechua text and French translation. A fundamental work, profusely illustrated and thoroughly documented.

Markham, Clements Robert. Cuzco and Lima. London, Chapman and Hall, 1856. 419 p. F3429.M34 [2350]

Yaravís, p. 105-197, with words to 3 songs. Quichua language of music, p. 403 (Indian words for various instruments).

——. Reisen in Peru. Leipzig, G. Senf. 1865. 316 p. F3423.M341 [2351]

Yaravís, p. 103-108. Translation of item no. 2350.

Mejía Baca, José. El nacimiento de "el triste" (canción costeña del Perú). *Tres,* no. 2 (1939), p. 63-68. [2352]

Romero, Fernando. Instrumentos musicales de la costa zamba. *Turismo* (Mar. 1939). [2353]

——. Ritmo negro en la costa zamba. *Turismo* (Jan. 1939). [2354]

Sánchez Málaga, Carlos. Música popular. Supplement of the review *Tres,* no. 7 (Dec. 1940). [2355]

Four dance tunes collected by Leonardo Cerrón and edited by Carlos Sánchez Málaga.

Sas, Andrés. Consideraciones sobre la música autóctona. *Antara,* v. 1, no. 1 (July 1930), p. 1-2 and 7. [2356]

Discusses the problem of finding a suitable technique for the artistic utilization of indigenous Peruvian Indian music. The conventional European technique of composition is declared unsuitable for this purpose.

———. La formación del folklore peruano. *Bol. lat. am. mús.,* v. 2 (1926), p. 97-103. **[2357]**

Includes a chart showing the development of folk music in Peru from · prehistoric times to the present.

———. La música popular en el Perú. Traducción, notas y comentario de Daniel Castañeda. *Música,* v. 1, no. 2 (-5 May 1930), p. 11-23. **[2358]**

Translation of an article which appeared originally in *Le Courrier musical* (see item no. 2859).

———. La musique populaire au Pérou. *Cour. mus.,* v. 32, no. 2 (15 Jan. 1930), p. 39-41. il. **[2359]**

Uriel García, José. El Jharahui. *Antara,* v. 1, no. 2 (Aug. 1930), p. 4. **[2360]**

Reproduced from the author's book. *El nuevo Indio* (see item no. 2464). The Jharahui among the Peruvian Indians of the pre-Columbian epoch was the song used for sacred rites and for prayers to the gods. After the Conquest it became part of the *mestizo* music of Peru under the name of *yaraví.*

Vásquez, Emilio. Orígenes del huayno. *Garcilaso* (Apr. 1941), p. 10. **[2361]**

Vega, Carlos. La supuesta escala mestiza de Perú y Bolivia. *La Prensa,* año 65, no. 23,282 (26 Nov. 1933), sec. 3, p. 2. **[2362]**

Vizcarra Rozas, Abraham. Bosquejo del proceso de la música en el Perú. Tésis presentada en la Universidad nacional del Cuzco, para optar al título de doctor en la facultad de filosofía, historia y letras. Universidad nacional del Cuzco, 1940. 65 p. **[2363]**

Treats extensively of Indian and Peruvian folk music, with 7 brief musical examples.

———. Folklore musical peruano. *Rev.*

univ. Cuzco, v. 29, no. 78 (1940), p. 163-198. **[2364]**

Zevallos Quiñones, Jorge. Un romance español del siglo xviii en el Perú. *Tres,* no. 7 (Dec. 1940), p. 63-70. **[2365]**

Gives the text and melody of a ballad collected in the Peruvian village of Usquil, and compares it with versions of the same ballad found in Spain in the 17th and 18th centuries.

(B) DANCES

Bailarines e instrumentistas en la feria nacional. *Turismo,* v. 15, no. 154 (Aug. 1940). **[2366]**

Description of the national festival of music and dance organized by Benjamin Roca Muelle. Includes 9 illustrations of dancers and instrumentalists.

Hernández, Francisco. Some Latin American festivals. 1. Fiestas in Perú. *Bull. pan amer. union* v. 52, no. 11 (Nov. 1939), p. 643-648. **[2367]**

References to musical instruments, and 6 photographs of dances.

Jiménez Borja, Arturo. Coreografía colonial: acuarelas mandadas hacer por D. Baltasar Jaime Martínez Compañon y Bujanda, siglo xviii. 12 p. inserted in *Tres* (Lima), no. 5 (June 1940). **[2368]**

8 plates.

———. Danzas de Lima. *Turismo* (Jan. 1939). **[2369]**

———. Folklore de Puno: la danza de las Choquelas. *El comercio* (23 June 1940). **[2370]**·

———. Máscara y música de la danza los Tistiles. *Turismo* (Sept. 1939). **[2371]**

———. Máscaras y danzas del Perú. *Turismo,* v. 13, no. -33 (1938). **[2372]**

Brief descriptions of 4 Peruvian folk dances, with 8 illustrations of dance masks. The dances are *Jija, Legión, Diablos de Cajabamba* and *Cunchos* .All are associated with local festivals.

Mejía Baca, José. Algunas noticias sobre la "conga". Lima, 1938.   [2373]
The Peruvian *conga* (now obsolete) is not to be confused with the Cuban dance of the same name. Concerning the origins of the *conga*, see Jorge Basadre, *Historia de la República* (Lima, 1939), p. 395-397. Cf. Pereira Salas, *Los orígenes del arte musical en Chile* [no. 1230], p. 293-294.

——. Las marineras chiclayanas. *El comercio* (26 Dec. 1937).   [2374]

——. El tondero. *El comercio* (1 Jan. 1938).   [2375]

Middendorf, E. W. Peru. Lima. Berlin, Robert Oppenheim, 1893. 638 p. F3408.-M62 v. 1   [2376]
Music, balls and the *zambacueca*, p. 262-263.

Pulgar Vidal, Javier. Tres danzas simbólicas de síntesis histórica: la danza garahuanca. El carodanza o cahuallo-danza. Los negritos. *El comercio* (4 May 1939).   [2377]

Romero, Fernando. Cómo era la zamacueca zamba. *Turismo*, no. 146 (1939).   [2378]

——. De la "samba" de África a la "marinera" del Perú. *Estud. afrocub.*, v. 4, nos. 1-4 (1940), p. 82-120. [2379]
An important study, tracing the ancestry of the modern folk dance of Peru called *marinera* from the colonial *zamba* and the *zamacueca* of the 19th century, and showing the Negro influence on these dances. Contains much incidental data on colonial music in Peru.

——. La zamba, abuela de la marinera. *Turismo* (July 1939).   [2380]

Ugarte de Landívar, Zoila. Y va de exámenes; baile indígena. Quito, La universidad, 1923. 10 p. plates. [2381]

Uriel García, José. La ciudad de los Incas. Cuzco, Librería Imp. H. G. Rozas, 1922. 253 p. F3611.C9G27   [2382]
El baile, p. 99-101 (with notes on music).

——. El coloniaje y las danzas indígenas. *La prensa*, v. 66, no. 23,783 (14 Apr. 1935), sec. 2, p. 1.   [2383]
Discusses the *Siclla, buenahechura*, and *general* dances, with illustrations of the dancers in action, and posing with their guitars.

Valcárcel, Luis E. Por Tawantinsuyu. La fiesta de la luna. *La prensa*, v. 67, no. 24,173 (10 May 1936), sec. 3, p. 1.   [2384]
References to the dances in this old Incan festival.

(c) AMERINDIAN

1. *Pre-Columbian (Inca and Pre-Inca)*

a. Music and Dance

Alviña, Leandro. La música incaica. Lo que es, y su evolución desde la época de los Incas hasta nuestros días. *Rev. univ.*, Cuzco, v. 13 (1929), p. 299-328.   [2385]

Ancient music and its connection with the origin of the Incas. *Inca chron.* (Lima), v. 3 (Feb. 1911), p. 15-16.   [2386]

Arróspide de la Flor, César. Valoración de la música como expresión cultural en el imperio de los Incas. *Rev. univ. cat. Perú*, v. 8, nos. 2-3 (May-June 1940), p. 124-132.   [2387]
A general aesthetic discussion.

Arte antiguo peruano. Música, composición y acotaciones de Theodoro Valcárcel. ¿Fué exclusivamente de 5 sonidos la escala musical de los Incas? *Rev. museo nac.*, v. 1, no. 1 (1932), p. 115-121.   [2388]
Includes music (voice and piano) of *Sankayo-ta*, fragment of the opera-ballet *Gran Kuraka* by Valcárcel. Also 5 examples of Peruvian Indian music.

Béclard d'Harcourt, Marguerite. ¿Existe una música incaica? *Gaceta mus.*, v. 1, no. 1 (Jan. 1928), p. 21-28.   [2389]

Berard, Carol. La música de los Incas.

Alma latina, v. 1, no. 1, (Aug. 1930).
[2390]
Based largely on the studies of the d'Harcourts. With one musical example.

Buenos Aires. Universidad. Facultad de filosofía y letras. Instituto de literatura argentina. Sección folklore, 2ª serie. Cancionero incaico, por Victor Guzmán Cáceres. Con introducción de Vicente Forte. Buenos Aires, Imprenta de la Universidad, 1929. 57 p. **[2391]**
Contains 200 melodies.

Cáceres, Esteban M. Origen de la música incaica. *Mús. de Amér.,* v. 2, no. 10 (1921). **[2392]**

Castro, José. Sistema pentafónico en la música indígena pre-colonial del Perú. *Bol. lat. am. mús.,* v. 4 (1938), p. 835.
[2393]
Includes the notation of 2 *yaravis* and a *kashua* (Kechua melodies), imperfectly transcribed. This article was written in 1908.

Comettant, Jean Pierre Óscar. La musique en Amérique avant la découverte de Christophe Colomb. *In* International congress of Americanists. *1st, Nancy, 1875.* Compte-rendu de la première session, Nancy-1875. Paris, Maisonneuve et cie., 1875, v. 2, p. 274-301. E51.I51
[2394]
Contains 3 Peruvian Indian tunes arranged for saxophone, from the collection of C. E. Soedling; and 3 *yaravis* harmonized for 3 saxophones by Ambroise Thomas.

——, La musique, les musiciens et les instruments de musique chez les différents peuples du monde. Paris, Michel Lévy frères, 1869. 737 p. il. ML38.P-2E8 **[2395]**
Discusses the *quena* and the pre-Columbian melodies of Peru, p. 577-584. Two Peruvian tunes aranged for 3 saxophones by Ambroise Thomas, p. 585.

——, La quena: les chants de l'ancien Pérou; le beau en musique. *Bull. soc. comp. musique,* v. 1, (1863), p. 149-157. **[2396]**
Includes "Deux chants de l'ancien Pérou,

joués par les Indiens sur la quena, harmonisés pour 3 saxophones par Ambroise Thomas."

Dumnesnil, Maurice. Music in Peru, the land of the Incas. *Etude,* v. 59, no. 4 (Apr. 1941), p. 223, 280-281. **[2397]**
Includes music of a *yaravi* from the collection of D. Alomía Robles.

Durán, Sixto M. La música incásica. *Mús. de Amér.,* v. 1, nos. 2-4 (1920).
[2398]

Enciclopedia universal ilustrada Europeo-Americana. Bilbao, Madrid, Barcelona, Espasa-Calpe, s. a., 1925. v. 28. AE61.E5 **[2399]**
Sub voce *Inca,* brief reference to music, p. 1148, with music of *Huayno incaico,* transcribed for piano by Felipe Urquieta.

Enock, C. Reginald. Peru. New York, Charles Scribner's sons, 1908. 320 p. F3408.E59 **[2400]**
Incan music, p. 24.

Fleck, W. L. Traditions and music of ancient Peru. *West coast leader* (4 Dec. 1923). p. 16-17. **[2401]**

Forte, Vicente. El lirismo en el imperio de los Incas. *Alma latina,* v. 8, no. 136 (9 July 1938), p. 16, 60. **[2402]**
Deals with the religious content of the music and dance of the ancient Peruvians; contains several notes on musical instruments, and a list of bibliographical references at the end of the article.

Garcés B., Miguel. La música incaica no es pentafónica. *Rev. univ.,* Cuzco, v. 25, 2º trim. (1936), p. 54-60. **[2403]**

Garcilaso de la Vega. Historia general del Perú, o los comentarios reales de los Incas. Madrid, Impr. de Villalpando, 1800-1801. 13 v. F3442.G245.
[2404]
Garcilaso, born at Cuzco in 1539 of Indian and Spanish parents, was an historian of the New World, particularly Peru. Known as *the Inca,* and devoting most of his literature to the Incas, Garcilaso spent the greater part of his life, not in

Peru, but in Spain. His first historical work *La Florida del Inca ó Historia del Adelantado Hernando de Soto,* was published in Lisbon in 1695. In the *Comentarios,* see part 1, bk. 2, ch. 14, which deals with the geometry, geography, arithmetic and music known to the Indians. A more recent edition of this work is the following: *Comentarios reales de los incas.* Edición al cuidado de Angel Rosenblat. Prólogo de Ricardo Rojas; con un glosario de voces indígenas. Buenos Aires, Emecé editores s. a. [1943]. 2 vols. An English translation by Sir Clements R. Markham was published in London for the Hakluyt Society, in 2 vols., 1869-71, as *The First Part of the Royal Commentaries of the incas.*

Harcourt, Raoul d'. Les instruments de musique des Mexicains et des Péruviens; place que tenait la musique chez ces peuples. *In* Encyclopédie de la musique et dictionnaire du conservatoire, partie 1, p. 3337-3353, Paris, Librairie Delagrave, 1922. il. ML100.E5. **[2405]**

This is part of a general study entitled *La musique indienne chez les anciens civilisés d'Amérique* [cf. item no. 210]. It consists of a detailed account of the musical instruments of the ancient Mexicans and Peruvians, with numerous illustrations, followed by a general survey of music and dancing in relation to the social organization of these peoples.

————, **and Marguerite d'.** La musique des Incas et ses survivances. Paris, P. Geuthner, 1925. 2 v. ML3575-H27. **[2406]**

Index bibliographique, v. 1, p. 545-556. Part 4 includes 204 musical examples, of which 141 are from Peru, 54 from Ecuador, and 9 from Bolivia. Most of these are melodies with Kechua text and French translation. A fundamental work, profusely illustrated and thoroughly documented.

Hornbostel, Erich von. D'Harcourt, R. et M.: La musique des Incas et ses survivances. *Anthropos,* v. 22 (1927), p. 657-661. **[2407]**

A detailed critical review of this important work [no. 2406], with a discussion of Incan music.

The Inca dance. *Inca chron.,* v. 2 (Oct. 1910), p. 9-10. **[2408]**

Klatovsky, Richard. Music in the realm of the Incas. *Mus. times,* v. 75, no. 1098 (1934), p. 696-700. il. **[2409]**

Description of musical instruments, with illustrations of the *tinya,* the *quena* and the *antàra.* Part 2 is a discussion of pre-Columbian music, with 12 brief musical examples. Also touches on *música mestiza.* Gives the Kechua text, with English translation, of two love-songs.

Lach, Robert. Die musik der Inkas. *Der auftakt,* v. 6, nos. 5-6 (1926), p. 124-126. **[2410]**

Book review of *La musique des Incas,* by Raoul and Marguerite d'Harcourt (see item no. 2406).

Markham, Clements Robert. Inca civilization in Peru. *In* Winsor, Justin, Narrative and critical history of America. New York, Boston, Houghton, Mifflin & co., 1889, v. 1, p. 209-282. E18.W76 v. 1. **[2411]**

Mention of dancing and *huayllinas* (songs) in sacrificial ceremony, p. 237; *yaravís* and musical instruments, p. 242.

Mortimer, William Golden. Peru. History of coca, "the divine plant" of the Incas, and of the Andean Indians of today. New York, J. H. Vail & co., 1901. 576 p. il. RS165.C5M8 **[2412]**

Description of Incan music and musical instruments, p. 438-443, with an Indian tune arranged for piano.

The music of the Incas. *South American,* v. 8, no. 7 (1920), p. 14-15. il. **[2413]**

Reprinted from the Kansas City Star.

Nolan, Patrick J. Tracing the "lost continent" through music's aid. Researches yield rich harvest of Incan music. *Mus. Amer.,* v. 38, no. 4 (1923), p. 3, 37. il. **[2414]**

Poindexter, Miles. The Ayar-Incas. New York, H. Liveright, 1930. 2 v. il. F3429.P75 **[2415]**

Deals with music, v. 1, p. 246-247.

Rivero, Mariano Eduardo de, and Juan Diego de Tschudi. Antigüedades peruanas. Viena, Impr. imperial de la corte y del estado, 1851. 328 p. il. F34-29.R47   **[2416]**

Includes 3 Peruvian Indian melodies arranged for piano, p. 135-141. For an English translation of this work, see item no. 2417.

Rivero, Mariano Edward, and John James von Tschudi. Peruvian antiquities. New York, A. S. Barnes; Cincinnati, H. W. Derby, 1855. 306 p. F-3429.R48.   **[2417]**

Haravís, p. 115; music to 3 *haravís*, p. 137-143; instrumental music (with 3 musical examples), p. 143-145. In the chapter on religious ceremonies, there are many brief comments on music and dance. Another edition of this work was published by G. P. Putnam at New York in 1853. This is a translation of item no. 2416.

Rodríguez del Busto, N. Del ambiente incaico. Buenos Aires, Talleres gráficos argentinos L. J. Rosso, 1936. 128 p. F3429.R655   **[2418]**

Includes: Danzas incaicas.

Sas, Andrés. Aperçu sur la musique inca. *Acta musicol.* v. 6, no. 1 (1934), p. 1-8.   **[2419]**

An analytical study of the modal structure of Incan music, with 11 musical examples.

——. Ensayo sobre la música inca. *Bol. lat. am. mús.,* v. 1 (Bogotá, 1935) p. 71-77.   **[2420]**

Includes 7 tunes. The following are the main points in this article: Peruvian Incan music, as it survives today, is essentially monodic; all evidence leads to the conviction that polyphony was unknown to the Peruvians in pre-Hispanic times. The Andean indigenes had only a few rudimentary musical instruments, of the types common to all primitive peoples. Their only melodic instruments were the *quena* (or *ḳena*), a vertical flute: the *antara*, or panpipes; and a kind of ocarina called *pinḳullo*. Other instruments, such as whistles, trumpets and conch-shells, could not play melodies. They also had a variety of drums and other

percussion instruments. Upon the basis of a minute analysis of over 400 melodies Sas puts forth the theory that the Incan pentatonic scale contains two dominants, one *melodic* (on the 4th degree of the scale), and the other *harmonic* (on the 2nd degree of the scale). The normal harmonic cadence, then is II-I.

——. Ensayo sobre la música Inca. *El momento musical,* v. 2, no. 7 (June 1937), p. 4-6.   **[2421]**

Reprinted from *Boletín latino-americano de música* (see item no. 2420).

——. Ensayo sobre la música nazca. *Bol. lat. am. mús.* v. 4 (1938), p. 221-233. il.   **[2422]**

Description of the primitive Peruvian musical instruments (antaras) in the Museo Nacional de Arqueología at Lima. Illustrated and with 25 examples of scale notations.

——. Ensayo sobre la música nazca. *Rev. museo nac.,* Lima, v. 8, no. 1 (1939), p. 123-138. Also printed separately, ML-3547.S28E5   **[2423]**

For comment, see item no. 2422.

Sobre música incaica. *Nosotros,* v. 23, no. 245 (Oct. 1929), p. 145-147.   **[2424]**

Quotes from an article by Atilio Sivirichi in reply to a criticism by Carlos Vega.

Uriel García, José. La música incaica. *Revista Amauta,* no. 2 (Oct. 1926).   **[2425]**

Valcárcel, Luis Eduardo. Arte antiguo del Perú. Danzas. *La prensa,* v. 69, no. 24,891 (1 May 1938), sec. 3, p. 1.   **[2426]**

Illustrations of ancient Peruvian (Mochica) ceramics, with bas-relief representing forms of dances and musical instruments. The article is a description of the dances as determined from these ceramics.

——. De la vida inkaica. Lima, Editorial Garcilaso, 1925. 132 p. F3429.V26   **[2427]**

Peruvian folk-lore. Music, p. 77-78.

Valcárcel, Theodoro. Composición musical Sankayota. ¿Fué exclusivamente de

5 notas la escala musical de los Incas? *Rev. museo nac.,* v. 1 (1932), p. 115-121. **[2428]**

Vega, Carlos. Escala con semitonos en la música· de los antiguos peruanos. *Cursos y conferencias,* año 3, v. 5, no. 1 (July 1933), p. 1-45. **[2429]**

A well-documented study upholding the thesis that scales with semitones (in addition to the pentatonic scale) were used in South America in pre-Hispanic times. With numerous diagrams and three tables.

——. Escalas con semitonos en la música de los antiguos peruanos. Actas y trabajos científicos del XXV Congreso internacional de americanistas (La Plata, 1932), v. 1 (Buenos Aires, 1934), p. 349-381. **[2430]**

Also published in *Cursos y conferencias* (for comment, see no. 2429).

——. La música incaica y el doctor Sivi-richi. *Nostros,* año 23, v. 64, no. 239 (Apr. 1929), p. 72-85. **[2431]**

——. El sistema musical de los antiguos peruanos. *La prensa,* v. 64, no. 23, 198 (3 Sept. 1939), sec. 3, p. 3. **[2432]**

——. Tonleitern mit halbtonen in der musik der alten Peruaner. *Acta musi-col.,* v. 9, no. 1-2 (Jan.-June 1936), p. 41-53. **[2433]**

Cf. nos. 2429 and 2430.

Velazco Aragón, Luis. La música incaica. *Verbum,* v. 17, no. 62 (Dec. 1923), p. 41-57. **[2434]**

Includes description of several instruments, with special reference to the *quena.* Dance, p. 45-47.

Villalba Muñoz, Alberto. La canción y de sus diversos géneros en la música incaica. *Mús. de Amér.,* v. 2, no. 6 (1920), **[2435]**

——. El sistema tonal de la música incaica. *Mús. de Amér.,* v. 2, no. 7. (1921). **[2436]**

——. The tonal system of Incan music. *Inter-America,* v. 5 (New York 1922), p. 257-265. **[2437]**

Wiesse, Carlos. Las civilizaciones primitivas del Perú. Lima, Tipografía "El Lucero", 1913. 291 p. F3429.W654 **[2438]**

Dance, music and poetry, p. 281-284.

——. Historia del Perú prehispánico. 8 ed. Lima, Librería Rosay, 1937. 132 p. il. F3429.W658 **[2439]**

b. Instruments

Campana, Domenico del. Notizie intorno all'uso della "siringa" o "flauto di Pane". *Arch. antrop. etnol.,* v. 39 (1909), p. 46-62. **[2440]**

Contains a plate showing 14 varieties of primitive pan-pipes, including some from Peru.

Chirre Danos, Ricardo. Variaciones sobre la kena. *Sustancia* (Tucumán), v. 2, no. 7-8 (1941), p. 561-575. **[2441]**

Engel, Carl. Musical instruments. Rev. ed. London, Wyman and sons, 1908. 146 p. il. ML460.E64 **[2442]**

References to the music of the Indians of Peru and Mexico, p. 78-80.

Harcourt, Raoul and Marguerite d'. La musique des Incas et ses survivances. Paris, P. Geuthner, 1925. 2 v. il. ML3575.H27 **[2443]**

Index bibliographique, v. 1, p. 545-556. Part 4 includes 204 musical examples, of which 141 are from Peru, 54 from Ecuador, and 9 from Bolivia. Most of these are melodies with Kechua text and French translation. A fundamental work, profusely illustrated and thoroughly documented.

Joyce, Thomas Athol. South American archaeology; an introduction to the archaeology of the South American continent, with special reference to the early history of Peru. London, Macmillan and co., ltd., 1912. 292 p. il. F2-229.J7 **[2444]**

Passing references to musical instruments, p. 21, 31, 32, 46. Illustration of a Quimbayan gold whistle, Pl. 4, no. 6.

Larco Herrera, Rafael. Civilizaciones de la costa peruana. *Rev. univ.* (Cuzco),

v. 11, 4° trim. (1926), p. 1-28.
[2545]

Illustration of 15 quenas found in *se-pulturas de Pachacamac*, opposite p. 16.

Mead, Charles Williams. The musical instruments of the Inca. New York, American museum press, 1924 (Anthropological papers of the American museum of natural history, v. 15, pt. 3), p. 313-347, il. GN2.A27 v. 15, pt. 3 ML4867.P3M36 **[2446]**

"Most of the text in this paper appeared under the present title in 1903, as a Guide leaflet, supplementary to the American museum journal".

——. Old civilizations of Inca land. New York, American museum press. 1924. 117 p. F3429.M46 **[2447]**

Musical instruments, p. 76-77, 92, 95, 96.

Ruth-Sommer, Hermann. Alte musikin-strumente, ein leit-faden für sammler. 2d. ed. Berlin, R. C. Schmidt & co., 1920. 214 p. il. ML489.R92 **[2448]**

Includes illustrations of Mexican and Peruvian flutes, p. 94-95.

Safford, William E. Pan-pipes of Peru. *Jour, Wash. Acad. scien.,* v. 4 (1914), p. 183-191. **[2449]**

Schmidt, Max. Kunst und kultur von Peru. Berlin, Im prophyläen, 1929. 622 p. F3429.3A7S3 **[2450]**

Photographs of musical instruments, p. 541-543, with explanations of these plates, p. 611.

Trimborn, H., and P. F. Vega. Arte Inca. Madrid, 1935. 160 p. F3429.3.-A7L18 (Organizada bajo los auspicios de la Academia de la historia y el Patronato de la Biblioteca nacional) **[2451]**

List of 11 musical instruments found in Peru, p. 145-146.

Varcárcel, Luis Eduardo. Arte antiguo de Perú. Músicos, *La prensa,* v. 67. no. 24,193 (31 May 1936), sec. 3, p. 1. **[2452]**

Illustrated with ceramic figures playing

various instruments, with descriptions of these instruments in the text.

——. Músicos ... Lima, imprenta del Museo nacional, 1938. 5 p. il. (Cuadernos de arte antiguo del Perú, no. 6). **[2453]**

With 5 illustrations of ancient Peruvian instruments.

See also nos. 2405, 2409, 2411, 2412, 2420, 2426, 2434.

2. *Post-Columbian (Primitive and Modern)*

a. Music and Dance

Argüedas, José María. Canto Kechwa; con un ensayo sobre la capacidad de creación artística del pueblo indio y mestizo. Lima, Ediciones "Club del libro peruano", 1938. 65 p. PM6308.A7 **[2454]**

Kechua and Spanish on opposite pages. Spanish versions of Kechua folk songs, with some discussion of the musical background.

Borchers, Philip, ed. Die weisse kordillere. Berlin, Verlag Scherl, 1935. 396 p. F3451.A5B7 **[2455]**

Music of the Cholo Indians, p. 246. See also p. 252-256 for an animated description of the festivals and an unusually fine account of their musical instruments.

Clément, Félix. Histoire de la musique ... Paris, Hachette et cie., 1885.819 p. il. ML160.C63 **[2456]**

La musique chez les Péruviens, p. 144-151. Mentions a work by Le Gentil de la Babinais, *Nouveau voyage autour du monde,* Amsterdam, 1728, which gives an account of singing among the Peruvian Indians, Music of a "mélodie péruvienne", p. 147-148, and of two *haravis (sic)* from Rivero's *Antigüedades peruanas* [no. 2416]. Two illustrations of musical instruments and musicians.

Farabee, William C. Indian tribes of eastern Peru. Cambridge, Mass., The Museum, 1922. 194 p. il. E51.H337 vol. 10 F3430.F21 **[2457]**

Refers to music, p. 11, 84, and to dancing, p. 123, 140.

Hardy, Osgood. The Indians of the department of Cuzco. *Amer. anthrop.*, v. 21, no. 1 (Jan.-Mar. 1919), p. 1-27. **[2458]**

New Year's dance festivities, p. 20; Feast of the Trinity dances, with descriptions of musical instruments, p. 22-23.

Karsten, Rafael. The head-hunters of Western Amazonas; the life and culture of the Jibaro Indians of eastern. Ecuador and Peru ... Helsingfors, 1935. 598 p. il. (incl. music). (Finska vetenskaps-societeten, Helsingfors. Commentationes humanarum literrarum. VII. 1). P9.F5 v. 7, no. 1 F3722.J5K2 **[2459]**

Poetry and music are discussed in Ch. 14, p. 496-502, with 2 tunes. There are also 9 other tunes: p. 135, 137, 200, 323, 325, 415, 467.

Mejía Xesspe, M. Torobio. Costumbres indígenas. *Inca.* v. 1, no. 4 (Oct.-Dec. 1923), p. 884-903. **[2460]**

The locale is the Andean region of Peru (departamento de Arequipa). "Las fiestas populares", p. 886. "Fiestas religiosas", p. 888. Description of numerous native dances. Words of songs, p. 897-898.

Middendorf, E. W. Peru. Das hochland von Peru. Berlin, Robert Oppenheim, 1895. 603 p. F3408.M62 v. 3 **[2461]**

Music and dance of the Indians, p. 103-104.

Sargeant, Winthrop. Music of the Incas survives in tribal melodies of the Andes. *Mus. Amer.*, v. 52, no. 2 (25 Jan. 1932), p. 25, 169. **[2462]**

A discussion of musical instruments; the music of the Kechua Indians; the importance of music in all festivals; the use of the pentatonic scale (with 3 musical examples); and a translation of a "melodic lament".

———. Types of Quechua melody. *Mus. quart.*, v. 20, no. 2 (April 1934), p. 230-245. **[2463]**

With 13 tunes, all but one collected by the author in Peru.

Uriel García, José. El nuevo indio. Cuz-co, H. G. Rozas sucesores, 1937. 2nd ed. 192 p. F3430.G3 1937. **[2464]**

Music of the *Indio antiguo*, p. 70-75, with a note on the change of the music of the Indians since the advent of modern civilization.

Verrill, A. Hyatt. Old civilizations of the new world. New York, The New home library, 1942. 393 p. il. E58.V55 1942 **[2465]**

First published in 1929. Refers to Indian music, p. 340-342. Examples of Peruvian Indian music, for piano, and for voice and piano, p. 343-355.

Yabar Palacio, Luis. El ayllu de Queros (Paucartambo). *Revista universitaria*, Cuzco, v. 11 (Sept. 1922), p. 3-26. LE-66.C8 **[2466]**

Las fiestas, p. 12-26. La música, p. 12-14. Se emplean el tambor, el bombo, la antara, y las quenas, p. 14.

b. Instruments

Forbes, David. On the Aymara Indians of Bolivia and Peru. *Jour. ethnol. soc.*, n. s., v. 2 (1870), p 193-298. **[2467]**

Mentions musical instruments, p. 233.

Izikowitz, Karl G. Le tambour à membrane au Pérou. Paris, 1931. **[2468]**

Tessman, Günter. Die indianer nordost-Perus. Hamburg, Friederichsen, de Gruyter & co., 1930. 856 p. il. F3430.-T31 **[2469]**

Important scientific notes on the instruments of each Indian tribe, with drawings of them, and charts comparing the level of culture of the various tribes.

———. Menschen ohne Gott. Stuttgart, Strecker & Schröder, 1928. 244 p. F34-30.T33 **[2470]**

Ucayali musical instruments, p. 40, 105.

Wiener, Charles. Pérou et Bolivie. Paris, Hachette & cie., 1880. 796 p. il. F3423.-W64 **[2471]**

Description of Peruvian Indian instruments, p. 690-692.

See also nos. 1334, 2455, 2456, 2458, 2462, 2466.

Considerable advance has been made in laying the foundations for the musical history of Peru, largely by the researches and publications of the American musicologist Dr. Robert Stevenson, of the University of California in Los Angeles, who spent the academic year 1958-59 in Peru as a research scholar under the Fulbright exchange program. He has published articles on *Ancient Peruvian musical instruments* (item 928a) and on *Opera beginnings in the new world* (item 963a), subsequently incorporated in an important monograph on *The music of Peru: aboriginal and viceroyal epochs,* published by the Pan American Union in 1960 (item 962a). This work has a wealth of bibliographical data.

The Peruvian composer and musicologist Andrés Sas has continued his researches in local archives, and some of the results have been published in articles dealing with Peruvian musicians active in the 18th century (items 959a and 961a). To these should be added the biobibliographical data based on contemporary sources collected by Rodolfo Barbacci (item. 942a).

In the immediate past, the analytical catalog of the works of Daniel Alomía Robles compiled by Rodolfo Holzmann is an extremely useful guide to the vast but rather disorganized body of folk music of the Andean region collected by that musical folklorist and composer. The preparation of such systematic catalogs is a basic requirement for the musical history of Latin America.

The eminent Peruvian music critic and scholar, Carlos Raygada, died in 1952, leaving a void that it has been difficult to fill. His exhaustive monograph on the history of the Peruvian national anthem was published posthumously (item 955a).

BIBLIOGRAPHY

(A) PRIMITIVE, FOLK, AND POPULAR MUSIC

Argüedas, José María. Songs of the Quechuas. *Américas,* v. 9, no. 8 (Aug. 1957), p. 30-34.　　**[904a]**

　　About *harawis,* ballads, love serenades. Considerable detail about music instruments. 8 song texts, in Quechua or Spanish, and English. No music. 5 photographs; of women chanting a *harawi,* with mouths covered; of man playing *pinkullu;* of man playing *charango;* of man playing *wak' rapuku,* made of bull's horn; of men performing the Dance of the Condors.

———. La fiesta de la cruz; danza de los sijillas. *Revista del Instituto americano de arte* (Cuzco, Peru), v. 1, año 2, no. 2 (1. y 2. semestre de 1943), p. 18-21.　　**[905a]**

　　Quechua text only of 4 couplets of accompanying songs.

Barbacci, Rodolfo. Bases para el estudio del folklore musical peruano. *Cult. peruana,* año 5, v. 5, no. 22 (Aug. 1945).　　**[906a]**

　　Stresses importance of scientific collection as over against that of amateurs. Recommends plan of organization of folklore study in Peru. (C.S.)

Bernal, Dionicio Rodolfo. El huaino. *Peruanidad* (Lima), v. 4, no. 18 (July-Aug. 1944), p. 1438-1445. **[907a]**

Includes texts of various *huainos*.

Brainerd, George W. A Peruvian whistling jar. *Masterkey*, v. 25, no. 1 (Jan.-Feb. 1951), p. 18-22. **[908a]**

Describes a late Chimú double bottle with a miniature modelled group on one of the necks. Includes also notes on whistling (J.H.R.)

Bustamante, Manuel E. Apuntes para el folklore peruano. Ayacucho, Imp. "La miniatura", 1943. 178, iv p. il. **[909a]**

Música indígena. Instrumentos musicales. El otro corneta. El *jarahui*. Breves referencias sobre la música vernacular: p. 134-145. Contains wood-cut of *toro corneta*.

Cabrera, Ana S. de. Instrumentos musicales indígenas. *Palabra americana* (Lima, Perú), v. 13 (April 1944), p. 61-64. **[910a]**

Carvallo de Núñez, Carlota. Canciones infantiles peruanas. *Ipna*, año 3, v. 5, no. 5 (Jan.-Apr. 1946), p. 43-61. **[911a]**

Eight songs scored for voice and piano. (C.S.)

Digby, Adrian. The technical development of whistling vases in Peru. *In* Tax, Sol, *ed*. The civilizations of ancient America. Selected papers of the XXIX international congress of Americanists. Chicago, Univ. of Chicago press, 1951, p. 252-257. (J.H.R.) **[912a]**

Farfán, José M. B. Cantos quechuas de Ancash *Rev. museo nac.*, Lima, v. 13 (1944, i. e., 1945), p. 145-152. **[913a]**

Fifteen songs with Quechua and Spanish texts. No music notations. (C.S.)

Folklore musical del siglo xviii. Lima, Scheuch, 1946. (No pagination) 18 pl. (Instituto de investigaciones artísticas de la Universidad católica del Perú, Lima.) **[914a]**

Fuentes, Manuel A. Lima or sketches of the capital of Peru, historical, statestical (sic), administrative, commercial and moral. Paris, Firmin Didot, brothers, sons & co., 1866. ix, 224 p. illus. **[915a]**

Deals with Negroes in Peru, their brotherhoods, music and dances, p. 79-86, with mention of the marimba as a typical musical instrument. National dances of Peru are discussed, p. 147-153, with mention of the *zamacueca, londú, cachucha,* waltz. States that the *zamacueca* has been variously known as *maiseto, ecuador,* etc., "and at present the *zanguaraña".* Also gives *Polka de cajón* as one of the names for the zamacueca at that time (from the big drum called cajón). On p. 152 there is an illustration captioned "Negroes dancing the Zamacueca", which has been reproduced by Vega and other modern writers. The popular orchestra, says the author, is composed of a harp and a guitar, to which is added "a kind of drum, usually made of a wooden box, the boards of which are partially unnailed to render it more sonorous".

Gálvez, José. La marinera. *Ipna* (Sept.-Dec. 1944), p. 20-30. **[916a]**

The late Peruvian poet writes impressionisticaly of this dance.

Garrido, Pablo. The singing stone. *Américas*, vol. 11, no. 6 (June 1949), p. 30-31. il. **[917a]**

An Incan wall in Cuzco which has three holes that produce different tones. The author disagrees with the finding of Augusto D. León Barandiarán, published in *El Comercio* of Lima on June 30, 1948.

Guamán Poma de Ayala, Felipe. Las primeras edades del Perú. Ensayo de interpretación por Julio César Tello. Lima, Empresa gráfica T. Schneck, 1939. 109 p. **[918a]**

Jiménez Borja, Arturo. La danza en el antiguo Perú, época inca. *Rev. museo nac.*, Lima, v. 15 (1946), i. e. 1947), p. 122-161. **[919a]**

Discussion of references in the chronicles relative to ritual, economy, costumes, masks, musical instruments. Seven plates, all from Guamán Poma. (C.S.)

———. Instrumentos musicales p e r u a n o s. *Rev. museo nac.* v. 19-20 (1950-1951), p. 37-190.   **[920a]**

Description and classification of musical instruments used in ancient and modern Peru, with abundant and important illustrations, many of archeological specimens in Peruvian collections that have not previously been published. (J.H.R.)

Jorge, Fray José Pacífico. Melodías religiosas en Quechua. F r e i b u r g i/B, Herder & Co., 1924. vii, 220 p.   **[921a]**

Contains 76 melodies, some composed by Pedro Ovalle, Paulino Cáceres, and Ascension Mayorga. (R.S.)

Navarro del Águila, Víctor. Danzas populares del Perú. *Revista del Instituto americano del arte,* Cuzco (1943), p. 24-44.   **[922a]**

Pacheco Garmendia, Elsa. Aspectos d e l arte incaico; música y danza. Cuzco, H. G. Rozas, 1943. 56 p.   **[923a]**

Thesis for doctorate in Faculty of letters, National university of Cuzco. Describes some dances still current. (R.S.B.)

Pozo, Manuel Jesús. La m ú s i c a v e r - nacular ayacuchana. *Huamanga, Ayacucho* (Oct. 1944), p. 1-7.   **[924a]**

Reichlen, Henry. Fêtes, d a n s e s et rites des indiens de Cajamarca, Pérou. *J. soc. amer.,* n. s., v. 42 (1953), p. 391-413, 5 pl.   **[925a]**

Romero, Fernando. Instrumentos musicales de posible origen africano en la costa del Perú. *Afroamérica,* v. 1, no. 1-2 (Jan.-July 1945), p. 51-62.   **[926a]**

Brief notes upon 22 instruments. (C.S.)

Sánchez Málaga, Carlos. Folklore musical. *In* Diez charlas sobre f o l k l o r e . Lima, Ediciones de la Dirección de educación artística y extensión cultural, Sección de folklore y arte populares, Ministerio de educación pública, 1946, 51 p. (Mimeographed).   **[927a]**

This publication also includes the texts of talks on various aspects of folklore by A.

Jiménez Borja, E. Romero de Valle, M. A. Ugarte, J. C. Muelle, and Luis E. Valcárcel.

Stevenson, Robert. Ancient P e r u v i a n instruments. *Galpin soc. jour.,* no. 11 (May 1959), p. 17-43.   **[928a]**

A very important study based on primary sources.

———. Early Peruvian folk music. *Jour. Am. folklore,* v. 73, no. 288 (Apr.-June 1960), p. 112-132.   **[929a]**

———. Music instruction in I n c a l a n d. *Jour. research mus. educ.,* v. 8, no. 2 (Fall 1960), p. 110-122.   **[930a]**

Detailed, scholarly study.

———. The music of Peru; aboriginal and viceroyal epochs. W a s h i n g t o n, Pan American union, n. d. [1960], xii, 331 p. (music).   **[931a]**

For comment, see introduction to this section.

Taquies según Guaman P o m a. L i m a , Cuadernos de Cocodrilo, 1941 (no pagination). il.

"Las danzas en el antiguo Perú se llamaban taquies." The importance of the *taquies* was great. The chronicles tell of kings dancing in public on ceremonial occasions. The essay assembles the references to dances in the illustrated chronicle of Guaman Poma (8 illustrations are reproduced with the text) and makes comments thereon, with some references to other sources. The essay is signed A. J. B. and was doubtless written by Arturo Jiménez Borja. A headnote says that the work was undertaken *"con la colaboración de J. M. B. Farfán."*

Ugarte, Miguel A. Juegos, canciones, dichos y otros entretenimientos d e l o s niños. Recogidos en la ciudad de Arequipa. Colaboración musical de José L. García y Alejandro Koseleff. Arequipa, Tipografía Portugal, 1947. 96 p.   **[933a]**

Apéndice musical :p. 97-92.

Varallanos, José. El genio e s p a ñ o l e n

nuestro cantar popular. *El comercio,* Lima (1 Jan. 1944), p. 14. **[934a]**

Evaluates erudite Spanish origins of Peruvian folksong.

Vargas Ugarte, Rubén, César Arróspide de la Flor, and Rodolfo Holzmann. Folklore musical del siglo xviii. Lima, Scheuch, 1946. 16 p. il. (Universidad católica del Perú, Instituto de investigaciones artísticas.) **[935a]**

Reproduces music of 18 *yaravíes* from Quito reported by Marcos Jiménez de la Espada in 1881, with words and comments on each. (R.S.B.)(Cf. item 1567).

Vásquez, Emilio. Coreografía titicaca. Los chokelas. *Rev. museo nac.,* Lima, v. 13 (1944, i. e., 1945), p. 65-83. **[936a]**

Comments upon this ancient dance. Illustrations, and four music notations for piano. (C.S.)

————. La pandilla. *Rev. museo nac.,* Lima, v. 15 (1946, i. e., 1947), p. 81-121. **[937a]**

Detailed study by careful observer. Four full-page drawings. Four full-page music notations, piano score. (C.S.)

Verger, Pierre. Fiestas y danzas en el Cuzco y en los Andes. Buenos Aires, Ed. Sudamericana, 1945. 199 p. il. **[938a]**

Villareal Vara, Félix. Las afinaciones de la guitarra en Huanuco-Perú. *Rev. mus. chil.,* v. 12, no. 62 (Nov.-Dec. 1958), p. 33-36. **[939a]**

Gives 6 different tunings.

Vivanco, Moisés. Melodías peruanas: Peruvian folksongs; album de 7 composiciones para piano, del folklore peruano. Buenos Aires, Ed. internacionales Fermata, 1944. 11 p. **[940a]**

Zárate, Fidel A. Los lares iluminados. Lima, Empresa editora peruana, 1941. 366 p. il. **[941a]**

Literary description of land of Contumazá, in the Andes of central Peru, containing a valuable miscellany of folklore:

Pablo the local minstrel; carnival; songs; dances; Christmas; etc. (R.S.B.)

(B) ART MUSIC AND MISCELLANEOUS

Barbacci, Rodolfo. Apuntes para un diccionario biográfico musical peruano. *Fénix,* no. 6, 1949, p. 414-510. **[942a]**

Unique and invaluable reference for the study of music in Peru. Sources used were contemporary documents and newspapers. Some of the work was done before the burning of the National Library. (C.S.)

Bolaños, César. ¿Conservatorio? *Música,* v. 1, no. 1 (July 1957), p. 2. **[943a]**

The need for a complete reform in the Conservatorio Nacional de Música.

Holzmann, Rodolfo. Aporte para la emancipación de la música peruana. ¿Es posible usar la escala pentáfona para la composición? *Rev. estud mus.,* v. 1, no. 1 (Aug. 1949), p. 61-80. **[944a]**

Ingenious critique of the use of Peruvian-Andean folk music in the composition of concert music. 20 musical notations. Originally publ. in *Nuestro Tiempo,* Lima, in abbreviated form.

————. Catálogo de las obras de Daniel Alomía Robles. *Bol. bibliog.,* Lima, año 16, v. 13 ,nos. 1-2 (July 1943), p. 25-78. **[945a]**

The task of making this catalog was complicated by the circumstance that data regarding informant, date, and place of origin are often missing from the immense MS. collection (650 melodies notated at dictation) assembled by Alomía Robles as "Folklore del Peru". However, the province or "department" is usually given, which allows an index "por departamentos". The catalog also includes 125 arrangements for piano of Peruvian folksongs, and over 200 compositions by Alomia Robles, of which most are in MS. This is a very valuable contribution to Peruvian musical bibliography.

————. Ensayo analítico de la obra musical del compositor peruano Theodoro Valcárcel. *Eco musical,* v. 2, no. 6 (March 20, 1943), p. 23-33. **[946a]**

Informative and detailed analysis, illustrated with 26 musical notations contained in a "suplemento musical" inserted in this issue, which is entirely devoted to the life and works of Valcárcel (q. v.).

——. Classified chronological catalog of the works of the Peruvian composer Rodolfo Holzmann. *Bol. interam. mús.,* no. 3 (Jan. 1958), p. 59-64.　　**[947a]**

Holzmann was born in Breslau, Germany, in 1910.

Iturriaga, Enrique. Apuntes sobre música peruana. *B. A. mus.,* v. 12, no. 197 (Oct. 1, 1957), p. 13.　　　**[948a]**

General aesthetic discussion rather than factual survey.

More, Ernesto. Con Daniel Alomía Robles. *Universal* (Lima), 19 July 1942, p. 15.　　　　　**[949a]**

"Charla retrospectiva", personal reminiscences and conversations, published the day following the death of this Peruvian musician and folklorist. Portrait.

Orquesta Sinfónica Nacional, Lima. Relación de las actividades durante el sexto año de labores, 11 de diciembre de 1938-, 11 de diciembre de 1944. Lima, Imp. Gmo. Lenta, 1944. 11 p.　　　　　**[950a]**

A set of programs of the period covered, said to be complete, is to be found in the Columbus Memorial Library of the Pan American Union.

——. Relación de las actividades desde su creación, diciembre de 1938 — diciembre de 1945. Lima, Imp. Gmo. Lenta, 1945. 24 p.　　　**[951a]**

List of works performed, of conductors and of soloists in 108 concerts.

Peralta Barnuevo, Pedro de. Obras dramáticas con un apéndice de poemas inéditos. Publicadas con introducción y notas por Irving A. Leonard, Ph. D. Santiago de Chile, Imprenta universitaria, 1937. frontis. 384 p.　　**[952a]**

Peralta y Barnuevo (1633-1743), the most eminent Peruvian scholar and author of the Baroque period, wrote a number of works for the stage, most of which were performed with music (vocal and instrumental) and dances. For example: *Loa que se cantó en forma de Ópera en la comedia Afectos vencen Finezas.* Also: *bailes, fines de fiesta, entremeses, comedias,* all with music ("cuatros de empezar", etc.) corresponding to the Spanish peninsular lyrico-dramatic forms of that period. As far as known, none of the music for these plays has been preserved.

[Pozzi-Escot, Charlotte]. *Música,* v. 1 no. 2 (Aug. 1957), p. 4-5. il. (port.)　　　　　　　**[953a]**

Biographical data and list of works of this Peruvian composer.

Pozzi-Escot, Inés. Medio siglo de educación musical en la escuela peruana a través de los programas de educación primaria y secundaria. *Bol. conserv. nac. música,* v. 5, no. 17 (July-Sept. 1948) p. 63-77.　　　　　**[954a]**

Brief historical summary from the first official course (1905) results in recognition of two distinct aims: education of the professional musician and music in general education. Bibliography. (C.S.)

Raygada, Carlos. Historia crítica del himno nacional. Lima, J. Mejía Baca y P. L. Villanueva, 1954. 2 vols. il. ports., facs., music).　　　　　　**[955a]**

Includes analyses of 50 different versions, a biographical appendix, and a documentary appendix. Prologue by Jorge Basadre.

——. Peru: A decade of orchestral growth. *Mus. amer.,* v. 69, no. 12 (Oct. 1949), p. 12.　　　　　**[956a]**

The *Orquesta sinfónica nacional* celebrated its tenth anniversary.

Sánchez Málaga, Carlos. La música en el Perú. *Nuestra música.* v. 2, no. 6 (April 1947), p. 72-77.　　**[957a]**

A brief historical survey.

——. Música peruana. *Boletín de la Academia nacional de música Alcedo.* Lima, v. 2, no. 6 (1945), p. 115-120.　　　　　**[958a]**

Sas, Andrés. Los primeros músicos indoperuanos de cultura europea, en el siglo xvi. *Música,* v. 1, no. 1 (July 1957), p. 3. **[959a]**

Comments on certain musical references in Garcilaso de la Vega and Gutiérrez de Santa Clara.

———. Tomás de Torrejón y Velasco (1644-1728). *Música,* v. 1, no. 3 (Oct. 1957), p. 3-6. **[960a]**

Important documentation on the life of this musician, who was choirmaster at the Cathedral of Lima.

———. Una familia de músicos peruanos en el siglo xvii: Los Cervantes del Águila. *Música,* v. 1, no. 2 (Aug. 1957), p. 2-4. **[961a]**

Based on documents in the archives of the Cathedral and of the Iglesia del Sagrario in Lima.

Stevenson, Robert. The music of Peru: aboriginal and viceroyal epochs. Washington, D. C., Music division, Pan American union, 1960. 334 p. **[962a]**

An important study, based on firsthand research in Peru during 1958-59. For comment, see introductory section above. Includes numerous musical notations and copious bibliographical data.

———. Opera beginnings in the new world. *Mus. quart.,* v. 45, no. 1 (Jan. 1959), p. 8-25. **[963a]**

Based on research undertaken chiefly in Lima, discusses Tomás de Torrejón's *La púrpura de la rosa* (1701), to a text by Calderón de la Barca, with 7 music notations and 2 facsimiles. Valuable and authoritative.

Stubbs, Eduardo Walter. José María Valle Riestra. *Peruanidad* (Lima), v. 4, no. 18 (July-Aug. 1944), p. 1434-1437. **[964a]**

Biographical notes.

Valcárcel, Edgar. Francisco Pulgar Vidal. *Tempora,* no. 7 (Dec. 1955), p. 2. **[965a]**

Deals with the First String Quartet of this young Peruvian composer, which was awarded the National music prize "Luis Duncker Lavalle" in 1955.

[Valcárcel, Theodoro]. In memoriam Theodoro Valcárcel. *Eco musical* (Buenos Aires), v. 2, no. 6 (March 20, 1943), 33 p. il. (ports.) **[966a]**

"Homenaje a la memoria del compositor peruano Theodoro Valcárcel, fallecido el 20 de marzo de 1942." Includes an important article on his music by R. Holzmann (q. v.). A biographical study, p. 11-20, is signed "C. V."

Valle-Riestra, José María. Ollanta, Ópera en 3 actos. Lima, Orellana y cía. 1923. 33 p. **[967a]**

Libretto.

Vargas Ugarte, Rubén. Notas sobre la música en el Perú. *Cuaderno de estudio* (Pontificia universidad católica del Perú, Instituto de investigaciones históricas), v. 3, no. 7 (1949). **[968a]**

———. Un archivo de música colonial en la ciudad del Cuzco. *Mar del Sur,* año 5, no. 26 (March.-Apr. 1953), p. 3 and 7. **[969a]**

PUERTO RICO

Even a cursory glance at the following bibliography reveals the predominance of material on folk and popular music, to the neglect of other aspects of music in Puerto Rico, especially its history during the early colonial period. The history of music in Puerto Rico remains to be written.

Aguinaldos populares. Ponce, Puerto Rico, Otero y sobrino, 1901. 3 p. [2472]

Anonymous collection of Puerto Rican Christmas carols.

Alonso, Manuel A. Aguinaldos. *Arch. folklore cub.* v. 5, no. 2 (1930), p. 164-169. [2473]

Extract from the book *El Gíbaro,* Barcelona, 1849.

Balseiro, José A. El vigía, ensayos. Madrid, Editorial "Mundo latino", 1925-28. 2 v. PQ6039.B25 [2474]

Vol. 1 includes *Juan Morel Campos y la danza portorriqueña.*

Cadilla de Martínez, María. Juegos y canciones infantiles de Puerto Rico. San Juan, Baldrich, 1940. 250 p. ML3565. C33J8 [2475]

With music (unaccompanied melodies). *Bibliografía mínima,* 4 p. following text. Description of children's singing-games.

———. Más juegos tradicionales de Puerto Rico. *Ateneo puertorriqueño,* v. 4, no. 3 (1940), p. 224-240. [2476]

Excellent illustrated world comparative notes on the same group *of Recotin, recotán, Asserín, asserán, How many horns has the buck?* and others. [R. S. Boggs]

———. Poesía popular en Puerto Rico. Madrid, Universidad de Madrid, 1933. 306 p. [2477]

Ph. D. dissertation. Comprehensive treatment of all types of Puerto Rican folk poetry.

Cadman, Charles Wakefield. Music in Puerto Rico. *Music news,* v. 31, no. 10 (18 May 1939), p. 11, 22. [2478]

Callejo Ferrer, Fernando. Música y músicos portorriqueños. San Juan, Tipografía Cantero Fernández & co., 1915. 313 p. il. ML315.P83C15 [2479]

Espinosa, Aurelio M. Romances de Puerto Rico. *Rev. hisp.,* v. 63, no. 104 (1918), p. 309-364. [2480]

The text of 36 ballads (including variants) taken from the collection of J. Alden Mason, with commentary. Spanish text only.

Fewkes, Jesse Walter. Aborigines of Porto Rico and neighboriing islands. *In* Bureau of American ethnology, 25th report, Washington, Government printing office, 1907, p. 18-296. F1969.F4 [2481]

Includes: instruments of the West Indian islanders, p. 210; dance and music in Antillean ceremonies, p. 64-65; modern dances of the Gibaros, p. 68-69; Porto Rican music, p. 69; description of an Arawak burial dance, p. 72 (quoted from W. H. Brett, *The Indian tribes of Guiana*); for many other references to dances, see index under *areitos.*

Hare, Maud Cuney. Porto Rican streetcries; a musical menu of the tropics. *Mus. Amer.,* v. 49, no. 22 (25 Nov. 1929), p. 5. il. [2482]

Includes 9 tunes.

Luce, Allena, ed. Canciones populares. Boston, etc., Silver, Burdett & co., 1921. 138 p. M1681.P6L9 [2483]

Traditional semi-popular songs edited and arranged for voice and piano. Section 1: 28 songs of Puerto Rico. Section 2: 12 songs of Cuba, Spain and Mexico. Section 4: 22 song and singing games (unaccompanied melodies and Spanish text).

Malaret, Augusto. Panorama folklórico de Puerto Rico. *Rev. univ. cat. boliv.,* v. 3, no. 7 (1938), p. 72-82. **[2484]**
Treats of the music, dances and folk songs of the *jíbaros.*

Mason, J. Alden. Porto-Rican folk-lore. Décimas, Christmas carols, nursery rhymes, and other songs. Edited by Aurelio M. Espinosa. *Jour. amer. folklore,* v. 31, no. 121 (1918), p. 289-450.
[2485]
Contains the words (Spanish only) of

373 traditionnal songs of Puerto Rico, with introductory comment.

Roberts, Helen H. Spanish romances from Porto Rico. *Jour. amer. folklore,* v. 33, no. 127 (1920), p. 76-79. **[2486]**
Includes 2 tunes, collected by J. Alden Mason and transcribed by Helen Roberts.

Rodríguez, A. Historia de la danza portorriqueña. *Isla,* v. 1, no. 3 (1939), p. 13-15. **[2487]**
See also no. 2692.

SUPPLEMENT TO 1960

Coen, Augusto. La fiesta de cruz. Música y letra del "Rosario cantao". Recopilación y anotación original de ... San Juan, P. R., Editado por "El santo rosario en el aire", n. d. (1951). Pages unnumbered. **[970a]**
A preface by Pablo Garrido tells about the Fiesta de Cruz of Puerto Rico and the "Rosario cantao" — i. e., the "sung rosary". The compiler and annotator of this booklet, Augusto Coen, was born in Ponce in 1895 and studied music with Dr. Angel del Busto in New York. The music consists of 19 numbers. Illustrations by the Spanish artist Guillermo Sureda.

Lamb, Elizabeth Searle. Song of the Jíbaro. *Américas,* v. 2, no. 8 (Aug. 1950), p. 20-21,45. **[971a]**
Good account of rural singing in Puerto Rico. Excellent photographs of people singing and playing drums and band instruments.

Fouche, Ruth Allen. Translational qualites in Puerto Rican folk music. *Jour. Amer. mus. soc.,* v. 9, no. 3 (Fall 1956), p. 232-234. **[972a]**
Abstract of lecture read in Chicago.

Matilla, Alfredo. Musicalia en Puerto Rico. *B. A. mus.,* v. 12, no. 197 (Oct. 1, 1957), p. 3. **[973a]**
General survey of musical activities and institutions.

Martínez, María Cadilla de. La histórica danza de Puerto Rico en el siglo xvi y sus posteriores evoluciones. *Rev. mus. chil.,* v. 6, no. 37 (Autumn 1959), p. 43-77. (music). **[974a]**
An important historical study.

UNITED STATES

THERE is no intention in this section of dealing with music in the United States as a whole. Yet it is fitting that in a work devoted to Latin American music, some attention should be given to Hispanic elements in the music of the United States. This section, then, is concerned primarily with Spanish-American musical traditions and survivals in the Southwest, beginning with the musical activities of the Spanish missionaries who penetrated that region in the seventeenth century. This approach to the subject has necessitated a radical change in the method of arranging the bibliography for this section. The arrangement adopted has been chosen with a view toward presenting the data on Hispanic music in the United States in a convenient and orderly sequence.

The first section, Mission Music, enables us to trace the beginnings of Hispanic musical activity in the Southwest through the efforts of the early Spanish missionaries to teach European music to the Indians. Lota M. Spell's monograph on *Music teaching in New Mexico in the seventeenth century* [no. 2498] deals with the activities of such musically-minded missionaries as Cristóbal de Quiñones (probably "the first music teacher who worked within the confines of the present United States"), who entered New Mexico between 1598 and 1604; Bernardo de Marta (1605), García de San Francisco y Zúñiga (ca. 1630) and Alonso de Benavides, whose Memorial, written in 1630, mentions that in New Mexico there existed "schools of reading and writing, singing, and playing of all instruments" (cf. *The Memorial of Fray Alonso de Benavides,* transl. Ayer, Chicago, 1916). The monograph by Sister Joan of Arc, C. D. P. [no. 2491] and the article by Anna B. McGill [no. 2495] continue the account of mission music in the Southwest and contain several musical examples, chiefly of the *alabados* and *alabanzas,* songs of praise which the missionaries taught to the Indians. The *alabado* is especially associated with the famous Mexican missionary Antonio de Margil (cf. no. 1974), who journeyed through what is now Louisiana and Texas. The literature on mission music was greatly enriched with the publication in 1941 of the volume entitled *Mission music of California* [no. 2489], being "a collection of old California mission hymns and masses" transcribed and edited by Rev. Owen da Silva. This contains an introductory section tracing the historical development of mission music in California (p. 3-16); brief biographies of musical missionaries (p. 19-26); a translation of the prologue written by Narciso Durán to his manuscript collection of church music (MS. in Bancroft Library; the editor calls this "the most valuable document extant bearing on the church music of the

348

California missions"); transcriptions of the music into modern notation; and bibliography.

After a brief section dealing with the religious folk theatre, of which the best-known example is the Christmas play called *Los pastores* [nos. 2500, 2501, 2503] we turn to the field of Spanish-American folk song. Arthur Leon Campa's monograph [no. 2508] and Lota M. Spell's article in Spanish [no. 2520] serve as a good introduction to this subject. Eleanor Hague's collection, *Spanish-American folksongs* [no. 2513] contains nearly a hundred tunes, with Spanish words and English translations. For an interesting comparison of these songs with their Spanish peninsular counterparts, see the article by the Spanish musicologist Julián Ribera [no. 2518]. Although some entries in this section are grouped separately under California, New Mexico and Texas, this is done primarily for the sake of convenience and does not necessarily indicate any fundamental distinction in the type of material covered. The entries on Portuguese-American folk music [nos. 2564 and 2565] are included for the sake of comparison with Brazilian folk music of Portuguese origin.

It may seem strange that a separate section should be devoted to one musician, the pianist and composer Louis Moreau Gottschalk (1829-1869). But from the point of view of inter-American musical relations, Gottschalk is the most important musician produced by the United States. A native of New Orleans, he studied in Paris and won brilliant success as a pianist all over Europe as well as in North and South America. He spent some time in Cuba and he died in Rio de Janeiro while on a South American tour. He began to be attracted by the exotic aspects of American folk music in his early youth, writing the Negro dance *Bamboula* at the age of fifteen. Later he drew on Latin American themes for several of his compositions, including *El cocoyé, grand caprice cubain de bravura; La gallina, danse cubaine; Ojos criollos,* another Cuban dance; the romantic symphony *A night in the tropics;* the symphony *Montevideo;* the *Escenas campestres cubanas* for orchestra. His variations on the Brazilian national anthem for piano added greatly to his prestige and popularity in Brazil (cf. item no. 2569). He also composed a *Gran marcha solemne* dedicated to the Emperor of Brazil. Recently other North American composers have been turning for material to the field of Latin American folk and popular music, which Gottschalk explored as a pioneer.

The final subdivision in this section, beginning with no. 2570, is intended to present some Latin American views of musical life in the United States. In this connection the articles by Mario de Andrade and Luiz Heitor Corrêa de Azevedo are of special interest [nos. 2570 and 2571]. Attention is also drawn to item no. 2578, *Invincible America, the national music of the United States,* by Guillermo M. Tomás, published at Havana in 1919, one of the most unusual items in the field of inter-American musical bibliography.

Latin American readers who wish to acquaint themselves with other aspects of musical activity in the United States can turn to the fifth volume of the *Boletín latinoamericano de música,* edited by Francisco Curt Lange in collaboration with Charles Seeger (cf. item no. 35). This issue contains forty-five articles dealing with every aspect of music in the United States, written by authoritative persons in their respective fields. The articles were written in English and translated into Spanish for this volume, which is dedicated to the United States. Distributed in Latin America by the Instituto Interamericano de Musicología at Montevideo, and in the United States by the Music Division of the Pan American Union, Washington, D. C., this volume of the *Boletín,* consisting of 637 pages, supplies a long-felt need in making available to Latin American readers information on United States music. A musical supplement of 167 pages, issued separately, contains a representative selection of compositions by contemporary composers of the United States, for piano, for voice, and for various chamber music combinations.

MISSION MUSIC

Blackmar, Frank W. Spanish institutions of the southwest. Baltimore, The Johns Hopkins Press, 1891. 353 p. il. H-31.J62 and F799.B62.   **[2488]**

References to Spanish-American music, p. 258, 259.

Da Silva, Owen Francis. Mission music of California; a collection of old California mission hymns and masses. Los Angeles, Warren F. Lewis, 1941. 132 p. il. (music) M2.D22   **[2489]**

For comment see introductory section above.

Engelhardt, Zephyrin. Santa Barbara mission. San Francisco, James H. Barry co., 1923. 470 p. F864.E65   **[2490]**

Includes music.

Sister Joan of Arc. Catholic music and musicians in Texas. San Antonio, Texas, Our Lady of the lake college, 1936. 64 p. ML3011.J6C2   **[2491]**

The introduction, entitled *Mission music,* deals with the *alabado.* Ch. 2, *Oral traditional music,* deals with the *matachines, Los pastores* and the *posadas.* There are musical examples of these 4 types.

——. Mission music of the southwest. *Cath. choirm.,* v. 26, no. 3 (13 Sept. 1940), p. 102-104.   **[2492]**

Koehler, Erna Buchel. Our musical beginnings in the southwest. *Etude,* v. 59, no. 1 (Jan. 1941), p. 7, 64-65, il.   **[2493]**

An account of Spanish pioneer musical activities in the Southwest and in Mexico, with references to *Los pastores* and other aspects of folk music.

Kroeber, A. A. A mission record of the California Indians. *In* University of California, Publications in American ethnology, no. 8 (1908), p. 1-27.   **[2494]**

Musical instruments, p. 6, 12, 19.

McGill, Anna Blanche. Old mission music. *Mus. quart.,* v. 24, no. 2 (Apr. 1938), p. 186-193   **[2495]**

Deals with the *alabados* and *alabanzas,* songs of religious praise taught to the Indians by the Spanish missionaries in the Southwest. Mentions especially Fray Antonio de la Ascención and Fray Antonio Margil. Includes 6 tunes.

Shaver, Lillie Terrell. Spanish mission music. *Mus. observer,* v. 19, no. 4 (1920), p. 11. **[2496]**

Spell, Lota M. Music in Texas. Austin, Tex., 1936. 157 p. il. ML200.7.T486 **[2497]**

"Spanish-American folk music", p. 14-22, includes 6 songs with Spanish words and English translation.

——. Music teaching in New Mexico in the seventeenth century. Santa Fe, El Palacio press, 1927. 12 p. ML210.S7 **[2498]**

Reprinted from the *New Mexico historical review,* v. 2, no. 1 (Jan. 1927).

See also no. 2528.

RELIGIOUS FOLK THEATRE

Campa, Arthur L. Spanish religious folktheatre in the southwest. Albuquerque, New Mexico university press, 1934. 71 p. (The University of New Mexico bulletin, language series, v. 5, no. 1) PQ7270.R4C32 **[2499]**

Cole, M. R., ed. Los pastores, a Mexican play of the nativity. Boston and New York, Houghton, Mifflin, and co., 1907. 234 p. (Memoirs of the American folklore society, v. 9, 1907). GR1.A5 v. 9 PQ7279.A1P2 **[2500]**

Text and music, with English translation and notes.

Rourke, John G. The miracle play of the Rio Grande. *Jour. amer. folklore,* v. 5, no. 21 (Apr.-June 1893), p. 89-95. **[2501]**

Description of *Los Pastores,* with quotation of some verses.

Van Stone, Mary R., and E. R. Sims. Canto del niño perdido. Publications of the Texas folk-lore society, no. 11 (1933), p. 48-89. GR1.T4 **[2502]**

The text of an old New Mexican religious folk play, with 5 tunes to which the words (in Spanish) are sung. An English translation is printed opposite the Spanish text.

Van Stone, Mary R., ed. Los pastores; excerpts from an old Christmas play of the southwest as given annually by the Griego family, Santa Fe, New Mexico. Cleveland, Gates press, 1933. 44 p. il. PQ7297.A1P2 1933. **[2503]**

Includes music.

SPANISH-AMERICAN FOLK SONGS

(A) BIBLIOGRAPHIES

Buchanan, Annabel Morris. American folk music. Ithaca, N. Y., National federation of music clubs, 1939. 57 p. Reproduced from type-written copy. ML120.U5B8 **[2504]**

Bibliography and list of music, including Mexican and Spanish-American songs, p. 56.

Campa, Arthur Leon. A bibliography of Spanish folklore in New Mexico. Albuquerque, University of New Mexico, 1930. 28 p. (The University of New Mexico bulletin. Language series, v. 2, no. 3, Sept. 1930, whole no. 176). P-25.N5 v. 2, no. 3. **[2505]**

Lomax, Alan, and Sidney Robertson Cowell. American folk song and folklore; a regional bibliography. New York, Progressive education association. 1942. 50 p. ML120.U5L7 **[2506]**

Section 10, Spanish-American, p. 49-52.

(B) MISCELLANEOUS

Boggs, Ralph S. Spanish folklore in America; Folklore in Pan-Americanism; Latin American folklore awaits conquistadores. Univ. of Miami, Hispanic-American studies, 1939, v. 1 (1940), p. 122-165. **[2507]**

Campa, Arthur L. The Spanish folksong in the southwest. Albuquerque,
N. M., The University of New Mexico,
1933. 67 p. (The University of New
Mexico bulletin. Modern language series. v. 4, no. 1. ML3558.C3 **[2508]**
Bibliography, p. 67. Without music.

Dickinson, Charles A., comp. Las posadas. Claremont, California, Padua
hills theatre, 1935. 16 p. il. M1682.D-
55P5 **[2509]**
Songs of Christmas in Mexico as re-
membered and sung by Miguel Vera.
Piano accompaniment, Spanish text. Descriptive foreword (signed by Bess A.
Garner).

Elliot, Gilbert, Jr. Our musical kinship
with the Spaniards. *Mus. quart.,* v. 8,
no. 3 (July 1922), p. 413-418.
[2510]
Traces the Spanish influence in American folk and popular music.

Espinosa, Aurelio M. The field of Spanish folklore in America. *South. folk.
quart.,* v. 5, no. 1 (Mar. 1941), p. 29-
35. **[2511]**
Popular and traditional ballads, p. 31;
Folk music, p. 32-33.

Garfías, Carlota. Mexican folklore collected in New York City. *Jour. amer.
folklore,* v. 51 (1938), p. 83-91.
[2512]
With 4 tunes.

Hague, Eleanor, comp. Spanish-American folksongs. Lancaster, Pa., and New
York, The American folk-lore society,
1917. (G. E. Stechert & co., New York,
agents). M1680.H2 **[2513]**
95 melodies, with Spanish and English
words.

Herzog, George. Research in primitive
and folk music in the United States.
American council of learned societies.
Bulletin, no. 24 (Apr. 1936), 97 p.
[2514]
Includes a list of record collections of

Spanish-American folk music, a brief bibliography, and much useful matter of general interest to the folklorist.

Lummis, Charles Fletcher. Catching
our archaeology alive. *Out-West,* v. 22
(1905), p. 35-45. **[2515]**
Deals with the activities of the Southwest Society of the Archaeological Institute
of America in collecting Spanish and Indian folk songs of the Southwest.

McMaster, Ann H. Creole songs. *In*
Thompson, Oscar, *ed.,* The internatio-
nal cyclopedia of music and musicians,
New York, 1939, p. 601-602. ML100.-
T4715 **[2516]**
Includes a reference to the *habanera.*

———. Spanish folksong in America. *In*
Thompson, Oscar, *ed.,* The internatio-
nal cyclopedia of music and musicians,
New York, 1939, p. 604-605. ML100.-
T4715 **[2517]**

Ribera, Julián. Para la historia de la
música popular. *Boletín de la Real academia de la historia,* v. 90 (Jan.-Mar.
1927), p. 47-65. **[2518]**
Refers to Spanish-American folk songs
published by Eleanor Hague in *Memoirs
of the American folklore society* [item no.
2513], and studies in detail the following: No. 63, *El demonio en la oreja;* no.
78, *Arrullo;* no. 12, *La paloma blanca;*
no. 55, *A cantar una niña;* no. 61, *La
jaula de oro;* no. 8, *Pregúntale a las
estrellas;* etc. Discusses the Spanish peninsular elements in these songs.

Schinhan, Jan Philip. Spanish folklore
from Tampa, Florida. VI, Folksongs.
South. folk. quart., v. 3 (1939), p. 129-
163. **[2519]**
Analysis of children's singing-games and
other Spanish and Cuban songs, with
transcriptions of some tunes (p. 154-163).

Spell, Lota M. Las canciones populares
hispano-americanas en los Estados Unidos. *Bol. lat. am. mús.,* v. 5 (Montevideo, 1941), p. 210-206. **[2520]**
Bibliography, p. 205-206.

(c) CALIFORNIA

Cowell, Sidney Robertson. The recordings of folk music in California. *Calif. folk. quart.*, v. 1, no. 1 (Jan. 1942), p. 7-23 **[2521]**

Also reprinted separately. References to Spanish-California songs, p. 10, 12, 16-17, 21; to Portuguese songs, p. 17-18.

Espinosa, Aurelio M. Traditional ballads from Andalucía. *In* Flügel memorial volume, Stanford University, Calif., 1916, p. 106-107. P26.F6L4 **[2522]**

These Spanish ballads were collected in California.

Farwell, Arthur. Folk-songs of the west and south, Negro, cowboy and Spanish Californian. Newton Center, Mass., The Wa-Wan press, 1905. 11 p. (The Wa-Wan series of American comps., v. 4, no. 27). M1.W35 **[2523]**

Hague, Eleanor. Spanish-American folksongs. *Jour. Amer. folklore*, v. 24, no. 93 (1911), p. 323-331. **[2524]**

The words (Spanish only) and melodies of 15 songs collected in California. Most of them are from Mexico.

——. Spanish songs from southern California. *Jour. amer. folklore*, v. 27, no. 105 (1914), p. 331-332. **[2525]**

Words (Spanish only) and melody of *El sombrero blanco*, and of a *Jota valenciana* from Spain showing melodic and poetic analogies with the California song.

Lummis, Charles Fletcher, comp. Spanish songs of old California. Pianoforte accompaniments by Arthur Farwell. Los Angeles, Calif., 1923. 35 p. M16-29.L94 **[2526]**

Contents: 1, La hamaca. 2. La barquillera. 3. El quelele. 4. La noche está serena. 5. El capotín. 6. Chata cara de bule. 7. Peña hueca. 8. El zapatero. 9. La primavera. 10. Mi Pepa. 11. Es el amor mariposa. 12. La mágica mujer. 13. El charro. 14. Adios, adios amores.

McCoy, William J. Folk songs of the Spanish Californians. San Francisco,

Sherman, Clay & co., 1926. 31 p. M16-29.M14F5 **[2527]**

Ten songs with piano accompaniment; Spanish words with the music, English translation below.

Music of the gold rush era. History of music project. Prepared with the assistance of the Works progress administration of California; sponsored by the city and county San Francisco, 1939. 212 p. 5 mounted photos. (facsims). (History of music in San Francisco series , v. 1) Mimeographed .ML-200.8.S2H4 v. 1 **[2528]**

Ch. 1, *Music of Mission Dolores*, p. 1-9, deals with Indian singers and primitive orchestras. Ch. 2, *Fandangos and fiestas*, p. 10-20, deals with the music and dances of the Spanish Californians. Music on inside cover includes part of tune *La noche está serena* (Spanish serenade).

Some California songs. I *The masterkey*, v. 8, no. 1 (Jan. 1943), p. 15-18. **[2529]**

This is the bulletin of the Southwest Museum in Los Angeles, Calif., which owns a collection of records of Spanish-Californian songs made by C. F. Lummis about 40 years ago. Eleanor Hague has transcribed some of these songs, 2 of which are reproduced here: *No hay en la brisa* and *Tu florido abril* (melodies with Spanish text).

——. II. *The masterkey*, v. 8, no. 4 (July 1934), p. 115-117. **[2530]**

Two songs, *Yo te juro, mi bien,* and *Golondrinas de Becquer* (melodies with Spanish text), transcribed by Eleanor Hague from recordings made by C. F. Lummis.

Spizzy, Mable Seeds, and Hazel Gertrude Kinscella. La fiesta; a unit of early California songs and dances. Lincoln, The University publishing co., 1939. 45 p. diagrs. MT950.F43 **[2531]**

With music (unaccompanied melodies).

Van der Voort, Antoni, comp. Old Spanish songs as sung by sra. da María Jimeno de Arata. Santa Bárbara, Calif.,

Santa Bárbara music shop, 1928
[2532]

19 songs of the early Californians, for voice with piano accompaniment (Spanish text only).

Watkins, Frances E. "He said it with music" — Spanish-California folk songs recorded by Charles L. Lummis. *Calif. folklore quart.*, v. I, no. 4 (Oct. 1942), p. 359-367. **[2533]**

(D) NEW MEXICO

Curtis, F. S., Jr. Spanish songs of New Mexico. *In* Publications of the Texas folk-lore society, no. 4 (1925), p. 18-29. GR1.T4 **[2534]**

Contains the words and tunes of 8 Spanish-American folk songs recorded in New Mexico. English translations are given for 7 of the songs.

Espinosa, Aurelio M. España en nuevo Méjico. New York, Boston, etc., Alyn and Bacon, 1937. 73 p. il. PC4127.H5-E7 **[2535]**

Textbook. *Los matachines* (dance), p. 48-49. *Coplas*, p. 61-63. Song, p. 68, with music.

———. New Mexican Spanish "coplas populares". *Hispania*, v. 18 (1935), p. 135-150. **[2536]**

———. New-Mexican Spanish folklore. X. Children's games. XI. Nursery rhymes and children's songs. *Jour. amer. folklore*, v. 29, no. 114 (1916), p. 505-535. **[2537]**

———. Romancero nuevomejicano. *Rev. hisp.*, v. 33, no. 84 (1915), p. 446-560. **[2538]**

A study of Spanish folk songs in New Mexico, with the words (Spanish only) and melodies of 9 ballads.

———. Romancero nuevomejicano. Addenda. *Rev. hisp.*, v. 40, no. 97 (June 1917), p. 215-227. **[2539]**

See item no. 2538.

———. Romances españoles tradicionales que cantan y recitan los Indios de los

pueblos de Nuevo Méjico. Santander, 1932. **[2540]**

Reprinted from *Boletín de la biblioteca de Menéndez y Pelayo*.

Freire-Marreco, Barbara. New Mexican Spanish folk-lore. *Jour. amer. folklore*, v. 29, no. 114 (1916), p. 536-546. **[2541]**

Includes the words (Spanish only) of a *cantico* and 2 *oraciones*, as sung by Pueblo Indians (vigil for the saints). The last two are characterized as "real traditional Spanish ballads".

Guitar method with guitar arrangements of Spanish-American folk songs of New Mexico. Work projects administration; music project (New Mexico), New Mexico, 1939. Mimeographed. **[2542]**

Includes 9 Spanish songs collected in New Mexico (Spanish words only). The guitar method was worked out by Eudora Garrett.

Lummis, Charles Fletcher. The land of poco tiempo. New York, C. Scribner's sons, 1925. 310 p. il. F801.L96 **[2543]**

Includes "New Mexican folk-songs" with 12 tunes, transcribed by Henry Holden Huss.

Miller, Emily Maverick. Four Mexican songs. Austin, Texas, 1917. 9 p. M16-83.M **[2544]**

Contents: Out on the waves (*Allá por los mares*); Brown eyes (*Ven a mis brazos, morena*); Alone (*Qué triste estoy*); Vaya con dios. Piano accompaniment. Spanish and English words.

Rael, Juan B. New Mexican wedding songs. *South. folk. quart.*, v. 4, no. 2 (June 1940), p. 55-72. **[2545]**

Gives the text (Spanish only) of verses sung for the *entrega de novios* and quotes a typical melody (in waltz time).

Spanish American folk songs of New Mexico. Works progress administration, Federal music project, unit no. 1, 1936-37. Mimeographed. **[2546]**

13 songs, arranged for piano with inter-

linear Spanish text; some descriptive comments in English, Introductory material by A. L. Campa and Helen Chandler Ryan.

——. Works progress administration, Federal music project, unit no. 2, 1936-37. Mimeographed. **[2547]**

18 songs arranged for piano with interlinear Spanish text. Some descriptive notes in English.

Spanish American singing games of New Mexico. Works progress administration, Federal music project, unit no. 3, 1940. 27 p. Mimeographed. MT-948.U5S6 **[2548]**

Spanish and English text, with directions for playing the games.

The Spanish-American song and game book. New York, A. S. Barnes, 1942. 87 p. M1993.W92S7 **[2549]**

Songs (with and without music) and games for children. Spanish and English text. Based on material originally compiled by the Federal music project of the WPA.

Strickroth, Flavia G. de, comp. Songs my nana sang, folklore melodies of Mexico with words and translations and their historical settings ... Ms., 1934. 14 l. M1682.9S5 **[2550]**

"Unrecorded melodies dictated from memory by señora Flavia de Strickroth, written and given musical settings by Lue Alice Keller." 12 songs with piano accompaniment; Spanish text only.

Three Spanish-Ameican folk songs from New Mexico. Bull. pan amer. union, v. 75, no. 5 (May 1941), p. 297-299. **[2551]**

From "Spanish American singing games" published by the WPA music project, 1940. The 3 songs are "Naranja dulce", "Doña Ana no está aquí" and "Víbora de la mar". With Spanish text, English translations, and directions for playing the games.

Van Stone, Mary R. Spanish folk songs of New Mexico. Chicago, R. F. Seymour, 1926. **[2552]**

(E) TEXAS

Dobie, J. Frank. Versos of the Texas vaqueros. In Publications of the Texas folk-lore society, no. 4 (1925), p. 30-43. GR1.T4 **[2553]**

Contains the words (with English translation) and tunes of 3 ballads and 1 love song found among ranch Mexicans of the Texas border.

González, Jovita. Folk-lore of the Texas-Mexican vaquero. In Publications of the Texas folk-lore society, no. 6 (1927), p. 7-22. GR1.T4 **[2554]**

Includes the Spanish text and English translation of 3 Mexican folk songs, Las mañanitas, Mi querida Nicolasa, and Mi caballo bayo.

——. Tales and songs of the Texas-Mexicans. In Publications of the Texas folk-lore society, v. 8 (1930), p. 86-116. GR1.T4 **[2555]**

Includes the words and music (incomplete) of 5 Mexican popular songs frequently heard in Texas. Spanish texts with English translations.

Lomax, John A. Two songs of Mexican cowboys from the Rio Grande border. Jour. amer. folklore, v. 28, no. 110 (1915), p. 376-378. **[2556]**

Spanish text only.

——, and Alan Lomax. American ballads and folk songs. New York, The Macmillan co., 1935. 625 p. M1629.L-85A52 **[2557]**

With music (unaccompanied melodies). "Bibliography ... compiled by Harold W. Thompson", p. 613-621. Includes 5 songs of the "Vaqueros of the southwest"; Allá en el rancho grande; El amor que te tenía; El abandonado; Cuatro palomitas blancas; Tragedia de Heraclio Bernal, p. 361-371. Spanish text and English translation. Descriptive notes.

Pan American union. Music division. 14 traditional Spanish songs from Texas; transcribed by Gustavo Durán. Washington, D. C., Pan American union, 1942. 20 p. Reproduced from type-written copy. (*Its* music series, no. 4). **[2558]**

These songs were transcribed from recordings made in Texas, 1934-1939, by John A., Ruby T. and Alan Lomax, and which are in the Archive of American folk song in the Library of Congress. There is a foreword by Charles Seeger, a preface by Alan Lomax, and an introduction by the compiler. Each song is preceded by an historical note. The melodies are unaccompanied. Spanish words only.

Taylor, Paul S. Songs of the Mexican migration. *In* Dobie, J. Frank, *ed.,* Puro Mexicano, Austin, Texas, 1935, p. 221-245. (Publications of the Texas folklore society, no. 12). GR1.T4 **[2559]**

Contains the words (Spanish and English) of 10 songs of the *corrido* type, and the music of 3 songs (voice and piano).

SPANISH-AMERICAN FOLK DANCES

Brewster, Mela Sedillo. Mexican and New Mexican folk dances, n. p., 1937. 50 p. il. Mimeographed. MT950.B84M3 **[2560]**

With the music for the New Mexican dances. Includes detailed dancing directions and costume sketches.

Lucero-White, Aurora. Folk-dances of the Spanish-colonials of New Mexico ... Music transcribed by Eunice Hauskins ... Patterns and descriptions of dances by Helene Mareau ... Rev. 2d ed. Santa Fe, Examiner publishing co., 1940. 46 p. diagrs. MT950.L95F6 1940. **[2561]**

With music (unaccompanied melodies).

Shafter, Mary Severance. American Indian and other folk dances for schools, pageants and playgrounds ... music arranged by Josephine Condon. New York, A. S. Barnes and co., 1927. 77 p. il. GV1743.S5 **[2562]**

Includes music for the *jota* and the *jarabe.*

Shambaugh, Mary Effie. Folk festivals for schools and playgrounds; folk dances and melodies ... music arranged

by Anna Pearl Allison. New York, A. S. Barnes & co., 1932. 155 p. il. diagrs. GV1743.S54 M1450.S4 **[2563]**

"Fiestas of the Spanish and Mexicans in California", p. 31-48, with music for *La Contradansa* and for *La Jota,* arranged for piano by A. Pearl Allison.

PORTUGUESE-AMERICAN FOLK MUSIC

Hare, Maud Cuney. Portuguese folk-songs from Provincetown, Cape Cod, Mass. *Mus. quart.,* v. 15, no. 1 (Jan. 1928), p. 35-53. **[2564]**

Contains 14 melodies, with Portuguese words and English translation.

Lang, Henry R. The Portuguese element in New England. *Jour. amer. folklore,* v. 5, no. 16 (Jan.-Mar. 1892), p 9-18. **[2565]**

Includes quotations of folk song texts, and references to music and dancing. Refers especially to the Chama-Rita, the popular dance of the Azores.

BIOGRAPHY (L. M. GOTTSCHALK)

Bolling, Ernest L. Our first musical ambassador. *Etude,* v. 50, no. 2 (Feb. 1932), p. 97-98, 142. **[2566]**

Short biography of Gottschalk as performer, composer and writer. Portrait, and one musical example.

Fors, Luis Ricardo. Gottschalk. Habana. La propaganda literaria, 1880. **[2567]**

Howard, John Tasker. Louis Moreau Gottschalk, as portrayed by himself. *Mus. quart.,* v. 18, no. 1 (Jan. 1932), p. 120-133, **[2568]**

Or, — d'. O grande compositor norte-americano, Gottschalk e o hymno nacional brasileiro. *In* Brasil-Estados Unidos, Rio de Janeiro, Ed. do Diario de noticias, 1930, p. 297-298. E183.8.B7B84 **[2569]**

LATIN AMERICAN VIEWS

Andrade, Mario de. A música na América do norte. *In* Brasil-Estados Unidos, Rio de Janeiro, Ed. do Diario de noticias, 1939, p. 287-291. E183.8B7 B84 **[2570]**

Azevedo, Luiz Heitor Corrêa de. Impressões norte-americanas. *Res. mus.*, v. 4, no. 37 (Sept. 1941), p 8-14; v. 4, no .41 (Jan. 1942), p. 9-15; v. 4, no. 42 (Feb. 1942), p. 7-12. **[2571]**
The author devotes these articles to his experiences in 5 cities: Washington, Chapel Hill, N. C., Syracuse and Rochester, N. Y., and Philadelphia, reviewing musical activities in these cities, and describing those which he attended. He has met a number of prominent musicians and musicologists, and gives his impressions of them.

Barreto, Ceição de Barros. Educação musical nos Estados Unidos *In* Brasil-Estados Unidos, Rio de Janeiro, Ed. do Diario de noticias, 1939, p. 293-296. **[2572]**

Guiomar Novaes fala sobre a arte musical nos Estados Unidos. *In* Brasil-Estados Unidos, Rio de Janeiro, Ed. do Diario de noticias, 1939, p. 299-303. E1-83.8.B7B84 **[2573]**
Interview.

Orquesta sinfónica de México. Notas por Francisco Agea. Programa 7, temporada 1937, p. 8-9. Salón México [Copland]. MT125.M307. **[2574]**
Aaron Copland's work, based on Mexican folk tunes, received its first performance on this occasion (27 Aug. 1937). An arrangement for two pianos, however, was played in New York in October 1935. The orchestration was completed in 1936. Some of the notes for this program were supplied by the composer.

Pereda Valdés, Ildefonso. Línea de color. Santiago de Chile, Ed. Ercilla, 1938. 248 p. E185.6.P44 **[2575]**
Includes: Negro music in the United States, p. 68-76. Bibliography at end of book.

Ponce, Manuel M. La música norteamericana. *Rev. mus. Méx.*, v. 1, no. 2 (15 June 1919), p. 22-23. **[2576]**
Points out that American composers have been able to make themselves heard, thanks to a vigorous campaign of action.

Ramos, Arthur. O negro nos Estados Unidos. *In* Brasil-Estados Unidos, Rio de Janeiro, Ed. Diario de noticias, 1939, p. 323-326. E183.B7B84 **[2577]**
Negro folklore, with notes on music, p. 325.

Tomás, Guillermo M. Invincible America. The national music of the U. S. Havana, "El siglo xx", 1919. 205 p. ML3551.T65 **[2578]**

SUPPLEMENT TO 1960

Chase, Gilbert. America's music: from the pilgrims to the present. New York, McGraw-Hill, 1955. xxiii, 733 p. (incl. music). **[975a]**
Cf. especially chapter 15, "The exotic periphery", with reference to West Indian musical influences in Louisiana.

Dobie, James Frank. Puro mexicano. Austin, Texas folk-lore society, 1935. 261 p. il. (incl. music). (Texas folk-lore society publications, no. XII). **[976a]**
Spanish-American folklore of the southwest.

Kennedy, Stetson. La paloma in Florida. *South. folk. quart.*, v. 7 (1943), p. 163-164. **[977a]**
Cites Ortega's opinion that this song derives from an ancient Aztec funeral song (*sic!*), and the report of Spanish governor of Florida in 1717 that Indians

there had a song by this name, and wonders if the two are related. (R.S.B.)

Mendoza, Vicente T. La canción hispanoamericana en Nuevo México. *Unit. Méx.,* v. 1, no. 2 (Nov. 1946), p. 21-22. **[978a]**

Brief survey. Illustrated.

———. La canción hispano-mexicana en en Nuevo México. *Nuestra música,* v. 2, no .3 (Jan. 1947), p. 25-32. il. **[979a]**

Religious music, *romance, décima, copla, trovos, corrido, sones, jarabes, canción,* etc. Two photographs.

———. La décima. (Sus derivaciones musicales en América.) *Nuestra música,* v. 2, no. 6 (Apr. 1947), p. 78-113. (music) **[980a]**

The *décima* in Colorado and New Mexico, in Mexico, Cuba, Santo Domingo, Puerto Rico, Panama, Colombia, Peru, Brazil, Chile, and Argentina. With 11 musical notations.

Orrego Salas, Juan. Aaron Copland's vision of America. *Américas,* v. 7, no. 6 (June 1955), p. 17-21. **[981a]**

Mainly on the composer's own development, there is considerable reference to his trips to Latin America, and use of Latin American melodic and rhythmic elements.

Ortiz Oderigo, Néstor R. Panorama de la música afroamericana. Buenos Aires,

Ed. Claridad, 1944. 298 p. il. (Biblioteca musical, v. 4) **[982a]**

Deals chiefly with Jazz in the United States.

Rael, Juan B. Un cantar hallado en Tucumán. *Revista ibero-americana,* v. 9, no. 17 (1945), p. 73-77. **[983a]**

Cites 5 variants of song beginning "Mira, mira pecador": one from Salta, Argentina, and 2 from New Mexico and 2 from southern Colorado, U. S. A. Gives texts of one from Salta and one from New Mexico. All are preserved in ms. and their uniformity indicates a literary source. (R.S.B.)

———. The New Mexican *alabado.* With transcriptions of music by Eleanor Hague. Stanford University press, 1951. 154 p. il. (Stanford university publications, University series, Language and literature, v. 9, no. 3). **[984a]**

Sedillo, Mela. Mexican and New Mexican folk dances. Albuquerque, New Mexico, University of New Mexico press, 1945. 47 p. **[985a]**

Valenti Ferro, Enzo. Estados Unidos, país musical. *B. A. mus.,* número extraordinario dedicado a la música en los Estados Unidos de América (Dec. 1959), p. 7-10. **[986a]**

Vega, Aurelio de la. La música de norteamérica, hoy. *B. A. mus.,* número extraordinario dedicado a la música en los Estados Unidos de América (Dec. 1959), p. 13-15. **[987a]**

URUGUAY

THE folk and popular music of Uruguay, characterized by such forms as the *triste*, the *estilo*, the *pericón* and the tango, is closely related to that of its neighbor, Argentina. Of these traditional dances, the one which has become most closely identified with Uruguay is the *pericón*, a rural dance of the *gauchos*, which Ricardo Escuder calls "the national dance of Uruguay" [no. 2606]. Around 1887 an "official" arrangement of the *pericón* for military band was made by Gerardo Grasso.

In the realm of art music, Uruguay has made a distinctive place for itself among the countries of South America. The country's leading composer, Eduardo Fabini (b. 18 May 1883), is considered one of the outstanding creative figures of Latin American music (see items no. 2599 and 2601). Other Uruguayan composers who enjoy international prestige are Vicente Ascone (b. 16 Aug. 1897), Alfonso Broqua (b. 11 Dec. 1876), Luis Cluzeau Mortet (b. 16 Nov. 1893) and Carlos Pedrell (1878-1941), who became an Argentine citizen. Among the younger men may be mentioned Carlos Estrada (b. 15 Sept. 1909) and Luis Pedro Mondino (b. 19 Nov. 1903). For the names of other contemporary composers, see the comment under items no. 2593 and no. 2600.

César Cortinas was a composer of much promise whose activities were cut short by death in 1918, at the age of twenty-five. Among his works are a Concerto for piano and orchestra, sonatas for piano, and songs (see item no. 2598). The late León Ribeiro was an important national composer who left a large body of unpublished music; he was born in Montevideo, 11 April 1854, and died there, 12 March 1931 (see item no. 2596).

The musicologist Francisco Curt Lange (b. Eilenburg, Germany, 12 Dec. 1903) has contributed much toward making Montevideo an important center of inter-American musical activity (see also items 78, 79, 80, 2588, 2595), particularly as founder and editor of the *Boletín latino americano de música* (see item no. 35). He is also founder and director of the Instituto Interamericano de Musicología at Montevideo, officialized by government decree in 1940, and of the Editorial Cooperativa Interamericana de Compositores, a publishing enterprise for bringing out the music of contemporary American composers (publication commenced in 1941). In addition, Lange as librarian of the Servicio oficial de difusión radio eléctrica (state broadcasting service, commonly caled SODRE), supervised a record collection of more than twenty thousand items. The SODRE also has a symphony orchestra under the direction of Lamberto Baldi (see item no. 2588), a chorus, various chamber music groups, and schools for music and for ballet.

GENERAL AND MISCELLANEOUS

Beattie, John W., and Louis Woodson Curtis. South American music pilgrimage. IV. Argentina and Uruguay. *Mus. educ. jour.*, v. 28, no 5 (Apr. 1942), p. 22-27. il. **[2579]**

Berrien, William. Some considerations regarding contemporary Latin American music. *In* Griffith, Charles C., *ed.*, Concerning Latin American culture, New York, Columbia university press, 1940, p. 151-180. F1408.3.G75 **[2580]**

The activities of Francisco Curt Lange receive considerable attention.

Calderón de la Barca, E. G. Apuntes de historia de la música. *Sudamérica. Correo mus. sud-am.*, v. 1, no. 22 (25 Aug. 1915), p. 4-6. **[2581]**

References to music of Brazil, Argentina and Uruguay.

Castro, Manuel de. Lámpara, vigilias de la cruz y la flauta. Montevideo, Imprenta Florenza, 1938. 59 p. PQ8519.C35L3 **[2582]**

Includes three of the author's poems set to music by the Uruguayan composers Vicente Ascone and Apolo Ronchi, for voice and piano (p. 37-46).

Dumesnil, Maurice. Musical advance in Uruguay and Brazil. *The Etude*, v. 59, no. 7 (July 1941), p. 469, 498. il. **[2583]**

Escuder, Esmeralda. El canto coral en Alemania y sus proyecciones en el Uruguay. *Bol. lat. am. mús.*, v. 4 (Oct. 1938), p. 375-386. **[2584]**

Hanson, Simon G. Music and radio in Uruguay. *Bull. pan amer. union*, v. 69, no. 11 (1935), p. 831-834. il. **[2585]**

Includes a "Triste do campo" adapted and harmonized by Eduardo Fabini, p. 834.

Inter-American reviews: Politics and international influence; Montevideo.

Mod. music, v. 20, no. 3 (March-Apr. 1943), p. 199-202. **[2586]**

Signed: R. U. A. Review of musical activities in Montevideo. Includes "a résumé of everything important heard in Montevideo for the first time in 1942".

Lange, Francisco Curt. La educación musical infantil en el Uruguay. Una nueva orientación. *Bol. lat. am. mús.*, v. 5 (Oct. 1941), p. 619-629. **[2587]**

———. Organización musical en el Uruguay: La Ossodre. *Bol. lat. am. mús.*, v. 1 (Apr. 1935), p. 111-132. **[2588]**

The Ossodre is the Orquesta sinfónica del Servicio oficial de difusión radio eléctrica, founded in 1931. "Estado demonstrativo de las obras ejecutadas de 1931 a 1934" (p. 118-131), chart of compositions performed by this orchestra from 1931 to 1934, inclusive.

Memoria de la labor artística desarrollada por la Asociación coral de Montevideo en el año 1930. [Montevideo, 1930] 18 p. ML238.8.M6A8 **[2589]**

Includes titles of Latin American compositions sung by this choral society.

Mondino, Luis Pedro. La ronda del sonido; resumen de historia de la música. Montevideo, Editorial Libertad, [1935?] 85 p. ML161.M82R6 **[2590]**

"Responde al programa de música de los institutos normales."

Montevideo musical; órgano defensor de los intereses artísticos. Director; Francisco Sambucetti. Montevideo. ML5.M54 **[2591]**

"Este periódico aparece los días 1º y 15 de cada mes." Library of Congress has año XVIII, Número 226 (1 Jan. 1903) through año XX Número 7 (1 July 1906). Beginning with no. 254 (1 Apr. 1904), issued once instead of twice a month. Includes musical supplements.

Oribe, Emilio. Un proyecto sobre historia estética de la música y el canto y teoría e historia del arte ... Buenos Aires-Montevideo, Palacio del libro, 1930. 47 p. MT3.A8O8 **[2592]**

Contents: Proyecto; Resolución del Consejo n. de enseñanza primaria y normal, 19 de septiembre 1929; Opiniones; Aclaraciones.

Pereda Valdés, Ildefonso. La música nativa en el Uruguay. *Nosotros,* v. 20, no. 58 (Buenos Aires, 1926), p. 517-521. **[2593]**

The title does not refer to folk music, but to the art music of Uruguay based on native themes. Discusses the work of the contemporary composers Eduardo Fabini, Alfonso Broqua, Luis Cluzeau Mortet, Telémaco Morales and Carlos Giucci.

Ramis, Cesáreo E. Apuntes y ensayos sobre estética musical. Montevideo, A. Monteverde y cía., 1939. 128 p. ML-3845.R25A6 **[2594]**

BIOGRAPHY AND CRITICISM

[Francisco, Curt Lange]. *Rev. bras. mús.,* v. 1, no. 3 (Sept. 1934), p. 265-266. **[2595]**

A biographical sketch of the director of the Instituto Interamericano de Musicología of Montevideo.

Lange, Francisco Curt. León Ribeiro. *Bol. lat. am. mús.,* v. 3 (1937), p. 519-536. **[2596]**

In 1934 the Sección de investigaciones musicales of the Instituto de estudios superiores of Montevideo acquired the library and private papers of the Uruguayan composer León Ribeiro (1854-1931), who wrote copiously in many forms. This is a list of his musical manuscripts pertaining to his life and work.

Morandi, Luis. León Ribeiro. *Bol. lat. am. mús.,* v. 3 (1937), p. 517-518. port. **[2597]**

A tribute to the late composer (see item no. 2596). "León Ribeiro es para mí el compositor uruguayo de su época... más completo, más fecundo, más digno de llevar merecidamente el título de Maestro."

Muller, María V. de. César Cortinas. *Rev. nac.,* v. 2, no. 21 (1939), p. 386-401. **[2598]**

A highly appreciative account of the work and life of the Uruguayan composer,

whose death in 1918 cut short his many activities at the age of 25. The outstanding compositions of Cortinas are analyzed and a list of all his known works is given. [Wm. Berrien].

Negro, Romeo. Uruguay. *Rev. música,* v. 1, no. 1 (15 July 1927), p. 56-58. **[2599]**

Deals with the artistic personality of Eduardo Fabini, especially in relation to his symphonic poems *Campo* and *La Isla de los Ceibos.*

Revista musical argentina. Número dedicado al Uruguay musical, v. 2, no. 11 (Jan. 1937). **[2600]**

Contains biographical sketches of Vicente Ascone, Lamberto Baldi, Alfonso Broqua, Benone Calcavecchia, Luis Cluzeau Mortet, Domingo Dente, Carlos Estrada, Eduardo Fabini, Francisco Curt Lange, Luis Pedro Mondino, José Tomás Mujica, Vicente Pablo, Carlos Pedrell, Ramón Rodríguez Socas, Virgilio E. Scarabelli, Eric Simón.

Slonimsky, Nicolas. Music in Uruguay. *Christian scien. mon.,* 18 Sept. 1943. **[2600x]**

Viñoly, S. Roman. Eduardo Fabini, músico. *Bol. lat. am. mús.,* v. 3 (Apr. 1937), p 113-120 **[2601]**

An impressionistic rather than critical sketch of the Uruguayan composer Fabini (b. 18 May 1883), among whose major works are the symphonic poems *Campo* and *La isla de los ceibos;* the ballet *Mburucuyá;* and *Melga sinfónica.* Fabini is considered the oustanding composer of Uruguay.

NATIONAL ANTHEM

Fávaro, Edmundo J. Los antecedentes del himno nacional. *Rev. nac.,* v. 1, no. 9 (Sept. 1938), p. 413-434. **[2602]**

——. Ensayo histórico sobre los antecedentes del himno nacional. *Bol. lat. am. mús.,* v. 4 (Oct. 1938), p. 571-634. **[2603]**

Himno nacional de la república O. del Uruguay. Letra de Francisco Acuña

de Figueroa; música de Fernando Quijano y Francisco J. Debali. Ministerio de
instrución pública. 7 p. M1688.U6Q

[2604]

"Oficializado por Decreto de poder ejecu-
tivo el 14 de mayo de 1934."

FOLK MUSIC

"Elisabetta" [E. M. P. de Pate]. Uruguayan music. *Bull. pan amer. union,*
v. 66, no. 11 (Nov. 1932), p. 763-778

[2605]

References to aboriginal music, and to
folk music of the Gauchos. The author
states that the *pericón* is the most characteristic type of Uruguayan folk music.
Includes several examples of "composed"
music, with some folk influence.

Escuder, Ricardo. El pericón, baile nacional del Uruguay. Montevideo, Claudio García y cía., 1936. 24 p. il. ML34-
17.E75P4 **[2606]**

Around 1887, when an official arrangement of the music (for military band)
was made by Gerardo Grasso, the *pericón*
became the national dance of Uruguay.

Rossi, Vicente. Martín Fierro, su autor
y su anotador. Rio de la Plata, 1940.
84 p. (Folletos lenguaraces, no. 25).

[2607]

On reverse of inside title-page; Casa editora, Imprenta argentina, Córdoba. Deals
with origins, choreography and etymology
of the *pericón*, p. 52-80. Rossi states that
the *pericón* is a dance of Uruguayan origin, derived from a combination of the
huella and the *gato con relaciones*.

Vignali, Marcelo. Danzas regionales del
Uruguay y manual de baile. Montevideo, Ed. Orsini Bertani, 1910. **[2608]**

SUPPLEMENT TO 1960

The indefatigable musicologist Lauro Ayestarán(q. v.), whose energy
and scholarship are exclusively concentrated on documenting and clarify-
ing the musical history of Uruguay, has been fully productive during
this period, as a glance at the bibliography below will reveal (it is not
complete but includes at least his major contributions). His *magnum
opus* is the work entitled *La música en el Uruguay* (item 990a), a work of
over 800 pages (and this is only Volume I!) containing an exhaustive
documentation of the foundations and early development of music in
Uruguay. Since Ayestarán is equally at home, and equally interested, in
folk, primitive and popular music, as in art music, his work covers the
whole range of musical expression in society. As director of the SODRE,
his influence is widely felt.

Ayestarán has, moreover, published specialized studies of folk and
popular music in Uruguay, including such widespread types as the *cielito,*
the *media caña* and the *pericón.* He has very wisely elected to concen-
trate on the gathering of first-hand and authentic documentation which
is the great need in Latin American musical historiography at present.
Speculation as to origins and influences are idle unless they are based
on a complete documentation.

For a succinct account of the development of musical composition in Uruguay, the reader is referred to Ayestarán's essay, *Evolución del pensamiento musical uruguayo,* published in *Buenos Aires Musical* in 1957) (item 999a). Beginning with the composer Manuel Ubeda (1760-1823), the author traces the culmination of "musical nationalism" in the work of Eduardo Fabini (1882-1950) and Alfonso Broqua (1876-1946), and then discusses the contemporary scene and the work of such composers as Carlos Estrada and Hector Tosar (b. 1923). In addition to Fabini and Broqua, the composers Benone Calcavecchia (1886-1953) and Luis Cluzeau Mortet (1889-1957) also died during this period.

The composer Eduardo Fabini is the subject of a large biographical work by Roberto Lagarmilla, published in 1956 (item 1008a).

BIBLIOGRAPHY

(A) PRIMITIVE, FOLK, AND POPULAR MUSIC

Ayesterán, Lauro. Del folklore musical uruguayo. *El Día,* Jan. 25, 1948, May 23, 1948.   **[988a]**

Scholarly treatment of the history of 2 dances (6 music notations).

——. El minué montonero. Montevideo, Universidad de la República, Facultad de humanidades y ciencias, 1950. (Separata from *Rev. de la Facultad de humanidades y ciencias,* no. 6, p. 225-237, with 9 additional pages of music).   **[989a]**

The history, music and choreography of this dance, with the music (in facsimile) of 9 versions from the mid-19th century, and several brief music notations in the text.

——. La música en el Uruguay. Vol. I. Montevideo, servicio oficial de difusión radio eléctrica, 1953. 818 p. il. (music, facs.)

Part I: "La música primitiva". ch. 1, "La música indígena". Ch. 2, "La música negra".   **[990a]**

——. La música indígena en el Uruguay. Montevideo, 1949. 40 p. il.   **[991a]**

Reference is to sources from 1531 to the 19th century, with special reference to the musical bow, of which the distribution is estimated on a map. Bibliogra-

phy and 12 plates. A scholarly work. Reprinted from *Revista de la Facultad de Humanidades y Ciencias,* Montevideo, v. 3, no. 4 (Dec. 1949), p. 239-282. (C.S.)

——. La primitiva poesía gauchesca en el Uruguay. Tomo 1. 1812-1838. Montevideo, Imprenta "El Siglo Ilustrado", 1950. 245 p. il. (music). (Apartado de la *Revista del Instituto Nacional de Investigaciones y Archivos Literarios,* año I, no. 1.)   **[992a]**

Includes "Referencias musicales", p. 50-64, with 2 brief musical examples, with special reference to the *cielito,* the *media caña,* and the *pericón* Plate IX is facsimile of a page of the holograph score of the fantasia *La Batalla de Cagancha* written by Francisco José Debail between 1839 and 1844 (music of the media caña). Plates X and XI, facsimiles of music of *media caña* from MS. album copies, and presumably composed, by F. J. Debali.

——. Temas bíblicos en el folklore musical uruguayo. *Escritura,* v. 1, no. 1 (Oct. 1947), p. 61-65.   **[993a]**

Text and melody of an estilo, "Cuando el mundo se formó" transcribed from a field recording.

Carámbula, Ruben. Negro y tambor. Poemas, pregones, danzas y leyendas sobre motivos del folklore afro-rioplatense. Melodías y anotaciones rítmicas del autor. Buenos Aires, Privately printed, 1952. il. (music).   **[994a]**

Not a systematic or scholarly work, but contains some brief melodies and much background material on Negro customs and traditions in the region of La Plata.

Carvalho Neto, Paulo de. La obra afrouruguaya de Ildefonso Pereda Valdés. Ensayo de crítica de antropología cultural. Montevideo, Centro de estudios folklóricos del Uruguay, 1955, 141 p. (Bibliográficos). **[995a]**

Contains important essays on Afro-Uruguayan cultural history: "El negro rioplatense y otros ensayos" (1937), "Línea de color" (1938), and "Negros esclavos y negros libres" (1941).

Pereda Valdés, Ildefonso. Cancionero popular uruguayo: materiales recogidos en los departamentos de Montevideo, Cerro Largo, Durazno, Canelones y Lavalleja, y ensayo de interpretación de los mismos, con una introducción al estudio de ciencia folklórica. Montevideo, Florensa y Lafón, 1947. 204 p. il. **[996a]**

760 items, with individual and section notes, including worksongs and ballads.

——. Negros esclavos y negros libres; esquema de una sociedad esclavista y aporte del negro en nuestra formación nacional. Montevideo, Gaceta comercial, 1941. 173 p. il. **[997a]**

Discusses the evolution of African dances in Montevideo from colonial times. Also contains data on tales and songs.

(B) ART MUSIC AND MISCELLANEOUS

Ayestarán, Lauro. Crónica de una temrada musical en el Montevideo de 1830. Montevideo, Ed. Ceibo, 1943. 108 p. il. (music). **[998a]**

Research on music activity during 1830, the year of the first operatic performance in Montevideo. One music notation.

——. Evolución del pensamiento musical uruguayo. B. A. mus. v. 12, no. 197. (Oct. 1, 1957), p. 4. **[999a]**

A substantial historical survey, beginning with the composer Manuel Úbeda (1760-1823) and giving special attention to the composers Eduardo Fabini (1882-1950), Alfonso Broqua (1876-1946), César Cortinas (1892-1918), and Héctor Tosar.

——. Fuentes para el estudio de la música colonial uruguaya. Montevideo, Impresora uruguaya, 1947. 57 p. Offprint from Rev. fac. hum. cien., v. 1, no. 1 (April 1947), p. 315-358. **[1000a]**

This work was undertaken as a research project in the course on musicology given under the Faculty of Sciences and Humanities of the University of Uruguay, and was carried out cooperatively by the students under the direction of the author. It consists of an annotated list of 147 documents covering the years 1573-1833, arranged chronologically under 9 headings.

——. La música en el Uruguay. Vol. I. Montevideo, Servicio oficial de difusión radio eléctrica (SODRE), 1953. 818 p. il. **[1001a]**

A fundamental work, culmination to date of the author's extensive researches in the history of music in Uruguay over the past 25 years. See the review by José Pereira Rodríguez in Américas, v. 6, no. 3 (March 1954), p. 38-39.

This volume contains Parts I and II of the projected work in 4 parts (Part III: La música folklórica; Part IV: Antología y ensayo crítico sobre el pasado y el presente de la música uruguaya). Part I deals with primitive music, Part II with "La música culta" (up to 1860). The latter includes music of the *salon* type, patriotic songs, military music, etc.

——. La música escénica en el Uruguay. Rev. mus. chil., v. 3, no. 19 (April 1947) p. 17-26. **[1002a]**

——. Panorama del folklore musical uruguayo El Día, Montevideo, v. 16, nos. 774, 776, 778, 780 (1947). **[1003a]**

Approximately half-page newspaper articles entitled respectively *Panorama, El Estilo, Antecedentes históricos, La polka,* Illustrations and music notations, latter mostly transcriptions of melodies recorded on discs in the field. (C.S.)

Balzo, Hugo. Divulgación musical en Uruguay. B. A. mus., v. 12, no. 197 (Oct. 1, 1957), p. 5, 14. **[1004a]**

Survey of musical organizations, including the SODRE (official broadcasting service).

———. Divulgación de la música en Uruguay. *Bol. interam. mús.,* no. 3 (Jan. 1958), p. 11-12.   **[1005a]**

A reprint of the preceding item.

Becerra, Gustavo. Sinfonía no. 2 para cuerdas de Héctor Tosar. *Rev. mus. chil.,* v. 11, no. 55 (Oct.-Nov. 1957), p. 5-23.   **[1006a]**

A detailed analysis, with 21 musical examples.

Herrera, Carlos A. El canto uruguayo, en la música de Broqua y Cluzeau-Mortet. *Rev. mus. chil.,* v. 2, no. 14 (September 1946), p. 19-26.   **[1007a]**

Lagarmilla, Roberto E. Eduardo Fabini, músico nacional uruguayo. Montevideo, Organización Medina, n. d. [1953], 241 p. il.   **[1008a]**

An important biographical study of this composer, regarded as the leading exponent of the "national" movement in Uruguay.

———. Eduardo Fabini ante la historia. Montevideo, Medina editor, n. d. (1955), 31 p.   **[1009a]**

"Conferencia pronunciada en la sala de actos del Jockey Club de Montevideo el viernes 10 de junio de 1955."

Uruguay; new Uruguayan opera. *Interamer. mus. bull.,* no. 7 (Sept. 1958), p. 5.   **[1010a]**

Account of first performance of *El Regreso* by Ricardo Storm, on April 17, 1958 in Montevideo, with information on cast, plot, and quotations from two newspaper reviews of the performance.

Uruguay's musical prospector. *Américas,* v. 1, no. 2 (Apr. 1949), p. 25, 47.   **[1011a]**

About the musicologist Francisco Curt Lange, and his studies of Latin American music. Photograph.

VENEZUELA

THE first teacher of European music in Venezuela appears to have been Luis Cárdenas Saavedra who, on July 16, 1591, received a subvention from the Ayuntamiento de Caracas for establishing a school whose curriculum included the teaching of plain song. In 1593, a further subsidy was granted to a certain Juan de Arteaga for the continuation of this same school. In 1698, we find that the regulations of the Colegio Seminario provided for the services of a music master to instruct the seminarians in music for a half hour each day. When the Universidad de Santiago de León was founded at Caracas in 1725, it included a chair of music whose first incumbent was Francisco Pérez Camacho.

The musical movement in Colonial Venezuela owed a great deal to Padre Pedro Palacios y Sojo, a member of the Congregation of the Oratory, who was a notable patron of the arts and of music in particular. Around the year 1770 he journeyed to Rome for the purpose of obtaining permission from the Pope to establish a monastery in Caracas. He brought back with him to Venezuela a collection of musical scores and several musical instruments, including the first European wind instruments to be introduced in Venezuela. Shortly after his return Padre Sojo established an Academy of Music which flourished and produced a brilliant school of composers. The most celebrated member of this school was José Angel Lamas, whose compositions include the famous *Popule Meus*, composed in 1806, which, to this day, is frequently performed in Venezuela and is looked upon by Venezuelans as a sort of unofficial national anthem. Lamas, like most of the musicians of the school, wrote chiefly religious music. Other important members of this group, known as the School of Chacao because that was the name of the suburb where Sojo's Academy was located, were: Atanasio Bello, José Antonio Caro de Boesi, José Cayetano Carreño (grandfather of Teresa Carreño), Juan Bautista Carreño, Rafael Isaza, Juan José Landaeta (composer of the Venezuelan National Anthem), Juan Francisco Meserón, José Lorenzo Montero, Pedro Nolasco Colón, Juan Manuel Olivares and José Francisco Velázquez.

The foregoing are the composers whose works have been preserved in the greatest quantity. Other composers represented in the archive of the Escuela de Música at Caracas are: Casimiro Arias, Juan Bautista Carreño, Domingo Ramón Hernández, Manuel E. Hernández, José María Isaza, Francisco Isturriaga, Manuel Larrázabal, Sebastián Lozano, Francisco Marcos y Navas, José María Mendible, José Ángel Montero, José María Montero, Juan Francisco Pereira, Manuel Toledo Hernández, Hermógenes

Tovar and José María Velásquez. To these should be added the names of Lino Gallardo, Marcos Pompa and José Rodríguez, who were active toward the end of the eighteenth century and the early part of the nineteenth.

Precise biographical data are lacking for most of these composers. Olivares was born in 1760. We know that Lamas, thirty-five of whose-compositions have been preserved and identified, died in 1814. Juan José Landaeta died as a result of the earthquake of 1812, and Cayetano Carreño lived from 1774 to 1836. These dates indicate approximately the period within which the early Venezuelan school reached its maximum development. The composers of Caracas in this period attained a remarkable technical maestery of their craft, and both the quality and abundance of their production gives to Venezuela a prominent place in the early history of American music.

In 1883, General Ramón de La Plaza, in his *Ensayos sobre el arte en Venezuela* [no. 2615] published a selection of compositions, both sacred and secular, by several of the composers mentioned above, including Olivares and Lamas. But many of the compositions by these and other composers of the period remained virtually unknown to the modern public until they were unearthed from the archives of the Escuela de Música of Caracas by Juan Bautista Plaza in the 1930's. Plaza catalogued the manuscripts and had many of them copied for performance. In 1942 a selection of this music, patronized by the Venezuelan government, was being published in Montevideo.

Most of the composers with whom we have been dealing lived to witness the beginnings, if not the final achievement, of Venezuelan independence. Caracas, birthplace of Simón Bolívar the Liberator, was the fountainhead of revolt against Spain, and several of the most prominent Venezuelan composers joined the Sociedad Patriótica and took an active part in the revolutionary uprising which led to the declaration of independence on July 14, 1811. Among these musicians were Lino Gallardo, Juan José Landaeta, Marcos Pompa and José Rodríguez. Landaeta composed the patriotic song, *Gloria al Bravo Pueblo,* which in 1810 was already the most popular revolutionary song and which eventually was officially adopted as the national anthem of Venezuela (during the regime of Guzmán Blanco, in the 1870's). Although the Venezuelans declared themselves independent in 1811, Spanish power was not broken until Bolívar won his decisive victory at Carabobo in 1821, and it was not until 1845 that Venezuelan independence was formally recognized by Spain. This long period of struggle produced many patriotic songs, of which *Gloria al Bravo Pueblo* is the most famous example. The brothers Landaeta composed another popular revolutionary song called *Sincamisa* (literally, "without a shirt", cor-

responding to the *sans-culotte* of the French Revolution), while Lino-
Gallardo composed a *canción patriótica* celebrating the heroic exploits
of Bolívar (printed by Ramón de La Plaza, *op. cit.,* musical supplement,
p. 38-43). Gallardo was one of the most active musicans of this period,
and one of the few who devoted himself mainly to secular rather than
to religious composition. In 1818 he obtained permission to establish a
music school, which was formally constituted in the following year under
the protection of General Morillo. In conjunction with the school, Gallardo organized a Philharmonic Society for giving orchestral concerts, which
he conducted.

The year 1830, approximately, marks the end of what may be termed
the classical phase of Venezuelan music. For the remainder of the nineteenth century the Romantic influence was predominant. The outstanding
composers of this period were Felipe Larrazábal (1816-1873), José Ángel
Montero (1839-1881) and Federico Villena (1885-c.1900). In the field of
popular music the leading figures were Juan José Tovar and later the
brothers Román and Rafael Isaza, who toward the middle of the century
enjoyed a virtual monopoly of dance music in Caracas. José María Velásquez, a viola player, was especially active in the realm of chamber music.
Other composers who may be mentioned are José Marmol y Muñoz, author
of a hymn in honor of General Guzmán Blanco; Jesús María Suárez, composer of many *aires nacionales* and marches for piano; his brother, Cesáreo
Suárez (b. 1837), a celebrated pianist who toured in the United States and
invented an instrument called the *melovitro;* José María Gómez Cardiel,
who wrote several patriotic songs, including *Himno a Bolívar;* Antonio
Jesús Silva, composer of the overture *La Esperanza;* Paz Abreu, who established himself as a music teacher in Barquisimeto; and José G. Nuñez,
author of a treatise on musical theory.

As regards the lyric theatre the first operatic troupe to appear in Caracas of which there is definite notice was a French company which gave
some performances at the Teatro El Conde in 1808. The company was
not large enough to give complete operas, so only excerpts were sung.
The works from which selections were sung included Mozart's *Don Gio-
vanni* and *Die Zauberflöte,* and an opera entitled *Pizarre ou la Conquête
du Pérou,* by the French composer Pierre Joseph Candeille, written in 1751.

In the orchestra of the Teatro El Conde were some of the most no-
table musicians of Caracas, including Juan Landaeta, Cayetano Carreño,
Lino Gallardo, José Ángel Lamas, the brothers Bernabé, José María and
Dionisio Montero, José Luis Landaeta, José Antonio Caro de Boesi, and
Juan Meserón. The conductor was Juan Manuel Olivares.

In 1836, there are notices of complete operatic performances in Caracas. Among the works performed in that year were *Il Barbieri di Seviglia* and *La Gazza Ladra* by Rossini. The first regular operatic company to function in Caracas appeared in 1843. Its repertoire included Bellini's *Norma* and Donizettti's *Lucia di Lammermoor*. This company came to Venezuela from Puerto Rico, and according to the advance publicity it had previosuly appeared in Cuba and the United States. It was an Italian company.

With the inauguration of the Teatro Caracas on October 22, 1854 (rebuilt in 1888), the lyric theatre acquired a more solid status in the Venezuelan capital. The work chosen for the opening performance was Verdi's *Hernani,* given by a French company from Paris. The Teatro Caracas, of course, was used for the spoken drama as well as for opera. Caracas never had a permanent resident opera company, but operatic performances continued to be given by visiting troupes. After the opening of the Teatro Municipal in 1881, operatic companies began to appear in Caracas with more regularity.

As regards the national lyric drama the only opera by a Venezuelan composer to be produced in the nineteenth century was *Virginia* by José Ángel Montero, performed at the Teatro Caracas in 1873. Andrés Delgado Pardo wrote two operas, neither of which was produced. José María Ponce de León wrote the sacred opera *Ester* in 1874. Shortly after 1900, Lucio Delgado attempted to produce a national opera entitled *Guaicaipuro,* but it never passed beyond the phase of rehearsal.

In the field of comic opera, which in Spanish is called *zarzuela,* Venezuelan composers have been more productive. Composers active in this field include José Ángel Montero (*Doña Inés o la política en el hogar*), José G. Nuñez, Federico Villena (*Las dos deshonras*), José María Ponce de León (*El castillo misterioso*), Sebastián Díaz Peña, Domingo Martínez, Rivera Vaz (*El Rey del Cacao*), and Pedro Elías Gutiérrez (*Percances en Macuto, Un Gallero como pocos, El inglés de la guayana, Alma llanera,* etc.)

We have aready traced the beginning of musical education in Venezuela from the teaching of plain song in 1591 to the Academia de Música founded by Padre Sojo in the last third of the eighteenth century and the similar academy organized by Lino Gallardo in 1819. In 1868-69, Felipe Larrazábal founded a noteworthy but shortlived conservatory. When the Instituto Nacional de Bellas Artes was founded in 1877, it included as one of its sections an Academia de Música whose first president was the distinguished politician, writer and musician Eduardo Calcaño.

The activities of the Academia embraced the teaching of music, for which purpose two instructors were engaged for the first academic year, when the number of students matriculated in the music courses was forty-six. Musical theory was taught by Antonio Jesús Silva. In 1878 a musical grammar by Francisco M. Tejera was adopted as an official text. For details regarding the organization of the Instituto de Bellas Artes and the Academia de Música, see R. de La Plaza, *op. cit.,* p. 235-255. Ramón de La Plaza was the first director of the Instituto.

The foregoing survey of musical activity in Venezuela is based on the monograph by Ramón de La Plaza already mentioned, on José Antonio Calcaño's *Contribución al estudio de la música en Venezuela* [no. 2611], on Juan José Churión's *El teatro en Caracas* [no. 2614], and on J. B. Plaza's article, *Music in Caracas during the colonial period* [no. 2621]. The last-mentioned writer is completing a book entitled *Historia de la música en Caracas durante la época colonial,* which will give a complete account of colonial music in Caracas.

For the contemporary musical scene in Venezuela, the reader should consult the articles by Mario de Lara [no. 2616], Eduardo Lira Espejo [no. 2617] and Carlos Vidal [no. 2622]. In the comments on these items the names of numerous contemporary Venezuelan composers are mentioned. Here we many mention that Vicente Emilio Sojo (b. 1887) is director of the Escuela de Música y Declamación and conductor of the Orfeón Lamas, an excellent choral group. Nor must we overlook the famous Venezuelan pianist Teresa Carreño (1853-1917), of whom there exists a full-length biography in English [no. 2619].

The works by R. de La Plaza and J. A. Calcaño mentioned above contain extensive sections on the primitive and folk music of Venezuela. Fray Baltasar de Matallana has written a valuable study of the music of an Indian tribe from the "Gran Sabana" [no. 2642]. The folk music of Venezuela may be divided into two main sections; that of the interior and that of the coast. In the former the Spanish element is predominant; in the latter there is a strong Negro influence. The most characteristic type of Venezuelan folk song and dance is the *joropo* ($^3/_4$ time). Calcaño refers to the *tono* as the most typical song of the *llanero* or plainsman, generally sung by three voices without accompaniment. Sometimes the *tono* is accompanied by the *cuatro,* a four-stringed guitar.

GENERAL AND MISCELLANEOUS

Asociación venezolana de literatura, ciencias y bellas artes. Primer libro venezolano de literatura, ciencias y bellas artes, ofrenda al gran mariscal de Ayacucho. Caracas, Tip. El cojo, 1ª parte; Tip. moderna, 2ª parte, 1895. PQ3581.A7   **[2609]**

Includes: El arte en Venezuela, por Ramón de La Plaza y la "Asociación", Tercera parte. La música, p. 271-301. Eight pages of music at end, including the *Popule meus* of José Angel Lamas; *Impromptu* for piano by María M. de Letts; *Melopeya* for vioce and piano by Isabel P. de Mauri; *Rondel de l'adieu* by Adina Manrique. Contains portraits of 35 Venezuelan musicians. Together with La Plaza's *Ensayos sobre el arte en Venezuela*, this is one of the main sources for the history of music in Venezuela.

Bello, Francisco R. Páez en Buenos Aires. Caracas, "Hogar americano", 1941. 44 p. F2322.8.P173 **[2610]**
"Apéndice" (music), p. 31-44.

Calcaño, José Antonio. Contribución al estudio de la música en Venezuela. Caracas, Editorial "Elite", 1939. 127 p. fold. plates (music). ML239.C2C6 **[2611]**
Contents. Historia: Exaltación y melodía. Efectos de la independencia en la música venezolana. En torno a Lamas. Anotaciones para el estudio de nuestra música romántica. Eslabones ausentes. Música indígena: Posición del investigador ante la música aborigen. Las maracas. Los botutos. Silbatos y flautas del Tacarigua. Folklore: Folklore Negro. Folklore llanero. El "tono" de los llanos. Baile de tambor en Borburata. Los tambores de Venezuela.

Catálogo general de las principales obras musicales del maestro Pedro Elías Gutiérrez. Recopiladas en sus diversos estilos por Mariano Hernández Laue y Pedro Arcilla Ponte. Caracas, 1940. 28 p. port. **[2612]**
Gutiérrez (b. La Guaira, 1870) is conductor of the Banda Marcial del Distrito Federal de Caracas and inspector of military mands. This pamphlet includes a biographical sketch.

Chase, Gilbert. Juan Bautista Plaza and Venezuelan music. *Int. amer. monthly*, v. 1, no. 4 (Aug. 1942), p. 28-29. **[2614]**

Churión, Juan José. El teatro en Caracas. Caracas, Tip. Vargas, 1924. 230 p. PN2552.C3C5 **[2614]**
Part 3, *La lírica y la ópera*, is important for the history of the lyric theatre in Venezuela. See also Part 4, *Teatro nacional*, p. 218-220.

La Plaza, Ramón de. Ensayos sobre el arte en Venezuela. Caracas, Impr. al vapor de "La Opinión nacional", 1883. 262 p. il. N6730.L2 **[2615]**

Lara, Mario de. Renacimiento de la música nacional. Detached from *Rev. nac. cultura*, no. 23 (Oct. 1940), p. 105-118. ML239.L2 **[2616]**
Deals with the following Venezuelan composers; Franco Medina, Andrés Delgado Pardo, Manuel Leoncio Rodríguez, Vicente Emilio Sojo, J. B. Plaza, José Antonio Calcaño, Joaquín Silva Díaz, Ángel Sauce, Antonio Estévez, Evencio Castellano, etc. Discussion of popular music, p. 113-118.

Lira Espejo, Eduardo. Realidad de la creación musical venezolana. *Rev. nac. cultura*, v. 2, no. 28 (July-Aug. 1941), p. 127-134. **[2617]**
The author, who is secretary of the Asociación Venezolana de Conciertos, traces the well-defined musical tradition of Venezuela from the composers of the 18th century, such as Lamas, Olivares, Velázquze and Caro de Boesi, to the leading contemporary figures such as Juan Bautista Plaza, Vicente Emilio Sojo, Moisés Moleiro and José Antonio Calcaño. Among the younger composers are mentioned Eduardo Plaza, José Antonio Estévez and Evencio Castellanos. Mention is also made of the folkloristic studies of P. Baltazar de Matallana and María Luisa Escobar.

Mathews, William Smythe Babcock. Teresa Carreño. Biographical and critical. Chicago, Curtis & Mayer, 1885. 11 p. ML417.C4M4 **[2618]**
Includes excerpts of press reviews.

Milinowski, Marta. Teresa Carreño, "by the grace of God". New Haven, Yale univ. press; London, H. Milford, Oxford univ. press, 1940. 410 p. il. ML417.C4M6 **[2619]**
'Sources", p. 399-403.

Morales Lara, Julio. Panorama musical venezolano. *Bol. lat. am. mús.*, v. 3 (1937), p. 81-82. **[2620]**
Touches on the rôle of folklore in the development of Venezuelan music.

Plaza, Juan Bautista. Music in Caracas during the colonial period (1770-1811). *Mus. quart.*, v. 29, no. 2 (Apr. 1943), p. 198-213. mus. facs. **[2621]**
This paper was read before the Greater New York Chapter of the American Musi-

cological Society at New York on 27 March 1942. Plaza (b. 1898), librarian and archivist of the Escuela de Música in Caracas, has compiled a catalogue of the manuscripts by Venezuelan composers discovered *circa* 1932 by Ascanio Negretti, at that time director of the school. For the names of these composers, see p. 233.

Vidal, Carlos. Indagación de la música venezolana. *Rev. nac. cultura,* no. 13 (1939), p. 95-99. **[2622]**

Influence of the *generation of 1930* (Plaza, Sojo, Moleiro) in the development of a truly Venezuelan music; importance for this music of the Orfeón Lamas; presence of a new attitude which seeks to help native composers who seek a freedom from mere servile imitation of established European masters. [Wm. Berrien].

Villanueva, Laureano. Apoteosis de Páez. Caracas, Imp. & litografía del gobierno nacional, 1888. 254 p. F2322.8.-P2 **[2623]**

Words to *La gloria de Páez,* an epic song by Felix Soublette, p. 226-235.

NATIONAL ANTHEM

Ofrenda de Venezuela en el primer centenario de la batalla de Ayacucho. Caracas, Litografía del comercio, 1924. 130 p. M1686.O35 **[2624]**

Includes the music of the national anthems of Venezuela, Bolivia, Colombia, Ecuador and Peru. Music for voice and piano, and band scores. Includes also the music of the hymns of the Venezuelan states (voice and piano only).

FOLK AND PRIMITIVE MUSIC
(A) GENERAL

Blaya Alende, Joaquín. El folklore musical argentino. *Alma latina,* v. 10, no. 208 (25 Nov. 1939), p. 17, 55. **[2625]**

Touches also on Venezuelan folk music.

Bolívar Coronado, Rafael. El llanero. Madrid, Editorial América, 1919. 208 p. F2313.B82 **[2626]**

Ch. 3 and 4 provide material on the music and songs of the *llanero.* Also printed in Caracas, Venezuela, Tip. *Cultura venezolana,* 1922.

Celis Ríos, Trino. Anotaciones marginales. Cantares llaneros. *Cult. venezolana,* v. 10, no .82 (July-Aug. 1927), p. 83-94. **[2627]**

Sobre la psicología del cantador llanero.

Lara, Mario de, and M. L. Escobar. Ritmo y melodía nativos de Venezuela. *Bol. lat. am. mús.* v. 3 (1937), p. 121-129. ML199.B64 **[2628]**

Includes music for the Danza de la Punta, as danced by the Indians of Venezuela; also rhythms of the *tanguito* and *merengue.*

Lira Espejo, Eduardo. El estado Lara y su riqueza musical. *El universal,* Caracas (19 Jan. 1941). **[2629]**

Points out the most important forms of musical expression in the state of Lara, which is one of Venezuela's richest in dance, music and folklore. [E. Planchart.]

———. Expresión musical y popular venezolana. *Revista del Caribe,* Caracas, Dec. 1941. **[2630]**

Survey of the various traditional musical manifestations of Venezuela, as follows; Expresiones indígenas; expresiones negras (tambores, fulías, quitiplás, etc.); expresiones criollas: el joropo, danza nacional; pasaje, corrido, golpe, galerón, etc. Aguinaldos y villancicos de Navidad. Décimas, salves y tonos religiosos. Las gaitas, canciones típicas de Maracaibo; la música del oriente de Venezuela: malagueñas, jota, polo margariteño, etc. Fiestas religiosas: El tamunangue en honor de San Antonio, las de San Benito en Mucuchíes de los Andes, etc. Citation from Enrique Planchart (Biblioteca Nacional, Caracas).

Liscano, Juan. Folklore venezolano. *Rev. mus. mex.,* v. 3, no. 5 (7 May 1943), p. 99-103. **[2630x]**

Reprinted from the *Boletín del Instituto cultural venezolano-británico,* no. 6 (Aug. 1942).

Machado, José E. Cancionero popular venezolano. Caracas, L. Puig Ros & Parra Almonar, 1922. 2d ed. 191 p. M1687.V3M2 **[2631]**

Includes 5 melodies with Spanish words,

and the song *Alma Llanera* by Pedro Elías Gutiérrez, for voice and piano.

——. Viejos cantos y viejos cantores. Caracas, Tipografía americana, 1921. 122 p. PQ8544.M3 **[2632]**

Mejía Baca, José. La barraca. *El comercio* (5 Dec. 1937). **[2633]**

Citation from Federico Schwab, Biblioteca central, Universidad mayor de San Marcos.

——. La saña. *El comercio* (30 Jan. 1938), **[2634]**

Citation from Federico Schwab, Biblioteca central, Universidad mayor de San Marcos.

Meneses, Guillermo. Excursión hacia el negro venezolano. *Élite*, v. 72, no. 836 (1941). **[2635]**

Illustrations of Afro-Venezuelan musical instruments.

Puchi, Emiro. Músicas de Margarita. *Presente*, Caracas, no. 1 (1941). **[2636]**

This article, taken from a radio speech, is illustrated with verses belonging to Juan Liscano's collection.

Sojo, Juan Pablo. Tierras del estado Miranda. Caracas, Cooperativa de artes gráficas, 1938. **[2637]**

El músico venezolano, p. 49-53, See also p. 18-19. Includes brief references to Venezuelan folk music and description of an Afro-Venezuelan *tambor* (drum). Citation from Enrique Planchart (Biblioteca Nacional, Caracas).

Tamayo, Francisco. Memorandum folklórico: Mi real y medio. *Revista Cubagua*, Caracas, v. 1., no. 2 (1938). **[2638]**

General observations on folklore, with special reference to the folk song, *Mi real y medio* [E. Planchart.]

——. Raíces del folk-lore venezolano; lo español en nuestra poesía espontánea. *Revista Cubagua*, Caracas, v. 1, no. 1 (1938). **[2639]**

Compares Venezuelan popular poetry in its *corrido* aspect with the Spanish *roman-ce*, or ballad. Includes an example. [E. Planchart.]

(B) AMERINDIAN

Alvarado, Lisandro. Noticia sobre los Caribes de los llanos de Barcelona. *Cult. venezolana*, v. 6, no. 47 (Mar. 1923), p. 225-250. **[2640]**

Musical instruments, p. 234-237; dance, p. 237-238.

Febres Cordero, T. Canto guerrero de los aborígenes de Mérida. *An. univ. Santiago*, v. (1934), p. 305-309. **[2641]**

Matallana, Baltasar de. La música indígena taurepán; tribu de la gran Sabana (Venezuela). Conferencia [Caracas], Editorial Venezuela, 1939. 36 p. il. ML-3575.B34M8 **[2642]**

The region known as La Gran Sabana is in the extreme south-east of Venezuela. This study is divided into 4 main sections: Conceptos sobre la música taurepán; canciones amatorias; canciones de baile. Music of 12 songs, following page 36.

——. La música indígena taurepán. *Bol. lat. am. mús.*, v. 4 (Oct. 1938), p. 649-664. **[2643]**

(C) COLLECTIONS OF MUSIC

Sojo, Vicente Emilio, ed. Primer cuaderno de canciones populares venezolanas. Caracas, 1940. 44 p. (Ministerio de educación nacional, Dirección de cultura) M1687.V3S6 **[2644]**

Most of these are "composed" songs that attained wide popularity in Venezuela during the 19th century. They are for voice and piano, with Spanish words only.

——. Segundo cuaderno de canciones populares venezolanas. Caracas, 1942. 47 p. (Editado por la Radio Caracas). M-1687.V3S6 v. 2 **[2645]**

Contains 20 songs, for voice and piano, some by known composers, others anonymous.

——, and R. Olivares Figueroa. Pequeñas canturias y danzas venezolanas.

Caracas, 1942. 20 p. (Editado por la Radio Caracas) M1687.V3S62 [2646]

15 songs, collected by Figueroa and harmonized by Sojo. The songs are suitable for children in the primary grades.

(D) COLLECTION OF TEXTS

Angarita Arvelo, Rafael. Ilustraciones del romancero castellano, cancionero y romancero venezolano (poesía popular). *Cult. venezolana,* v. 13, no. 106. (Sept.-Oct. 1930), p. 65-93. [2647]

Contains the verses of several popular corridos (no music), principally those from the *guerras de la Independencia* and the *guerra federal.*

Cantares llaneros. *Cult. venezolana,* v. 11, no. 75 (Sept. 1926), p. 361-362. [2648]

Cantares populares llaneros. *Cult. venezolana,* v. 10, no. 78 (Jan.-Feb. 1927), p. 129. [2649]

———. *Cult. venezolana,* v. 11, no. 76 (Oct. 1926), p. 117-119. [2650]

———. Galerón corrido. *Cult. venezolana,* v. 11, no. 77 (Nov.-Dec. 1926), p. 265. [2651]

Coplas populares venezolanas. *Boletín de cultura "Presente",* Caracas no. 2 (1941). [2652]

Folk song texts collected by Juan Liscano.

Corridos de Zaraza. *Cult. venezolana,* v. 13, no. 107 (Nov. 1930), p. 247-249. [2653]

Ernst, Adolf. Para el cancionero popular de Venezuela. *El cojo ilustrado* (2 Jan. 1893). [2654]

———. Proben venezuelanischer volksdichtung. *Verhandlungen der Berliner gesellschaft für anthropologie, ethnologie und urgeschichte* (20 July 1889), p. 525-535. [2655]

Gives the Spanish (with German translation) of two well-known Venezuelan songs,

with a page of music of the second song (taken from Ramón de La Plaza, no. 2615). There is one additional musical, example.

Folk-lore venezolano. *Cult. venezolana,* v. 12, no. 94 (May-June 1929), p. 151-152. [2656]

Poems.

———. v. 12, no. 96 (Aug. 1929), p. 427-429. [2657]

Words of songs.

———. v. 12, no. 98 (Oct. 1929), p. 276-277. [2658]

Poems from the collection of José E. Machado.

———. v. 13, no. 97 (Sept. 1929), p. 124-127. [2659]

Words of several songs from the José E. Machado collection.

———. v. 13, no. 99 (Nov.-Dec. 1929), p. 320-322. [2660]

Poems from José E. Machado's collection.

———. v. 13, no. 101 (Feb.-Mar. 1930), p. 310-211. [2661]

Text of some folk songs. Collection of José E. Machado.

———. v. 13, no. 103 (May 1930), p. 123-124. [2662]

Text of several songs. Collection of José E. Machado.

Gaitas o cantos populares zulianos. *Cult. venezolana,* v. 11, no. 70 (Mar.-Apr. 1926), p. 234-235. [2663]

Text of these *gaitas zulianas* (folk songs from the State of Zulia).

———. v. 11, no. 71 (May 1926), p. 139-140; v. 11, no. 72 (June 1926), p. 271. [2664]

Lyrics of these songs.

———. v. 11, no. 73 (July 1926), p. 104. [2665]

Text of folk songs from the State of Zulia.

———. v. 11, no. 74 (Aug. 1926), p. 234. [2666]

El galerón de No Marcos. *Cult. venezo-lana,* v. 10, no. 80 (Apr. 1927), p. 109-110. **[2667]**

Words to a *galerón.*

Liscano, Juan. Aspectos de la música popular venezolana. *Ahora,* Caracas (3 Mar. 1941). **[2668]**

Comments on popular Venezuelan music in its Negro, Hispanic, mestizo and indigenous aspects. [E. Planchart.]

——. El cante popular. *Acción democrática,* Caracas (14 Feb. 1942). **[2669]**

Studies the Hispanic element in Venezuelan popular song, giving as examples numerous folk song texts. [E. Planchart.]

Machado, José E. Aires populares. *Cult. venezolana,* v. 11, no. 89 (Sept. 1928), p. 268-270. **[2670]**

Gives an account of the *conga del Tuy y Aragua.* With excerpts from accompanying verses.

——. Cancionero popular venezolano... Caracas, Emp. El Cojo, 1919. 251 p. PQ8545.M3 **[2671]**

Cantares y corridos—galerones y glosas, con varias notas geográficas, históricas y lingüísticas para explicar o aclarar el texto. Introduction of 21 pages by way of explanation of sources, types, etc., of these songs. The second edition of this work include music (see item no. 2631).

——. Centón lírico, pasquinadas y canciones, epigramas y corridos... Caracas, Tip. americana, 1920. 244 p. PQ8545.-M32 **[2672]**

Political ballads and folk songs.

Montesinos, Pedro. Dos romances viejos. *Rev. nac. cultura,* v. 2, no. 24 (Nov.-Dec. 1940), p. 45-53. **[2673]**

Gives the text, with variants and commentary, of two traditional Spanish ballads found in Venezuela.

Nombres propios, allá arriba el amor. *Cult. venezolana,* v. 12, no. 95 (July 1929), p. 287-288 **[2674]**

Texts for several songs.

Pardo, I. J. Investigaciones folklóricas. Viejos romances españoles en tradición popular venezolana. *Rev. nac. cult.,* v. 5, no. 36 (Jan.-Feb. 1943), p. 35-74. **[2675]**

The author includes many *romance* texts, giving various Spanish versions as well as the popular Venezuelan forms.

Planchart, Enrique. Observaciones sobre el cancionero popular venezolano. *Cult. venezolana,* v. 4, no. 28 (Aug. 1921), p. 153-167; v. 4, no. 29 (Sept. 1921), p. 250-257. **[2676]**

Pages read to a group of North American school teachers. Includes *Romance de negro primero.*

Recepción académica. *Cult. venezolana,* v. 7, no. 56 (Apr.-May 1924), p. 30-61. **[2677]**

Discurso de recepción de José E. Machado en la Academia nacional de la historia, por el doctor Santiago Key Ayala. This discourse includes quotations of several song texts.

Serpa P., Domingo A. Del cancionero popular. *Rev. nac. cultura,* v. 2, no. 28 (1941), p. 135-139. **[2678]**

Selections from Venezuelan folk poetry, with comments.

(E) DANCES

Calcaño, Eduardo. El tiburón; mimodrama folklórico. *Élite,* v. 17, no. 858 (1942), **[2679]**

Describes a carnival pantomime danced by Venezuelan sailors, disguised and accompanied by the music of *cuatros* (4-stringed guitars), *maracas* and *güiros.*

Golpe de asamblea. *Cult. venezolana,* v. 11, no. 87 (May-June 1928), p. 245-246. **[2680]**

Words to this *golpe,* a dancing step.

Lara, Mario de. Rhythms in Venezuela. *Bull. pan amer. union,* v. 82, no. 11 (Nov. 1938), p. 646-649. **[2681]**

Describes with choreographic details the ceremonial Corn Dance of the Indians of

Mérida, and the Dance of the Macuchíes. Includes musical examples.

Lira Espejo, Eduardo. El tamunangue. *El universal,* Caracas, Jan. 26, 1941. **[2682]**

A study of the choreographic, musical and historical aspects of this dance from the state of Lara. "La danza, la letra y la música exhiben la influencia de los elementos hispánicos y negros, con predominancia del primero". The *tamunangue* is danced in honor of St. Anthony and consists of several numbers, beginning with *La batalla* and ending with a *Salve* of archaic musical character. Citation from Enrique Planchart (Biblioteca Nacional, Caracas).

——. Las turas, baile indígena del Estado Lara. *El universal, Caracas,* 2 Feb. 1941. **[2683]**

The *turas* is an Indian dance from the state of Lara in Venezuela. "La importancia y transcendencia que el Baile de las Turas tiene y ha tenido para esta tribu lo revela la existencia de todo un código de ceremonias, de un protocolo que se ha venido transmitiendo de generación en generación y que se respeta y cumple con la fidelidad de los grandes rituales". Citation from Dr. Enrique Planchart, Biblioteca Nacional, Caracas.

López Ruiz, Juvenal. Una danza larense, y la opinión de un musicólogo chileno. *Élite,* v. 16, no. 802 (15 Feb. 1941), p. 20. **[2684]**

Interview with the Chilean musicologist Eduardo Lira Espejo, who relates historical data about this dance, the *tamunangue,* the Negro and Spanish influence upon it,

etc. He relates the number called *La batalla* to certain Basque dances.

Méndez, Agustín José. El tamunangue. *Élite,* v. 16, no. 803 (22 Feb. 1941), p. 27. **[2685]**

Describes the atmosphere of the town El Tocuyo, where this dance originated, and goes into further discussion of the *tamunangue,* its formation, development, etc.

Prat, Domingo. Diccionario biográfico, bibliográfico, histórico, crítico, de guitarras, guitarristas, danzas y cantos, Buenos Aires, Casa Romero y Fernández, 1934. 468 p. ML128.G8P7 **[2686]**

The section on *Danzas* (p. 425-452) includes many descriptive notes on Venezuelan dances. See *cachupín, cambullón, charandé, joropo, para, sambe,* etc.

Silva Uzcátegui, R. D. El tamunangue *El universal,* Caracas (12 Feb. 1941). **[2687]**

Studies the popular *El tamunangue.* From the chapter *Música y músicos del estado Lara,* of the *Enciclopedia Larense.* [E. Planchart.]

Trujillo, Teófilo. El tamunangue, tema de actualidad. *El universal,* Caracas (8 Mar. 1941). **[2688]**

Studies the dance *El tamunangue,* of the state of Lara, covering its origin and the etymology of its name. The author cites various historical facts of folkloric value, which explain the formation of this popular Venezuelan dance. [E. Planchart.]

SUPPLEMENT TO 1960

An extremely valuable contribution to the musical history of Venezuela was made by the publication in 1958 of José Antonio Calcaño's *La ciudad y su música: Crónica musical de Caracas* (item 1064a). While, as the title indicates, this is limited to a chronicle of music in Caracas, it is virtually a compendium of Venezuelan musical history, since this has been so largely concentrated in the capital. In his preface the author begins by observing that "Music is essentially a social art". He maintains, therefore, that its history is inseparable from that of its social setting. His work purports to be *una crónica de la ciudad y su música* —"a chronicle of the city and its music".

Emphasizing the importance of Padre Pedro Palacios y Sojo (*vide supra*), Calcaño entitles his first and second chapters, respectively, "Antes del Padre Sojo", and "La época del Padre Sojo", The first important musical figure is that of Francisco Pérez Camacho (1659-*ca.* 1725), who was the first Professor of Music at the University of Caracas. The first member of a famous musical family, Ambrosio Carreño, was born in 1721. During "The Period of Padre Sojo", musical activity in Caracas developed rapidly, and more than thirty composers flourished in his circle, together with fifty executants. "Por esto ocupa el Padre Palacios y Sojo en nuestra historia musical el alto sitio de un verdadero patriarca del arte."

We cannot here trace in detail the course of Calcaño's chronicle, especially since it covers very much the same ground that was described in the original introduction to this section of the *Guide* (*vide supra*). Suffice it to say that Calcaño's work is more thoroughly documented and therefore more reliable, than previous works on this subject (such as Ramón de la Plaza's). Through it we are able to follow the course of musical activity throughout every phase of Venezuelan history, including the vicissitudes of the War for Independence and the civil struggles of the republican era. The references to the growth of urban popular music are numerous and illuminating (e. g., the section on the *valse criollo*, pp. 382-289).

Calcaño's work contains an appendix on Historical Sources, an extensive bibliography, an index of names, and a detailed table of contents. Not to be overlooked are the numerous interesting illustrations. The volume, it should be added, is printed on exceptionally fine paper (a heavy, glossy stock).

An authoritative monograph on Padre Sojo was published in 1958 by Juan B. Plaza (item 1068a) with a reproduction of a very fine portrait of the composer made during his visit to Rome in 1769. Various documents relating to Padre Sojo are published in the Appendix, together with two facsimiles. Plaza's history of music during the Colonial period has not yet been published as of this writing.

In the field of folk music, mention must he made of an important monograph by Luis Felipe Ramón y Rivera, titled *El Joropo, baile nacional de Venezuela,* published in 1953 (item 1052a). Although dealing specifically with a single type of dance, this study sheds much light on Venezuelan folk music as a whole, and indeed does a great deal to clarify the whole question of *criollo* folk music and its evolution. Excellent photographs, numerous musical notations, and a scrupulous documentation, make this monograph a model of its kind. In the same category of value is the monograph on the *polo* by Isabel Aretz (no. 1017a). Both of these eminent folklorists (husband and wife) have published many more articles than it has been feasible to include here.

BIBLIOGRAPHY

(A) PRIMITIVE, FOLK, AND POPULAR MUSIC

Álbum de música folklórica del estado Táchira; edición ordenada por el Ministerio de relaciones interiores, con ocasión de la exposición nacional celebrada en conmemoración del centenario del traslado de los restos del Libertador a Caracas. Caracas, 1943 (?), 10 p. **[1012a]**

Arrangements of 17 *bambucos, valses, canciones* and a *pasillo.*

Alvarado, Lisandro. Música y danza entre los aborígenes venezolanos. *Rev. nac. cultura,* v. 7, no. 50 (1945), p. 17-37. **[1013a]**

Two chapters from the author's book, *Datos etnográficos de Venezuela.*

Aretz, Isabel. Correlaciones entre las flautas de pan venezolanas y las andinas de alta cultura. *Bol. indigenista venez.,* v. 6, nos. 1-4 (1958). **[1014a]**

——. Das dreitonsystem in der sudamerikanischen volksmusik. *Sudamerica,* v. 1 (July 1950), p. 43-47. **[1015a]**

——. El maremare como expresión musical y coreográfica. *Bol. inst. folk. ven.,* v. 3, no. (July 1958), p. 45-108. **[1016a]**

The entire issue is devoted to this important and authoritative study of the *maremare,* an indigenous dance of Venezuela which has undergone many transformations since colonial times (it is more a generic term than a specific designation). With 27 music notations and 3 photographs. Bibliography.

——. El polo. Historia — música — poesía. *Bol. inst. folk.,* v. 3, no. 6 (Dec. 1959), p. 227-273. **[1017a]**

This entire number of the *Boletín* is devoted to a detailed and densely documented study of what has become a widely diffused type of Venezuelan folk music. Contains textual and musical analyses, with 33 musical notations, a catalog of field recordings, and a bibliography. The author concludes that the Venezuelan *polo* is recognizable only by its music, since it has no specific poetic pattern. Its relationship to the Andalusian *polo* of Spain is tenuous, consisting mainly of the use of a somewhat similar cadence, which is considerably modified in the Venezuelan version.

——. El tamunangue. Separata from *Folklore americano,* Lima, 1956. 96 p. **[1018a]**

——. La fiesta de los diablos. *Rev. ven. folk.,* v. 1, no. 2 (July-Dec. 1947), p. 91-110. **[1019a]**

——. La Fiesta de San Juan en Cúpira. *Bol. inst. folk.,* v. 2, no. 2 (Aug. 1955), p. 57-61. **[1020a]**

Festival of St. John the Baptist, in Cúpira, State of Miranda, Venezuela. Details of official celebrations, and popular ones, with particular attention to dances. No music.

——. Música de los Estados Aragua y Guárico. Los tonos de velorio. *Rev. ven. folk.,* v. 1, no. 2 (July-Sept. 1947, i. e., 1948), p. 47-78. **[1021a]**

Summary of the study of a field collection trip undertaken in November 1947 by the author and her husband, Luis Felipe Ramón y Rivera. 160 disc recordings were made. 29 music notations, several of three-voice singing, with accompaniment of *cuatro.* (C. S.)

——. Músicas pentatónicas en Sudamérica. *Arch. ven. folk.,* año 1 (July-Dec. 1951), p. 283-309. **[1022a]**

——. Organización del archivo y de la sección de musicología del Servicio de investigaciones folklóricas nacionales. *Rev. ven. folk.*, v. 1, no. 1 (1947), p. 165-172. **[1023a]**

On methods in field working and collecting, organizing and studying materials, bibliographical investigation, collections of books, music and recordings, and popular diffusion of materials. (R. S. B.)

——. Reseña de las investigaciones sobre las músicas del pueblo venezolano. *Educación*, Caracas, v. 8, no. 147 (Feb.-Mar. 1947), p. 98-108. **[1024a]**

Survey of work done in collecting and studying Venezuelan folkmusic, including a few of the older publications, beginning with Ramon de la Plaza's Ensayo sobre el arte in Venezuela, 1883, and ending with current activity of the past 10 years. (R. S. B.)

——, L. F. Ramón y Rivera, and Abilio Reyes. Baile de la candelaria. *Bol. inst. folk. ven.*, v. 2, no. 8 (Nov. 1957), p. 294-303. **[1025a]**

Description of the dance, with diagrams and 6 photographs.

Calcaño, José Antonio. La música folklórica del llano. *El país* (Caracas), 16 March 1947, 2nd part, p. 9-10. **[1026a]**

Carreño, Francisco, and Abel Vallmitjana. Comentarios sobre el origen indígena del Mare-Mare criollo. *Rev. venez. folklore*, v. 1, no. 1 (Jan.-June 1947), p. 67-78. il. (music). **[1027a]**

It has generally been assumed that there are two types of *Mare Mare*, the indigenous and the *criollo*, unrelated to each other. The authors of this paper maintain, on the contrary, that there is a close relation between the two types; more precisely, that the *Mare Mare* is essentially a *criollo* species with aboriginal antecedents. To document this thesis, they demonstrate the process whereby the "criollización" of an indigenous *Mare Mare* takes place. The *Mare Mare* may be sung or danced, or both together. Its name is derived from the indigenous type of pan-pipes, called *mare* in Venezuela. Seven music notations and 2 photographs.

Domínguez, Luiz Arturo. Aspectos del folklore del Estado Falcón. *Rev. ven. folk.*, v. 1, no. 1 (Jan.-June 1947), p. 91-119. **[1028a]**

About 30 folk practices, including songs and dances. One briefly described. (C. S.)

Fiesta de San Benito. *Bol. inst. folk. ven.*, v. 2, no. 5 (Dec. 1956), p. 149-187. **[1029a]**

The entire issue is devoted to the description of the Fiesta of San Benito ("Benito el Moro" or San Benito de Palermo), which is celebrated in various regions of Venezuela. Illustrated with photographs, line drawings, diagrams. and music notations.

Lauro, Antonio. Orfeones estudiantiles y restauración de nuestro folklore. *Rev. nac. cultura*, v. 4, no. 32 (1944), p. 138-140. **[1030a]**

Appeals to student choruses or singing societies to nurture the truly Venezuelan element of their folk music and spurn foreign influences and local decadence. (R. S. B.)

Laya, J. C. La gaita. *Bol. inst. folk. ven.*, v. 2, no. 7 (July 1957), p. 227-254. **[1031a]**

Authoritative study of this type of Venezuelan folksong, with 25 music notations.

Liscano, Juan. Apuntes para la investigación del negro en Venezuela. Sus instrumentos de música. *Acta ven.*, v. 1, no. 4 (Apr.-June 1946), p. 421-440. **[1032a]**

Brief account of historical background and of some instruments. Some critical conclusions. Eight reproductions of photographs of drums and drummers. (C. S.) Also published separately (see next item).

——. Apuntes para la investigación del negro en Venezuela. Sus instrumentos de música. Caracas, Tipografía Garrido, 1947, 22 p. il. **[1033a]**

The book is divided into two parts. The first deals with the historical process of acculturation of the Negro in Venezuela. The second is a description of popular instruments, most of them drums, from the North-Central coast of the country.

——. Baile de tambor. *Bol. soc. venez. cien. nat.*, v. 8, no. 55 (Apr.-June 1943), p. 245-251.   **[1034a]**

Information on Afro-Venezuelan folk traditions in song and dance in the coastal region from Zulia to Sucre. (C. S.)

——. Hear the people sing. *Américas,* v. 1, no. 5 (July 1949), p. 12-15, 34-35.   **[1035a]**

The author describes various experiences while collecting in the field. Excellent photographs.

——. Las fiestas del solsticio de verano en el folklore de Venezuela. Caracas, Venezuela, Imprenta de la Dirección de cultura, Ministerio de educación nacional, 1947. 32 p. il.   **[1036a]**

Separata de la *Rev. nac. cultura,* no. 63, julio-agosto de 1947.

——. Poesía popular venezolana; colección, notas y selección. Caracas, SVMA, eds. al servicio de la cultura, 1945. 62 p. (Cuaderno no. 16).   **[1037a]**

Words only of 101 *coplas, 9 décimas, 3 corridos,* collected by the author.

——. Venezuela's devil dancers. *Américas,* v. 4, no. 8 (Aug. 1952), p. 24-25 and two pages of photographs.   **[1038a]**

Brief account of the tradition of devil dancers on the day of the Corpus Cristi festival, tracing it from the early Middle Ages to Venezuela today. 12 photographs of the dancers of San Francisco de Yare, in Miranda State, Venezuela.

——, **and Charles Seeger.** Venezuelan folk music. Washington, D. C., The Library of Congress, Music Division Recording Laboratory ,n. d. 26 p.   **[1039a]**

Notes for Album XV of Folk Music of the Americas issued from the Collections of the Archive of American Folk Song.

Machado, José E. Cancionero popular; nota biográfica y comentario de Alberto Arvelo Torrealba. Caracas, Ed. del Ministerio de educación nacional, 1946. 117 p.   **[1040a]**

Olivares Figueroa, Rafael. Cancionero popular del niño venezolano; segundo volumen. Caracas, Ministerio de educación nacional, 1946. 25 p. (Biblioteca venezolana de cultura)   **[1041a]**

Words and music of 20 well-selected folksongs and ballads, children's and game songs, lullabies, etc., for use in schools, to initiate Venezuelan children from an artistic point of view, into a national atmosphere and good taste, in material most suitable for their comprehension and assimilation. (R. S. B.)

——. Cancionero popular del niño venezolano; 1º y 2º grados. Caracas, Ministerio de educación nacional, 1946. 20 p.   **[1042a]**

Words and music of 15 folksongs for Venezuelan school children.

——. Diversiones pascuales en Oriente. *Rev. ven. folk.*, v. 1, no. 1 (Jan.-June 1947), p. 81-90.   **[1043a]**

On the kind of *comparsa* that appears at Christmas time in the eastern states of Venezuela, founded upon the indigenous theme of *El pájaro guarandoly.* Two music notations. (C. S.) (Cf. next item)

——. Diversiones pascuales en Oriente y otros ensayos. Caracas, Ed. Ardor. 1949. 191 p. il. (music).   **[1044a]**

All the essays in this volume are of interest from the aspect of musical folklore in Venezuela. Among the topics dealt with are the *aguinaldo,* the carnival in Venezuela, the *tamunangue* (a religious folk dance and song), and music for the festival of St. John the Baptist. There are illustrations (drawings) showing typical musical instruments. Includes 11 music examples, most of them arranged by V. E. Sojo and previously published in other collections. Contains the words of numerous other songs.

——. Folklore venezolano. El folklore en la escuela. *Onza, tigre y león,* v. 8, no. 79 (1946), p. 5-7, 22; 80, p. 6-7, 22-24; no. 81, p. 21-24; no. 83, p. 20-22; no. 84, p. 17-21; no. 85, p. 16-22; no. 88, p. 14-17; v. 9, no. 89, p. 21-23.   **[1045a]**

A series of short articles upon various aspects of folklore, most of them involving music. No music notations, however, are given. (C. S.)

———. Observaciones sobre el sentido y letra de El tamunangue. *Farol*, v. 9, no. 100 (Sept. 1947), p. 16-20. **[1046a]**
Semi-ritual dance observed in the state of Lara. Brief bibliography. (C. S.)

———. Reflexiones sobre la canción de coro en Venezuela. *Rev. nac. cultura*, v. 7, no. 52 (Sept.-Oct. 1945), p. 145-151. **[1047a]**
Brief but careful notes on some children's game songs with special reference to "La Viudita" and its variants. (C. S.)

Ramón y Rivera, Luis Felipe. Aguinaldos venezolanos. *Nosotros Caracas*, no. 98 (Dec. 1956). **[1048a]**

———. Cantos de trabajo del pueblo venezolano. Caracas, Fundación Eugenio Mendoza, 1955. 55 p. il. (music). **[1049a]**
The able director of the Folklore Institute of Venezuela has written here an admirable monograph on the work songs of Venezuela, including an introduction on the environment and function of these songs, analysis of 22 melodies (plus 6 cries of street vendors), and photographs illustrating the various tasks associated with the songs.

———. Consideraciones sobre un instrumento y música de los indios guajiros. *Acta ven.*, v. 2, no. 1-4 (July 1946-June 1947), p. 104-115. **[1050a]**
The *uótoroyo*, a free-wind instrument, with some relation to the bombard and the Venezuelan gaita zuliana, is thought by the author to produce sounds in inferior resonance. Six notations (transcribed from recordings of singing) are given. (C. S.)

———. Dos cantos de Apure. *Elite*, no. 981 (22 July 1944). **[1051a]**

———. El joropo: baile nacional de Venezuela. Caracas, Ministerio de Educación, Dirección de cultura y bellas artes 1953. 92 p. plus 31 pages of music, unnumbered. **[1052a]**

———. El pasaje apureño. *Bol. inst. folk.*

ven., v. 2, no. 4 (June 1956), p. 125-138. **[1053a]**
The designation *pasaje* is given to "a type of music that is executed alternately by the harpist and the singer, in all the region of the valleys of Aragua and Miranda..." This music is "de cultísima ascendencia". Illustrated with 5 music notations.

———. El seis. *Bol. inst. folk. ven.*, v. 3, no. 4 (March 1959), p. 1-38. **[1054a]**
The entire issue is devoted to this careful study of various musical species that are used to accompany the dance known as *joropo*, and which have different names, such as *Seis por ocho, Seis figurao, Seis corrido*, etc. With 16 music notations and numerous texts.

———. El vals venezolano. *Rev. shell*, Caracas, no. 22 (March 1957). **[1055a]**

———. Historia de las vacas. *Bol. inst. folk. ven.*, v. 2, no. 8 (Nov. 1957), p. 267-270. **[1056a]**
Includes words and melody of the *Canto de "La historia de las vacas"*, which has to do with the legendary character called Florentino, who appears in Venezuelan folklore as a man who competed with the Devil in a singing contest —and won.

———. La anonimia en el folklore musical. *Educación*, no. 44 (Aug.-Sept. 1946). **[1057a]**

———. La música popular de Venezuela. Buenos Aires, Publicación de la embajada de Venezuela, n. d. unpaged. (music). **[1058a]**
A very concise introduction to the subject, consisting of 18 pages, with 3 musical examples.

———. La polifonía popular de Venezuela. Separata de la *Revista del Instituto Nacional de la Tradición*, Dic. de 1949, no. 2 (i. e., v. 1, entrega 2, July-Dec. 1948, p. 168-208). Buenos Aires, 1949. 29 p. (music). **[1059a]**
Data based on field recording trip made in 1947 toward the central region of Venezuela. "Cuadro sinóptico de la investigación realizada", p. 29. Distribution map,

tonos (three voices) and 9 briefer musical notations. A careful and thoroughly documented study.

——. Los negritos. *Bol. inst. folk. ven.,* v. 2, no. 8 (Nov. 1957), p. 303-306. **[1060a]**

Text of this traditional dramatic dance, with music of the part that is sung.

——. Un auto sacramental venezolano. *El farol,* Caracas, no. 167 (Nov. 1956) **[1061a]**

——, and **Isabel Aretz.** Viaje de investigación a Pregonero. *Bol. inst. folk.,* v. 2, no. 1 (June 1955), p. 1-37. (entire issue). **[1062a]**

Pregonero is the capital of the Uribante district in the State of Táchira, Venezuela. Most of the material related to Christmas celebration, as observed there Dec. 16, 1954 to January 6, 1955. Song texts of Procesión de Posadas, verses for the Canto de Aguinaldas (p. 14-18). Analysis of music (p. 18-24) includes 6 melodies. Brief observations added on local beliefs, dialect, customs, games, domestic industries, food, etc. 4 photographs and many drawings.

Reyes Ochoa, Abilio. Descripción del baile del joropo. *Bol. inst. folk. ven.,* v. 3, no. 1 (March 1958), p. 26-31. **[1063a]**

Choreographic directions, with diagrams.

(B) ART MUSIC AND MISCELLANEOUS

Calcaño, José Antonio. La ciudad y su música. Crónica musical de Caracas. Caracas. Caracas. Edición y distribución "Conservatorio Teresa Carreño", 1958. 518 p. il. (music). **[1064a]**

A monograph that studies with lavish detail and impressive erudition the musical activity of Caracas from colonial times to the present. Starting from the premise that "Music is essentially a social art", the author relates all musical events to their historical and social background. An Appendix lists the historical sources for each chapter. There is a bibliography and an index of proper names. (See the Introduction to this section, above.)

Estévez y Gálves, Camilo Antonio. Historia y teoría de la música elemental y superior. Caracas, Tip. americana, 1916. 44 p. **[1065a]**

A general elementary history of music, with the following paragraphs on Venezuelan music: p. 22 — "El arte musical venezolano en la época colonial"; p. 24 — "La música moderna en Venezuela"; p. 28 — "Artistas venezolanos de actualidad" and p. 37 — "La música en diversos estados venezolanos".

Milinowski, Marta. This was Carreño. *Américas,* v. 5, no. 9 (Sep. 1953), p. 10-12,, 44-45. **[1066a]**

Short biographical account of world-famous Venezuelan pianist Teresa Carreño. 7 photographs.

Plaza, Juan Bautista. Don Bartolomé Bello, músico. *Rev. nac. cultura,* v. 5, no. 39 (July-Aug. 1943), p. 5-14. **[1067a]**

The father of Andrés Bello was for 13 years a singer in the choir of the cathedral of Caracas.

——. El Padre Sojo. Caracas, Imprenta del ministerio de educación, 1958. 56 p. il. (port.) **[1068a]**

Separata from the *Revista nacional de cultura* (no. 124, Sept.-Oct. 1957). An important monograph on "the patriarch of Venezuelan music".

——. Juan Manuel Olivares, el más antiguo compositor venezolano. *Rev. nac. cultura,* v. 8, no. 63 (July-Aug. 1947), p. 105-123. **[1069a]**

Careful study, making public for the first time discovery of the date of birth of the composer (1760), who died in 1797. Two facsimile reproductions, one of music notation, the other of handwriting of the composer. (C. S.)

——. Música colonial venezolana. *Bol. progr. Col.,* v. 19, no. 187 (Feb. 1960), p. 71-76. **[1070a]**

With 3 illustrations. A concise but authoritative account.

Rojas, Aristides. Estudios históricos. (Serie primera). Caracas, Lit. y tip. del comercio, 1926, 337 pp. **[1071a]**

"Noticias sobre el arte musical en Caracas", p. 304-309, includes data on the origins of musical instruction in Caracas, with the formation of a school of plainsong by the Cabildo Metropolitano in 1640; the first choirmaster of the cathedral, P. Gonzalo Cordero, appointed in 1671; the "school of Chacao" grouped around the personalities of Padre Sojo and Don Bartolomé Blandin; the musical influence of the German naturalists Bredemeyer and Schultz; and the leading composers up to the revolution of 1810.

"Orígenes del teatro de Caracas", p. 310-325, also contains brief references to music in the theatre, e. g., in the *Auto a nuestra señora del rosario*.

Valenti Ferro, Enzo. Venezuela: Entusiasmo y búsqueda. *B. A. mus.,* v. 12, no. 197 (Oct. 1, 1957), p. 8, 14.

[1072a]

Traces historical background of musical composition in Venezuela, then deals with various contemporary composers, among them J. B. Plaza,, Carlos E. Figueredo, J. A. Calcaño, Blanca Estrella, Angel Sauce, J. C. Laya, E. Castellanos, Antonio Estévez, A. Lauro, A. Sandoval, G. Castellanos, and Inocente Carreño.

WEST INDIES

Bowles, Paul. Calypso—music of the Antilles. *Mod. music,* v. 17, no. 5 (1940), p. 154-159. **[2689]**

Charlevoix, Pierre François Xavier de. Histoire de l'isle espagnole ou de St. Dominique. Amsterdam, F. L. Honoré, 1733. 4 v. F1911.C47 **[2690]**

Vol. 1, p. 51-52 treats of the songs and dances of the Antilleans, with a description of a large cylindrical drum used in their ceremonies.

Clark, Evans. Catalogue of Latin American and West Indian dances and songs in the record collection of Evans Clark. [New York?], 1941. 114 p. ML138.C54 **[2691]**

Reproduced from type-written copy.

Cunard, Nancy, comp. Negro anthology ... 1931-1933. London, Wishart & co., 1934. 854 p. il. HT1521.C8 **[2692]**

Porto Rico, p. 400-401, West Indies, 346-400. Contains music.

Dunn, Henry. Guatimala [sic]. New York, G. & C. Carvill, 1828. 318 p. F-1464.D92 **[2693]**

West Indian dancing, p. 20; making of musical instruments, p. 111.

Encyclopedie van Nederlandsch West-Indië onder redactie van Dr. H. D. Benjamins en Joh. F. Snelleman. 's-Gravenhage, M. Nijhoff, 1914-17. **[2694]**

Muziek-instrumenten en muziek, p. 494-499.

Fewkes, Jesse Walter. Aborigines of Porto Rico and neighboring islands. *In* Bureau of American ethnology, 25th report. Washington, Government printing office, 1907, p. 18-296. F1969.F4 **[2695]**

Includes: instruments of the West Indian islanders, p. 210; dance and music in Antillean ceremonies, p. 64-65; modern dances of the Gibaros, p. 68-69; Porto Rican music, p. 69; description of an Arawak burial dance, p. 72 (quoted from W. H. Brett, *The Indian tribes of Guiana);* for many other references to dances, see index under *areitos.*

Hearn, Lafcadio. Two years in the French West Indies. New York and London, Harper & brothers, 1923. 460 p. il. F2081.H442 **[2696]**

Appendix: Some Creole melodies.

Heilner, Van Campen. Beneath the Southern Cross. Boston, R. G. Badger, 1930. 203 p. il. F1611.H46 **[2697]**

"Folk songs of the West Indies", p. 193-202.

Schomberg, A. A. West Indian composers and musicians. *Opportunity,* v. 4 (1926), p. 353-356. **[2698]**

Shedd, Margaret. Carib dance patterns. *Theatre arts monthly* (Jan. 1933), p. 65-77. il. **[2699]**

See also entries under CUBA, DOMINICAN REPUBLIC, HAITI, JAMAICA, PUERTO RICO.

SUPPLEMENT TO 1960

Adams, Alton A. Whence came the calypso? *The Caribbean,* v. 8, no. 10 (1953), p. 218-220, 230, 235. **[1073a]**

Beckwith, Martha Warren. Jamaica folk-lore. With music recorded in the field by Helen H. Roberts. New York, G. E. Stechert Co., 1928. 137 p. il. (Memoirs of the American folklore society, v. 21). **[1074a]**

In a brief introduction the author discusses the English and Scottish origins of the folk games of the Jamaican Negroes and their significance in the social life of these people. The book is divided into two parts, one on Folk-games and the other on the festivities of *Christmas numming* (cf. items 1673 and 1674, *supra*). Numerous music notations are included.

Biguines et autres chansons de la Martinique. *Les temps modernes* (Paris), v. 5, no. 52 (Feb. 1950), p. 1397-1407.
[1075a]

Material from Coridun, *op. cit.* (item 1077a).

Braithwaite, Lloyd. The problem of cultural integration in Trinidad. *Soc. ec. stud.,* v. 3, no. 1 (June 1954), p. 82-96.
[1076a]

An interesting discussion of the quest for foci of cultural integration in an economically and ethnically differentiated society. Carnival and the steel band "movement" are among the cultural phenomena described. (S. W. M.)

Coridun, Victor. Folklore martiniquais. Le carnaval de Saint Pierre (Martinique). Fort-de-France, Imprimerie R. Illemay, 1930.
[1077a]

Espinet, Charles S., and Harry Pitts. Land of the calypso; origin and development of Trinidad's folksong. Port-of-Spain, Guardian commercial printery, 1944. 75 p. il.
[1078a]

Attempts to define calypso, to trace its origins through African, French and Spanish sources, and to set forth its history since 1898. There is also a general discussion of Afro-Caribbean rhythms in various types of dances and folksongs of Trinidad.

Holder, Geoffrey. That fad from Trinidad's folksong. Port-of-Spain, Guardian commercial printery, 1944. 75 p. il.
[1079a]

"It is Calypso, a joyous, sorrowful,

scandalous music, here defined by a man who first heard it from his mother".

Lindstrom, Carl E. The American quality in the music of Louis Moreau Gottschalk. *Mus. quart.,* v. 31, no. 3 (July 1945), p. 356-366.
[1080a]

Includes a few brief references to Gottschalk's ancestors of Haiti, his stay in the West Indies, and an anecdote about Acapulco, Mexico.

Ortiz Orderigo, Néstor R. El 'calipso', expresión musical de los negros de Trinidad. *In* Miscelánea de estudios dedicados al Dr. Fernando Ortiz por sus discípulos, colegas y amigos (La Habana, 1960).
[1081a]

Parsons, Elsie Clews. Folklore of the Antilles, French and English, Part II. New York, G. E. Stechert Co., 1936. 586 p. Part III, 1943. 487 p. (Memoirs of the American folklore society, v. 26).
[1082a]

Pearse, Andrew C. While Carriacou makes music and dances, we study... *Carib quart.,* v. 3, no. 1 (1953), p. 31-34.
[1083a]

Photographs and comments based on a brief visit to Carriacou in the Grenadines to collect data on the African-derived music and dances of that island. (S. W. M.)

Simpson, George E. Jamaican cult music. Introduction and notes. N. Y., Ethnic Folkways Library. (Album P461), 1954. 10 p.

A description of various types of cult music recorded in West Kingston, Jamaica, with some information on the historical and cultural background of the cults, musical forms, instruments, etc. (S. W. Mintz.)

Key to Periodicals

Acción social. Santiago, Chile. HD4835.C5A5 1926
Actualidades. Guatemala City, Guatemala
Acta musicol. Acta musicológica. Copenhagen, Denmark. ML5.16
Allgem. mus. zeit. Allgemeine musikalische zeitung. Leipzig. Germany. ML5.A43
Alma latina. San Juan, Puerto Rico. AP63.A543
Amer. anthrop. American anthropologist. New York, New York. GN1 A5
Amér. mus. América musical. Buenos Aires, Argentina. ML5.A51
América, Habana. Revista de la asociación de escritores y artistas americanos. Habana, Cuba
An. acad. nac. artes. let. Anales de la academia nacional de artes y letras. Habana, Cuba. AS71.H14
An. bibl. nac. Annaes da bibliotheca nacional. Rio de Janeiro, Brazil. Z1675.R58
An. inst. etnog. amer. Anales del instituto de etnografía americana. Mendoza, Argentina. E51.M45
An. inst. invest. est. Anales del instituto de investigaciones estéticas. México, D. F.
An. inst. pop. conf. Anales del instituto popular de conferencias. Buenos Aires, Argentina. AS78.16
An. museo nac. arqueol. hist. etnol. Anales del museo nacional de arqueología, historia y etnología. México, D. F. F1219.M7
An. soc. geog. hist. Guatemala. Anales de la sociedad de geografía e historia de Guatemala. Guatemala City, Guatemala. F1461.S67
An. univ. cent. Ecuador. Anales de la universidad central del Ecuador. Quito, Ecuador. AS83.Q8
An. univ. Santiago. Anales de la universidad de Chile. Santiago, Chile. AS81.S3
Andean monthly. Santiago, Chile
L'anthropologie. Paris, France. GN1.A68
Anthropos. Vienna, Austria. GN1.A7
Anuario brasileiro de literatura. Rio de Janeiro, Brazil. PQ9501.A6
Arch. anthrop. etnol. Archivio per l'antropologia e la etnologia. Florence, Italy. GN1.A8
Arch. folklore cub. Archivos del folklore cubano. Habana, Cuba. GR121.C8A15
Arch. musikf. Archiv für musikforschung. Leipzig, Germany. ML5.A628
Ars. Revista ars. Buenos Aires, Argentina
L'art musical. Paris, France. ML5.A655
Atenea. Revista mensual de ciencias, letras y artes. Concepción, Chile. AP63.A73
Atti. soc. rom. antrop. Società romana di antropologia, atti. Rome, Italy
Azul. Buenos Aires, Argentina. AP63.A92

Baes-arch. Baessler-archiv. Liepzig, Germany. GN1.B3
Báhoruco. Santo Domingo, Dominican Republic
Bol. acad. arg. letras. Boletín de la academia argentina de letras. Buenos Aires, Argentina. AS78.B55
Bol. ariel. Boletím de ariel. Rio de Janeiro, Brazil. AP66.B6
Bol. bibliog. antrop. amer. Boletín bibliográfico de antropología americana. Instituto panamericano de geografía e historia. Tacubaya, D. F., México. F1401.P153
Bol. bibliog., Lima. Boletín bibliográfico. Universidad mayor de San Marcos Lima, Peru. Z782.L77B
Bol. bim. com. chil. coop. intel. Boletín bimestral de la comisión chilena de cooperación intelectual. Santiago, Chile
Bol. inst. musicol. Boletín del instituto mexicano de musicología y folklore. México, D. F. ML27.M417

Bol. lat. am. mús. Boletín latino-americano de música. Montevideo, Uruguay. ML199.B64

Bol. O. S. M. Boletín de la orquesta sinfónica de México. México, D. F. ML5.B668

Bol. soc. mex. geog. estad. Boletín de la sociedad mexicana de geografía y estadística. México, D. F. F1201.S67

Brazil. New York, New York. F116.B85

Brotería. Lisbon, Portugal. QH7.B87

Bull. hisp. Bulletin hispanique. Bordeaux, France. AS162.B73

Bull. mém. soc. anthrop. Bulletins et mémoirs de la société d'anthropologie de Paris. Paris, France. GN2.S61

Bull. pan amer. union. Bulletin of the pan American union. F1403.B955

Bull. soc. comp. musique. Bulletin de la société des compositeurs de musique. Paris, France. ML5.S578

Caecilia. Mainz, Germany. ML5.C12

Calif. folklore quart. California folklore quarterly

Caras y caretas. Revista semanal ilustrada. Buenos Aires, Argentina. AP63.C27

Christian scien. mon. Christian science monitor. Boston, Massachusetts

Claridad. Buenos Aires, Argentina. AP63.C466

The commonweal. New York, New York. AP2.C6897

Contemporáneos. México, D. F. AP63.C525

Correo mus. sud-am. Correo musical sud-americano. Buenos Aires, Argentina. ML5.C71

Cour. mus. Le courrier musical. Paris, France. ML5.C71

Crisol. México, D. F. AP63.C646

Cromos. Bogotá, Colombia. AP63.C665

Cuad. amer. Cuadernos americanos. México, D. F.

Cuad. cult. teatral. Cuadernos de cultura teatral. Instituto nacional de estudios de teatro. Buenos Aires, Argentina. PQ7683.A3

Cult. venezolana. Cultura venezolana. Caracas, Venezuela. AP63.C83

Cursos y conferencias. Revista del colegio libre de estudios superiores. Buenos Aires, Argentina. AS78.B7

Dancing times. London, England. GV1580.D34

Der Auftakt. Prague, Czechoslovakia. ML5.A68

Diario de la marina. Habana, Cuba.

Elite. Caracas, Venezuela. AP63.E55

Ensayos. Montevideo, Uruguay

Estud. afrocub. Estudios afrocubanos. Revista trimestral. Habana, Cuba.

Estudio. Barcelona, Spain. AP60.E87

Estudios acad. lit. del Plata. Estudios de la academia literaria del Plata. Buenos Aires, Argentina. AP63.E733

Ethnos. México, D. F. F1201.E84

Etude. The etude music magazine. Philadelphia, Pennsylvania. ML1.E8

Eurindia. Eurindia, panoramas de México. Revista de izquierda, de asuntos sociales y política continental. México, D. F. AP63.E8

Folklore. Boletín del departamento de folklore del instituto de cooperación universitaria. Buenos Aires, Argentina

Fomento agric. Fomento y agricultura. San Salvador, El Salvador.

Gaceta mus. Gaceta musical. Paris, France

Geog. rev. Geographical review. New York, New York. G1.G35

Globus. Brunswick, Germany. G1G57
Guide concert. Le guide du concert. Paris, France. ML5.G77

Harper's. Harper's monthly magazine. New York, New York. AP2.H3
Hisp. amer. hist. rev. Hispanic american historical review. Durham, North Carolina.
F1401.H66
Hisp. rev. Hispanic review. University of Pennsylvania. Philadelphia, Pennsylvania.
PQ6001.H5
Hispania. George Washington university. Washington, D. C. PC4001.H7

Ibero-amer. archiv. Ibero-amerikanisches archiv. Berlin, Germany. F1401.I24
Ibero-amer. rund. Ibero-amerikanisches rundschau. Hamburg, Germany. F1401.I25
Illus. bras. Ilustração brasileira. Rio de Janeiro, Brazil. AP66.I58
Illus. mus. Ilustração musical. Rio de Janeiro, Brazil
Ilus. peruana. Ilustración peruana. Lima, Perú
Inca. Revista trimestral de estudios antropológicos. Lima, Perú. F3402.I36
Inca chron. Inca chronicle. Lima, Perú
Int. amer. The inter-American. Washington, D. C. (Title changed from *The inter-
American monthly,* with v. 2, no. 1, Jan. 1943)
Int. amer. quart. The inter-American quarterly. Washington, D. C. F1401.I67 (Title
changed from *Quarterly journal of inter-American relations,* with v. 2, no. 1,
Jan. 1940)
Int. arch. ethnog. Internationales archiv für etnographie. Leiden, Holland. GN1.16
Isla. San Juan, Puerto Rico

Jour. amer. folklore. Journal of American folklore. New York, New York. GR1.J8
Jour. ethnol. soc. Journal of the ethnological society of London. London, England
GN2.E84
Jour. Negro hist. Journal of Negro history. Washington, D. C. E185.J86
Jour. Phila. orch. Journal of the Philadelphia orchestra. Philadelphia, Pennsylvania
MT125.P53
Jour. soc. amér. Journal de la société des Américanistes. Paris, France. E51.S
Jour. Wash. acad. scien. Journal of the Washington academy of sciences. Washington
D. C. Q11.W32

Kollasuyo. Revista mensual de estudios bolivianos. La Paz. Bolivia. F3301.K6

Lanterna verde. Boletím da sociedade Felipe d'Oliveira. Rio de Janeiro, Brazil. AP66.L3
Lasso. Buenos Aires, Argentina. F2801.L36
Letras. Letras de México. México, D. F.
Letras, Brazil. São Paulo, Brazil
Letras, Méx. Publicación literaria y bibliográfica. México, D. F.
El libro de la cultura. Barcelona, Spain
Lippincott's mag. Lippincott's monthly magazine. New York, New York. AP2.L55
Lit. digest. The literary digest. New York, New York. AP2.L50

Masterkey. Bulletin of the Southwest museum. Los Angeles, California. E51.M42
Mens. jorn. com. Mensario do jornal do comercio. Rio de Janeiro, Brazil. AP66.J66
Mercurio mus. Mercurio musical. Buenos Aires, Argentina. ML5.M23
Mex. folkways. Mexican folkways. México, D. F. F1201.M5
Mex. life. Mexican life. México, D. F. F1201.M54
Mex.mag. Mexican magazine. México, D. F. F1201.M56
Méx. mus. México musical. México, D. F.
Mod. music. Modern music. New York, New York. ML1.M178

Modern Mexico. New York, New York. HC131.M6

Mon. educ. común. El monitor de la educación común; órgano del consejo nacional de educación. Buenos Aires, Argentina. L45.M6

Monde mus. Le monde musical. Paris, France. ML5.M53

Montevideo musical. Montevideo, Uruguay. ML5.M54

Month. mus. record. Monthly musical record. London, England. ML5.M6

Mundo mus. Mundo musical. Buenos Aires, Argentina. ML5.M63

Mus. advance. Musical advance. New York, New York. ML1.M357

Mus. Amer. Musical America. New York, New York. ML1.M384

Mus. cour. Musical courier. New York, New York. ML1.M43

Mús. de Amér. Música de América. Buenos Aires, Argentina. ML5.M714

Mus. digest. Musical digest. New York, New York. ML1.M44

Mus. educ. jour. Music educators journal. Chicago, Illinois. ML1.M234

Mus. monitor. Musical monitor. New York, New York. ML1.M678

Mus. observer. Musical observer. New York, New York. ML1.M696

Mus. opinion. Musical opinion. London,England. ML5.M78

Mus. quart. Musical quarterly. New York, New York. ML1.M725

Mus. record. The musical record. Philadelphia, Pennsylvania. ML1.M736

Mus. times. Musical times. London, England. ML5.M85

Mús. viva. Música viva. Rio de Janeiro, Brazil. ML5.M7517

Museum jour. Journal of the museum of the university of Pennsylvania. Philadelphia, Pennsylvania. AM101.P34

Music news. Chicago, Illinois. ML1.M27

Música. Buenos Aires, Argentina. ML5.M7133

Música, Bogotá. Órgano de la orquesta sinfónica nacional. Bogotá, Colombia. ML-5.M715

Música, Chile. Música; publicación mensual. Santiago, Chile. ML5.M713

Música, México. Música, revista mexicana. México, D. F.

Musicalia. Habana, Cuba. ML5.M874

Musik und volk. Kassel, Germany. ML5.M905

Musique. Musique; revue mensuelle. Paris, France. ML5.M974

La nación. Buenos Aires, Argentina

Nat. geog. mag. National geographic magazine. Washington, D. C. G1.N27

The nation. New York, New York. AP2.N2

Nativa. Buenos Aires, Argentina. F2801.N27

Neue musikzeitung. Stuttgart, Germany. ML5.N32

New Mex. anthrop. New Mexico anthropologist. Albuquerque, New Mexico. E77.N45

New Mex. hist. rev. New Mexico historical review. Santa Fe, New Mexico. F791.N65

New mus. rev. New music review. New York, New York. ML1.N36

Neza. Revista de cultura zapoteca. México, D. F.

Norte. Revista continental. New York, New York

Nosotros. Buenos Aires, Argentina. AP63.N6

Nouv. arch. miss. scien. litt. Nouvelles archives des missions scientifiques et littéraires. Paris, France. AS162.F82

Nuestro México. México, D. F.

Opera. The opera. New York, New York. ML1.O45

Orbe. Habana, Cuba. AP63.O7

Palacio. El palacio. Santa Fe, New Mexico. E791.P15

Panam. mag. Panamerican magazine. New York, New York

Panorama. Pan American union. Washington, D. C.

Para todos. San Salvador, El Salvador. AP63.P34

Plus ultra. Buenos Aires, Argentina. AP63.P687

Preludios. Órgano de la asociación argentina de música de cámara. Buenos Aires, Argentina. ML5.P7

La prensa. Buenos Aires, Argentina

Progressive education. Washington, D. C. L11.P935

Pro-musica. Pro-musica quarterly. New York, New York. ML1.P78

Quarterly journal of inter-American relations. See Inter-American quarterly

Quetzalcoatl. México, D. F.

Rep. diario Salvador. Repertorio del diario de Salvador. San Salvador, El Salvador. AP63.R45

A república. Fortaleza, Brazil

Res. mus. Resenha musical. São Paulo, Brazil. ML5.R196

Rev. acad. letras. Revista das academias de letras. Rio de Janeiro, Brazil

Rev. am. lat. Revue de l'Amérique latine. Paris, France. F1401.R45

Rev. amauta. Revista amauta. Lima, Peru

Rev. amer. Revista americana de Buenos Aires. Buenos Aires, Argentina. AP63.R485

Rev. arch. bibl. nac. Revista del archivo y biblioteca nacionales. Tegucigalpa, Honduras. F1501.R45

Rev. arg. Revue argentine. Paris, France

Rev. arq. mun. São Paulo. Revista do arquivo municipal de São Paulo. São Paulo, Brazil. F2651.S2R4

Rev. arqueol. Lima. Revista de arqueología. Lima, Perú

Rev. arte. Revista de arte. Santiago, Chile. N3.R37

Rev. arte, bol. mens. Revista de arte, boletín mensual. Universidad de Chile. Santiago, Chile

Rev. assoc. bras. mus. Revista da associação brasileira de música. Rio de Janeiro, Brazil. ML5.R2

Rev. bim. cub. Revista bimestre cubana. Habana, Cuba. AP63.R5

Rev. bras. mús. Revista brasileira de música. Rio de Janeiro, Brazil. ML5.R198

Rev. Brasil. Revista do Brasil. Rio de Janeiro, Brazil. AP66.R55

Rev. chil. hist. geog. Revista chilena de historia y geografía. Sanitago, Chile. F3051.R45

Rev. Chile. Revista Chile. New York, New York

Rev. circ. altos estud. Revista del círculo de altos estudios. Rosario, Argentina

Rev. Españas. Revista de las Españas. Madrid, Spain

Rev. fac. cien. jur. soc. Revista de la facultad de ciencias jurídicas y sociales. Guatemala City, Guatemala. H8.G8

Rev. fac. letras cien. Revista de la facultad de letras y ciencias. Habana, Cuba. AS-71.H2

Rev. folklore chileno. Revista de folklore chileno. Santiago, Chile. GR1.R3

Rev. geog. amer. Revista geográfica americana. Buenos Aires, Argentina. G1.R4

Rev. hisp. Revue hispanique. Paris, France. PQ6001.R5

Rev. hisp. mod. Revista hispánica moderna. Columbia university. New York, New York. PQ6001.R47

Rev. Indias. Revista de las Indias. Bogotá, Colombia

Rev. inst. etnol. univ. Tucumán. Revista del instituto de etnología de la universidad de Tucumán. Tucumán, Argentina. F2801.T93

Rev. inst. hist. geog. bras. Revista do instituto histórico e geográphico brasileiro. Rio de Janeiro, Brazil. F2501.I6

Rev. inst. hist. geog. Rio Grande do Sul. Revista do instituto histórico e geográphico do Rio Grande do Sul. Porto Alegre, Brazil. F2621.I55

Rev. int. mus. danse. Revue internationale de musique et de danse. Paris, France. ML5.R57

Rev. mex. estud. hist. Revista mexicana de estudios históricos. México, D. F. F1201.R46
Rev. mex. soc. Revista mexicana de sociología. México, D. F. H8.R53
Revista militar del Perú. Lima, Perú. U4.P5
Rev. min. instr. púb. Revista del ministerio de instrucción pública. San Salvador, El
 Salvador
Rev. mus. arg. Revista musical argentina. Buenos Aires, Argentina. ML5.R255
Rev. mus. cat. Revista musical catalana. Barcelona, Spain. ML5.R255
Rev. mus., Costa Rica. Revista musical. San José, Costa Rica. ML5.R218
Rev. mus., Guatemala. La revista musical. Guatemala City, Guatemala. ML5.R22
Rev. mus. mex. Revista musical mexicana. México, D. F. ML5.R288
Rev. mus. Méx. Revista musical de México. México, D. F.
Rev. museo nac., Lima. Revista del museo nacional. Lima, Perú. F3401.L56
Rev. música. Revista de música. Buenos Aires, Argentina. ML5.R21
Rev. musicale. La revue musicale. Paris, France. ML5.R613
Rev. nac. Revista nacional. Montevideo, Uruguay. AP63.R676
Rev. nac. cultura. Revista nacional de cultura. Caracas, Venezuela. AP63.C83
Rev. nac. turismo. Revista nacional de turismo. México, D. F.
Rev. soc. amigos arqueol. Revista de la sociedad de amigos de la arqueología. Monte-
 video, Uruguay. F2701.R63
Rev. sud.-am. Revue sud-américaine. Paris, France. AP20.R65
Rev. univ. cat. boliv. Revista de la universidad católica bolivariana. Sucre, Bolivia
Rev. univ. cent. Revista de la universidad central. Tegucigalpa, Honduras. AS67.T4
Rev. univ. Chuquisaca. Revista de la universidad de Chuquisaca. Sucre, Bolivia
Rev. univ., Cuzco. Revista universitaria. Cuzco, Perú. LE66.C8
Romance. Revista popular hispanoamericana. México, D. F.

Samlb. int. mus. gesell. Sammelbände der internationalen musikgesellschaft. Leipzig,
 Germany. ML5.I66
Schola cantorum. Revista de cultura sacro musical. Morelia, México. ML5.S27
Senderos. Órgano de la biblioteca nacional de Bogotá. Bogotá, Colombia. AP63.S47
Signale. Signale für die musikalische welt. Berlin, Germany. ML5.S57
Síntesis. Buenos Aires, Argentina. AP63.S5
El sonido 13. México, D. F. ML65.S65
South. folk. quart. Southern folklore quarterly. Gainesville, Florida. GR1.S65
Southw. mus. Southwestern musician. Arlington, Texas. ML1.S85
Surv. graph. Survey graphic. New York, New York. HV1.S82

Tres "3". Lima, Perú
Turismo. Revista peruana de viajes, artes y actualidad. Lima, Perú

Univ. Méx. Universidad de México. México, D. F. AS63.U6
El universal. México, D. F.

Verbum. Buenos Aires, Argentina. AP63.V43
Villa-Lobos. Mensário de cultura. Baurú, Brazil

Weco. Organ of Carlos Wehrs e companhia. Rio de Janeiro, Brazil

Ymer. Stockholm, Sweden. GN1.Y5

Zeit. ethnol. Zeitschrift für ethnologie. Berlin, Germany. GN1.Z4
Zeit. musik. Zeitschrift für musik. Leipzig, Germany. ML5.N4
Zeit. vergl. musikw. Zeitschrift für vergleichende musikwissenschaft. Berlin, Germany
 ML5.Z39

SUPPLEMENTARY LIST

Acta anthrop. Acta antropológica. México, D. F.
Afroamérica. México, D. F.
Americas. Pan American union, Washington, D. C. (published in English, Spanish and Portuguese editions)
Amér. indígena. América indígena, México, D. F.
An. museo nac. Anales del museo nacional "David J. Guzmán". San Salvador, El Salvador
An. soc. folk. Mex. Anuario de la sociedad folklórica de México. México, D. F.
Antártica. Santiago, Chile
Antr. hist. Antropología e historia de Guatemala. Guatemala City, Guatemala
Arch. ven. folk. Archivos venezolanos de folklore. Caracas, Venezuela
Arg. news. Argentine news. Buenos Aires, Argentina
Arte. Tolima, Colombia
Ateneo. Chiapas, México
Atica. Buenos Aires, Argentina

B. A. lit. Buenos Aires literario. Buenos Aires, Argentina
B. A. mus. Buenos Aires musical. Buenos Aires, Argentina
Bohemia. Habana, Cuba
Bol. arch. gen., México. Boletín del archivo general de la nación. México, D. F.
Bol. dep. mus. inst. nac. Boletín del departamento de música del instituto nacional de bellas artes. México, D. F.
Bol. inst. folk. ven. Boletín del instituto de folklore. Caracas, Venezuela
Bol. inst. invest. folk. Boletín del instituto de investigaciones folklóricas, Panamá
Bol. mus. artes. Boletín de música y artes visuales. Washington, D C.
Bol. museos. bibl. Boletín de museos y bibliotecas. Guatemala City, Guatemala
Bol. sem. cult. mex. Boletín del seminario de cultura mexicana. México, D. F.
Bol. soc. venez. cien. nat. Boletín de la sociedad venezolana de ciencias naturales. Caracas, Venezuela
Bol. unión panamer. Boletín de la unión panamericana. Washington, D. C.
Brasil mus. Brasil musical. Rio de Janeiro, Brazil
Bull. bur. d'ethnol. Bulletin du bureau d'ethnologie de la République d'Haiti. Port-au-Prince, Haiti

Car. mus. Carnet musical. México, D. F.
Car. quart. Caribbean quarterly. Port-of-Spain, Trinidad
Casa cult. ecuat. Casa de la cultura ecuatoriana. Quito, Ecuador
Clave. Bogotá, Colombia
Colombia. Bogotá, Colombia
Conservatorio. Habana, Cuba
Cuadernos. Cuadernos del congreso por la libertad de la cultura. Paris, France
Cult. peruana. Cultura peruana. Lima, Perú
Cult. polít. Cultura política. Rio de Janeiro, Brazil

Diario oficial. México, D. F.

Educación, Caracas. Caracas, Venezuela
Elite. Managua, Nicaragua
Escritura. Montevideo, Uruguay
Estud. amer. Estudios americanos. Sevilla, Spain
Estudios. Habana, Cuba

Folk-lore. London, England

Galpin soc. jour. Galpin society journal. London, England

Interamer. mus. bull. Inter-American music bulletin, Washington. D. C.
Ipna. Órgano del instituto cultural peruano-norteamericano. Lima, Perú

Jour. Amer. mus. soc. Journal of the American musicological society. (U. S. A.)
Jour. research mus. educ. Journal of research in music education, Ann Arbor, Mich.
(U. S. A.)

La música. Revista trimestral publicada por la sociedad de ediciones cubanas de música. Habana, Cuba
Lyra. Buenos Aires, Argentina

Mem. rev. ac. nac. cien. Memorias y revista de la academia nacional de ciencias
México, D. F.
Musica (Kassel). Kassel, Germany
Música, Lima, Perú
Mensuario. Mensuario de arte, literatura, historia y crítica. Habana, Cuba. (N. B.
Takes the name of the month in which it is published)
Micro. Bogotá, Colombia

Numen. México, D. F.

Oesterreichische musikzeitschrift. Vienna, Austria
Orientac. mus. Orientación musical. México, D. F.

Prod. camp. El productor campechano. Campeche, México
Prov. S. Pedro. Provincia de São Pedro. Porto Alegre, Brazil

Rev. América. Revista de América. Bogotá, Colombia
Rev. educ., Asunción. Revista de educación. Asunción, Paraguay
Rev. educ., Santiago. Revista de educación. Santiago, Chile
Rev. fac. hum. cien. Revista de la facultad de humanidades y ciencias. Universidad
de la República, Montevideo, Uruguay
Rev. fed. estud. Chuquisaca. Revista de la federación de estudiantes de Chuquisaca.
Sucre, Bolivia
Rev. Habana. Revista de La Habana. Habana, Cuba
Rev. I. F. A. L. La revue de l'institut français de l'Amérique latine. México, D. F.
Rev. mex. estud. antrop. Revista mexicana de estudios antropológicos. México, D. F.
Rev. museo nac. Guatemala. Revista del museo nacional de Guatemala. Guatemala
City, Guatemala
Rev. soc. escritores Chile. Revista de la sociedad de escritores de Chile. Santiago, Chile
Rev. univ. nac. Córdoba. Revista de la universidad nacional de Córdoba. Cordoba,
Argentina
Ricordiana. Milan, Italy

Soc. ec. stud. Social and economic studies. University college of the West Indies. Mona,
St. Andrew, Jamaica

Temas elegidos. Buenos Aires, Argentina
Tempo. London, England
Tempora. Revista de arte. Lima, Perú

Universidad, Santa Fe. Santa Fe, Argentina

Index of authors

Abascal Brunet, Manuel, 1268, 1268x
Abelardo Guerra, Nicolás, 1553
Abreguí Virreira, Carlos, 544
Acevedo Hernández, Antonio, 1276, 1277, 1278
Acquarone, F., 877
Acuña, Luis Alberto, 1396, 519a, 520a
Acuña Escobar, Franco, 870a-874a
Adalid y Gamero, Manuel de, 1184, 1662, 658a, 659a
Adams, Alton, 1073a
Adams, Franklin, 143
Adán, Elfego, 2084
Agea, Francisco, 1253, 1767, 1768, 1769, 1800-1819, 1851, 1902, 2574, 753a
Aguayo, Samuel, 2289
Agüero (y Barreras), Gaspar, 1476, 1480, 1481, 1481x, 573a
Águila, Luis A., 1272
Aguilar, Miguel, 424a, 425a
Aguilar Machado, Alejandro, 1413
Aguirre, Julián, 367
Aimes, Herbert H. S., 1083
Akora, C. R., 231
Alarcón P., Esperanza, 1681, 1905
Alas, Ciriaco Jesús, 1580
Alba, Antonio, 1349
Alcaráz, Angela, 2085
Aldunate C., María, 1217
Alejo, Benjamín, 251a
Alessio, Nicolás Alfredo, 302
Alfaro González, Anatasio, 1427
Almeida, Benedito Pires de, 703
Almeida, Renato, 704, 705, 785, 876, 960, 1105, 35a, 268a, 323a, 372a
Alonso, Manuel A., 2473
Altamirano, Ignacio M., 1738
Alvarado, Lisandro, 2640, 1013a
Alvarenga, Oneyda, 25, 706, 961, 1126, 269a-274a, 324a
Alvarez, Juan, 457, 541, 610
Alvarez, Manuel J., 1563
Alvarez de la Cadena, Luis, 662a
Alvarez de Toledo, Federico C., 2086
Alviña, Leandro, 2385
Alzedo, José Bernardo, 2306
Allende (Sarón), Adolfo, 426a-429a
Allende (Sarón), Pedro Humberto, 126, 1273, 1279, 1280, 1281
Amador, Armando C., 1906
Amador, Graciela, 2087
Amaral, Amadeu, 962, 1138, 1139
Amberga, Jerónimo de, 1320
Ambrosetti, Juan Bautista, 532, 593, 594, 1036
Ambrosetti Villa, Victoria, 429, 458

Amengual, René, 430a, 431a
Americano do Brasil, A., 1140
Amézquita Borja, Francisco, 663a, 664a
Amunátegui, Miguel Luis, 1269
Amunátegui y Solar, Domingo, 1243
Anaya A., Franklin, 252a
Ancona, Eligio, 1907
Andrade, Mário de, 25, 83, 707-715, 786, 787, 834, 835, 963-971, 996, 1106-1112, 1118, 1176, 2570; 325a, 326a
Andrade, Martins de, 836
Andrade, Victor, 648
André, José, 303
Angarita Arvelo, Rafael, 2647
Angulo A., José, 1282
Anson, George, 36a
Antoine, Le Roy, 1645
Apel, Willi, 37a
Aprile, Bartolomé R., 624, 625
Aragón, Arcesio, 1353
Aramburu, Julio, 459, 459x
Aranda, Hugo, 1739
Araujo, Alceu M., 275a
Araya R., José Rafael, 1414, 546a
Archanjo, Samuel, 716
Arconada, César N., 368
Ardévol, José, 574a-582a
Ardoino Pose, Alfredo, 431
Aretz-Thiele, Isabel, 144, 460, 461; 1a, 143a-146a, 1014a-1025a, 1062a
Argüedas, Alcides, 214
Argüedas, José María, 2329, 2330, 2331, 2454; 904a, 905a
Arias Anduaga, Clotilde, 2332
Arias-Larreta, Abraham, 2333
Arinos, Affonso, 973
Arinos, Afonso, 972
Arista, A. S., 2036
Armitage, Marie Teresa, 2334
Arona, Juan de, 2335
Arriaga, J. J., 2164
Arróspide de la Flor, César, 2387; 935a
Artel, José, 521a
Arvey, Verna, 145, 1442, 1821
Arzeno, Julio, 1537
Arzoz, P., 2037
Assiz, Pedro de, 788
Asuar, José Vicente, 38a, 432a
Atl, Dr. See Murillo, Gerardo.
Augusta, Félix José de, 1301
Austin, Leonard, 232
Ayala, Santiago Key, 2677
Ayarza de Morales, Rosa Mercedes, 2336
Ayestarán, Lauro, 370; 988a-993a, 998a-1003a

DATE DUE